CANADIAN FOREIGN POLICY

SELECTED CASES

DON MUNTON

University of British Columbia

JOHN KIRTON

University of Toronto

Prentice-Hall Canada, Inc.
Scarborough, Ontario

In memory of
Margaret Ann Munton

Canadian Cataloguing in Publication Data
Munton, Don, 1945-
    Canadian foreign policy
Includes index.
ISBN 0-13-118654-X

1. Canada - Foreign relations - Case studies.
I. Kirton, John J.   II. Title.
FC242.M86 1991   327.1   C91-095178-0
F1029.M86 1991

Prentice Hall, Inc., Upper Saddle River, NJ 07458
Prentice-Hall International, Inc., London
Prentice-Hall of Australia, Pty., Ltd., Sydney
Prentice-Hall of India Ptv., Ltd., New Dehli
Prentice-Hall of Japan, Inc., Tokyo
Prentice-Hall of Southeast Asia (Pte.) Ltd., Singapore
Editora Prentice-Hall do Brasil Ltda., Rio de Janeiro
Prentice-Hall Hispanoamericana, S.A., Mexico

ISBN 0-13-118654-X

Acquisitions Editor: Michael Bickerstaff
Developmental Editor: Maryrose O'Neill
Production Editor: Valerie Adams
Production Coordinator: Anna Orodi
Cover Design: Olena Serbyn
Interior Design: Olena Serbyn
Page Layout: Anita Macklin

1 2 3 4 5 RRD 96 95 94 93 92

Printed and bound in the U.S.A. by R.R. Donnelley and Sons

TABLE OF CONTENTS

PREFACE

This book emerged from our experiences in teaching undergraduate and graduate courses in Canadian foreign policy and in locating Canadian-oriented material for courses on comparative foreign policy and international relations—experiences shared, we believe, by many of our colleagues across and outside Canada.

This book is very much a testimony to the legacy of John W. Holmes who popularized the case study method as a principal approach to studying Canadian foreign policy and whose impact is still felt in the organization and conduct of courses in this area. The policy-oriented nature of much teaching in the Canadian foreign policy field also led to case studies becoming a vital component of courses organized around competing theoretical traditions or major thematic debates. Yet, despite this emphasis on case material in the teaching of Canadian foreign policy, on the one hand, and despite a rich array of textbooks, readers and collections of primary documents, on the other, there was no book which brought together any significant number of the cases fundamental to

understanding Canadian foreign policy in the post World War II period. At a time of growing need to expand courses beyond the traditional St. Laurent, Diefenbaker, Pearson, and Trudeau periods, to include the important Mulroney years, the lack of such a collection of critical cases was even more apparent.

Available materials for courses in international relations and comparative foreign policy are similarly deficient. Here there is a recurrent desire from instructors and students to incorporate content relating to Canada—as either a country of immediate interest, a representative middlepower, or a consequential actor—into the analysis of the major events in postwar international politics. The founding of the United Nations and NATO, the management of the Suez and Cuban missile crises, the waging of the Korean and Vietnam wars, the responses to the Soviet invasion of Afghanistan and the Iraqi invasion of Kuwait, the campaign against apartheid in South Africa, and efforts for Third World development—in all of these Canada was a participant, and often played a key world role. General textbooks and readers of international politics and comparative foreign policy, however, rarely even refer to Canada. There was no comprehensive source of relevant materials to which instructors and students could turn for material on Canada's involvement in these and other events.

This book is designed to meet the needs of students of both Canadian foreign policy and international relations courses. It brings together in a single volume introductory treatments or overviews of major cases which are at the centre of both Canadian policies and international politics in the post World War II period. Each case study provides, first, a reasonably comprehensive description of a major decision, or set of decisions, in Canadian policy, and, second, an analysis of the major factors and motivations which led the Canadian government to act as it did.

Taken together the cases thus cover highlights of Canadian foreign policy from 1945 to 1991. Although this volume will not render unnecessary the writing at some point of a single-volume comprehensive history of Canadian foreign policy over the postwar years, it should help fill that gap. It is chronologically organized and has introductions to historical periods (as defined largely by government changes). It includes an appended chronology of important events over these years to provide essential background and to allow students to put the specific events of any one case into the broader stream of postwar international politics. While selected cases do not a coherent history make, they can perhaps serve as a foundation on which

a solid historical understanding can be built.

Why cases? As instructors of foreign policy and international politics courses have long recognized, the case study approach has much to recommend it as an organizing device for pedagogical purposes. It can convey a sense of the full historical context in which important international events take place. It provides the specificity and detail, about both key actions and their antecedents, that are necessary if students are to connect causes to effects, assess competing explanations, and begin the task of evaluating or constructing more general theories of foreign policy behaviour. And, because the case study method permits the analyst to recreate the world of the decision-maker at the time, it facilitates the consideration of the costs and benefits of alternative—exisiting and imagined—policy choices.

Why these cases? The cases selected for inclusion in this volume were chosen primarily for their importance in defining the direction of Canada's foreign policy in the years since 1945. Each of the cases included has as its focus a reasonably tightly time-bound, high-level decision or interrelated set of specific decisions that mark a major change in policy or characterized a durable pattern or trend (either intellectually or institutionally) in the management of Canada's relations with the outside world.

These cases embrace both the traditional realms of peace and security and the more recent concerns about economic, environmental, and humanitarian issues. They cover

Canada's compelling and complex interactions with other key actors, its multilateral as well as bilateral relationships with the first, second, and third worlds, and its activities both within formal international institutions and through more informal diplomatic forums. The cases deal relatively equally with the four periods into which Canada's postwar experience can be, perhaps, most conviently divided: the "golden decade" of the St. Laurent years; the disruptive "tenth decade" of the Dienfenbaker-Pearson years; the challenge of the Trudeau years and Clark interlude; and the rediscoveries and departures of the contemporary Mulroney era.

Why these selections? The articles selected for the cases included in this volume were chosen, usually after competitive assessment and much debate between the co-editors, with several criteria foremost in mind. We attempted to select articles or chapters that in the first instance provided a more or less chronologically-structured, descriptive, historical treatment of each case, accounts that focused on what the Canadian government actually did, or decided to do, with the issues at hand. Our central goal was to provide the best introductory interpretive overview of each case, on the assumption that this would be students' first, but not last, exposure to material on the particular case. In making these selections we assumed students would have some knowledge of the general events in postwar international politics, but not of Canada's involvement in them. Under the assumption that readers will want to read further, we have provided "Suggested Readings" after each chapter. These suggest additional sources which provide alternative interpretations and deeper or more refined analyses. With the conviction that at least some of these events can be clarified through the use of maps, we have provided these where most helpful. We make no claim that the resulting collection represents the full range of theoretical or thematic traditions at work in the field of Canadian foreign policy or international relations at present.

Despite the lack of existing anthologies of case studies in Canadian foreign policy, there is no lack of case study material in the literature. It was thus possible in our selections to include a substantial number of previously published studies, many of which have alearly become classics in their own time. Some gaps remained however. There were a number of critical cases which, for some reason or other, had never been the subject of published accounts. These gaps were particularly acute in the 1980s. There were a number of other cases for which the available accounts were in various ways incomplete or unsatisfactory as short overviews. For each of these cases we commissioned the writing of, or obtained, or wrote ourselves, a new account. Thus, published here for the first time are case studies on the Columbia River Treaty by Neil Swainson, Canada and Vietnam by John English, the response to the Afghanistan invasion by James Bayer, the conclusion of the Canada-United States Air Quality Agreement by Don Munton and Geoffrey Castle, and the waging of the Gulf War by John Kirton. Two additional chapters—on the formation of NATO by Escott Reid and the Cuban missile crisis by Jocelyn Ghent-Mallett and Don Munton—represent such substantial overhauls of earlier material as to be virtually new articles. Thus, almost one-third of this volume comprises previously unpublished chapters.

We fully realize that any selection of the twenty, or twenty-five, or thirty, "most critical cases" in Canadian foreign policy is a set of decisions on which reasonable women and men will disagree. We think that the cases we have selected each merits this label, but recognize that other cases might have been included as well, or perhaps substituted for some of those we selected. In addition to the intrinsic importance of each of these cases, however, there were other criteria which argued particularly strongly for the inclusion of certain of those found here. One such criterion, noted above, was coverage of non-traditional, non-diplomatic security issues. Another was to show the domestic face of Canadian foreign policy. While it has become commonplace to give lip service to the idea that foreign policy has both domestic determinants and a domestic audience, not all cases in Canadian foreign policy demonstrate equally well this conventional wisdom. These criteria made even more compelling the argument to include, for example, the Columbia case, a resource development issue in which the province of British Columbia took a key role, the Afghanistan case, which uniquely was played out during a federal election campaign, and the air quality or acid rain case, which was both the major environmental issue of the 1980s in Canada and a federal-provincial problem as well as a Canada-United States problem. One additional criterion, of course, dictated which previously published studies could be re-printed—the permission of authors and publishers.

Why the editing? A final word or two ought to be said about the editing done on most of the case studies. In some cases this editing was rather light. In others it was considerable, to an extent that even a most reasonable author might regard it as excessive abuse of his or her carefully crafted prose. The heaviest-handed editing was inflicted, although always reluctantly, upon material from books where the story in which we were interested spanned a number of chapters. The original writing and analysis in such material is not designed to provide, and is thus less suited to the demands and constraints of, the short succinct overview case study. For each such case we have endeavored to preserve the character of the material while adapting it to rather rigid page length limits. In these and some other cases what we have edited out is most often extensive background information about the world situation, detail about events in Canada, and/or extensive explanatory analysis of factors behind the policies adopted by Canada.

ACKNOWLEDGMENTS

Assembling this volume has left us with a long list of individuals whose contribution we gratefully acknowledge. Neil Swainson kindly agreed to write a new chapter-length account of the Columbia River development saga. John English and James Bayer generously allowed us to use previously unpublished materials they had written on the Vietnam and Afghanistan cases, respectively. Michael Hart updated an earlier published analysis of the free trade negotiations. Jocelyn Ghent-Mallet graciously accepted our rather presumptuous suggestion that her fine analysis of the Diefenbaker government in the Cuban Missile Crisis could benefit from some "revisionist" thoughts in the light of recent fascinating revelations and newly released documents. Louis Pauly, David Wolfe, Ted Cohn, James Bayer, and about fifty colleagues who responded anonymously to a survey we conducted all suggested and evaluated candidate cases. This assistance provided invaluable guidance to us in designing this book. We owe a great debt, of course, and offer many thanks to the authors of the materials we are re-printing here and to their publishers. For assembling the raw material, locating relevant maps, researching the chronology, photocopying endless articles and versions of chapters, and retyping some of these, we are grateful to our hard-working research assistants: Mana Naghibi, Natasha Tiosajvlejvic, Laura Hurst, Naina Sloan, Julia Grossman, and Sarah Ann Munton. Catherine Lu, Brian Job, Karen Guttieri, Escott Reid, Neil Swainson, James Bayer, David Welch and Jocelyn Ghent-Mallet read one or more chapters at or before the proof stage. For their faith in this project and their tireless efforts in overseeing this book to fruition we thank our friends at Prentice-Hall, Patrick Ferrier, Maryrose O'Neill, and Valerie Adams.

Our families, Mary, Michael and Joanna Kirton, Ann and Sarah Munton, gave up many hours with us as the original idea of this book slowly became a reality. Though they may have wondered whether this was The Book we should have been working on, they provided priceless support. Our deepest gratitude is to them, for being them.

CREATING THE POSTWAR ORDER

anadian foreign policy obtained its
contemporary style and content, to
a very significant extent, in the
transformation of the international system
wrought by World War II. Canada emerged
from the war a stronger nation—militarily, economically, and politically—and had
shed lingering semi-colonial attitudes. Its
leadership emerged virtually unanimously
rejecting the pre-war pursuits of quasi-isolationism and fully committed to the sort
of active involvement in world affairs that
has been a consistent theme in subsequent
postwar policy.

To be sure, some of the pre-war concerns did not entirely disappear. As in the
pre-1939 period, Canadian leaders after
1945 were still concerned with the country's international "status." Prior to the
war, this concern was focused largely on
the pursuit of legal independence and recognition of sovereignty; after the war, it became more focused on the pursuit of
international influence. As it had even after
the Statute of Westminster and through
the 1930s, when struggling against the
pressures from London to adopt a common
imperial policy, Canada spent much of the
war and much of the postwar period trying
to ensure that great power decisions did
not ignore Canadian interests. To a substantial degree, these continuing concerns
are those of any non-great power in a world
largeley run by great powers. For Canada,
however, there was also the particular ongoing concern with national unity, the need
to ensure that active international involvements did not re-create the bitter domestic divide between English- and
French-speaking Canadians that had arisen
in the conscription crises of 1944 and 1917.

The watchword of the shift in policies
after 1945 became "internationalism." This
term was never to be defined precisely by
diplomats or politicians. But the fact that it
still took pride of place in the rhetoric of
the Mulroney government in the mid- and
late-1980s shows clearly its staying power
as the central idea of postwar Canadian
policy. While other countries and traditions
give different meanings to this term, for
Canada it seems to have come to mean not
only an active involvement in world affairs
but also, initially, support for effective international organizations and, eventually,
a search for mechanisms and opportunities
to help resolve international conflicts.
"Internationalism," in the Canadian context, thus came to be tied inextricably to
the notion of Canada as a "middle power,"
not only in the sense of a country neither
at the top nor the bottom of the international power hierarchy, but also in the sense
of seeking a middle ground or compromise
in the peaceful settlement of inter-state
conflicts.

One related idea first articulated publicly by Canada's wartime Liberal prime minister, William Lyon Mackenzie King, in 1943, was what became known as the "functional principle." Often confused, mistakenly, with the "functional approach" to international cooperation popularized by David Mitrany, the Canadian "functional principle" argued that international responsibilities and influence in any particular issue area ought to be afforded to those with expertise and capabilities, and interests, in the area. Thus, although Canada did not see itself as a great power in military terms, it was, for example, a significant economic power and trading nation, and should thus be included in decision-making on matters of international economy and trade.

These tendencies and themes are borne out well in the case studies in this section. Canada's role in the formation of the United Nations, although a modest one in global terms, reflectd both its middle power status and its concerns for a peaceful postwar order managed by effective international organizations. The shift from quasi-isolationism toward "internationalism" is traced by Soward and McInnis, as is the position Canadian policy makers took to a variety of issues about the form and powers of the United Nations and the extent to which these positions were influenced by official Ottawa's "functional principle" thinking. What is also evident there, and in the other cases in this section, is an over-arching pragmatism about the desirable shape of this postwar order. Canadian officials seldom took unyielding, dogmatic stands on these matters, perferring, for example, to give the five permanent UN Security Council members the veto they insisted on having, rather than opposing its adoption and having one or more of them opt out of the organization.

As the other case studies in this section show, Canada's desire to protect its interests by playing a consequential role in creating strong multilateral institutions extended well beyond the central political and security organs of the United Nations. Inspired by the Mitranyian spirit of cooperation in functional areas as well as Canada's own principle of functional representation, it focused importantly on the core economic areas of money and trade, through the establishment of the International Monetary Fund (IMF) in 1945 and the General Agreement on Tariffs and Trade (GATT) in 1948. Moreover, propelled by the looming Cold War, and the transatlantic and indeed global affiliations flowing from Canada's longstanding Commonwealth connections, it lead to Canada's interest and initiatives in the creation of the North Atlantic Treaty in 1949.

Canada played a leading, and mediatory, role in creating the IMF, the only country apart from the United States and the United Kingdom to have a fully developed plan for the world monetary organization. Its plan, reflecting its awareness of thinking in Washington and London and its skilled civil service in Ottawa, was useful in harmonizing the British and American schemes into a final blueprint, if one notably tilted toward the American pole. And Canada's position as a major financial power—indeed, the world's second creditor country (after the United States)—succeeded in securing for it a permanent (if constituency-based) seat on the IMF's Executive Committee, alongside the world's normal array of great powers.

In creating the GATT, as Robert Spencer describes, Canada's strong position as the world's third largest trading power at the time was again offset by its immediate need to reconcile different American and British orientations.

Canada's large imports from the United States could not be paid for by its traditional exports to the United Kingdom and the Commonwealth, as long as the United States remained adamantly opposed to the system of Commonwealth preferences and exclusive sterling area that had grown up in previous decades, and as the US Congress's sentiment shifted from the immediate postwar enthusiasm for strong international institutions to more traditional American isolationism and protectionism. Canadian pragmatism once again reaped its reward as Canada succeeded in obtaining a provisional set of rules and tariff reductions that enhanced its access to its key American and British (as well as other) markets, preserved its existing Commonwealth preferences, and avoided the need to negotiate in desperation a bilateral free trade agreement with the United States.

The negotiation of the North Atlantic Treaty, recounted by Escott Reid, who was a participant in the process, again showed Canada's interest in moving beyond the United Nations' framework to create effective international institutions. In the face of threatened Soviet expansionism in Europe and Soviet obstructionism at the UN, Canada joined with the United States and the United Kingdom to pioneer a formal arrangement for collective self-defence. In part because Canada's new multilateral Liberal Prime Minister, Louis St. Laurent, was anxious to overcome the historic, self-absorbed isolationism of francophone Quebec, and make it a full and willing participant in shouldering Canada's enlarged international responsibilities, Canada pushed for a political and economic role for the alliance and for the inclusion of France within the founding coalition. Working with sympathetic Atlanticists within the US administration (one of the keys to Canada's postwar foreign policy success), it pursued. The first was a genuinely multilateral alliance in which every member would support every other member, rather than a unilateral American security guarantee. The goal of an institution that would be not just a military alliance to counter a Soviet threat, but also a permanent forum for political, economic and social consultation and coordination, was only partially realized. Like the UN itself, NATO was to evolve under the influence of power realities and events in the 1950s.

chapter 1

FORMING THE UNITED NATIONS, 1945

F.H. Soward and Edgar McInnis

When the Canadian delegation set out for San Francisco to participate in drafting the Charter of the United Nations, it brought along the experience of a quarter century in the League of Nations. That experience had been neither particularly commendable nor satisfying. Initially, membership in the League had been sought as a proof of Canada's recognition as an independant entity in international affairs. Yet Sir Robert Borden and his colleagues who fought the battle for status in Paris were at the same time uneasy about some of the implications of League membership. They disliked the commitments set out in Article 10 of the Covenant which, in their judgment, required too much from countries like Canada that were secure from danger and had limited interests but were expected to act like great powers with universal responsibilities. "Let the mighty, if they will, guarantee the security of the weak" was the essence of one Canadian memorandum at the time.[1] Although the parliamentary debates upon ratification of the Treaty of Versailles were largely concerned with wrangles over how much real advance had been made in obtaining international recognition, there were a few, like a Liberal member from Quebec, who disliked the prospect of being governed in military matters "by and from Geneva."

When it was subsequently realized that the United States, the principal author of Article 10, was not going to enter the League, Canadian delegates at four successive meetings of the League Assembly did their best to destroy or whittle down the provisions for sanctions contained in the Covenant. Their efforts were only partially successful. By 1928, in the false dawn that followed Locarno and the Kellogg Pact, Canadians were optimistic about the prospects of world peace, but were still emphasizing the League's value primarily as "an indispensable and continuing agency of international understanding."[2]

In the timid thirties, when the League was openly defied in Asia and Africa, the Canadian government tried to cling to its advocacy of public opinion as "the final and effective sanction for the maintenance of the integrity of international engagements."[3] While Geneva grappled with the problem of upholding the principle of collective security in the Italo-Ethiopian conflict, Canada pursued a "back seat policy" and remained firmly opposed to automatic commitments, especially of a military character.

Such a policy, cautious rather than cowardly, but certainly undistinguished, commanded the support of most Canadians. Like other democratic peoples, they dreaded the prospect of a return to war. They feared

4   F.H. Soward and Edgar McInnis, "Canada Enters the United Nations," from *Canada and the United Nations*, Canadian Institute of International Affairs and Carnegie Endowment for International Peace, Manhattan Publishing Co., 1956. Portions of the text have been deleted. Some footnotes have been removed; those remaining have been renumbered.

as well that participation in war might place an intolerable strain upon Canadian unity. They remembered how the application of conscription for military service during the latter part of the First World War had been so bitterly resented by French-speaking Canada, which regarded the conflict as "British, alien and remote." Its necessity had then been just as passionately upheld by the great majority of English-speaking Canadians. The conscription issue had split the Liberal party, whose great leader Sir Wilfrid Laurier (Prime Minister, 1896-1911) had remained true to his people in Quebec and had refused to join the wartime coalition which enforced conscription.

After Laurier's death in 1919 the Liberals chose as his successor William Lyon Mackenzie King, whom Quebec solidly supported as one "toujours fidèle à Laurier." It was Mackenzie King's lot to head the Canadian government for all but five years (1930-1935) of the period between 1922 and 1948. In view of this heritage from Laurier, it is not surprising that throughout that period Mackenzie King constantly stressed the supreme importance of preserving Canadian unity. As he told the House of Commons on March 23, 1936: "I believe that Canada's first duty to the League and to the British Empire, with respect to all the great issues that come up, is, if possible, to keep this country united."[4] In keeping with this attitude the Prime Minister told the League Assembly in September 1936 after the League's failure in the Italo-Ethiopian crisis, that Canada must consider any decision to participate in resistance to aggression "in the light of all existing circumstances: circumstances of the day as they exist in Canada as well as in the areas involved."[5]

By May 1938 he was publicly asserting that so far as Canada was concerned "the sanctions articles have ceased to have effect by general practice and consent and cannot be revived by any state or group of states..."[6] Confronted by the failure of leadership on the part of the great powers in the democratic camp and the corresponding increase in aggressiveness by Germany, Italy, and Japan, the Canadian government strongly supported the Chamberlain policy of appeasement, welcomed the Roosevelt assurances of American aid "if domination of Canadian soil was threatened by any other Empire,"[7] and reluctantly embarked upon a modest program of rearmament. As the international horizon grew darker, Mackenzie King bitterly expressed in the House of Commons on March 30, 1939, Canadian resentment at the painful dilemma of a country which could not effectively influence the trend of events that were to affect so profoundly its own destiny.

> The idea that every twenty years this country should automatically and as a matter of course take part in a war overseas for democracy or self-determination of other small nations, that a country which has all it can do to run itself should feel called upon to save periodically a continent that cannot run itself, and to these ends risk the lives of its people, risk bankruptcy and political disunion, seems to many a nightmare and sheer madness.[8]

Yet, in less than six months, the harsh sequence of events in Europe which reached its climax in the Nazi invasion of Poland had impelled the Prime Minister to summon a special session of Parliament at which approval was given for a declaration of war on Germany. Because of the time required to do so, the Canadian declaration of war on September 10 came a week later than that of the United Kingdom. By taking this step, Canada had asserted the reality of her status as an independent state, a fact which the United States significantly recognized by not considering Canada as having been bound by the British declaration (as was the case in 1914) and consequently not invoking the terms of its neutrality legislation against Canada until after September 10. At the same time, in rallying to meet the danger of Nazi aggression in Europe, Canada had once again demonstrated her solidarity with the United Kingdom.

This solidarity was all the greater in English-speaking Canada because of its appreciation of the sincerity with which Chamberlain had previously striven, however ineffectively, to avert war. Those who had preferred the views of Churchill and Eden and those who had supported Chamberlain before Munich could now unite on a policy on which all three British leaders were in agreement. But for many of British stock it was still the impulse of the heart rather than the logic of the head which had governed their actions, as those of French origin were well aware. In Quebec the traditional dislike of being involved in a "British imperialist" war in Europe was still powerful, but the majority were not prepared to provoke another domestic crisis over an issue on which English-speaking Canada felt so strongly. They were also reassured in 1939 by the pledge against conscription for overseas service which had been taken by all the Quebec members of the cabinet. Moreover, the obvious complicity of an atheistic, communistic Russia in the Nazi attack on a Catholic Poland carried great weight with the leaders of the Roman Catholic Church in Quebec.

Canadian unity, therefore, was not immediately imperilled by the descent into war.[9] That it could still be threatened by sectional and racial differences was, however, to be demonstrated in the manpower crisis of 1944, when the desirability of maintaining the Canadian Army in Europe at full strength necessitated the despatch overseas of conscripted troops who had previously not been required to serve outside the Western Hemisphere.

. . .

The disastrous sequence of events in that unhappy period had tended to drive some English-speaking Canadians into a disgusted variant of American isolationism. Others sought comfort in greater reliance upon the familiar comradeship of the British Commonwealth of Nations. Only a minority, for whom the late J.W. Dafoe of the *Winnipeg Free Press* was the ablest and greatest spokesman, remained convinced that the policy of collective security had not failed because it had never been effectively tried. They were prepared, under more favorable auspices, to resume the struggle to erect a firm structure of international organization.

During the early years of the war, especially in its grimmest period when the British Commonwealth faced Hitler alone, Canadians necessarily concentrated their undivided attention upon the mobilization of the country's resources, human and material. In so doing they surprised themselves, and perhaps the world, by the extent of their contribution. As Mr. Glazebrook has put it, "Canada was in the somewhat ambiguous position of a minor power playing, for a time at least, a major role.[10] As a consequence, Canada acquired a greater feeling of self-confidence, attained membership with the United States and the United Kingdom in combined boards on the allocation of food and the co-ordination of war production, and obtained a prominent position in such organizations as UNRRA (the United Nations Relief and Rehabilitation Administration).

By 1943 the impact of the war had changed the nature of Canadian thinking in both governmental and unofficial circles upon the character of Canadian participation in international affairs. The fond delusion of the twenties, epitomized in Senator Raoul Dandurand's famous description of Canada's living "in a fireproof house remote from inflammable materials" had little appeal to Canadians living in the brutal world of the forties. As the Prime Minister told the nation in February 1942, during an appeal for support of a Victory Loan:

> The fortunes of battle since the outbreak of war; the fate of nations that lie prostrate beneath the heel of the aggressor; the terrific tasks which face the nations still battling for their freedom—all these go to show that neutrality has become a snare and isolation an illusion.[11]

Seven months later Mr. King again drove home the lesson, declaring:

> If we, on this continent, have thus far escaped invasion, either by Japanese forces from across the Pacific or by German forces from across the Atlantic, it is because of the resistance of other nations....However questioning we may have been in the past, there can be no doubt that from the very first day of the war, whatever our motives, we have in very truth been fighting for our own preservation, for our own survival.[12]

Holding this conviction and fortified by the growing interest of the United States in international organization (which Prime Minister King had three times during 1941 declared should be "on its way" before the war was over) the Canadian people supported the re-emergence of some system of world order. In a Gallup poll, released on November 20, 1943, 78 per cent of those interviewed supported Canada's playing an active part in maintaining world peace, even though it involved the despatch of Canadian forces to other parts of the world.

But cautious as always, Prime Minister King evaded too precise a description of Canadian policy until the political horizon was clearer both at home and abroad. Thus, in March 1943, when the opposition demanded a clarification of Canadian policy, Prime Minister King was content to take his stand on a statement made in May 1938, which he considered was still the basis of Canadian policy:

> Our foreign and external policy is a policy of peace and friendliness, a policy of trying to look after our own interests and to understand the position of other Governments with which we have dealings. It is a policy which takes account of our political connections and traditions, our geographical position, the limited numbers and racial composition of our people, our stage in economic development, our own internal preoccupations and necessitates in short a policy based on the Canadian situation.[13]

The fact that speakers from both the Progressive Conservative party and the CCF (Co-operative Commonwealth Federation) criticized the declaration as inadequate, and urged that Canada, because of her enhanced position, should give leadership in creating a new and better League of Nations may have persuaded the Prime Minister to emerge guardedly from his entrenched position. He may also have been encouraged by advance information that the foreign ministers of the United States, the United Kingdom, and the Soviet Union were going to meet in Moscow in October to discuss, among other topics, problems of postwar organization.

Accordingly, in July the Prime Minister took advantage of the annual debate on the estimates of the Department of External Affairs to make a statement which reflected a second trend in Canadian opinion: the conviction that Canada's growth in stature as a result of her wartime efforts entitled her to greater recognition than she had yet achieved. After describing the organization and planning of the United Nations war effort, which had been almost entirely in the hands of the great powers since Pearl Harbour, the Prime Minister declared that "the time is approaching, however, when even before victory is won the concept of the united nations will have to be embodied in some form of international organization." He conceded that authority could not be divided equally among the thirty or more nations then linked together against the Axis powers, but he rejected the alternative concept of vesting authority exclusively in the largest powers. What Mr. King advocated was adequate representation for Canada in the various new international institutions which it seemed likely would be set up on a functional basis after the war. As he put it:

> In the view of the government effective representation on these bodies should be neither restricted to the largest states nor necessarily extended to all states. Representation should be determined on a functional basis which will admit to full membership those countries large or small which have the greatest contribution to make to the particular object in question. In the world there are over sixty sovereign states. If they all have nominally an equal vote in international decisions, no effective decisions are likely to be taken. Some compromise must be found between the theoretical equality of states, and the practical necessity of limiting representation on international bodies to a workable number. That compromise can be discovered, especially in economic matters, by the adoption of a functional principle of representation. That principle is likely in turn to find many new expressions in the gigantic task of liberation, restoration and reconstruction.[14]

This ingenious argument, which drew attention to a dilemma in international organizations that still remains largely unresolved, was in keeping with the Canadian experience during the war and was to remain implicit in Canadian policy at the San Francisco Conference. It was well received in the House of Commons and by those outside whose attention was not distracted by the exciting news that Canadian troops had landed in Sicily. It was felt that this "new and wholly Canadian concept," as the *Montreal Gazette* of July 10 termed it, might serve to avert the danger which a Progressive Conservative M.P. envisaged "of a Big-Four set-up in international affairs with Canada as one of the smaller nations waiting around outside."[15]

After the Moscow Conference the foreign ministers of the Big Four powers issued a declaration on October 30, 1943, in which they recognized "the necessity of establishing at the earliest practicable date a general international organization, based on the principle of the sovereign equality of all peace-loving states, and open to membership by all such states, large and small, for the maintenance of international peace and security." They made no reference to the functional principle. The Canadian government made no further public comment at that time. But in providing the Chairman (Mr. L.B. Pearson) for the Interim Commission of the Conference on Food and Agriculture which established the framework of the Food and Agriculture Organization, and by playing an active part at the Atlantic City session of the UNRRA Council in November, Canadians were demonstrating that they believed in practicing what they preached. Indeed, the authors of *Canada in World Affairs, September 1941 to May 1944*, subsequently went so far as to claim that:

Conscious of her magnificent war effort, her new industrial prowess, her great stocks of foodstuffs, her vastly augmented activities as a world trader, and her strategic position as an air power, her delegates and advisers were able to speak with such confidence, conviction and competence that Canada seemed often to be automatically regarded at the conference table as occupying a position only less important than the three great powers. That the matter of her full national status and indeed her position as a world power of middle rank seemed never in question proved a pleasant surprise to many Canadian participants and observers.[16]

When the Canadian Prime Minister next surveyed external policy before the House of Commons on August 4, 1944, he had behind him the gratifying experience of the Conference of Commonwealth Prime Ministers of the previous May. The conference had agreed that it was essential to create a world organization for the maintenance of peace and security which should be "endowed with the necessary power and authority to prevent aggression and violence."[17] Advocates in London of a single voice in foreign policy for the Commonwealth, or of a more centralized Commonwealth, had been routed. Rather, the emphasis was placed upon continuous consultation among the governments to ensure as far as possible a parallelism in the foreign policies of the various countries. The phrase "foreign policies" appeared for the first time in a conference communiqué. There was general acceptance of the Canadian view that the stability and cohesion of the Commonwealth was linked with the creation of a strong international organization.

At the time he made his policy statement in the House of Commons, Mr. King was also aware that a conference of representatives of the great powers was to meet shortly at Dumbarton Oaks. He assured the House that, although Canada was not invited, as some members argued should have been the case, the government was kept fully informed and knew "the line which will be presented...in regard to the world organization by the officials who are discussing matters there."[18]

In his comments on the Canadian attitude toward the projected new organization, the Prime Minister suggested that Canadians should have as their goals the adoption of the most effective possible methods for ensuring security and the safeguarding of Canadian interests in a manner which would ensure steady public support throughout the country. He did not object to the great powers taking the initiative. On the contrary, that seemed to him "a correct application of the functional principle." Nor did he question the concentration of wide powers in the council of the organization and permanent membership in it of the great powers. What did concern the Prime Minister was the manner in which the other powers were to be represented. It was here that his functional principle should apply, in accordance with which "those countries which have the most to contribute to the maintenance of peace should be most frequently selected." Bearing in mind what had happened since 1939, the Prime Minister maintained that one good working basis for selecting council members would be an examination of the military contribution actually made during the war—a yardstick admirably suited to the record of the Commonwealth countries but less favorable to the aspirations of the Latin American states.

Mr. King did not, however, wish to see too much emphasis placed either on the possession of power as the yardstick for participation in the United Nations, or on the maintenance of a large superiority in power as the basis for security. What was also needed—and this point, too, was to be stressed by the Canadian delegation in San Francisco—was the staking out of "a large and fruitful area of collaboration" in such fields as trade, social welfare, and transportation. By developing collaboration in these fields, the Prime Minister thought, it might be possible to lower the temperature of nationalism while maintaining its constructive features. In answering comments by other speakers, Mr. King made it clear that Canada was prepared "to do its full part in carrying out agreed security schemes, whether they involved the creation of an international police force, or, alternatively, of measures for seeing that there will always be an overwhelming preponderance of power available to protect the peace."[19]

During the Dumbarton Oaks conversations, which began on August 21 and continued for almost two months, the Canadian Embassy in Washington kept the government fully informed of developments. Each day United Kingdom officials, who participated in the talks, briefed the representatives of other Commonwealth governments in Washington on what had taken place. It is not known whether Canadian comments to the United Kingdom representatives had any effect upon the talks. The proposals, which were released in October, would certainly indicate that the representatives of the great powers were naturally and markedly concerned with safeguarding their own interests.

. . .

There was a marked willingness among Canadians to favor membership in the new organization. According to a Gallup poll of January 1945, it had the support of 90 per cent of the population. This willingness was coupled with a noticeable emphasis upon the new position of Canada as a leader among the middle powers. Such a claim for recognition was justified by the type of argument advanced by the *Windsor Star* that Canada was "a country large enough to have world interests but small enough to be free of any suggestion that she is seeking to rule." The lesson of the war was also reflected in the willingness of 76 per cent of those polled to favor the principle of punitive sanctions. On this question the usual sectional deviation was reflected, the majority in favor of the principle falling to 51 per cent in the province of Quebec.

A significant reflection of official opinion, despite the speaker's emphasis that his views were those of an individual Canadian citizen, was afforded by Mr. L.B. Pearson, then Canadian Ambassador to the United States, in an address on December 26, 1944, to the Winnipeg Canadian Club. He agreed with the recommendation that each member of the Organization should not, as in the League of Nations, possess a veto on policy questions. He accepted the necessity of a great power veto in the Security Council, but he thought that a great power should be barred from exercising a veto in disputes to which it was a party. Mr. Pearson recognized that the existence of a great power veto was simply one method of spelling out the fact that "the only chance of survival of the organization depends upon the agreement of the Great Powers." Everything depended upon their close and friendly co-operation. However, he pointed out that these concessions to the great powers put their position in striking contrast to "the almost completely unprotected and unnecessarily subordinate position of other powers such as the Netherlands, Brazil, Belgium and Canada," which he obviously grouped as middle powers. Unless some concessions were made to their position, there was a danger that the new League of Nations would be considered as "not much more than an alliance of Great Powers for two things; to keep Germany and Japan down and to keep the middle and smaller powers in order."

To offset that danger, Mr. Pearson wished to vest greater power in the new General Assembly as the agency which would best represent "the universal, collective, and permanent character" of the organization. One method of increasing the General Assembly's power and prestige would be to require that decisions on collective security taken by the Security Council must be ratified by a majority of the General Assembly before they became binding upon members. In rebuttal of the anticipated argument that such a procedure would delay speedy action and thereby give aid and comfort to the aggressor, the ambassador argued that the Council could by itself promptly mobilize "95 per cent of the effective strength of the world" against an aggressor, and the Assembly could readily meet in a week and take a decision a few days later. If the Assembly shared in the indictment and punishment of the aggressor, each member state would be made to feel itself an actual participant in the formulation of policy. Such a belief was of great importance since "there really can be no other basis for general international cooperation than that feeling." Although Mr. Pearson described the Security Council as the most important single agency of international action yet proposed, he took pains to lay great stress upon the possibilities of the proposed Economic and Social Council and to advance Canada's claim to membership in such a body.

Mr. Pearson's comments upon the role of the Security Council in holding down Germany and Japan will evoke a wry smile today. But his forecast of the possible role of the General Assembly was to find unexpected confirmation in the Acheson proposals of 1950 which were provoked by the danger of an impasse over Korea in the Security Council.

During this period, the government busied itself in exchanging views on the blueprints for the new organization with those countries where Canadian missions were established. It also despatched a formal submission to the great powers which contained suggestions for improving the effectiveness of the new organization. These suggestions were not made public, but the diplomatic correspondent of *The New York Times* in a despatch dated December 11, 1944, claimed that they were designed to increase the authority of the middle powers without flouting the position of the larger ones or reducing the effectiveness of the organization. Early in March 1945 the Prime Minister also visited Washington and was able to discuss the Canadian proposals with President Roosevelt.

In the same month, and in accordance with its policy of keeping public opinion in step with the government, Parliament was asked in a formal motion to approve the acceptance of the invitation to attend the San Francisco Conference to draft the Charter of the United Nations. The motion also asked the legislators to accept the principles embodied in the Dumbarton Oaks proposals as a "satisfactory basis for a discussion of the charter of the proposed international organization," and to agree that it was of vital importance to Canada that an effective international organization for the maintenance of international peace should be established. Such a resolution offered a wide field for discussion of external policy of which the House of Commons took full advantage. Over one quarter of the members took part in the week-long debate,[20] the most sustained of its kind in parliamentary experience. The fact that the motion was endorsed by all parties, approved by the overwhelming majority of 200 to 5 in the House of Commons,[21] and unanimously approved in the Senate, gave the Prime Minister ample encouragement for his hope that Canada would be able to speak "with a clear, strong, and united voice" at San Francisco. After watching the debate from the press gallery, a reporter described it as being "as convincing a display of internationalism as the most enthusiastic idealist could wish."[22] In accordance with his stress on unity, Mr. King announced that the government proposed to have Canada represented at the Conference by spokesmen from the chief parties in Parliament.

During the debate the Prime Minister solemnly warned that "if we have another conflagration such as we have had in this war this country stands to lose more than any other country on earth." With such a possibility in mind the government appreciated the importance of securing the support of the great powers for the new organization. Failure to do that had been the great defect of the League of Nations. The government was also aware that it would be unrealistic to expect the immediate establishment of an international system strong enough to coerce any great military power bent on attaining its aims by force. On the other hand, while accepting the guiding principle that "power and responsibility should as far as possible be made to coincide," the government felt that it was advisable to seek at San Francisco clarification of the constitutional position of what the Prime Minister called "the important secondary states." Some method of selection for representation in the Security Council which would have due regard for the power and responsibility of these states would undoubtedly make it a stronger and more efficient body.

The Prime Minister was also anxious that the Conference should embody in a for-

mal rule what he believed would become in any event the probable practice in respect to the method of applying sanctions. He argued that states should not be called upon for "serious enforcement duties" without having first participated in the discussions of the Security Council, or without having previously negotiated an agreement to co-operate in enforcing the decisions of that body.

In dwelling on this last stipulation, Mr. King conjured up the ghosts of Canadian policy in the thirties when he assured the House that the present plans would "in no way commit Canada to send forces beyond Canadian territory at the call of the Security Council" until an agreement had been freely negotiated and approved by Parliament. For invoking once again his favorite maxim, "Parliament must decide," he was subsequently criticized by Progressive Conservative speakers for having appealed to "the same old isolationism of a minority" which in the past had led Canada to "whittle down" her responsibilities. As Mr. Pearson had already done, the Prime Minister emphasized Canada's willingness to take "a prominent and useful part" in the social, economic, and humanitarian activities of the new international body. This attitude was strongly supported by the CCF party which stressed the value of the proposed Economic and Social Council. Mr. King also hoped that adequate provision would be made for a general review of the Charter after a period of years.

. . .

The San Francisco Conference opened on April 25, 1945, and ended on June 26. Since a general election in Canada had been fixed for June, the M.P.'s in the delegation were obliged to leave the Conference after being present for only a relatively short time. The Prime Minister, for example, was absent from May 14 to June 23. Even that brief experience appears to have been a disillusioning one. His recent biographer, Mr. Bruce Hutchison, claims that within a week Mackenzie King had become convinced that "the United Nations simply would not work," and that "secretly he had written it off as a failure." He summarized the Prime Minister's views as follows:

> It might be worth establishing as a forum of discussion and to perform certain international chores. It might grow gradually into something better. In the foreseeable future it could not hope to keep the peace. If there were to be peace, it would be maintained by some new balance of power in which, as usual, Canada's position would be difficult.[23]

As a result of the enforced absence of the M.P.'s, the responsibility for expounding the Canadian position was necessarily shouldered for the greater part of the time by the permanent officials. For that reason the Canadian delegates were less conspicuous in the public debates than might otherwise have been expected. However, since Canada was one of the fourteen states elected to the Executive Committee and was also a member of the Coordination Committee which passed upon the final wording of the clauses of the Charter, these officials were able to render valuable, if inconspicuous, service. An index of their competence is afforded by the fact that two of them were among those originally considered for the post of Secretary-General of the United Nations.

At the second plenary session of the Conference, Prime Minister King sounded the keynote of Canadian policy. He emphasized his country's anxiety to bring into being as soon as possible a charter of world security which would ensure "an overwhelming preponderance of power on the side of peace." But he rejected the thesis that power was exclusively concentrated in the hands of four or five states and said

bluntly that "the Conference should not act on the assumption that it is." If it did so, he foresaw the danger of a "new type" of isolationism, characterized by the feeling in many smaller countries that the task of preserving the peace could be left in the hands of the great powers. (Parenthetically it may be noted that this type of isolationism was not "new," but the normal attitude of the smaller European powers in the nineteenth century.) If such an attitude developed, it would be difficult for the smaller powers to serve the new organization effectively. Mr. King deplored this possibility on the ground that "experience has shown that the contribution of smaller powers is not a negligible one, either to the preserving of the peace or to its restoration when peace has been disturbed." His emphasis upon the desirability of a positive role for the smaller nations in the United Nations when contrasted with his previous preference for a "back seat policy" in the League of Nations was an indication of how much the Second World War had altered the thinking of Canadian leaders.

Throughout the discussions in San Francisco, the Canadian delegation pursued the sort of middle course which environment and tradition seem to have made almost instinctive in Canadian policy. Thus in their desire to further the role of middle powers in the new organization the Canadians never forgot the limitations inherent in that status. They were consequently more realistic, if less spectacular, in their advocacy of reforms in the Dumbarton Oaks proposals than some of the other spokesmen for the smaller powers. A typical reflection of this attitude at San Francisco was later given by Mr. St. Laurent in January 1947, in an address at the University of Toronto:

> We have, of course, been forced to keep in mind the limitations upon the influence of any

secondary power. No society of nations can prosper if it does not have the support of those who hold the major share of the world's military and economic power. There is little point in a country of our stature recommending international action, if those who must carry the major burden of whatever action is taken are not in sympathy. We know, however, that the development of international organizations on a broad scale is of the very greatest importance to us, and we have been willing to play our role when it was apparent that significant and effective action was contemplated.[24]

Such an attitude accounts for the fact that Canada was less vehement or obdurate than Australia or Argentina in the debates at San Francisco upon such questions as the exercise of the veto by the great powers. Similarly, the reticence upon such questions as trusteeship (which did not directly affect Canada as a non- colonial power but might embarrass the United Kingdom) and the paucity of comment upon the role of regional organizations (since Canada belonged to none) were in keeping with the caution of a country disinclined to argue over controversial matters not of apparent direct concern. But this discreet reserve did not mean that when it was essential to make a point the Canadian views were not firmly expressed, although never to the point of sullen recalcitrance.

Thus the Canadians did their best, by advocating the functional principle, to gain for the middle powers more effective representation on the Security Council than seemed likely to result under the Dumbarton Oaks proposals. In accordance with their belief that power should be combined with responsibility, they suggested that the General Assembly be required to draw up rules governing the election of nonpermanent members of the Security Council which would ensure that "due weight be given to the contribution of the members to the maintenance of international peace and security and the performance of their obligations to the United Nations."[25]

This formula aroused opposition since it might hamper the aspirations of those states which were unlikely to make such a contribution but valued Council membership for prestige and other reasons. The views of such states soon found support among the sponsoring powers, as the authors of the Dumbarton Oaks proposals termed themselves. Accordingly, they successfully introduced an amendment, which appears in the first paragraph of Article 23 of the Charter. This amendment omitted any reference to the Canadian proposal for rules, but directed that, in elections to the Security Council, due regard should be specially paid "in the first instance" (the Canadians would have preferred the adverb "primarily") to the contributions of members along the lines suggested by Canada. At the same time, it was emphasized that equitable geographical distribution should also be taken into account. Although the sponsoring powers argued at the time that geographical distribution would be "a secondary consideration," such has certainly not proved to be the case in elections to the Security Council.

Another partial victory for Canada was the inclusion in the Charter of Article 44 concerning participation by states not members of the Security Council in decisions of that body which involved the use of their armed forces for punitive measures. Acting on the principle of "No Taxation without Representation," a phrase which heads the summary of the discussion on this question in the Canadian delegates' report on the Conference,[26] Canada suggested that such states should be invited by the Security Council to participate in any discussions involving the use of their forces. In defense of this suggestion, Prime Minister King pointed out that the great powers had already amply safeguarded their own positions by the fact that any one of them could veto the imposition of sanctions. They also would have the advantage of participating from the outset in the discussion of any dispute. But the secondary powers, whose active collaboration might well be required, could be committed by a vote of seven Council members including all the permanent members. What Canada wanted was to "be consulted rather than ordered to take action."[27] The Conference did not go as far as Canada would have wished toward what a writer in *The Round Table* described as her "most important objective,"[28] but it did adopt what Secretary of State Stettinius subsequently commended as "a significant and constructive change."[29] It agreed that any state asked to participate in the application of force should be given the right to take part in the decisions of the Security Council concerning the employment of contingents of that member's armed forces.

Chapter IX of the Dumbarton Oaks proposals deals in somewhat cursory fashion with the important problem of international economic and social co-operation. The Canadian delegation submitted a complete revision of that chapter for the purpose of arranging its provisions more logically and clarifying its intent.[30] In a series of proposals (which eventually became Articles 55, 56, 62, 64, and 66 of the Charter) Canada sought to strengthen the position of the proposed Economic and Social Council. This body was to be entirely elective and its members were to possess no veto powers. Here too the Canadians were anxious to have the functional principle applied in order that states of major economic importance should have adequate representation. Their desire was met, in large part, by Article 60, paragraph 2, which, in contrast

to the provisions for election to the Security Council, permits retiring members of the Economic and Social Council to be eligible for immediate re-election.

Five other proposals (now contained in Articles 57, 59, 63, 64, and 70) were designed to clarify the relationship between the new Council and the various specialized agencies. Because of a belief in what one Canadian speaker described as "the antiseptic quality of light" an attempt was made throughout to enhance as much as possible the fact-finding powers of the Economic and Social Council. In practice, this laudable aim of using the Council primarily as a body of experts for the investigation and analysis of international economic and social questions was not realized. Like so many other agencies, the Council was used as a platform for rhetorical battles between spokesmen for the Soviet bloc and the free world which generated more heat than light.

In general, the Canadian interest in furthering the non-political activities of the United Nations was consistent with the attitude earlier displayed at Geneva in League meetings. It was subsequently to reappear in the drive in support of Article 2 of the North Atlantic Treaty. Such an attitude was in keeping with the position of a country whose well-being is so largely dependent upon a stable and prosperous world in which international trade has more prospects of expansion. Stress on economic and social co-operation was further buttressed by the realization that, in this field of activity, middle powers endowed with ample resources of raw materials or technical competence, or both, might approach more closely the level of great powers whom they could not hope to emulate in the military sphere. As a country which had made such remarkable progress economically during the war, a progress which contributed to Canada's becoming the third or fourth ranking country in foreign trade during the fifties, it was to be expected that Canada should stress as much as possible the obligation incumbent upon the United Nations to promote international economic and social co-operation.

It should not be inferred that the Canadians at San Francisco did not frequently pool their efforts to secure Charter improvements with other delegates. Although they did not carry their objections against the almost unlimited scope of the veto power by the great powers as far as did the Australians, they shared in the fight to limit the scope of that power.[31] In common with Brazil and other countries, Canada tried in vain to obtain a more flexible method for amending the Charter than the great powers were ready to concede. They worked with New Zealand delegates in attempting to protect the international character of the Secretariat.

Cautious approval was displayed in the debate upon the Charter which took place in the Canadian Parliament in October 1945. By that time the war was at an end in both Asia and Europe, but had been brought to a direful close in Asia by the use of the atomic bomb. In contrast to the manner in which it had treated the Covenant of the League of Nations, the United States Senate ratified the United Nations Charter by a huge majority. This step was particularly welcome to Canada. But the hoped-for unity of the great powers, which was perceptibly sagging in San Francisco, had largely vanished during the meeting of the Council of Foreign Ministers at London in September 1945. It fell to the lot of Mr. St.

Laurent, then Minister of Justice, to present on October 16 the government's case for ratifying the Charter.

Mr. St. Laurent commended the Charter as a great improvement upon the Dumbarton Oaks proposals, but he significantly declined to go further than to describe it as "a first step in the direction of that co-operation between nations which appears to be essential to the survival of civilization."[32]

There was evidence in the debate an even greater realization than in the preceding March of the impossibility of isolation. For this heightened emphasis the release of the atomic bomb was largely responsible. The same desire that Canada should play a worthy part in the United Nations was again conspicuous. "It is our feeling," said Mr. St. Laurent at the close of the debate, "that the majority, the very large majority, if not the whole, of the Canadian people wish Canada to be a part of the international organization and to do whatever may be required in order to be a full partner in it. I believe that whatever may be required is a price that Canada is prepared to pay to make the organization effective, if it can be made effective."[33]

A reporter for the *Ottawa Journal*, who had been at San Francisco, aptly described the mood of the sixteen speakers in the House as ranging "from prayerfulness to a rather sour brand of cynicism."[34] Nevertheless both Houses of Parliament gave unanimous approval of the government's motion. With more disquiet than optimism they waited to see how the new organization would make its mark upon world society.

NOTES

1. Quoted in G.P. de T. Glazebrook, *A History of Canadian External Relations*, Canadian Institute of International Affairs (Toronto: Oxford, 1950), p. 312.
2. From the Canadian government's note accepting the Pact of Paris, 1928. Quoted in R.A. Mackay and E.B. Rogers, *Canada Looks Abroad*, Canadian Institute of International Affairs (Toronto: Oxford, 1938), p. 331.
3. Prime Minister R.B. Bennett. Canada, Parliament, *House of Commons Debates*, February 24, 1933, p. 2430.
4. *Ibid.*, March 23, 1936, p. 1333.
5. Quoted in Mackay and Rogers, *op. cit.*, p. 367.
6. Quoted in F. H. Soward, J. F. Parkinson, N. A. M. Mackenzie, and T. W. L. MacDermot, *Canada in World Affairs: The Pre-war Years*, Canadian Institute of International Affairs (Toronto: Oxford, 1941), p. 97.
7. *Ibid.*, p. 107.
8. Canada Parliament, *House of Commons Debates*, March 30, 1939, p. 2419.
9. Nevertheless, shortly after the outbreak of war, when the Premier of Quebec, Mr. Maurice Duplessis, staged an election in which he began by declaring that a vote for him would be a vote against conscription and participation in the war, it took the most strenuous efforts of the Liberal party to secure his defeat. Cf. Robert MacGregor Dawson, *Canada in World Affairs: Two Years of War 1939-1941*, Canadian Institute of International Affairs (Toronto: Oxford, 1943), pp. 17-19.
10. Glazebrook, *op. cit.*, p. 424. For a brief description of the Canadian contribution, cf. F.H. Soward, *Canada in World Affairs: From Normandy to Paris 1944-1946*, Canadian Institute of International Affairs (Toronto: Oxford, 1950), Chapters I, III, and IV.
11. *The Inauguration of the Second Victory Loan* (Ottawa: King's Printer, 1942), p. 3.
12. *Three Years of War* (Ottawa: King's Printer, 1942). p. 11.
13. Canada, Parliament, *House of Commons Debates*, March 19, 1943, p. 1396.
14. Canada, Parliament, *House of Commons Debates*, July 9, 1943, p. 4558.
15. *Ibid.*, p. 4565.
16. C.C. Lingard and R. G. Trotter, *Canada in World Affairs: September 1941 to May 1944*, Canadian Institute of International Affairs (Toronto: Oxford, 1950), pp. 268-69.
17. Commonwealth Prime Ministers Meeting, 1944: *Declaration of 16 May 1944* (London: Dominions Office).
18. Canada, Parliament, *House of Commons Debates*, August 11, 1944, p. 6416.
19. *Ibid.*
20. For the debate, see Canada, Parliament, House of Commons Debates: March 1945.
21. All five of the dissenters were independent members from Quebec. It should be noted that those most conversant with the trend of opinion in Quebec believed that these five represented a much more substantial element of public opinion than their numbers indicated.
22. *Saturday Night*, April 7, 1945, p. 8.

23. Bruce Hutchison, *The Incredible Canadian* (Toronto: Longmans, Green, 1952), p. 403.

24. Louis St. Laurent, *The Foundations of Canadian Policy in World Affairs* (Toronto: University of Toronto Press, 1947), p. 33.

25. *UNCIO Docs., op. cit.*, Vol. III, p. 589.

26. Canada, Department of External Affairs, *Report on the United Nations Conference on International Organization*, Conference Series, 1945, No. 2 (Ottawa, 1945), p. 37.

27. *UNCIO Docs., op. cit.*, Vol. XII, pp. 297, 303.

28. *The Round Table*, No. 140 (September 1945), p. 362.

29. U.S. Department of State, *Charter of the United Nations, Report to the President on the Results of the San Francisco Conference*, Publication 2349, Conference Series 71 (Washington: U.S. Government Printing Office, 1945), p. 94.

30. *UNCIO Docs., op. cit.*, Vol. X, pp. 205-8.

31. In justification of the Canadian unwillingness to go the whole way with Australia in opposing the great powers' refusal to broaden the Yalta voting formula, the report of the Canadian delegation on the San Francisco Conference explains that it was the view of the delegation that "while they could not accept the interpretation of the voting procedure as satisfactory, it was not too high a price to pay for a world organization which was good in other respects." *Report on the United Nations Conference on International Organization, op. cit.*, p. 32.

32. Canada, Parliament, *House of Commons Debates*, October 16, 1945, p. 1202.

SUGGESTED READINGS

Eayrs, James, "'A Low Dishonest Decade': Aspects of Canadian External Policy, 1931-1939," pp. 59-80, in Hugh L. Keenleyside, ed. *The Growth of Canadian Policies in External Affairs*. New York: Knopf, 1952.

Eayrs, James, *In Defence of Canada, Volume III: Peacemaking and Deterrence*, Toronto: University of Toronto Press, 1972, pp. 137-167.

Glazebrook, G. de T., "The Middle Powers in the United Nations System," *International Organization* 1 (1947): pp. 307-315.

Holmes, John W., *The Shaping of Peace: Canada and the Search for World Order, 1943-1957*, Volume 1, Toronto: University of Toronto Press, 1979.

McNaught, Kenneth, "Ottawa and Washington Look at the U.N.," *Foreign Affairs* 33 (1955): pp. 663-78.

Stacey, C.P., *Canada and the Age of Conflict, Volume 2: 1921-1948, The Mackenzie King Era*, Toronto: University of Toronto Press. 1981, pp. 374-386.

c h a p t e r 2

RESTORING MULTILATERAL TRADE, 1948

Robert Spencer

Towards the Restoration of Multilateral Trade

Canada's long range aim was to develop "a high level of multilateral trade on the broadest possible basis,"[1] and to this end Canada's postwar economic foreign policy had two main lines: the economic restoration of Europe, and the development of liberal trade and currency arrangements.[2] Canada had a stake in the restoration and extension of world trade that was greater than size or population would indicate. Even before 1939 Canada ranked fifth among exporters and eight among importers.[3] During the war commodity trade soared to the record level of $5,000 million. This was in large measure the result of heavy defence procurement spending in Canada, and it was recognized that to sustain industry at the greatly increased wartime levels normal trading relations with the rest of the world must be re-established as soon as possible.

The other striking feature of Canada's trade position lay in the fact that Canada's economy had grown up in large part to supply needs of Europe and the sterling area, while proximity and similarity of tastes and problems made Canada dependent on the United States for imports of many raw materials as well as industrial and manufactured goods. In the past the heavy deficit with the United States had been balanced by a corresponding surplus with the United Kingdom and Europe, the historic North Atlantic Triangle which was in fact but a part of an international trading system extending to the four corners of the earth.[4] It was these two factors—the importance of foreign trade in her economic life and the fundamental unbalance in trading relationships with the United Kingdom and Europe on the one hand and with the United States on the other—which impelled Canada to take all steps possible for the early re-establishment of multilateral (or price) trading and the convertibility of currencies which it implied. "Fundamentally," Mr. King could tell the Commons on December 9, 1947, "we are concerned not only over the level of our external trade, but we have also a fundamental concern for the level of external trade of other countries. The character of our trade, with surpluses of exports to certain countries and excesses of imports from other countries, requires a condition in which surpluses on one account can be converted to offset deficiencies on another account. This means that a bilateral approach to trade is not enough."[5]

Interest in multilateral trade led Canada to participate actively in organizations designed to promote order and stability in international economic affairs.

Robert Spencer, "Towards the Restoration of Multilateral Trade," from *Canada in World Affairs, 1946-1949*, Canadian Institute of International Affairs, Toronto, Oxford University Press, 1959. Portions of the text have been deleted. Some footnotes have been removed; those remaining have been renumbered.

There was a general feeling that world trading relations during the interwar period, particularly after 1929, had been most unsatisfactory.[6] Unstable exchange rates, import quotas, quantitative controls, high tariffs and other restrictive practices had constituted barriers by which Canada, as one of the largest *per capita* exporters of goods, had been penalized more than helped. The Canadian government was therefore determined that postwar trading arrangements should be more sensible and workable, and was prepared to support American attempts to re-establish a viable system of multilateral trade, based on relatively stable and interchangeable currencies, moderate tariff barriers, non-discriminatory trade practices, and a healthy flow of investment capital.[7]

Planning for improved arrangements by the United States, the United Kingdom and Canada began early in the war; and at the Bretton Woods Conference in the summer of 1944 two of the cornerstones of postwar economic collaboration, the International Bank for Reconstruction and Development, and the International Monetary Fund, were devised and came into being on December 31, 1945. The negotiations for the creation of the third, the International Trade Organization, came only later, and after postwar economic dislocation had placed new obstacles in the way of liberalizing and expanding trade.

. . .

After the Bretton Woods agencies were created, the next step involved a twofold (though simultaneous) attack on trade barriers by attempts to lower tariffs and to create an International Trade Organization. The negotiations towards both these objectives had their origin in the obligation contained in Article VII of the Lend-Lease Agreement to eliminate "all forms of discriminatory treatment in international commerce, to the reduction of tariffs and other trade barriers...." Canada was not a recipient of lend lease, but was committed in precisely the same way through notes exchanged in 1942.[8] In February 1946 the UN Economic and Social Council adopted an American resolution calling an International Conference on Trade and Employment, and a Preparatory Commission was instructed to prepare an annotated agenda, including a draft charter for an International Trade Organization. Canada was among the eighteen states named to the Commission which met between October 15 and November 26, 1946 in London. Canada approached these meetings with trepidation, but the results exceeded expectations. Canada gave provisional agreement to the preliminary draft charter which was completed at Geneva in August 1947. It was described as "a triumph of definition of conflicting desires and ideas rather than a conclusive common accord."[9]

A more immediate interest at Geneva lay in the negotiations towards widespread tariff reductions which took place independently of, though concurrently with, the drafting of the charter. The procedure followed in these ambitious negotiations was dictated by the U.S. Trade Agreements Act. It was described not unfairly as "madly complex."[10] The twenty-three participating governments carried on bilateral tariff negotiations. Usually bargaining on a particular item was conducted by the principal supplier. However, on the principle of non-discrimination, each country was entitled as a matter of right to every tariff reduction made by every other participating country. Bilateral negotiations would thus lead to multilateral agreements. In the course of the meetings at Geneva 123 agreements were drafted, over 45,000 tariff items were affected, and half the world's trade was involved in the twenty schedules drafted. Despite the fact that the conception of tariff negotiations on so vast a scale seemed to be too ambitious for practical accomplishment, twenty-three nations signed the General Agreement on Tariffs and Trade (GATT) on October 30.

At Geneva Canada emerged as one of the most active and aggressive proponents of a world trade scheme, and the Canadian delegation, led by Mr. L. Dana Wilgress, Canadian Minister to Switzerland, took an active part in negotiations with seven of the twenty-three participating countries.[11] Ranking as one of the "Big Three" of the trading world, Canada undertook to make concessions on about 1,000 out of 2,000 items on her list of tariffs. Of these, 600 represented reductions in most-favoured-nation rates, and over 500 a binding of existing rates against increase. On the basis of 1946 trade, it was expected that nearly two-thirds of Canada's imports would be affected in some way by these concessions. In return, three-quarters of Canada's exports were involved in concessions granted by other countries. Of particular importance were the concessions exchanged with the United States. On the basis of 1939 trade, only 5 per cent of Canada's exports would not benefit by American concessions; 25 per cent would enjoy bound tariff rates; 70 per cent would be subject to tariff reductions; and 60 per cent would be entitled to reductions from the prohibitive levels of 36 and 50 per cent. In return, Canada conceded reductions or bindings on 70 per cent of imports from the United States.[12]

In a broadcast from London, soon after the close of the Geneva Conference, Mr. King described the negotiations as "the most comprehensive, significant and far-reaching" ever undertaken in the history of world trade.[13] The General Agreement,

he later told the Commons, embodied "the widest measure of agreement on trading practices and for tariff reductions that the nations of the world have ever witnessed."[14] Especially promising were the terms of the Protocol of Provisional Application, by which the contracting parties were to bring into effect provisionally the new tariff rates on January 1, 1948, establish the most-favoured-nation treatment among themselves, and follow the rules governing trade relations laid down in the general provisions of the Agreement. Contracting parties were not required to amend existing legislation or to promulgate new legislation in order to adhere more closely to the Agreement. They were, however, expected not to enact any new legislation that was inconsistent with it.

It was both ironical and unfortunate that the General Agreement and the Protocol of Provisional Application came before the House of Commons in December 1947, at the same time as approval was sought for the emergency dollar conservation programme. The delay in announcing these measures was in itself further evidence of the seriousness with which the Canadian government viewed the gains to be won at Geneva. The case for the General Agreement was put before the Commons by the Prime Minister and Mr. Howe. Mr. King suggested that its importance for Canada could scarcely be exaggerated.[15] Mr. Howe declared that Canada had actually gained more from the agreements than any other country, and would derive great benefits from the new international commercial code, from the opportunities afforded by the American tariff concessions, and from the restoration of freedom for negotiations in the matter of Imperial preferences. Even if the Havana Conference, then in session, should fail to produce an acceptable charter for the proposed ITO, the code and the principles agreed upon in the twenty articles of the draft character which had been included in Part II of the General Agreement, would be of great assistance in removing administrative barriers to trade which were often more formidable than tariffs. As regards the United States practically the entire range of restrictions against Canadian goods had been reviewed and very substantially reduced; and the largest tariff reductions would apply to exports which were already entering the United States on a competitive basis in spite of existing restrictions.[16]

Both Ministers were at pains to indicate that the system of Imperial preferences had been modified, not abandoned. At Geneva, Canada had favoured working towards equality of treatment for all nations and achieving general tariff reduction through a diminution of the margins of preference. In only one instance (tin) was a preferential margin narrowed by the device of raising preferential tariff rates. The principles underlying the General Agreement were that no new preferences were to be created; no existing preferences were to be enlarged; and remaining preferences were to be negotiable. The last provision meant that the contractual policy of bound margins, inaugurated with the Ottawa agreement of 1932, was abrogated, and Canada recovered complete control of her tariff policies so far as relations with Great Britain were concerned. This provision, evidently the result of Canadian initiative, was in line with the historic Canadian attitude that preferences should be concessions, freely given, rather than permanent, binding obligations. The new position had been set forth in an exchange of notes on October 30 in which Canada and the United Kingdom mutually agreed to recognize the right of each to reduce or to eliminate the preferences remaining after

the conclusion of the General Agreement, but each undertook not to raise tariff rates above the level in force under the 1937 agreement. In any event, the items in the schedules to which preferences would henceforth apply had been drafted so broadly that neither Canada nor any other Commonwealth country had given up any preferential position which it regarded as important.[17]

The agreements reached at Geneva met with little favour on the Opposition benches, however.[18] Mr. Bracken, the Progressive Conservative leader, could see no benefit in the reduction of American duties on cattle, which was nullified by short term measures such as the Canadian embargo; nor on wheat, when the United States had an annual surplus of hundreds of million bushels. But "the chief folly of the government" was the loss of preferences on items such as apples, and the "death knell" to the whole remaining system of preferences implied by the exchange of October 30. For the CCF, Mr. Coldwell argued that until European recovery had proceeded much further there was no possibility of multilateral trade on a world basis. For the Social Credit, Mr. Blackmore saw the Geneva agreements as one more step in the attempt to force acceptance of the American interpretation of non-discrimination: "Each of these trade conferences was aimed to add threads to the spider web of intrigue wrapped around Britain and the members of the British Commonwealth." After two days of debate, the urgency which had led to the early recall of the House appeared to evaporate. The government evidently had little hope of securing approval of the agreements before they were put into effect by Order-in-Council on January 1, 1948. Even the more limited aim of setting before the House the larger objectives which it was expected the Geneva agreement would serve, before turning to the more immediate and more urgent task of restoring the dollar position, met with only limited success. Mr. Howe complained of "the lack of appreciation of the importance" of "the most far-reaching lowering of trade barriers ever accomplished in the history of international trade," and for this the competition of the dollar conservation measures was chiefly to blame.

There is much to suggest that the government, both led and assisted by a gifted company of expert advisers, had moved ahead of Canadian public opinion. The correspondent of the *Winnipeg Free Press* might declare that the General Agreement placed Canada in "a better trading position than ever before,"[19] and the *Montreal Star* might headline its editorial "The Best News Ever,"[20] but the country was more interested in the programme of restrictions with which Mr. Abbott had unwisely coupled the term "austerity." The debate was not proceeded with after the Christmas recess. Although Mr. Abbott suggested that the resolution would be brought forward in the 1949 session,[21] the Geneva agreement remained without parliamentary ratification.[22]

The General Agreement was provisionally brought into effect on January 1, 1948, by Order-in-Council.[23] Similar action was taken by Australia, Belgium, Cuba, France, Luxembourg, the Netherlands, the United Kingdom and the United States. Until the other countries with whom reductions were negotiated made their concessions available to Canada, a small number of items in the Canadian schedule was withheld. At the end of the first year, Mr. Abbott claimed that the initial experience had been satisfactory, and that the trade figures for 1948 constituted a strong endorsement of the government's policies vis-à-vis GATT.[24]

The International Trade Organization was variously described as a capstone, a keystone, or a cornerstone, but whatever the metaphor, it was widely accepted that an agreement on trade principles and an organization to supervise their application was to be an essential part of the American-inspired structure of economic co-operation.[25] "Without it," Mr. Abbott declared, "the International Monetary Fund and the International Bank would be left incomplete and unable to fulfil effectively the functions for which they were established."[26] Once the draft Charter was completed at Geneva in August 1947, the way was open for the United Nations Conference on Trade and Employment, which opened at Havana, Cuba, on November 21, 1947. In the course of 800 meetings a revised charter was worked out, incorporating some of the hundreds of amendments which had been put forward, chiefly by small nations interested in protecting nascent industries from British and American competition. In addition, two major problems, the distribution of voting power and the relations of members with non-members had been left for solution. Although Canada had put forward no amendments, the Canadian delegation, led by Mr. Wilgress, played an active and effective role in the final steps of this titanic programme. Canada was among the fifty-four nations which signed the Final Act on March 24, 1948. The Charter was to come into effect sixty days after a majority had ratified it, or, after the elapse of one year, sixty days after it had been ratified by twenty countries. In any event, it was hoped that the Charter would come into effect before the end of 1949. In the meantime, an Executive Committee of the Interim Commission was instructed to prepare the way for the first session of the Organization. Mr. Wilgress was its chairman.[27] The Havana draft charter had two main features. It set forth rules designed to govern commercial policies and to limit, to the greatest extent possible, trade restrictions which had developed in the interwar years. It also provided for the creation of an Organization to administer, interpret and, if necessary, to amend these rules.

For the immediate future, the prospects for ITO were not bright. By the spring of 1948, emphasis was on emergency measures such as the Marshall Plan which could be counted upon to show early returns, rather than on comprehensive schemes designed for a "normal" world.[28] By the time Congress began hearings in 1950, American policy was moving away from the free trade principles which had inspired Bretton Woods, GATT, and ITO. In a subordinate clause in a long mimeographed statement at the time of the Torquay negotiations in December 1950, the State Department announced that "the proposed Charter for an International Trade Organization would not be resubmitted to the Congress...." This was a death-blow, and ITO was quietly buried with only a "second class funeral." The Canadian government had earlier announced its intention to seek parliamentary approval for the Charter in the 1949 session; but nothing more was heard of it in the face of the American withdrawal.

Yet the demise of ITO did not mean the end of the principles embodied in the Charter. Certain of its provisions had acquired a form of shadow existence through incorporation in the agreements creating the OEEC and the European Coal and Steel Community. Its principal survivor, however, was the General Agreement on Tariffs and Trade. Conceived as an advance instalment of the Charter, GATT became the instrument through which, temporarily in the first instance, most of the Charter's chapters on commercial policy have been put into effect. By the end of 1949 it was firmly established as the most important multilateral instrument in the field of commercial relations. The main event of 1949 was the second round of tariff negotiations at the Annecy Conference, held under the chairmanship of Mr. Wilgress, where Canada concluded agreements with ten more countries, bringing the total up to 33.[29] A year later at the Torquay Conference, GATT was extended for another three years. Thus, despite the fate which overtook ITO, the General Agreement, appropriately described as ITO *manqué*, was able to make considerable progress towards completing the original pattern, in part because it was largely limited to subjects of traditional commercial policy, and so required little, if any, legislative action by its signatories.[30]

NOTES

1. Statement of Mr. King, *Can. H. of C. Debates*, December 9, 1947, Vol. I, p. 100.

2. L. Rasminsky, *Statements and Speeches*, No. 48/4, January 30, 1948, p. 6.

3. Bank of Nova Scotia *Monthly Review*, April 1948.

4. J. Douglas Gibson, "Canada Depends on Price Trading," *Canadian Business*, May 1949, pp. 27-28.

5. *Can. H. of C. Debates*, December 9, 1947, Session 1948, Vol. I, p. 99.

6. M. C. Urquhart, "Post War Trading Arrangements," *Canadian Journal of Economics and Political Science*, Vol. XIV, No. 3, August 1948, p. 373.

7. D.C. Abbott, *Statements and Speeches*, No. 47/9, May 15, 1947, p. 2. In 1937 Canada's *per capita* exports amounted to $91, as against $62 for the United Kingdom and $25 for the United States. See Department of External Affairs, *Reference Paper No. 30*, August 8, 1948.

8. Wilson, "The External Background of Canada's Economic Problems," p. 8.

9. Hebert Feis, "The Geneva Proposals for an International Trade Organization," *International Organization*, Vol. II, No. 1, February 1948, p. 50.

10. *Round Table*, Vol. XXXVII, No. 148, September 1947, p. 394. There is a brief description of the method of negotiation in *The Attack on the Trade Barriers: A Progress Report on the Operation of the General Agreement on Tariffs and Trade from January 1948 to August 1948*, (Interim Commission for the ITO [1949]), pp. 10-11.

11. K.R. Wilson, "Geneva and the ITO," *International Journal*, Vol. II, No. 3, Summer 1947, p. 249.

12. Department of External Affairs, *Reference Paper No. 30*, August 9, 1948, p. 12. The official press release, summarizing the changes in considerable detail, is reproduced in *Foreign Trade*, November 22, 1947.

13. *Statements and Speeches*, No. 47/20, November 17, 1947, p. 2.

14. *Can. H. of C. Debates*, December 9, 1947, Session 1948, Vol. I, p. 99.

15. *Ibid.*

16. *Ibid.*, pp. 119-20; and December 10, 1947, pp. 130-36.

17. *Ibid.*, December 9 and 10, pp. 100-102 and 132-33. See the analysis of the Geneva agreements in the *Financial Post* of November 29, 1947.

18. *Can. H. of C. Debates*, December 9, 1947, Session 1948, Vol. I, pp. 104-12.

19. November 18, 1947.

20. November 18, 1947.

21. *Can. H. of C. Debates*, March 18, 1949, Vol. II, p. 1624.

22. On February 28, 1950, Mr. Abbott told the Commons that as the Agreement was subject to ratification by the United States, it would be just as well not to "rush" it through parliament until Congress had acted. But the Agreement had been printed in *Canada. Treaty Series, 1947*, No. 27 and 27A.

23. P.C. 5270, December 23, 1947.

24. *Can. H. of C. Debates*, March 22, 1949, Vol. II, p. 1801.

25. Cf. William Diebold, Jr., *The End of I.T.O.*, (Princeton, 1952), p. 2. On the ITO generally see J. B. Condliffe, "International Trade and Economic Nationalism," *International Conciliation*, December 1951, pp. 569-76.

26. *Statements and Speeches*, No, 47/9, May 15, 1947, p. 6.

27. *Report of the Department of External Affairs*, 1948, pp. 14, 43 and 44.

28. Raymond Vernon, "Organizing for World Trade," *International Conciliation*, November 1955, pp. 186-87. "When the fox is being chased by the hounds," it was said at the time, "long-run planning consists of deciding where next to jump."

29. *Report of the Department of External Affairs*, 1948, pp. 45-47. See also *The Attack on the Trade Barriers*, for a review of operations from January 1948 to August 1949.

30. Diebold, *The End of ITO*, pp. 28-29.

SUGGESTED READINGS

Angus, H. P., "Canada's Interest in Multilateral Trade," pp. 54-91, in J. Douglas Gibson, *Canada's Economy in a Changing World*. Toronto: Macmillan, 1948.

Bothwell, Robert and John English, "Canadian Trade Policy, 1943-1947," pp. 145-157, in Jack Granatstein, (ed.), *Canadian Foreign Policy: Historical Readings*, Toronto: Copp Clark Pitman, 1986.

Bothwell, Robert, Ian Drummond, and John English, *Canada Since 1945: Power, Politics, and Provincialism*, Toronto: University of Toronto Press, 1981, pp. 78-90.

Muirhead, Bruce, "Perception and Reality: The GATT's Contribution to the Development of a Bilateral North American Relationship 1947-1951," *American Review of Canadian Studies*, 20 (Autumn 1990): pp. 279-302.

Stone, Frank, *Canada, the GATT, and the International Trade System*, Halifax: The Institute for Research on Public Policy, 1984.

chapter 3

FORMING THE NORTH ATLANTIC ALLIANCE, 1949

Escott Reid

The ideas which led to the discussions in 1948 of the possibility of a North Atlantic alliance started coming to the surface in the summer of 1947. One reason was a desire to head off a campaign which was gathering strength in the United States, Britain, Canada and other countries for amending the United Nations Charter to exclude the great power veto over sanctions and other matters even though this would mean driving the Soviet Union and the Eastern European states out of the United Nations. The main reason was, of course, the advance of Soviet power in Europe.

In 1944 and 1945 the Western powers did not have high hopes of cooperation with the Soviet Union in dealing with the problems of the postwar world. They did not, however, assume that the borderline in Europe between the Soviet troops advancing from the east and the Western troops advancing through France and Italy would become a borderline between a Soviet Empire and the Western world. They believed that a buffer zone would be created between the two spheres consisting of Poland, Czechoslovakia, Hungary, Rumania, and Bulgaria. These states would be friendly to the Soviet Union but they would not be dominated by it. In 1947 and the first few months of 1948, however, these states fell one by one under Soviet domination in a pattern which became frighteningly clear: first, a government of national unity; then a popular front government; then a communist government; and finally a purge of communists who were not considered reliable by the Soviet government, which usually meant liquidating those who had not spent the war years in the Soviet Union. The communist takeover of Czechoslovakia on February 25, 1948, seemed final, conclusive proof that the Soviet Union was not content with friendly states on its borders, but demanded that the border states should become satellite members of its empire. The suspicious death of Jan Masaryk, the pro-Western Czech foreign minister, on March 10, 1948 was an intense emotional shock. Western leaders became afraid in the first three months of 1948 that the pattern of the Soviet Union's takeover of the countries east of the ceasefire line would be reproduced west of the line, especially in countries such as Italy and France where the communist parties were strong and subservient instruments of the Soviet government. It seemed that an increasing number of influential people in Italy and France had concluded that the accession to power of a Soviet-controlled communist government in their country was inevitable, that Soviet power was the wave of the future, and that they had better ingratiate themselves with, or at least not offend, those who would take

From M. Fry (ed), *Freedom and Change: Essays in Honour of L.B. Pearson*, Toronto, McClelland and Stewart, 1975. This essay has been edited to suit the needs of this volume.

GREENLAND
(Denmark)

Norwegian Sea

ICELAND
Reykjavik

NORTH ATLANTIC OCEAN

Faeroe Is.(Den.)

SWEDEN

FINLAND

NORWAY

Helsinki

Oslo

Stockholm

Moscow

Baltic Sea

U.S.S.R.

DENMARK
Copenhagen

Dublin

IRELAND

UNITED KINGDOM

London

Amsterdam
NETHERLANDS
Brussels
BELGIUM

Berlin
(G.D.R.)

POLAND

Warsaw

GERMANY
Bonn
(F.R.G.)

Prague

CZECHOSLOVAKIA

Paris

FRANCE

SWITZERLAND
Bern

Vienna

AUSTRIA

Budapest

HUNGARY

ROMANIA

Bucharest

Black Sea

Belgrade

YUGOSLAVIA

BULGARIA
Sofia

ITALY

Corsica

Rome

Tirane
ALBANIA

Ankara

TURKEY

SPAIN

PORTUGAL
Lisbon

Madrid

Sardenia

GREECE

Athens

Mediterranean Sea

Sicily

Algiers

Tunis

Rabat

MOROCCO

ALGERIA

TUNISIA

NATO members* as of 1955
(in addition to Canada and the United States)

Tripoli

Cairo

LYBIA

EGYPT

* shown in white

control very soon and who would then liq-
uidate any opponents of importance. The
fear at the time, as Charles Bohlen has put
it, was less an "all out military attack" by
the Soviet Union "than the use of Soviet
armed force to encourage and give direct
support to the Communist parties of
Western Europe in case of an attempted
[Communist] take-over."[1] This increasing
fear of Soviet power was accompanied by
mounting revulsion against the nature of
Soviet rule, as the West learned more about
the atrocities of Soviet armies in occupied
territories, Soviet treatment of their own
people returning from German prisoner of
war and displaced persons camps, their
treatment of leaders of social-democratic
and agrarian parties in eastern Europe, and
the nature of the society which had been
created in the Soviet Union.

To understand the mood in Ottawa at
the time of the negotiation of the North
Atlantic treaty, it is necessary also to com-
prehend how our feelings about the United
States and about our own country differed
from feelings a quarter of a century later.
The United States of 1948 and 1949 was
the pre-imperial United States; the United
States government was interested in and
influenced by the views of friendly governments. The United States was a great
power. It had not yet become a super-power.
The United States presidency was the pre-
imperial presidency; the State Department
was powerful under George C. Marshall,
Robert A. Lovett, and Dean Acheson.
Canada was just emerging from the period
when it was the third most important country in the "free world."

In August 1947, at the Couchiching
Conference of the Canadian Institute of
Public Affairs, I tentatively put forward the
idea that the people of the Western world
might consider creating a regional security
organization, open to any Western country,

in which each member state would undertake "to pool the whole of its economic and
military resources with those of the other
members if any power should be found to
have committed aggression against any one
of the members."

I was then L. B. Pearson's second-in-
command in the Department of External
Affairs where he was Under-Secretary. I
asked him for permission to include this
proposal in my speech. Most heads of foreign offices would have refused permission
on the ground that it was inapporprite for
a foreign service officer to make in public
a proposal so far in advance of government
policy. Mr. Pearson gave me permission but
suggested that it would be just as well if
this particular passage were omitted from
the copies of the speech given to the press at
the conference. (The speech was, however,
published in full by the Department of
External Affairs at the end of September.)

At the U.N. General Assembly in the
middle of September I wanted Mr. St.
Laurent to say in the opening debate very
much what I had said at the Couchiching
Conference. Mr. Pearson, with his shrewd
sense of timing, argued that it would be
wiser for Mr. St. Laurent to mention both of
the methods by which nations might deal
with the problem created by what we considered to be the Soviet Union's abuse of
its veto privilege in the Security Council,
without coming down definitely on either
side. Mr. St. Laurent accepted Mr.
Pearson's advice. In his speech to the
General Assembly, he said that one way
was to change the voting procedures and
practices in the Security Council by voluntary abandonment, by agreed conventions,
or understandings which would regulate
them "or, if necessary, by amendments of
the Charter"; and that the other way was a
supplementary security pact—"an association of democratic and peace-loving states

willing to accept more specific international obligations in return for a greater measure of national security."

In November 1947, United States, British, and Canadian politicians and civil servants started talking with each other, very privately and confidentially, informally and tentatively, about these matters in groups of two or three in Washington and in New York. There seemed to emerge a general feeling that we should explore what might be done under Article 51 of the U.N. Charter which refers to the inherent right of individual or collective self-defence.

A top-secret, "prime minister to prime minister" telegram from British Prime Minister Clement Attlee to Canadian Prime Minister Mackenzie King arrived in mid-January 1948, in which Mr. Attlee spoke eloquently of the urgent necessity of rallying the forces of Western civilization to stem further encroachment of the Soviet tide in Europe. This telegram was an opening gun of the successful British campaign led by Mr. Attlee and Ernest Bevin which finally resulted in the creation of the Western European Union by the Brussels Treaty of March 17, 1948. The telegram also sparked the discussions which resulted in the North Atlantic Treaty.

Mackenzie King had by this time become incalculable on major issues of foreign policy. During the war he had urged the creation of an effective collective security system but as soon as the war was over he began to retreat to his pre-war isolationism. We, in the External Affairs Department, never knew which way he would jump. Because of this, we, of course, did our best to take advantage of opportunities to get him to put himself on record against a retreat to isolationism.

The British prepared the way for their initiative by sending us an appreciation of the dangerous international situation.

Within the next few weeks developments took place which persuaded the British government that the propitious moment had arrived. It can reasonably be assumed that these developments were the Soviet coup in Czechoslovakia on February 25, the opening of the discussions on the Brussels treaty on March 7, and a message from the Norwegian government on March 8 that it feared that Norway might soon face Soviet demands for a pact which would reduce Norway to the level of a satellite.

On March 11 Attlee proposed to the United States and Canada that officials of the three countries should meet without delay to study the establishment of a regional North Atlantic pact of mutual assistance under Article 51 of the UN Charter. All the countries threatened by a Soviet move on the Atlantic could participate—Norway, Denmark, Iceland, Ireland, France, Portugal, Great Britain, the United States, Canada, and Spain, once it established a democratic regime. Attlee, as Pearson records, "warned that 'failure to act now may mean a repetition of our experience with Hitler.'"[2]

Mackenzie King was shocked by the news of Jan Masaryk's death. He wrote in his diary that night, March 10: "One thing is certain. It has proven there can be no collaboration with Communists."[3] The next day he was greatly impressed by the British appreciation of the dangers of the international situation. He read it on March 11 and 12 to the leaders of the three opposition parties and on March 15 to the Cabinet. We received Attlee's proposal on March 11. That same day, Louis St. Laurent, Secretary of State for External Affairs, Brooke Claxton, Minister of National Defence, and Lester Pearson, Under-Secretary of State for External Affairs, cabled Attlee, accepting his proposal.

Clearly, the British Labour government, not the Truman administration, launched the tripartite discussions which resulted in the North Atlantic treaty. A British, not a United States, appreciation of the dangers of the international situation in March 1948 provided the background against which the Canadian government decided to participate in those discussions. The British pressed persistently for a North Atlantic treaty during the first six months of the intergovernmental discussions when opinion in the United States administration was divided and support in Western Europe was lukewarm. The one thing the North Atlantic treaty of 1949 is not is an example of Canada being persuaded by the United States to support its Cold War policies.

Mackenzie King, St. Laurent, Claxton, and Pearson, who were responsible for the decision on March 11 to accept the British proposal to participate in discussions on an Atlantic security pact, had lived through two world wars. They were convinced that Canada could not escape being an active belligerent in a third world war. They had come to believe that the First and Second World Wars would not have broken out if Germany had known that it would eventually face a coalition of the United States, Britain, and France. They concluded that the way to prevent a third world war was to convince Stalin that in such a war he would face from the outset an even stronger coalition than the coalitions of 1917 and 1941. The grand coalition, therefore, should be created before and not after the outbreak of war. If created before it might deter Stalin; if created after, all it could do would be to defeat him.

On 19 June 1948 Mr. St. Laurent replied to a question in the House of Commons by referring to a statement in the *Ottawa Journal* that Canada had been conducting a crusade for a North Atlantic pact. "That title of crusade," he said,

> perhaps justly describes the attitude we have adopted. We feel that, should war break out that affected the United Kingdom and the United States, we would inevitably be involved and that there might be great value in having consummated a regional pact...whereby these Western European democracies, the United Kingdom, the United States and ourselves agreed to stand together, to pool for defence purposes our respective potentials and coordinate right away our forces, so that it would appear to any possible aggressor that he would have to be prepared to overcome us all if he attempted any aggression.

That was strong medicine for June 1948. It went beyond anything which had been said in public by the United States Government, the British Government or any Western European Government. But, warming to his subject, carried away by the fervour of his crusade, Mr. St. Laurent went further. He said that if the United States was willing to join in an alliance with Great Britain, France, and the three Benelux countries, "we think the people of Canada would wish that we also be associated with it." This was the first unambiguous public statement of Canada's willingness to enter a North Atlantic military alliance.

He sat down. He leaned across to me and said, "I wonder how that will go down." I said, "I think it will go down very well in the country." Mr. St. Laurent said: "I wasn't thinking of the country. I was thinking of Laurier House"—Mr. King's residence in Ottawa.

Mr. St. Laurent had made his decision in favour of a North Atlantic treaty by the end of March of 1948. Once he made up his mind, he became the leader of a crusade for the treaty, with L. B. Pearson as his senior partner and Brooke Claxton as his junior partner. The task was not easy. It meant for Canada a complete break with the past. Up to then we had resolutely rejected any proposal from any source that we enter into any kind of military treaty, even with our mother country, Great Britain. Opposition to such proposals was nation-wide but it was especially strong in French Canada. It was, therefore, especially difficult for a French Canadian to lead a crusade for a North Atlantic treaty. Yet Mr. St. Laurent did.

The tradition of Canadian diplomacy not only at that time but for many years after was that on an issue of this kind Canada should not get out in front either in private talks or in public. It was up to the three principal Western powers to take the initiative. It would be presumptuous for Canada on an issue like this to force itself to the front. Moreover, if we played an active role in the negotiation of the treaty, this would increase the danger that we would be expected to make a large contribution to the common defence effort. So went the traditional argument.

A cautious man would not have got out in front in an international crusade for the North Atlantic Treaty. A cautious man in the private diplomatic negotiations would have thrown his weight on the side of those who wanted a weak treaty, with ample provision for every nation to decide for itself what it should in fact do if one of its allies were attacked. There were plenty of opportunities to do this during the negotiation of the treaty. Instead, Mr. St. Laurent campaigned in private and in public for a strong treaty—in speeches, in cabinet and in instructions to our representatives in the international negotiations.

The North Atlantic Alliance of 1949 was to a very great extent the creation of Britain, the United States and Canada. In this it is similar to a number of other international agencies established from about 1943 to about 1949, notably the International Monetary Fund, the World Bank, the International Civil Aviation Organization, and, I think, the Food and Agricultural Organization. They were established at a time when, because of a peculiar and temporary set of circumstances created by war and occupation and reconstruction, the European governments were, unfortuantely, not able to play the major role in world affairs which they had played before the war and which they are playing today.

It is a mistake to believe that those who conceived the North Atlantic Alliance were obsessed with the possibility of an open armed attack by Russia. Indeed there was no assessment in the summer of 1948 that the Russian Government was planning a military aggression as an act of policy—though we, of course, recognized that in the tense situation then existing, war might break out either because of some incident or because the Russians might miscalculate Western intentions and, in the false belief that the United States was about to launch an atomic attack on them, strike a pre-emptive blow in Western Europe with their conventional forces.

Those who conceived the North Atlantic Alliance were mainly concerned with the expansion of Russian power in Western Europe not as the result of armed attack by the Russians, but as a result of a weakening of self-confidence in Western Europe, of an increasing belief among Western Europeans that Russian communism was the wave of the future.

By March of 1948 the Soviet Union had consolidated its position in Eastern Europe. It had secured complete control of Czechoslovakia. It looked as if it was about to secure complete control of Finland. There were grave indications that it might soon make demands on Norway. Russian pressure on Northern Europe had been accompanied by threats to Greece and Italy. A war-weary West was being pushed back by what seemed to be a remorseless advance of Russian power. It is not surprising that at this time one of the chief British advocates of a North Atlantic treaty said that Russia's allies in Western Europe were not so much the communists as the forces of despair, apathy, doubt, and fear. The atmosphere at the beginning of 1948 was apocalyptic. We saw the tide of Russian power moving across Europe, the threat of Stalinism to the virtues and values of Western civilization, the natural but almost paralyzing obsession in Western Europe, and especially in France, with the dangers of a Russian occupation from which Western Europe would probably never recover.

In this apocalyptic atmosphere a military alliance was essential but a military alliance was clearly not enough.

This was recognized by the framers of the Western European Union Treaty which was signed at Brussels on March 17, 1948, by Britain, France, and the Benelux countries. That treaty was the precursor and pattern of the North Atlantic Treaty. It reflected the determination of the British Labour Government, under Clement Attlee and Ernest Bevin, that the treaty should rally not only the military and economic resources of Western Europe but also its spiritual resources in a dynamic, liberal and democratic counter-offensive against Russian totalitarianism. For this reason it reaffirmed the tenets of the creed of Western liberalism: faith in human rights and fundamental freedoms, the worth and dignity of man, the principles of parliamentary democracy, personal freedom and political liberty, and it provided for economic, social, and cultural cooperation between the signatories of the treaty.

The intergovernmental discussions and negotiations in Washington on the North Atlantic treaty were spread over twelve months, from March 22, 1948 to March 15, 1949. The discussions went through three phases. The first was confined to representatives of the United States, Britain, and Canada. It lasted from March 22 to April 1, 1948 and was kept secret from the public and possibly from the United States Congress and the French government.[4] In the second and third phases France, Belgium, and the Netherlands also took part. Luxembourg was represented by Belgium in the second phase and participated directly in the third phase. The second phase lasted from July 6 to September 10 (the day Pearson entered the cabinet),[5] the third phase from December 10 to March 15, 1949.[6] Norway joined the talks on March 4 and the treaty was made public on March 18. It was signed on April 4 by Denmark, Iceland, Italy, and Portugal as well as by the countries which had participated in the discussions: Belgium, Britain, Canada, France, Luxembourg, the Netherlands, Norway, and the United States. It came into force on August 24, 1949.

Canada pursued four main objectives in the negotiations on NATO. The first was that there should be a treaty and not just a declaration by the President of the United States, even a declaration accompanied by a congressional resolution and followed by massive arms aid to Western Europe. The second was that the guarantee article in the treaty should be strong, and the third that there should be a strong article on nonmilitary cooperation. The fourth was that Italy should not be a member of the alliance and that the guarantee provisions of the treaty should not extend to Algeria; on these last two issues St. Laurent, when he became Prime Minister, took a stronger line than Pearson. A fifth Canadian objective was that the North Atlantic treaty should contain an undertaking by the parties to submit to the International Court of Justice all justiciable disputes which they might have with each other. We hoped for an unqualified acceptance of the jurisdiction of the Court over justiciable disputes between the parties; the Brussels treaty made possible the continuance of reservations to that jurisdiction.

We succeeded in our first objective in the negotiations; there was a treaty. We had only limited success in our second and third objectives; the guarantee clause and Article 2 were not nearly as strong as we wanted them to be. We failed to realize our fourth and fifth objectives. On the first objective we were lined up alongside the British and part of the State Department. On the second we were aligned with the Brussels treaty powers (Britain, France, and the Benelux countries). On the third we were toward the end of the negotiations isolated, but eventually, successful.

One of the most revealing aspects of the early discussions of the possibility of a North Atlantic Treaty was that a number of the most intelligent and influential Americans who were involved in these discussions were skeptical about the necessity of a treaty. Their initial preference was for a unilateral declaration by the United States that the United States would consider an attack upon any free Western European country as an attack on itself. The Monroe Doctrine would be extended to Western Europe. Canada, it was suggested, might make a similar unilateral declaration. One American opposed to the idea of an alliance established by a treaty was George Kennan, the head of the State Department policy planning staff. The farthest he was prepared to go, and that with reluctance because he saw "no real neces-

sity" for it, was that the United States, "in partnership with Canada, if Canada were willing," would give countries which joined the Brussels Treaty a unilateral political and military guarantee plus a "readiness" to extend to these countries "whatever was necessary in the way of assistance in military supplies, forces, and joint strategic planning."[7]

In the first tripartite phase of the discussions the pro-treaty group in the State Department won a victory over the anti-treaty group. But immediately after the first phase was over, the anti-treaty group started pressing their views. The result was that on April 12, only eleven days after the end of the first phase, Pearson was seriously concerned at

> the possibility that the United States Government might decide that no pact of any kind is necessary and that the situation can be met by a unilateral guarantee of assistance by the President...to a selected group of states (in Western Europe)...given after Congressional approval....

Pearson asked me to prepare a memorandum setting forth our reasons for believing that a treaty was preferable to a unilateral guarantee. The memorandum was revised by Wrong and Pearson and became the brief for our discussions with the United States. Later we incorporated most of the memorandum along with additional arguments in letters of instruction to our ambassadors in Paris, Brussels, and The Hague. St. Laurent incorporated parts of the first draft of the memorandum in his speech in the House of Commons on April 29.

Kennan came to Ottawa at the beginning of June where, after a dinner given by the United States ambassador, Pearson, Claxton, John W. Pickersgill, Special

Assistant to the Prime Minister, and others launched at him the reasoning set forth in the memorandum. The main argument ran as follows. Because a treaty would have to be ratified by the Senate, it would commit the United States much more firmly. It would embody the element of mutual assistance. Why should the United States and Canada come to the assistance of European countries if those countries were not willing to accept similar obligations to us? A unilateral guarantee gave unnecessary prominence to the dependence of the European states and seemed to underline the satellite character of their relationship to the United States. As such, it might unnecessarily offend their pride. Moreover, the United States and Canada needed the assistance of the Western European democracies just as they needed ours. A Russian conquest of Western Europe would mean for us war and war on most unfavourable terms. A unilateral guarantee smelled of charity (in the worst sense of the word); the Western European democracies were not beggars asking for our charity, but were potential allies whose assistance we needed in order to be able to defend ourselves. A pact would be an important demonstration that security arrangements could be worked out under the Charter, in this case under Article 51. Eventually other arrangements could be negotiated for other areas until all free countries might be brought in. Most important of all, a unilateral guarantee would be nothing more than a pledge of military assistance.

Pickersgill added two specifically Canadian arguments. In the last two world wars Canada had gone to war two years before the United States; a treaty commitment by the United States would be more likely than a presidential declaration to lessen the danger that this would happen again. Second, Canada and a number of other North Atlantic countries would find it politically easier to grant defence facilities to a North Atlantic alliance than to the United States.

In a telegram of June 3 to Hume Wrong, I reported that Kennan had said that he was impatient with the pressure from the United Kingdom and the Western European states to make a formal treaty commitment. Those states did not seem to realize that if the United States gave this guarantee it would be doing something which would be in the interests of Western Europe but not necessarily in the interests of the United States itself, since it could at any time make a deal with the Soviet Union.

We naturally took him up on this and he withdrew from this exposed position. However it did give me a feeling that if you scratch almost any American long enough, you will find an isolationist. They suffer, and you can hardly blame them, from a homesickness for isolation.

When we debated with Kennan in Ottawa, we did not know that on May 24, a week before he came to Ottawa, Kennan had informed Marshall, the Secretary of State, that St. Laurent's speech of April 29 in the House of Commons had added "a new and important element" to the problem and that, in the light of this speech and of arguments advanced by Ernest Bevin in a confidential message of May 14, "we must be very careful not to place ourselves in the position of being the obstacle to further progress toward the political union of the western democracies."[8]

By the time the second phase of the negotiations opened in Washington on July 6, the United States administration was pretty well convinced of the advantages of a treaty over a unilateral guarantee, though it was still not firmly committed.

The central provision in the North Atlantic Treaty is the provision on armed attack contained in Article 5. This provision constituted a revolution in United States foreign policy and in Canadian foreign policy. Up to then, each of us had refused in time of peace to make a military alliance with any country. Article 5 of the Treaty made the North Atlantic Treaty a military alliance.

If Canada's first objective, then, was securing a treaty, the second objective was that the guarantee article in the treaty should be a strong one. In order to reduce the possibility of opposition in the Senate, the United States wanted a guarantee article as close as possible to that in the Rio treaty which the Senate had already approved.[9] The United States therefore suggested the following text:

> An armed attack by any state against a Party shall be considered as an attack against all the Parties and, consequently, each Party undertakes to assist in meeting the attack in the exercise of the inherent right of individual or collective self-defence recognized by Article 51 of the Charter.

The European representatives wanted a text as close as possible to that in the Brussels treaty and suggested:

> If any Party should be the object of an armed attack in the area covered by the Treaty, the other Parties will, in accordance with the provisions of Article 51 of the Charter, afford the Party so attacked all the military and other aid and assistance in their power.

The deadlock remained even at the end of the second phase of discussions on September 10. The United States continued to press the Rio formula; the Brussels treaty powers still preferred the Brussels formula; and Canada wanted a compromise it had put forward in March.

On December 24, 1948, four weeks before Acheson became Secretary of State, the ambassador's group in Washington had tentatively agreed to a compromise which represented a substantial weakening of the Brussels treaty formula. After using the Rio treaty language of an attack on one being an attack on all, the parties to the treaty would undertake to

> assist the party or parties so attacked by taking forthwith such military or other action, individually or in concert with the other parties, as may be necessary to restore and assure the security of the North Atlantic area.

On February 18, Acheson persuaded the Senate Foreign Relations Committee to accept this draft of the guarantee article with one change. The words "as it deems necessary, including the use of armed force" were substituted for the words "such military or other action...as may be necessary." Article 5 as agreed to thus read:

> The Parties agree that an armed attack against one or more of them in Europe or North America shall be considered an attack against them all; and consequently they agree that, if such an armed attack occurs, each of them, in exercise of the right of individual or collective self-defense recognzied by Article 51 of the Charter of the United Nations, will assist the Party or Parties so attacked by taking forthwith individually and in concert with the other Parties, such action as it deems necessary, including the use of armed force, to restore and maintain the security of the North Atlantic area.

On balance the pledge in the North Atlantic treaty was somewhat stronger than the pledge in the Rio treaty. After eleven months of negotiation, Canada, the British, and the Western Europeans had won a partial victory. How far Canada contributed to that victory and, in particular, how far

Ottawa helped Acheson to resist more erosion of the pledge than that which took place, is impossible to say.

The third Canadian aim was to try to ensure that the alliance emphasized non-military cooperation. We were trying in 1948 to do something in a formal treaty to cover not just the unlikely event of an open armed attack by the Russians, but also the more likely event of indirect aggression. We did it in two ways—by Article 2 and by Article 4. These articles set forth three distinct but related undertakings, dealing with democracy, economic collaboration, and consultation.

Each of the allies undertook in Article 2 to

> contribute toward the further development of peaceful and friendly international relations by strengthening their free institutions (and) by bringing about a better understanding of the principles upon which those institutions are founded.

These principles were defined in the preamble as "democracy, individual liberty and the rule of law." The second non-military undertaking, also set forth in article 2, was to "contribute to the further development of peaceful and friendly international relations...by promoting conditions of stability and well-being," to "seek to eliminate conflicts in their international economic policies," and to "encourage economic collaboration between any or all of them." The preamble made clear that the reference to conditions of stability and well-being was to conditions "in the North Atlantic area."

The purpose of Article 2 was to strengthen the ability and will of the West to resist Russian pressure—Russian indirect aggression. The purpose of Article 4 was to provide a basis for meeting Russian threats with counter-threats. In Article 4 the member states promised to consult together whenever any one of them considered that its territorial integrity, political independence, or security was threatened. This required all the allies, at the request of any one of them, to consult together on any threat which an ally perceived in any part of the world to its territorial integrity, political independence, or security. The threat might arise from indirect aggression by the Soviet Union or any other country anywhere in the world, or unwise action by the United States or any other member anywhere in the world.

From the earliest informal preliminary discussions of the possibility of a North Atlantic Treaty, Mr. Pearson pressed for inclusion in the Treaty of provisions similar to those which the British Government had succeeded in having included in the Western Union Treaty—and for the same reasons. When I prepared for him our first draft of the preamble and of Article 2 of the North Atlantic Treaty, I borrowed the language from the Brussels Tready. The language in the final text of the North Atlantic Treaty reflects the language of the Brussels Treaty.

Article 2 is in the North Atlantic Treaty because we and our friends believed that Stalin's principal allies in the Western World were fear that Soviet communism was dynamic and Western liberalism passive, apathy about our historic beliefs, and doubts that the West had enough vigour in it to provide a dynamic counter-attraction to Russian totalitarianism.

We believed that the Western World would be less likely to be overwhelmed by Russia if it strengthened its free institutions and if its peoples understood better the principles upon which those free institutions were founded. We believed that the Western World would be less likely to be overwhelmed if its governments cooperated in promoting conditions of economic sta-

bility and well-being. We also believed that
if the members of the North Atlantic alliance were constantly quarrelling over such
matters as tariff and non-tariff barriers to
trade, competitive currency devaluations,
aviation rights, and access to raw materials,
they would be less likely to be willing and
able to cooperate in political and security
matters to the extent necessary to make
the military guarantees credible. We therefore considered that pledges of military co-
operation should be accompanied by pledges
of economic cooperation.

Mackenzie King, at the outset of discussions on the treaty, thought that a commitment there to reduce trade restrictions
might assist Canada in the top secret discussions then also being conducted with
Washington on the possibility of a bilateral
free trade agreement. In his diary King
states that on March 22, 1948, the day the
first phase of the NATO treaty discussions
opened, he told some of the Cabinet ministers and officials involved that he felt trade
proposals might be made to fit, as it were,
into the larger Atlantic Pact. That if, for
example, the Atlantic Security Pact were
agreed upon and were brought before
Parliament and passed as it certainly would
be, we might immediately follow thereafter
with a trade agreement as being something
which still helped to further the object of
the Pact, namely the removal of restrictions
to trade within the area arranged by the
Pact.[10] King thus assumed that the North
Atlantic treaty would contain an undertaking by the parties to remove restrictions
to trade between them.

Our belief that a North Atlantic treaty
which contained a strong Article 2 would
start a movement towards the political and
economic unification of the North Atlantic
community is the one which has properly
received the most attention in discussions
of the Canadian approach to the treaty.

What has received insufficient emphasis
was our belief that the farther the North
Atlantic Community moved towards political and economic unification, the more protection it would give Canada from the
power of the United States. We believed
that the more developed the constitutional
structure of the Community became, the
more the power of the United States would
be restrained by the influences of its allies,
especially Britain and France. The alliance
would provide for Canada a countervailing
force against the United States; the alliance
would call in Britain and Western Europe
to restore the balance in North America.
As Pearson put it in his memoirs: "[I]n one
form or another, for Canada, there was always security in numbers. We did not want
to be alone with our close friend and neighbour."[11]

There was another motive for Canadian
insistence on Article 2, which was not mentioned in public speeches by St. Laurent
and Pearson, but which was pressed hard
in the private discussions in February 1949
between Wrong and Acheson, and between
St. Laurent and Truman. This motive was
that the treaty would secure much more
public support in Canada if it were more
than a military alliance. From my knowledge of St. Laurent and Pearson I think it
is highly likely that this consideration did
not even occur to them during the first six
months or so of the discussions on the
treaty. During those six months they constantly emphasized, in all their public
speeches, the importance of these non-military aspects because they believed in them
for reasons not connected with the political necessity of getting public support in
Canada for the treaty. They gradually came
to realize that their emphasis on the non-
military aspects was one of the reasons for
the widespread support for the treaty in
Canada. This enabled St. Laurent, in his

talks with Truman in February 1949, when all other arguments had failed, to bring forward an argument which was appropriate for one practical politician to put to another, the argument that the realities of domestic party politics in Canada made it essential for him to have substantial non-military provisions in the treaty.

The draft of Article 2 agreed to on December 24 was a compromise between the Brussels treaty powers, which did not want an article on economic, social, and cultural cooperation, and the United States and Canada, which wanted a strong article. The compromise was:

Article 2 (General Welfare). The parties will encourage co-operative efforts between any or all of them to promote the general welfare through collaboration in the cultural, economic and social fields. Such efforts shall, to the greatest possible extent, be undertaken through and assist the work of existing international organizations.

Dean Acheson took office as Secretary of State on January 20, 1949. He was not able to look at the papers on the North Atlantic treaty discussiosn until January 29. Early in February he informed the negotiating group in Washington that the United States was opposed to any Article 2. In reporting this Wrong said that he had learned that Acheson did not like Article 2 because it meant "next to nothing," and that Senators Vandenberg and Connally, whom Acheson had consulted, might wish to have it deleted.

Faced with the possibility of complete defeat we took three steps to strengthen our position. On February 8, at a meeting of the ambassadors' group in Washington, Wrong, on Pearson's instructions, formally proposed amendments to strengthen the December draft. Second, St. Laurent on his visit to Washington on February 12, put to

Truman the pratical domestic political Canadian arguments for Article 2. He said that it was most important to him that the treaty should not be a military alliance only, but should hold out the prospect of close economic and social collaboration between the parties. An article to this effect would be of the greatest value to him politically in securing the full acceptance of the treaty by the Canadian people. Third, Norman Robertson of London, and the Canadian ambassadors in Paris, Brussels, and the Hague, were instructed to try to persuade the government to which they were accredited to support our position on Article 2. The result was that the Consulative Council of the Brussels treaty powers at its meeting on February 23, unanimously agreed to support the Canadian draft of Article 2. After more discussions with the Americans, and pressure from supportive State Department officials, Acheson finally agreed to the following text (in the treaty):

The Parties will contribute toward the further development of peaceful and friendly international relations by strengthening their free institutions, by bringing about a better understanding of the principles upon which these institutions are founded, and by promoting conditions of stability and well-being. They will seek to eliminate conflict in their international economic policies and will encourage economic collaboration between any or all of them.

Acheson has claimed that he "defused" the Canadian draft of Article 2.[12] A comparison of the two texts demonstrates that he was mistaken. Acheson did not defuse the Canadian draft of Article 2; by the vigour of his opposition he helped to infuse new life into it.

It is clear that without Canada there would have been no Article 2 in the North

Atlantic treaty. Where we failed was that we were not able to put into the Treaty additional provisions which might have sped up the growth of a sense of North Atlantic community, and we did not, in the years following the signing of the Treaty, make sufficient use of the fact that the members of the Alliance had entered into solemn treaty obligations embodied in Article 2.

The coming into force of the treaty did not result in any substantial increase in the defence expenditures of the allies. In the United States, in the spring of 1950, the highest figure suggested for the defence budget was $14 billion. In the year ending March, 1950, Canada's expenditures on defence were $385 million. The creation of the North Atlantic treaty did not result in Canada sending armed forces to Western Europe, nor did it result in the creation of a military structure for the alliance. Rather, the Korean war precipitated these developments. This was because the North Atlantic countries believed that North Korea would not have attacked South Korea without at least the blessing of the Soviet Union, and that Stalin must have realized how shocked the West would be by this first attempt to change by force of arms the *de facto* boundaries between them. The North Atlantic countries, therefore, concluded that the attack on South Korea demonstrated a dangerous willingness on the part of the Soviet Union to risk a general war. The willingness of the Soviet Union to run such risks would, it was thought, be diminished if the Western powers were to rearm; rearmament would be a deterrent. The Korean war, therefore, led to vast rearmament in the North Atlantic countries. Their total defence expenditures increased from $20 billion in 1950 to $64 billion in 1953. Canada's outlays increased from $30 million a month in June 1950 to $150 million a month in June 1952. The Korean war also led to

United States insistence on the admission of Greece and Turkey to the alliance, on the rearmament of Western Germany and its inclusion in the alliance, on the creation of a military structure for the alliance and the appointment of a supreme commander; in fact on the metamorphosis of the North Atlantic alliance into the North Atlantic Treaty Organization. The Korean war led to what Bohlen in his memoirs calls "the militarization of NATO," to what Pearson in July 1951 called "the growing NATO concentration on the military aspects of the alliance."[13] Without these developments, there might have been a world war in the 1950s. With these developments, the chances of the North Atlantic alliance providing a starting point for the economic and political unification of the North Atlantic community became remote.

The purpose of the military clauses was deterrence, not war; the purpose of the military build-up was negotiation, not a standstill. As Dean Acheson put it at the time; "We arm to parley."

Here I will hazard a generalization about the subsequent development of the North Atlantic Alliance. We armed sufficiently. We did not parley sufficiently with the Russians. We didn't even parley sufficiently among ourselves as a first step to parleying with the Russians.

The advocates in the United States of a multilateral treaty of alliance won the argument over those who favoured a unilateral declaration; but they did not wholly convert some of the most influential of the sceptics in Washington. Some of these people never really liked, or even understood, the very idea of an alliance. They weren't very anxious to learn the complex and subtle art of how the leader of an alliance conducts its relations with the other members of the alliance. They hankered after unilateral declarations, unilateral decision-making, unilateral actions. If they were out of step with all their allies, they were apt to believe that it was their allies who were out of step with them. In any alliance where the leader has a great preponderance of power, this strain of thinking is likely to be strong among those who bear part of the Atlantean burden of responsibility which falls on the shoulders of the leader of the alliance. My impression, however, is that this strain of thinking has, from the beginning, been particulary strong in Washington, and that its existence has helped to make the operation of the North Atlantic Alliance even more difficult than it otherwise would have been.

NOTES

1. Charles E. Bohlen, *Witness to History*, New York, 1973, p. 267.

2. Lester B. Pearson, *Mike: The Memoirs of the Rt. Hon. Lester B. Pearson*, Vol. II, Toronto, University of Toronto Press, p. 42.

3. J. W. Pickersgill and D. F. Foster, *The Mackenzie King Record*, Vol. IV, 1947-48, Toronto, 1970, p. 165.

4. Secrecy enabled the United States government to pretend to Congress that the second phase grew out of the Vandenberg resolution, adopted by the Senate on 11 June, whereas in fact the State Department was securing by that resolution *ex post facto* legitimation of the results of the first phase of the discussions. Secrecy also enabled Britain, Canada, and the United States to pretend to France and the Benelux countries that they had participated in the negotiations from the outset. As part of this pretence, the "heads of agreement" of 1 April were drafted in the form of tentative proposals by the United States government. On balance, I feel that secrecy aided the negotiations. Publicity about disputes between the negotiators might have helped produce a better treaty; it probably, however, would have resulted in no treaty.

5. This phase resulted in an agreed statement dated September 9 "on the nature of the problems discussed and the steps which might be practicable to meet them"; and an annex outlining possible provisions for inclusion in a North Atlantic Security Pact.

6. The Presidential elections delayed the start of this phase. Until the treaty was almost in final form, the participating governments insisted that no formal negotiations were taking place.

7. George F. Kennan, *Memoirs, 1925-50*, Boston, Little Brown, 1967, pp. 401-3 and pp. 406-7.

8. *Foreign Relations of the United States*, 1948, Vol. III, p. 128.

9. The 1947 "Rio Treaty", or more formally, the Inter-American Treaty of Reciprocal Assistance, established the mutual defence alliance of the US and the Latin American states. Concerning the North Atlantic treaty, from April 1948 the State Department was constantly sounding out Senatorial opinion, especially through Senators Vandenberg and Connally. Dean Acheson, in February and March 1949, conducted two sets of formal negotiations, one with governments and the other with the Senate Foreign Relations Committee. The State Department was justifiably concerned with Senate opinion, but, in my view, made more concessions than were necessary to ensure Senate ratification.

10. Pickersgill and Foster, *op cit.*, p. 264.

11. Pearson, *Memoirs*, Vol. II, *op cit.*, pp. 32-33.

12. Dean Acheson, *Present at the Creation*, New York, 1969, p. 277.

13. Bohlen, *op cit.*, p. 304 and Pearson, *op cit.*, p. 70.

SUGGESTED READINGS

Eayrs, James, *Canada in World Affairs, 1955-1956*, Toronto: Oxford University Press, 1959, pp. 52-74.

Eayrs, James, *In Defence of Canada, Volume 4, Growing Up Allied*, Toronto: University of Toronto Press, 1980.

Harrison, W.E.C., *Canada in World Affairs, 1949-1950*, Toronto: Oxford University Press, 1959.

Page, Don and Don Munton, "Canadian Images of the Cold War, 1946- 47." *International Journal*, 32, 1977, pp. 577-604.

Pearson, Lester B., *Mike: the Memoirs of the Rt. Hon. Lester B. Pearson*, Volume 2, 1948-1957, Toronto: University of Toronto Press, 1973, pp. 66-106.

Reid, Escott, "Canada and the North Atlantic Alliance," *Behind the Headlines*, Vol. 28, No. 3, 1969, pp. 13-16.

Reid, Escott, *Time of Fear and Hope: The Making of the North Atlantic Treaty, 1947-1948*, Toronto: McClelland and Stewart, 1977.

section 2

IMPLEMENTING
INTERNATIONALISM

If the mid and late 1940s were dominated by the creation of the institutions of the postwar order, Canadian policy in the 1950s and early 1960s was, to a considerable extent, dominated by the implementation of many of the ideas behind this order. The themes were there—"internationalism," support for effective international action on world problems, and "middlepowermanship"; but their pursuit had to be balanced with alliance ties and traditional friendships. The realities of world politics necessitated pragmatism in the actions taken.

One of the first tests of the principle of collective security, the basic principle underlying both the UN and the old League of Nations, came when war broke out in divided Korea in 1950. Denis Stairs's analysis of the Canadian response to this development in distant Asia shows well how Canadian officials tried to apply many of the ideas they now held dear. Chief among these were the importance of the UN playing a major role in resolving the conflict but also the need for western unity, even while allies like Canada worked together to constrain the tendency of the United States to take unilateral actions, to depend overly on the use of military force, and to accomplish American rather than collective objectives.

The Suez crisis, which broke out in 1956, provided Canada with its best opportunity in the postwar period to apply diplomatic skills and secure a strong and effective UN involvement in peaceful dispute resolution. As the account by Robert Reford suggests, the popular notion of Canada as a mediating middle power really grew out of the successful efforts of Canada's Secretary of State for External Affairs, Lester B. Pearson, to design and apply the mechanism of an international peacekeeping force. This mediatory and peacekeeping tradition, sanctified by the award of a Nobel Peace Prize to Pearson, depended for its success on both Canada's wide array of international connections, and its close association with American interests.

One of the most difficult international assignments ever accepted by Canada was membership on the international supervisory commissions for Laos, Cambodia and, in particular, Vietnam. Originally asked to serve on these bodies as a result of the 1954 Geneva Conference on Indochina, which negotiated a settlement to the long-standing Indochina war fought against French colonial power, Canada continued its participation through the breakdown in the Geneva process during the late 1950s and then through the buildup of American forces during the early 1960s. This shift to US involvement naturally brought for Canada a new set of difficulties to the "peace" supervision task and to Canadian foreign policy in general. Increasing Canadian concerns about the escalation of the war under US President Lyndon Johnson led to a rare public disagreement with the Americans in 1965 when Pearson, now prime minister, spoke out against continued US bombing of North Vietnam and advocated a negotiated settlement. John English's discussion of this case captures well the dilemmas for Canada concerning a neighbour and ally engaged in a unpopular and vicious conflict.

The Cold War was at its height during the 1950s and early 1960s, and for Canada it importantly defined its approach to regional conflicts such as those in the Middle East or Asia. While the Korean and Indochina Wars were widely interpreted in western countries as struggles with international communism, the focus of the period was more on security in Europe. The dominant threat was that of an apparently aggressive Soviet Union; the dominant issues were those of defence and alliances. The ultimate Cold War crisis, and the turning point in the Cold War, the point at which it is possible to perceive the emergence of some elements of the later period of détente, was the Cuban missile crisis. But for Canada the decision by Soviet leader Nikita Khrushchev to deploy ballistic missiles in Cuba did more than create a superpower confrontation. Situated so close to the United States, being so much affected by both its internal moods and external actions, and having an extensive set of formal institutional links in matters of continental defence, especially the 1958 North American Air Defence Command (NORAD), meant that this crisis assumed a major Canada-US dimension. While

Canada was suddenly on the front lines of an east-west conflict, closer and more involved than any other US NATO ally, its geographic and political position led to a distinctly different confrontation of sorts with Washington. As shown in the case study in this section, authored by Jocelyn Ghent-Mallet and Don Munton, what emerged was a crisis that for America's small, and often taken-for-granted, northern neighbour was as much a crisis in Canadian-American defence cooperation as in east-west relations. They take into account new information and insights into the crisis and argue for a new evaluation of Canadian policies and leaders.

Another major defence-related issue of this period was the agonizing 1963 decision to acquire nuclear weapons for the Canadian armed forces and to deploy other US nuclear weapons on Canadian soil. Some of these weapons were intended for the defence of North America; the rest were a part of Canada's other international commitment in the security field, its role in a new NATO nuclear-reliant defence posture in Europe. As is clear here, Canadian "internationalism" never meant an exclusive concern with the United Nations and collective security, and certainly never implied any sort of nonalignment. Reconciling concerns about arms control and Canada's image with the need to fulfill alliance commitments, however, did not prove easy.

There are clear links between the two security cases. Responsibility for their resolution resided not with the Liberal government architects of Canada's postwar foreign policy, but with the Progressive Conservative Government of John Diefenbaker that had come to power in 1957. The decision to cancel the AVRO Arrow left Canada without a modern interceptor for the defence of North America, and required the Diefenbaker government to acquire a replacement aircraft from the United States. The replacement eventually announced, the CF-101 (Voodoo), was part of a package of weapons systems adopted by Canada during the late 1950s, all of which required nuclear weapons for maximum effectiveness. And the Cuban missile crisis, which occurred at the point when these systems had not yet been armed with their nuclear warheads and were therefore quite useless. The crisis thus greatly increased pressure on the Diefenbaker government to decide whether or not to accept the nuclear warheads, as the chapter on this case by Jocelyn Ghent-Mallet and Don Munton shows.

But there is also a link across these cases in more abstract terms. In each, Canadian officials can be seen to be struggling with the definition and limits of an active international involvement, with the trade-offs between different dimensions of "internationalism," and with the dilemmas of maintaining influence in the international system. One of the major arguments against acceptance of nuclear weapons, voiced by Howard Green, Diefenbaker's Secretary of State for External Affairs during the early 1960s, was that joining the nuclear club would greatly undermine Canada's campaign in the UN for disarmament negotiations.

Despite the primacy of defence matters during this period, the Canadian diplomatic agenda also included issues that had nothing to do with security, at least with security as conventionally defined in military terms. Many of these, especially the economic and resource issues, had, not surprisingly, a strong Canada-US transborder element. One of the most significant was the Columbia River Treaty. While NORAD reflected the integrated nature of North American defence, the Columbia project represented joint development of water resources and electricity production. Neil Swainson's treatment of this complex issue, a chapter written especially for this volume, sorts out the often torturous planning and negotiation process and highlights a new element in Canadian foreign policy— the key role that can be played by the provinces. The Columbia case also foreshadows the emergence in the late 1960s of a wide range of non-military security-related international issues—one of the themes of the cases in the next section of this volume.

c h a p t e r 4

CONTAINING COMMUNISM IN KOREA, 1950-53

Denis Stairs

C anadian security policies are prone to quick births and slow deaths. Born in times of urgent peril and crisis, when there are premiums on haste, they die in periods of tranquillity, the victims of indifference, neglect and the infirmities of old age. In their middle years, they are sustained as much by inertia as by purpose— creatures partly of genuine perceptions of external menace, but partly too of static habits of decision-making and unchallenged habits of mind.

The most recent crisis to generate spurts of major innovation in Canada's external affairs was not, as some are wont to suppose, the coming to power of Pierre Elliott Trudeau as Prime Minister in 1968, or even the appointment in 1963 of Paul Hellyer as Minister of National Defence. Nor was it the Cuban missile crisis of 1962; nor any of the peacekeeping episodes of the late 1950s and early 1960s. It was instead the outbreak of the Korean War, which in Ottawa and other capitals in the West served to confirm and entrench, where it did not actually create, alarming perceptions of the Soviet Union and its "satellites" as aggressively hostile powers, ominous and threatening, not only politically but militarily as well. The members of the North Atlantic pact, hitherto an alliance in support more of morale than of military capa-

bilities, looked accordingly to the expansion of their armies, and Canada's was among them.

In the winter of 1950-51, the Federal Government embarked upon a program of military expenditures that was to cost $5 billion over three years. On its completion, the Canadian defence establishment had assumed dimensions that it was to maintain without major change for nearly two decades. This, taken together with the range and intensity of the policy community's rapidly-expanding linkages with other members of the alliance (notably the United States) and the strength and persistence of its perceptions of hostile Soviet intent, set parameters to the conduct of Canada's external relations which have begun only recently to display the symptoms of senility, weakening and giving way under the pressure of changing conditions abroad.

Of these latter transformations, the current advances in negotiations between the governments of North and South Korea are both a symbol and a part. But they are a reminder, too, of the only occasion since 1945 on which Canadian armed forces have been despatched abroad for the explicit purpose of combat.[1] Canada's role in the diplomacy of the Korean War may thus warrant brief review.

 Denis Stairs, "Canada and the Korean War: The Boundaries of Diplomacy," from *International Perspectives*, (Nov./Dec. 1972).

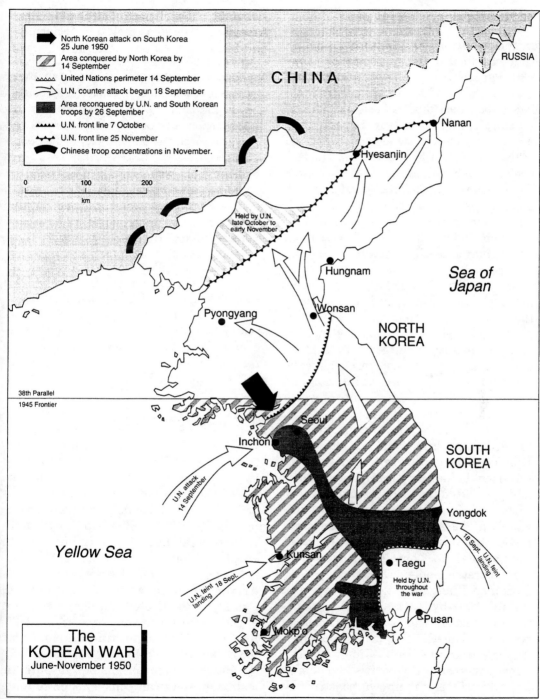

Legend:

- North Korean attack on South Korea 25 June 1950
- Area conquered by North Korea by 14 September
- United Nations perimeter 14 September
- U.N. counter attack begun 18 September
- Area reconquered by U.N. and South Korean troops by 26 September
- U.N. front line 7 October
- U.N. front line 25 November
- Chinese troop concentrations in November.

0   100   200
km

CHINA

RUSSIA

Nanan

Hyesanjin

Held by U.N. late October to early November

Hungnam

Sea of Japan

Wonsan

Pyongyang

NORTH KOREA

38th Parallel

1945 Frontier

Seoul

Inchon

SOUTH KOREA

U.N. attack 14 September

Yongdok

Yellow Sea

Kunsan

Taegu

18 Sept. U.N. feint landing

U.N. feint 18 Sept. landing

Held by U.N. throughout the war

Pusan

Mokp'o

The
KOREAN WAR
June-November 1950

Source: Adapted from M. Gilbert, *Recent History Atlas: 1870 to the Present Day*, London, Weidenfeld and Nicolson, 1966.

Hardening of Division

In the spring of 1950, the Korean peninsula was divided into two parts along the 38th Parallel, a politically convenient but economically and topographically meaningless boundary that had been established as the demarcation line between the American and Soviet zones of occupation at the end of the war with Japan. The failure of the occupation authorities to agree on procedures for the creation of a unified and independent Korean state, and the differences in their respective policies of occupation, had resulted (as in Germany) in a hardening of the division between the two sectors.

In the autumn of 1947 the Americans, as a last resort, had raised the matter in the United Nations General Assembly, and at their request a Temporary Commission on Korea had been charged with the task of supervising an election throughout the peninsula as a prelude to unification and independence. The Commission, of which Canada was a member, was denied effective access to the Soviet zone and, much to the disgust of Prime Minister Mackenzie King (whose opposition to Canada's involvement in the Commission's proceedings had generated for a time a major crisis within the Canadian Cabinet), it had ultimately decided to accede to an American proposal that it proceed with elections in the South alone. There duly emerged an administration under the leadership of Dr. Syngman Rhee, and it was followed in August 1948 by the transfer of governmental functions from the American occupation authorities to what was now described as the "Republic of Korea." Shortly thereafter the Soviets had administered elections of their own, constructing in the area north of the 38th Parallel a "People's Democratic Republic." In December the United Nations General Assembly passed a resolution declaring:

> that there has been established a lawful government (the Government of the Republic of Korea), having effective control and jurisdiction over that part of Korea where the Temporary Commission was able to observe and consult and in which the great majority of the people of all Korea reside; that this Government is based on elections which were a valid expression of the free will of the electorate of that part of Korea and which were observed by the Temporary Commission; and that this is the only such Government in Korea.

The resolution also created a new United Nations Commission on Korea, of which Canada was not this time a member. It was directed to continue the work of its predecessor by observing the withdrawal of occupation forces and by generally facilitating the process of political transition and eventual (it was hoped) unification.

Hostile Relations

During the ensuing months, relations between the two Korean regimes, supported by their respective great-power patrons, were hostile and uneasy, with indications on both sides of acquisitive intent. In the first half of 1950, military and para-military skirmishes of ambiguous origin erupted along the border areas with such frequency that when John W. Holmes, the Acting Permanent Representative of Canada to the United Nations, first heard of the North Korean invasion on June 25, he assumed that nothing unusual was afoot.

Revisionist historians now dispute the claims of American policymakers to innocence in the events leading up to the North Korean attack, assigning them at least partial responsibility for the developing conditions of conflict. In some of the more extreme versions they are accused of connivance and conspiracy too. Of these two classes of argument, the first is far more convincing than the second, but in either event they have little bearing on the Canadian case. For whatever one believes of Washington, there can be little doubt that in Ottawa the outbreak of major hostilities in Korea came as a complete surprise.

So did the American response. Policymakers in Washington had been making it clear for some time that they considered the Korean (and Formosan) theatres to be outside their strategic defence perimeter in the Pacific and, as recently as February 1950, General Douglas MacArthur had advised the Canadian Secretary of State for External Affairs during a visit to Tokyo that Korea was strategically unimportant to the United States, and therefore did not fall within the American protective umbrella. In consequence, External Affairs Minister Lester Pearson assumed that the U.S. Government would respond with little more than verbal protests, a view which was shared by John Holmes in New York and by Hume Wrong, the Canadian Ambassador in Washington.

Soviets Absent

In the absence from the Security Council of the Soviet Union (which since January had been boycotting the proceedings on the matter of Chinese representation), the United States secured the passage of a resolution on the afternoon of Sunday, June 25, calling for an immediate cessation of hostilities and the withdrawal of North Korean forces. The resolution also requested reports on developments in the theatre from the United Nations Commission on Korea, and asked "all members to render every assistance to the United Nations in the execution of this resolution and to refrain from giving assistance to the North Korean authorities." This initiative received Mr. Pearson's support in the House of Commons on June 26, when he expressed the hope "that as a result of the intervention of the United Nations some effective action may be possible to restore peace." But in an off-the-record press conference some hours later, he told reporters that he did not anticipate that military measures would be taken by either the Americans alone or the United Nations as a whole.

As early as Sunday evening, however, President Truman had authorized General MacArthur to evacuate American nationals from Korea, under the protection south of the Parallel, if necessary, of the United States Air Force. He was authorized also to offer logistical support to the South Korean forces, and to assume operational command of the Seventh Fleet. Late the following day he was ordered in addition to give combat air and naval support to the South Koreans in Republic of Korea territory, and to despatch the Seventh Fleet to patrol the Formosa Strait. These measures were to be made legitimate in the name of the United Nations, from which an authorizing resolution would be pursued at a meeting of the Security Council scheduled for Tuesday afternoon.

Throughout the early phase of the war, the principal concern of the Canadian authorities was that the American response (upon which depended the postures of all the other Western allies, Canada included) be conducted under United Nations auspices. This was partly because it was felt that the strength of the organization as an agent for the maintenance of collective security depended on its being used, or at least on its being *seen* to be used, as the primary vehicle for countering aggression. If actions in constraint of "aggressor" powers were taken unilaterally, such promise as the United Nations still held out for international methods of security enforcement would be lost. More immediately, however, it was also because the Canadians realized that, if the Americans acted unilaterally, there would be little opportunity for constraining their behaviour, whereas if they responded through the United Nations, their policies would be exposed (within limits) to inhibiting multilateral influences, of which Canada's was one.

This was regarded as particularly important in the Korean context because it was possible, in the absence of such constraints, that the Americans, by a mixture of distorted perceptions of self-interest and inflexibly ideological conceptions of their opponents, would be drawn into a major Asian war, thereby involving the Soviet Union and/or the Communist Chinese. This would be a disaster in itself. In addition, it would mean that American attentions and resources would be diverted away from Western Europe, which in the Canadian view—as that of the other Western allies— was a far more vital theatre.

When, on Tuesday morning, Mr. Pearson was informed by the U.S. Ambassador of the President's decisions, therefore, he telephoned Hume Wrong in Washington to stress the importance of urging the Americans to bring their action under United Nations auspices, and to withhold public announcements of their initiative until the Security Council's authorization had actually been obtained. When Mr. Wrong raised the matter at a late morning meeting of State Department officials with the Washington ambassadors of the NATO powers, however, he was advised that the American view was that the June 25 resolution had provided them with all the authority required. On the apparent assumption that the Soviet Union would continue to boycott the Security Council, they believed in any case that the matter of timing was not serious since their informal discussions with other Council members had revealed that their proposal for a more explicit resolution would pass that afternoon without great difficulty—as indeed it did. In it, the Council recommended "that the members of the United Nations furnish such assistance to the Republic of Korea as may be necessary to repel the armed attack and to restore international peace and security in the area concerned." Later in the week, on June 30, President Truman ordered General MacArthur to impose a naval blockade on the Korean coast and to make full use of the ground forces under his command in responding to the North Korean assault.

Had the Americans decided to intervene against the North Koreans entirely without the blessing of the United Nations (as the State Department's George Kennan would have liked them to do), Canadians would have had as little to do with the war in Korea as they had subsequently had to do with the war in Vietnam—perhaps less, given that Canada was not a member of the UN Commission on Korea whereas it was a member of the International Control Commission. With the passage of the resolutions of June 25 and 27, however, the Canadian Government acquired on the one hand a battery of pressures, from constituents at home and abroad alike, to contribute to the conduct of the hostilities themselves (an outcome of which the Americans heartily approved), and on the other a licence to intervene in the making of decisions (a consequence with which the Americans were naturally displeased).

Restricted Involvement

To the extent that payment of dues buys access to the club, the second of these acquisitions was contingent on the first and, like buyers in every market, the Canadians sought to maximize their marginal utilities. Their military expenditures came, therefore, in dribs and drabs, constrained in part by the poverty of their resources (early in July the Director of Military Operations and Plans was to advise the Minister of National Defence that, if all the units of the Active Force Brigade Group were brought up to strength and allowed to concentrate on training, they would be reasonably efficient after a period of six months), in part by the fear—soon dispelled—that such dabblings in overseas wars would not go down well in Quebec, in part by a reluctance to divert Canada's meagre defences away from the North Atlantic area, and in part by the simple sluggishness of the mechanics of collective military effort.

The first instalment, as it happened, came easily. Three Canadian destroyers sailed for the Western Pacific on July 5 and were ultimately assigned to General MacArthur's Unified Command on July 12. But in Korea, armies, not navies, were in the greatest jeopardy and hence in greatest need. On July 14, therefore, UN Secretary-General Trygve Lie despatched a message to 53 member governments asking them to examine their "capacity to provide an increased volume of combat forces, particulary ground forces," and his multilateral plea was supported by American bilateral pressure. On July 19 the Canadian Cabinet accordingly deliberated again. And again it settled on equipment, not men.

A squadron of RCAF long-range transport aircraft was assigned to service in the Pacific airlift (its efforts were later augmented by civilian flights chartered from Canadian Pacific Airlines). But of ground forces there were none. Not until August 7, under steadily-increasing pressure at home and abroad, did the Government finally announce its intention of recruiting a brigade-size Special Force of volunteers "for use in carrying out Canada's obligations under the United Nations Charter or the North Atlantic Pact." The full deployment of the brigade in the Korean theatre was even then not finally determined until late in February 1951.

But, if the Canadians paid their dues with reluctance, they exercised their privileges with enthusiasm. Their principal concern throughout the diplomacy of the war was to constrain and to modify American behaviour (since they could not hope themselves to modify the behaviour of America's opponents) with a view ultimately to containing the scope and duration of the hostilities. Their principal dilemma was to find a way of doing so without alienating the Americans entirely from their practice of acting in concert with their allies in the United Nations. For Mr. Pearson in particular, therefore, the exercise of diplomatic judgment involved not merely decisions with regard to the timing and tactics of diplomatic manoeuvre but also calculations with respect to the limits of American patience.

On what issues did the maintenance of allied pressure on Washington offer some possibility of success? On what issues did it not? And precisely when in particular cases was it "better" to give in to American resistance and fight again another day than to persist in one's opposition? Such preoccupations reflect a utilitarian morality upon which it is possible for good men to differ, but their importance for the conduct of

Canada's diplomacy in the Korean War was so central as to warrant illustration.

The pattern of Canadian behaviour became very evident, for example, in the first few days after the passage of the resolutions of June 25 and 27, when State Department officials turned their attention to drafting yet a third Security Council proposal—this one authorizing the United States to establish a United Nations Command. Hume Wrong was deluged with instructions from Ottawa.

To emphasize the "United Nations" character of the commitment in Korea, he was to recommend to the Americans that they reduce in their draft the number of references to the "United States." To diminish the possibility of UN forces becoming involved in issues other than the purely Korean, he was to suggest that they improve upon the precision of such casual phrases as "in the area," which were used in their resolution to define the scope of UN objectives. To secure the explicit exclusion of Formosa from the sphere of UN Command operations, he was to propose that they include in the draft a geographically-defined boundary around Korea within which General MacArthur would be acting on UN authority, and beyond which he would not.

On receiving the last of these directives, Mr. Wrong gave vent to his exasperation. In a reply which accorded well with the opinion of Mr. Holmes in New York, he advised Ottawa that so complex an amendment might seriously delay the progress of proceedings at the United Nations. The Americans, in any case, had made it clear that their "neutralization" of Formosa was an ingredient of their own policy, which was quite independent of the UN. They would not react favourably to a suggestion that implied scepticism about the reliability of their guarantees, and which was redundant besides. There was, moreover, a limit to the number of "treks" he could undertake with dignity to an already harassed Department of State.

In consequence of Mr. Wrong's complaints, this particular "trek" appears not to have been taken at all, while the ones that were proved ultimately to have been in vain. But the episode nonetheless exemplifies not only the substance of the Government's intent but also the tactical calculations to which the pursuit of its intent was constantly subject.

Two Requirements

To provide another example, if late June and early July, when Canada had still to announce a significant contribution to the conduct of the war, was an inappropriate time to influence the course of American policy, then an appropriate time was when the Government was in the process of paying its dues. Hence, when Mr. Pearson flew on July 29 to Washington to inform the Americans of plans then being developed for the recruitment of a Canadian Army Special Force and to discuss the conditions under which it might be made available, he used the occasion to insist on two requirements. The first was that the troops would not be ordered into combat before they had been trained to the satisfaction of their Canadian officers. The second was that under no circumstances would they be involved in the defence of Formosa. To these, the Americans readily agreed (although in connection with China their inability later to control effectively the public utterances of General MacArthur subsequently led, on more than one occasion, to additional Canadian protests).

Definition of Objectives

Once MacArthur had reversed the fortunes of the war after his amphibious attack through Inchon in mid-September (see map), there ensued a new series of policy questions which, until then, had not been explicitly considered. These related in particular to the definition of the UN's general objectives in the theatre. The resolution of June 27, devised while the North Koreans were still hurtling down the peninsula, had made vague reference only to the need "to repel the armed attack and to restore international peace and security in the area." On the face of it, this suggested that the UN's task would be completed once the security of South Korea had been re-established at the 38th Parallel. At the same time, however, the United Nations had been committed since the winter of 1947-48 to the ultimate objective of Korean unification, and it did not officially recognize the government in the North as a legally-constituted regime. Now that the North Korean army was in total disarray, therefore, the temptation to occupy the northern zone and settle the matter once and for all was difficult to resist. The danger was that an advance into North Korean territory would escalate the conflict beyond manageable proportions by inciting the intervention of the Communist Chinese.

General MacArthur had advised the American Army Chief of Staff, General J. Lawton Collins, as early as July 13 that his intention was to destroy the North Korean forces entirely, and not merely to drive them out of South Korea, and he was not long in persuading his colleagues to a similar view. On September 7 the American Joint Chiefs of Staff recommended that ground operations be carried "beyond the 38th Parallel as necessary" to ensure the destruction of the North Korean forces. President Truman, after discussions with his National Security Council, agreed on September 11 that MacArthur should be authorized to proceed into North Korean territory, subject to there being "no indication or threat of entry of Soviet or Chinese Communist elements in force." In the more detailed directives which the General received later in the month, he was instructed also to ensure that "no non-Korean ground forces" would be used in areas of North Korea bordering on Soviet or Chinese territory.

There remained the question of the involvement in these decisions, *post hoc*, of the United Nations. At first, the Americans argued that a formal resolution would not be necessary because the Security Council had already authorized the restoration of "international peace and security *in the area*," an ambiguity to which the Canadians had objected from the beginning, and to which they—among others—were not now disposed to fall victim. Fearful of a Soviet or Chinese intervention, they at first strongly opposed any crossing of the Parallel, and when after several days of informal discussions the Americans succeeded in having Britain and seven other countries sponsor a resolution recommending, among other things, that "all appropriate steps be taken to ensure conditions of stability throughout Korea." Mr. Pearson was urged by his senior staff not to support their initiative. Assured privately by the Americans, however, that the advance would not be allowed to proceed beyond the narrow waist of the Korean peninsula (roughly half-way between the 38th Parallel and the Manchurian border), and anxious to support the implementation of other features of the new resolution (which recommended procedures under United Nations auspices "for the establishment of a unified, independent and democratic Government in the sovereign state of Korea"), Mr. Pearson ultimately decided to support it.

An informally-expressed Canadian suggestion that the passage of the resolution be postponed until there had been diplomatic contact with the North Korean regime was rejected by the American Secretary of State, and Canadian plans for proposing modifications in the draft in order to win the support of the Indians had to be abandoned because of the swiftness of events. On October 7 the resolution carried by a vote of 47 (Canada reluctantly included) to 5 (Soviet bloc) with 7 abstentions (India's among them). Within hours, American units in Korea had followed the earlier example of their South Korean counterparts and had crossed the 38th Parallel.

China's Entry

Their sojourn in North Korea was to be short-lived. By the end of the month, General MacArthur's headquarters were receiving sporadic reports of contacts with Chinese forces. On November 5 he filed a special report to the United Nations advising the members that his troops "in certain areas of Korea" were "meeting a new foe." Three days later President Truman authorized him to bomb bridges linking North Kora and Manchuria across the Yalu River.

Throughout the preceding weeks there had been repeated attempts by the British, French and Canadians at the United Nations and elsewhere to obtain explicit agreement from the Americans to establish an unoccupied "buffer zone" in Korea's northernmost provinces, but to no avail. General MacArthur was in any case unreceptive to such restrictions, and his superiors in Washington were not disposed to insist. When on November 14 the Truman

Administration requested allied approval of the "hot pursuit" of enemy aircraft into Manchurian air-space, it was discouraged by the vehemence of the response (Canadian opposition was conveyed to American officials within two hours of the arrival in Ottawa of their inquiry).

Now that there was evidence that the Chinese were already in the field, Hume Wrong was instructed yet again to press upon the State Department the need to keep United Nations forces well away from the northern areas and to exercise the greatest possible degree of military restraint. In advising an audience in Windsor, Ontario, on November 15 of his view that "nothing should be done in the establishment of a united and free Korea which would carry the slightest menace to Korea's neighbours," Mr. Pearson suggested that it was still possible that the Chinese were engaged only in a "protective and border mission," and a case could therefore be made for the United Nations attempting to get in touch with them "to find out their intentions," But it was much too late. On November 26, the Chinese "volunteers" launched a major offensive, and by December 15 the United Nations Command had been driven in a chaotic 120-mile retreat down the peninsula to lines located once again in the general vicinity of the 38th Parallel.

In thus so rude a fashion were the allied powers compelled to abandon their plans for a Korea unified and "democratized" by force of United Nations arms. All they could hope for now was an eventual securing of the peace, if necessary on terms reflecting no more than the restoration of the *status quo ante bellum*. But here, too, the Americans and their colleagues in the United Nations were prone to quarrel. For, in the case of the United States, the intervention of the Chinese had made the war more, not less, difficult to resolve. This was partly in consequence of the political pressures to which it gave rise at home, but more because in the American perspective it escalated the international significance of the crisis as a "Communist" challenge which could not safely be ignored. For the allies and the "neutrals," on the other hand, it strengthened immeasurably the argument that every effort should be made to contain the hostilities and to treat the issues involved as if they were reflective of nothing more than a localized breach of the international peace. From this vantage-point it was essential to restore the limited character of the UN's objectives in the theatre, and to persuade the Peking regime that the security of Chinese territory was not under threat.

Chinese Position

There ensued a complex series of negotiations among the Americans and other members of the United Nations, focusing on the question of whether discussions might usefully be initiated with the Chinese. The essence of the American position was that no progress could be expected until the military fortunes of the UN Command had improved at the front, and that concessions ought not to be granted in any event under military pressure. The British view, shared in general if not in detail by the Canadians among others, was that an intensification of United Nations military and other sanctions would harden, not soften, the Chinese position, and that Peking, therefore, ought to be approached instead in a spirit of accommodation. Certainly there could be little harm in making the attempt. If a cease-fire could be arranged, a conference in pursuit of a political settlement might shortly follow (the British, in fact, were prepared to make a number of the political

concessions in advance, but the Americans would have none of this and the Canadians thought it futile to press them).

Confronted by these insistent demands, and convinced in any case that the Chinese would not agree to a cease-fire without advance political concessions, the Americans finally gave their blessing to an attempt "to seek an end to the hostilities by means of negotiation." They made it clear, however, that in the event the negotiations failed, a resolution labelling the Chinese as aggressors would be brought before the General Assembly for its approval.

Cease-Fire Group

The immediate result was the passage of a resolution in the General Assembly authorizing the creation of a Cease-fire Group to initiate discussions with the Communist Chinese. Its members included Nasrollah Entezam of Iran, Sir Benegal Rau of India and Mr. Pearson.

The history of the group's activities need not be recorded in detail here. Suffice it to say that the American requirement that a cease-fire precede, rather than follow, negotiations on the unification of Korea, the recognition of the Peking regime, and other political issues appeared to be unacceptable to the Chinese. At the same time, however, Peking's communications in response to the Cease-fire Group's inquiries were sufficiently ambiguous to lead a number of UN powers—notably Britain, Canada, France and several of the Arab and Asian states—to conclude that there was still room for manoeuvre.

In consequence, when the Americans ultimately introduced on January 20 a resolution in the General Assembly declaring that the Chinese People's Republic had "itself engaged in aggression in Korea," they encountered stiff resistance. In the meantime, the Canadians and the British had gone independently in search of a clarification of the Chinese position. A series of questions conveyed to Peking by Prime Minister Louis St. Laurent through New Delhi produced a reply which suggested that the mainland government might be prepared to consider at least a short-term, conditional cease-fire pending negotiation of some of the more immediately important political issues. Thus encouraged, the Asian powers, under the leadership of India, introduced an Assembly resolution calling for a 48-hour adjournment of the Korean proceedings in order to permit further study. To the fury of the Americans, whose condemning resolution had been ready to come to a vote when the Chinese reply to Mr. St. Laurent's private inquiries arrived in New York, the Indian proposal was adopted. The American delegation subsequently complained with some bitterness that the Canadians had been negotiating with Peking behind their backs. Such was their resentment that Mr. Pearson was to recall the episode in later years as one of the most serious in the history of Canadian-American relations.

But, in the end, the Americans were to have their way. Peppered throughout the ensuing week by the pleas and propositions of diplomats representing the full spectrum of neutral and allied United Nations powers, they would agree only to minor modifications of the wording in their own draft. They were paying the piper, and they were calling the tune.

Since "the methods of peaceful negotiation" had not yet been "completely exhausted," Mr. Pearson confessed that he thought the measure "premature and unwise." But like the British, the French, and other sceptics in the Western camp, he ultimately voted in its favour. The demands of "allied unity," and the need to avoid alienating the United States entirely from the machinery of UN decision-making, were factors that he considered too important to ignore. In the utilitarian calculus of foreign policy, the strategy of constraining the Americans had passed, for Canada if not for India, beyond the point of productive return.

Armistice Negotiations

With the Chinese thus diplomatically condemned, the contest was left for a time with the military, and it was not until July 10, 1951, that armistice negotiations finally began. They endured for more than two years, and in them the United Nations played only a sporadic part. Even here, however, the pattern was the same, with the United States again the object of concerted diplomatic manoeuvres in which the Canadians assumed a prominent role. In the autumn of 1952, for example, the American authorities were compelled to accept a General Assembly resolution incorporating proposals for the repatriation of prisoners-of-war of which they did not entirely approve. Advanced initially by the Indians, it had been moulded only in part to American taste by the attentions of the Canadians, British and French, and it left Dean Acheson with so prolonged a sense of irritation that years later he was to write of Lester Pearson and India's Krishna Menon as "adroit operators" against whose proposals it had been necessary to maintain a constant guard.

Although little was achieved by the resolution at the time of its initial passage—it did not then appeal to the Chinese—it was later mobilized again in constraint of United States behaviour at the climax of the armistice negotiations in May and June of 1953, and the Americans were compelled once more to accede to its provisions. Within a month the war in Korea was over. The lines of demarcation had shifted a little, but the peninsula was as divided at the end as it was at the beginning.

Perhaps the most central feature of Canada's diplomacy throughout was the fact that its targets were friends rather than enemies. For the United States, the most important actors in the conflict were the North Koreans, the Chinese and potentially, at least, the Soviet Union. The allied and neutral powers that were so active in the United Nations were relevant, too, but more as restive constituents than as primary targets of policy. They complicated America's diplomatic life; they did not determine its central direction.

For the Canadians, on the other hand, these conditions were reversed. Since the "enemy" powers were clearly beyond the reach of Canadian influence, they could not be made the immediate object of Canadian policy. In the final analysis, their behaviour could be directly affected only by the United States. Hence, if the Canadians wished to modify the dynamics of East-West relations, they had little choice but to concentrate on the behaviour of the Americans, amplifying Canada's influence wherever possible by acting in concert with the governments of other powers. For the pursuit of such strategies, the United Nations was a convenient instrument.

NOTES

1. For a comparison and contrast with the war in the Persian Gulf, see Chapter 24 in this volume.

SUGGESTED READINGS

Pearson, Lester B., *Mike: The Memoirs of the Right Honourable Lester B. Pearson, Volume 2, 1948-1957*, Toronto: University of Toronto Press, 1973, pp. 107-133.

Soward, F. H., and Edgar McInnis, *Canada and the United Nations*, prepared for the Canadian Institute of International Affairs and the Carnegie Endowment for International Peace. New York: Manhattan Publishing Co., 1956.

Stairs, Denis, *The Diplomacy of Constraint: Canada, the Korean War, and the United States*, Toronto: University of Toronto Press, 1974.

Thorgrimson, Thor and E.C. Russell, *Canadian Naval Operations in Korean Waters, 1950-1955*, Ottawa: Queen's Printer, 1965.

Wood, Herbert F., *Strange Battleground: Official History of the Canadian Army in Korea*, Ottawa: Queen's Printer, 1966.

c h a p t e r 5

PEACEKEEPING AT SUEZ, 1956

Robert W. Reford

On July 26, 1956, Egypt's President Gamal Abdel Nasser nationalized the Suez Canal Company.

In retrospect, it is astonishing that no one seems to have seriously anticipated that Nasser would seize the Suez Canal. His nationalistic policies were well-known. His plans for the development of his country were ambitious and obviously needed money. He was negotiating with the United States, Britain and the World Bank for loans to finance construction of the Aswan high dam. If these were not forthcoming, it was generally assumed that he would turn to the Soviet Union. There does not seem to have been any anticipation that he might look to the Canal as another possible source. Apart from the financial aspects, Nasser might well have been expected to react in the way he did to the crude and peremptory manner in which US Secretary of State John Foster Dulles withdrew the possibility of an American loan. He was the leader of a nation with a civilization dating back thousands of years, whose people had been treated as inferiors and with contempt by the Europeans who had governed them for the previous century. His pride was naturally stung by what he felt to be the insulting way that Dulles had behaved. In fact, Nasser had been looking into the idea of taking over the Canal since October, 1954.

What Nasser had nationalized was not the Canal but the Compagnie Universelle du Canal Maritime de Suez. This was a joint stock company which was promoted in the 1850s by Ferdinand de Lesseps to build the Canal and which had been granted a concession by Egypt for 99 years from the date the Canal was opened. That was in 1869, and so the concession was due to expire in 1968. It was an Egyptian company, though its head office was in Paris. The concession stipulated that 15 per cent of the profits would be paid to Egypt, 10 per cent to the founders and 75 per cent to the shareholders. The British interest dated from 1875, when Disraeli agreed to purchase the 176,602 shares held by the Khedive of Egypt to enable him to pay his debts. Thus, the British government became a stockholder, possessing 44 per cent of the company's stock. Nasser's decree nationalized the company, rather than the canal, though the company's main business at the time was operating the waterway. It included provision for the compensation of the stockholders and could not therefore be described as an outright seizure.

When the British Cabinet considered the issue next day, it was decided that Britain's essential interests "must be safeguarded, if necessary by military action, and that the needful preparations must be made."[1] The Chiefs of Staff were instructed

 Robert Reford, *Canada and Three Crises*, Toronto, Canadian Institute for International Affairs, 1966. This article has been edited to suit the needs of this volume.

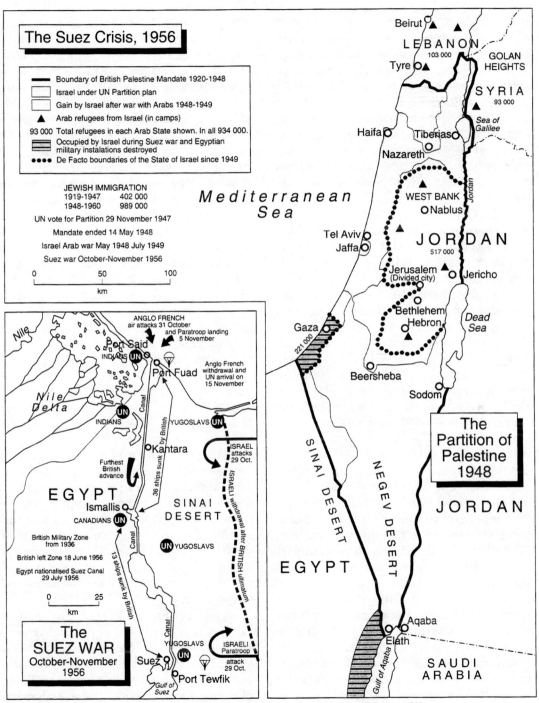

The Suez Crisis, 1956

▬▬▬	Boundary of British Palestine Mandate 1920-1948
☐	Israel under UN Partition plan
☐	Gain by Israel after war with Arabs 1948-1949
▲	Arab refugees from Israel (in camps)
93 000	Total refugees in each Arab State shown. In all 934 000.
▤	Occupied by Israel during Suez war and Egyptian military instalations destroyed
●●●●	De Facto boundaries of the State of Israel since 1949

JEWISH IMMIGRATION
1919-1947	402 000
1948-1960	989 000

UN vote for Partition 29 November 1947

Mandate ended 14 May 1948

Israel Arab war May 1948 July 1949

Suez war October-November 1956

0   50   100
km

Mediterranean Sea

Beirut
LEBANON
103 000
Tyre
GOLAN HEIGHTS
SYRIA
93 000
Sea of Galilee
Haifa
Tiberias
Nazareth
WEST BANK
Nablus
Jordan
Tel Aviv
Jaffa
JORDAN
517 000
Jerusalem (Divided city)
Jericho
Bethlehem
Hebron
Dead Sea
Gaza
221 000
Beersheba
Sodom

The Partition of Palestine 1948

SINAI DESERT
NEGEV DESERT
EGYPT
JORDAN
Aqaba
Elath
Gulf of Aqaba
SAUDI ARABIA

Nile

ANGLO FRENCH air attacks 31 October and Paratroop landing 5 November

Port Said
INDIANS UN
Port Fuad

Anglo French withdrawal and UN arrival on 15 November

Nile Delta
Canal
UN
INDIANS

YUGOSLAVS UN

ISRAEL attacks 29 Oct.

by British

36 ships sunk

Kantara

Furthest British advance

EGYPT

Ismallis
CANADIANS UN

British Military Zone from 1936

British left Zone 18 June 1956

Egypt nationalised Suez Canal 29 July 1956

0   25
km

SINAI DESERT

Canal

UN YUGOSLAVS

ISRAELI withdrawal after BRITISH ultimatum

13 ships sunk by British

Canal

The SUEZ WAR October-November 1956

Suez
YUGOSLAVS UN
Port Tewfik
Gulf of Suez

ISRAELI Paratroop attack 29 Oct.

Source: Adapted from M. Gilbert, *Recent History Atlas: 1870 to the Present Day*, London, Weidenfeld and Nicolson, 1966.

to get ready a plan and a timetable for an operation designed to occupy and secure the canal, should other methods fail. Britain, France and the US met and decided to summon a conference. They invited the eight nations which were parties to the Suez Canal Convention of 1888 and 16 countries "largely concerned in the use of the canal either through ownership of tonnage or pattern of trade." Canada was not among them. It did not meet any of these criteria.

The tripartite meeting marked the emergence of a difference in approach between London and Washington. UK Prime Minister Anthony Eden had decided immediately that it would probably be necessary to use force and had set military preparations in motion. France's representative, Christian Pineau, supported him. US President Dwight Eisenhower had his sights set on a negotiated solution. Eden was ready to try negotiating, but if it failed, then he would use force. Eisenhower and Dulles wanted to exhaust every possible avenue of negotiation, with force only as a very last resort. The key to the Americans was whether Nasser could operate the canal. If he could, then the situation would be different. The British, on the other hand, felt that Nasser had his thumb on their windpipe, and to them this was intolerable. Eden seemed to feel this was an occasion when the Americans should support him, where he had the right to take the lead. The Middle East was an area vital to Britain, less so to the United States. If the special relationship between the two countries meant anything, then he should be able to count on American support. Eisenhower, on the other hand, was sensitive to the reactions of the newer nations which had emerged from colonialism to what they would regard as a return to gunboat diplomacy of the Victorian Age. Then

also, this was a Presidential election year. Eisenhower had won the Presidency in 1952 on a peace platform, which included an end to the Korean war. Running for a second term, he was hardly likely to favour a policy which would lead to an outbreak of fighting in another part of the world.

The Canal was not a vital issue to Canada. It was remote geographically, and free passage was not essential to Canadian trade. Indeed, the Middle East as a whole was an area where Canada had no involvements. In the past, it had carefully remained aloof from ventures into this part of the world, dating back to Sir John A. Macdonald's remark when Gladstone asked for Canadian help in the Sudan in 1885. "The Suez Canal is nothing to us," he said. "Our men and money would merely be sacrificed to get Gladstone and Co. out of the hole they have plunged themselves into by their own imbecility."

However, as the summer of 1956 drew on, Ottawa became increasingly concerned about the growing differences between Washington and London and Paris. The Secretary of State for External Affairs, Lester Pearson, aware of the gap developing between his country's two closest allies, knew it represented a potential disaster for Canada. The recurrent nightmare in Ottawa was a situation in which London and Washington were on opposite sides of the fence. Despite efforts, they were unable on this occasion to play what was regarded as Canada's rightful role of interpreter between the two.

The first Suez conference opened in London on August 16. Egypt and Greece refused to attend. After a week's deliberations, 18 of the 22 nations present reached agreement on what should be done. (Those dissenting were Ceylon, India, Indonesia and the Soviet Union). In essence, they asked Nasser to hand over the Canal to an international organization to operate. But, Nasser announced that he would negotiate only on the basis of Egyptian ownership and control of the Canal.

It is now known that the first plans for the invasion of Egypt had set September 15 and 16 as the dates for the armada of landing ships to sail from Malta. Guy Mollet, the French Prime Minister, and Christian Pineau flew to London on September 10, both determined to press for action.... On September 11, the Suez Canal Company authorized its non-Egyptian employees to cease work by September 15. Nasser made no attempt to keep them, and his reason soon became obvious. The Egyptian pilots, aided by new recruits from other countries including Russia, successfully passed 40 ships through the Canal on the first day. This was more than the daily average and exposed the alleged expertise of the job to be little more than a boast or, at best, a bluff. Lloyd's of London, which had imposed a 15 per cent surcharge on ships using the Canal, soon withdrew it.

The Security Council began its debate on October 5. No one really expected that the Council would be able to solve the dispute. Britain and France introduced a resolution endorsing the proposals agreed to by the 18 nations at the first London conference and recommending that Egypt cooperate by negotiation in working out a system of operation for the Canal on the basis of these proposals. Egypt, as might be expected, opposed the resolution, and the Soviet Union joined in this opposition. The Council then adjourned to allow direct talks among Britain, France and Egypt, in which the Secretary-General, Dag Hammarskjold, participated. From these emerged what became known as the Six Principles:

1. There should be free and open transit through the Canal without dis-

crimination, overt or covert, this to include both political and technical aspects.
2. The sovereignty of Egypt should be respected.
3. The operation of the Canal should be insulated from the politics of any country.
4. The manner of fixing tolls and charges should be decided by agreement between Egypt and the users.
5. A fair proportion of the dues should be allotted to development.
6. In cases of disputes, unresolved affairs between the Suez Canal Company and the Egyptian Government should be settled by arbitration with suitable terms of reference and suitable provisions for the payment of sums found to be due.

These principles were endorsed by all concerned, including Egypt. Egyptian Foreign Minister Mahmoud Fawzi left New York thinking that a further round of direct talks would follow. There was general expectation that they would open in Geneva on October 29.

But the first steps had already been taken which would make peace almost impossible. France and Israel had found common cause against the Arabs. As it had been since the Arab-Israeli war of 1948-49, following its declaration of independence, Israel was concerned with Egypt, and France was involved in combatting an insurrection in Algeria, which she believed to have the backing of Nasser. They were about to cement an alliance which would have far-reaching repercussions.

On October 10, Israel launched one of its retaliatory raids on a border police post in Jordan. It was a particularly savage affair, in which heavy artillery was used, and

U.N. observers subsequently counted 48 dead Jordanians. Jordan protested to the Security Council, which debated the issue on October 19, appealing to both sides to abstain from acts which might aggravate the situation. Soon afterwards, the establishment of a joint military command among Egypt, Jordan and Syria was announced.

In fact, Israel's actions against Jordan were largely a cover plan. The real enemy was Egypt, and in the greatest secrecy, Israel was cementing its alliance with France and co-ordinating military plans. Even as the prospects of negotiations through the U.N. were opening, Eden and Mollet confirmed their decision to intervene. On October 16, the two Prime Ministers and their Foreign Secretaries met in Paris. It was a secret gathering, with no advisers present. France was admitting its determination to work with Israel in attacking Egypt, but the British ministers still shrank from the idea of collusion. They were anxious to appear to be reacting to an Israeli invasion of Egypt. Whether or not Eden and Lloyd were advised of the full extent of the French plans to help Israel, they seem to have approved in principle the idea of co-operation between them. The British Cabinet met two days later to consider the Paris discussions. In his memoirs, the Prime Minister says he described the growing tensions in the Middle East and "the growing danger that Israel, under provocation from Egypt, would make some military move."

Four days later, on October 22, the climactic act of the conspiracy opened in the Paris suburb of Sèvres. There, Ben Gurion, his Chief of Staff, Gen. Dayan, and Simon Peres, the Secretary-General of the Israeli Defence Ministry, met with Mollet, Pineau and Maurice Bourges-Maunoury, the French Defence Minister, to confirm the entire operation. Next day they were joined by two British representatives. A formal document was signed by the three nations.[2]

...

Four days before Israel invaded Egypt, the British Cabinet decided on the terms of the ultimatum it would send to both sides. But no word of this was passed to the United States or to the Commonwealth. It made a mockery of the principle of consultation so important during times of crisis.

On the afternoon of October 29, Israel began its attack on the Egyptian forces in the Sinai peninsula. Paratroops were dropped at the Mitla pass, 30 miles east of the Suez Canal, and armoured columns roared across the border into the desert. By coincidence, the Israeli attack occurred less than one week before Soviet tanks rolled into Hungary to quell a popular uprising there. Next morning, the British cabinet met and approved the terms of the ultimatum to Egypt and Israel, which it had accepted in principle a few days before. Mollet and Pineau came over for consultations, and the document was handed to the ambassadors of the two countries at 4:15 p.m. that afternoon. The British Prime Minister made a statement in the House of Commons 15 minutes later.

As always under such circumstances, many members of the Canadian Parliamentary Press Gallery wanted an interview with Pearson. The requests were so numerous that he held a press conference on the evening of October 30. The first question was blunt: was Canada likely to be involved in a war?[3] Pearson replied: "I don't think we need to go quite so far as that at the moment," but the tone of his other answers showed he was worried and saw no reason to be cheerful. He gave the first word that the normal channels of Commonwealth consultation had broken down. Asked about the Anglo-French ultimatum, he said: "We weren't warned." Later, he added that there had been no opportunity for an exchange of views on the desirability of the British action.

While Canada may have regretted what Britain and France had done, it did not condemn them. As Pearson explained later to the House, "we expressed our regret and we began to pursue a policy, both here by diplomatic talks and diplomatic correspondence, and later at the United Nations, which would bring us together again inside the Western alliance and which would bring peace in the area on terms which everybody could accept."[4] The simplest way to regain the confidence of London and Paris would have been to support their action. However, there was also Washington to consider, and Canada was conscious of the rest of the world as well, especially Asia where India was a key nation besides being a member of the Commonwealth. Obviously, the United Nations was going to play a key role in the crisis, and Canada had placed great emphasis on the role of the organization in the search for peace and settlement of outstanding disputes.

The Security Council met late in the day, and the United States pressed immediately a resolution calling for the withdrawal of Israeli forces to the armistice line and asking all members to refrain from the threat of force or the use of force or from aiding Israel as long as it had not complied with these terms. Britain and France cast their veto. (This was the first time Britain had used the veto, and only the third time France had done so.)

The deadline of the ultimatum expired in the early hours of the morning of October 31. By that time, Israel had announced that it would accept, provided Egypt did likewise. To no one's great surprise, Egypt did not do so, and as a result, the Anglo-French military operation was launched. The bomb-

ing of airfields and military targets in Egypt by British aircraft began the same day. In New York, the Security Council met again, and Yugoslavia introduced a resolution under the Uniting for Peace formula, which would refer the issue to the General Assembly. It was approved, despite negative votes by Britain and France. Because the issue was a procedural one, these did not count as vetoes.

Meanwhile, Eden had written a letter to the Commonwealth Prime Ministers in which he had explained the motives for his actions and appealed for their understanding and support. The reply he received from St. Laurent has been described[5] as the most blistering personal message ever to pass between two Prime Ministers. In substance, it sympathized with Britain's predicament, regretted the absence of prior consultation, refused to recognize Israel's justification to attack Egypt or the Anglo-French justification to intervene, and deplored the serious divergence of views between London and Washington. But as at the time of the Canal's nationalization, the Canadian Prime Minister did not voice his support for Eden's policy. St. Laurent's temper was plainly aroused.

At a 31 October Cabinet meeting, the idea of a U.N. Emergency Force was first discussed in tentative terms. It was still too early to see how events would develop, but that evening Pearson got in touch with Canada's representatives in London and in Washington, asking that they sound out the governments to which they were accredited on the general idea. The replies next morning were to the effect that the concept was fine but too complicated to establish under present circumstances.

When Pearson flew down to New York to attend the General Assembly meeting on the evening of November 1, his general idea was that British and French troops should form the nucleus of a U.N. force. These two countries had men ready—it was still not known that they were actually at sea—and they had proclaimed their intention of separating the belligerents. Why not take them at their word, and let them do this for the U.N.? Contingents from other countries could follow in due course. But when he arrived in New York, Pearson soon realized this would not be possible. The Afro-Asian countries would not accept such a plan because, in their eyes, it would give respectability to a policy with which they strongly disagreed. India's Prime Minister Nehru had already sent a telegram to Hammarskjold accusing Israel of aggression and Britain and France of violating the Charter. Prime Minister Bandaranaike of Ceylon had said there was no justification for either the Israeli invasion or the Anglo-French ultimatum.

When Pearson arrived at the General Assembly, he found an American resolution under debate. It called for a cease-fire, a prompt withdrawal behind the old armistice lines, a halt to all arms shipments into the area and, as soon as this was done, the reopening of the Suez Canal. It proposed that the Assembly remain in session until these terms had been met and asked Hammarskjold to report on progress toward compliance. Pearson immediately asked to have his name added to the speakers list, but there were 21 others ahead of him. Since Dulles was pressing for a vote as soon as possible, obviously Pearson would not be able to speak before it took place. Under the circumstances, this did not disturb him. As he saw it, the American resolution was inadequate. Of course Canada supported the call for a cease-fire and the reopening of the Canal, but the problems which led to the crisis were not recognized. Nor were there any provisions for supervising the cease-fire. Very quickly, he concluded he

should abstain and use the occasion to press for the establishment of a U.N. force. As he explained subsequently, "We were anxious not to give our support at the first meeting of the Assembly to a resolution which might seem to bring the fighting to an end but to do nothing else, or even to recognize the importance of doing something else."[6] Just before the dinner recess, Pearson went over to talk to Dulles at his desk in the Assembly Hall. He outlined his thinking, and the Secretary of State agreed that it was desirable to establish some sort of machinery to supervise the cease-fire and pave the way for negotiations. If Pearson wished to make a move to this end, he would support it. But there was not time to work it out then, and the important thing was to get a cease-fire resolution approved.

After their talk, Pearson telephoned St. Laurent in Ottawa and proposed that Canada abstain when the U.S. resolution was put to vote. This, he explained, would enable him to preserve his freedom of manoeuvre to put forward his own proposal for an international force. After consulting with the Cabinet, the Prime Minister called back to approve this approach. And so it was that when the vote came, the American resolution was approved by 64 in favour and five opposed (Britain, France, Israel, Australia and New Zealand) with six abstentions (Canada, Belgium, the Netherlands, Laos, Portugal and South Africa). Then Pearson spoke, ostensibly to explain his vote but in fact to put forward his own ideas.

We support the effort being made to bring the fighting to an end. We support it, among other reasons, because we regret that force was used in the circumstances that face us at this time. As my delegation sees it, however, this resolution which the General Assembly has thus adopted in its present form—and there was very little chance to alter that form—is inadequate to achieve the purposes which we have in mind.... This resolution does provide for a cease-fire, and I admit that is of first importance and urgency. But, alongside a cease-fire and a withdrawal of troops, it does not provide for any steps to be taken by the United Nations for a peace settlement, without which such a cease-fire will be only of temporary value at best. Surely we should have used this opportunity to link a cease-fire to the absolute necessity of a political settlement in Palestine and for the Suez, and perhaps we might also have been able to recommend a procedure by which this absolutely essential process might begin.

. . .

I would therefore have liked to see a provision in this resolution—and this has been mentioned by previous speakers—authorizing the Secretary-General to begin to make arrangements with member governments for a United Nations force large enough to keep these borders at peace while a political settlement is being worked out. I regret exceedingly that time has not been given to follow up this idea, which was mentioned also by the representative of the United Kingdom in his first speech, and I hope that even now, when action on the resolution has been completed, it may not be too late to give consideration to this matter. My own government would be glad to recommend Canadian participation in such a United Nations force, a truly international peace and police force.

Dulles immediately took the floor to admit the imperfections of his resolution and endorse Pearson's approach. The United States, he said, would be very happy if the Canadian delegation would introduce a concrete suggestion along these lines. The Assembly adjourned at 4.20 a.m. and Pearson had a brief conversation with Hammarskjold before they went home. They met again at lunch the following day,

together with a small group of advisers. Pearson was anxious to have the principle of a U.N. force accepted as soon as possible. He could see no other way to stop the fighting. Hammarskjold appeared skeptical. His concern was with the practicalities, and his usual approach to a problem of this kind was to adopt the attitude of "Show me how it can be done." The only force in the area not engaged in the fighting was the U.S. Sixth Fleet, and the Secretary-General wondered whether it might be asked to intervene. He knew full well all the reasons why this would not be a wise move, and the idea was soon dropped. "Early in the fish course, however, Pearson was able to convince Hammarskjold that the obstacles could be overcome; and the rest of the meal was spent planning an approach to the General Assembly and deciding immediate next steps. By demi-tasse time, the Secretary-General had been fully persuaded...."[7] Then Pearson returned to Ottawa to consult the Cabinet.

The Cabinet had discussed the idea in general terms before Pearson went to New York, and now the opportunity had arisen to put it into practice. According to one report,[8] Pearson simply reported what had happened so far in the General Assembly. When he had finished, the Prime Minister thanked him and said that he should go back to New York. As the meeting was breaking up, Pearson told St. Laurent he would like to introduce a resolution as soon as possible to establish an international force, and the Prime Minister replied that he should do what he thought best and "I will support you here." Pearson has been quoted[9] as explaining that he had to get his instructions informally that way "because one or two of our Cabinet colleagues opposed us taking the initiative. They thought it might prove politically embarrassing." However, in this Cabinet, St.

Laurent was very much the Prime Minister. When he decided that Pearson should go ahead, none felt inclined to object. In addition, time was short and there was no opportunity for long discussion.

Armed with this approval, Pearson proceeded with his plan. The first essential step was to advise London and Washington of his intentions because while something might be desirable in principle, there would be no point in putting it forward at the U.N. if it were not going to get any support. The guidelines for Pearson's actions were to refrain from condemning Britain and France as aggressors, thus giving them an opportunity to withdraw gracefully when a U.N. force could take over. At the same time, he wanted to work toward a peace settlement and not simply a return to the *status quo* in the Middle East. That too would help ensure that Britain and France did not lose face.

The initial reaction from London and Washington was encouraging and ideas were exchanged with those and other governments on what might be included in a resolution. The first proposal was for the Assembly to appoint a Committee of Five to prepare a plan for an international force, but this was changed to give the executive responsibility to Hammarskjold. The phrase "with the consent of the parties concerned" was added. That caused a certain amount of confusion, but its very vagueness had the advantage of allowing different delegations to use their own interpretations in supporting the resolution. It was also a phrase which almost boomeranged against Canada.

Norway had indicated its support early in the game and its ambassador to the U.N. Hans Engen, was a key man in the preliminary discussions with the Canadian delegation. He agreed to act as a co-sponsor of the resolution, as did Colombia. The actual text did not take final shape until almost the last minute. Shortly before he introduced it, Pearson sent a note to Hammarskjold, who was sitting on the rostrum, and the two men met in the Secretary-General's office behind the Assembly Hall. Only then did Hammarskjold learn exactly what he would be asked to do.

Pearson would have liked to include India as one of the co-sponsors, but its own advocacy of another resolution made that difficult. This motion was sponsored by 19 Afro-Asian nations. It noted that the U.S. resolution had not been complied with and authorized the Secretary-General to arrange for its implementation, asking him to report within 12 hours. In effect, it was an attempt to get Israel, Britain and France out of Egypt overnight.

When Pearson talked to Arthur Lall, head of the Indian delegation, they agreed that their two resolutions could complement each other. The Canadian proposal for a U.N. force held out the prospect of international supervision of a cease-fire, while the Afro-Asians were asking an immediate end to the fighting. If this was to work, each move needed the maximum support, and therefore the two men agreed to ask their supporters to vote for the other's resolution. It was a reasonable bargain. Tempers were running high and there was a real danger of Britain and France being publicly condemned. While Pearson wished to avoid this, he had no objection to a little pressure being applied. Perhaps as important, one of the 19 Afro-Asian sponsors was Egypt, whose opposition would be ruinous if a U.N. force were to operate. But as some of Pearson's colleagues in the Cabinet had feared, there were to be political repercussions. Canada's vote in favour of the Afro-Asian resolution was the basis for the charge made later by the Progressive Conservatives during the Special Session of Parliament that Canada had indulged in gratuitous condemnation of Britain and France. It was a delicate game then and throughout the next weeks. If the Canadian plan were to succeed, it had to have the support of the Afro-Asians, including the Arab countries. It also had to be acceptable to Britain and France and to the United States. To achieve this was a real balancing act, and at times the Canadians felt that by trying to keep both sides happy, they were playing a double game.

And so, on November 3, the Canadian resolution was introduced. It was, as Pearson said, very short:

> The General Assembly, bearing in mind the urgent necessity of facilitating compliance with the (U.S.) resolution of 2 November, requests, as a matter of priority, the Secretary-General to submit to it within forty-eight hours a plan for the setting up, with the consent of the nations concerned, of an emergency international United Nations force to secure and supervise the cessation of hostilities in accordance with the terms of the above resolution.

This resolution was voted on first, and it was approved by 57 votes in favour and none opposed, with 19 abstentions (including Britain, France, Israel, Egypt, Australia, New Zealand, South Africa and the Communist bloc). Then came the vote on the Afro-Asian resolution, which was passed by 59 in favour and five opposed (Britain, France, Israel, Australia and New Zealand) with 12 abstentions (including the Scandinavians, the Benelux countries and South Africa).

So it was that the idea of a U.N. peace force was accepted by the General Assembly. Yet it was still only an idea. A great deal of work remained to put it into practice. While no one involved was blind to

the problems to be overcome, perhaps no one anticipated how difficult some would be.

The reaction of the Canadian press was divided over the Anglo-French military action, some condemning and others supporting it. One amusing comment, accurately summing up the feelings of many, appeared in *The Economist*, which described Canadian reaction as "almost tearful...like finding a beloved uncle arrested for rape." However, the Canadian papers were virtually unanimous in welcoming Pearson's plan for a peace force. The *Globe and Mail*, a staunch supporter of British policy, praised him for linking a cease-fire with a political settlement. The *Vancouver Province* called his a remarkable performance of diplomacy.

The planning for UNEF began on the morning of Sunday, November 4, in Hammarskjold's office. The first meeting was attended by Pearson, Engen, Lall, Dr. Francisco Urrutia, head of the Colombian delegation, and Dr. Ralph Bunche, who had helped negotiate the 1949 armistices between Israel and the Arab countries and who was now Under Secretary in charge of Special Political Affairs. At this meeting certain fundamental decisions were made. The first was that the Assembly be asked to establish a U.N. Command and to designate General E.L.M. Burns, a Canadian then currently serving the U.N. as the Chief of Staff of the United Nations Truce Supervisory Organization (UNTSO), to head it. A second was that the five permanent members of the Security Council should not contribute troops. This was determined partly by Afro-Asian opposition to British and French participation. There was also, no doubt, a general desire not to allow the Soviet Union to muddy the waters, as it was already attempting to do with talk of sending volunteers to Egypt's aid.

If the Soviet Union were out, then obviously the United States would have to be as well. But as a general principle, it was obvious that if one of the Big Five were unacceptable, then they all should be. And so, less than 24 hours after Pearson's resolution had been approved, Hammarskjold presented his first report to the Assembly. It proposed giving Burns the authority to recruit his staff initially from the present truce observers and then directly from member countries. The Secretary-General was authorized to "take such administrative measures as would prove necessary" and the selection of troops to make up the force was to be left in his hands. Canada, Norway and Colombia introduced a resolution endorsing this report, and it was approved by the same vote as the original resolution asking Hammarskjold to draw up a plan.

Speaking on the resolution, Pearson said, as St. Laurent did in his broadcast to the Canadian people the same day, that Canada was ready to participate in the force if it were established. Even at this early date, there was no doubt that it would be created. Hammarskjold had been given 48 hours to submit a plan for the force and he presented his first report in less than half that time. The speed with which he acted was deliberate. His purpose was to impress on everyone—on Israel, Britain and France, on Egypt, and on the General Assembly itself—that the U.N. Emergency Force was a credible project and that the Secretary-General was determined to press ahead with it.

On November 7, an announcement from the Prime Minister's office in Ottawa said that Canada was prepared to offer a contingent of battalion strength, with appropriate supporting troops to make it self-sufficient. In all, there would probably be over 1,000 men. Canada was ready to fly them to the Middle East in RCAF aircraft and the aircraft carrier HMCS *Magnificent* would carry their vehicles and stores, acting subsequently as a temporary mobile base.

A key factor for the next step was Egypt's attitude. It had abstained on both the original Canadian resolution and the second one which established the U.N. command. Still unknown was whether it would agree to allow U.N. troops on its territory. On November 5, Egypt accepted the resolution establishing the U.N. command. However, the situation was further complicated by the landing of British and French paratroops that day and by a seaborne assault on November 6. Moscow sent notes to Britain, France and Israel warning that the U.S.S.R. was prepared to resort to force if necessary to halt aggression against Egypt, and a similar one was sent to the United States. They mentioned the possibility of rocket weapons showering down on London and Paris. In London, Eden rejected the note. In Washington, Eisenhower warned that he would oppose Soviet intervention in the Middle East, terming Soviet-American action there unthinkable. In Ottawa, St. Laurent was asked for his reaction and replied: "I did not tremble in my shoes." In fact, the Western powers did not take this threat very seriously. The Soviet Union was heavily involved in suppressing the Hungarian revolt.

The Anglo-French landings led to heightened tension at the U.N. and the Afro-Asians began pressing for a resolution which would condemn Britain and France as aggressors and invoke sanctions against them. Meanwhile, Hammarskjold wasted no time in drafting his second report, and he consulted very closely with Pearson in doing so. For his part, the Canadian telephoned St. Laurent and suggested he send a personal appeal to Eden asking him to accept the cease-fire immediately. This the Prime Minister did. Eden replied that he had talked to the French leaders and they agreed the operation had to continue or else the whole area would relapse into chaos. Once again, he appealed for Canadian support. And once again, St. Laurent refused to give it. He answered that while he sympathized with Britain's position, he regretted the decision to continue. He pointed out that just as Eden was saying he was acting to restore peace and order, so was the Soviet Union using this argument to justify its actions in Hungary. While the parallel might not be exact, it certainly complicated any condemnation of the Soviet Union.

When the Assembly met again on November 6, it had before it Hammarskjold's second and final report. It was a remarkable document, prepared under great pressure and presented just a little more than 48 hours after the Assembly had approved his first report. It laid down the principles which have guided U.N. peacekeeping operations ever since:

- The great powers would not be included in the force.
- There should be an advisory committee in New York. (Its membership would be Brazil, Canada, Colombia, India, Norway and Pakistan. Iran was originally nominated but withdrew in favour of Ceylon.)
- The force would not be a fighting army and it would not seek to impose its will on anyone.
- It would be neutral.
- The sovereign rights of the nation on whose soil it was stationed would be respected.
- A nation providing troops would be responsible for paying them and

providing their equipment. Other costs would be borne by the U.N.

As Pearson said later, the Secretary-General did not attempt to go into detail. For one thing, there was not time. But perhaps more important, "if we had attempted to do it in detail, we would still be arguing about what those functions should be."[10]

Then Britain announced that its forces had been given the order to cease fire at midnight, November 6. Eden explained in his memoirs that the fighting between Israel and Egypt had stopped, and therefore the reason for the intervention no longer existed. Perhaps more decisive, however, was the run that had developed in world financial markets on the British pound. In the background was the possibility that he could no longer count on the support of Parliament and that there would be resignations from the Cabinet. There was also the unknown quantity of the Soviet threat to intervene. Britain attached three conditions: that Egypt and Israel also agree to the cease-fire; that a competent U.N. force be established to secure and supervise the cessation of hostilities; and that British and French technicians be permitted to help clear the Canal.

Meanwhile, the Afro-Asians had introduced another resolution. It affirmed the previous calls for a cease-fire and called upon Israel, Britain and France to withdraw their forces "immediately." Thus, on November 7, the Assembly had two items before it: this resolution, and another to approve Hammarskjold's second report. The latter was approved by a vote of 64 to none with 12 abstentions (including the Soviet bloc, Israel and Egypt). Perhaps its most interesting feature was the sponsors. They were Argentina, Burma, Ceylon, Denmark, Ecuador, Ethiopia and Sweden, an indication of the wide support which the idea of an international force had gained. By this time, Hammarskjold had on his desk offers of troops from Canada, Ceylon, Colombia, Czechoslovakia, Denmark, Finland, India, New Zealand, Norway, Pakistan, Rumania and Sweden.

In a sense, the Afro-Asian cease-fire resolution was redundant, but by this time feelings were running high. There was, perhaps, one consolation: it contained no reference to sanctions. A question mark was the definition of the word "immediately" which it included, and various delegations put forward their own interpretations. For Canada, Pearson noted the close interrelation between the two resolutions and the impossibility of separating one from the other. "In our mind," he said, "there is a relationship bearing on this word 'immediately' between the withdrawal of the forces referred to in the resolution and the arrival and the functioning of the United Nations forces." On this basis, he voted for the Afro-Asian resolution, which was passed by 65 in favour and one against (Israel) with 10 abstentions (including Britain and France). Explaining subsequently to Parliament, Pearson said that accepting this resolution had helped in the rejection of extreme demands. He also expressed his belief that Britain and France were wise to accept the cease-fire at this time, instead of pressing on until they had occupied the entire Canal.

> By this time both Israel and Egypt had accepted the cease-fire. Therefore the original reason given by the United Kingdom and French forces for intervening had been removed. If (they) had continued fighting at that time...I suggest that the Commonwealth might not have been able to stand the strain; that the Asian members might not have been able to remain in it in those circumstances. There is evidence from New Delhi, Karachi and Colombo to support that statement. I suggest also that a continuation of the fighting, even if it had immediately successful military results, would have created even a deeper and more permanent split between the Western European and the Arab world. It might well have led to the occupation of Egypt, which was not an original objective of the British-French intervention. It would have been a standing invitation to the Egyptian government to invite in at that time, when the fighting was going on, Soviet volunteers.[12]

On November 8, Israel announced that it would agree to the U.N.'s demand for a withdrawal from the Sinai peninsula. It did not, however, mention either the Gaza strip or the vital territory controlling access to the Gulf of Aqaba. Nor was timing mentioned, except for a reference to the need for satisfactory arrangements for a U.N. police force to be introduced into the area first. On the same day, Egypt agreed to the entry of ten truce observers to watch over the cease-fire.

One of the key sentences in Hammarskjold's second report was that the force would "enter Egyptian territory with the consent of the Egyptian government." There was to be considerable controversy over how far this gave Egypt a veto on the composition of the force and where it should be stationed. This first became evident when Burns flew to Cairo on November 8. At this stage, while Egypt had agreed to the establishment of a U.N. command, it still had not formally agreed to admit the troops to its territory. Burns saw Fawzi, the Egyptian Foreign Minister, who began raising all kinds of questions. The most startling was his hint that Egypt might not admit a contingent from Canada. His argument was that because Canadian soldiers wore similar uniforms to the British and were subjects of the same Queen, the average Egyptian might not understand the difference between them. Burns pointed to Pearson's role in the formation of the force, and Fawzi replied that he appreciated these helpful efforts as well as Canada's independence in foreign policy, but Canadian troops might not be acceptable. Burns was firm in opposing this—as was Hammarskjold when he heard about it—and told Fawzi that under these circumstances "I should naturally not be able to act as commander." The Foreign Minister said this would be regrettable, but he still maintained that there might bé objections to the Canadians. Fawzi was undoubtedly acting under instructions and, as he so often has done, was testing the ground for Nasser. When Burns saw the President next day, he met the same argument. More important, Nasser raised questions about the role of UNEF itself, and Burns returned to Jerusalem on November 10 still uncertain whether Egypt would permit the entry of any troops.

(Ironically, Nasser's suspicions of the Canadians would have been strengthened had he known that the battalion earmarked for UNEF was from the Queen's Own Rifles. When Pearson heard this, he asked whether any other unit was available. Wasn't there something like the 1st East Kootenay Anti-Imperialistic Regiment? While he was trying to be funny, the joke was not appreciated at National Defence Headquarters where people wondered if the External Affairs Minister was trying to change the name of one of Canada's most historic regiments.)

The issue of Canadian troops for UNEF was an important one. From the Canadian point of view, the refusal by Egypt was a severe blow to national pride. It represented an apparent failure—or a deliberate refusal—to recognize the key contribution the country had made to the formation of the force in the first place. It would also be politically embarrassing to the St. Laurent government, which had already stuck its neck out to a considerable degree. This was shown clearly when Parliament debated the subject later in the month. One of the points in the opposition motion of no confidence was that the government had placed Canada "in the humiliating position of accepting dictation from President Nasser." In wider terms, it raised the whole question of how far the host country could exercise a veto over the operations of a U.N. force. Burns never hesitated in opposing the Egyptian refusal to accept Canada, and he was promptly supported by Hammarskjold. The Canadian ambassador in Cairo, Herbert Norman, took up the issue with Nasser and Fawzi immediately when he heard about it. Word of this crisis reached Ottawa on November 10, when Hammarskjold's executive assistant phoned Pearson. As well as informing him of Nasser's objections to Canadian troops, he said he believed the difficulties could be overcome and that the government should not change its plans. Pearson went to New York and saw Hammarskjold on November 13. He emphasized that it was essential that neither Egypt nor any other country should be able to impose conditions about the composition of the force. As far as Canada was concerned, "on this matter we would negotiate only with him, the Secretary-General, although we recognized, of course, that it was right and proper that he should discuss these matters with Egypt in order to avoid, if possible, subsequent difficulties."[13] Hammarskjold agreed completely and told Pearson Canada should go ahead with its plans. The advisory committee held its first meeting next morning, and Pearson insisted that Egypt could not have a veto over the force.

As Canada saw it, nations were being asked to contribute units to a U.N. force. Once the U.N. had accepted them, they became U.N. bodies, accepting orders from the U.N. commander and not from their own government. The issue was not settled by the advisory committee, but Hammarskjold left immediately afterwards for Cairo, intending to take the matter up directly with Nasser.

Meanwhile, pressure on the Egyptian President was coming from another quarter. India's foreign minister Krishna Menon supported Pearson, and on November 15, he was able to report that the Egyptian government had relented to the extent of agreeing to accept Canadian air transport and a field ambulance unit. Pearson insisted in cables and phone calls to Hammarskjold in Cairo that this was still not good enough, that the host country did not have the right to decide on the size or type of national contributions, and the Secretary-General took the same stand. By this time, Burns had arrived in New York for consultations with the Secretariat. He found most of the troops offered him were infantry battalions but he was short of air transport and supporting troops such as signallers, engineers, supply and medical units. Thus, he decided that the most valuable contribution Canada could make would be to provide these. As he said subsequently, "Nasser's refusal was a blessing in disguise, for the administrative and supporting troops Canada provided then and subsequently were absolutely essential, and the force could not have operated without them." A way had been found for everyone to save face without anyone sacrificing a point of principle.

In all the controversy over Egypt's attitude, too little attention seems to have been paid to what Israel might do. At this stage, the pressure had to be on Nasser because his country had been the scene of the fighting. If UNEF were to supervise the withdrawal, it must go to Egypt. However, after the withdrawal, it would have to patrol the old armistice line between Egypt

and Israel. The logical thing would be to station units on both sides, some on Egyptian and some on Israel territory. However, from the very beginning, the Assembly had accepted the principle that the force could only operate "with the consent of the parties concerned." Considerable pressure would be put on Israel, but it never showed any sign of agreeing to let UNEF inside its boundaries. As seen through Israeli eyes, this was sensible. The presence of U.N. troops would inevitably circumscribe its freedom of action, and even the UNTSO observers stationed there had had their difficulties. However, it was unfortunate for the peace of the world, as events a decade later would show.

In New York, Hammarskjold and his advisers were conscious of the need to get UNEF into Egypt as soon as possible. If that did not happen, there was a danger of the cease-fire breaking down. On November 11 he announced that Egypt had agreed in principle to the entry of the U.N. force and that he would be flying to Cairo to work out details directly with the Egyptian government.

Thus the United Nations Emergency Force was born. It was a remarkable feat. Credit belongs to many people, but two can be singled out: Pearson for sensing that this was the occasion to establish an international force, and Hammarskjold for his drive in putting the concept into concrete terms. Pearson showed the brilliant sense of timing which was a hallmark of his diplomacy. His abstention on the U.S. resolution on the first day's debate enabled him to speak at a time when the Assembly had called for a cease-fire but had taken no action to enforce it. The idea of a U.N. force would fill this need, as well as holding out the prospect of something better than a return to the *status quo*. Thus, it was proposed at precisely the moment when it was most likely to be accepted. Hammarskjold may have been doubtful at first, but he was soon convinced that this was the only way of halting the fighting. With that, he became determined to overcome the seemingly insuperable obstacles.

Within 14 days, the troops were on the ground. It was an outstanding example of what the United Nations could achieve when the nations composing it had the will and determination to use its unique capacities.

The great disappointment, of course, was that the Suez crisis was not followed up by any political negotiations to bring about a permanent settlement in the Middle East. This was not for want of urging by Canada. Its spokesmen were constantly pressing for something to be done, but somehow the occasion never seemed propitious. There was no fighting, even if there was not a final settlement. And in any case, there were so many other more pressing issues—Berlin, Cuba, the Congo, Kashmir, Cyprus, Rhodesia, or Vietnam. So the time-bomb was left ticking over because no one attempted to defuse it, and in 1967 it exploded once more.

Canada's Parliament met in special session on November 26, 1956. There were just two items of business in the Speech from the Throne: approval of the necessary expenditures for Canada's contributions to UNEF and for relief of the victims of the Hungarian rebellion. The government had waited until it knew exactly what troops Canada would be sending to UNEF. Once that had been decided and the order-in-council passed by Cabinet, Parliament was summoned to approve the government's actions.

Acting Conservative leader Earl Rowe made a scathing attack on the government's policy. He did say that there would be no disagreement over the desirability of form-ing a U.N. force to police the Suez canal area, recalling that Diefenbaker had put forward the idea early in the year.[14] He had pungent criticism of the way Nasser appeared to have been allowed to decide the composition of the force, especially its Canadian component. This, he said, was the result of the weak and vacillating policy which the government had followed, and the Egyptian leader now seemed well on the way to converting a military defeat into a political victory. As it was, no one knew how the force would function, nor where it was going, nor how long it would stay. The British, French and Israeli troops should not be asked to withdraw without any guarantee of a settlement of the Suez Canal issue or without a permanent political settlement.

But the central theme of Rowe's argument was the traditional one of an old-line Canadian Tory—the government's failure to support Britain. Not only had the government failed to provide support, it had gone further and actually repudiated Britain by its voting at the United Nations. The acting Conservative leader introduced a motion of no confidence charging that the government

1. had followed "a course of gratuitous condemnation of the action of the United Kingdom and France which was designed to prevent a major war in the Suez area";
2. had "meekly followed the unrealistic policies of the United States," thereby encouraging a truculent and defiant attitude on the part of "the Egyptian dictator";
3. had "placed Canada in the humiliating position of accepting dictation from President Nasser."

When the Prime Minister rose to reply, his Irish was up. After disposing of the constitutional arguments and explaining why the government had waited until now to call Parliament, he plunged straight into the Opposition's attack. Originally, the U.N. had been faced with a resolution which, in effect, placed some of the blame on Israel, some on Britain and some on France, for having taken the law into their own hands when the issue was already before the Security Council. The nations of the world, he continued, had signed the U.N. Charter, thereby undertaking to use peaceful means rather than force to settle their disputes. Then he used words which would come back to haunt him:

> I have been scandalized more than once by the attitude of the large powers, the big powers as we call them, who have all too frequently treated the Charter of the United Nations as an instrument with which to regiment smaller nations and as an instrument which did not have to be considered when their own so-called vital interests were at stake....

The second speaker from the official opposition was Howard Green. He began by saying he was shocked at the stand taken by the government, and he quoted a newspaper dispatch to prove his point: "Canada Turns Her Back on U.K." were the headlines. That was on October 31, and then Pearson went to New York and voted "with Russia and the United States against the United Kingdom and France..." It was high time the country had a government "which will not knife Canada's best friends in the back." The present policy could well be disastrous. The United States, he added, "would have far more admiration for Canada if this government stopped being the United States' chore boy."

The Secretary of State for External Affairs followed. Just as St. Laurent had been goaded by Rowe, so now was Pearson

stung by Green's words. The record of the last few years would show that Canada was no chore boy of Washington, he said. "It is bad to be a chore boy of the United States. It is equally bad to be a colonial chore boy running round shouting `ready, aye, ready'." Then Pearson launched into a lengthy account of the crisis and of the government's reaction and actions at each stage.[15] Pearson answered the various points brought up by opposition speakers. At one point he said he did not "for one minute criticize the motives of the governments of the United Kingdom and France in intervening in Egypt at this time. I may have thought their intervention was not wise, but I do not criticize their purposes." In fact, one of his main motives throughout the weeks of negotiation at the U.N. was to help the British and French get out of the corner into which they had painted themselves. The Conservatives had misinterpreted what he was trying to do. The last words of the session came from the Prime Minister.

> The goal we have been pursuing ever since the very first of these resolutions came before the United Nations (was) to work toward what we regard as almost essential for the peace and security of the free world; that is to say, the reliance on Commonwealth relations and the reuniting of this alliance in an effective way between the United Kingdom, France and the United States.... I think it is and should be the purpose of the Canadian government to put forth its very best efforts to (these) ends.... We have felt that to do that we had to speak our considered views frankly to all our friends, in no "blistering" terms.

In working to achieve this, St. Laurent continued, the government felt it had to speak very frankly to all its friends, but just because they were friends, this did not mean that "everything done by every one of our allies was the wisest course and decision that could be taken."

Thus was the pattern of debate set. It continued until Thursday, when the Conservative motion was defeated by a vote of 171 to 36.

No issue of foreign affairs affected Canada as deeply as Suez. Ten years later, one could still meet Canadians who would not vote Liberal because that party refused to support Britain's action and who regarded Pearson less as a man who won the Nobel Peace Prize than as the man who stabbed Britain in the back. Yet the political repercussions of Suez are difficult to analyze precisely. In the long run, the pipeline debate was far more decisive in contributing to the defeat of the Liberals in 1957. The Progressive Conservatives did see in the crisis an opportunity to embarrass the government and to make an emotional appeal to Canadians who still regarded Britain as the mother country. Prof. John Meisel, in his study of the 1957 election, did not consider Suez a major factor in the government's defeat.[16]

Suez brought honour to Canada and to the architect of its policy during the crisis, Lester B. Pearson. The award of the Nobel Peace Prize to him was announced the following year, ironically on the day the new Parliament opened when, for the first time, he was to sit on the opposition benches. It was a proud achievement. Yet, in the long run, it turned out to have some aspects of an albatross round Canada's neck. Winning this prize seemed to become the goal of successive Secretaries of State for External Affairs and at times appeared to be the driving force behind their actions. An honourable ambition at times took on the aspect almost of an obsession. This was equally true of the general public. They too expected their government to continue the major role it had played during the Suez

affair, and every time a new crisis burst upon the world, there was a cry for a Canadian initiative that would bring its resolution. The Canadian role at the time of Suez was possible because of an unusual coincidence of circumstances. This opened the door for the middle powers, and Canada had the qualifications to step in. One of the major reasons why Canada was able to play such a decisive role in the crisis of 1956 arose from its detachment and its impartiality. Not only that, it had the men trained and equipped to seize advantage of the opportunity available to them. The result is history. But the following decade showed how unusual the occasion had been.

One result of Suez, 1956, was that Canadians began to see themselves in the chosen role of peace-keeper. It is an honourable one, and Canada's performance in keeping the peace is equally honourable. Its troops have taken part in virtually all the U.N. operations, from Suez to Cyprus, from the Congo to Kashmir. But the major part Canada had played in the Suez crisis of 1956 had created an illusion. In the eyes of the public, it had marked the emergence of Canada as a power to be reckoned with, and they expected their government to be able to continue in this role. In fact, it marked the peak of Canadian influence. In the post-war decade, Canada had been able to play an important part in many aspects of world affairs. It had led the cry for the formation of NATO and had an influential role in the complicated negotiations to bring about a cease-fire in Korea. It had played a constructive part in the creation of the new Commonwealth by helping to devise the formula whereby India could become a republic and still remain a member. It had broken the stalemate on the admission of new members to the U.N. Its record in the Colombo Plan and in the operations of the U.N. specialized agencies was a proud one.

But much of this had been played out behind closed doors. Not until Suez did Canada emerge from the corridors of quiet diplomacy to play its part in the spotlight and gain public acclaim for its contribution to the peace of the world. One starring role inevitably breeds expectations of a repeat performance, especially when it brings with it the award of an Oscar, in this case the Nobel Peace Prize. What was not evident at the time was, as one commentator put it, that this was "a one-night stand, an exceptional turn staged and circumstances unlikely to occur."[17]

NOTES

1. This and other quotations are taken from Anthony Eden, *Full Circle: The Memoirs of the Rt. Hon. Sir Anthony Eden, K. G., P. C., M. C.*, London, Cassell & Co. Ltd., 1960.
2. *Crisis* by Terence Robertson, pp. 157-63.
3. This account and the quotations are taken from a transcript prepared by the Department of External Affairs.
4. *Canada, House of Commons Debates*, (hereafter cited as "*Hansard*"), 4th (Special) Session, p. 53. The account of the development of Canadian policy is taken largely from this speech.
5. By Patrick Gordon-Walker, a prominent member of the British Labor Party. See Eayrs, *Canada in World Affairs, 1955-57*, Toronto, Oxford University Press, 1959, p. 184.
6. *Hansard*, 4th (Special) Session, p. 56.
7. William R. Frye, *A United Nations Peace Force*, p. 5.
8. Robertson, *op. cit.*, p. 199.
9. *Ibid.*, p. 199.
10. *Hansard*, 4th (Special) Session, p. 59.
11. In all, 24 nations eventually offered to contribute men to UNEF.
12. *Hansard*, 4th (Special) Session, p. 60.
13. *Ibid.*, p. 63.
14. John Diefenbaker, the Conservative party's foreign affairs spokesman, had raised the question of an international force to police Israel's boundaries with the Arab countries when he spoke during a House of Commons debate on January 31, 1956. Pearson answered him the following day. He said he had discussed the idea with representatives of both the Arab and Israeli governments, as well as Gen. E.L.M. Burns, then Chief of Staff of the U.N. Truce Supervisory Organization.
15. *Hansard*, 4th (Special) Session, pp. 51-66. This speech is the most detailed account of government policy, both its motives and its execution.
16. John Meisel, *The Canadian General Election of 1957*, Toronto, University of Toronto Press, 1962.
17. Eayrs, *The Commonwealth and Suez*, p. 386.

SUGGESTED READINGS

Burns, E.L.M. *Between Arab and Israeli*, Toronto: Clarke, Irwin, 1962.

Eayrs, James, *Canada in World Affairs, 1956-1957*, Toronto: Oxford University Press, 1959, pp. 182-93.

Eayrs, James, *The Commonwealth and Suez*, London, Oxford University Press, 1964.

Eden, Sir Anthony, *Full Circle: The Memoirs of the Rt. Hon. Sir Anthony Eden, K. G., P. C., M. C.*, London: Cassell & Co. Ltd., 1960.

Pearson, Lester B., *Mike: The Memoirs of the Rt. Hon. Lester B. Pearson*, Vol. 2, Toronto: University of Toronto Press, 1973, pp. 239-315.

Robertson, Terence, Crisis: *The Inside Story of the Suez Conspiracy*, Toronto: McClelland and Stewart, 1964.

Taylor, Alastair and David Cox, *Peacekeeping: International Challenge and Canadian Response*, Toronto: Canadian Institute of International Affairs, c. 1968.

c h a p t e r 6

CONFRONTING KENNEDY AND THE MISSILES IN CUBA, 1962

Jocelyn Ghent-Mallet and Don Munton

The international crisis that developed in October 1962 over the deployment of Soviet nuclear missiles to Cuba was both the most serious superpower confrontation in the postwar period and a major turning point in the Cold War. It was also a crisis for the Canadian government, but at least as much one in its relations with the United States as a Cold War crisis. And it precipitated domestic crises of different sorts in both Canada and the United States.

For decades before the Cuban revolution brought Fidel Castro to power and began the process of turning Cuba into a Soviet ally and military outpost in the Caribbean, Canadian governments, though no less firmly opposed to Soviet expansionism, had taken a view of the struggle with Communism somewhat at variance with that prevalent in the United States. Canadian officials, even in the early postwar period, did not perceive an aggressive ideological element in the Soviet threat to the same extent as most of their American counterparts. Many, but not all, also had misgivings about what they saw as an excessively ideological and emotional drive to policies of the leader of the western forces.[1] Canadian governments supported containment of the USSR but preferred moderation to needless confrontation, military or diplomatic. This wariness, however, was seldom publicly articulated. The differences in approach were there, however, but largely behind the scenes during the Korean War in the early 1950s.[2] It was perhaps thus almost inevitable that Ottawa and Washington would not see eye to eye when the Kennedy administration decided it would respond firmly to the discovery of Soviet nuclear missile sites secretly under construction in Cuba.

Further complicating Canadian-American harmony were clear and public differences over policies toward Castro's Cuba. Beyond the simple fact of geography—Cuba lies not ninety but well over a thousand miles from Canada—Canadians have not shared in the long history of American military and political involvement in Cuban affairs. Where the United States owned eighty percent of the utilities and ninety percent of the mining wealth in pre-1959 Cuba, Canadian investments were small and were not jeopardized by the Castro revolution.

Although generally sharing the American antipathy towards communism, the majority of Canadians did not agree with the United States on the tactics of dealing with communist governments. Living in a nation more dependent on trade than most, they had little use for economic sanctions as a weapon of statecraft and held the view that maintaining normal relations did not signify approval of a particular regime. In Cuba's case, it was widely believed that isolating Castro from western trade and diplomatic contact could not bring about his downfall, but would instead drive him to further reliance on less desirable associations.[3]

Trade relations, moreover, represented one area of foreign policy formulation in which Canadians believed they could and should, if necessary, exercise judgement independent of the United States. In trade relations with Cuba, Canada's normal sensitivity to any interference with its foreign policy was intensified; some Canadians felt that they shared with Cuba the status of economic satellite to American industry. A large part of Castro's offence had been in expropriating the properties of American corporations. If policies should be adopted someday which were displeasing to the American owners of Canadian industries, would Canada too become the target of a United States boycott? This possibility, however remote, was not absent from Canadian minds.[4]

The Kennedy administration inherited not only the problem of Castro's Cuba from its predecessor, but also the plan which eventually resulted in the Bay of Pigs fiasco. Even before the ill-fated Bay of Pigs invasion, "US policy toward Cuba was widely thought to be mistaken and both Prime Minister Diefenbaker and External Affairs Minister Howard Green certainly subscribed to that view."[5] Many Canadians regarded the Central Intelligence Agency's sponsorship of the invasion as irresponsible behavior and deplored the presumed American right to forceful intervention as a means of blocking "Communist penetration" of the hemisphere.[6]

Despite these misgivings, the Prime Minister made a personal effort to offset public and parliamentary criticism. With the President due to visit Ottawa in a month's time, Diefenbaker apparently had no wish to discomfit further the already embarrassed Kennedy administration. On April 19, 1961—two days after the invasion had been launched—the Prime Minister spoke to the House of Commons. Cuba, he said, had become "the focal point" in an ideological contest which was spreading into every corner of the world. He was following events with "much anxiety and deep concern."[7] Diefenbaker's expression of solicitude, and especially his accompanying characterization of Cuba as "a bridgehead of international communism threatening the Hemisphere, a danger to which Canada could not be indifferent," was gladly recorded by the State Department. The President was informed that the Prime Minister's statement had been his own idea, had been expressed "contrary to the advice of External Affairs," and had been "undertaken at some political risk."[8] While his motivation for offering this political support is not clear, it is now known that Diefenbaker also privately voiced to American officials his hope that, given his "difficult domestic political situation," he would be informed of any future plans "involving drastic action with respect to Cuba."[9] This hope was to be dashed.

While Diefenbaker had expressed misgivings about Kennedy's inexperience and rashness before and during the 1960 presidential election campaign, there was no apparent personal antagonism at this point. Indeed, the meeting with Kennedy in February went well. But the relationship between the two men soon soured. Through 1961 Diefenbaker, by nature suspicious and prone to harbouring slights, "formed an irrational prejudice against Kennedy and Rusk."[10] The animosity was soon reciprocated.

Of considerable irritation to the Americans in May 1961 was a public suggestion by Howard Green that Canada might effectively mediate the Cuba-United States dispute.[11] According to a State Department communication, President Kennedy was "concerned" over Green's statements; in the American view, they reflected a "distressing lack [of] awareness of [the] facts of [the] Cuban situation."[12] The problem was not lack of facts. Nor was the difference of views solely with Howard Green. Officials in External Affairs shared with their minister grave concerns about "the American tendency to go off half-cocked."[13] Nevertheless, the government subsequently denied that Canada had any intention of playing the role of mediator.[14]

Canada had been cooperating with the United States, since late 1960, to the extent of banning the export of strategic materials to Cuba, as well as the re-export of American products covered by the United States embargo. American officials correctly recognized, however, that Canada "probably would not comply with a US request to impose a total embargo on Canadian goods."[15] And with Canada so "extremely sensitive to U.S. public display of our right to control subsidiaries," US policy makers considered it inadvisable to try to pressure Canada by invoking the Trading With the Enemy Act with respect to goods exported to Cuba by Canadian branches of United States corporations.[16]

In spite of continued Canadian assurances that no bootlegged or strategic goods were being exported, criticism from various sources in the United States intensified during 1962. By this time, the US had orchestrated the expulsion of Cuba from the Organization of American States, cut off Cuba's foreign exchange, and extended economic sanctions to include all Cuban imports. Emotions were also running high over the fate of the Bay of Pigs prisoners. In the press, Canada was widely accused of pursuing a "fast buck" policy.[17]

Relations with Cuba, moreover, were not the only issue on which Canada and the United States were at odds in the latter half of 1962. There was, for one thing, Ottawa's reluctance to accept American nuclear weapons, an issue then moving rapidly to the open, public dispute it became in early 1963. And there was External Affairs Minister Howard Green's continuing efforts to promote nuclear disarmament and, in particular, a ban on nuclear testing. Only days before the crisis over the missiles in Cuba broke, President Kennedy had taken the unusual step of signing a personal letter to Diefenbaker in which he expressed his "distress" over Canada's apparent intention to support an upcoming UN resolution calling for an unverified moratorium on nuclear tests. The Canadian vote, Kennedy wrote, "will be tantamount to Canada's abandoning the Western position" and "will be seen by the Soviet Union as a successful breach" of Western solidarity. Thus, if the Canadians did not reconsider their vote, they would "damage, and damage seriously, the Western position on an essential issue of Western security."[18]

These differences were all consequential factors behind the events which unfolded in Canada during and after the Cuban missile crisis, a crisis which forced to a head in Canada the nuclear weapons controversy, which in turn led to the fall of the Diefenbaker government.

Prelude to Crisis

Growing American concern with the Russian buildup of Cuban military power was expressed by President Kennedy on September 4, 1962 and reiterated in a second statement on September 13. Noting the presence of anti-aircraft defence missiles, Soviet-made torpedo boats and Russian military technicians, Kennedy stated that there was no immediate evidence of a "significant offensive capability." Were this to change, however, the United States would "do whatever must be done to protect its own security and that of its allies."[19]

Kennedy's warning did not succeed, and was arguably too late. Khrushchev had decided, likely in May, to deploy the medium- and intermediate-range ballistic missiles and their nuclear warheads. The first shipment of missiles had already left the USSR by the time of the President's speech; they arrived in Cuba on September 15.[20] The objectives behind Khrushchev's decision are still a matter of much debate. One likely goal, and the one long favoured by strategic analysts, was that Krushchev was attempting to narrow the substantial American advantage in long-range nuclear weaponry by moving shorter-range missiles close enough that they could reach targets in the United States. Another possibility, as Krushchev himself claimed after the crisis broke, was that the missiles would help defend Cuba against an American invasion. Kennedy advisers at the time and most American analysts since have dismissed this claim, in part because in the US view the missiles were offensive not defensive in nature and in part because such an action by the US was so implausible that Krushchev's claim seemed to be a rather lame, *ex post facto* excuse. Scholars currently give this concern greater credence.[21] It is now known that there was a covert operations campaign against Castro's Cuba organized by the CIA (code named "Mongoose"), there had been "pin-prick" raids by exile groups against Havana harbour and other targets (four of them in the weeks preceeding the missile crisis), there had been large-scale U.S. naval manoeuvres in the Caribbean, and there were, in fact, contingency plans for such an invasion under continuous review.[22] The Soviets,

however, were not alone in their perception of the danger of an American invasion. Presidential adviser Arthur Schlesinger reported after a European trip in mid-1961 that a number of those he spoke with "believe ... an American invasion of Cuba is a distinct and imminent possibility."[23]

Since the Soviet buildup on Cuba had been acknowledged to be of a purely defensive nature, Canadians tended to view Americans fears as yet another exaggeration of the potential Cuban threat. Calls for an invasion of Cuba, such as those from Senators Homer Capehart and Strom Thurmond seemed too reminiscent of the Bay of Pigs. It was also widely believed in Ottawa that Washington was being pushed into a more extreme position by Republicans campaigning in the off-year elections. Richard Nixon, then involved in an ultimately unsuccessful campaign for the California governorship, accused Kennedy of appeasement and, along with Senator Barry Goldwater, suggested a blockade to stop the movement of armaments to Cuba.[24] There was, in short, "a major partisan fight going on, and a struggle over public opinion," a Kennedy administration official has acknowledged. "The Republicans were really heating Cuba up as the November elections drew closer ... Things in Congress were getting out of hand. An extreme resolution was even introduced which called for military action against Cuba."[25] A Canadian diplomat posted to the American capital found that the crisis took on an all-consuming, single-minded quality reminiscent of a capital at war. "I was struck," Basil Robinson wrote, "by the extraordinary force of Washington's preoccupation with Cuba and the arch-villain, Fidel Castro."[26]

The *Financial Post* typified the reaction of many Canadians to such statements by terming the demands for invasion a case of "irresponsibility rampant," and by commenting that "emotional anti-Castro jingoists in the U.S. press and the Congress" did enormous harm in deflecting the focus away from Berlin, which was the real Cold War front.[27] Prime Minister Diefenbaker was one of those more worried about an impending confrontation in Berlin than about one in Cuba. As late as October 16, he warned the House of Commons that there were some indications the Russians might soon precipitate a new crisis in that city. Concerning Cuba, he commented that the United Nations was providing "an opportunity to ensure that all possible steps are taken to arrive at a peaceful solution," and that the Canadian government would not fail to do "everything within its power to achieve this objective."[28]

The Crisis Breaks

On the morning of the same day that Diefenbaker made this statement, President Kennedy was informed by his national security adviser, McGeorge Bundy, of the presence of nuclear ballistic missiles in Cuba. Aerial reconnaissance photographs, taken on October 14, revealed that the Russians were in the process of completing launching sites for both medium- and intermediate-range ballistic missiles (MRBM's and IRBM's), capable of reaching targets in Canada as well as the United States and Latin America. The President asked Bundy to assemble in absolute secrecy a group of select advisers who came to be known as ExCom, the Executive Committee of the National Security Council.

The ExCom, in an intensive series of meetings over the next six days, explored the pros and cons of a range of possible American responses, from diplomatic approaches to Khrushchev or Castro to an air strike against the missile sites or a full-scale invasion of Cuba. Both diplomacy ("talking 'em out," as one participant later labelled it) and military force ("taking 'em out") had their proponents amongst the advisers. Ultimately, the President decided that attacking the missile sites was too likely to escalate the crisis, and thus was too dangerous, at least as a first step. On the other hand, diplomacy by itself was unlikely to be productive and, equally important, was certain to be seen by critics of the administration as a weak, insufficient response. The decision was made to establish a naval blockade of Cuba to prevent the shipment of further missiles and nuclear warheads and to demand that the Soviets dismantle the sites already under construction and withdraw the existing missiles.[29]

There is no question that the President and his advisers were very much aware of the risk of nuclear war and much concerned with Soviet objectives and possible responses. At the same time, they were very mindful of American public opinion and its receptivity to the kind of hawkish arguments being made by right-wing congressmen and Republican candidates such as former Vice-President Richard Nixon. As one of the President's closest advisers put the matter at an early ExCom meeting: "I'll be quite frank. I don't think there is a military problem here ... This, this is a domestic, political problem ... we said we'd *act*."[30]

Although students of the Cuban Missile Crisis tended initially to emphasize its strategic and foreign policy implications, increasing attention has been paid recently to the domestic side. "The President felt he had to take decisive military action if his Presidency was not to be severely challenged and his political credibility undermined," one analyst has written. "While the risks of escalation pushed the decision down the ladder to the blockade, the President's domestic political interests favored military action over diplomacy.... From a domestic political standpoint, the blockade was a less risky course of action."[31]

On Saturday October 20, the group acquiesced in the draft of a blockade speech, although Kennedy did give some last-minute reconsideration to an air strike in a meeting with USAF bombing experts on Sunday morning. With Kennedy scheduled to deliver the public address Monday at 7 p.m., the American government then proceeded to notify the allies. Dean Acheson was dispatched to Paris to brief President De Gaulle and to assist in explaining the situation to the North Atlantic Council. Personal messages from the President were also conveyed to Chancellor Adenauer of Germany and Premier Fanfani of Italy.

Prime Minister Harold Macmillan had already been advised on October 19 that a crisis was imminent in Cuba through David Ormsby-Gore, British ambassador to the United States and a close friend of John Kennedy.[32] In a personal message on Sunday October 21, Kennedy told the Prime Minister that while the American ambassador in London would brief him more fully the next day, he wanted him "to have this message tonight, so that you may have as much time as possible to consider the dangers we will now have to face together." Kennedy explained that he had found it "absolutely essential in the interests of security and speed to make my first decision on my own responsibility," but from that point on he and Macmillan would "have to act most closely together." In a subsequent message, Kennedy added, "I wanted you to be the first to be informed of this grave development, in order that we should have the opportunity should you wish it, to discuss the situation between ourselves by

means of our private channel of communication."[33] Immediately after the televised broadcast, the President telephoned Macmillan, the first of many such calls through the duration of the crisis.

Although the missiles were, in the British Prime Minister's words, "a pistol pointed at America and Canada," no such offers of consultation were made to the Canadian Prime Minister. Canada was treated like the other allies, and was deliberately not informed until shortly before the President made his public statement. In a message delivered to Diefenbaker an hour and a half before his address, Kennedy said only that "we should all keep in close touch with each other," and that "I will do all I can to keep you fully informed of developments as I see them."[34] To Macmillan, on the other hand, Kennedy wrote that "it is a source of great personal satisfaction to me that you and I can keep in close touch with each other," and that "I intend to keep you fully informed of my thinking as the situation evolves."[35]

Canadian Responses

The emissary chosen to deliver the message to Diefenbaker was the distinguished former ambassador to Canada, Livingston Merchant. Accompanied by the American Embassy's Charge d'Affaires and two intelligence officers, Merchant met with the Prime Minister, External Affairs Minister Howard Green and Defence Minister Harkness around 5:30 p.m. on Monday October 22. Merchant thought that Diefenbaker behaved rather coolly towards him, possibly because of his being "tired, harassed and wrapped up in other things,"[36] but possibly also because of the stern letter Diefenbaker had received from Kennedy only days before. In the message now handed to him by Merchant, Kennedy said first of all that the United States had "clear evidence," to be explained by the ambassador, "that the Soviets have secretly installed offensive nuclear weapons in Cuba, and that some of them may already be operational." The situation called for "certain quarantine measures whose object is to prevent the introduction into Cuba of further nuclear weapons, and to lead to the elimination of the missiles that are already in place." Kennedy noted that a personal communication was being sent to Khrushchev, making it clear that the actions in Cuba constituted "an unacceptable threat to the security of this hemisphere" but expressing "the hope that we can resume that path of peaceful negotiation." The longest part of the presidential communication, however, dealt with a proposal to be placed before the United Nations:

> I am also requesting an urgent meeting of the United Nations Security Council. I have asked Ambassador Stevenson to present on behalf of the United States a resolution calling for the withdrawal of missile bases and other offensive weapons in Cuba under the supervision of United Nations observers. This would make it possible for the United States to lift the quarantine.

Kennedy then specifically asked the Prime Minister to "instruct your representative in New York to work actively with us and speak forthrightly in support of the above program in the United Nations."[37] This paragraph in the President's message was identical to one sent to Macmillan, but it was not preceded as in Macmillan's case by a lengthy exposition on the dangers of the crisis or by offers of private discussion.[38] In the much shorter message to Diefenbaker, therefore, the President appears to be placing a greater emphasis on a solution through the United Nations. Since turning to the UN was the traditional

Canadian instinct in time of crisis, this undoubtedly struck a chord with the Canadians.

After Diefenbaker had read the message from Kennedy, the ambassador showed the ministers the photographic evidence, outlined to them the American actions, and read them the text of the President's speech.[39] The Prime Minister asked that one sentence from the speech—a sentence characterizing Soviet Foreign Minister Gromyko in unflattering terms—be deleted. Merchant telephoned Washington and, reaching Dean Rusk, told him that he agreed with Diefenbaker's objection. The offending phrase was removed. Merchant brought no specific requests for Canadian government action, aside from the matter of supporting the US initiative in the UN. After the Americans departed, the Prime Minister went home for dinner and watched Kennedy's address on television.

Opposition Leader Pearson, after conferring with House Conservatives, telephoned the Prime Minister to ask him to make a statement, in view of the Kennedy announcement, when the House of Commons resumed sitting at 8 p.m. Mr. Diefenbaker agreed. Indicative perhaps of the little time he had been given to think about this important statement, the Prime Minister said that it was "impossible to say much" in response, but characterized Kennedy's address as a "sombre and challenging one." Noting that the "construction of bases for the launching of offensive weapons" constituted a threat to most of North America, "including our major cities in Canada," the Prime Minister urged calmness and the avoidance of panic. "Our duty as I see it," he said, "is not to fan the flames of fear but to do our part to bring about relief from the tensions, the great tensions of the hour."[40]

The Prime Minister made no comment on the blockade and, of the other measures announced by Kennedy, noted only the call for a resolution to be placed before an emergency session of the Security Council, the step which had been emphasized in the personal presidential letter to him. "The determination of Canadians," the Prime Minister stated, "will be that the United Nations should be charged at the earliest possible moment with this serious problem." He went on to suggest how the United Nations might help:

> I think what people all over the world want tonight and will want is a full and complete understanding of what is taking place in Cuba. What can be done? Naturally there has been little time to give consideration to positive action that might be taken. But ... if a group of nations, perhaps the eight nations comprising the unaligned members of the 18 nation disarmament committee be given the opportunity of making an on-site inspection in Cuba to ascertain what the facts are, a major step forward would be taken.[41]

Diefenbaker then asked for the views of, and possible suggestions from, the leaders of the other parties. Lester Pearson, a former External Affairs Minister and now the Liberal leader, noting that the matter was being brought before the OAS as well as the UN, concurred with the Prime Minister that "international organizations should be used for the purpose of verifying what is going on." Like the Prime Minister, he offered no comment on the blockade. Neither did the spokesmen for the two minor parties.[42] The national leader of the New Democrats expressed some skepticism ("we have only the statements of the Americans") but then pointed to precisely the point that Kennedy and his advisers wanted to avoid. "Before we get too excited," he said, "we should remember that for fifteen years the Western powers have been ringing the Soviet Union with missile and air bases."[43]

To turn to the United Nations for assurance was not only consistent with Diefenbaker's own position before the crisis broke but also a typical Canadian response. Canada had consistently supported the UN, Canadian statesmen had played a major role in strengthening it, and the UN was one area of world politics where the Canadians believed they could exert some influence.[44] Canadian doubts, latent or implied, about the wisdom of American actions were a reflection of perceptions of the Cuban-American issue. Some Canadians, their suspicions raised by the original American denials of involvement in the Bay of Pigs operation, may have had doubts about US claims as to the existence of an offensive base. Many, including some Canadian officials, feared that the United States might once more be overreacting. The close circle of advisers around Kennedy, of course, did not see the matter this way. Preoccupied with hawks within ExCom pressing for an attack on the missile sites and worried about right-wing critics in Congress pressing for an all-out invasion, they regarded themselves justifiably as moderates trying to prevent a military escalation of the crisis.[45]

In any case, skepticism was not a uniquely Canadian reaction. Others in the United States and abroad, while accepting the existence of the offensive missiles, questioned the appropriateness of the response. Former President Eisenhower, for example, suspected that Kennedy might perhaps "be playing politics with Cuba" on the eve of the off-year elections.[46] Harold Macmillan, Kennedy's staunchest ally at the time, later wrote in his memoirs that one "had to remember that the people of Europe and the people of Britain had lived in close proximity to Soviet missiles for several years."[47]

The Alert

Meanwhile, a request to raise the alert status for the Canadian component of NORAD—the North American Air Defense Command—had been received through military channels after the President's speech. Merchant had provided no warning that such a request would be made. Air Chief Marshall Frank Miller, the Chairman of the Canadian Chiefs of Staff Committee, arrived at Defence Minister Harkness's home to inform him that the entire military apparatus of the United States had gone on "Defcon 3" alert.[48] Canadian units in NORAD, Miller advised, should be brought to the same state of readiness. At the time NORAD was established, an informal "agreed procedure" had been adopted whereby, in the event of an alert, the President and the Prime Minister would consult about the "risks and repercussions" of recommended joint military proposals.[49] But Harkness had attended the Merchant briefing and knew that Kennedy had not even informed Diefenbaker of the proposed alert, let alone consulted him. Nevertheless, the Defence Mnister was in no doubt that some action would have to be taken. He asked Air Chief Marshall Miller to call an immediate meeting of the Chiefs of Staff committee.[50] There were, it emerged, two questions: first, what procedure should be followed when US forces had been put on a Defcon 3 alert and, second, who was the appropriate authority to order it?

Although the first question of what procedure should have been followed would become a contentious one politically, Harkness and his senior military advisers came to a quick agreement on the necessity for an alert. The degree of military integration between the United States and Canada and communality of interest de-

manded, in their view, that the Canadian forces in NORAD be brought to equivalent status immediately.[51]

The second question of who had the appropriate authority to implement an alert proved more difficult. Initially, the Chairman of the Chiefs thought he had the authority, because the alert was "low-level," equivalent to those he had approved during NORAD exercises.[52] Harkness, however, was not so sure. On checking the Canadian War Books, they found themselves in a complete hiatus. The old War Books, which were no longer in use, gave the authority to the Prime Minister and the cabinet. The new War Books, not yet approved by the cabinet, gave it to the Defence Minister. Harkness decided therefore that he must consult Diefenbaker. Telling the Chiefs to "get ready," he left to confer with the Prime Minister, completely confident that the matter was a mere formality.

Diefenbaker disagreed. He refused to give his permission for an alert until the cabinet could meet and discuss the situation the next monring. Harkness, believing that he had no other choice, returned to the Chiefs of Staff meeting and, in effect, authorized the alert on his own. Apart from a few minor details, such as official announcement of the alert and the recall of men on leave which would, of course, have attracted the attention of both the public and the Prime Minister, all of the requirements were met.[53] The Canadian army, although not involved in NORAD, was also authorized to take whatever steps it could "without putting the country in turmoil." The Canadian navy was a special case. Ships are not as easily dispersed as aircraft, and they must not be caught in harbor. The Chief of Naval Staff, therefore, having received information through his own channels, acted on personal initiative and ordered the Atlantic fleet based in Halifax to get ready for sea. In this case, it was necessary to recall men on shore leave, but further actions were specifically not taken for fear of creating public alarm.[54] The naval alert was approved some hours later by the Defence Minister.[55]

While the close cooperation of the Canadian and American air forces under the aegis of NORAD is well known, the extent of naval coordination under the cover of NATO is not. The integration of the Canadian Atlantic fleet into NATO's SACLANT (Supreme Allied Command Atlantic), headed by an American admiral, meant that the Canadian navy played a key and active role in the Cuban missile crisis, a role that has been either ignored or mistated in all existing accounts of this crisis.[56] The deployment took the covering form of repeating a major SACLANT exercise of a month before, which had simulted a situation very much like the actual Cuban crisis. "In effect," Canadian Admiral Dyer has stated, "We went to our war stations." According to newly released US documents, a "submarine barrier" was established "south of Newfoundland" by October 27, and there seems little doubt that the ships on this "barrier" were Canadian.[57] The purpose was the detection and tracking of Russian submarines, but a close eye was also kept on the Russian fishing fleet which was known to possess communication abilities. The Canadian Navy deployment permitted units of the American navy to move south into the blockade zone.

Given the central role of the United States Navy in the missile crisis, this Canadian contribution was arguably a more significant measure of military support than the alert of Canadian forces in NORAD.[58] Canada was the only ally to

order its forces into active duty to aid the Americans. By contrast, Harold Macmilan, who offered the most forthright political support of all the allies, refused to order an alert of British forces.[59]

When the cabinet met to discuss the situation the next morning, Prime Minister Diefenbaker and his colleagues, with one exception, were under the impression that the decision to support or not support the United States militarily still rested in their hands. The debate was pitched. Although they met twice on October 23 and again on the 24th, no formal decision about the alert ever emerged. The government, however, on its own initiative, did officially inform the Soviet embassy in Ottawa Tuesday morning that it was withdrawing landing rights for Soviet planes using Gander as a stopover en route to Cuba.

Although some accounts of this crisis have blamed the lack of a cabinet decision on Prime Minister Diefenbaker and to a lesser extent on External Affairs Minister Green, there was, in fact, a substantial cabinet split. One group within the cabinet agreed immediately with Harkness that, given Canada's NORAD commitment and an apparent Russian threat to the entire continent, the nation's security interests could best be served by declaring an alert. A second group, which included three other ministers (Alvin Hamilton, J. Waldo Monteith, and Richard Bell), as well as Diefenbaker and Green, felt those interests would be better served by avoiding any action that might appear provocative to the Soviet Union. Between these two groups lay approximately half the cabinet, who were at first uncertain as to how to proceed. Although these ministers came eventually to support Harkness, their varying degrees of resentment over the United States' failure to consult Canada initially strengthened the position taken by Diefenbaker and Green. A majority of ministers resented the American failure to consult and the lack of recognition of Canadian sovereignty.

When the ministers gathered together on the morning of October 23, most knew only what they had seen on television or read in the newspapers. None of them, except the three ministers who had been briefed by Merchant, had seen the photographic evidence. Thus they were being asked to reach a decision concerning the advisability of supporting the Americans on the basis of essentially second-hand information. This information had to be fitted, moreover, into existing images of the Cuba-United States issue, images which centered on the belief that the Americans had been overestimating and overreacting to the Cuban threat. Additional information from Washington through open channels of political communication might have revised negative attitudes, but the President never followed through on his implied promise of further contact. It now appears that the two leaders did talk once on the telephone, but it is not clear who initiated the call or what was discussed.[60]

Although little new information was being received from the United States, the Prime Minister was not without trusted sources of advice. Diefenbaker telephoned Harold Macmillan who told him that the United Kingdom had not gone on alert and would not, at this stage, since additional mobilization could easily be interpreted as a provocative measure by the Russians. This was, moreover, not the first time the two prime ministers had discussed this very problem. At a meeting in 1959, Diefenbaker himself had expressed to Macmillan his own similar misgivings about the US Stategic Air Command being placed on increased readiness at times of tension, in the context of a discussion of the Berlin issue.[61]

Macmillan's caution was an important consideration and it bolstered some Canadian predispositions. Actions taken now also had implications for the government's nuclear dilemma. Approval of the alert could have meant that the United States would request the movement of nuclear-equipped interceptors to their bases in Canada, an action that might both appear provocative and compromise the decision on deploying nuclear weapons on Canadian soil. Given the uncertain status of his minority government, voter approval was certainly one of Diefenbaker's concerns if not the rest of the cabinet's. The Prime Minister was sure that the majority of the electorate would not approve of Kennedy's action or want to be militarily involved in the Cuban affair. He was, on this score, quite wrong.[62]

The Crisis Continues

As the cabinet debate wore on, international tension heightened. On October 23, the OAS approved the quarantine with only three countries abstaining from that section of the resolution which authorized OAS members to use force against Cuba. Early on Wednesday October 24, the naval blockade went into effect. Russian ships continued to advance steadily towards Cuba. By the end of the third cabinet meeting in Ottawa on the morning of the 24th, three-fourths of the ministers had set other considerations aside and supported the Harkness position. As one former minister initially sympathetic to a non-alert stated: "We had reason to resent the lack of consultation, but it would have been foolish not to temper it with an understanding of the situation."[63]

During the afternoon of the 24th, Harkness received "a lot of intelligence on Russian preparations." He also learned that certain elements of the United States forces had moved from a "Defcon 3" to a "Defcon 2" alert, indicating full-war footing, just one step removed from actual hostilities.[64] The Defence Minister tried once more to get the political authorization he wanted. This time he succeeded. Diefenbaker was convinced that Canada's security was now gravely endangered by the reported preparations of the Soviet Union.[65] Diefenbaker still delayed formal proclamation of the alert until the next day, Thursday October 25.

During parliamentary question periods on the previous two days, government spokesmen had adroitly circumvented any lengthy discussion of Canadian response to the crisis. Harkness later admitted that he had "very carefully" phrased his answers to opposition queries. When asked by the Liberal defence critic on October 23 if Canadian units assigned to NORAD had been alerted, or if "special orders" had been transmitted to naval units, Harkness replied that "by and large the answer to that question is no."[66] The Defence Minister also denied on October 24 that Canada was taking any part in the quarantine. These answers were of course misleading, but technically correct. No alert had been proclaimed. Naval units were not actually blockading Russian ships—they were merely repeating a NATO exercise. On the other hand, when asked if Canada had defaulted on its NORAD agreement, Harkness could truthfully say "emphatically no, we have not defaulted."

Opposition members had also pressed the Prime Minister for information. One plea for assurance that the government was "doing everything possible to halt this race toward international suicide" was ruled out of order, but to other requests for informa-tion, Diefenbaker responded by asking for restraint. "Were we to place before the House various matters that might be spoken of at this time," he suggested, it would not benefit Canada's security situation, "...and might indeed be provocative." The theme of non-provocation runs through all of Diefenbaker's statements during the crisis. It was also a constant in the responses of External Affairs Minister Green during a half-hour television interview on the evening of October 24. "We're going to do everything we can to get this crisis settled," he said; "we don't want a nuclear war."[67]

In proclaiming the alert to the Commons on October 25, the Prime Minister's choice of words revealed the differing perceptions of Canada's national security interests which had plagued two days of cabinet discussion. Now conceding the arguments of the Harkness group, he accused the Soviet Union of reaching out across the Atlantic "to challenge the right of free men to live in peace in this hemisphere." He declared the weapons in Cuba "a direct and immediate menace to Canada...and indeed to all the free world, whose security depends to such an extent upon the strategic strength of the United States." In light of the "new and immediate threat" posed by the Soviet Union to the security of the continent, Diefenbaker dismissed arguments over the legality of the quarantine as "largely sterile and irrelevant. We have a situation to face," he emphasized. In order to deal with that situation, he announced that "all Canadian military forces have taken precautionary measures," and that NORAD's Canadian component had "been placed upon the same level of readiness" as the forces of the United States. It was later made clear, however, that the same level of readiness did not mean that Canada's weapons systems had been nuclear-armed.

Observing then the arguments of that group in the cabinet who had opposed the alert, the Prime Minister made the following statement:

> It has been necessary and will always remain necessary to weigh the risks of both action and inaction in such circumstances.... Canadians stand by their allies and their undertakings, and we intend in the present crisis to do the same. On the other hand, we shall not fail to do everything possible to seek solutions to these problems without war. We shall seek to avoid provocative action. Our purpose will be to do everything to reduce tension.

Taking encouragement from the fact that some Soviet ships had turned back from Cuba, Diefenbaker still cautioned that "it would be dangerously premature to assume that the critical phase" had passed. Returning to the basic theme of his statement on October 22, he stated that the "greatest hope" of finding a peaceful solution lay in the United Nations. While avoiding any expression of personal confidence in American leadership, Diefenbaker praised U Thant both for the way in which he was discharging his responsibilities, and for his proposal of a standstill which would permit time for negotiation.[68]

Opposition Leader Pearson spoke even more intensely of a debt to the United Nations ("the world organization . . . stands between humanity and destruction") and was less supportive than Diefenbaker had been of the quarantine as a security measure. Backing the United States, he suggested, did not necessarily mean that "all the details of that action are to be approved without qualification." Pearson also put forth the idea of a UN naval inspection force to guard against possible Russian evasion of a standstill resolution. The New Democratic Party leader expressed disdain

for the "fetish that Canadians must never rock the boat of United States foreign policy," and voiced the belief that the present American course "is likely to land us on the rock of international suicide." He was also sharply critical of the American failure to consult Canada, NATO or the UN before taking unilateral action.

The Superpowers Deal

Quite oblivious to the turn of events in Ottawa, the crisis was entering a new, even more dangerous phase. The same day as Ottawa's halfhearted support was offered, President Kennedy ordered the loading of nuclear weapons on US aircraft in Europe and the open preparation of US troops for the invasion of Cuba many Americans were calling for. The Kremlin meanwhile had ordered work on the missile sites in Cuba to be stepped up. On Friday, October 26, a letter from Khrushchev arrived in Washington that appeared to be offering to withdraw the missiles in return for a US pledge not to invade Cuba. The following day, however, another, tougher message arrived demanding that the United States agree to withdraw its Jupiter missiles in Turkey as well. The same day an American U2 spy plane was shot down over Cuba by a Soviet anti-aircraft surface-to-air missile.

Although Kennedy had said he would retaliate if any US planes were shot down, faced with a mounting crisis, he chose not to do so. The ExCom decided to pursue the terms of the first Khrushchev letter and the President sent his brother to meet secretly with Soviet Ambassador Anatoly Dobrynin. Robert Kennedy told Dobrynin that the United States was prepared to agree formally to the non-invasion guarantee, warned of the mounting pressure on the White House for direct military action, and insisted on a response from Moscow by the following day. He also suggested pointedly that, while the President could not now undertake publicly to withdraw the Jupiter missiles from Turkey, he was prepared to remove them in the near future in return for the Soviet missiles being removed immediately. The next morning, in an extraordinary broadcast over Radio Moscow, Khrushchev agreed to remove his missiles from Cuba. The deal was done.[69]

Recent evidence suggests that John Kennedy may have been willing by the 27th to accept a *public* trade of the Jupiters for the Soviet missiles, but only as the alternative to a military escalation such as an attack on the missile sites. The President told the ExCom on 26 October that the Americans could get the missiles out of Cuba only by an invasion or by trading.[70] The strong preference though, for political reasons, was not to link publicly the American missiles in Turkey with those the USSR had been deploying in Cuba. To one of the president's closest advisers, Defence Secretary Robert McNamara, publicly "buying 'em out" was so politically dangerous it was "not much different" from allowing the Soviet missiles to stay in Cuba, at least in the sense that "people would have interpreted this as caving in . . . including a lot of congressmen and our allies."[71]

It is clear from this perspective and mounting other evidence that a dominant concern, if not *the* dominant concern, of the President and his closest advisers was the domestic political reaction in the United States itself. The extent to which the Soviet buildup in Cuba had become a congressional election issue was no doubt a major factor in this preoccupation. A failure to deal forcefully with the missiles, coupled with the 1961 disaster at the Bay of Pigs, would have allowed opponents to brand Kennedy convincingly as a weak and ineffective president, and thus would have dealt

him a personal political blow from which he might not have been able ever to recover.[72]

In October 1962, John F. Kennedy appeared victorious. Bold headlines announced Khrushchev had "backed down." Force had, apparently, won the day. The Canadian government's concerns about escalation and provocation appeared, by contrast, weak and inadequate. Across Canada, the censure was widespread and even included important elements within the Conservative Party. External Affairs Minister Green's television appearance on October 24 provoked the first outcry. Both Green and Diefenbaker had been pleased with the interview, but prominent Conservatives across Canada expressed disappointment and anger at what had seemed a confusing and evasive performance. The Young Progressive Conservatives of Manitoba sent the Prime Minister a telegram denouncing the government's position and urging open support for the quarantine.[73] In the afterglow of the successful conclusion of the crisis, disapproval within the party grew and criticism in the nation's press intensified. The Associate Minister of Defence later wrote in his memoirs that the government's behaviour "led a great many staunch Conservatives to doubt Diefenbaker's ability to lead the nation in the event of an international crisis."[74] Much of the censure focused on Canada's alleged delay in backing the United States militarily. One report claimed that Canada had "flunked" its first major NORAD test.[75] Another charged that American defence officials were "furious" over Canada's "sluggish reaction."[76] Various accounts accused the cabinet of refusing the United States request to move nuclear-equipped interceptors into Canada, to allow more US bomber flights over Canada, and to arm the squadrons at American bases in Labrador and Newfoundland with nuclear weapons.[77] Defence Minister Harkness has since said that the request was not in any event specific, but was more in the nature of a "feeler," and that the crisis was over before a decision became necessary.[78] There is also some question whether any such requests were, in fact, authorized by the American political leadership, which was at the time doing much to avoid provocative military moves, or stemmed solely from the American military, which was not displaying the same level of concern.

Given the extent of the military support offered by Canadian forces in NATO and NORAD, however, the Americans had few grounds for complaint. Although government spokesmen in the United States immediately voiced their complete satisfaction with Canadian cooperation during the missile crisis, those in the Kennedy administration who noticed Ottawa's political response were probably disappointed by it.[79] But the Canadian rhetoric, or lack of it, had exposed no weakness and posed no threat to national security interests. The Americans may also have realized that they too were vulnerable to criticism. Under the NORAD agreement, the "agreed procedure," was that the President and the Prime Minister were supposed to consult about the "risks and repercussions" of recommended joint military proposals during a crisis. This, of course, had not been followed in the case of the Cuban alert.

In his first response to the critics within his party and the press, the Prime Minister took aim at this failure:

> Canada and the United Sates are members of NORAD... As I look back on the Cuban crisis I believe that it emphasized more than ever before the necessity of there being full consultation before any action is taken or policies executed that might lead to war ... Consultation is a prerequisite to joint and contemporaneous action being

taken for it could never have been intended that either of the nations would automatically follow whatever stand the other might take.[80]

Diefenbaker's criticism was echoed not only in the press[81] but also by the Liberal leader. "Cuba," Pearson stated, "re-emphasizes the danger of one ally acting alone without consultation with others, though those others are bound to be involved in any results from the decision taken."[82] A formal memorandum written shortly after the crisis by the Under-Secretary of State for External Affairs, Norman Robertson, similarly argues that the provisions of the NORAD agreement, as Canada understood them, had not been followed by the US.[83]

Conclusion

The Cuban missile crisis was not John Diefenbaker's finest hour. But it was also not as thoroughly wrong-headed and lamentable a performance as has been portrayed. His critics have suggested Diefenbaker misjudged the seriousness of the crisis, misunderstood the strategic threat presented by the missiles, misread the concerns of Washington, and misconceived Canadian policy. On all of these points some reassessment is required by the new evidence now available. Diefenbaker cannot be criticized for Canada being slow to put forces on alert (since they were, in effect, on alert virtually from the beginning), for not providing military support (since Canada played an active role in the naval operations), and for not providing an official statement of support, given that this expression was eventually forthcoming. To be sure, it did not come forth immediately or enthusiastically, but it came.

It is also now clear that those Canadians, including Diefenbaker, who worried about American emotionalism over

Cuba were quite justified in doing so. Washington's adoption of the blockade option was necessitated not just by the international situation created by the Soviet deployment but also, and perhaps even more, by the internal political situation in the United States. The dangerous state of American public and elite feelings about Cuba made the discovery of the missiles at least as much a domestic political crisis for the Kennedy administration as an international crisis for the superpowers.

Though it is doubtful how much John Diefenbaker thought through the strategic implications, it is clear he had misgivings about the wisdom of Kennedy's publicly announced course of action. It is also arguable that these were justifiable misgivings. The missile crisis did not come to a peaceful conclusion through the resolute coercive action which had worried the Canadian government. Though the blockade forced the issue of the missiles, the crisis was peacefully concluded ultimately by flexible diplomacy. In the end, Kennedy, fearful of escalation and the dangers inherent in the unfolding events he and Khrushchev had precipitated, not only accepted but offered the Soviets the sort of deal he and his advisors had soundly rejected a few days before. The misgivings about the course of action pursued initially by Washington were thus not only to be found in Ottawa.

The missiles in Cuba precipitated more than an east-west crisis and a domestic political crisis for the President. Canadians found themselves at the brink without consent—or even consultation. While the Kennedy administration was very much concerned about the views of the OAS, the views of Canada aroused little interest or attention.[84] The required measure of cooperation seems to have been simply assumed. The realization of this situation in Ottawa created an acute crisis in Canadian-American relations inextricably linked to the broader international crisis.

Canada, the only NATO ally to back the United States militarily, yet ironically criticized for insufficient support, would suffer other repercussions as a result of the missile crisis. In the next months, the government was subjected to increasing pressures both from domestic sources and from outside Canada, to come to a decision on the acquisition of nuclear arms for the Canadian military. The impotence of Canada's weapons systems during the crisis came as a shock to the many Canadians who had not previously focused on the nuclear issue. The crisis also seriously damaged the credibility of Diefenbaker's promise that nuclear warheads, while shunned in peacetime, would be made quickly available in time of war.[85] Within the cabinet, the nuclear split hardened and became more sharply defined. At the same time, with the world having come so close to nuclear catastrophe, those who opposed nuclear arms were more than ever determined to keep them out of Canada. The major political crisis of the Diefenbaker era was now brewing.

NOTES

1. See Don Page and Don Munton, "Canadian Images of the Cold War 1946-7" *International Journal*, Vol. XXXII, No. 3, Summer 1977, pp. 577-604.

2. See Chapter 4 in this volume.

3. See, for example, (Toronto) *Globe and Mail*, December 10, 1960; *Toronto Telegram*, February 5, 1962; Denis Stairs, "Confronting Uncle Sam, Cuba and Korea," *An Independent Foreign Policy for Canada?* ed. Stephen Clarkson (Toronto, McClelland and Stewart 1968), p. 62. These differences in views and the pressures brought to bear against Canada by US officials were evident, for example, at the July 1960 closed-door meeting of the Canada-US Ministerial Committee on Joint Defence. See H. Basil Robinson, *Diefenbaker's World: A Populist in Foreign Affairs*, Toronto, University of Toronto Press, 1989, p. 146.

4. See "Why We Won't Join the Blockade to Starve Castro Out of Cuba," *Maclean's*, LXXV (April 21, 1962), p. 2. A similar comment was offered by John Holmes, "Canada and the United States in World Politics," *Foreign Affairs*, XL (October, 1961), 107. "A small country," Holmes said, "somewhat concerned itself with the overweening power of the United States has a certain sympathy with aspects of Castroism."

5. Robinson, *Diefenbaker's World*, p. 147. In mid-1961 Diefenbaker remarked to Robinson on "the acute nervousness of the US administration on Cuba" (p. 196).

6. Richard Preston, *Canada in World Affairs, 1959-1961* (Toronto: Oxford University Press, 1965), p. 181.

7. *House of Commons Debates*, April 19, 1961, p. 3795.

8. "The Cuban Situation," May 12, 1961, POF: Countries: Canada Security, JFK Trip to Ottawa, 5/16-8/61, folder (B), Kennedy Papers, John F. Kennedy Library. (Hereafter cited as Kennedy Papers.)

9. "The Cuban Situation," May 12, 1961, POF: Countries: Canada Security, JFK Trip to Ottawa, 5/16-18/61, folder (B), Kennedy Papers.

10. Robinson, *Diefenbaker's World*, pp. 166, 168.

11. *Washington Post*, May 12, 1961, clipping included with briefing papers, POF: Countries: Canada Security, JFK Trip to Ottawa, 5/16-18/61, folder (D), Kennedy Papers. Canada was also involved at this time to a certain degree in what have been described by the Prime Minister's foreign policy adviser as "low key attempts" with Brazil and Mexico to reduce the growing tensions between Washington and Havana. (Robinson, *Diefenbaker's World*, p. 146.)

12. Department of State Telegram from Acting Secretary Chester Bowles to Secretary Rusk, American Consulate Geneva, May 12, 1961, POF: Countries, Canada Security, JFK Trip to Ottawa, 5/16-18/61, folder (D), Kennedy Papers.

13. Canada's senior diplomat at the time, Norman Robertson, was very much of this view. See J.L. Granatstein, *A Man of Influence*, Ottawa: Deneau Publishers, 1981, pp. 343, 345.

14. *Debates*, May 19, 1961, p. 5039.

15. "Trends in Canadian Foreign Policy," National Intelligence Estimate Number 99-61, May 2, 1961, POF: Countries: Canada Security, JFK Trip to Ottawa, 5/16-18/61, folder (D), Kennedy Papers.

16. "Cuban Situation," May 12, 1961, POF: Countries: Canada Security, JFK Trip to Ottawa, 5/16-18/61, Folder (B) Kennedy Papers.

17. John T. Saywell (ed.), *Canadian Annual Review for 1962* (Toronto, 1963), p. 81. In an article entitled "How Canada Helps Keep Castro Going," *U.S. News and World Report* asserted that "food, machinery, aircraft engines and other goods from Canada— even explosives—are being used by Cuba's Communist masters to stave off any internal crisis that might spark an uprising." LII (February 26, 1962), p. 6.

18. Department of State Telegram to American Embassy in Ottawa, "Text of Letter from President to Prime Minister," October 19, 1962, POF: Countries: Canada Security, 1961-1963, Kennedy Papers.

19. *American Foreign Policy, Current Documents 1962* (Washington, 1966), pp. 369, 374.

20. James G. Blight and David A. Welch, *On the Brink: Americans and Soviets Reexamine the Cuban Missile Crisis*, New York, Noonday, 1990, pp. 407, 409.

21. See Graham T. Allison, *The Essence of Decision*, Boston, Little Brown, 1971 and Blight and Welch, *On the Brink*.

22. Various material, Cuba General, 4/63-11/63, Kennedy Papers. See also Blight and Welch, *On the Brink*, and Raymond L. Garthoff, *Reflections on the Cuban Missile Crisis*, Washington, D. C., Brookings, 1987, pp. 17, 78-9. Although the hard evidence is not conclusive, some recently available materials suggest the possibility that the Kennedy administration was "moving toward a military attack on Cuba in the fall of 1962, even before it discovered the Soviet strategic missiles." See James G. Hershberg, "Before 'The Missiles of October': Did Kennedy Plan a Military Strike against Cuba?" *Diplomatic History*, Spring, 1991.

23. Memorandum to the President, "Reactions to Cuba in Western Europe," May 3, 1961, Cuba Security—1961, Kennedy Papers.

24. On the role of Congressional critics, see Robert A. Divine (ed.), *The Cuban Missile Crisis* (Chicago, 1971), pp. 7, 9, 14; Louise Fitzsimmons, *The Kennedy Doctrine* (New York, 1972). pp. 129-39.

25. Abram Chayes in Blight and Welch, *On the Brink*, p. 40.

26. Robinson, *Diefenbaker's World*, p. 283.

27. September 22, 1962.

28. Debates, October 26, 1962, p. 567.

29. These deliberations have been described by various participants, including Robert F. Kennedy, *Thirteen Days; A Memoir of the Cuban Missile Crisis*, New York, Norton, 1969; Theodore C. Sorenson, *Kennedy*, New York, Harper and Row,1965; and analyzed at length by Allison, *Essence of Decision*, pp. 185-210. Unknown to most of the participants, however, the ExCom meetings (and numerous other White House meetings of this period) were secretly tape-recorded. Transcriptions of these tapes are now available at the John F. Kennedy Library in Boston, and have been excerpted. See "White House Tapes and Minutes of the Cuban Missile Crisis," *International Security*, Vol. 10, No. 1, Summer 1985, pp. 164-203 and "October 27, 1962: Transcripts of the Meetings of the ExComm," *International Security*, Vol. 12, No. 3, Winter 1987-88, pp. 30-92.

30. Robert McNamara in "White House Tapes...," *International Security*, pp. 164-203. A confidential memorandum to the President from Lou Harris, his political pollster, focusing on the election campaign and drafted only days before the missile crisis developed warned Kennedy that, while he was doing well on some other issues such as the racial problem, the balance of American public opinion on his policies toward Cuba was overwhelmingly negative. Over 80% in some key states were in favour of a blockade. The domestic political message was presumably clear. (Memorandum to the President from Louis Harris, "Subject: The New Shape of this Campaign," 4 October 1962, POF, Polls, General, Kennedy Papers). Former President Eisenhower suspected that domestic politics might be involved. See Elie Abel, *The Missile Crisis*, New York, Bantam, 1966, p. 64. So did some Canadians; "There was a nagging worry here which no one put into words publicly but which some responsible people expressed privately...that the American reaction...may not be completely separate from the American election campaign." *Montreal Star*, October 23.

31. Fen Osler Hampson, "The Divided Decision-Maker: American Domestic Politics and the Cuban Crises," *International Security*, Vol. 9, No. 3, Winter 1984-5, pp. 149, 141.

32. The Ormsby-Gore-Kennedy friendship has been described as a "unique relationship between an Ambassador and a President with no parallel in modern times." David Nunnerley, *President Kennedy and Britain* (New York, 1972), p. 43.

33. Harold Macmimllan, *At the End of the Day 1961-1963* (London, 1973), pp. 182, 186.

34. Message from President Kennedy to Prime Minister Diefenbaker, October 22, 1962, POF: Countries: Canada Security, 1961-1963, Kennedy Papers.

35. Macmillan, *End of the Day*, p. 186.

36. Interview with the Hon. Livingston Merchant, June 18, 1974.

37. JFK message to Diefenbaker, October 22, 1962, POF: Countries: Canada Security, 1961-1963, Kennedy Papers.

38. Macmillan, *End of the Day*, pp. 185-887.

39. Although Merchant thought that the Prime Minister had probably been briefed by his own military on the activity in Cuba, Diefenbaker gave no sign he knew anything at all. It appears, however, that Diefenbaker, in fact, did know by Sunday, 21 October, the day before the Merchant visit and the Kennedy speech, that a serious crisis over Cuba was brewing and that it concerned Soviet missile installations. (Robinson, *Diefenbaker's World*, p. 285.) He almost certainly knew no details, however.

40. *Debates*, October 22, 1962, pp. 805-06.

41. This proposal, contained in a memorandum drafted before the US photo-reconnaissance evidence had been revealed, came from the Under-Secretary of External Affairs, Norman Robertson. This document also drew an explicit analogy with the Suez siuation, which, as Diefenbaker was well aware, had led to Lester Pearson's receipt of the Nobel Peace Prize. (Robinson, *Diefenbaker's World*, p. 288) Although Diefenbaker was subsequently much criticized for this proposal, the US State Department was at this time working on a UN-centred plan for the withdrawal of the missiles which would have involved an "observer corps" of inspectors in Cuba and UN-supervised inspection of all nuclear missile sites. Secretary of State Dean Rusk presented these plans to the ExCom on Friday 26 October.

42. The above quotations are all from *Debates*, October 22, 1962, pp. 806-07.

43. Saywell, *Review 1962*, p. 128.

44. This concern for working within the UN is very much evident in such cases as the Korean War and the Suez crisis. See Chapters 4 and 5 of this volume.

45. This asymmetry of perceptions is one of the most common observations of research on perceptions that members of one group tend to perceive those of another group as like-minded even when they are not. The moderation of the Kennedy administration was recognized by officials in the Canadian embassy in Washington, but not initially by their political masters in Ottawa.

46. Abel, *The Missile Crisis*, p. 64.

47. Macmillan, *End of the Day*, p. 187.

48. Defense Condition 3 indicates very serious international tension. Defcon 5 is normal; Defcon 1 is war.

49. Charles Foulkes, "The Complications of Continental Defence," *Neighbors Taken for Granted*, ed. Livingston Merchant (New York, 1966), p. 121.

50. Except where notes indicate otherwise, the account of this meeting, which lasted until approximately 2 a.m. on October 23, has been put together from interviews with Harkness, Miller, Dunlap and an interview with General G. Walsh (Chief of General Staff), October 25, 1974.

51. As a briefing memorandum prepared for President Kennedy in 1961 had stated, "loss or dimunition of U.S. use of Canadian air space and real estate and the contributions of the Canadian military, particularly the RCAF and Royal Canadian Navy, would be intolerable in time of crisis." Memorandum for the President, February 17, 1961, POF: Countries: Canada Security, 1961-1963, Kennedy Papers.

52. Miller interview, October 31, 1974.

53. NORAD headquarters announced on January 1, 1963 that Canadian units had been on alert since the beginning of the crisis. *Globe and Mail*, January 2, 1963.

54. For example, the recall of men on longer leave and evacuations. Interview with Rear Admiral Kenneth Dyer, October 28, 1974.

55. Harkness interview, July 22, 1974.

56. None of the accounts written from the US point of view mention it. Of Canadian accounts, only Peyton Lyon and Robert Reford comment. Lyon states that "The movement of RCN ships out of Halifax freed ships of the U.S. Navy to take up positions further south in the quarantine area." (*Canada in World Affairs, 1961-63*, Toronto, Canadian Institute of International Affairs, Oxford, 1968, p. 42.) Reford makes a similar statement but neither source deals with the NATO implications. (*Canada and Three Crises*, Toronto, Canadian Institute of International Affairs, p. 213.)

57. Blight and Welch, *On the Brink*, p. 61. Rear Admiral Kenneth Dyer, who held the "triple-hatted" position of Atlantic Maritime Commander responsible for the Chairman of the Chiefs of Staff, Atlantic Flag Officer responsible to the Naval Chief, and most importantly, Canadian Atlantic Area Commander responsible to SACLANT's Admiral Wright in Norfolk, proudly notes in his career résumé that a major operational test of our effectiveness was achieved during the Cuban missile crisis when all available maritime forces were deployed at short notice in accordance with NATO plans." (Résumé copy provided by Admiral Dyer.)

58. It can be argued that the NORAD contribution mattered far less. One critic of Canadian participation in NORAD, writing under the impression that there had been no alert until the 24th, poses the following question: "Did this hesitancy expose the United States to a possible devastating nuclear attack and did it make the Strategic Air Command vulnerable? The answer is clearly, "no." If the Russians had launched a nuclear attack, missiles would have been launched first, and there "was and still is no defence against missiles." SAC missiles were alerted; SAC bombers—not under NORAD control— were dispersed. "The deterrent was protected as well as it could have been." John W. Warnock, *Partner to Behemoth: The Military Policy of a Satellite Canada* (Toronto: New Press, 1970), p. 176.

59. Macmillan recorded in his diary conversations he had with General Lauris Norstad, NATO's Supreme Allied Commander in Europe, on October 22, in which Norstad agreed that NATO forces ought not go on alert. See Macmillan, *End of the Day*, pp. 190, 195.

60. Diefenbaker's memoirs make reference to a phone call with Kennedy on Monday, 22 October, but most other sources contradict this claim. Basil Robinson, citing Diefenbaker's secretary as the source, states there was a "bad-tempered" call with the President on Tuesday, 23 October. (Robinson, *Diefenbaker's World*.)

61. Robinson, *Diefenbaker's World*, p. 176.

62. A poll taken in the first two weeks of November showed that 79% of Canadians approved of Kennedy's action. *Globe and Mail*, November 23, 1962. At the same time, in the US, approval of Kennedy's presidential performance climbed to "nearly 80%." Robert A. Divine (ed.), *The Cuban Missile Crisis*, Chicago, 1971, p. 58.

63. Interview with the Hon. E. Davie Fulton, July 11, 1974.

64. Canadian apprehensions about American tendencies to provoke the Soviets would not have been allayed had they known that the chief of the US Strategic Air Command had deliberately and without authorization sent the order to move to Defcon 2 status (imminent enemy attack expected) "in the clear," rather than in secret, precisely to ensure the Russians would know about it. This was, incidently, the highest alert level *ever* of American forces. (Blight and Welch, *On the Brink*, pp. 3, 75).

65. Although the source of this intelligence about Soviet preparations is not known, it is now clear that it was false, or at least greatly exaggerated. The Soviet military were not at any point during the crisis put on heightened alert. See Marc Trachtenberg, "The Influence of Nuclear Weapons in the Cuban Missile Crisis," *International Security*, Vol. 10, No. 1, (Summer 1985), pp. 137-63. It is unclear whether or not Diefenbaker, in fact, knew that Harkness had already, in effect, put the Canadian forces on alert. Although Diefenbaker himself consistently denied he did, a former senior staffer suspects he did know. "Not much" he says, "escaped the Diefenbaker antennae." (Robinson, *Diefenbaker's World*, p. 288.)

66. These and following comments are from *Debates*. October 23 and 24, 1962, pp. 822, 883. 884-5.

67. From a transcript provided by the Canadian Broadcasting Corporation, Green interview, July 9, 1974. A good part of the questioning in the interview was an attempt to elicit a satisfactory response as to the degree of support Canada was offering the United States, but Green avoided any endorsement of Kennedy's blockade. He stated that he didn't know what history would say about the President's action, "but that action has been taken now, and I think the important fact is what's done from now on."

68. For these and following comments, see *Debates*, October 25, 1962, pp. 911-917.

69. None of the early accounts of the missile crisis, including those by Robert Kennedy, *Thirteen Days*, and White House aide Ted Sorenson, *Kennedy*, portray the withdrawal of the Jupiter missiles as an explicit provision of the agreement which ended the crisis. Ambassador Dobrynin has recently argued that Robert Kennedy proposed it explicitly to him and represented it as a significant US concession. (In one sense it was, but in another sense it was not, as the administration had, in fact, explored months earlier the possibility of removing these missiles from Turkey.) Soviet Foreign Minister Andrei Gromyko has made it clear that he and Khrushchev so perceived the agreement. Moreover, Sorenson has recently acknowledged that, as the editor of *Thirteen Days*, he revised the relevant account from Robert Kennedy's diary prior to the book's publication to make it appear there had been no explicit American undertaking (Blight and Welch, *On the Brink*, p. 341). Sorenson's explanation for what thus was a deliberate act of misrepresentation is that only a very few key officials then knew of the secret provision, but he was presumably conscious that revelation of any such agreement would be, even a few years after the event, still extremely sensitive politically. The importance of this piece of new information can hardly be overestimated; at the very least it discredits the popular notion that Khrushchev "backed down." In fact, Moscow agreed to remove the missiles in return for two important concessions by the US.

70. Blight and Welch, *On the Brink*, pp. 102, 108, 190; "White House Tapes," p. 195.

71. Blight and Welch, *On the Brink*, p. 190.

72. This point is reinforced in a number of ways. Blight and Welch, for example, argue that a basic cause of the crisis was Khrushchev's lack of understanding of the potency of American public opinion on both Cuba *per se* and the extent of increasing Soviet influence there. (Blight and Welch, *On the Brink*, p. 303).

73. Green interview, July 9, 1974.

74. Pierre Sevigny, *This Game of Politics* (Toronto, 1965), p. 253.

75. Warner Troyer, "We Flunked the NORAD Test," *Commentator*, VI (December 1962), 6-7. It might be noted here that the text of the agreement itself stresses the "fullest possible consultation...on all matters affecting the joint defence of North America," but formally left open the question of whether such consultation was a prerequisite during an emergency or only during the stage of contingency planning. *Canada Treaty Series*, No. 9.

76. *The Financial Post*, November 3, 1962.

77. "Canada: Defensive Gap," *Time*, LXXX (November 9, 1962), 41. For Harkness's response to a similar report see *Debates*, November 2, 1962, p. 1218.

78. Harkness interview, July 22, 1974. According to Harkness, some confusion arose because the Americans did request extra flights, but not during the crisis. An increase above the usual number was requested for the month of November, and this was approved by Harkness.

79. *Globe and Mail*, November 5, 1962. Theodore Sorenson refers to "some wavering by Canada" (*Kennedy*, p. 705).

80. Canadian Institute of International Affairs Library: Canada- Foreign Relations—Cuba. Notes for Diefenbaker Address to Zionist Organization of Canada, Toronto, November 5, 1962.

81. See the *Globe and Mail*, November 7, 1962, and *Toronto Star*, November 1, 1962, quoted in Saywell, *Review 1962*, pp. 134-35.

82. *The Nation's Business*, October 31, 1962, quoted in Reford, *Three Crises*, p. 210.

83. Department of External Affairs, file 50309-40, NAR to Minister, 7 November 1962, cited in Granatstein, *A Man of Influence*, p. 353.

84. A summary of the foreign press response to the blockade, found in President Kennedy's office files, makes it clear that a differing perception was not expected from the Canadians. The nine-page résumé covers the press reaction of Europe, Latin America, Asia, Africa and the Middle East but does not mention a single Canadian newspaper. USIA Summary of Foreign Press, October 23, 1962, POF: Countries: Cuba 1962, Kennedy Papers.

85. Lyon, *Canada in World Affairs, 1961-63*. p. 119. As one Ottawa commentator wrote on October 27, the crisis "laid at rest for all time the government's theory that the time to acquire nuclear weapons is on the eve of actual hostilities." Quoted in Saywell, *Review 1962*, p. 135.

SUGGESTED READINGS

Diefenbaker, John G., *One Canada: The Tumultuous Years, 1962-1967*, Toronto: Macmillan, 1977, pp. 77-90.

Lyon, Peyton V., *Canada in World Affairs, 1961-1963*, Toronto: Oxford University Press, 1968, pp. 77-90.

Nicholson, Patrick, *Vision and Indecision: Diefenbaker and Pearson*, Toronto: Longmans, 1968, pp. 145-78.

Reford, Robert, *Canada and Three Crises*, Toronto: Longmans, Canadian Institute of International Affairs 1968, pp. 147-218.

Stursberg, Peter, *Diefenbaker: Leadership Lost, 1962-67*, Toronto: University of Toronto Press, 1976.

c h a p t e r 7

DEPLOYING NUCLEAR WEAPONS, 1962-63

Jocelyn Ghent-Mallet

On the evening of 5 February 1963, a motion of no-confidence in the government of John Diefenbaker, based on "lack of leadership, the breakdown of unity in the cabinet, and confusion and indecision in dealing with national and international problems," was carried by a majority of 142 to 111. The only nationally elected Progressive Conservative government in four and a half decades of recent Canadian history was toppled by vote of the House of Commons, the second government since Confederation to be so defeated.

. . .

The problem which provoked both domestic upheaval and political tension between Canada and the United States centred on the question of whether the Diefenbaker government should accept a nuclear role, within the American alliance system, for Canada's armed forces. Analysts are agreed that the nuclear controversy in Canada came to a head following the October 1962 crisis over emplacement of Soviet missiles in Cuba. In the aftermath of the Cuban confrontation, public discussion of Canada-United States interaction during the crisis broadened into a widespread realization that Canada's Bomarc missiles had stood unarmed throughout the period of continental alert, and that Canada's Voodoo interceptors had lacked the nuclear weaponry which their American counterparts possessed. In editorials and from public platforms, the Diefenbaker government was accused of failing not only in its commitments to NORAD (the North American Air Defence Command), but also in its obligations to NATO (the North Atlantic Treaty Organization). Observers pointed out that the Honest John launcher and rocket system, deployed by the Canadian army in Europe, was as impotent as the Bomarc, and that the Starfighter aircraft was now being delivered to overseas units of the Royal Canadian Air Force without the nuclear agreement needed to make it operational.

From November 1962 through the collapse of the government in February and the election of a Liberal prime minister in April 1963, defence policy was the subject of unremitting public debate. Strong voices were raised for the first time in support of the acquisition of nuclear weapons. Influential segments of the Canadian press, once vehemently opposed to the arms, now condemned the government for obfuscation and delay. The shift in attitude was hastened by the missile crisis, but had actually begun some months before, as the press became aware that three of the four weapons systems acquired by the government could not be fitted with conventional armament. Rejection of a nuclear role,

Jocelyn Ghent-Mallet, "Deploying Nuclear Weapons," from *The International History Review*, Vol. 1, No. 2, April, 1979.

101

therefore, risked the scrapping of hundreds of millions of dollars worth of military hardware, as well as new problems with respect to Canada's future contribution to collective security. The Toronto Globe and Mail moved from a declaration of firm opposition in May 1961 to the assertion on 5 January 1963 that Canadians were committed to the acceptance of nuclear warheads, and must either honour that commitment or withdraw from NATO and NORAD. Similarly, Maclean's magazine, which had organized a nation-wide, anti-nuclear letter-writing campaign in 1960, censured the government in October 1962 for "coquettish indecision" and insisted that Canada live up to its obligations.

Gallup and other polls taken during the last two months of 1962 confirmed this shift in mood. A November survey by the Canadian Peace Research Institute revealed that sixty per cent of the electorate supported a nuclear role for Canada's armed forces.[1] Prime Minister Diefenbaker placed absolutely no credence in these samples of public opinion. "Polls (or poles)," in his oft-expressed view, were "for dogs." Anti-nuclear demonstrations staged in the wake of brinksmanship over Cuba, and a steady flow of anti-nuclear letters and telegrams to his office, impressed the prime minister far more.

To dissension within the country was added dissension within cabinet. Upon assuming the national defence portfolio late in 1960, Douglas Harkness stated a view in direct conflict with that held by Howard Green, secretary of state for external affairs. Harkness sought outright acceptance of the nuclear armament needed to make all systems operational and effective. Green was resolutely opposed to Canadian acquisition of nuclear weapons, because he feared such action would compromise Canada's search for a means to global disarmament.

The majority of ministers had no strong sentiments one way or the other and paid little heed to the nuclear question until after the Cuban crisis. The weapons systems had been acquired in the first place without full cabinet consideration or understanding of the nuclear implications, primarily as consequence of the close relationship between the Canadian and American bureaucracies. Heavy economic and allied pressures, the absence of appropriate political counsel, poor civilian-military communication, and a general lack of ministerial interest in defence matters were all factors contributing to quick cabinet acquiescence in what had seemed merely a series of technical decisions. Thus ministers generally concur that before November 1962 there had been virtually no discussion of nuclear weapons in cabinet.

After the missile crisis, cabinet discussion focused on the nuclear question to the effective exclusion of everything else. The ministers eventually agreed that Canada could negotiate acceptance of nuclear weapons for the systems in Europe, but the minister for external affairs insisted that the government must continue to take a lead in the pursuit of disarmament, and that the ability to do so would be irreparably impaired by the presence of a nuclear force in Canada. Green hoped that warheads stored in Europe for the Canadian army and air division in NATO would be interpreted in world councils less as a national possession, and more as a non-proliferating contribution to an existing multilateral capability. As American intelligence experts had correctly predicted the year before, the external affairs minister would be likely to seize on any sign of disarmament progress "to justify continued refusal to accept nuclear weapons on Canadian soil," but given his commitment to the principles embodied in the Atlantic

Alliance, the government under pressure "probably would not...refuse nuclear weapons for Canadian NATO forces in Europe."[2]

American officials regarded Green's attitude as part of a "naive and parochial approach" to global politics, but they conceded Green's influence on Diefenbaker and his ability to exercise "a voice in the cabinet second only to that of the prime minister."[3] Green drew support for his views from ministers who were concerned about the implications for Canadian autonomy in weapons control arrangements. The Americans insisted that the so-called two-key system, already negotiated between the United States and other NATO powers, was a bilateral control arrangement fully consistent with allied sovereignty. Under the terms of American legislation passed in 1958, custody of the weapons in Canada would remain with the United States, but once the weapons had been released by order of the president, the decision whether to use them would belong to the Canadian government. Canada would control the second key, but American custody would mean detachments of US troops at Bomarc and Voodoo bases. The stationing of American soldiers in Canada was an old grievance, a felt infringement of sovereignty dating back to the Second World War. Hence the separate concepts of custody and control, of possession and autonomy, tended to muddle—an effect exacerbated by the simultaneous American demand for storage in Canada of nuclear weapons, not only for Canadian forces, but for United States forces as well. Declassified presidential papers reveal what prime ministerial memoirs now also confirm: the Kennedy administration sought Canadian territory as a nuclear base not just for squadrons under NORAD's bilateral command, but also for military units under exclusive United States control—

Polaris submarine and Strategic Air Command forces at United States bases in Argentia, Newfoundland, and Goose Bay, Labrador. American insistence on negotiating, as part of a single nuclear package, the question of weapons for Canadian systems and the question of Canadian facilities for a US nuclear strike force under sole US command clouded the issue of control.[4] "The basic problem in any Canadian acquisition of nuclear weapons," Diefenbaker wrote, "assumed a greater importance after the Cuban crisis than before. Canada had to achieve the maximum degree of political control.... I felt that Canadian public opinion, rightly or wrongly, attached a special significance to nuclear weapons, and that the acceptability of [an affirmative] decision...would be greatly influenced by the degree of control the Canadian government exercised over those weapons."[5]

If some members of cabinet leaned towards Green's point of view because they were worried about questions of sovereignty and control, others supported Harkness because they were concerned with the possibility of American economic redress, and the fate of defence production-sharing. They were also sensitive to the dissatisfactions being expressed by other NATO allies. One minister reported that he was "horrified" to discover that discussions with the Americans had not been going on all along. After the Cuban crisis, he declared, "cabinet gave Green specific instructions to negotiate, to seek practical alternatives."[6] "The cabinet was virtually unanimous," Defence Minister Harkness similarly recalled, "in agreeing that negotiations were necessary. Even Green concurred...."[7] Talks with the United States began, but the character of the discussion was shaped by the conflict in ministerial judgement, and by Diefenbaker's conviction that a majority of Canadians would not accept outright acquisition of nuclear weapons. As one cabinet colleague explained, "a minority government is always sensitive to public opinion." With parliamentary opposition so strongly anti-nuclear, a decision in favour of the weapons would also have meant "a very delicate situation" in the Commons.[8] Yet with spreading domestic criticism, mounting pressure from the allies, and his own cabinet pleading for resolution of the issue, Diefenbaker knew he had to find some sort of answer. Perhaps the Americans could be persuaded to accept a compromise.

Kennedy's Secretary of State, Dean Rusk, later told members of the United States senate foreign relations committee that on the prime minister's insistence, the negotiations were conducted on a "top-secret" basis. There did seem to be, Rusk acknowledged, "a serious internal problem and differences within the Cabinet." Government officials wanted to be able to say "somewhat different things" to two different kinds of audience. For the benefit of one group, they wished to confirm defence arrangements "which the United States considers fully effective, [but they also] wanted to be able to say to the Ban the Bomb people, 'We have no operational nuclear weapons on Canadian soil'."[9] One idea—that the warheads be quickly obtained from the Americans if an emergency arose—had been suggested publicly by the prime minister as early as February 1962, but the scheme was rejected by the Americans as too time-consuming and costly to be feasible. Another Canadian idea, one which was never disclosed to the press or parliament, involved American retention of a crucial piece of the weapon near the border, where it could be held in readiness and then airlifted to Canada more rapidly and less expensively than could the weapon itself. According to the prime minister, the American negotiating team pre-

sented studies, on 4 December 1962, which showed that all Bomarcs and Voodoos in Canada could be armed with the missing part in two hours and ten minutes or less. Since the "likely warning time of bomber attack" was estimated at three hours, the prime minister considered the plan "capable of meeting the requirements of effective North American defence."[10] According to Secretary Rusk, however, the American negotiators "could not figure out any way" to meet time requirements or, "most critically," to avert "the chance of an actual nuclear explosion in the process of putting [the] pieces into the weapons...under conditions of great urgency."[11] The defence minister had a similar view. None of the schemes, Harkenss later complained, "would provide a really satisfactory solution."[12]

While discussions with the United States wore on through the last two months of 1962 and into the new year, the Diefenbaker government edged unknowingly closer to defeat. Although the Conservatives largely succeeded—right up to the start of a month-long Christmas recess on 21 December—in keeping the nuclear issue from reaching the floor of the House of Commons, public pressure continued to intensify. On 3 January 1963, the farewell visit to Canada of General Lauris Norstad, NATO's newly-retired supreme allied commander [in] Europe, interjected a new and dramatic voice into the Canadian domestic debate. Upon his arrival in Ottawa, Norstad paid a formal call on the governor-general, lunched with senior military officials, and then met the press. In his opening statement, Norstad complimented his hosts by observing that there were "no finer troops made available to NATO than those that Canada has sent to Europe." But in the question and answer period that followed, Norstad contradicted the government's public position. He declared his belief that Canada would not be fulfilling its obligations to NATO unless nuclear weapons were provided. The general appeared to grow increasingly uncomfortable under the intense questioning, and observed finally that the press was "spending too much time" on the topic of nuclear commitments. "Certainly," he added, "there must be something else interesting to Canadians."[13]

Norstad's seeming reluctance to respond to some questions and his apparently minimal awareness of their potential political significance have led some to suppose that the general was inadequately briefed on the sensitivity of the nuclear issue. The press conference transcript, according to one account, "and the man's own reputation for integrity and independence, tend to disprove" the theory that Norstad's visit was the first step in a Pentagon campaign "to bully the unwilling Canadians into relinquishing their nuclear virginity."[14] The general's "integrity and independence," however, would not have precluded him from expressing an opinion that he shared not only with other NATO officials and the Pentagon, but also with the Canadian military. The prime minister regarded Norstad's action as evidence of "what amounted to a supra-governmental relationship between the Canadian military...and the Pentagon.... The Norstad visit was part of this pattern; it was the Canadian military that organized his press conference."[15]

One analyst, examining Norstad's comments in this context, judged his action "an attempt to influence the conclusion of the Canadian nuclear debate...in a manner satisfactory to the organization with which he was associated." As the first top-level NATO officer to take a public position, the general's opinion of Canada's commitment "car-ried great weight in influencing Canadian opinion." The fact that it was expressed in Canada tossed it into the increasingly agitated Canadian public debate. This then tended to fortify the U.S. position on the Canadian acquisition of nuclear weapons and armed those Canadians who opposed the government's policy.[16] As Diefenbaker remarked, Norstad "had held the most politically sensitive military command in the NATO structure. It is impossible to accept that he innocently wandered into Canada's nuclear debate."[17]

Although Diefenbaker is on less solid ground when he additionally insists that Norstad's visit to Ottawa "could only have been at the behest of President Kennedy," it is certainly possible that the Kennedy administration encouraged Norstad to express his views.... It is clear that the Kennedy administration generally availed itself of every possible diplomatic opportunity to exert pressure.

In any case, as even orthodox accounts concede, "the General did not appear to regret his words."[18] Five days later, Norstad told a reporter in Washington that the alliance "would suffer a great loss" if Canada did not fulfil its nuclear commitment to NATO.[19] Although many Canadians thought it inappropriate and even presumptuous for an American general to come to Canada and tell Canadians of their nuclear obligations, the majority tended to believe the military assessment. The Liberal leader of the opposition, Lester Pearson, "who knew Norstad well and had a great admiration for him," thought that the general had perhaps gone too far in making a public statement. Nevertheless, Pearson added, Norstad "judged it his duty as our Commander, as well as the American Commander in NATO, to express his views.... The series of events leading to the collapse of the government really began," he observed, with Norstad's 3 January press conference.[20]

The next step was Pearson's. In a Toronto speech on 12 January, the Liberal party leader offered his own view of the government's commitments and announced that Canada must honour them by accepting nuclear arms. In his speech and in his memoirs, Pearson emphasized the alliance considerations that led him to reverse, completely, his long-held anti-nuclear position. He had been influenced, in particular, by a report prepared for him by Paul Hellyer, the Liberal defence critic, upon Hellyer's return from a NATO parliamentarians conference in November 1962. Hellyer's pro-nuclear recommendations, in turn, had been inspired by a lengthy private chat with General Norstad. Hellyer subsequently asserted that he had been shaken by the "low morale and downcast attitude" of Canada's NATO forces.[21] But in the memorandum he wrote for Pearson, it is the references to warnings offered by officials at NATO military headquarters and the views expressed by Norstad as supreme allied commander that stand out. Hellyer informed Pearson that "the military people" were very concerned. "They have not reported to the [NATO] Council in a way which will bring the matter into the international political arena, [but] if a decision is not reached, it will not be long before they consider such a report unavoidable." If Canada did not fulfil its nuclear commitments, Hellyer added, "there will be intense pressure on us to withdraw and turn the facilities over to others. Our influence in NATO will be reduced to negligible." To an internationalist like Pearson, who had helped develop the North Atlantic Treaty, this was a powerful argument. The Liberal leader also found the economic considerations persuasive. Rejection of nuclear weapons would mean not only the casting aside of a substantial

investment in existing systems, but also the purchase of new and expensive conventional equipment. Hellyer further warned his chief of the "considerable" economic consequences if Canada should fail to meet its NORAD obligations. The Americans, he stated, "are almost certain to reduce or terminate their production-sharing arrangements with us."[22] Thus Canadian-American military influence was critical to Pearson's change of heart.

The timing of Pearson's announcement was exquisite, for the government was still reeling from the impact of Norstad's press conference. In his speech, the leader of the opposition had disclaimed a partisan motivation, but a decade later he admitted that the nuclear decision was the moment "when I really became a politician."[23] Now, for the first time since the onset of the nuclear controversy, the voters would be able to determine a real difference between the parties. Pearson encountered some opposition from within his own ranks. He had made the decision independently, without consulting his closest political colleagues or the top Liberal leadership. Most anti-nuclear members eventually fell into line, but the party suffered some embarrassing temporary defections. Pierre Trudeau, for one, decried the new policy and declined a Liberal nomination to a seat in the Commons. Pearson acknowledged subsequently that he had also been the recipient of "very bitter letters," accusing him of turning Canadians into "American toadies," and charging him with "shameless immorality." But he discounted this "thoughtless criticism" as the failure to understand that Canada had accepted a NATO strategy and "hence accepted responsibility for the use of nuclear weapons as part of that strategy."[24] A Gallup poll majority and the bulk of the press agreed with him.

Prime Minister Diefenbaker regarded the Opposition leader's *volte-face* as testimony to a Pearson-Kennedy conspiracy aimed at ousting his government. Disquieting evidence of collusion seemed to be accumulating. Pearson had delivered his 12 January speech immediately upon returning from a trip to New York City. Nevertheless, it is important to note that the prime minister *thought* he had detected a conspiracy. The Norstad press conference and Pearson's New York excursion lent new significance to earlier impressions of a very special Kennedy-Pearson warmth and rapport. Together, all seemed clear demonstration of the president's developing determination "to fix things so that he would no longer be obliged to deal with me or my government. It is interesting," Diefenbaker added, "that on 11 January, the day before Mr. Pearson's...speech, the United States administration informed us that they regarded the 'missing part' approach to arming the Bomarcs in Canada as impracticable."[25]

Diefenbaker's perception of collusion between Pearson and Kennedy, and his unshakable conviction that a majority of Canadians held anti-nuclear views, led him to decide on further delay. Defence Minister Harkness had expected that the government would find it easier to accept nuclear weapons, now that the New Democratic party remained the only strong parliamentary opposition. To his dismay, Harkness discovered that Pearson's change of policy had produced quite the opposite effect. The reason lay in the prime minister's faith that his voluminous anti-nuclear correspondence accurately reflected public opinion. Diefenbaker was similarly swayed by a large and growing number of anti-nuclear letters to the editors of major Canadian newspapers. Many letters to the editor, and probably much of Diefenbaker's

mail, also roundly condemned Pearson for political expediency and demanded that his 1956 Nobel peace prize be revoked. Such attitudes helped to persuade the prime minister that Canadians would never elect a Liberal government pledged to the acceptance of nuclear arms. Increasingly, he was coming to feel that the nuclear issue was one on which he could fight a campaign and win back the majority he had lost in 1962. The evidence of a Liberal Party-Kennedy administration conspiracy angered him, and spurred his determination to defeat the Liberals by appealing to the people. "To my complete surprise," Harkness reported, the prime minister "took the position that we must now oppose the position taken by Pearson and delay any decision on acquiring the warheads."[26]

At a cabinet meeting on 20 January, Harkness threatened to resign if the prime minister continued to insist on "delay and no definite policy until an election was over."[27] And there were six or seven other cabinet ministers, according to information received by Dean Rusk, who wanted "a defense policy and not an election."[28] Party discontent, openly revealed at the 18-19 January meeting of the Progressive Conservative Association, added to the challenge. In the light of these fresh confrontations, and of the urgency presented by the reconvening of parliament on 21 January, Diefenbaker agreed to the appointment of an ad hoc cabinet committee. The committee would investigate, once and for all, the question of nuclear commitments, and on the basis of the findings recommend a policy. After detailed examination over two days and nights of all cabinet and other relevant documents, the four-member committee, which included both Harkness and Green, finally came to a compromise. On 25 January, in a major defence policy address, Diefenbaker used the words of the ad hoc committee report to concede, for the first time, Canadian nuclear obligations. However, the prime minister also listed a number of reasons why the government would have to postpone their implementation, and perhaps eventually change their nature. The speech led to a public contradiction by the United States government, to Defence Minister Harkness's resignation, and to Diefenbaker's parliamentary defeat.

In outlining the nature of Canada's defence obligations to NATO and NORAD, the prime minister's statement seemed in general agreement with the new Liberal position except on one vital point. Pearson regarded the storage of nuclear weapons on Canadian soil as part of the Canadian commitment. Diefenbaker did not, and he revealed the existence of negotiations with the United States to show that the Americans had been willing, over the past three months, to discuss the idea of making the warheads readily available in case of need. As subsequent events would demonstrate, the Americans were disturbed by Diefenbaker's revelation of confidential negotiations, and by the implication that the United States regarded quick availability schemes as practicable. On Canadian insistence, Dean Rusk later complained, the United States "had held [the talks] very closely indeed." The public revelation was of "some embarrassment," for the administration "had not discussed the fact of these negotiations with any of the other governments interested in such problems." As to the usefulness of the Canadian proposals, Rusk protested that "we did not feel...we should be a party to a fraud."[29]

The Americans would display even greater irritation, however, over Diefenbaker's understanding of the Nassau agreement—reached a month earlier by President Kennedy and Prime Minister Harold Macmillan of Britain—as justification for a few more months of delay in arming Canadian weapons systems. The American decision to cancel development of its Skybolt air-to-surface missile had plunged Anglo-American relations into a December crisis. The British had been counting on the Skybolt to prolong the life of their Royal Air Force bombers. After three days of bargaining at Nassau, Kennedy and Macmillan had agreed that the United States would furnish, instead, Polaris missiles for British-built submarines, with the weaponry pledged to NATO in a multilateral nuclear force. The Americans would also contribute to the new force, and it was hoped that other allies would too. Diefenbaker, briefed by Macmillan on the outcome of the Anglo-American talks, regarded the latter discussions as pertinent to his own defence dilemma. In his 25 January speech, the prime minister used the aborted Skybolt to illustrate how the defence "decisions of today are often negatived tomorrow," and employed the concept of a multilateral nuclear force to suggest "a vast alteration in all the defensive techniques that we have accepted in the last few years." "If ever there was a reason," he added in his memoirs, "to seriously re-examine every Canadian defence commitment, this was it."[30]

Diefenbaker regarded the Skybolt cancellation as evidence that technological advance, and hence growing dependence on the ballistic missile deterrent, meant "the day of the bomber is phasing out." Since the Bomarc was an anti-bomber weapon, the obvious implication was that Canada should reassess its commitment to that system. "Should we," he asked the Commons, "carry on with what we have done in the past, merely for the purpose of saying, 'Well, we started, and having started...we will continue?' Should we do this in an area where mistakes are made?" The prime minister also noted the Kennedy-Macmillan emphasis on the importance of strengthening conventional forces. He declared that on the basis of the Nassau communiqué, he had reached these conclusions:

> that there should be no further development of new nuclear power anywhere in the world; that nuclear weapons as a universal deterrent is a dangerous solution. Today an attempt is being made by the United States to have the NATO nations increase their conventional arms. The Nassau agreement seemed to accept these...principles as basic....

For Diefenbaker, both in his speech and in his memoirs, the stress on conventional arms and the concept of a multilateral nuclear force added up to a "tremendous step—a change in the philosophy of defence; a change in the views of NATO." Canada must wait, therefore, for the upcoming NATO ministerial meeting before deciding whether to fulfil its commitments. At the NATO conference, to be held in Ottawa from 21 to 23 May 1963, "we shall secure from the other member nations their views, and on the basis of that we shall be in a position to make a decision...first to maintain our undertakings and second, to execute, if that be the view, the maintenance of our collective defence."[31] In the meantime, the government could continue the negotiations with regard to NORAD. Clearly, the prime minister was playing for time, time to call an election, win it, and rid himself of an incapacitating minority government. The almost two-hour speech reflected his effort to hold together his Conservative party and cabinet, while securing the blessing of what he believed to be the country's anti-nuclear majority.

"Throughout the speech," Defence Minister Harkness recalled, "I sat on ten-

terhooks, waiting to see if the pro-nuclear position would be stated. It was, therefore, with great relief that I heard the terms of the (ad hoc committee report) given. I took this to mean that the prime minister had accepted this position and that the battle was over.[32] Harkness was dismayed, however, to find that the press had focused largely on the anti-nuclear elements of the address and had missed what he felt were its salient points. Thus on 28 January, he took the unprecedented step of issuing a clarifying statement for the press. Harkness asserted that Diefenbaker's speech had set out in a few summary paragraphs "a definite policy for the acquisition of nuclear arms." He noted the prime minister's statement of Canada's commitments. He reiterated, in stronger language, Canada's intention to equip its NATO forces with nuclear weapons should NATO, at the upcoming ministerial meeting, "reaffirm" a Canadian nuclear role. Harkness's final point dealt with NORAD and revealed more than a simple difference of emphasis between his and Diefenbaker's statements. The defence minister announced that Canada had been negotiating over the past months "in order that nuclear weapons will be made available for our...Bomarcs and for the F101 [Voodoo] interceptor squadrons."[33] Diefenbaker had declared, in contrast, that the negotiations were being carried out so that "in case of need nuclear warheads will be made readily available."[34]

The Liberals immediately seized on this evidence of ministerial disarray. Indeed, to both the opposition and the press, it seemed obvious that the cabinet was in deep crisis and increasingly apparent that the government probably would not be able to carry on much longer. As Harkness later acknowledged, his "clarification" had been deliberate. He felt abused by Diefenbaker, and was now persuaded that he had been wrong to compromise at all, that he should never have accepted the idea of postponing a final decision until after the NATO ministerial meetings in May. Thus his statement was "intended" to bring things to a head. "Cabinet either had to accept it, or accept my resignation."[35] But the final filip to Harkness's resignation, and the government's collapse, came from a source outside Canada. On 30 January, the United States' department of state issued a press release which contradicted the basis of the prime minister's 25 January address.

The state department note coldly challenged the prime minister on several important points. Diefenbaker's effort to appease his party's pro-nuclear faction by revealing the existence of nuclear negotiations to arm the systems committed to NORAD was undercut by American insistence that discussions had been merely "exploratory" in nature, and that the government had not proposed any arrangement "sufficiently practical to contribute to North American defense." The prime minister's use of the Nassau agreement as a rationale for further delay before deciding to arm the systems committed to NATO was countered by the assertion that the Kennedy-Macmillan accords had been "fully published" and raised "no question of the appropriateness of nuclear weapons for Canadian forces in fulfilling their [alliance] obligations." Similarly, Diefenbaker's emphasis on the new significance of conventional armament was disputed by the American statement that while a "balanced defense requires increased conventional forces...[these] are not an alternative to nuclear-capable weapons systems." The state department press release also stressed that the Soviet bomber fleet remained a threat, and that a nuclear-armed Bomarc was therefore necessary to an "effective continental defense."[36]

Canadian press and parliamentary reaction to the Kennedy administration's open intervention in a domestic political debate was an angry one. "To put it in the bluntest terms," wrote one Ottawa paper, "the State Department publicly called Prime Minister Diefenbaker a liar." Parliament "was stunned.... Tempers were flaming. President Kennedy was being called a 'bully' among other things.... The immediate and general reaction was that Washington had gone much too far."[37] However, the US embassy in Ottawa reported three days after the issuance of the press release that the "initial psychological reaction...including statements of political leaders, has toned down now—after [the] first shock—to a predominantly positive attitude. [The] feeling is that what [the] U.S. said *had* to be said."[38] In the Commons, all political parties concurred with the prime minister's assertion that the press release had constituted an "unwarranted intrusion in Canadian affairs," but the Liberals charged Diefenbaker with acting "improperly" by disclosing unilaterally the existence of secret negotiations. The Liberals also described the American statement as but "a further link in the chain of evidence which exposes the confusions, the contradictions, the weakness and the indecision of Canadian defence policy."[39]

Prime Minister Diefenbaker's official response was the immediate recall of Charles Ritchie, Ottawa's ambassador to Washington. The prime minister's intent was to deliver a severe rebuke to the United States, and Diefenbaker was furious. The state department note represented the ultimate example of blatant American interference with Canada's sovereign right to determine its own policy. It offered him final proof, it seemed, of a Liberal party-Kennedy administration conspiracy. On the floor of the house, the prime minister did not hesitate to note a "striking resemblance" between the American statement and earlier statements by Mr. Pearson, or to ask the opposition leader "when he was going back for further instructions."[40] American intervention had hardened the prime minister's resolve to appeal to the people, to fight and defeat the Liberals on the nuclear question.

From Defence Minister Harkness's point of view, the press release was "a piece of complete stupidity....a terrible blunder." The Americans, he later reflected, "could have done nothing better to prejudice my case."[41] With Diefenbaker now determined to campaign on an anti-nuclear platform, the defence minister's position became completely untenable. After a highly emotional cabinet session on 3 February, Harkness handed in his long-contemplated resignation, citing differences with the prime minister "not capable of reconciliation."[42] He was the first Canadian cabinet minister to resign on a matter of principle in almost twenty years. To Harkness's surprise, his supporters in cabinet did not follow suit.

The Liberals had known from the moment of the state department's intervention that they had the government "on the ropes." As Pearson recalled, the opposition had read about the cabinet split, "and heard about it, but now we could see it happening before us.... [We] would not let them escape." The Harkness resignation delivered "the crucial blow."[43] On the afternoon of 4 February, the opposition leader moved the no-confidence amendment and on the following evening the government was defeated. During the debate on the motion, the prime minister gave one of the most eloquent and inspiring speeches of his political career, but outside the chambers of the commons he apparently made no attempt to secure the support of the smaller parties. Social Credit, who were also divided on the nuclear issue, would have backed the government according to most accounts, for very little in return.

. . .

Whatever the subconscious motivations, the political maneuverings and plottings, the fact remains that the Canadian domestic crisis had been set off by a United States government action. While the Canadian press did not generally blame the state department, or the Pentagon, or the Kennedy administration for bringing Diefenbaker down, much of the American press did. American criticism of Diefenbaker's ambiguous nuclear speech, declared the 7 February *Winnipeg Free Press*, was the "occasion" and "not the reason" for the government's fall. "It fell because Parliament and nation had lost all confidence in it."[44]

. . .

Contemporary press reports quoting "informed officials" claimed that the idea [of issuing the press release] had originated in the Ottawa embassy. An interview with the former US ambassador, Walton W. Butterworth, later confirmed the assertion. "We decided we had to set the record straight," Butterworth declared. "There was too much at stake. We decided to do it that way because Canadian statements had not come in polite notes, through channels, but on the floor of the House. If you want to play rough," he added, "then we'll play rough too. They chose the weapon." The embassy draft, Butterworth concluded, was dispatched to Washington where it was polished by George McGhee, checked by under secretary George Ball, and quickly approved by Rusk.[45] White House clearance came from McGeorge Bundy, Kennedy's adviser on national security affairs. The president never saw the press release.

. . .

Butterworth was fully aware of the profound divisions within cabinet, and knew that it would take very little to push Harkness into resigning, and the government over the brink. Personally frustrated by the character of the negotiations, irritated by the government's failure simply to accept "its alliance responsibilities," and angered by Diefenbaker's denial of a United States right "to put nuclear weapons on our own bases in Canada," it is certainly possible that Ambassador Butterworth had a dual purpose in mind when he forwarded the embassy draft to the state department. The record of Rusk's testimony before the Senate seems to indicate that Washington officials, on the other hand, simply acted in haste and were primarily motivated by NATO considerations. They appear to have seized on Butterworth's draft as a way of easing concern over Nassau within the alliance, and either did not care about, or give much thought to, the measure of its political impact on Canada. But the one policy-maker most assuredly, and ironically, innocent of any attempt to force the collapse of the government was President Kennedy.

Although Kennedy would have liked little better than to see Diefenbaker overthrown, he was very upset when he learned of the state department's action, considering it a stupid blunder.[46] The president's anger, of course, was based on the fear that Diefenbaker would now be able to campaign on an anti-American theme and win an anti-nuclear majority. United States embassy officials had known better. Butterworth's cables to the state department, detailing Canadian public and private reaction from US consulates across the country, indicate that the Americans in Ottawa understood that most Canadians were not anti-American, that they were weary of Diefenbaker's ambiguity on the nuclear issue, and that a preliminary wave

of anger would be tempered by an awareness of provocation.

The nuclear issue dominated the campaign, but never more than in its last week... Nine days before the April 8 polling, the Americans inadvertently gave Diefenbaker the very opportunity he needed to exploit anti-nuclear sentiment, to sway the undecided, and perhaps even to change the minds of some who had no objection to nuclear arms. On March 29, the United States Department of Defense released testimony which Defense Secretary Robert McNamara had given before a congressional appropriations committee in February. In his testimony, McNamara had conceded that the Bomarcs were "ineffective" weapons, offering only a minimum of protection, but he told the committee that the operational costs were justified because the Bomarcs would be useful in drawing Russian missiles that "would otherwise be available for other targets."[47] "It was almost," one Conservative stated, "as if a prayer had been answered."[48]

The Prime Minister exultantly jumped on the McNamara testimony, not only as a vindication of his view of the Bomarc, but as proof that the Liberals intended to make Canada into a "burnt sacrifice," a "decoy duck in a nuclear war."[49] Pearson attempted to counter Diefenbaker's charges by observing that the Bomarc had been acquired over Liberal objections to its dubious strategic value, and that it was "strange, indeed," to see the Prime Minster gloating over "the discovery that the weapon he took on in 1958-59 is of no use."[50] The Pentagon gave Pearson a hand by issuing a clarifying statement which asserted that Canada's two Bomarc bases were far less vulnerable to attack than their more numerous American counterparts.

Lacking a complete analysis of voter attitudes, historians have not been able to assess, properly, the direct impact of the nuclear issue on the outcome of the 1963 election. In any event, it seems apparent that the great majority of the electorate did not consider nuclear weapons to be the nation's most pressing problem. When asked by Gallup surveyors in March 1963 what that problem was, 34 percent cited unemployment, and only 17 percent, nuclear weapons or defense. Indeed, unemployment and other economic considerations emerged as the primary concerns of 47 percent of those Canadians polled. Indirectly, however, the nuclear issue significantly influenced the outcome of the election. The incessant, bitter debate within cabinet over nuclear arms had contributed to the government's ineffective parliamentary performance in the months before collapse. This evidence of ineptitude, combined with the apparent delay during the Cuba crisis and the public realization that the government could not make up its mind over nuclear weapons, led to a cry for strong and decisive government.

Whatever benefit Diefenbaker may have accrued from the Pentagon slip, it was not enough to give him a plurality. On April 22, 1963, Lester Pearson became the fourteenth Prime Minister of Canada. Kennedy confidentially expressed his "heartiest congratulations and best wishes," adding that he looked forward to "an early opportunity to talk." In his message, the President stressed that "the early establishment of close relations between your administration and ours is a matter of great importance to me."[51]

Pearson met with Kennedy at Hyannisport on May 10-11, less than three weeks after being sworn in as Prime Minister.[52] According to a memorandum prepared for the President, External Affairs was already at work drawing up "a single document based on copies of draft stockpile agreements which U.S. representatives

[had] furnished" the Diefenbaker government during the post-Cuba negotiations.[53]

The Prime Minister had immediate reservations, and did hesitate, when he learned about the other half of the nuclear question—the United States demand for nuclear storage facilities in Canada for its own forces. Within two weeks of his return from Hyannisport, Pearson had forwarded to the State Department the cabinet-approved draft of a stockpile agreement for Canada's Bomarc, Voodoo, Starfighter and Honest John. But ... [to] American dismay, the Liberal government insisted, like the Conservative government before them, that the American storage proposals must be considered separately after an agreement had been concluded with regard to nuclear warheads for Canada's own systems.

That agreement was reached in the summer of 1963, and announced to Canadians on August 16 [after Parliament had recessed]. Custody of the warheads for the Bomarc and Voodoo, Starfighter and Honest John, would remain with detachments of United States troops at Canadian bases in Canada and Europe. Joint control was ensured by the provision that the weapons could not be used without the authorization of the Canadian government. Pearson told the press that a "hot line" would probably be established between his office and the White House.

Then, on October 9, Prime Minister Pearson informed the House that a second agreement had been concluded, an agreement permitting the storage of air-to-air nuclear missiles for USAF interceptors assigned to Goose Bay, Labrador and Harmon Field, Newfoundland, under NORAD command.[54] Pearson's emphasis was all on the complementary nature of the two agreements, on the fact that the second would now permit all NORAD forces stationed in Canada, "regardless of nationality," to be equipped with the weapons needed "to fulfil effectively their role of protecting this continent against bomber attack." Although he refused to table either the August 16 or October 9 agreements on the grounds that they were executive understandings which could not be made public for reasons of national security, Parliament was given to understand that Canada's autonomy had been protected.

NOTES

1. John Paul and Jerome Laulicht, *In Your Opinion: Leaders and Voters Attitudes on Defence and Disarmament* (Clarkson, Not. 1963).

2. "Trends in Canadian Foreign Policy," National Intelligence Estimate Number 99-61, 2 May 1961, President's Office Files: Canada Security: JFK Trip to Ottawa, 5/16-18/61, folder (D), John F. Kennedy Library, Boston, Massachusetts, (hereafter cited as "Kennedy Papers")

3. "Biographic Material," President's Office Files (POF): Canada Security: JFK Trip to Ottawa, 5/16-18/61, folders (C) and (F), Kennedy Papers.

4. American policy-makers apparently did not understand the problem for Canadian sovereignty implicit in the demand for a US nuclear base in Canada. Hence they never perceived the significance of negotiating the issue separately. After the election of the Liberals, the White House was surprised to learn that they, too, regarded the provision of nuclear facilities at Goose Bay and Argentia as a different question from that of securing nuclear arms for Canadian forces. Memorandum for McGeorge Bundy from L.J. Legere, 27 May 1963, Staff Files: Feldman Files: Canada, Kennedy Papers.

5. John G. Diefenbaker, *One Canada: The Tumultuous Years, 1962-76*, Toronto, Macmillan, 1977, (Hereafter cited as "Diefenbaker, *Memoirs*,"), p. 92.

6. Interview with the Hon. Richard A. Bell (Ottawa, Ontario), 18 January 1974.

7. Interview with the Hon. Douglas Harkness (Gleaneagle, Quebec), 22 July 1974.

8. Interview with the Hon. E. Davie Fulton (Vancouver, British Columbia), 11 July 1974.

9. US Congress, Senate, Subcommittee on Canadian Affairs of the Committee on Foreign Relations, *Hearing, Relating to the Supplying of Nuclear Arms to the Canadian Forces*, 4 February 1963 (Washington, DC 1963), pp. 11-13.

10. Diefenbaker, *Memoirs*, III, p. 94.

11. Senate, Subcommittee on Canadian Affairs, *Hearing*, 4 February 1963, pp. 13-14.

12. "The Harkness Papers," *The Citizen* (Ottawa), 22 October 1977. The comment was contained in this first of three articles, originally written by Harkness shortly after the collapse of the government and deposited in the archives. Harkness decided to publish his account in 1977 as a response to the publication of Volume III of the Diefenbaker *Memoirs*.

13. Transcript of the press conference held by General Lauris Norstad, Ottawa, 3 January 1963 (copy provided by the Department of National Defence).

14. Lyon, *Canada 1961-63*, p. 136.

15. Diefenbaker, *Memoirs*, III, p. 3. In the opinion of at least one reviewer, the assertion of "supra-governmental" activity indicated that the prime minister's reconstruction of events "should

be treated with suspicion." Charles Lynch, "Dief's Harsh Judgement," *The Citizen* (Ottawa), 11 October 1977.

16. Roger Frank Swanson, "An Analytical Assessment of the Canada-United States Defense Issue Area," *International Organization*, XXVIII (Autumn 1974), p. 795.

17. Diefenbaker, *Memoirs*, III, p. 2.

18. Lyon, *Canada 1961-63*, p. 136.

19. Quoted in John T. Saywell, ed., *Canadian Annual Review for 1963* (Toronto 1964), p. 286.

20. Pearson, Lester B., *Mike: The Memoirs of the Rt. Hon. Lester B. Pearson*, Vol. III, 1957-1968, Toronto, University of Toronto Press, 1975, (hereafter cited as "Pearson, *Memoirs*"), p. 72.

21. Interview with the Hon. Paul Hellyer (Ottawa, Ontario), 28 January 1974.

22. The text of the Hellyer memorandum is reprinted as Appendix A, in Peter C. Newman, *The Distemper of Our Times* (Toronto 1968), pp. 426-9.

23. Interview with the Rt. Hon. L.B. Pearson, quoted in Denis Smith, *Gentle Patriot: A Political Biography of Walter Gordon* (Edmonton 1973), p. 119.

24. Pearson, *Memoirs*, III, p. 71.

25. Diefenbaker, *Memoirs*, III, pp. 106-7.

26. "Harkness Papers," *Citizen*, 22 October 1977. Elsewhere, Harkness added that Diefenbaker received "thousands of letters" and gave them "a great deal of importance.... He didn't seem to realize that this was an organized campaign.... He became convinced that the majority...were against our having any nuclear warheads and that if we actually got them at this particular time the result would be electoral defeat." Peter Stursberg, *Diefenbaker: Leadership Lost 1962-1967* (Toronto 1976), pp. 25-6.

27. "Harkness Papers," *Citizen*, 24 October 1977.

28. Senate, Subcommittee on Canadian Affairs, *Hearing*, 4 February 1963, p. 8.

29. Senate, Subcommittee on Canadian Affairs, *Hearing*, 4 February 1963, pp. 37, 24.

30. Diefenbaker, *Memoirs*, III, p. 104.

31. Above quotations from the speech are all from *Debates*, 25 January 1963, pp. 3125-37. See also *Memoirs*, III, pp. 101-6.

32. "Harkness Papers," *Citizen*, 24 October 1977.

33. Quoted in Saywell, *Review 1963*, p. 292.

34. *Debates*, 25 January 1963, p. 3136.

35. Harkness interview, 22 July 1974.

36. United States, Department of State, *Press Release No. 59*, 30 January 1963. Also reprinted in Diefenbaker, *Memoirs*, III, pp. 13-15.

37. *Ottawa Journal*, 31 January 1963.

38. Memorandum for Mr. Kilduff, White House, from Dean Chamberlin, USIA Duty Officer, 2 February 1963, White House Central Subject Files: Countries: Canada CO43, 8/1/62, Kennedy Papers.

39. *Debates*, 31 January 1963, pp. 3289, 3304, 3314.

40. *Debates*, 31 January 1963, pp. 3289-90.

41. Harkness interview, 22 July 1974.

42. The letter was released on 4 February and printed in the Toronto *Globe and Mail* on 5 February 1963. Harkness also explained his position to the House. *Debates*, 4 February 1963, p. 3377. For Diefenbaker's written response to Harkness's letter, see *Memoirs*, III, p. 161.

43. Pearson, *Memoirs*, III, p. 74.

44. Memorandum and Canadian Press Round-Up for McGeorge Bundy from I.J. Légère, 13 February 1963, President's Office Files: Countries: Canada Security 1961-3. Kennedy Papers.

45. Butterworth interview, 2 August 1974.

46. Kennedy's outright hostility towards, and complete disdain of, Prime Minister Diefenbaker is well known. See for example, his comments in Benjamin C. Bradlee, *Conversations with Kennedy* (New York 1975), p. 183.

47. The relevant portion of McNamara's testimony is reprinted in McLin, *Canada's Changing Defense*, pp. 164-65.

48. *Globe and Mail*, April 5, 1963.

49. Quoted in Saywell, *Review 1963*, p. 312.

50. *Globe and Mail*, April 5, 1963.

51. Telegram from the State Department to American Embassy, Ottawa, April 22, 1963, POF: Countries: Canada Security 1963-1963, Kennedy Papers.

52. In addition to nuclear weapons, the two men discussed at Hyannisport a wide range of bilateral questions: defense production-sharing, Canadian oil exports, maritime labor difficulties on the Great Lakes, a proposed extension of the Canadian fishing zone, and lumber tariffs. The Americans had been especially pleased with Pearson's willingness to act promptly on the Columbia River Treaty problem. The treaty, which had been ratified by the United States in 1961, was still pending in Canada two years later because of unresolved difficulties between the federal and British Columbia governments.

53. Memorandum of Actions Required: Follow-up on Hyannisport Meeting May 10-11, 1963; May 13, 1963, White House Staff Files: Feldman Files; Canada, Kennedy Papers.

54. Canada, House of Commons, *Debates*, October 9, 1963, p. 3345. See also "Nuclear Storage Plans," *Canadian Aviation*, XXXVI (November 1963), 37.

SUGGESTED READINGS

Diefenbaker, John G. *One Canada: The Tumultous Years, 1962-76*, Toronto, Macmillan, 1977.

Foulkes, Gen. Charles, "The Complications of Continental Defence," in Livingston Merchant (ed.), *Neighbours Taken for Granted*, Toronto, Burns and MacEachern, 1966, pp. 101-6.

Heeney, A.D.P., *The Things That Are Caesar's: Memoirs of a Canadian Public Servant*, Toronto, University of Toronto, Press, 1972.

Lentner, Howard H., "Foreign Policy Decision Making: The Case of Canada and Nuclear Weapons," *World Politics*, Vol. 29, No. 1, 1976, pp. 29-66.

Lyon, Peyton. V., *Canada in World Affairs, 1961-1963*, Toronto: Oxford University Press, 1968, pp. 76-222.

McLin, Jon B., *Canada's Changing Defense Policy, 1957-1963: The Problems of a Middle Power in Alliance*, Baltimore: Johns Hopkins Press, 1967.

Pearson, Lester B., *Mike: The Memoirs of the Rt. Hon. Lester B. Pearson,* Vol. III, 1957-1968, Toronto: University of Toronto Press, 1975, Chapter 2.

Stursberg, Peter, *Diefenbaker: Leadership Lost, 1962-1967*, Toronto: University of Toronto Press, 1976.

Warnock, John W., *Partner to Behemoth: The Military Policy of a Satellite Canada*, Toronto: New Press, 1970, pp. 183-201.

chapter 8

HARNESSING THE COLUMBIA RIVER, 1964

Neil Swainson

The Columbia River Treaty of 1964 committed Canada and the United States to at least sixty years of collaborative development of a magnificent natural resource.[1] The process was unusual in two respects: twenty years of investigation, analytic effort and bargaining preceded the ratification of the treaty, and it was only the second time in the postwar period that a bilateral agreement between Canada and another country was incorporated into a formal treaty.[2] Perhaps most significant from the perspective of students of Canadian foreign policy, however, is the fact that the treaty deals in large measure with a resource belonging, under the Canadian constitution, to a province. It thus required in its inception and implementation the cooperation of the governments of Canada and British Columbia.

The Columbia River begins in the towering mountains of southeastern British Columbia, flows northwest for about 150 miles, and then turns to flow southwards, past the town of Trail, and into the United States, and then on to the Pacific Ocean. The Canadian drainage area of the Columbia (only about 13 percent of the total Columbia watershed) produces disproportionately about 30 percent of the river's total run-off, and substantially more than that in flood years. Furthermore, in the river's natural state, 70 to 90 percent of

this water crosses the international border in the five months between April and August, with peak flows in May and June. In short, the run-off of the Columbia was notably variable from month to month as well as from year to year. These characteristics had two consequences. First, flooding was a recurrent problem in both countries. Second, the output of the power projects built on the mainstream of the Columbia in the United States, beginning as early as 1928, was severely limited by their inability to use excessive mid-summer flows (when local domestic power demand was low) and by the progressive decline in flow available to them annually from September to March.

Nature of the Columbia River Treaty

Technical experts in both countries came to recognize as early as the 1930s the exceptional significance of the Canadian Columbia watershed as a potential site of storage projects which could help even out the river's flow within years and between years. Ensuring the construction of such works soon became a major objective of American policy. In time, the Canadian government became committed to cooperative development also, but with the qualifica-

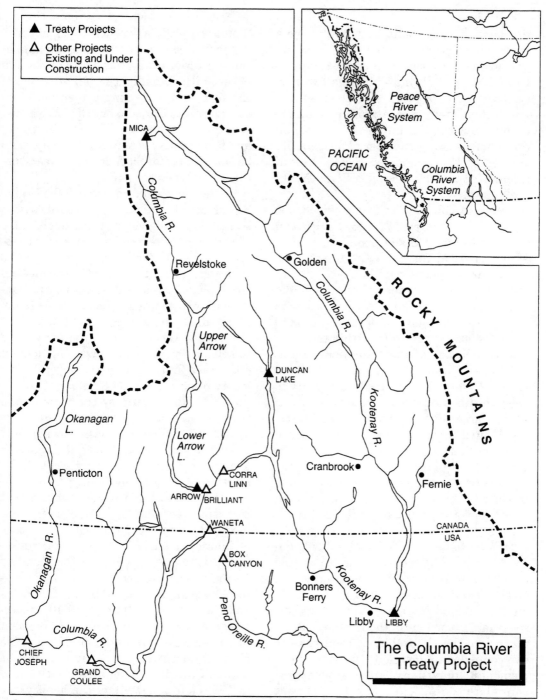

The Columbia River Treaty Project

Source: Neil Swainson, *Conflict over the Columbia*, Montreal, McGill-Queens University Press, 1979.

tion that Canada would have to receive a reasonable share of the benefits, from upstream storage, derived downstream in the United States. Ultimately these two perspectives had to be reconciled. The resulting agreement involved, on the one hand, evening out the Columbia's flow and, on the other, sharing the costs and benefits created by these modifications. This, in essence, is what the Columbia River Treaty is all about.

More specifically, the treaty, which was signed on January 17, 1961, required Canada to build three projects, on the Arrow Lakes, at Duncan Lake and at Mica Creek on the upper Columbia, providing in all 15.5 million acre-feet of storage. (One acre-foot is the amount of water it takes to cover one acre of land to a depth of one foot.) Some 8,450,000 acre-feet of this total (almost entirely behind the Arrow and Duncan Lake dams) was to be operable for flood control. Canada agreed under the treaty to operate this storage to produce a downstream power benefit in the United States. The United States agreed to give Canada credit for this storage when calculating the downstream power benefit, and to give Canada title to one half of the power thus produced. The United States also agreed to compensate Canada (for flooded land, etc.) in the amount of $64.4 million (US) estimated to be one-half of the flood control benefits. The treaty made it possible for Canada to dispose of portions of its power benefit in the United States, and, after 20, 60 and 80 years, to divert successively larger portions of the Kootenay River north into the Columbia. It required the two countries to designate entities to implement its provisions, and to appoint personnel to a four-member Permanent Engineering Board to supervise the implementation process and to report to the two national governments. As well, the United

States was given a five-year option in which to commence the construction of a dam at Libby in Montana on the (US) Kootenai River, with Canada absorbing the cost of the forty-two mile long projection of its reservoir into Canada, but the US was not required to share the downstream power and flood control benefits. The treaty could be cancelled after 60 years on 10 years' notice given by either party.

After the treaty was signed, the United States Senate quickly approved it, with a single dissenting vote, on March 16, 1961. Three years were to pass, however, for reasons discussed later, before it was presented to the Canadian parliament. Ottawa—and British Columbia—did not give final approval until further agreements were negotiated. In one of these, an "Attachment Relating to Terms of Sale," Canada agreed to sell its downstream power entitlement during the first thirty operative years of its treaty projects for $254.5 million (US) prepaid in a lump sum at the time of the treaty's ratification. A protocol to the treaty also clarified certain provisions which had been the subject of internal debate in Canada and modified a few others without altering its major provisions.

The protocol and the sale attachment were signed on January 22, 1964. The now modified treaty was presented to the House of Commons early in April, 1964, subsequently reviewed in detail by the Standing Committee on External Affairs over a six-week period, and passed by the Commons and the Senate on June 5 and 10, respectively. After a power purchase agreement had been signed by the British Columbia Hydro and Power Authority (which was named Canada's designated treaty entity in 1963) and a new American agency, the treaty was ratified and proclaimed. Concurrently, the purchase agreement was made operational (in diplomatic terms, by a further "exchange of notes") on September 16 of that year. Two other agreements, exclusively between Canada and British Columbia, arrived at in 1963 and 1964, complemented the international agreement.

Behind these seemingly straightforward undertakings lay a complex and politically tortuous process. Serious consideration of the prospect of cooperatively developing the Columbia really dates from the period of World War II. Faced with soaring demand for electrical energy from the defence industries in the US Pacific Northwest, Canada and the United States jointly asked the International Joint Commission (IJC) in 1944 to determine if further development of the river was practicable and in the public interest of both countries.[3] If such developments were desirable, the Commission was asked to identify the interests likely to be affected in the process, to estimate relevant costs, and to determine how they might be apportioned.

The IJC was performing here an investigative role under Article IX of the Boundary Waters Treaty of 1909. Other provisions of that landmark accord give the Commission the authority to license developments on boundary rivers or their tributaries which affect the "levels and flows" at the boundary. Article 2 of the Boundary Waters Treaty, it might be noted, provides great freedom of action to upstream riparians on trans-boundary waters (in the case of the Columbia, Canada). Given the province of British Columbia's authority over its lands and resources, Victoria and Ottawa worked closely together concerning the preparation of this reference to the Commission.

The IJC created an International Columbia River Engineering Board to produce a draft response to the reference. The Board established an Engineering Committee, which in turn called into being

a working group of engineers and other federal and provincial officials. In the early postwar years work on the IJC reference moved rather slowly, as the pressure of wartime energy use disappeared, and new projects were launched in the American watershed. While the US Army Corps of Engineers already had hydrologic and geologic studies of the American section of the Columbia watershed, similar investigative effort had to be undertaken by the province's Water Resources Branch, the federal government's Water Resources Bureau and its Department of Public Works. A real stimulus to the investigations was a very severe 1948 flood on the Columbia, which caused extensive damage in both countries, and took fifty lives in a major tragedy at Portland, Oregon. As a consequence, the Corps of Engineers sought Congressional authorization to build a major storage project at Libby in Montana which (subject to IJC approval) would create a reservoir flooding back upstream into Canada.

The essence of the American proposal to the IJC was that in return for permission to go ahead, the United States would pay all of the cost of acquiring the Canadian portion of the reservoir, but would not be required to share with Canada any of the very sizable power and flood control benefits which Libby would produce in the United States. On the other hand, the downstream benefits produced by the Libby project's flooding into Canada would not have to be shared. British Columbia's response to the Americans' Libby application was to ask for part of the hydro power output of Libby itself and part of the downstream benefit produced by it in the United States, in return for the head, flow, and storage on the Kootenay which Canada would be committing to this project. In effect, Libby would be a test case of American willingness to accept a general Canadian right to compensation for downstream benefits stemming from Canadian storage.

Neither the American government nor the three American IJC commissioners were prepared in the early 1950s to accept the Canadian claim. The Americans also pointed out that, in another current IJC case, involving a Canadian application to build a dam on the Pend d'Oreille River, Canada stood to benefit in a major way from upstream American storage yet was not offering to pay compensation for it. Although Ottawa at first seems to have had doubts about British Columbia's tough stand on Libby, it soon came to accept it; the upshot was a deadlock in the IJC over both Libby and the generalized Canadian claim for downstream benefit compensation which lasted until the late fall of 1957.

In the early 1950s, Canada's new IJC co-chairman, General A.G.L. McNaughton, began both within the IJC and publicly to outline his vision of desirable Columbia River development. On occasion he did this without consulting British Columbia. In 1954 he endorsed a major diversion of water from the Kootenay River to the Columbia (which would make Libby unfeasible), and in 1955 suggested that Canada could divert part of the Columbia's flow into the Fraser River watershed—without incurring an American claim for damages arising from the loss downstream of this diverted water.

The winds of change were also blowing in British Columbia. Since 1952 a new Social Credit government under a flamboyant premier, W.A.C. Bennett, reviewed the province's approach to Columbia River development. It quickly became impatient at the deadlock within the IJC and skeptical about General McNaughton's insistence that nothing should happen in the Canadian watershed until the IJC's master plan had emerged. Early in 1954 it indicated a willingness to consider incremental development. Two serious proposals were made, both by American concerns offering to build storage dams in BC on the Columbia. A tentative 1954 agreement between the US-based Kaiser Aluminum and Chemical Company and British Columbia to pursue one of these, a Low Arrow Lakes dam, became the subject of a major domestic controversy both within the province and between its government and Ottawa. The federal government quickly announced its intention to block the project, and did so, in 1955, by piloting through parliament the International Rivers Improvements Bill—which required a federal license for works on any such stream.

The provincial government ultimately accepted Ottawa's right to regulate works on international rivers, but Mr. Bennett and his colleagues came out of this experience rather affronted by the federal government's treatment of them, and determined to ensure that the province's basic prerogatives concerning the use of the resource in question were preserved. Particularly unhappy at the role played by General McNaughton in opposing the Kaiser plan, they were also determined that the General not assume responsibility for reconciling differing views between Ottawa and Victoria over Columbia River development. They felt that these differences would have to be worked out in direct exchange between the governments in question and also insisted that the downstream benefit concept warranted more of a review than it had actually received from the national government.[4] The IJC remained stalemated over the Canadian downstream benefits claim, and in the late fall of 1955 became bitterly divided over the merits of General McNaughton's assertion of a Canadian right to divert (without compensation) some part of the Columbia's flow to the Fraser.

Eventually the governments at Ottawa and Victoria recognized that they both had veto power over Columbia development and that they would simply have to cooperate. Thus in the spring of 1956 they quietly agreed that while the IJC should be left to work on its Columbia investigation, an attempt should be made via diplomatic channels to exchange views with Washington which might help break the deadlock within the IJC. In July 1956, they publicly agreed to halt their earlier debate over Columbia development strategy, and to commission major independent studies of the Columbia to augment their own staff and the IJC-led efforts. Ottawa invoked the assistance of the Montreal Engineering Company, and Victoria turned to the Crippen Wright Engineering Company of Vancouver.

The Canada-US diplomatic-level exchange did not take place until May of 1957, and then was hardly productive. Only national government personnel participated directly, although a British Columbia minister and two of his advisors were present in Washington and met with Ottawa's representatives before and after these meetings. The British Columbians returned home convinced that the national government now acknowledged that the province would have to play a dominant role on the Canadian side.

In June 1957 a federal election brought to an end thirty-two years of continuous Liberal Party rule. During the campaign, Mr. Diefenbaker suggested in British Columbia that his Progressive Conservative party would be more sensitive to the province's objectives and role than the Liberals had been. The new government in Ottawa moved cautiously at first in developing its approach to the Columbia. It decided to halt further diplomatic level exchanges on the question and to rely on the IJC. The October 1957 Speech from the

Throne acknowledged the need to resolve international difficulties around the Columbia, but referred only in general terms to the prospect of the river's "joint" development. The federal cabinet seemed to have decided to develop its own view of what an optimal Columbia policy for Canada should be without consulting British Columbia. It held the province at arm's length on this issue until the end of 1958. In doing so, it ignored the advice of its own Department of External Affairs which, in July 1957, advised that basic responsibility for engineering decisions concerning the Columbia "were almost solely a matter of provincial government responsibility."[5]

In the fall of 1957 Ottawa established a Cabinet Committee on the Columbia and in November received the report of the Montreal Engineering Company, which strongly endorsed the concept of working cooperatively with the Americans, placed great emphasis on the case for storage on the Arrow Lakes, expressed major reservations about a diversion of more than modest proportions from the Kootenay to the Columbia, and saw merit in an international agreement allowing for the Libby project. The extent to which these recommendations differed from those advanced for years by General McNaughton was noteworthy. The federal cabinet's response was to seek a further assessment of Canada's options produced by an objective team of economists headed by the retired governor of the Bank of Canada. Somehow, when he declined, that chairmanship went to General McNaughton. The Economic Committee study extended through virtually all of 1958.

Meanwhile, in British Columbia, the province's largest utility, the BC Electric Company, was running out of hydro sites and opted to build a major thermal (natural gas-fired) power station. In another significant development, in October 1957, Victoria and an international financial group led by Sweden's Axel Wenner Gren agreed to study the feasibility of a very large hydro power project, with possibly the largest man-made reservoir in the world, on the Peace River in northern BC. Mr. Bennett's enthusiasm for this initiative on the Peace River was manifest as was his impatience with the delays on the Columbia. "Surely now," he declared, "both Ottawa and the United States will realize that we mean business." From this point onward the province's power-planning horizon was substantially expanded; henceforth Mr. Bennett, who dominated his government, had as his goal the concurrent development of the Peace and the Columbia watersheds. What puzzled so many at the time about his enthusiasms was the fact that the provincial electricity market could not absorb the power output of the two rivers developed simultaneously. Selling power to the Americans would alter the equation mightily, but such sales were contrary to national policy. The federal government—due to a World War I era experience with the Americans—had long assumed that power once exported could not be recovered and thus had banned such long-term sales. Through 1960, and even beyond, as the provincial premier reaffirmed his objective, he and it were widely discounted.

Whether or not the Peace River studies helped prompt a change of thinking in Washington (as Mr. Bennett believed until his death) American policy with reference to the Columbia quickly began to change. Late in 1957 a new American co-chairman of the IJC made clear his country's willingness to have that body's forthcoming engineering report deal with the case for a Kootenay to Columbia diversion and, by January 1958, was conceding that Canada was entitled to

a share of the capacity in a Libby project. Nor did the changes in American policy stop here. By midsummer the US IJC commissioners were hinting that, if the downstream flood control and power benefits were defined fairly, there was a good chance that the United States would agree to an equal split of them.

Through 1958 no significant advances were made in developing an agreed-upon international approach to the Columbia, nor did the governments of Canada and BC get beyond agreeing in October that their staffs would have to meet to harmonize their perspectives on one. In November the federal cabinet received its own Economic Committee's report which, not surprisingly, proposed a programme of development for Canada which reflected General McNaughton's well-known preferences. This report had a considerable impact on some members of the Canadian cabinet. Eventually, in January 1959, Ottawa agreed with Washington on a new reference to the IJC, asking it (as the 1940 reference had not) to draft a set of principles for identifying the benefits stemming from cooperative Columbia development, and for dividing them. Notably, in contrast to the 1944 reference, there was this time no prior consultation with the province.

There were four other significant developments apropos the Columbia early in 1959. Mr. Bennett announced that the BC Power Commission was to be the provincial agency responsible for the development of the Canadian watershed. The province also received from its Crippen Wright consultants a sophisticated report which in many ways anticipated the shape of the ultimate international bargain. Ottawa and Victoria established a Policy Liaison Committee of cabinet personnel and a Technical Liaison Sub-Committee of Canadian federal, provincial and IJC staff which over the next two years contributed greatly to synthesizing federal and provincial perspectives. Finally in March, after 14 years of effort, the IJC's Engineering Board presented to the IJC a massive response to its 1944 reference. Produced from a system perspective, ignoring the boundary, it advanced no one preferred development scenario, but identified a number of merit, and referred to others. One of the very few authoritative documents placed at this time in the public domain, it was widely referred to for years to come.

The Policy Liaison Committee was immediately assigned two tasks. One was to develop an agreed federal-provincial position on the forthcoming IJC negotiations dealing with the "principles." The other was to seek agreement on a set of Canadian objectives to be pursued in international negotiations once agreement on the principles had been reached. As matters developed during 1959, progress was made on only the first of these objectives. By far the greatest difficulty emerged when the IJC, as it sought to identify the true benefits from cooperative development, began to take into account related development costs. Initially both Washington and Ottawa felt that some such procedure (termed "netting") would be necessary. By mid-1959, however, provincial personnel became convinced that any attempt to do this would render the entire enterprise politically infeasible, and ultimately persuaded Ottawa of this proposition. This modified Canadian view was eventually if reluctantly accepted in the IJC by the Americans before the principles were relayed to the two national governments in December 1959.

The IJC had identified three general, seven power, and six flood control principles. Those which were specific, as many were, eventually emerged in the treaty to come, but not all of them were precise. On some issues, such as storage on the East Kootenay River, the IJC (and the governments behind it) had simply concluded that agreement would have to come from direct bargaining between the parties involved. From that point the IJC role faded.

At this time there was still considerable ambiguity about Ottawa's financial participation in Columbia development. Howard Green, a BC member of the federal cabinet, speculated in December 1959 about a 50-50 sharing of Columbia costs, but nothing was said of the precise nature of federal assistance. Mr. Bennett had for some time made no secret of his objective— a direct grant. The federal government also raised with Victoria the prospect of establishing a joint federal-provincial agency to develop the Columbia in Canada. The province's response at the time had been enigmatic, although it was, in fact, opposed to direct involvement by Ottawa in the management of a provincial resource.

A further complication late in 1959 was the mounting concern in Ottawa over Mr. Bennett's continuing endorsement of early development on the Peace River. (There was little enthusiasm for this idea in Washington, D.C. The American government was anything but keen over the prospect of seeing its domestic capital markets having to finance concurrently the Peace River as well as the Columbia River development). There were reservations also about the Peace River proposal, felt not just in Ottawa but also amongst governmental technical staff in Victoria, based on the realization that, in a sense, Canadian Columbia storage was a wasting asset. If the Americans, frustrated by delay, were to authorize storage construction on their Columbia tributaries, the result would be significant reduction in the utility to the US of subsequently built Canadian storage. These concerns were only heightened when both national governments learned that the Peace River Power Development Company had met its deadline, and on December 30, 1959, had filed a comprehensive report in Victoria proposing to construct not one but two projects on the northern river with over 3,000 megawatts of installed capacity.

Concerned about losing the project entirely if there were further delays and, in the face of a slowdown in the Canadian economy, keen to hasten the arrival of the anticipated economic stimulus associated with construction on the Columbia, the federal cabinet took a crucial decision. It approached the United States suggesting a commencement of negotiations leading to a treaty. Not only did Ottawa do this without informing British Columbia, it did so before reaching an agreement with Victoria concerning either the objectives to be sought or the strategies to be utilized in negotiations with the United States. BC had expected and requested consultation, but to no avail. The province formally protested, and suggested a delay, but the federal government insisted on maintaining the momentum derived from the 1959 IJC discussions on principles. In the end, British Columbia once again agreed to cooperate. It was convinced of the merit of the technical analysis available to it, and convinced that the strength of its position constitutionally meant that ultimately it would be able to shape the Canadian position in the international negotiations ahead. In this it proved to be correct.

The imminence of international negotiations quickly led to federal-provincial cooperation. British Columbia's Deputy Minister of Lands and Forests was appointed to join two senior federal public servants and the Minister of Justice, E. Davie Fulton, on the team of Canadian treaty negotiators, which Mr. Fulton was to lead. Cooperation was also pursued in meetings of the Policy and Technical Liaison Committees which backed up and guided the negotiators between February 1960, when the international negotiations began, and the early days of January 1961, when they were concluded. Although the Canadian technical personnel did not reach a consensus on all matters they agreed on a great many, and were able to clarify the likely consequences of many of the options from which the politicians, in conjunction with the treaty negotiators, had to choose.

Federal-provincial agreement still came slowly on three major issues. One, which had to be worked at during the first four months of the international negotiations and which became more important as the bargaining evolved, concerned the projects which Canada would be prepared to accept in a treaty. The crux of the disagreement here was the case (made by the federal Economic Committee in 1958) for the early construction of storage on the Upper Kootenay in Canada, and the prospect of diverting water from the Kootenay storage into the Upper Columbia. This diversion, which would have rendered the construction of an American project at Libby infeasible, and would have had a major environmental impact, was strongly supported from February through June 1960 by at least some federal members of the Policy Liaison Committee and by General McNaughton. Provincial officials, on the other hand, opposed it. BC insisted on incorporating storage on the Arrow Lakes into an international agreement, along with a possible development at Libby. This project selection issue was referred back to both Canadian cabinets in June. The province refused to budge; Ottawa had to give way.

The second disagreement concerned federal financial involvement in the Columbia's development. Although Mr.

Bennett's request for a direct grant had been ruled out, the Diefenbaker cabinet was still divided on the question, as it was on so many other issues. Early in 1960, Ottawa offered a loan, conditional on its approval of project selection. It dropped this position in July, but subsequently tied its offer of a loan to the province's acceptance of a joint federal-provincial development agency. In December Mr. Bennett angrily denounced the concept of a joint development instrument as an unwarranted intrusion into a provincial prerogative.

By October of 1960, the forces of accommodation between Canada and the United States, and within Canada, had produced general agreement on a draft treaty. There was still a third problem, however, for British Columbia since 1959 had insisted that negotiating a treaty could not bypass the public hearing and licencing requirements of its Water Act. The province had assumed that, after basic agreement had been reached, the international negotiations would be adjourned until the provincial hurdles had been cleared. They would then be resumed for the final drafting and signature stages. By mid-November, however, there was pressure from Ottawa and Washington to "wrap up" the Columbia agreement. The Republicans had lost the White House in that month's presidential election, and not finishing by January could mean having to renegotiate the treaty with the new Kennedy administration. British Columbia agreed to defer the application of its project approval process on the understanding that it would be carried out before the treaty's ratification.

Thus the momentum of the negotiations was continued, and final refinements to the treaty were pursued through December. The circumstances on the Canadian side were unusual, however. After attempts to reach an Ottawa-Victoria accord on project financing and on a supervisory agency failed, the goal of obtaining overall federal-provincial agreement on the treaty's implementation, before its signature, was abandoned.

Real nervousness developed in Ottawa in the opening days of 1961 at the news that the province's cabinet had asked the British Columbia Energy Board for a comparative evaluation of the merits of Peace and Columbia River development. Apparently reasonable explanations of this move by provincial ministers at Policy Liaison Committee meetings in January 1961 eased this concern, as did a letter sent by Ray Williston, the provincial minister most directly involved with the Columbia's development, to Mr. Fulton on January 12. These were frequently thereafter referred to by Ottawa—with some reason—as having given it a clearance to go ahead with the treaty signing.

Mr. Bennett, however, had not finished playing his hand. On January 13, without informing Mr. Williston, Mr. Bennett wrote an enigmatic letter to Donald Fleming, the federal minister of finance. While seemingly relaying the province's intent to proceed with Columbia development, if it proved to be feasible "from engineering and financial standpoints," he went on to query the low cost estimates of Columbia River power. Clearly this was intended as a warning, although what action on it Mr. Bennett expected was never made clear. (Later he was often to argue that the treaty had been signed too soon.) But this was not the end to the mystery. While the Bennett letter arrived in Ottawa at least a day before Diefenbaker and Fulton left to sign the treaty in Washington, it was not shown to the Prime Minister before his departure.

After the treaty signing on January 16, an impasse quickly emerged between Victoria and Ottawa over its implementation. Indeed, for over a year, ministerial and technical level contact between the two Canadian governments on this issue virtually ceased, although a good deal of relevant engineering work was quietly continued. This hiatus stemmed from the fact that Premier Bennett had come to envelop Columbia development in a larger plan, designed both to stimulate his province's economy and to move its centre-of-gravity away from southwestern British Columbia. He had become committed to the concurrent development of both the Peace River in BC's north and the Columbia in the south, and was determined not to let Ottawa's preoccupation with the Columbia pre-empt his vision.

One feature of the strategy which he gradually developed in the spring of 1961 was a decision to seek to sell in the United States all of the power to which Canada was entitled under the treaty. He could then use the proceeds of the sale to finance the province's capital commitments on the Columbia. A second and essential element in his strategy was his public advocacy of a new national policy allowing the long-term export of surplus Canadian electrical energy. Such a change had been recommended by the Gordon Royal Commission in the previous decade, and provisions for it had been included in the 1959 National Energy Board Act. But, to that point in time, the idea had not been actively endorsed by any of the country's national political parties. By early spring of 1961 Mr. Bennett had "gone public" with both of these positions. A third strategic decision was not publicly revealed until August 1961. At a special session of the provincial legislature, Mr. Bennett's government expropriated the privately owned B.C. Electric and Peace River Power Development Companies. The provincial government thus assumed dominant control of the

power market in the province, and this put Mr. Bennett in a position where he could dictate whether or not there would be a market in BC for Columbia power. The cabinet then gave instructions to proceed immediately with construction on the Peace.

With these bold moves, Mr. Bennett had gone a long way to launching development on the northern river and determining the shape of development on the southern one. Reviving progress on the Columbia, however, proved more difficult. The federal cabinet, already dismayed at the delay in the treaty's implementation, was subjected over the 1961-62 winter to an amazing range of often conflicting pressures from residents of British Columbia concerning the premier's power planning. It was not prepared to approve either power exports generally or the downstream power benefit sales which, it assumed, would mean foregoing a quick reduction in the province's domestic power costs. For the balance of 1961 there was no meeting of minds at cabinet level on these issues. Indeed, Mr. Fulton and Mr. Bennett had a major row in the fall of 1961 over the merits of the Columbia River Treaty as negotiated. All was not inaction, however.

Federal cabinet ministers, including Mr. Fulton, quietly sought to investigate the feasibility of selling power in the United States—as did Mr. Bennett himself. In September-October 1961, British Columbia held public hearings related to the three treaty storages. In April 1962 licenses were issued, paving the way for the dams. In November Mr. Bennett took an opportunity to meet President Kennedy in Seattle and assure him of the province's commitment to the basic compact in the treaty.

Washington was obviously frustrated by the delayed approval of the treaty in Canada. During the 1961-62 winter it moved quietly to see if, by helping find a market for Columbia (not Peace River) energy in the US, it could help the two Canadian governments with their problems. At the same time, it moved to approve a new storage project in the American Columbia watershed, and received a task force report strongly recommending the construction of a transmission intertie from the American Northwest to the Southwest. Both of these initiatives provided alternate routes to achieving some of the major benefits sought by the United States under the treaty. An American diplomatic note arrived in Ottawa offering help, urging early treaty ratification, but also stressing the serious consequences of further delay.

Mr. Bennett decided on March 12, 1962 that the province would be able to finance the Peace and Columbia developments on its own. In this light, and with an impending federal election, the federal cabinet came close to a tentative but unpublicized decision to allow the sale of part of the downstream power entitlement. The forces of accommodation in Canada were now moving. A halt was called late in March to federal-provincial feuding over the province's power planning, and in April technical representatives from Ottawa and Victoria met for the first time in fourteen months. On this occasion the British Columbians argued vigorously the merits of a compromise plan which they presented.[6] Ultimately, however, the federal government simply deferred acting on it, and further bargaining had to be deferred until after the June 1962 election.

Two months after this election, in which the Diefenbaker government lost its working majority, Mr. Bennett visited Ottawa, seeking permission to test formally the American market for a power sale. This time the federal cabinet agreed, although it deliberately refused to commit itself to approving any agreement which might be reached. When parliament reassembled in the fall, the Speech from the Throne appeared to herald a new federal policy on the export of electrical energy. The Diefenbaker cabinet was nevertheless unable to reach agreement on the principle involved in this issue. Three major bilateral meetings on the question of a power sale were held between September and December 1962. No Canadian cabinet ministers participated in any of these, and the four federal public servants present were there with only a watching brief. The initiative from the Canadian side thus came from the province, whose team was led by the two co-chairmen of the new BC Hydro and Power Authority. The four months of bargaining which ensued clarified a great many issues inherent in the concept of a downstream benefit sale, and led to an American proposal on December 19 of that year which the Canadian technicians involved felt warranted very serious consideration in the two Canadian capitals.

But the Diefenbaker cabinet was distracted by other more pressing issues. Bedeviled by an inability to reach definitive decisions, not only on the sale of downstream benefits and power exports but also on Canada's acquisition of nuclear weapons, it was defeated in the House of Commons in February 1963. An election was called for April. The treaty, British Columbia, and the Americans, who earlier had suggested that March 31 was their deadline before they turned to alternative options, simply had to wait.

The last stage in the evolution of the treaty, which stretched from May 1963 to the treaty's ultimate ratification on September 16, 1964 involved a return to the close federal-provincial liaison over Columbia River development which had existed almost two decades earlier. The new Prime Minister, Lester Pearson, and his colleagues quickly reached three decisions. No renegotiation of the treaty would be sought, but a protocol containing some refinements and modifications would be. In the context of a reasonable bargain, a downstream power benefit sale would be permitted. (In October 1963 the Pearson government dropped the long-standing ban on the long-term export of Canadian-generated electricity.) Finally, no formal diplomatic approaches to the United States would be made until a definitive agreement had been reached and signed with British Columbia.

This federal thinking was quickly endorsed in Victoria and informally relayed to President Kennedy in May. A six-page Canada-British Columbia Agreement was negotiated early in June, and formally signed on July 8, 1963. In it all property rights, title and interests arising under the treaty in Canada were declared to belong to the province. Canada agreed to nominate BC Hydro as the Canadian entity responsible for the treaty's implementation, to allow the province to nominate one of the two Canadian members of the Permanent Engineering Board to be established under the treaty, to approve a power benefit sale, and to seek the province's concurrence before taking a number of other specified actions. For its part, British Columbia undertook to meet all the construction and operating requirements of the treaty, to indemnify Canada in respect of any liabilities incurred because of its actions or inactions, and to exempt Ottawa from any financing obligations arising therefrom. Both governments agreed to do everything possible to expedite the issuance of necessary licences and permits. The way was at last prepared for the deal Mr. Bennett had sought.

Subsequent international negotiations focussed on the protocol in August 1963,

and then, between September and December 1963, on the power sale. Paul Martin, the new Secretary of State for External Affairs, headed the Canadian team in both negotiations. He had two of the 1960 negotiators, Gordon Robertson and Edward Ritchie, working with him. From British Columbia, Hugh Keenleyside, co-chairman of BC Hydro (and a former External Affairs officer), also participated. The team was well coordinated. Fundamentally, federal personnel took the lead in drafting the protocol, on which agreement came quickly. Provincial staff on the other hand played a major role in the more protracted and difficult negotiations over the power entitlement, which ultimately led to the sale agreement in the form of an attachment to the treaty.

The only stress in the otherwise amicable federal-provincial collaboration in these negotiations emerged late in December 1963 when American representatives drew attention to the risk they were taking in prepaying a very large sum of money up to thirty-nine years before the benefits they were purchasing were to be received. Their concern was real in spite of the fact that BC had already formally agreed to meet Canada's legal obligations. When Ottawa insisted on its right to recover (out of payments it was making to Victoria) funds which might be claimed if the province did not fulfill its treaty obligations, Mr. Bennett reacted vigorously to the implication that the province might not be trustworthy. He was only reconciled to the drawback provision (which was included in a second federal-provincial agreement) by a proviso that any alleged default would have to be recognized by the courts.

In two additional ways British Columbia was involved in this treaty-making exercise before it was completed in

1964. While the federal government assumed major responsibility for the presentation, explanation and defence of the treaty before the House of Commons External Affairs Committee between April and May 1964, Mr. Williston and Dr. Keenleyside made major presentations to that body, and provincial technicians helped prepare an extensive descriptive monograph for it. Secondly, technical personnel from the Government of British Columbia and BC Hydro played a significant role in the negotiation of the detailed power sale—between BC Hydro and a new American entity, the Columbia Storage Power Exchange, on August 13, 1974.

Mr. Bennett joined Prime Minister Pearson and President Johnson to proclaim the treaty ceremonially on September 16, 1964 at Blaine, Washington. As provided for under the July 1963 Canada-British Columbia Agreement, BC Hydro was designated as the Canadian entity under the treaty. The province has since 1964 regularly nominated one of its employees as one of the two Canadian members of the Permanent Engineering Board which supervises the implementation of the treaty. Hydro completed all three of the Canadian treaty projects on (or before) the revised treaty deadlines, and had operated this storage in accordance with the Assured and Detailed Operating plans, agreed to by both countries' entities. The Peace River project also went ahead as promised; on completion, its colossal dam was, fittingly enough, named after the premier who had championed it.

Conclusion

The important role British Columbia played in the making of Canadian foreign policy in the Columbia case is clear. What is less clear is how it was that, although the governments of Canada and British Columbia recognized from 1944 onward that their efforts concerning the Columbia had to be integrated, they ended up on collision courses intermittently over the next twenty years. What were some of the major results of this extraordinary intermixing of cooperative and competitive behavior? Were the disagreements really necessary? What can be said of the international agreement which was finally achieved, and what lessons can be derived from this experience with respect to Canada's rather distinctive handling of the "treaty power"?

One explanation for the intermittent federal-provincial conflict was the political upheaval which brought the BC Social Credit Party to power in 1952 and which left a legacy of intense partisan competitiveness both in British Columbia itself and between the provincial government and the major federal political parties. For at least a decade after 1952, one important dimension of this tension was a notable coolness in the personal relations between Mr. Bennett and a few former colleagues of his in the Conservative Party who, after 1957, were key members of the federal cabinet from British Columbia.

Some considerable responsibility for the competitiveness also has to be attributed to General McNaughton, the co-chairman of the IJC, and his determination to pursue the Canadian interest as he saw it. His conviction that the federal government's influence in international river development had to be the dominant one was, in the context of Canadian domestic law, simplistic at best and (where major costs were not being imposed on other provinces let alone another country) notably vulnerable.[7] If maximizing power generation in Canada (ignoring costs) had been the Canadian goal, there was a logic to his conviction and plans. But a decision on that question, on the inevitable flooding of valleys, on the projects to be built, and their sequencing and timing, really was one for the province to make.[8] In a sense the General made himself into the self-appointed architect of an optimal Canadian strategy, into an agent of Canada. The problem here was that this agent role was one which IJC commissioners, pursuing a binational perspective, traditionally have sought to avoid. The General's significant impact on some key federal ministers compounded the problem.

A further explanation for this federal-provincial competition is rooted in the approach to Columbia River development of the Diefenbaker government between 1957 and 1963. The federal cabinet was concerned about the prospective Peace River development, and was convinced through 1960 and 1961 that the end result of cooperative development on the Columbia should be the earliest possible reduction in the cost of electricity in BC. Unfortunately, from 1957-58 onward, these considerations co-existed with an extraordinary insensitivity to the province's responsibility for the development of its own resources. Ottawa failed to inform British Columbia of the 1959 IJC reference, failed to consult with it before commencing international negotiations a year later, and failed to secure the province's agreement either on what Canada should hope to obtain through these negotiations or on what it did obtain. These were not just notable oversights; they were unnecessary provocations.

Part of the problem here was also that the BC premier was simply not taken seriously on his pet scheme of a two-river policy. Even where due allowance is made for the fact that Mr. Bennett could be a difficult man to work with, it is hard to escape the conclusion that the federal cabinet sought to shape the physical development of the Columbia in ways which the province clearly did not want, and that it badly misread the practical implications of the Canadian constitution. In a real sense it defied the logic of that constitution, which in dividing jurisdiction over policy-making between two basic levels of government clarified responsibility both for the country's politicians and the public at large.[9] While some members of the Diefenbaker cabinet accepted this view and advanced it in cabinet, this group did not include two of the most senior ministers from BC. In sum, much of the dissonance in the federal-provincial exchanges between 1958 and 1962 over the Columbia need not and ought not to have occurred.

It is remarkable, in view of the circumstances out of which the treaty evolved, that it has been as effective as it has in creating and conferring significant benefits on both countries. As is always the case with hydro-electric development, there have been intangible opportunity costs (e.g., along the foreshore of the Arrow Lakes), and some material ones, especially involving forestry income foregone. The United States eventually attained two of its major objectives, Canadian storage to regulate the Columbia's mainstream runoff and approval for the Libby project—even though it had not wanted originally to pay for the former. Both countries have acquired access to enhanced power resources at a lower cost than would have been possible without the treaty, and both have enjoyed significant flood control benefits as a result of it. Because the downstream power benefit has not declined as much as was expected in 1963, the United States enjoyed a bonus from the power sale. When British Columbia reacquires title to this residual benefit between 1998 and 2013, it will also gain. In November, 1989 the province announced its intent to bring this energy back to Canada—presumably for the remaining life of the treaty. The power will belong to the province which will be free to sell it and to use the proceeds as it pleases. (Interestingly, during the last thirty years, the retail price of electricity in British Columbia has moved from being one of the highest to being one of the lowest in Canada). BC Hydro and the American entity have generally worked out solutions to problems not identified in the treaty.

The fundamental lesson to be learned from all of this is that Canada's approach to the making of treaties involving provincial classes of subjects is workable, notwithstanding reservations raised on this issue, for example, during the 1960s.[10] The de-

gree of federal-provincial cooperation required in such circumstances is attainable. When reflecting on his experience retrospectively, Mr. Bennett vigorously defended the existing constitutional arrangement.[11] Ultimately, if belatedly, the necessary mix of jurisdictional modesty, intelligent cooperation and common sense emerged to produce an international agreement of real benefit to one province and to Canada. Notwithstanding the difficulties faced by the Canadian federal system at the beginning of the 1990s, there is no reason to assume that these attributes cannot be applied when treaties are required to resolve analogous problems in the future.

NOTES

1. The account in this chapter, which has been written specially for this book, is drawn from N.A. Swainson, *Conflict Over the Columbia*. (Montreal: McGill-Queen's University Press, 1979).

2. A.E. Gotlieb, *Canadian Treaty Making*. Toronto: Butterworths, 1968, p. 84.

3. For background on the IJC, see William Willoughby, *The Joint Organizations of Canada and the United States*, Toronto: University of Toronto Press, 1979.

4. See C.D. Howe on the second reading of the International Rivers Improvements Bill, Canada, House of Commons, *Debates*, 22nd Parliament, 2nd Session, February 4, 1955, p. 871.

5. Summary Memorandum for Mr. Fulton, as Acting Minister, from J.W.H. (Office of the Under-Secretary), 3 July, 1957, p. 4.

6. See N.A. Swainson, *Conflict Over the Columbia*. (Montreal: McGill-Queen's University Press, 1979), pp. 223-224.

7. See his argument in—Canada, House of Commons, Standing Committee on External Affairs, *Minutes of Proceedings and Evidence: Columbia River Treaty and Protocol*, 26th Parliament, 2nd Session, April 21, 1964, p. 545.

8. Building the high altitude Kootenay to Columbia storage McNaughton favoured would have displaced some 500 fewer people than Arrow Lakes storage, but it would have flooded almost three times as many acres in creating a reservoir almost 150 miles long.

9. J.A. Corry, *Difficulties of Divided Jurisdiction*. (Ottawa: King's Printer, 1939).

10. See Laurier LaPierre, "Quebec and Treaty-Making," *International Journal*, Vol. XX (Summer, 1965), pp. 362-366. Louis Sabourin, "Politique etrangere et 'Etal du Quebec'" *International Journal*, Vol. XX, (Summer, 1965), 353. J.V. Morin, "Vers un nouvel equilibre constitu-

tionnel au Canada," in P.A. Crepeau and C.B. Mcpherson, *The Future of Canadian Federalism*. (Toronto: University of Toronto Press, 1968), pp. 147-168.

11. W.A.C. Bennett, "Opening Statement to Planning Session of the Federal-Provincial Conference," Ottawa, February 5, 1968. See also *The Victoria Daily Times*, July 15, 1967, 7.

SUGGESTED READINGS

Fox, Annette B., *The Politics of Attraction*, New York: Columbia University Press, 1977.

Girard, Charlotte S.M., *Canada in World Affairs, 1963-1965*, Volume 13, Toronto: Canadian Institute of International Affairs, 1980, pp. 79-97.

Higgins, Larratt, "The Alienation of Canadian Resources: The Case of the Columbia River Treaty," in I. Lumsden (ed.), *Close the 49th Parallel*, Toronto: University of Toronto Press, 1970, pp. 224-40.

Higgins, Larratt, "The Columbia River Treaty: A Critical View," *International Journal*, Vol. 16, 1961, pp. 399-404.

Krutilla, John, *The Columbia River Treaty: The Economics of an International River Basin Development*, Baltimore: Johns Hopkins Press, 1967.

Le Marquand, David G., *International Rivers: The Politics of Cooperation*, Vancouver: Westwater Research Centre, University of British Columbia, 1977.

Lyon, Peyton, *Canada in World Affairs, 1961-1963*, Toronto: Oxford University Press, 1968, pp. 371-91.

McNaughton, A.G.L., "The Proposed Columbia River Treaty," *International Journal*, Vol. 18, pp. 148-165.

Swainson, Neil, *Conflict Over the Columbia: The Canadian Background to an Historic Treaty*, Montreal: McGill-Queen's University Press, 1979.

Swettenham, J., *McNaughton*, Volume 3, 1944-1966. Toronto: Ryerson, 1968-9.

Waterfield, Donald, *Continental Waterboy: The Columbia River Controversy*, Vancouver: Clarke, Irwin, 1970.

chapter 9

SPEAKING OUT ON VIETNAM, 1965

John English

The Vietnam War affected Canadians more than any other war they did not fight. It profoundly altered Canada's view of the United States and American goals. The buoyant, appealing vision of the Kennedy New Frontier dissolved into a surreal collage of dark exits, strobe colours, and blinding napalm. The change was too sudden to understand. Startled, the Canadian government and Canadians in general hesitated between the role of consoler and critic, and between a nationalism that called for the closing of the 49th parallel and a fascination with the unfolding American drama in which they thought they had a part.

Unlike Charles Taylor's *Snow Job: Canada, the United States and Vietnam [1954 to 1973]*, this chapter does not seek "to establish what went wrong" and "with the benefit of hindsight" suggest "other courses of action that would have been more consistent with Canadian self-interest."[1] The compass here is narrower, enclosing mainly the decisions made by Canadian government officials between 1965 and 1967 about Indochina and the United States. The account of these decisions will provide much raw material for the future historian of the Vietnam War's profound effect upon Canada, at a later time when hindsight's benefits are more bountiful.[2]

Canada's interest in Indochina began with the Geneva Conference of 1954 when Canada reluctantly agreed to serve upon the International Control Commissions (ICC) in Vietnam, Laos and Cambodia.[3] The first work of the Commission in Vietnam, resettling refugees and establishing lines of division, went reasonably well, but soon the Canadians became frustrated with the North Vietnamese refusal to accommodate the Commission in its resettlement work. The attitude of the Poles, who seemed to collude with the North Vietnamese, also upset Canadian commissioners. There developed, not surprisingly, a Canadian sympathy with the South and a Canadian suspicion of Northern motives. Canadian representatives continued to regard themselves as objective assessors of the Vietnamese turmoil, but, in the fifties, there was no doubt who the Canadians deemed to be the instigator of the troubles. For example, Paul Martin, a visitor to Saigon in November 1956, reported favourably on President Ngo Dinh Diem's attempts "to restore life and sense of purpose to that half of Viet Nam which he has been left by the Geneva settlement." Martin added, "he thinks it useful to have the International [Control] Commission present to help maintain stability provided that it does not lend itself too much to

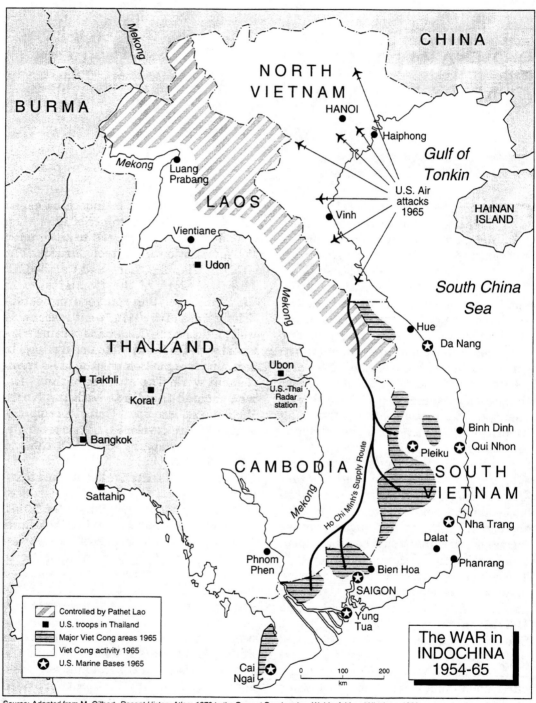

CHINA

NORTH VIETNAM

BURMA

Mekong

Mekong

Luang Prabang

LAOS

HANOI

Haiphong

Gulf of Tonkin

U.S. Air attacks 1965

HAINAN ISLAND

Vientiane

Vinh

Udon

THAILAND

South China Sea

Hue

Da Nang

Takhli

Korat

Ubon

U.S.-Thai Radar station

Bangkok

Binh Dinh

Pleiku

Qui Nhon

CAMBODIA

SOUTH VIETNAM

Sattahip

Mekong

Ho Chi Minh's Supply Route

Nha Trang

Dalat

Phanrang

Phnom Phen

Bien Hoa

SAIGON

Controlled by Pathet Lao

U.S. troops in Thailand

Major Viet Cong areas 1965

Viet Cong activity 1965

U.S. Marine Bases 1965

Yung Tua

Cai Ngai

0   100   200
km

The WAR in INDOCHINA 1954-65

Source: Adapted from M. Gilbert, *Recent History Atlas: 1870 to the Present Day*, London, Weidenfeld and Nicolson, 1966.

Vietminh propaganda or facilitate their subversive activities...."[4]

And so the Commission stayed. When Martin became Secretary of State for External Affairs in 1963, the unification of Vietnam was still unachieved, and the Commission's life was increasingly difficult as North Vietnam and the United States built up their forces in clear violation of the Geneva Agreement and in apparent preparation for a major test. In November 1963, Diem died, the victim of a coup encouraged by his American allies. In the election campaign of 1964, President Johnson reiterated his aim "to get the boys in Vietnam to do their own fighting—we are not going north and drop bombs at this stage of the game."[5]

Johnson's words cheered Pearson and Martin, who were both well informed about, and fearful of, American involvement in Vietnam. In the spring of 1964, the Canadian chief diplomat to the ICC, Blair Seaborn, had acted as an intermediary between Washington and Hanoi. Martin had apparently suggested this use of Seaborn in a conversation with Rusk early in the year. The Americans quickly appropriated the notion as their own, and prepared a message for Seaborn to convey. The Canadians, however, were sensitive to the charge that they were simply errand boys, and the American "message" was recast as Canadian views of American policy. Moreover, the Canadian government warned the Americans—this was possible partly because of Seaborn's role—that the war was becoming unpopular in Canada and that a wider war might compel the government to disagree openly with American policy. This Canadian reserve did not affect American decision-making at all. In fact, Seaborn's report in June 1964 that North Vietnam was "not now interested in negotiation" probably hardened American attitudes and fostered deeper involvement.[6]

In his August 1964 visit to Hanoi, Seaborn, according to the Pentagon Papers, "transmitted a blunt U.S. refutation of the [North Vietnamese] Tonkin Gulf account and an accusation that [North Vietnamese] behaviour in the Gulf sought to cast the U.S. as a paper tiger or to provoke the U.S." Canadian sources claim that Seaborn expressed not an "American message" but the American appreciation of the situation; no matter what the true case, Seaborn's listener, Prime Minister Pham Van Dong, responded angrily, denouncing the Americans for carrying the war to the north and calling for a return to the 1954 Geneva agreements. Seaborn reported that Pham Van Dong

> gave no indication of being worried by firmness of U.S.A. message I delivered and in fact its immediate effect was to produce(?) anger rather than desire to discuss way out. But I find it mildly encouraging that he did calm down as he talked further and significant that (he?) should state unequivocally that he wanted to keep DRVN-USA channel of communication.

The channel remained open—but just barely.[7]

In December 1964 Seaborn returned to Hanoi with no new message from the Americans, only a reiteration of the "carrot and stick" policy presented in August and June. Seaborn was nevertheless asked to "convey attitude of real *personal* concern over the growing possibility of direct confrontation between GVN and DRV." This time Seaborn's access to North Vietnamese officials was limited, and the information he relayed was of minimal interest. The Americans seemed to care little. The Canadian channel became obsolete.

The importance of the Seaborn missions in 1964 and 1965 lies not in their substance but in their style. They illustrate Canada's rather complex attitude toward, and peculiar involvement in, the war. First, although Seaborn did not convey American messages as an American representative, he did, judging from his reports to the American government, express Canadian sympathy with US aims. The Canadian government in 1964 thought that the US course was fundamentally correct although it did fear a protracted and extended conflict. In short, Pearson and Martin were worried, but they trusted the American leadership in 1964. Johnson seemed, Pearson wrote in his diary, "calm and moderate" in his approach to "cold war problems—except Cuba and Sukarno."[8] The Canadians could only encourage this moderation, and it was thought that the Seaborn missions did so. Secondly, the Seaborn missions were an attempt to salvage some usefulness for Canada from the ICC which was increasingly scorned by the principals in Southeast Asia and even by Canadian ICC diplomats who found the Poles and Indians most difficult to deal with. Thirdly, the missions betray a Canadian eagerness to play the traditional intermediary-interpreter part at a time when the opportunities for such a role were disappearing. The ICC was a curious and dubious instrument to use, but, for Indochina, it was the only one Canada had. Fourthly, the Seaborn missions reveal Canadian misunderstanding of American aims and policy and American insensitivity to Canadian purposes and politics. The Canadians, for example, were not told of American rejection of (Secreary-General of the United Nations) U Thant's mediation attempt in 1964. Had they known, they might have been less inclined to think that Seaborn's missions could encourage negotiation. The Seaborn missions, in the view of Paul Martin and External Affairs officers, were directed towards a solution to the conflict through increasing information and eliminating misperception on both sides, especially the American side.

Seaborn's reports were pessimistic, warnings of North Vietnamese determination. They might reasonably have been thought to be a deterrent upon further American involvement in Vietnam. In fact, the effect was the opposite.

In the attempt to "save" South Vietnam, February 1965 seems in retrospect a "fateful" month. For many Americans, not only the soldiers and their families but the President and his advisers, the war became personal. Pearson and Martin knew this after their discussions with Johnson at the LBJ ranch in mid-January 1965. These discussions were a turning point in the Canadian perception of Amerian involvement. Before they flew to Texas, the Canadians were puzzled and disturbed by the direction of American policy on Vietnam. They knew that the South Vietnamese were weaker than ever before and that the existence of the regime depended more and more on American support. What the United States intended to do was a mystery to them and to Canadian officials who briefed them before departure. The Canadians were wary, not least because the United States Ambassador to South Vietnam, Henry Cabot Lodge, had spoken of "internationalizing" the war when he had visited Ottawa in September 1964. In December President Johnson himself had requested that some Canadian technical assistance be sent to Vietnam. Pearson and Martin both believed they could not possibly comply with this request, but they had not yet said no when their plane landed on the runway at the LBJ ranch in Texas.

The meetings got off to a bad beginning when President Johnson welcomed "Prime Minister Wilson" and his Canadian colleagues. He immediately took his visitors on a rambunctious tour of the ranch. The dinner which followed featured steak and catfish on the same plate and Johnson dominating conversation and interrupting others who ventured a few words. Pearson later wrote: "General MacArthur would definitely not have approved, nor, I suspect, John Kennedy." Neither did Lester Pearson. Pearson saw the style was not his own, but, more important, the substance also seemed flawed. Pearson and Johnson never found the easy familiarity that Kennedy and Pearson had at Hyannisport.

Vietnam was apparently not discussed in detail in Texas, but the Canadians knew that the Americans faced a critical decision about the war's future. The next month the decision was made. Advisors became soldiers; dependents went home; bombs rained on North Vietnam. An address by Prime Minister Pearson in early February betrays the fears he felt as the Americans sank into the mire. Pearson warned his countrymen against either "automatic support or captious criticism" of the United States: "We must protect and advance our national interests, but we should never forget that the greatest of these is peace and security. The achievement of this aim—it is chastening to realize—does not depend on our policies so much as it does on those of our neighbour." The remainder of the speech deserves careful reading:[9]

This will mean, in practice, that our official doubts about certain U.S. foreign policies often should be expressed in private, through the channels of diplomacy, rather than publicly by speeches to Canadian Clubs. It does not mean that we must always remain silent if there is strong disagreement on matters of great moment or principle. Not at all. Canadians in official positions have more than once spoken very frankly about policies and actions of our neighbour. Washington ruefully refers to it as arm-twisting from a close friend. But we must never do this merely for the purpose of rousing a chauvinistic cheer at home. Pulling the eagle's tail feathers is an easy, but a dangerous, way to get a certain temporary popularity, as well as a feeling of self-satisfaction at having annoyed the big bird.

It's a form of indulgence that we should keep strictly under control—for national and international reasons.

. . .

So the situation is full of danger and Canada is directly interested in it. We have naturally expressed our concern to our neighbour. But at this time, and following the precepts I have mentioned, that concern is most likely to have maximum influence if it is expressed responsibly through diplomatic channels.

In this speech Pearson speaks directly of the danger and hints broadly about his fears, "our concern" about American action. Mackenzie King could not have cloaked his message so skillfully as his one-time servant. Equal skill was demanded of Blair Seaborn, who on March 4 returned to Hanoi to pass on a statement of American intentions to North Vietnam. This time the premier would not see him, and the message was passed to a lower-ranking official, Ha Van Lau. The reception was cool. Seaborn reported his personal opinion that the North Vietnamese "have very little interest in CDN channel of communication with USA." His judgment was almost surely correct. Ten days after Seaborn's discussions, the "Rolling Thunder" bombing of the North became continuous, and each side's suspicions grew.

Seaborn had as little success with his Indian and Polish colleagues on the International Control Commission as he had in Hanoi. The Indians were ever more reluctant to act, ever more resentful of the Canadian charge that they were not acting impartially. The Canadians made representations in New Delhi and to the Indian High Commission in Ottawa urging that "Commission business" be cleared up and that "impartiality" rule in Commission judgments. The response was, from the Canadian viewpoint, unsatisfactory. On February 13, Canada dissented sharply from a majority ICC report declaring it "an oversimplified and misleading impression of the root causes of the dangerous instability in Vietnam."[10] Relations with India worsened, and the hope that the ICC might play a part in ending the conflict diminished greatly.

Canadians continued to look to Pearson for leadership. The *Globe and Mail* (5 March 1965) asked him to use his skill to persuade the Americans that the Vietnam War must come to an honourable end. Others, citing the sharp ICC minority report, demanded that Canada not be linked with American actions. On March 26, Martin spoke to the editors of Canada's foreign language press on the subject of Canada and Vietnam. He began with a defence of Canada's activities on the ICC, arguing that this Canadian presence had given Canadians "a pretty objective analysis" of events in Vietnam. This analysis had led Martin to blame the conflict in Vietnam upon "a process of subversion directed by authorities of North Vietnam against South Vietnam." To this point there was no evidence that there was a "genuine disposition" on the part of North Vietnam and China to approach negotiations with sincerity. Canada would continue to urge restraint and to pursue "openings" wherever they might appear. In conclusion, Martin emphasized the limits on Canadian action and expressed his disappointment at the ineffectiveness of the UN in Vietnam.[11]

Martin's speech reflected his Commons statement in which he expressed Canada's dissent from the ICC report that condemned the American air strikes.[12] This statement came on the day two US Marine corps battalions landed just north of Danang. These were the first American ground units in Vietnam.

Martin's tone was stronger, and his meaning less equivocal than the Prime Minister's had been in February and March. In his February 10 speech, Pearson had hinted broadly about Canada's disagreement with some aspects of American policy in Vietnam. In that same speech he had spoken openly about Canadian differences with the Americans on NATO. After the speech, Martin, who had not been informed about Pearson's comments, asked for clarification of the Prime Minister's meaning. Pearson reassured him that he had said nothing that disagreed with Canadian foreign policy, which was, of course, the responsibility of Martin's department. Indeed in the House of Commons, after it began to sit on February 16, Martin and Pearson never contradcited each other. Pearson left Vietnam to his foreign minister, and his statements were notably cautious. The Canadian government's stand gained the approval of all parties in the House of Commons except the New Democrats. The Conservatives asked for more outspoken support but generally supported the government's policy. The press, on the whole, thought the Canadian refusal to criticize American policy while urging negotiations and seeking methods by which these negotiations could take place was sensible. Pearson's proposal for an international police force to prevent border incursons won general approval. The Americans, it was said, welcomed this proposal.[13]

We do not know whether the Americans did, in fact, welcome this proposal or if they even noticed it. There is no evidence that the Americans thought that the Canadians would dissent in any way from their policy. In private, Martin and Pearson had warned of the dangers of an expanded war, but in February and March both Martin and Pearson had expressed sympathy for the American predicament and had emphasized the importance of disagreeing with American policy through "diplomatic channels." President Johnson had good reason to be thankful for the Canadians' willingness to use Seaborn to warn the North Vietnamese and for the Canadian dissent from the ICC majority report which condemned the bombing. In this spirit Johnson wrote to Pearson on 30 March 1965:[14]

Dear Mike:

I am delighted to join in sending my heartiest greetings to you on the occasion of your receiving the Temple University World Peace Award. Your long record in the struggle for peace needs no repetition from me, but I want to bear witness to the wisdom and courage that you have brought to bear on every question affecting world peace that you and I have worked on together in sixteen months of the closest cooperation.

With warmest personal good wishes,

Sincerely,

"LBJ"

On April 2 "Mike" Pearson accepted his award at Temple University in Philadelphia and tried to bring his "wisdom and courage" to bear upon the troubled Vietnam War. Once again Pearson lauded the honourable American motives in their Vietnam involvement. His government and the "great majority" of Canadians had supported US "peace-keeping and peace-making policies in Vietnam," Then significantly: "We wish to be able to continue that support." A negotiated peace was the only exit. The bombing "beyond a certain point" may "only harden [North Vietnamese] determination to pursue, and even intensify, their present course of action." Perhaps now we had come to that "point." After two months of bomb-

ing, "the message should ... have been received 'loud and clear'." Admitting that he might not know many factors, Pearson suggested that there might be "a possibility" that

a suspension of air strikes against North Vietnam *at the right time* might provide the Hanoi authorities with an opportunity, if they wish to take it, to inject some flexibility into their policy without appearing to do so as the direct result of military pressure. If such a suspension took place for a limited time, then the rate of incidents in South Vietnam would provide a fairly accurate way of measuring its usefulness and the desirability of continuing it. I am not, of course—I would not dare—propose any compromise on points of principle, nor any weakening of resistance to aggression in South Vietnam. Indeed resistance may require increased military strength to be used against the armed and attacking Communists. I merely suggest that a measured and announced pause in one field of military action at the right time might facilitate the developments of diplomatic resources which cannot easily be applied to the problem under the existing circumstances. It could at least, at the very least, expose the intransigence of the North Vietnam government if they remained intransigent.[15]

This proposal was much more than "a diffident aside" as Charles Taylor suggests; it challenged the clear direction of American policy at the time. Johnson noticed.

The speech ended, and the President called to invite Pearson to join him for lunch at his Camp David retreat. The invitation was presidentially proper, but Johnson's manners were not. During the lunch Johnson talked continuously and loudly on the telephone about Vietnam. Not even the normal pleasantries could be exchanged, and Canadian Ambassador Charles Ritchie recalls the occasion as "very strained."[16]

After lunch, Pearson and Johnson left the other diners to chat on the terrace. Then Johnson "simply exploded." Pearson's speech was "bad," and for the next hour Johnson berated his visitor. Pearson could scarcely say a word during the harangue. Johnson complained that Pearson

> had joined the ranks of the domestic opponents of his Vietnam policy: (Senator Wayne) Morse, (Walter) Lippmann, the *New York Times*, ADA (Americans for Democratic Action), the ignorant Liberals, the "know nothing," do gooders, etc. By doing so, (Pearson) had made it more difficult. He didn't expect that of me, etc.; that I would come into the United States and make a speech of this kind without consulting him or "Mac" Bundy or Dean Rusk.[17]

Pearson tried to explain his motives. A bombing pause "might be of help," and, moreover, "public opinion in [Canada] was profoundly disturbed by the implications of certain aspects of US policy and...some of us were having difficulty with public opinion in our complete support of that policy." Johnson could not see why these difficulties occured. There were three choices: the expansion of the war, perhaps even to Peking; withdrawal; and the policy that was being followed. Pearson managed to ask what in fact American plans were.

> The President said their plans were *not* for unlimited bombing but for the progressive destruction, if necessary, of military installations, communications and industrial facilities important in the assistance North Vietnam was giving the South. They would not bomb within a 50 mile radius of Hanoi, the distance beyond which Hanoi MIGs cannot operate and return. They would also do everything possible to avoid killing civilians, for which restraint, the President repeated with the bitterness he had previously shown on this matter, they would get no thanks even from their friends.

"It's hard to sleep these days," Johnson complained, "I'm beginning to feel like a martyr; misunderstood, misjudged by friends at home and abroad."

Johnson's public face did not conceal his unhappiness when Pearson and he met the press. Asked what he thought of Pearson's speech, Johnson answered: "It is not a matter for me to pass judgment on what other governments do. It is his expression. He has expressed it very well."[18] If any doubted what Johnson meant, his aides explained it clearly to the press "off the record." Still, many questions remain, about Johnson's reaction and Pearson's motives. Johnson's reaction is probably most easily explained. For Johnson's purposes the speech was badly timed. In mid-March Johnson had demanded that the Joint Chiefs of Staff find ways to "kill more VC." On April 1 and 2, he decided that only more Americans could "kill more VC" and save the deteriorating position of the South Vietnamese government. In National Security Memorandum 328, the President personally approved the deployment of two Marine battalions and several other measures recommended by the Joint Chiefs of Staff. This decision, the Pentagon Papers rightly declared, was pivotal: "It marks the acceptance by the President of the United States of the concept that U.S. troops would engage in offensive ground operations against Asian insurgents." Nevertheless, it also reveals Johnson's anxiety, shown in his decision to move slowly and to focus no publicity on the Marines' actions in order that "U.S. policy should appear to be wholly consistent."[19]

The telephone conversations about Vietnam which so rudely disrupted the April 3 lunch, therefore, concerned the most critical decision of American Vietnam involvement. Pearson's account clearly shows that he was *not* told the significance of what he overheard. He had spoken of restraint on the same day as Johnson had decided to throw off restraints. The fact that numerous American advisors, including Maxwell Taylor, had expressed private doubts about Johnson's decision surely increased his irritation when the Canadian Prime Minister publicly expressed these doubts. In Johnson's mind, moreover, the Canadians had no right to complain. Their own representative, Blair Seaborn, had told the Americans that the North Vietnamese were not interested in negotiations. The Canadian ICC minority report had also pointed to the North Vietnamese aggression in the South. Pearson and Martin had themsleves condemned the North Vietnamese in strong terms in February and March and had warned of the dangers of a South Vietnamese collapse.

Years later the State Department's William Bundy, who had become a major adviser to Johnson after late 1964, said that he could never understand Pearson's decision to make "that speech at that particular moment on American soil." The place and the time were, according to Bundy, "what really put Johnson over the boiling point." There is, however, another factor. Rufus Smith, who was then on the staff of the American Embassy in Ottawa, recalls that George Ball, the Under-secretary of State, had been invited to speak on a controversial subject in Canada. Ball refused because the Canadian government suggested he should. Pearson, it seemed, never took the courtesy to ask the Americans if they minded.

Pearson's sense of diplomatic timing and courtesy, so keenly developed in over three decades of international service, had failed him. It did so because the Americans had taken him for granted. Despite Seaborn's "valuable" work for the Americans and the private doubts but public support Canadians had expressed about expansion

of the Vietnam War, the Americans had not told Ottawa what they intended to do. Canadian records of the time show that the Canadians knew little more about Washington's intention than Moscow's. The signals changed hourly from storm to calm. It was in this changing climate that Pearson's action is best understood.

Personal relations also explain a great deal. Norman Mailer's fictional answer to the question of "Why are we in Vietnam?" was a Texan's hunting trip. It is a metaphor Mike Pearson would have understood after his ranch encounter with Lyndon Johnson. The roughness, the profanity, and the grasping ambition were not traits conducive to the delicate balancing of international diplomacy. This was especially so when the American military was becoming more dominant and when "hardliners" like William Bundy were heard more often in the Oval office. If the Americans were losing their balance, the Canadians, in the interests of America and the Western Alliance, thought they should try to correct them. As Pearson later said to Bruce Hutchison, he "decided on a constructive intervention, a piece of friendly advice from a good neighbour." Besides, he added to Hutchison, persons highly placed in the United States government who were loyal to Johnson but disagreed with his Vietnam strategy and hoped to moderate it "urged Pearson to speak out."[20]

Identifying these "persons highly placed" is difficult. In any case they probably strengthened what was Pearson's judgment already. On 30 March, three days before the speech, the prominent Washington journalist and Pearson friend, Marquis Childs, called on the Prime Minister who asked that Childs's views be recorded for use by the Department of External Affairs. Childs warned that Johnson faced a decision which might bring the United States close to war with Peking and even Moscow. Johnson's advice came from the military, and he was unaware of the diplomatic consequences of his actions. Canada, Childs urged, had an important part to play in presenting alternatives and restraining the hawks. There were those who agreed with Childs—Vice President Hubert Humphrey was cited—but they needed help, quickly. Childs's comments may not have influenced Pearson's thinking; they probably reflected it. Pearson shared Childs's concerns about Johnson, and like Childs, so many of Pearson's American friends, men like Walter Lippmann and James Reston, strongly opposed the expansion of the Vietnamese War. During the Korean War, Pearson had spoken out against the risks involved in American policy. He may not have affected American decisions then, but Pearson believed hindsight showed his judgment to have been correct. Pearson wrote in his diary after his Camp David quarrel: "This crisis over Vietnam is going to be a great test for LBJ. I'm not now certain that he is going to be successful in meeting it." Once again hindsight favours Pearson.

We must finally consider what influence "public opinion" had upon Pearson's action. Pearson himself told Johnson that he was having "some difficulty with public opinion." What did he mean? In February 1965 the voices of dissent were not strong, except on the left. President Johnson was a popular president in Canada: in late April 1964, 29 percent of Canadians thought him an "excellent" president and 43 percent ranked him as "pretty good." More thought him "excellent" in April 1965 than in February 1964, and it was clear that Vietnam had not harmed Johnson's reputation in Canada. And yet there were those who objected, and their voices were heard and respected by Pearson. Pearson's son and External Affairs

officer Geoffrey and his wife Maryon both thought the American policy dangerous. So did Walter Gordon, the Finance Minister and party manager. Gordon represented a left-wing faction in the Liberal Party that had more influence than numbers. Pearson needed this influence, and, in a minority Parliament, he also had to count on the New Democrats, the most vigorous opponents of Vietnam War. "Public opinion" in its traditional sense explains little. The "people" favoured a "harder line" than the politicians. But politics mattered, public opinion did not. The distinction is a difference.[21]

Paul Martin shared many of Pearson's doubts about American policy in Vietnam, but he did not share Pearson's belief that public expression of some of those doubts was wise. In February and March his speeches had supported the aims of the American effort in Vietnam, and he had, on one occasion, expressed scepticism about the success of any peace conference at this time. His public statements did not reflect his private feelings because he knew how sensitive the Americans were to criticism of Vietnam. Rusk had repeatedly told him that, in Vietnam, the United States was carrying alone the burdens that the West together should share.[22] Thus, when Pearson told him a few days before the Temple speech what he intended to say, Martin exploded. According to his later recollection, he told Pearson:[23]

> You can't make that speech! What you're doing is calling upon the president of the United States to stop the bombing. If you publicly criticize the United States like this, you're going to discount our influence in Washington and your own forever. And you must not do that.

Martin argued that the speech would destroy Canadian influence on other issues as well. It would make his position impossible; he would have to resign. He could not support Pearson's proposal, and neither could his department.

Martin, of course, did not resign, but his assessment of Johnson's reaction and of his department's attitude was largely correct. Although some later commentators have minimized the significance of Pearson's remarks, Martin's reaction indicates that Johnson's strong reaction was anticipated. Indeed, members of Pearson's staff had told reporters on the plane to Philadelphia that the speech was one of the most "serious" Pearson had ever made.[24] That certainly was his foreign secretary's and foreign office's feeling. Why did they differ so strongly with External Affairs' most distinguished former servant?

Comparison of the speeches of Martin in February and March with Pearson's Temple speech gives some indication why Martin was so annoyed. Pearson at Temple seemed to contradict what his foreign secretary had said only a few weeks earlier. Nor was this the first problem with independent initiatives. Pearson's comments on NATO in February 1965 had not been cleared with Martin, who had to explain to some Europeans and Americans that Pearson's remarks did not portend a policy change. Coming after this incident, the Temple speech surely offended Martin greatly, not least because consultation with him occurred at the last minute. When counselled to remain silent, Pearson rejected the counsel. Pearson had wisely refrained from regular dealings with the department because of his eminence in external affairs. He was, perhaps, more distant from the department than other prime ministers who had much less experience and knowledge. Thus his initiatives undoubtedly puzzled and frustrated Martin. That they reflected, in small part, the complaints of Martin's left-wing critics must

have infuriated Martin. Resignation was definitely an act that had to be considered. The absence of similar Pearson initiatives in the future indicates that Martin's threat may have had some effect.

Martin's attitude was also influenced by the difficulties with the Americans on other issues which in the spring of 1965 were mounting. His American desk officers in External Affairs were reporting on possible economic quarrels, and they were also warning that inconsistency in American policy was becoming marked as Vietnam absorbed so much attention and as divisions in the administration grew. Diplomatic finesse was required if Canada was to negotiate the rapids around the bend. The Pearson speech brought the rapids closer. Another group in External Affairs which opposed Canadian peace overtures was made up of those who had served in Southeast Asia. During their service in Southeast Asia, most officers came to believe that the American response should be strong. Having seen North Vietnamese intransigence, the flow of refugees, and the growth of infiltration, these officers returned to Ottawa as "hardliners." They were not blind admirers of South Vietnamese politics and politicians, but their emotions and their analyses favoured support for the southern side. Because they knew so much of Southeast Asia, these officers' influence exceeded their numbers. They certainly received a sympathetic hearing from the Undersecretary, Marcel Cadieux, and he, in turn, passed on their judgments to Martin.

The major work on Canada and Vietnam shows how the department's "liberal moderate" section declined in importance as the sixties progressed and how the "conservative" faction grew.[25] Although some department officers remained skeptical about or opposed to greater American involvement in Vietnam—especially those dealing with Europe or the Third World where America's Vietnam adventure was controversial—those who offered the "expert" advice tended to be "conservative" on the subject. Their advice Martin listened to even if he did not always follow it. This influence no doubt affected Martin's reaction to Pearson's speech. Thus when Martin, at Pearson's request, met Marquis Childs, he pointed out that Canada had privately tried to get negotiations started but that there was no indication at that time that negotiations could occur. He approvingly cited Dean Rusk's question: If we agreed to negotiate, with whom would we negotiate? Why then call publicly for an opening of the door when it led only into the night?

For the remainder of Pearson's years in office, Canada was in the darkness about Vietnam. Martin's warning that Canada would lose influence proved correct. As William Bundy later remarked, the speech "did seriously impair the relationship." Canada was not informed of new American initiatives or of various peace "feelers." Sources became "unofficial" and rumour became the common currency of Vietnam transactions. According to a prominent American official, Canada after Temple was told less than the United States' more "reliable" allies, nations such as Britain, Australia, and New Zealand. After April 1965, Canada's activities in Vietnam were of little significance in terms of international diplomacy although politically and culturally the effects of that war on Canada and on Canadian attitudes towards the United States were immense. Perhaps Pearson sensed this. Canada was changing along with the United States and Canadian-American relations could not be those of the past. The February speech where Pearson called for reassessment of NATO and NORAD thus leads directly to

the Temple remarks. Pearson was already taking that longer view of international development, which was later expressed in his report on international aid.

The Temple speech did not end Canadian involvement with the Vietnam War, although it did mean that what followed was a denouement. Canada did continue its International Control Commission membership although the Commission proved ever more ineffective. It also contributed indirectly to American military efforts through the sale of military goods under the Defence Production Sharing Agreement. Nor did diplomatic efforts to produce negotiations cease. Indeed, Blair Seaborn returned to Hanoi at the end of May 1965 during a short bombing pause.

This pause came about after seventeen non-aligned nations had presented an appeal for a peaceful end to the war through negotiation and after an important 7 April speech by Johnson, in which Johnson stated that the United States was prepared for unconditional discussions with Hanoi. Hanoi responded on 8 April with its "Four Points." The Hanoi plan seemed to some like an opening, and the Americans were obligated to see if it was. Consequently Johnson ordered a brief bombing pause on May 13 which he believed he "could use to good effect with world opinion."[26] The pause would not be announced, but Moscow and Hanoi would be told that the United States was "watching closely to see whether they respond." They did not.

Seaborn's visit followed this pause, and once again the Americans gave him a message to bear. This time Martin was especially reluctant and insisted on rewording what the Americans wanted to say. In any event, Seaborn's meetings brought little hope of negotiations. Foreign Minister Trinh denounced the American offer of unconditional discussion as "deceitful," and when asked whether Hanoi's "Four Points"

were preconditions to talks or simply ultimate goals, he was "deliberately vague."
With this mission, Seaborn's usefulness—
to Canada, the United States, and North
Vietnam—ended. There was a return trip to
Hanoi in the fall, but there was no
American message sent and, from the
North Vietnamese, no interesting comments given. Rusk privately told Martin
that publicity about the Seaborn missions
had made the Canadian "channel" no longer
valuable. New Canadian initiations would
be taken independently.

The news about the missions had
"leaked" in late May at which time debate
about Vietnam in Canada had intensified.
Opinions were divided, but as the poll about
Johnson's popularity in Canada suggests,
most Canadians continued to support
American action. In May as well, the
American intervention in the Dominican
Republic did not bring a critical Canadian
reaction. Even Tommy Douglas only questioned what the American intentions were,
not whether Americans had the right to intervene to support their own nationals. On
Vietnam, Douglas was harsher, attacking
the Americans for repressing "the legitimate aspiration of the people" for the right
to self-determination. He criticized Canada
for assuming "a deferential pose of supine
subservience." Douglas's attitude had already earned him righteous rebuke from
some Canadian newspapers. The *Globe and
Mail* claimed that "Mr. Douglas's obsession
could only help the side of Communist imperialism in the Southeast Asian power
struggle." If Douglas found few echoes in
the press, he did get some support in the
universities. It was still a time for civility in
dealing with the United States, however.
When about twenty-five University of
Toronto professors requested that the
University not grant an honorary a degree
to the United States Ambassador to the
United Nations, Adlai Stevenson, the re-

quest was dismissed by the Univeristy
Senate with only one member out of one
hundred and fifty supporting the request.
When Stevenson came to Toronto,
protestors met him with silence. The *Globe
and Mail* was not silent, denouncing the
protest as "plain and simple bad manners."[27]

By year's end the manners were worse
and the silence had ended. Martin and
Pearson had continued to believe during
1965 that negotiations were impossible.
Pearson kept his silence after the April
speech. He had apologized to Johnson in a
long letter sent after his return to Ottawa.[28]
Its importance lies in its statement that if
the North Vietnamese did not respond to
a bombing halt, the Americans could be
strengthened in their case for "planned and
limited air retaliation." After Pearson said
this and after the bombing pause "failed,"
he could say very little about Vietnam.
What little he did say caused confusion. On
July 20, Johnson sent a letter to the heads
of state of several nations asking for support of South Vietnam. Pearson reported
this, and in answer to a parliamentary
question implied that the United States
had asked for token Canadian military assistance. Almost simultaneously, Martin
denied this. To clarify what was said,
Pearson asked Washington to release the
exchange of letters. Johnson refused. Jack
Valenti, a White House aide, then warned
Johnson that Pearson was "getting beat
over the head from the opposition who accused him of lying about what he told the
President." To "cleanse" himself, Pearson
was going to release a paper explaining the
Canadian position and incorporating sum-
maries of the letters. Valenti asked whether
Pearson should be cautioned about doing
this. Pearson did release the statement, but
it was a bland restatement of previous positions which simply indicated that
Canada's contribution to South Vietnam

could come from economic assistance and participation on the ICC. Johnson had clearly not forgiven Pearson. The Washington *Daily News* (August 23) reported that in the Washington dog house, Pearson occupied the "No. 1 kennel." In the future, he would have to rescue himself when he was being beaten.[29]

This incident followed a major debate on Canadian-American relations that was provoked by the publication of the Merchant- Heeney Report on 12 July. This report grew out of the amicable Johnson-Pearson discussions of January 1964. The Report echoed the mood of that day rather than that of the summer of 1965. The authors of the report, the distinguished diplomats Livingston T. Merchant and Arnold Heeney, favoured closer institutional links between the two countries: indeed their mandate "to make it easier to avoid divergencies in economic and other policies" made such a thrust inevitable. Thus, Merchant and Heeney examined where "divergencies" had occurred and suggested methods of resolving them. They recommended, *inter alia*, expansion of the functions of the International Joint Commission, the establishment of a joint deputy minister level committee, the development of more cooperative energy policies, and the reinvigoration of the Permanent Joint Board on Defence. But with memories of Diefenbaker's relationship with Kennedy very much in their minds, Merchant and Heeney dwelt on style rather than substance. The style should not be Diefenbaker's:

It is important and reasonable that Canadian authorities should have careful regard for the U.S. Government's position in this world context, and, in the absence of Canadian interests or obligations, avoid so far as possible, public disagreement upon critical issues.

It is in the abiding interest of both countries that, wherever possible, divergent views between two governments should be expressed and if possible resolved in private, through diplomatic channels.

This statement brought upon the authors a fusillade of criticism.

The response was a measure of the ambiguity of Canadian attitudes towards the United States in 1965. As the *Canadian Annual Review* observed, the "admonitions" of Merchant and Heeney, "though written well before the Prime Minister's speech in Philadelphia, were examined with aftermath in mind."[30] The opposition responded angrily, with Conservative Alvin Hamilton excoriating the report as a sell-out that allowed Canada only a role in world affairs as an American lap dog. New Democrats were equally virulent in their criticism. Charles Lynch of Southam News used the report to criticize Lester Pearson's approach to diplomacy. The report, Lynch wrote, was a bureaucrat's dream: "Keep it quiet, boys, work it out, we will all keep out of trouble and things will go smoothly." Heeney, in Lynch's view, "has many of the characteristics of Lester B. Pearson—in fact he is the kind of man Mr. Pearson might have become had Mr. Pearson stayed out of politics." Lynch's comments draw attention to the image that Pearson was acquiring midway through his prime ministership. The aggressive peacemaker of the 1950s who had pulled the eagle's tail feathers when General MacArthur threatened to take the Korean conflict to a nuclear conclusion, and who had pushed the British towards sensible compromise during the Suez madness, now seemed curiously inactive, incapable of an imaginative response to clear, present dangers. Pearson's domestic political difficulties did much to transform the perception of his character and purposes, but so did his obvious ineffectiveness in dealing with the Americans. "Independence" had become a measure of diplomatic usefulness for many Canadian commentators. A.D.P. Heeney wrote to Merchant, in "a philosophical and optimistic vein," that their report would "be around for quite a long time." It was: It haunted Canadian policy-makers for several years.[31]

In the fall, the Canadian election diverted Canadian attention from international affairs. Unlike the 1963 election, the November 8, 1965 election focused almost exclusively on domestic affairs. This occurred because, in contrast to the pattern of 1963, John Diefenbaker was more supportive of American Vietnam policy than the Liberals were. The NDP and the Créditiste party did attack the government, but their major charge, that Canada was making plans to send troops to Vietnam, was easily denied by the Liberals.[32] The criticisms from the Créditstes and the NDP are nevertheless significant, because the election brought yet another minority government, where the support of those parties could be essential to the government. The Liberals, moreover, lost voters to the New Democrats, and in the future they had

to be concerned about erosion of support on the left. Several new members would ensure that this concern was genuine. Although Walter Gordon resigned from the cabinet after the election, many Gordon supporters, such as Donald Macdonald, were elected and would become prominent. Gordon's absence from the cabinet meant that his critical views on American policy could be more freely expressed. Most important were the new Quebec members, Jean Marchand, Pierre Trudeau, and Gérard Pelletier. They reflected the opposition to the Vietnam War expressed by such respected French Canadian intellectuals as André Laurendeau in *Le Magazine Maclean* and Claude Ryan in *Le Devoir*. Because Pearson's concern for Quebec became paramount in the 1965-67 period, the new voices from Quebec were more often heard and their recommendations were often followed.

Pearson and Johnson never repaired their relationship. In 1967, Canada called once again for a bombing halt, but its voice was one among many. In 1968, both Pearson and Johnson left political life. Vietnam had wounded both men and the relationship between the nations they led.

NOTES

1. (Toronto: Anansi, 1974), vii. Other studies of Canada and Vietnam are James Eayrs, *In Defence of Canada, Indochina: The Roots of Complicity* (Toronto: University of Toronto Press, 1983); and Douglas Ross, *In the Interests of Peace: Canada and Vietnam 1954-1973* (Toronto: University of Toronto Press, 1984).

2. See John Holmes "Geneva 1954," *International Journal*, Vol. xxii (Summer 1967), pp. 457-83.

3. The best account of the Commission is Ross, *In the Interests of Peace* and Eayrs, *Roots of Complicity*. The interpretations differ significantly.

4. Martin to Pearson, 24 November 1956, Martin Papers, volume 24, file L.B. Pearson (National Archives).

5. Quoted in Jack Shepherd and Christopher S. Wren, *Quotations from Chairman* LBJ (New York, Simon & Schuster 1968), p. 66.

6. Office of the Secretary of Defense, Vietnam Task Force, United States-Vietnam Relations 1945-1967, Diplomatic Papers, Section VI.C.1.

7. Forrestal to Rusk, 19 Aug. 1964; Report of Conversation with Prime Minister Phan Von Dong, 17 Aug. 1964; "Saigon to Sec. State," 18 Aug. 1964; all in the *U.S.-Vietnam Relations, ibid.* Also, *Snow Job*, ch. 2; Paul Martin, *A Very Public Life. Volume II. So Many Worlds* (Toronto: Deneau, 1985). For an earlier American account, see Chester Cooper, The Lost Crusade (New York: Dodd, Mead, 1970).

8. L.B. Pearson, *Mike, Volume III* (Toronto: Univ. of Toronto Press, 1975), p. 122. Arthur Schlesinger's claim that Pearson told John Kennedy to "get out" of Vietnam in 1963 cannot be corroborated and is almost surely false. Schlesinger got this story from Chalmers Roberts, *First Rough Draft* (New York: Praeger 1973), 195-96.

9. "Extracts from an Address by the Right Honourable Lester B. Pearson, Prime Minister of Canada, to the Canadian Club of Ottawa, February 10, 1965," External Affairs, *Statements and Speeches* 65/3. On American decision-making in this critical period, see Larry Berman, *Lyndon Johnson's War: The Road to Stalemate in Vietnam* (New York: Norton, 1989), chs. II-III

10. Quoted in J. Saywell, ed., *Canadian Annual Review for 1965* (Toronto: Univ. of Toronto Press, 1966), 220.

11. "Canada and Vietnam," 20 March 1965, External Affairs, *Statements and Speeches* 65/9.

12. Statement by Martin, 8 March 1965, on the Tabling of the Special Message of 13 February, 1965 of the International Commission for Supervision and Control in Vietnam. External Affairs, *Statements and Speeches*, 65/8.

13. *Toronto Star*, 6 March 1965.

14. Johnson to Pearson, 30 March 1965 (drafted by McGeorge Bundy), Johnson Papers, Johnson Library, MEVPCO43Ma2/T.

15. Quoted in C.I.I.A. Monthly Report, v. 4, no. 4 (April 1965), 30-2. This was not issued as one of the External Affairs Statements and Speeches.

16. L.B. Pearson, *Mike: The Memoirs of the Rt. Hon. Lester B. Pearson, Volume 3* (Toronto: Univ. of Toronto Press, 1975), p. 139. This is from the Pearson diary. Charles Ritchie's later comments suggest that the quarrel began before Pearson and Johnson went to the terrace. See Peter Stursberg, *Lester Pearson and the American Dilemma* (Toronto: Doubleday Canada, 1980), 220-1 and Charles Ritchie, "The day the President of the United States struck fear and trembling into the heart of our PM," *Maclean's* (January 1974), pp. 35, 40, 42. See also Charles Ritchie, *Storm Signals* (Toronto: Macmillan, 1983), pp. 81-4.

17. Pearson, *ibid.*, pp. 140-1.

18. C.I.I.A. *Monthly Report*, v. 4, no. 4 (April 1965), p. 32.

19. *Pentagon Papers*, III, 447. See also Guenter Lewy, *America in Vietnam*, (New York: Oxford, 1978) pp. 46-47; and Leslie Gelb with Richard K. Betts, *The Irony of Vietnam: The System Worked* (Washington: Brookings, 1979), 120 ff. The controversy about Vietnam as history is discussed in Berman, *Lyndon Johnson's War*, pp. 3-8.

20. Bruce Hutchison, *The Far Side of the Street* (Toronto: Macmillan, 1976), p. 354; See also Bundy's comments in Stursberg, *Pearson and the American Dilemma*, 222.

21. The poll on Canadian opinions of Johnson was sent to Johnson with the observation that a greater loss of support was expected because of "Vietnamese Policy." Johnson Papers, Executive FG1C043. The debate about public opinion and attentive publics continues. For the 1965 poll, see "Our Quiet War Over Peace: Politicians vs. the People," *Maclean's*, January 23, 1965, p. 18.

22. For a good illustration of Rusk's attitude, see his interview with Peter Stursberg in *Pearson and the American Dilemma*, pp. 210-11 where he accuses Canada of taking a "free ride."

23. *Ibid.*, p. 218.

24. *Montreal Star*, 3 April 1965.

25. Ross, "In the Interests of Peace," *passim*. See also John Holmes, "Canada and the Vietnam War," in J.L. Granatstein and R.D. Cuff, eds., *War and Society in North America* (Toronto: Nelson, 1971), pp. 184-99. Much of this section is based on confidential interviews which tend to support Ross's thesis.

26. Gravel, *Pentagon Papers*, pp. 111, 366.

27. C.I.I.A. *Monthly Report*, v. 4, no. 5 (May 1965), 45-50; *Canadian Annual Review* 1965, 230-3; and *Commons Debates*, May 1965. *The Annual Review*'s account of protest is detailed and balanced with the *Globe and Mail*, April-May 1965 *passim*. On Seaborn, see also, Geoffrey Steven's "Quiet Canadian and a Tale of Two Cities," *Globe Magazine* (31 July 1965) p. 2.

28. Pearson, *Mike*, III, pp. 142-3.

29. Valenti to Johnson, 14 Aug. 1965, Executive C043ND1900312, Johnson Library.

30. *Canadian Annual Review 1965*, 260. The *Review* gives a good summary of criticism.

31. A.D.P. Heeney, *The things that are Caesar's: Memoirs of a Canadian Public Servant* (Toronto: University of Toronto Press, 1972), p. 196. *Ottawa Citizen*, 14 July 1965. C.I.I.A. *Monthly Report*, v. 4, no. 7-8 (July-August 1965), pp. 79-81. American reaction to the report was more favourable and unremarkable. In September, eleven Republican members of the House of Representatives issued a "White Paper" on Canadian-American relations that reflected the thrust of Merchant-Heeney. See C.I.I.A. *Monthly Report*, v. IV, no. 9 (September 1965), p. 93.

32. The *Globe and Mail*, 22 October 1965. For an example of the increasing suspicion on the left, see J.W. Warnock, "Canada's Real Role in Vietnam," *Commentator* (October 1965), pp. 14-15, 25.

SUGGESTED READINGS

Anonymous, "Canada in the Pentagon Papers," *Canadian Forum*, September 1973, pages: 8-19.

Bridle, Paul, "Canada and the International Commissions in Indochina, 1954-1972," *Behind the Headlines*, Vol. 32, No. 5, (October 1973), p. 1-28.

Dai, Poliu, "Canada's Reluctant Participation in the International Commission For Supervision and Control in Vietnam in 1973," *Canadian Yearbook of International Law*, Vol. XI, 1973, pp. 244-57.

Dobell, William A., "A 'Sow's Ear' in Vietnam," *International Journal*, Vol. 29, No. 3, 1974, pp. 356-92.

Eayrs, James, *In Defence of Canada, Indochina: Roots of Complicity*, Toronto: University of Toronto Press, 1983.

Goldblatt, Murray, "Canada's Role in Vietnam," *International Perspectives*, (March/April 1973), pp. 47-51.

Holmes, J., "Canada and the Vietnam War," in J.L. Granatstein and R.D. Cuff (ed.), *War and Society in North America*, Toronto: Nelson, 1971, pp. 184-99.

Martin, Paul, *A Very Public Life*, Volume 2, "So Many Worlds," (Toronto: Deneau, 1985), pp. 421-457.

Ross, Douglas, *In the Interests of Peace: Canada and Vietnam, 1954-1973*, Toronto: University of Toronto Press, 1984.

Sharp, Hon. Mitchell, *Vietnam: Canada's Approach to Participation in the International Commission of Control and Supervision*, October 25, 1972-March 27, 1973, Ottawa: Information Canada, 1973.

Taylor, Charles, *Snow Job: Canada, the United States and Vietnam 1954-1973*, Toronto: Anansi, 1974.

Thakur, Ramesh, *Peacekeeping in Vietnam: Canada, India, Poland and the International Commission*, Edmonton: University of Alberta Press, 1984.

s e c t i o n 3

ADAPTING TO THE NEW
FOREIGN POLICY AGENDA

The decline of the Cold War was soon evident in the pattern of east-west relations after the Cuban Missile Crisis and through the mid-1960s. The creation of the Washington-Moscow hot line, the conclusion of the Partial Test Ban Treaty in 1963, and an improvement in superpower rhetoric all signaled the shift to a new era of détente. With mutual accommodation came a de-emphasis on the military-security and alliance issues that had been dominant. Partially as a reslt, a wide range of new issues began to thrust themselves into a more prominent place on the agenda of Canadian foreign policy. Some had immediate roots within Canada and the North American continent. These included Quebec's demand for a larger international presence, Pierre Trudeau's desire for a new foreign policy, Canada's need to protect its Arctic waters, Canada's effort to redefine its economic and energy relationship with the United States, and Joe Clark's attempt to move the Canadian embassy in Israel to Jerusalem.

Other new issues emerged more or less directly as a result of the warming east-west climate. The opportunity to reduce defence spending through reductions in NATO forces was one such example, as was the pursuit of a long-stalled initiative to establish diplomatic relations with the People's Republic of China and the negoti-

ation, during the 1970s, of a new comprehensive accord on security and cooperation covering all of Europe, the Conference on Security and Cooperation in Europe (CSCE). At the very end of the 1970s, however, the Soviet intervention in Afghanistan signaled the passing of the era of détente and, with the election of Ronald Reagan, there emerged a period of more confrontatational US-USSR relations.

The new Liberal government of Pierre Trudeau launched a comprehensive review of Canadian foreign policy, culminating in the 1970 "Foreign Policy for Canadians" white paper and marking the demise of Pearsonian "internationalism" as the key theme of the country's diplomacy. In part, as Denis Stairs argues in his chapter on the review, the launching of this soul-searching exercise can be explained as a response to the changing international system of the day as much if not more than by the change of government in Ottawa. In part, this was because (as John Schlegel describes in his chapter on the Gabon incident) the old internationalist formulae were no longer adequate to counter a Quebec now demanding a role in foreign affairs.

These international changes, notably the relative decline of the United States as an internationally dominant power, made economic matters, especially bilateral ones with the US, more prominent in Canadian foreign policy during the 1970s. One manifestation, as Peter Dobell details, was the development of the "Third Option" policy through a review of Canada-US relations which followed the release of "Foreign Policy for Canadians" and more immediately followed significant international economic policy changes announced by President Nixon in 1971. Another was the increasing salience of energy issues with the OPEC-inspired world oil price increases of the 1970s which, as David Leyton-Brown describes, led to the Trudeau government's announcement of a new "National Energy Program" in 1980. In both cases, the search for partners beyond the United States and for more national solutions within North America marked a departure from the continental approach that the traditional internationalism had favoured.

This Canadian shift from an emphasis on collaboration to greater national assertion was also evident as environmental problems forced their way into the public consciousness and onto the international agenda of the 1970s. The interplay of environmental concerns and national assertiveness was first revealed, as Kirton and Munton outline in their chapter, in the unilateral Canadian initiative to protect its claim to, and the ecological integrity of, the Arctic waters prompted by the voyages of the US oil tanker *Manhattan* through the Northwest Passage. Canada and the United States also negotiated at this time a pioneering agreement to control water pollution in the Great Lakes.

The ill-fated attempt by the short-lived government of Joe Clark to move the Canadian embassy in Israel from Tel Aviv to Jerusalem also shows much about changes internationally during the 1970s. As George Takach outlines, the decision to move the embassy reflected the inexperi-

ence of the Progressive Conservative Government of Joe Clark that came to office in 1979, and its assessment of the influence of Canada's Jewish community. The opposition that emerged in the wake of Clark's announcement took the form not only of protests from Arab countries, which had become much more influential and more important to Canada commercially as a result of their new oil wealth, but also of domestic pressure from Canadian companies with commercial links to the Arab world and from Canadians who saw this move as a particularly intolerable expression of a traditional pro-Israeli position by Canada.

The tendency to define foreign policy on the basis of domestic interests during the 1970s paralleled the receding assertiveness of the Soviet Union, the eroding power of the United States, and their waning ability to generate Cold War crises and tightly defined alignments. Thus, as Bruce Thordarson describes, a determined Prime Minister Trudeau was able in 1969 to secure a reduced Canadian military contribution to the European theatre of NATO, while entrenched Atlanticists within Ottawa were able to stave off a complete withdrawal. As John Harbron explains, Pierre Trudeau was successful in his unilateral announcement, upon his election in 1968, that Canada would recognize the People's Republic of China, which left others room only to find the particular formula by which this directive could be implemented.

By the mid-1970s the Trudeau government, in part propelled by its "Third Option" quest for expanded European involvements, enthusiastically took up the task of constructing the institutions of what came to be called the new post-Cold War international order. As Peyton Lyon and Geoffrey Nimmo describe, Canada helped to construct a new security regime in Europe in the CSCE, established its European credentials as a strong anti-communist crusader, highlighted the family reunification and human rights priorities dear to its large constituency of Canadians of East European origin, and included the environmental concerns of the new era in the mandate of the new organization.

Anti-communist attitudes were also evident in 1980, when the Soviet invasion of Afghanistan again presented Canada with the question of how much to pay, and how best to organize internationally, to counter aggression abroad. Jim Bayer explores the dilemmas of managing a foreign policy crisis while conducting an election campaign, and of harming particular groups of Canadians, such as grain farmers and Olympic athletes, for general foreign policy purposes. Externally, the case highlighted the Canadian challenge of how best to be loyal and to ensure an effective and distinctive Canadian foreign policy, while avoiding American unilateralism and domination.

chapter 10

CONTAINING QUEBEC ABROAD: THE GABON INCIDENT, 1968

John P. Schlegel

By 1968 cooperative federalism had stalled. There arose in the first three months of Canada's second century a number of unresolved disagreements concerning the respective roles of the Federal and Provincial Governments, notably in the area of international affairs.

The Quebec challenge to Ottawa's treaty-making prerogative was the first manifestation of the frustration French Canadians experienced when they realized the extent of the one-dimensional image projected by Canada in the international community. The presence of Charles De Gaulle in a supportive role on behalf of Quebec aspirations contributed to Ottawa's belief that France, with the connivance of its African allies, was engaged in a deliberate policy of encouraging Quebec's pretensions. It has been argued that Gaullist France did, in fact, have an acute interest in Quebec's international status.[1] Ottawa looked upon this foreign support as an attempt to destroy Canadian confederation or at the very least to challenge its stability by intervening in Canadian domestic affairs.

The pressures increased when Quebec went beyond the question of treaty-making powers and ventured into the realm of active and autonomous participation in international conferences.

Ottawa in 1967 could reasonably expect continued cooperation with the states of French Africa as its educational, technical and capital aid to that area increased, albeit at a slow rate. Coupled with this newly-emerging, if somewhat still undefined, bicultural image of Canada's nascent policy in the francophone world, came a new firmness in federal policies towards the provinces as indicated by Pearson's reaction to De Gaulle in 1967. A major benefit to the Federal Government emanating from Quebec's Quiet Revolution was the presence of dedicated anti-separatist French Canadians in the federal Liberal Party. The ascent of Pierre Trudeau into federal politics contributed to the new resolute federal position vis-à-vis the provinces.

Participation in foreign conferences provided a point of bitter contention between the two levels of government over a two-year period. Stemming from the first conference for education ministers of French-speaking states held in Gabon during February 1968, this tension continued through to the second Niamey Conference and the establishment of l'Agence de coopération culturelle et technique (ACCT) in 1970. The evolution of this controversy is complicated by the interjection of dramatic altercations within the triangular relationship between Ottawa, Paris and Quebec

 John P. Schlegel, S. J., from *The Deceptive Ash: Bilingualism and Canadian Policy in Africa: 1957-1971*, pp. 243-301, Lanham, Maryland, University Press of America, 1978.

and the personalities involved. In addition, the increased political prominence of Trudeau and his accompanying political philosophy greatly influenced the outcome of this question. The year 1968 proved to be a crucial one in this controversy. That year Ottawa joined in battle with Quebec over its claims for international autonomy, resulting in a federal offensive which successfully forced a Quebec retreat, although it did not terminate the war.

On 5 February 1968 Lester Pearson convened a constitutional conference in Ottawa composed of the Federal Prime Minister and the First Ministers of the provinces. With undisguised candor Pearson elucidated his views:

> We all know today that French Canada feels a deep dissatisfaction with its place in confederation. The reasons for that are complex...What is far more important is to admit that this dissatisfaction is fact and to recognize that, if it is allowed to continue without remedy, it could lead to separation and to the end of the confederation. For let me be explicit—what is at stake, in my opinion, is no less than Canada's survival as a nation.[2]

Quebec Premier Daniel Johnson agreed with Pearson that a crisis did exist, but argued that the genesis of the "crise canadienne" resided in Ottawa's infidelity to the entente of 1867. As the homeland and mainstay of French Canada, Quebec must assume responsibilities peculiar to it alone and Quebec must have power proportionate to these responsibilities.[3] Johnson considered an active participation in international affairs as essential to an authentic expression of Quebec's mission within Canada and the world.

. . .

Ottawa reiterated what had been its position on the matter since Paul Martin's statement in April 1965. Canada could have only one international personality. The Government was convinced that the majority of Canadians wanted their country to be seen as a single united entity abroad. To do this, Ottawa must continue to assume and implement the total responsibility for Canada's external policy and for the representation abroad of Canada's interests. Provincial goals and aspirations would be attained through cooperative arrangements between themselves and the Ottawa Government. To give provinces a separate presence in international organizations, for example, would serve to fragment a federal union into separate international entities. In Canada's case it would not only destroy its influence and its presence abroad, it would also undermine it's unity at home.[4]

. . .

In anticipating the attention given to the external policy issue in the process of constitutional review, and because of the tensions of the immediate situation, the Federal Government made public at the February Conference a second White Paper entitled "Federalism and International Relations." This document outlined for the first time legal and constitutional arguments supporting the exclusive international competence of the central government.[5]

. . .

L'Affaire du Gabon

The first overt confrontation emerging from Quebec's desire to participate autonomously in international conferences was precipitated by the Gabonese Government's invitation to Quebec to participate in a conference of Educational Ministers from French-speaking countries scheduled for February 1968.

Once it was ascertained that Quebec alone would participate as a peer of sovereign states without any reference to Ottawa,[6] Pearson wrote to Quebec Premier Johnson. Pearson suggested that arrangements should be agreed upon between the two governments with respect to la Francophonie in general, which would allow for full Quebec participation in all Canadian delegations. Conferences of a more general nature or in the realm of external aid would be attended by Canadian delegations headed by the Minister for External Affairs, although Quebec would be promised a strong representation. If, however, conferences dealt with specific questions such as education or cultural exchanges, then a Quebec minister could be a member or even the head of the Canadian delegation.[7] These arrangements were based upon an extension of the principle underlying arrangements worked out between Ottawa and the provinces for attendance at Commonwealth and UNESCO conferences on education.

Quebec's reactions to Ottawa's suggestions were non-committal. The conference took place without any reply from Quebec. Between 5-10 February France, Quebec, and fifteen independent francophone states met in Libreville with ministerial level delegations. Quebec's Minister of Education, Jean-Guy Cardinal, was accompanied by a delegation of three officials from the Quebec Government. On his return to Montreal Cardinal told a press conference that the Gabon meeting had set an important precedent which showed Quebec's desire to participate in la Francophonie and the world's willingness to accept such participation.[8]

The Federal Government's initial silence was broken on 4 March when Pearson tabled in the Commons a statement issued earlier announcing that Canada had suspended diplomatic relations with the Republic of Gabon. The announcement was delayed from 19 February, when Canada's newly-designated ambassador, Jean Thibault, had been instructed not to present his credentials in Libreville. In a diplomatic note handed to L.A. Bandinga, Gabon's ambassador-designate to Canada, Paul Martin declared that in attempting to interpret the Canadian constitution in their own way, as well as disregarding the responsibility of the Canadian Government, "Gabon has acted in such a way which is neither in conformity with international law nor with the maintenance of close and friendly relations between our two countries."[9] At the same time Pearson criticized the Quebec Government and regretted their inability to reach an agreement on sending one Canadian delegation to Gabon.

Gabon countered with a statement suggesting that Canada had suspended relations to divert Canadian public opinion from the reality of the Quebec problem and Ottawa's interference in provincial affairs.[10] The Gabonese Government also accused Ottawa of reneging on its promises of aid.[11]

Within Canada opinion was divided. Some supported Trudeau's allegations that the French were the real culprits and if they persisted in interfering in Canadian affairs, relations should be severed with Paris as well.[12] But Quebec was not without its supporters. Le Devoir summarized what it called the true feeling of Quebecers when it declared: "Nous croyons profondément, toutefois que dans le désir fondamental qu'il épouve de prolonger sans action sur le plan international sans être toujours chaperonné par Ottawa, le gouvernement de Québec expresse une aspiration trés réele du peuple québecois."[13]

With the next education conference of francophone countries scheduled for Paris in April, Ottawa again entered into communication with Quebec authorities with a view to arriving at an understanding on future meetings.[14]

A further silence and the imminence of the Paris conference prompted yet a third letter to Johnson.[15] Pearson's letter of 5 April broke with the two previous letters in that it specifically mentioned the Paris meeting and emphasized the importance of finding a mutually acceptable solution before the conference was convened.

A personal note from Johnson to Pearson constituted the only reply given to the three letters cited. Johnson wrote "there is nowhere in the Canadian constitution a disposition so fundamental and over which jurisdiction of the provinces has been so firmly established as education."[16] He went on to say that Ottawa was using its exclusive jurisdiction over international affairs as a counter argument. This would have to be settled by negotiation, but in the meantime Quebec could only assume all of its responsibilities.

The following day Jean Cardinal announced Quebec's decision to attend the Paris meeting. While the Ottawa Government was never officially informed of the status held by the Quebec delegation at that conference, the proceedings clearly indicate that Quebec was accorded the same basis of participation as other sovereign delegations.[17] At the close of the Paris session Cardinal affirmed reports that Quebec would open direct relations with French language countries in Africa. He indicated that Quebec felt itself better suited to handle French cultural ties with these states than was Ottawa because external aid from Ottawa had been traditionally orientated towards the Commonwealth states in Africa and Asia.[18]

This episode more than any other event before 1968 evoked a direct confrontation between Ottawa and Quebec over that province's aspirations to international cir-

cles. The fact that Gabon, a French African state supported by and deeply indebted to France,[19] was cast in the role of villain, animated Ottawa's preoccupations with implementing a positive bicultural image in French Africa. So precipitative was Ottawa's reaction to the Gabon affair that it disrupted Pearson's cherished principle of "Quiet Diplomacy," at least in Africa.

Ivan Head, then Professor of International Law at the University of Alberta, saw the invitation to Quebec as no less than a formal act of recognition of Quebec's international independence.[20]

Speaking retrospectively in 1974, Paul Martin has maintained that as an isolated incident, the Gabon affair presented little problem; the problem arose in that it was not an isolated event. Placed in the context of Quebec's strides towards a separate and special relationship with la Francophonie, this incident took on a new meaning and became very serious and politically threatening. Like Trudeau, Martin harbored suspicions that France was set on undermining the stability of the Canadian federation to the point of possibly separating Quebec from Ottawa's control. The threat was intensified as France worked through her minions in Africa to create the image of international support for Quebec's pretentions. Martin asserted that Gabon had been encouraged to exclude Ottawa from the conference. And as such this was a deliberate act inspired by personalities and forces in France and within the French Government aimed at creating for Canada a serious problem of national identity. Martin's contentions were partially verified in the attitude of the French delegate at Libreville, Alain Peyrefitte, who stressed the significant and unique contribution Quebec made in bringing about a truly worldwide concept of la Francophonie.[21]

A vocal advocate favoring Quebec's participation in the Gabon conference was found in Paul Gérin-Lajoie, former Quebec Minister of Education and a constitutional expert. Long a firm supporter of Quebec's international personality, Gérin-Lajoie defended Quebec's legitimate demands for an international personality so as to meet the very precise needs of the Quebec collectivity which devolved upon it under the terms of the 1867 constitution.[22]

The General Election of 1968

On 20 April 1968 Pierre Trudeau succeeded Lester Pearson as Prime Minister of Canada and Leader of the Liberal Party. Three days later Parliament was dissolved and an election called for 25 June.

On 8 May Trudeau made it clear that he would consider a Liberal victory as a mandate to challenge Quebec's extraterritorial ambition. He believed this to be the type of issue the Canadian people should have a right to pass judgment on because it ultimately would be detrimental to their federal form of government at home and abroad.[23]

On the same day the Government's long awaited study on provincial participation in international education conferences was issued.[24] This fifty-eight-page report, entitled "Federalism and International Conferences on Education," laid down proposals for attendance at such gatherings dealing with subjects under provincial jurisdiction. The proposals established were similar to those suggested by Pearson in the letters cited above. In addition, it noted that federal ministers should normally be attached to a Canadian delegation on education to "advise" on foreign policy but not to deal with the educational matters as such. In an important pre-election statement Trudeau said that

...at the present time our paramount interest is to ensure the political survival of Canada as a federal and bilingual sovereign state...It means reflecting in our foreign relations the cultural diversity and the bilingualism of Canada as faithfully as possible. Parallel to our close ties with the Commonwealth, we should strive to develop a close relation with the francophone countries...In order to exploit more fully the opportunities inherent in our bilingual country, it is our intention to open five new missions by 1969 in French-speaking countries. A substantially increased share of our aid will be allocated to francophone countries as an important investment both in improving bilateral relations and in contributing to national unity.[25]

There was widespread debate in the weeks preceding the election, centering on Quebec's role outside Canada's boundaries; such debates were kindled by a series of articles in La Presse which described the elaborate nomenclature of a sovereign state which Quebec was building itself. Under the joint control of the Ministre des Affaires Intergouvernementales and the Commissaire général de la coopération were several bureaus dealing with such matters as technical cooperation, education, culture and youth. The budget was in excess of $8 million for 1968. Quebec's delegation in Paris was enlarged and a liaison with the French-speaking citizens of Louisiana and French Indo-China was initiated; there was talk of Quebec establishing an office for African affairs.[26] France indirectly assisted the Quebec cause by inviting Premier Johnson to be De Gaulle's guest at the annual Bastille Day parade in Paris.

• • •

The Liberal victory of 25 June and the formation of a majority government toughened the Trudeau administration's attitudes towards Quebec's international pretensions and towards French intervention in Canada's domestic affairs.[27] In addition it served as an enlivened catalyst in accelerating the establishment of a federal presence in francophone Africa.

The Chevrier Mission

During 1968 continued efforts were made to strengthen relations with the French African states. That Ottawa now realized the significance, potential and necessity of establishing a powerful link with these countries was underlined by the dispatch of two ministerial missions to that part of the world during 1968. The first, led by Lionel Chevrier, was a special economic cooperation mission of a highly political nature originally scheduled to take place before the Gabon incident.

This mission, to investigate methods of improving and expanding Canadian aid programs in francophone Africa, had been planned months in advance of its actual realization in February-March 1968. It was initiated by Pearson and Martin as they viewed the long-term challenge of Quebec's forays onto the world scene.

The psychological pressures of this domestic challenge was heightened by the secessionist bid of Biafra culminating in the Nigerian civil war then in progress. A classified study of Canada's role in French-speaking Africa undertaken in 1970 noted that Canada had long realized the potential of its influence in this part of Africa, as well as the fact that Canada was respected by most French African states.[28]

The choice of Chevrier for this mission, like that of Dupuy and Trudeau before him, was highly significant. As a French Canadian, former Federal Cabinet Minster and High Commissioner to London, Lionel Chevrier had also served as the official "guest master" for visiting dignitaries dur-

ing "Expo '67." He thus had personal contacts with many African heads of state and could be assured of a warm welcome. An additional asset was Chevrier's chairmanship of the Commonwealth Committee which had studied sanctions and Britain's position on Rhodesia; hence he could be seen as a representative of Canada's new African policy, albeit in old clothing. The political nature of this mission was indicated by two unique aspects: Chevrier was directly responsible to the Prime Minister and the Cabinet; and secondly, the mission was empowered to pledge Canada to particular projects while in the field, thus rendering further ratification by the DEA unnecessary.

The mission, composed of Chevrier, Dr. Henri Goudifouy, an assistant director of the External Aid Office, and Jacques Dupuis from the DEA, visited seven francophone countries. The major objective was to study the Canadian aid programs in progress there and undertake the further funding of particular projects. With over $40 million committed to forty-nine projects in Morocco, Algeria, Tunisia, Cameroon, Ivory Coast, Senegal and Niger, the mission gave substance to Chevrier's announced interpretation of his objective: to broaden Canadian scope and increase contributions to Africa, rendering a more just distribution between French- and English-speaking states. Canada was to be second only to France in assistance and attention paid to French Africa.[29]

The Chevrier visit was delayed until after the Libreville conference had adjourned. At that time Gabon was taken from the itinerary. Chevrier was told by Martin to offer assistance to the francophone states for a specific political reason: to illustrate that Ottawa was the source of greater aid than Quebec could ever aspire to. However, there was to be no assistance to those African states who were following a course of action inimical to Canada's federal structure or sympathetic to Quebec's aspirations.

To illustrate this new approach, and because of the direct influence of De Gaulle on the Gabon episode and the subsequent suspension of diplomatic relations with that country, Ottawa halted all aid to Gabon, modest though it was. This action was not so much to punish Gabon but to warn other African countries that in the future, direct lines of contact between them and Quebec, without first consulting Ottawa, would result in a similar breaking of relations and suspension of aid.[30]

...

The success of Ottawa's policy in French Africa was attested to by Senator Martin upon his return from a tour of the Ivory Coast, Ruanda, Congo (K), Niger and Senegal. He reported that these states were desirous of closer and more advantageous cooperation with Canada.[31] The exact purpose of Martin's sojourn in Africa is now clearer. Martin asserts his major intention was to visit Niger and to challenge Quebec's autonomous participation at the pending Niamey conference. Before seeing the Niger President he gained the active support of Presidents Senghor of Senegal and Mobutu of Congo (K). Mobutu appreciated Canada's concerns about Quebec's actions as it would those of Katanga. While the Ivory Coast was desirous of closer relations with Ottawa, Houphouet-Boigny was indifferent to Canada's situation and more concerned that Canada support the Biafran cause. Martin's talks with Diori Hamani of Niger were successful in getting the conference postponed and new invitations issued which specified that Quebec was to participate within the Canadian delegation.[32]

Canada's new posture towards African affairs in a broader perspective visibly man-ifested itself in the autumn session (1968) of the UN.

On 25 October Canada voted with the majority, denying Rhodesian independence without majority rule. This was a break with Ottawa's traditional abstention policy. It represented a clear support of the majority African position, a position which went directly against most of Canada's European allies. In casting this vote Canada had resisted strong pressure from Britain.

A second manifestation of Canada's new African image was the vote of 20 November 1968 calling for the condemnation of Portugal's colonial policies. Again Canada voted with the Afro-Asian states in condemning one of its NATO allies. On this particular occasion Canada was credited with swaying Norway, Denmark, Iceland, Greece and Turkey to vote against Portugal.

Simultaneously, Canada was working out a pro-federal Nigeria stance in that civil war; this policy was in keeping with the wishes of the OAU and was supported by the majority of African states. Canada proved to be a key Western supporter of a non-interventionist policy. Britain and France, however, were overly-identified with one particular side. The most dramatic impact of this "new deal" for Africa appeared in the field of external aid, especially to francophone countries where grants, loans and food assistance rose in a single year 87% over the 1967 allocation.

While Ottawa was orchestrating this new deal for Africa, Canadian-French relations reached their nadir.

The visit of Phillippe Rossillon to Manitoba in late August elicited a strong rejoinder from Trudeau about French intervention in Canadian domestic affairs. Rossillon was described as the head of a committee for the expansion of the French language. Ottawa suspected Rossillon of playing a role in the "affaire du Gabon," arranging visits to France for Acadian leaders and meeting several times with Quebec separatists. He was also suspected of disrupting the Queen's visit to Quebec in 1964.[33] Neither the Canadian nor the Manitoban Governments had been informed of his visit. Rossillon quite obviously did not avail himself of the protocol arising from the Franco-Canadian accord of 1965 which stipulated conditions for visits of a political nature.

In a press conference Trudeau explicitly stated that many Canadians were greatly annoyed by this intervention.[34] If Quebec was going to play with secret agents of France, he said it would undoubtedly harm their cause nationally.

The feelings in Quebec, however, ran counter to those of Ottawa. Le Devoir saw this special Franco-Quebec relationship as an urgent need for Quebec's mission in North America and within Canada. It was "loath to have to submit, in developing these relations, to the jealous supervision of a mother-in-law, no matter how benevolent she may be."[35]

. . .

The Kinshasa Conference (January 1969)

In the wake of renewed federal-provincial antagonism there arose the question of both Ottawa and Quebec participating in a conference "of education ministers of French-speaking countries being planned for Niamey, Niger. The difficulty as before, resided in Quebec's invitation coming from Niger and not through Ottawa. Trudeau stressed the point that the Niamey conference was not simply for educational ministers, as the Libreville conference had been, but for French-speaking nations in

general. In consultation with Quebec officials, Trudeau hoped to implement the policy established by Pearson, namely, a single delegation to represent all Canadians, especially French Canadians. Having gained a two-month postponement through the visit of Paul Martin to Niger, Trudeau conceded that the Niger Government had particularly requested Quebec to attend. Ottawa was quite prepared to concur provided a formula could be worked out whereby a single Canadian delegation would be composed to provide adequate representation of the several provinces interested in la Francophonie.[36]

An education ministers' conference scheduled in Kinshasa for mid-January 1969 provided a dress-rehearsal for the first Niamey conference. Ottawa and Quebec had been invited separately. Trudeau insisted that the principle of a single Canadian delegation must be upheld. In an exchange of telegrams with the new Quebec Premier, Jean-Jacques Bertrand, Trudeau proposed the conditions under which Quebec's participation in the Canadian delegation would be acceptable to both Governments.[37] Quebec's Minister of Education or his proxy would serve as chairman or co-chairman of the Canadian delegation, a delegation composed of education ministers from interested provinces together with the delegates appointed by Ottawa. The minister from Quebec was to speak on behalf of Quebec on all questions falling within that province's constitutional jurisdiction, as would the other provincial representatives. The opinion of the Canadian delegation itself would be expressed by the chairman or the co-chairman.

Ottawa acknowledged receipt of Bertrand's acceptance of terms the next day. Bertrand stated that "a Quebec delegation duly identified will join with other representatives of the Canadian delegation."[38]

The presence of a single delegation left Canada's international integrity intact. This was done to the great annoyance of the French Government who reportedly had underwritten the entire cost of the conference as the price for a Quebec invitation. In fact, this invitation was issued three weeks after the invitation to Ottawa.[39]

The First Niamey Conference (February 1969)

The question of Canada's representation at the delayed conference to take place in Niamey during February 1969 remained unsettled at the end of January. Ottawa again was anxious to have a single unified delegation since this meeting was to discuss the possibility of establishing an international agency to coordinate aid and cultural exchanges among French-speaking states. Both Ottawa and Quebec had received invitations. Procedures were complicated as tensions ran high resulting from the visit to Paris by Quebec's Minister of Education, Jean-Guy Cardinal, at the end of January 1969. A series of agreements between Paris and Quebec covering joint work on a telecommunications satellite, assistance from France for the new University of Quebec and increased involvement by France in the provincial economy, sparked off a negative reaction in Ottawa and in the press. Critics claimed the Franco-Quebec agreements to be null and void unless entered into under the protocol of 1965. Others maintained that the Federal Government claimed constitutional responsibility in the field of telecommunications and it did not devolve into the provinces' realm of competency. De Gaulle's actions once again suggested that he was

the culprit, as he extolled the values of renewed and direct relations with "New France." The French press chided the General for deliberately provoking the Canadians on the eve of the Niamey Conference by directly interfering in domestic affairs.[40]

Preparations for Niamey were further complicated by the contradictory report from Paris that Quebec had advised the French that it would send an autonomous delegation to Niger.[41] Trudeau informed the Commons on 5 February that negotiations concerning the composition of a delegation were still under way, but it would not be similar to that sent to Kinshasa. Because the Niger conference dealt with subjects which were within the Government's constitutional jurisdiction, Ottawa intended to send federal ministers as delegates.

A glimmer of hope for a positive settlement was elicited from Bertrand's reported statement that Quebec would go to Niger and join the Canadian delegation, while retaining the representation of Quebec on matters of education and culture.[42] That same day Gerard Pelletier, Secretary of State, was named the sole leader of the Canadian delegation; he would exercise the single vote of the delegation, although in the event of disagreement among the delegates, he would abstain.

Quebec had sought acceptance of the two delegations concept within a single representation from Canada; Ottawa never acknowledged such an idea. Pelletier was to be the head of what Ottawa considered to be a single Canadian delegation which included Quebec's Minister Without Portfolio, Marcel Masse, and a five-man delegation from that province.

On the eve of the conference, however, Masse was reported to have denied any links with the Canadian delegation. He stated that not having a co-chairman, as at Kinshasa, implied that Quebec would not have to "consult" Ottawa on matters involving education and culture. This imbroglio was aggravated at the conference itself where Quebec, listed separately from Canada, was given the status of an autonomous participant. In a neo-Gilbertian comic-opera situation, the Canadian and Quebec delegations co-existed rather uneasily together within a common delegation, with two sets of flags and with each Government assuming the travel and related expenses of its delegation.

The main item on the agenda, the establishment of an agency for technical and cultural cooperation among French-speaking states, was achieved on 20 February. Jean-Marc Leger, a noted Canadian journalist, separatist and advocate of Quebec's international personality, was chosen, with French support, as provisional executive-secretary. His task was to assist President Diori in establishing a secretariat, preparing the constitution and defining the organization's future plans. Pelletier made it known that Canada, together with New Brunswick, Ontario and Quebec, had agreed to pay up to 30% of the new agency's budget.

. . .

The Quebec White Paper: A Final Quest for Provincial Sovereignty

The Quebec Government's claims for a greater role in international affairs was manifested on 12 February 1969 in the closing moments of the Federal-Provincial conference, when Premier Bertrand tabled a working paper on Quebec-Ottawa cooperation in international affairs.[43] This surprise move provided the long-awaited Quebec response to the Federal Government's position papers issued the previous year. This action poignantly indicated that the issue was far from dead and was, in fact, emerging as a principal issue again in 1969.

. . .

A final aspect of the White Paper was the proposal of five ground-rules for Quebec's participation in international conferences covering composition, identification and degree of activity of Quebec delegations. The key element was the presence of a Quebec delegation, headed by a provincial minister, within the overall Canadian delegation. At such conferences Federal officials would advise on foreign policy matters, allowing the running of the delegation to the Provincial minister.

. . .

The Federal Response

In preparing what was to be a firm rebuke to the Quebec White Paper, the Government was influenced in part by two events: the visit of President Diori Hamani of Niger to Canada and the "affaire Lipkowski." Both occasions elicited from Trudeau critical comments on "le désir d'un gouvernement provincial de se créer un petit empire."[44]

Le Devoir saw the visit of the President of Niger to Ottawa and Quebec as marking an important stage towards the resolution of this federal-provincial controversy.[45] As one of the leading proponents behind the establishment of the ACCT, as well as a principal spokesman for la Francophonie, Diori reflected in his visit the changing attitudes of the French African states towards Canada and Quebec. These countries, by late 1969, were less and less interested in dealing directly with Quebec. After speaking with Quebec officials Diori indicated that if any one of the Canadian provinces wanted to assist Niger in its development projects, their assistance would be most welcome, provided that it had been cleared and coordinated with Ottawa.[46]

Nor could it be denied any longer that Canada, all of Canada, was truly a part of the "communauté francophone."

Several French African leaders were aware that Ottawa was trying to rectify the imbalance in Canada's one-dimensional image abroad as well as at home. The Government's legislation of July 1969 making Canada a bilingual country by law was one such testimony to Ottawa's good intentions. To encourage the Government in this cooperative venture with Quebec, Diori informed Trudeau of the ACCT Secretariat's decision to utilize Ottawa's participation as the umbrella for Quebec's membership in that organization, thus settling, it was hoped, all further questions of Quebec's representation at Francophone conferences.

A second incident which forced Ottawa to re-assert a firm hand on Quebec's maneuvering in international relations was the visit of Jean de Lipkowski, the Deputy Secretary of State for Foreign Affairs. He visited Quebec in October 1969 at the invitation of Marcel Masse, a Quebec minister. Although Lipkowski had been invited by the Federal Government to visit Ottawa, this invitation was ignored. Ottawa interpreted this as a continuation of the Gaullist policy of giving priority to close exchanges with Quebec at the expense of Canadian national unity. Federal fears were soon realized.

In speaking of Quebec's struggle for survival, the Minister said that France could no longer remain indifferent but must assist Quebeckers in their lonely battle for national identity. To do this was in keeping with France's dedication to the self-determination of peoples. In commenting on Franco-Canadian relations, Lipkowski de-

clared that there had been no change in Paris's foreign policy towards Ottawa and Quebec since the departure of De Gaulle. He indicated the decision to by-pass Ottawa had, in fact, been made by President Pompidou himself, who did not recognize the Federal Government's monopoly over Franco-Quebec relations. Lipkowski concluded that "French cooperation with Quebec was the only cooperation France had in the world which enriches France as well as the government with which we cooperate."[47]

During this visit, the first open admission of French collusion with Gabon in 1967-1968 was made public when Lipkowski announced that Paris had indeed advised Gabon and other African countries that they could have direct relations with Quebec in the field of education.

Trudeau himself took the occasion to speak on the significance of Lipkowski's disclosures of foreign intervention in Canada's domestic affairs.[48] Ottawa issued a formal note of protest to France on 20 October, charging intervention in Canadian domestic questions and asked the Quai d'Orsay for talks on the nature of French official visitors to Canada. Paris did not reply to the Canadian note.[49]

The Rejection of Shared Foreign Policy

The Federal Government's response to the Quebec White Paper took the form of a lengthy, detailed and tightly-argued speech in the Commons on 30 October by Jean-Pierre Goyer, Mitchell Sharp's Parliamentary Secretary.[50] Goyer rejected the concept of "external sovereignty" for the provinces, corresponding to an extension of their fields of exclusive or shared internal competence.... The assertive tone of this statement presaged an even more decisive policy on Ottawa's part. This was significant considering that at this time negotiations were under way between the two levels of government seeking agreement on the composition of representation at the second Niamey conference.

The Second Niamey Conference (February 1970)

As a follow-up to the conference held in Niger earlier in 1969, this gathering of French-speaking countries was devoted to the examination and adoption of the statutes and programs of the ACCT, established in principle at the first Niamey conference. This was to be a meeting of sovereign states where the countries involved were called upon to undertake formally, by signature of a convention, the establishment of this new transnational agency with its permanent secretariat and budget. It marked the participation of Canada as a whole in an institutionalized and international Francophonie, similar in many ways to its participation in the Commonwealth.

An exchange of official correspondence from Quebec's Deputy Minister of Intergovernmental Affairs, Claude Morin, to André Bissonnette, Assistant Under-Secretary of State for External Affairs, clearly outlined Quebec's aims within the greater Canadian delegation.[51] Quebec sought a co-chairmanship, the ability to speak in the name of Quebec, and the right to be an active signatory to the accord.

Informing Quebec of the invitation to attend the Niamey conference, Trudeau urged an early agreement on such outstanding pre-conference issues as finance. He wrote to Bertrand indicating that since Canada's support of and contribution to the

ACCT would be an important factor in its success, it was up to them not to give their francophone friends the impression that the issue was a subject of controversy in Canada.[52]

Trudeau then indicated Ottawa's intentions of allowing the Quebec Government to play a major role within the Canadian delegation, both at the conference and within the Agency itself. In seeking Quebec's co-operation, he assured the Premier that his province would have both a voice in the negotiations leading to the establishment of the ACCT and an active participation in the major bodies within the new organization. These arrangements were intended to give full expression to the importance of the Government of Quebec in this field, while reflecting the full extent of Canada's intended contribution to the francophone world. They would also serve the singleness of Canada's personality in the international field. Trudeau discussed these questions with Bertrand during the Federal-Provincial conference in Ottawa on 16 February.

In the final stages of negotiations, the Premier disclosed for the first time four fundamental principles on which Quebec could not give way. In a letter of 10 March, Bertrand insisted on the following points.[53] First, Quebec Province must be able to speak in its own name and to enter into commitments of its own in areas within its competency. Secondly, Quebec's presence and activity must be adequately identified; and thirdly, the voting procedure must reflect this duality by providing for mandatory abstention in the event of disagreement on matters within Quebec's competency. Finally, the statutes of the ACCT must be based on the same principles and allow for direct participation by Quebec in the activities of the Agency.

There was a distinct tone of confusion and frustration in Bertrand's telegram, though he assured Ottawa of Quebec's honorable intentions of avoiding any grave crisis endangering la Francophonie. The letter stressed Quebec's deep-felt desire to see the francophone community organized.

The federal response put forward new proposals on certain details raised by Bertrand without making any direct reference to Quebec's four principles.[54] While commenting on the question of the vote and the possibility of the Quebec representative within the Canadian delegation to "speak in the name of Quebec," Trudeau stressed the truly international nature of this conference. While leaving it open to the province to express their point of view on proposals made at the conference which bore on matters of exclusive provincial competence, Ottawa would not agree that a province could prevent the Federal Government from using its right to veto if faced with a proposal at Niamey which involved external policy considerations and to which the Ottawa Government was firmly opposed.

The text suggested by Trudeau preserved the position of both Federal and Provincial representatives by providing that the delegation would abstain only if there was disagreement on a matter relating to the exclusive domestic competence of the provincial governments. Trudeau carefully explained that in the final analysis the vote of the delegation would be guided by Canadian external policy considerations. But, he continued, however useful abstention may be in resolving certain possible differences, it must not paralyze Canada's foreign policy or its policies on economic and technical cooperation.

As regards Quebec speaking in its own name, Trudeau was determined that such a small request should not be a stumbling block for a useful Quebec-Ottawa agreement, knowing full well it did not imply

any international recognition of an autonomous Quebec. He conceded this point. The Quebec delegate was allowed to speak in the name of Quebec on any subject within the constitutional competence of the Quebec Government.

Because the conference and the ACCT represented an important external policy function and because both dealt with matters which would go well beyond those of exclusive provincial jurisdiction, the chairmanship was to be held by a Federal Minister, Gerard Pelletier. For similar reasons Quebec was offered the vice-chairmanship, not a co-chairmanship as requested.

Bertrand accepted Trudeau's offer but he indirectly asserted that Ottawa had, in fact, accepted and acceded to Quebec's four fundamental principles.[55] The Federal Government denied this. Nothing in Trudeau's telegram supported this assertion.[56]

While the final composition of the Canadian delegation was still incomplete, Bertrand announced that an election would be held in Quebec. This election brought about the defeat of the Union Nationale Party and the return of the provincial Liberal Party under Robert Bourassa. The election campaign prevented any cabinet minister from leaving the country and Quebec was consequently represented at the second Niamey conference by Julien Chauinard, the Secretary-General of the Cabinet. As a public servant he had to work within the guidelines established by the Trudeau-Bertrand negotiations. Hence the unfortunate events of the 1969 conference were avoided.

In these last negotiations Ottawa played from strength. Not only had the federal position gained international support from the endorsement of the African Heads of State and psychological support from the

Lipkowski affair, but Ottawa also secured a seemingly unlikely ally in the person of the acting executive secretary of the ACCT, Jean-Marc Leger.

Before the conference convened, Ottawa was aware that the draft proposals prepared by Diori and Leger endangered Quebec's participation under the aegis of Ottawa. Leger's and Ottawa's view of the ACCT coincided in that they both understood that the purpose of the organization was to be a sharing of cultural and technical experiences with other French-speaking countries. It was not to be political nor was it to define the French language too narrowly.

One possible explanation for the conversion of Leger away from his strongly Quebec-oriented views to a stand closer to the Federalists can be seen in his genuine concern for the development of Africa. To secure this objective, one which Leger felt to be both legitimate and essential, he had temporarily to suspend, although not necessarily abandon, some of his attitudes regarding Quebec. He also had to face stiff French criticism. A strong, generous, and wealthy Canada would be of greater assistance to the Africans, he felt, than Quebec would be by itself. A single Canada would also provide a strong alternative to French aid and influence.

. . .

After three days of acrimonious debate, a compromise between the French and Canadian Governments was reached and inserted in the Agency's Charter. It provided for the participation of non-sovereign governments in the activities of the ACCT with the approval of their sovereign authorities.[57] Canada's head of delegation, Gerard Pelletier, stated that although this text did not give Quebec full membership in the organization, it did allow Quebec to play an original and important role.[58] This position was elucidated in an agreement reached by Ottawa and Quebec on 1 October 1971, before the meeting of the ACCT in Canada.

That Niger came under the influence of Canada through the Chevrier Mission, the visit of Senator Martin and President Diori's sojourn in Ottawa, cannot be denied. That Niger received extensive Canadian aid, in the form of the $13 million "La route de unité et d'amitié canadienne," funding for other projects, fifty technical experts and the designation of Niger as "a country of concentration" by CIDA, are also facts in the Canadian-Nigeran relationship which blossomed in the years after the Libreville conference. France was not pleased to see Canada make such a successful entrée into its "private preserve." Canada, for its part, was satisfied with Leger as Secretary-General of the ACCT. Ottawa could not be accused of having its man in the top spot since Leger still remained a separatist; he was also helping Africa and that came to involve Ottawa at every level; it also suited federal policy perceptions.

A Toronto paper set the tone when it stressed that while Quebec's brash insistence on playing a role in international affairs angered much of English-speaking Canada, the creative tension it built up gave the country an external thrust that was truly representative of its bilingual and bicultural nature. Canada's horizons had broadened considerably as it took an interest in the French-speaking nations without detracting from existing relationships with English-speaking countries.[59]

The Quebec-Ottawa Agreement of 1971

The institutionalization of the elusive concept called la Francophonie must be seen as a major accomplishment in a world environment where multilateral and multicultural groupings were taking on a new importance, in an international milieu where interdependence among the less than super-powers was becoming essential for economic, political and cultural survival. For Canada participation within the ACCT was a natural step in Ottawa's accelerated bilingual external policy. Relations between Canada and francophone Africa had become a subject actively affecting the internal political life of both Canada and Quebec.

The agreement reached between these two governments on the eve of the ACCT's second general conference in Canada during October 1971, formalized Quebec's status in that organization. This agreement gave Quebec the stature of a participatory government, but such status was not granted by the ACCT itself, rather only Canada enjoyed this privilege. Quebec did not participate in the organization as an independent delegation but as a part of the Canadian representation. Under Article 16, Quebec was given a wide scope, even an exceptional opportunity, to act within the ACCT; but Quebec was also charged with keeping

Ottawa informed of its activities within the organization.[60]

The Ottawa agreement, like so many other previous confrontations, was heavily conditioned by the political climate. The defeat of the Union Nationale Party by the Liberals in 1970 made room for a more moderate point of view emanating from Quebec. Robert Bourassa, the new Premier, was more amenable to a cooperative venture in external policy, at the same time insisting that Quebec's relations with France were fundamental for all of the reasons voiced over the previous decade. He was, moreover, somewhat diverted by political and economic conditions within his province. The "Front de Libération du Québec" (FLQ) was, at that time, a source of great concern. This gave both federal and provincial officials time to reflect and develop new approaches to their relationship. It may be noted also that France under Georges Pompidou had by late 1970 altered its attitudes towards both Quebec and Ottawa; Franco-Canadian relations were on the mend. Paris had come to recognize that an active Canada within the francophone world was not there to dislodge the French culture but rather to enrich it.

NOTES

1. Thomas Levy, "The French Connection: French Attitudes and Policies Relating to Canada and Quebec," 1977, p. 33.

2. Lester B. Pearson, "A Time for Crucial Decision," *Statement and Speeches*, No, 68/4, 5 February 1968, pp. 2-3.

3. Daniel Johnson, "Opening Statement," *Constitutional Conference Papers*, First Session, February 1968, p. 61.

4. Lester B. Pearson, Federalism for the Future: A Statement of Policy by the Government of Canada, February 1968, p. 10.

5. Paul Martin, *Federalism and International Relations*, 1968, pp. 12-15.

6. The Federal Government first heard of Quebec's status at Libreville in a Bernard Kaplan article, *Montreal Star*, 11 January 1968.

7. Letter from Pearson to Johnson, 1 December 1967, in M. Sharp, *Federalism and International Conferences on Education*, 1968, pp. 62-64.

8. *Le Devoir*, 14 February 1968.

9. *Canada: Debates*, 4 March 1968.

10. *Le Monde*, 5 March 1968; *Fraternité-Matin* (Abidjan), 6 March 1968.

11. *Sept Jours*, 10 March 1968, p. 11.

12. *Toronto Star*, 5 March 1968; *Ottawa Citizen*, 6 March 1968.

13. *Le Devoir*, 6 March 1968.

14. Pearson to Johnson, 8 March 1968 in M. Sharp, *Federalism and International Conferences on Education*, 1968, pp. 66-68.

15. Pearson to Johnson, 5 April 1968, *Ibid.*, pp.70-72.

16. *CIIA Monthly Bulletin*, Vol. 7 (May 1968), pp. 52-53.

17. *Le Monde*, 22 & 23 April 1968.

18. *Ottawa Citizen*, 26 April 1968.

19. President Albert Bango was always under strong French influence. He was particularly indebted to France for retaining him in power after an army uprising in February 1964. French troops were employed to quell the rebellion at a cost of twenty-five lives. It is tempting to say that an invitation to Quebec for a simple education conference was only as a partial re-payment of an outstanding debt to Paris.

20. Ivan Head, "Quebec in Gabon: Canadian Sovereignty Clear and Present," *Montreal Star*, 18 March 1968.

21. Government of France, *Textes et Notes*, 1re Semestre 1968, pp. 58-59.

22. Paul Gérin-Lajoie, "Quebec in International Affairs: Federal Position Anachronistic," *Montreal Star*, 19 March 1968. Developed in a series of extended articles.

23. *Ottawa Citizen*, 9 May 1968; *Vancouver Sun*, 9 May 1968. This statement was carried in most papers.

24. Mitchell Sharp, *Federalism and International Conferences on Education*, 1968, pp. 56-58.

25. Pierre Trudeau, "Canada and the World," *Statement and Speeches*, No. 68/17, 29 May 1968, p. 6.

26. Christopher Malone, "La Politique Québecois en Matière de Relations Internationales: Changement et Continuité, 1960-1972," unpublished MA Thesis, University of Ottawa, 1973, p. 324. See also Marcel Cadieux, "Quebec in World Affairs: Myth or Reality," *Statement and Speeches*, No. 68/10, 2 March 1968.

27. A convincing argument favoring a Trudeau victory is reflected in the attitude that "he was a Frenchman who would put the trouble-making Frenchmen in their place." J.M. Beck, *Pendulum of Power, Canadian Federal Elections*, 1968, p. 400.

28. "Sans passé colonial, ni visées impérialistes, le Canada peut élaborer sur ce continent une politique étrangère originale, neuve et se tailler rapidement une place honorable et enviable. Ses deux langues officielles sont aussi des langues de communications en Afrique et lui fournissent un instrument de travail essentiel dans cette tâche." *Classified Report*, "La Politique Canadienne au Meghreb et en Afrique Noire Francophonie dans les Années 1970," September 1972, p. 2 (hereafter: *Report*).

29. "Canada and Africa: Mission to the Francophone States," *Africa Report* (April 1968), pp. 21-23.

30. Louis Sabourin, "Le Canada et l'Afrique francophone," in *Revue Française d'Etudes Politiques Africaines* (July 1970), pp. 42-43.

31. *Canada: Journals*, 18 December 1968, pp. 795-796.

32. See Guy Cornier, "Une delicate partie," *La Presse*, 30 November 1968.

33. R.L. Tournoux, *La Tragédie du Général*, 1967, p. 660.

34. *CIIA Monthly Bulletin*, Vol. 7 (September 1968), pp. 92-93.

35. *Le Devoir*, 14 September 1968.

36. *Canada: Journals*, 18 December 1968, pp. 795-796.

37. Telegram, Trudeau to Bertrand, 8 January 1969 (DEA Library).

38. Telegram, Bertrand to Trudeau, 9 January 1969 (DEA Library).

39. Christopher Malone, "La politique Québecoise en Matière de Relations Internationales: Changement et Continuité, 1960-1972," unpublished MA Thesis, University of Ottawa, 1973, p. 64. See also Claude Morin, *Le Pouvoir Québecois...en Negotiation*, 1972, p. 90.

40. *Le Monde*, 22 January 1969.

41. *Globe and Mail*, 30 January 1969.

42. *Globe and Mail*, 10 February 1969.

43. Claude Morin, *Working Paper on Foreign Relations*, Government of Quebec, 5 February 1969, p. 5.

44. *Le Devoir*, 17 September 1969.

45. Paul Sauriol, "La Visite de M. Diori à Québec et nos relations avec l'étranger," *Le Devoir*, 23 September 1969.

46. Jean Charles Bonenfant, "Les Relations extérieures du Québec," *Etudes Internationales*, Vol. 1 (February 1970), 81-84. See also *Le Devoir*, 17 September 1969.

47. *Ottawa Citizen*, 15 October 1969.

48. Office of the Prime Minister, "Transcript of a Press Conference of the Rt. Hon. Pierre Elliott Trudeau," 15 October 1969, pp. 5-7.

49. When Ambassador J. Leger went to the Quai d'Orsay to deliver this note, the French Foreign Minister was absent and the note had to be delivered to the Deputy Minister, M. J. de Lipkowski.

50. Jean-Pierre Goyer, "Foreign Policy and the Provinces," *Statement and Speeches*, No. 69/18, 30 October 1969.

51. Letter, Morin to Bissonnette, 8 January 1970 (DEA Library).

52. Letters, Trudeau to Bertrand, 12 February 1970 and 6 March 1970 (DEA Library).

53. Telegram, Bertrand to Trudeau, 10 March 1970 (DEA Library).

54. Telegram, Trudeau to Bertrand, 12 March 1970 (DEA Library).

55. Telegram, Bertrand to Trudeau, 12 March 1970 (DEA Library).

56. Telegram, Trudeau to Bertrand, 13 March 1970 (DEA Library).

57. *Charte De L'Agence De Coopération Culturelle et Technique*, article 3:3, as printed in *Etudes Internationales*, vol. 1 (June 1970), 96.

58. Quoted in Louis Sabourin, "A Painful Birth of an agency to link French-speaking States," *International Perspectives* (January-February 1972), p. 27.

59. *Globe and Mail*, 20 March 1970.

60. Montreal Gazette, 12 October 1971.

SUGGESTED READINGS

Background Papers and Reports, *Ontario Advisory Committee on Confederation*, Vol. 3, (1967).

"Working Paper on Foreign Relations" in the *Quebec Delegation to the Constitutional Conference Continuing Committee of Officials*, Quebec, 1969.

Atkey, Ronald G., "The Role of the Provinces in International Affairs", *International Journal*, Vol. 26, (1970-71) pp. 249-73.

McRoberts, Ken, "Quebec: Canada's Special Challenge and Stimulus" in Thomas Hockin *The Canadian Condominium: Domestic Issues and External Policy*, Toronto: McClelland & Stewart, 1972, pp.38-59.

P.R. Johannson, "Provincial International Activities," *International Journal*, Vol. 33 (Spring 1978), pp. 357-78.

Leeson, Howard A. and Wilfrid Vanderlest, *External Affairs and Canadian Federalism: The History of a Dilemma*, Toronto: Holt Rinehart and Winston, 1973.

Martin, Hon. Paul, *Federalism and International Relations*, Ottawa: Queen's Printer, 1968.

McWhinney, E., "Canadian Federalism and the Foreign Affairs and Treaty Power: The Impact of Quebec's 'Quiet Revolution'," *Canadian Yearbook of International Law*, Vol. 7, pp. 3-32.

Morin, Claude, *Quebec versus Ottawa: The Struggle for Self- Government, 1960-1972*, Toronto: University of Toronto Press, 1976.

Patry, André, *Le Quebec dans le monde*, Ottawa: Lemeac, 1980.

Sabourin, Louis, "Quebec's International Activity Rests on Idea of Competence," *International Perspectives*, March/April 1977, pp. 3-7.

Sharp, Hon. Mitchell, *Federalism and International Conferences on Education*, Ottawa: Queen's Printer, 1968.

c h a p t e r   11

CUTTING BACK
ON NATO, 1969

Bruce Thordarson

Between 1948 and 1968 successive Canadian governments pursued a foreign policy that, with the exception of the period 1957-63, remained remarkably consistent in its orientation, goals, and underlying philosophy. Canadian foreign-policy-makers believed that contributing to collective security and world peace was their supreme task. These goals were to be attained through active support of the United Nations and, if the world organization was unable to provide these guarantees, through the regional security alliances of the North Atlantic Treaty Organization (NATO) and the North American Air Defence Agreement (NORAD).

With the accession to power of Pierre Elliott Trudeau in the spring of 1968, this foreign policy of twenty years' duration was suddenly thrown into question. Had the new prime minister merely wished to subject a few selected issues to review, there would have been little cause for surprise or alarm among the Canadian foreign-policy establishment. What Mr. Trudeau proposed to undertake, however, was a reassessment not only of issues but also of the whole underlying philosophy of Canada's external relations. "We wish," he said, "to take a fresh look at the fundamentals of Canadian foreign policy to see whether there are ways in which we can serve more effectively Canada's current interests, objectives and priorities."[1]

The result was that, between May 1968 and June 1970, the Canadian government undertook an extensive reassessment of its foreign and defence policies that for the first time went right back to basic principles. Indeed, it is unlikely that any government in any country has ever subjected its external relations to such scrutiny. During these twenty-five months foreign policy became in Canada what it had not been for years: a subject of contention and stimulated interest throughout much of the country.

When the dust had settled, the result of this two-year study was a document comprising six brightly coloured booklets called *Foreign Policy for Canadians*, in which the government set out what it referred to as the "conceptual framework" that should guide Canada's foreign relations in the years ahead.[2] The fundamental premise was that foreign and domestic policies are determined by, and must be used to promote, the same national aims. This emphasis on national interests in turn provided the justification for Canada's new foreign-policy priorities: policies designed to promote economic growth, social justice, and quality of life were henceforth to be given greater emphasis than those related to peace and security, sovereignty and in-

Bruce Thordarson, "Introduction"and"The NATO Decision," from *Trudeau and Foreign Policy*, Don Mills, Oxford University Press, 1972. Portions of the text have been deleted. Some footnotes have been removed; those remaining have been renumbered.

dependence, and a "harmonious natural environment." Foreign policy, the government advised, must be based on national interests rather than on an assumption that Canada's natural role was to be the world's "helpful fixer."

The "St Laurent-Pearson tradition in foreign policy" or "Pearsonian diplomacy" are terms that were used frequently in the course of the two-year review, even by commentators who associated them only with some vague concept of the status quo and who would have been hard-pressed to define them with any precision. If there is one term that best summarizes what both Mr. St. Laurent and Mr. Pearson sought in their approach to international affairs, it is "collective security." Having lived through two world wars caused by narrow nationalism and the refusal of states to cede part of their sovereignty to a universal peacekeeping organization, Mr Pearson in particular was a tireless crusader on behalf of collective security. "We also know, or should know," he said in 1948, "that there can be no political security except on the widest possible basis of co-operation. If that basis can be a universal one—so much the better. If it cannot, then on the broadest possible basis and inside the United Nations."[3] The firm support given by Canadian governments to the United Nations and its peacekeeping activities was one application of this principle; another was the Canadian commitment to NATO and NORAD, which successive governments considered to be important regional collective security alliances.

Another key concept in the St Laurent-Pearson tradition was a firm commitment to internationalism. Both prime ministers believed that Canada's first foreign-policy goal was world peace and security, which could be attained only if countries put aside their own narrow interests. "The last thing we Canadians should do," Mr. Pearson said,

"is to shut ourselves up in our provinces, or indeed, in our own country, on our own continent. If we are to be of service in the world and to ourselves and our own destiny, if we are to find our right place in the sun, we must look beyond our own national or local limits."[4] In its dealings with other countries, Canada was to seek to gain their confidence by not giving undue publicity to differences of opinion (an aspect of Canada's so-called "quiet diplomacy") and by making whatever contributions to regional collective security alliances that its allies considered appropriate. "We can most effectively influence international affairs," Mr. Pearson believed, "not by aggressive nationalism but by earning the respect of the nations with whom we co-operate, and who will therefore be glad to discuss their international policies with us."[5] Canada's natural allies in the quest for world peace were the countries of Western Europe and the United States. One of Mr. Pearson's dreams was the establishment of a "North Atlantic community" in which Canada, the United States, and Western Europe would cooperate in political, economic, social, and military matters. When this proved impossible to attain, he emphasized the creation of strong bilateral ties between Canada and these nations. In his dealings with the United States he spoke frequently of the special relationship that existed between the two countries, occasionally reminding the Americans that they must not, however, take their northern neighbour for granted.

This brief description indicates the main trends in Canadian foreign policy between 1948 and 1968: support for the UN, NATO, and NORAD in the quest for collective security; an internationalist approach based on the premise that peace and security must be the foremost goal of any country's foreign policy; "quiet diplomacy" in dealings with allies; and a belief that the United States and the countries of Western Europe were Canada's best and most natural friends. This is the foreign policy that Pierre Elliott Trudeau inherited in 1968 and that he decided to subject to intense scrutiny.

In spite of Prime Minister Trudeau's frequently expressed desire to ensure that Canada's defence policy flowed out of its foreign policy, the decision to revise Canada's military contribution to NATO and to set new defence priorities preceded by fourteen months the publication in 1970 of the government's papers outlining its new approach to foreign policy. Because of the exigencies of fiscal planning, the Cabinet needed to know as quickly as possible the size of the defence budget for the fiscal year 1969-70; only after a thorough review of defence policy could the government decide whether this budget should be reduced, increased, or frozen. Secondly, the annual review of NATO by all its members was approaching, when Canada and the other member-countries would be required to make firm military commitments for one year and tentative forecasts for the next five years. Finally, it can be surmised that the defence review was given priority because NATO was the issue that seemed to arouse the greatest interest among critics of Canadian foreign policy, and because it was one of the areas in which Mr. Trudeau himself appeared critical of existing policy.

For the proponents of a new Canadian foreign policy, NATO had become the symbol of the detested status quo—a military alliance dominated by the United States, a power bloc that lessened Canada's credibility in the Third World and as a peacekeeper, and a bottomless pit into which were thrown resources that could be put to better use in foreign aid. The advocates of existing Canadian foreign policy, on the other hand, saw NATO as a symbol of all that was laudable in Canada's approach to international affairs—its concern with contributing to the stability of Europe, the area in which world peace was most immediately threatened; its emphasis on gaining influence with its NATO allies, particularly the United States, and using it to encourage diplomatic imagination and military caution; and its search for counterweights to offset Canada's dependence on the U.S.

There were six courses of action open to the government:

1. Adopt a policy of non-alignment, which would mean withdrawal from both NATO and NORAD.
2. Withdraw from NATO but remain in NORAD.
3. Remain in NATO but withdraw all forces from Europe.
4. Remain in NATO but reduce the number of troops in Europe.
5. Remain in NATO with present force strength.
6. Remain in NATO and increase the size of the force in Europe.

During the course of the NATO review in Canada (between May 1968 and April 1969), there occurred two important events in the external environment that might have discouraged any decision to withdraw Canadian forces from Europe. One was the decision of the NATO ministers in Reykjavik in June 1968 to press for mutual and balanced force reductions (MBFR) with the Warsaw Pact countries, a move based on the understanding that no NATO member would take unilateral action that would reduce the overall military capability of NATO and thereby weaken the credibility of the MBFR approach. The second major international event was the Soviet-led invasion of Czechoslovakia in the fall of 1968, which greatly increased East-West tensions.

The fear and uncertainty that it created in the West remained for some months, and there was talk in NATO of the need to maintain and possibly increase the strength of its forces.

The NATO issue involved far more than military considerations, for it went to the very basis of Canada's philosophy of foreign policy. This may explain why, for the first time ever, the Canadian government made a conscious and serious attempt to involve Parliament, academics, and the public in the formulation of foreign and defence policy.

The NATO Review Process

One innovation of the NATO review process was the government's decision to look beyond the civil service for policy proposals. Another innovation that emerged in the course of the NATO review was the Prime Minister's encouragement of his Cabinet ministers to express in public their own differing views on the NATO issue.

. . .

Mr. Trudeau and his ministers made a concerted effort to familiarize themselves with the views of Canadian academics. The Prime Minister discussed foreign and defence policy with them on at least two occasions. Not long afterwards other ministers began to follow Mr. Trudeau's lead. Mr. Sharp met a group in Toronto in the fall of 1968. At that meeting James Eayrs reports that Mr. Sharp appeared to have already made up his mind that Canada would remain in NATO and the tenor of the conversation was that the academics "tried to persuade Sharp that if the government was reviewing foreign policy some changes in policy should result and it would not be enough to stand pat."[6]

. . .

In the first three months of 1969 the Commons' Standing Committee on External Affairs and National Defence undertook an extensive examination of Canada's NATO policy. Hearings were held twice weekly and reported in considerable detail by newspapers such as the Toronto *Globe and Mail*, an indication of the general enthusiasm and interest that surrounded the NATO debate.

For one of the first times in the history of this Parliamentary Committee, attendance was regular and the members took a real interest in its work.... Indeed, Chairman Ian Wahn announced at the beginning of the first hearing that the aim of the Committee's study was to hear from experts and to stimulte debate in the hope of influencing the current review of defence and foreign policies.

From the outset the Committee worked on the principle that the Committee should be exposed to as wide a variety of opinions as possible in order to arrive at the most favourable NATO policy for Canada. This deliberate search for people who would challenge existing views was highly unusual, but it was in keeping with the government's own predilection for exposing itself to all possible sources of advice.... For some witnesses the only way in which Canada could play an active and constructive role in international affairs was as a completely non-aligned country. A complete withdrawal from NATO and NORAD, said Michael Brecher of McGill, would create "a distinct image in the external world of an autonomous Canadian identity," while the resulting decrease in the defence budget would provide more resources for foreign aid and peacekeeping, as well as for the alleviation of financial problems within Canada. Other witnesses maintained that Canada could play a constructive role without withdrawing completely from its military alliances. Jack Granatstein of York University believed that peacekeeping should be the primary function of the Canadian Armed Forces. He noted that participation in NATO had not hampered Canada's role as a peacekeeper in the past; what was needed now was the withdrawal of Canada's forces from Europe and the establishment in Canada of a mobile force that, in addition to fulfilling any peacekeeping obligations, could also play a useful role in NATO in case of war.

. . .

To balance the testimony of these academic critics, the Committee heard from witnesses who were in varying degrees generally sympathetic to Canadian participation in military alliances and emphasized that NATO continued to perform an important military function, since it was in Europe that they perceived the greatest danger to world peace and security. They agreed that Canada's military contribution was primarily symbolic but still very important, and that any Canadian withdrawal of its forces might trigger a chain reaction of other withdrawals on the part of Holland, Denmark, Norway, and perhaps even the United States.

. . .

The Committee also heard from two members of Canada's military establishment. On February 4, Major-General Michael Dare presented a strictly factual description of the existing roles and capabilities of the Canadian Armed Forces. However, it was the testimony of General Charles Foulkes, former Chairman of the Joint Chiefs of Staff Committee, that seems to have particularly intrigued the Committee members. General Dare was prevented by his position from offering his personal views, but General Foulkes, who was then a university professor, was able to give not only impressive factual information but his own opinions as well. Although he believed that a Canadian military presence in Europe was still desirable, General Foulkes considered the present commitment to have "rather dubious" validity. He described the nuclear-strike capacity of the alliance as one "of doubtful and diminishing value under today's strategy," and advocated the handing over of the "wasteful" [Canadian] ground role to Britain or Germany. Canada, he said, should reorganize its contribution as a mobile formation based on Europe, for this would best suit Canadian aptitudes and would also provide the necessary flexibility to meet UN peacekeeping roles. General Foulkes went on to shock the Committee members by revealing for perhaps the first time publicly, that Canada's claim to ownership of the Arctic islands was not beyond dispute and that he had been informed recently that some American maps showed these Arctic islands as "disputed territory." Thus, he said, as the Arctic became more important economically, the necessity for "surveillance, control, and policing" would increase. His final argument against a posture of unarmed neutrality for Canada consisted of the warning that there was no guarantee that Canada would escape the civil disorders that had plagued other countries, and that it would be unwise to ignore the need for the means of controlling any such outbreaks of violence.

. . .

The Committee began a tour of Europe early in March as the final stage of its deliberations.... There appears to be little doubt that this two-week exposure to European views helped convince most members of the Committee who were still undecided that there was a need for Canada to remain in NATO and continue its military activity in Europe.

By mid-March the Committee members had developed clearly formed opinions.

Among the most passionate and articulate supporters of NATO were Douglas Harkness, Norman Cafik, and Perry Ryan, who were instrumental in convincing most of the other Committee members of the need for Canada to remain in Europe. Only two Liberal members opposed this view. One was the Committee Chairman, Ian Wahn, who was inclined to favour a complete withdrawal from NATO.

...

The Committee's Final Report to the House on March 25 contained five recommendations. First, it stated that Canada should remain a member of NATO because the organization was necessary for the security of both Europe and Canada, because membership did not impair Canada's effectiveness in peacekeeping or in the Third World, and because considerations of both geography and cost made non-alignment unfeasible. Secondly, Canada should maintain troops in Europe, for the Committee rejected the notion that Canada could take a "free ride" without losing freedom both of action and influence: it also discounted the idea that defence expenditures were disproportionately high. It saw no advantage to be gained from basing this force commitment in Canada and suggested that a Canadian withdrawal might "possibly" bring about other withdrawals of NATO members. Both the third and fourth recommendations, however, pointed in the direction of change. Canada should continue its present military roles in Europe until the equipment for its Air Division and Mechanized Brigade became obsolete in 1972, and a prompt review of possible future military roles should be undertaken so that new defence policies would be available for the post-1972 period. (The Report stated that the Committee did not have enough information to recommend what these future roles should be.) The final rec-

ommendation was an uncontroversial statement that Canada should in future emphasize the political functions of NATO and encourage it to seek détente and balanced force reductions with the Warsaw Pact countries.

At the same time as the NATO debate was stimulating the interest of Canadian academics and Parliamentarians, the civil-service departments involved in foreign activities were carrying on their own review of Canada's relations with Europe. The Prime Minister's statement of May 29, 1968, had revealed the government's intention to establish an interdepartmental Special Task Force on Relations with Europe, which would soon be known by the code name STAFFEUR. While its defence policy was being reviewed, the government wanted to reassess Canada's relations with Europe in the political and economic fields, which "are inevitably intermingled with our defence commitments."[7] The Special Task Force, therefore, was intended to investigate Canadian-European relations in their totality, with one aspect of this review dealing with NATO.[8]

The Task Force began its work in the summer of 1968. Although the Department of External Affairs supplied the secretariat and STAFFEUR was to report to the government through Mr. Sharp, the Force's twenty-five to thirty-five members were chosen from several departments. By the beginning of 1969, STAFFEUR had completed its study and submitted to the government a four-hundred-page report analysing Canada's past and present relations with the countries of Eastern and Western Europe. The report examined such matters as Europe's role in counteracting the influence on Canada of the United States and in promoting Canadian unity, Canadian-European defence and economic relations, and Canada's general relations with Eastern Europe. As for NATO, the Task Force concluded that Canada should continue to station troops in Europe since it was in Canada's economic and political, as well as military, interests to be actively involved on the continent.

While STAFFEUR was examining Canada's overall relations with Europe, the Departments of External Affairs and National Defence were conducting a joint study of a more specialized nature. Their report, known as the External-Defence Report and classified as "Secret, For Canadian Eyes Only," considered the problems and costs of maintaining and replacing military equipment, the international obligations to which Canada was committed, and analysed all possible options ranging from neutrality to increased support of NATO. The External-Defence Report reached conclusions that were almost idential to STAFFEUR's recommendations about NATO: maintain Canada's existing NATO forces, at least for the time being. The two reports differed in form, however. The External-Defence Report consisted mainly of little more than a set of options, while STAFFEUR adopted a more prescriptive approach and made definite policy recommendations. Nevertheless, since neither External Affairs nor National Defence were prepared to see their traditional policy of support for NATO rejected, the External-Defence Report clearly implied in its listing of options that a continuation of military activities in Europe was desirable.

At the same time, the fiscal constraints facing the government, coupled with a deteriorating economy and high inflation rates meant that the costs of Canada's NATO contribution could not be ignored. By 1972 new equipment costing $300 to $400 million would be needed for the NATO forces. It is signifcant that both the STAFFEUR and External-Defence reports agreed that Canadian participation in NATO would probably have to be curtailed by 1972, since not even the NATO supporters in the government and civil service were willing to spend the sums required to purchase the new equipment.[9]

Dissatisfied with the STAFFEUR and External-Defence reports, still awaiting the report of the Parliamentary Committee, and with the April 10 deadline rapidly approaching, Mr. Trudeau decided in late March to turn to his own advisers. The Prime Minister asked Ivan Head to take a fresh look at the whole question of Canada's military policy in the hope that he would be able to develop a satisfactory solution to what had become a much more difficult and contoversial issue than Mr. Trudeau had expected. Head chaired a small committee that examined both general and specific questions dealing with military policy. Working with him were senior civil servants who served as "resource people," answering any detailed questions that he raised in the course of his study. By March 29 Head had completed his special report, entitled "Canadian Defence Policy—a Study" but referred to by a few knowledgeable insiders as the "non-group report" (a somewhat caustic allusion to the large bureaucratic and parliamentary committees that had prepared the other NATO studies). The document was prepared with the utmost secrecy: neither Mitchell Sharp nor Léo Cadieux apparently even knew of its existence until it was distributed to Cabinet ministers only hours before the March 29 Cabinet meeting. It apparently contained the recommendations that Canada remain in NATO, retain in Europe approximately 3,000 men out of its existing 9,800-man contingent, and abandon its nuclear-strike role.

The Government's Decision

Throughout the review process Mr. Trudeau consistently refused to speculate about its outcome or take any action that might prejudge its results. In a CBC interview in January 1969 the Prime Minister said he did not know what the NATO review would lead to. Not until February 1969 did he even indicate when the review would be completed. The deadline, he told the House, had been March 15, since a decision was required before the meeting of NATO foreign ministers in Washington on April 10.[10] However, since the Commons' Committee had begun its work at such a late date that its ability to submit a report by the middle of March was doubtful, the government was prepared to delay its decision in order to include this report in its deliberations. As a result the Cabinet did not meet to decide on Canada's defence policy with respect to NATO until the weekend of March 29-30, and it continued its discussions into the next week.

One of the reasons why the NATO decision is so significant is that it was the first clear indication that the role of the civil service in foreign- and defence-policy formulation had changed drastically. During the St. Laurent and Pearson administrations, the Departments of External Affairs and National Defence had with few exceptions been able to convince the government to accept the policies they advocated. If senior civil servants expected that this approach would be continued in the Trudeau administration, their hopes were dashed when the Cabinet rejected the NATO recommendations of both the STAFFEUR and External-Defence reports. One major Cabinet criticism of both was that they took for granted the effectiveness of the existing weapons of Canada's NATO

contingent without offering the detailed proof that already-skeptical ministers demanded. The view expressed in the reports that Canada's CF-104 Starfighters provided an effective second-strike capability was typical of the kind of civil-service reasoning that the Cabinet regarded as faulty.

That the Prime Minister was able to reach a Cabinet consensus based on the "non-group report" stems from the fact that it presented new and compelling ideas that many ministers had not previously considered. According to one official, the realization that Canada's air element in Europe was likely to be perceived by the Soviet Union as a provocative first-strike force sent ministers "climbing the wall" in surprise. The logic of the arguments presented in the study and defended by the Prime Minister may have convinced some ministers of the need to alter Canada's contribution to NATO. One of Ivan Head's conclusions was that since Canada's CF-104s in Europe used too much fuel to be effective over long distances and were very vulnerable to surprise attack, they would be perceived by the Warsaw Pact countries as a first-strike attack force. In his Calgary speech Mr. Trudeau spoke in remarkably similar terms. "Is our squadron of CF-104s" he asked, "the right kind of contribution? Will it be used only as a second strike? Are the 104s soft targets? And are not the Soviets entitled to ask themselves, `They are soft targets, they are on the ground, we know where the airfields are. Isn't it likely that they might be used to attack us first?'" Convinced that the presence of Soviet missile bases only three hundred miles away made it unlikely that the aircraft would ever get off the ground in the event of war, Cabinet soon came to the conclusion that the civil service's NATO recommendations were based not only on a lack of imagination but also on faulty judgement.

. . .

On April 3, the Prime Minister announced the government's decision. The delay seems clearly attributable to a serious division of opinion that existed within Cabinet. The Prime Minister's April 3 statement began with the announcement of the government's rejection of a non-aligned or neutral role for Canada.[11] One of the most important reasons for staying in NATO, Mr. Trudeau explained, was Canada's desire to play a political role and to orient NATO towards seeking détente and arms reduction with the East. He said Canada shared the same values as the other NATO members; if he did not feel that Canada could have some influence in the policies that further Canada's interests, he would have recommended total withdrawal. But, although it would remain a member of NATO, Canada had decided to "bring about a planned and phased reduction of the size of the Canadian forces in Europe." Mr. Trudeau refused to divulge the size of this reduction, saying only that it would be decided "in consultation with Canada's allies," and that it would constitute the second phase of the NATO review. (The decision of April 3 was the conclusion of the first phase.) The withdrawal, the Prime Minister noted, was purely unilateral, occasioned not by any desire for a reciprocal reduction in Warsaw Pact forces or to weaken NATO, but rather by Canada's belief that there were better uses for its armed forces in Canada than in Europe. As for NORAD, the Prime Minister announced that Canada intended to continue to cooperate with the United States in the defence of North America, although the details of this joint defence effort had still to be discussed with the Americans.

As Mr. Trudeau himself observed, what had been decided was not so much the details of Canadian defence policy as the government's new "philosophy of defence." The most signifcant part of the April 3 statement was the announcement of the government's new defence priorities, based on the concentric-circle principle that money would be provided for low-priority activities only after those of high priority had been adequately financed. These priorities, which defined the future roles of the Canadian Armed Forces consisted of:

(a) the surveillance of our own territory and coast-lines—i.e., the protection of our sovereignty;
(b) the defence of North America in co-operation with United States forces:
(c) the fulfilment of such NATO commitments as may be agreed upon;
(d) the performance of such international peacekeeping roles as we may, from time to time, assume.

The reasoning behind the government's decision to downgrade Canada's NATO role became clear in Calgary on April 12 when the Prime Minister delivered a speech entitled "The Relation of Defence Policy to Foreign Policy."[12] Its theme was that NATO, a military organization, had in the past determined Canada's defence policy, which had in turn determined the country's foreign policy. We had "no foreign policy of any importance except that which flowed from NATO," Mr. Trudeau said, and "this is a false perspective for any country." What the government was attempting to do, he explained, was to "stand the pyramid on its base" instead of its head—"to review our foreign policy and to have a defence policy flow from that, and from the defence policy to decide which alliances we want to belong to, and how our defences should be deployed." And that, the Prime Minister concluded, "is why we gave a series of four priorities." Not until the government had presented its foreign policy to the country would it decide on its defence policy "in a final way."

Since the NATO ministerial meeting had obliged the government to announce its defence philosophy before it could complete its White Paper on Foreign Policy, Mr. Trudeau was able to announce only in general terms the foreign policy upon which his government had based its NATO decision. But he said that the aims of Canada's foreign policy were "to serve our national interests and to express our national identity abroad." This, it seems, is the explanation for the government's emphasis on sovereignty as Canada's first defence priority. "When we place sovereignty at the head of the priorities," Mr. Trudeau explained at his press conference on April 3, "it is because we believe this is essentially the role of a foreign policy and of a defence policy." It was far from clear, however, what he meant when he talked of sovereignty. In his April 3 statement he equated it with "the surveillance of our own territory and coast-lines"; during the press conference he expanded his definition to include "assistance to the civil power," protection of our "territorial waters," and the Gaullist line that the country should provide as large a part of its own protection as possible rather than "having the Americans do it for us." Then in Calgary he said simply that the government's first priority was the protection of Canadian sovereignty "in all the dimensions that it means." Although no one knew how far the government intended to carry its determination to defend Canadian sovereignty, the decision to emphasize sovereignty appears to have been inspired by the belief that defence policy had to be based on national interests that were more North American-oriented than were contributions to world peace and security through participation in NATO. Mr. Trudeau explained that the redefinition of the roles of the Canadian Armed Forces that this im-

plied was intended to reassure the CAF personnel, and "especially" to convince the public, that there was a valid role for armed forces in Canada.

A defence policy based on considerations of sovereignty was such a novelty on the Canadian scene that there was some concern that the government might be intending to regard it as an end in itself and as something that had to be defended in its entirety. The government's reluctance to specify what it meant by this new emphasis greatly contributed to such fears. When the long-awaited 1971 Defence White Paper was [later] published, however, it became apparent that the Cabinet had been thinking in far different terms. "Sovereignty" was an important concept of the paper, but it was defined with precision, and the idea that Canada's sovereignty had to be defended in its entirety was rejected. What the government meant by "sovereignty" was jurisdicion and internal security—the idea that any national government had to be capable of surveillance and control activities over its own land, territorial waters, and airspace. The first real indication that sovereignty was not viewed as an end in itself but rather as a means came in April 1970, when Canada asserted jurisdiction over its offshore waters; this was done for the specific and limited purpose of establishing pollution and fishing control. It soon became apparent that the government was also thinking in terms of asserting its jurisdiction in the Arctic for purposes of pollution control and economic growth. Government officials implied that the emphasis on sovereignty was designed to remind Canadians that they should be more moderate and realistic in their conception of Canada's international role, and think less in terms of "crusading."

The importance of the second aspect of sovereignty—internal security—became particularly apparent after the FLQ crisis in 1970, but the government was conscious of the need for more emphasis in this direction as early as April 1969. In both his April 3 statement and his press conference, Mr. Trudeau made it clear that his government considered support of the civil authority as one of the prime functions of the Canadian Armed Forces. And insiders report that during part of 1969, aid to the civil authority was the first priority within the Department of National Defence. After the FLQ crisis, Mr. Trudeau implied that considerations of internal security had been very much in the government's mind when the new defence priorities were being determined. One result of our more realistic approach, he said, "was the decision taken 20 months ago to re-align our military forces to make sure that they would be available for the defence of Canadian sovereignty and as an aid to civil authorities. That decision has been proven correct in recent weeks."[13]

The part played by financial and military considerations on the NATO decision is particularly difficult to determine. Mr. Cadieux said in the House that finances had definitely been considered and that he had told the NATO Defence Planning Committee in Brussels that Canada's NATO decision "was occasioned, in part, by a requirement for budgetary restraints on all Canadian government departments.[14] But he did not reveal how important these restraints were compared to other factors. No mention was made of financial difficulties in the Prime Minister's statement of April 3, in spite of the fact that the country's economic problems might have been one of the most effective arguments the government could have used to defend its controversial cutbacks.

One thing was clear, however: the government did decide to freeze the dollar value of the Canadian defence budget for at least the next few years and those who shaped Canada's defence policy would have to keep this limitation very much in mind. Mr. Cadieux told the House on June 23, 1969, that the goal of his department was to achieve the transition to a new defence posture "within a defence budget which will be maintained for the next three years at its current dollar level."[15] In a time of severe inflation this meant that cuts had to be made in some commitments, but it did not necessarily dictate an immediate cut in Canada's NATO contribution, since in the short run the withdrawal of some or even all of its troops from Europe would effect a relatively minor saving.

The Prime Minister realized that his statement of April 3 had aroused concern in Cabinet, among some segments of the articulate public, and among Canada's allies. It was therefore wise, for both political and diplomatic reasons, to offer assurance that Canada would contiue to play an active role in NATO. On the first day of the Commons debate on the government's new NATO policy, which took place on April 23 and 24, Mr. Trudeau delivered a speech that stressed a Canadian foreign and defence policy that was as active and internationally inclined as his earlier statements had been domestically oriented.[16] Gone was the emphasis on sovereignty as the prime goal of Canadian defence policy. Instead he stressed that Canada was continuing to participate in collective-security arrangements that were necessary for the peace and security of the world. He said that Canada was on the threshold of a new international role, one that would be characterized by participation in international peacekeeping forces, by a search for détente, by contributions toward arms limitation and disarmament, and by assistance to developing countries. Mr. Sharp told the

House the following day that the Prime Minister's statement "makes it very clear that Canada is broadening its horizons in every direction and is intent on playing a still more active role in world affairs."[17] The Prime Minister's principal foreign-affairs adviser, Ivan Head, was even more emphatic, suggesting that Mr. Trudeau's speech might well rank as one of the most internationalist statements ever made by a head of government while still in power.

It is difficult to assess the extent of the division in Cabinet over the NATO issue, but the fact that the decision was so long in coming indicates that it was considerable. The Prime Minister's April 23 speech was in part an attempt to repair this breach. It can also be assumed that he realized before April 3 that it would have been extremely difficult (as well as politically unwise) to ignore completely the "pro-NATO" views of the majority of his ministers. The decision to leave a token force in Europe appears to have been inspired at least in part by the need to reconcile through a compromise solution the varying views of members of Cabinet. As James Eayrs wrote later, the Prime Minister's April 23 statement was designed "to reconcile contending Cabinet factions, to allay public apprehension and to reduce anguish among allies.[18]

There were many questions that remained unanswered, however. How quickly would the NATO cuts take place? Would the withdrawal of forces from Europe be total? Would Canada's nuclear role be maintained? What would be the future size and role of the naval forces? Would the new priorities result in a reduction or increase in the defence budget? Some of these questions were dealt with in statements made by Defence Minister Cadieux on June 23 and September 19, 1969, but for the answers to other more tactical questions it was necessary to await the 1971 White Paper on Defence.

The government made it clear from the outset that the decision to reduce Canada's forces in Europe was not negotiable, and that only the size of the reduction would be a matter for discussion with Canada's allies. When Mr. Cadieux attended the May meeting of the NATO Defence Planning Committee in Brussels, he informed the ministers of Canada's intention to reduce the size of its forces in Europe. As had been the case during the April meeting in Washington, the withdrawals were criticized by other NATO members—particularly the British and West Germans—as "highly inadvisable" and likely to be "infectious." The other NATO members were so opposed to a Canadian cut-back that the European Defence Ministers, with American encouragment, met in caucus to decide in advance the arguments they would use. When Mr. Cadieux arrived in Brussels he was met with a well-co-ordinated stream of criticism that American Ambassador Harlan Cleveland later described as "the toughest talk I have ever heard in an international meeting."[19] British Defence Minister Denis Healey delivered a particularly scathing attack on Canada, accusing it of "passing the buck to the rest of us," a comment that was leaked to the press.[20] In the House a few days later Mr. Cadieux admitted that Canada's proposals had not been well received, but claimed that the principal objection concerned Canada's failure to conform exactly to prescribed procedures of consultation.[21] This, Mr. Cadieux said, Canada had agreed to do, and during the summer months there were several lenghty exchanges of notes between the Department of National Defence and NATO headquarters. Reliable sources indicate that the government had originally been thinking of a two-thirds reduction in the size of Canada's forces in Europe, but on September 19 Mr. Cadieux announced that only half the forces would in fact be withdrawn. Although reluctant at the time to say that the government had compromised, the Defence Minister admitted three months later in the House that, as a result of consultation with our allies, "we had modified considerably our original plan."[22]

Mr. Cadieux also announced in September that the remaining 5,000 man force in Europe would be organized by the autumn of 1970 into a land and air force located in the same area that would replace the separate brigade group and air divisions. Canada would also disengage gradually from all nuclear activities in Europe, dropping the "Honest John" nuclear role in 1970 and the nuclear-strike role for the air force in 1972. By 1972 and after the country would be maintaining in Europe a conventionally armed land and air element of approximately the same size (5,000 troops).[23] However, Mr. Cadieux did not explain how this decision, which seemed final, was consistent with the government's earlier promises that final defence commitments would not be made until the foreign-policy review had been submitted to the country.

One of the problems with a compromise solution that neither totally withdrew nor fully maintained Canada's forces in Europe, as the government soon discovered, was that it satisfied virtually none of the critics of Canadian defence policy. Among the Parliamentarians, for example, the government's decision of April 3 was interpreted in a variety of ways. For T. C. Douglas and the NDP, the government had committed itself to no real changes, since Canada was remaining in NATO and saying only that "at some indeterminate time there will be, possibly, some indeterminate reduction of Canada's forces in Europe." Douglas Harkness, on the other hand, concluded that "the Prime Minister intends to end our military contributions as quickly as possible."[24] Mr. Cadieux's September 19 announcement resolved some of the confusion, however, and interest in the NATO question rapidly declined. The government's new defence priorities also drew criticism on the grounds that they represented a swing toward "isolationism and continentalism" (according to Robert Stanfield) and ignored the vital role of the United Nations in contributing to world peace (according to Andrew Brewin). Only the Créditiste Party agreed with the government's emphasis on national interests, which it defined even more narrowly than Mr. Trudeau seemed inclined to do. Charity begins at home, said Créditiste leader Réal Caouette, and Canada should concentrate on solving its own economic problems rather than on worrying about such remote concerns as European security or international development assistance.[25]

One of the best indications of the Prime Minister's decisive role in the NATO review—whether it was direct or indirect—is the striking similarity between the 1969 defence-policy decisions and his personal beliefs. His lack of hostility to the Soviet Union helps explain why Canada could reduce its NATO commitment only half a year after the Soviet-led invasion of Czechoslovakia, while his belief that Canada's natural alliance is with the United States was reflected in the high priority given to NORAD. If, as Mr. Trudeau desired, Canada was to adopt a more modest international role and to be selective in its ventures, a partial withdrawal from Europe was very much in order. His longstanding antipathy to nuclear weapons is seen in the government's decision to phase out Canada's nuclear-strike role in Europe.

The only area in which Mr. Trudeau appears to have altered his original views during the NATO review was over the extent of the withdrawal of Canadian forces from Europe. His own opinion seems to have been that Canada should remain in NATO in order to increase Canada's political, economic, and cultural relations with Europe, but that it should terminate its military activity in Europe, concentrating instead on the North American security alliance.

Once Canada's main national interest was defined as "national identity and independence" rather than peace and security, it was inevitable that NATO would be accorded a lower priority in Canada's defence policy than formerly. It was this new "philosophy of defence" (to use Mr. Trudeau's expression of April 3), not financial considerations, that determined the money that would be made available for Canada's various military roles and the priorities given to them.

The compromise reflected in deciding to withdraw one half instead of two thirds of Canada's forces from Europe was, after all, of little importance compared to the decision that the country would henceforth concentrate its military efforts in Canada. The idea that defence policy should be determined by a foreign policy that was based on such national interests as the promotion of a Canadian identity explains why sovereignty became the country's first defence priority, a decision that seems to have no other source than the Prime Minister.

And the most notable change in foreign policy—the decision to relegate peacekeeping to last place in the new list of priorities, which was a conscious attempt to focus the attention of Canadians on more important national objectives than an idealistic search for international glory—seems clearly inspired by Mr. Trudeau.

NOTES

1. Canada, Department of External Affairs, *Statements and Speeches*. No. 68/17, May 29, 1968, p. 3.
2. Canada, Department of External Affairs, *Foreign Policy for Canadians*. Ottawa: Queen's Printer for Canada, 1970.
3. Lester B. Pearson, *Words and Occasions*. Toronto: University of Toronto Press, 1970, p. 69.
4. *Ibid.*, p. 292.
5. *Ibid.*, p. 69.
6. *Canadian Annual Review*, 1968, pp. 221-2.
7. Mitchell Sharp, "Canada's Relations with Europe." *Statements and Speeches*. No. 69/1, January 3, 1969.
8. See Albert Legault, *Le Devoir*, 25 novembre, 1969, pp. 1 and 6 for the most complete account available of this review.
9. See Legault, *loc. cit.* The real question, he writes, was only one of *when* there would be a new definition of Canada's NATO role.
10. *Debates*, February 21, 1969, pp. 5801-2.
11. Pierre Elliott Trudeau, "A Defence Policy for Canada," *Statements and Speeches*. No. 69/7, April 3, 1969; *Transcript of Press Conference*, Office of the Prime Minister, April 3, 1969 (hereafter referred to as *Press Conference, April 3*).

12. Pierre Elliott Trudeau, "The Relation of Defence Policy to Foreign Policy," *Statements and Speeches*. No. 69/8, April 12, 1969.

13. *International Canada*, November 1970, p. 254.

14. *Debates*, December 8, 1969, p. 1681.

15. *Debates*, June 23, 1969, p. 10518.

16. *Debates*, April 23, 1969, pp. 7866-70.

17. *Debates*, April 24, 1969, p. 7905.

18. James Eayrs, "NATO Policy tries to Reconcile the Cabinet and our Allies," *Toronto Star*, April 27, 1969.

19. Harlan Cleveland, *NATO: The Transatlantic Bargain*. New York: Harper & Row, 1970, p. 128.

20. *Globe and Mail*, May 30, 1969, p. 1; *Monthly Report*, May 1969, pp. 138-9.

21. *Debates*, June 2, 1969, p. 9327; June 3, 1969, p. 9382.

22. *Debates*, December 8, 1969, p. 1681.

23. Léo Cadieux, "Canada Adopts a New defence Posture," *Statements and Speeches*. No. 69/15, September 19, 1969.

24. *Debates*, April 23, 1969, p. 7876 (Douglas); April 26, 1969, p. 7908 (Harkness).

25. *Debates*, April 23, 1969, p. 7875 (Standfield); April 23, 1969, p. 7890 (Brewin); April 23, 1969, p. 7883 (Caouette).

SUGGESTED READINGS

Eayrs, James, "Future Roles For the Armed Forces of Canada," *Behind the Headlines*, Vol. 28, No. 1.2, pp. 1-13 (1969).

Gellner, John, *Canada in NATO*, Toronto: Ryerson, 1970, pp. 90-110.

Gray, C.S., *Canadian Defence Priorities: A Question of Relevance*, Toronto: Clarke, Irwin, 1972. Hertzman, Lewis, "Canada and the North Atlantic Treaty Organization," in L. Hertzman, J. Warnock and T. Hockin, *Alliances and Illusions*, Edmonton, Hurtig, 1969 pp. 3-35.

Stairs, Denis, "Pierre Trudeau and the Politics of the Canadian Foreign Policy Review," *Australian Outlook*, Vol. 26, No. 3, 1972, pp. 274-290.

c h a p t e r   12

REVIEWING FOREIGN POLICY, 1968-70

Denis Stairs

There is a great hazard in official foreign policy reviews, the hazard of taking them too seriously. Participants and spectators alike are drawn in fascination to an exercise which claims to apply comprehensive principles of "rationality" to external affairs and which consumes a substantial measure of highly paid time, energy and talent. Existing policies, regarded often as the stale and eclectic accumulation of old decisions and obsolete relationships, become the object of a harsh and critical scrutiny. The promise is that unless proven sound they will be displaced by new and coherent programmes rooted in first principles and priority needs. Habitual routines, flowing from years of bureaucratic inertia, are intended thus to be invigorated and transformed by a fresh political leadership—encouraged, perhaps, by an active and attentive public.

It is easy to believe in such an enterprise, and to expect much of it. And so it was with the Canadian foreign policy review conducted under the auspices of the government of Pierre Elliott Trudeau. Initiated in May 1968, it took twenty-five months to complete. Its progress ultimately absorbed the attentions of senior officials in almost every department of government as well as interested individuals and organizations from the public at large. In its service the Departments of External Affairs and National Defence together produced a classified report on Canadian defence policy, a multi-departmental Task Force of approximately 30 officials generated a 400-page review of Canada's relations with Europe, and independently of both these exercises the Prime Minister's Office compiled a critical analysis of existing military commitments. Quite apart from the usual peregrinations of the Prime Minister, the Secretary of State for External Affairs, and the Minister of National Defence, a battery of five Cabinet ministers and thirty civil servants embarked on an extensive tour of Latin America. Mr Trudeau personally consulted "on at least two occasions"[1] with academic specialists in foreign and defence policy, and with the help of the Canadian Institute of International Affairs the government sponsored four conferences in which various aspects of Canada's external relations were discussed by policy-makers, academicians, and other members of the attentive public.[2] More informally, the Secretary of State for External Affairs, Mitchell Sharp, debated foreign policy issues in a private session with a group of Toronto academics in the autumn of 1968, and the pattern was repeated in a meeting with six other Cabinet ministers in the following March. In the House of Commons, the Standing Committee on External Affairs and National Defence interviewed a

Denis Stairs, "Pierre Trudeau and the Politics of the Canadian Foreign Policy Review," *The Australian Outlook*, Australian Institute of International Affairs, 1972.

189

series of specialists from the public service, the armed forces, and the academic community as well as representatives of a number of interested pressure groups, and in March of 1969 it completed a major tour of western Europe. The *Minutes* of its proceedings for the two years from 1968 to 1970 came to an unprecedented total of 2,719 pages, and its activities were reported in some detail in the daily and periodical press. Following the publication in June 1970 of the resulting "white paper," moreover, there was considerable *post mortem* analysis in Parliament, the news media, and elsewhere, and by the time of this writing (October 1972) the exercise as a whole had already become the principal focus of three books.[3]

Foreign policy, however, is not the product of intellectual effort alone, but of intellectual effort applied to objective conditions—conditions established by the behaviour of other states, by the accidents of geography, the distribution of economic resources, the progress of military technology, the demands of domestic publics, and a multitude of other pertinent factors. Of these, some are prone to rapid change, others advance at a sluggish pace, and still others do not move at all. In the normal course of events, the more precipitate of environmental transformations come by surprise and necessitate a quick and pragmatic response on the part of policy-makers. Since such developments do not lend themselves to management by long-range plans, it is to the more gradual of alterations in external "reality" that reviewers of foreign policy are compelled to direct their analysis. And here, even if their respective perceptions coincide (they rarely do), they may discover that within the parameters of their existing political values, they have scant room for productive innovation. They may wish in any case to say little of substance in public, for excessive advance commitment to specific policies can lead to the articulation of inconvenient domestic demands, to the loss of tactical advantage to others and to a general diminution of future freedom of manoeuvre. In these circumstances the temptation is to convert review to rhetoric, reasoning to rationalization. The relevance of the outcome for the making of foreign policy decisions becomes in consequence obscure, conveying at times the Kafkaesque impression that the newly contrived "grand design" is not a design at all, that the proffered explanation of the government's external behaviour has essentially little to do with the behaviour itself, that the calculations came after, not before, the fact. While it would be unfair to advance this argument in so stark a guise with reference to the [1968-70] Canadian experiment, it bears reflection in any analysis of the significance of the review for the practical conduct of Canada's external affairs.

External Changes

The decision to conduct a thorough review of Canadian foreign and defence policy was taken in the first instance on the personal initiative of Prime Minister Trudeau, but it was related to fundamental changes in the international environment which had already come to the attention of the interested public. Some of these transformations challenged the premises of Canadian policy by appearing to diminish the government's capacity for performing its accepted roles in the international system. Others posed the issue of policy obsolescence more directly by casting doubt upon the accuracy and relevance of Canadian (and allied) perceptions of the conditions of contemporary international politics. In the first of these categories the most significant developments by far were, first, the final recovery of western Europe from the wreckage of World War II, and second, the emergence in the 1960s of a substantial array of new members of the international community. Taken together, these had the effect of reducing Canada's relative political influence in the very contexts that had hitherto provided the most hospitable arenas for the pursuit of Canadian diplomacy—namely, the NATO alliance and the United Nations.

The North Atlantic alliance had been regarded in Canada from the beginning in terms which were as much political as military. In 1948-49, when the organization was first created, the Soviet threat to western Europe was seen to derive more from the strength of indigenous communist movements in France, Italy and elsewhere than from the possibility of a direct Soviet attack, and initially the government in Ottawa did not assume that NATO membership would imply more than nominal increases in Canadian military expenditures. The essential purposes of the alliance from the Canadian point of view were, first, to acquire through co-operation with like-minded governments overseas the economies in defence spending and other advantages that would ensue from an efficient co-ordination of military effort; second, to strengthen the confidence and will of the western Europeans in confronting the challenge of "communism" both at home and abroad; third, to establish a vehicle for consultation and collective action in other potential areas of mutually beneficial endeavour; and fourth, to provide an organizational environment within which Canada's relations with the United States could be placed on a multilateral basis. It was a reflection of Ottawa's view of the matter that Article II of the NATO treaty, which obligates the signatories to strengthen "their free institutions" and "encourage economic collaboration," was in-

serted only under strong Canadian pressure. By the early 1950s the notion of a North Atlantic "community" of broadly co-operating powers had become part of the central rhetoric of Canadian foreign policy.

The outbreak in June 1950 of the Korean War, however, generated new and more alarming perceptions of the Soviet threat, and this naturally led to a heavy round of western military expenditures. From 1951 to 1953 Canada ranked fourth among the NATO allies—after the United States, Britain and France—in terms of per cent of GNP expended on defence. But 1953 was the post-war peak.[4] As the European powers recovered their strength, and as the cost of modern weapons technology began to outstrip the capacities of the Canadian defence budget, the military importance of Canada's alliance contribution diminished before long to marginal significance. By the late 1950s, moreover, the spirit of Article II had been exposed as a hopeless aspiration. Under these circumstances the government was compelled to articulate a new set of political justifications for its NATO policies. It was argued that Canada's participation provided access to sophisticated technology and intelligence data; that it purchased admission to advantageous weapons manufacturing and procurement arrangements; that it offered otherwise unattainable opportunities for the training of the Canadian armed forces; that it promoted Canadian diplomatic influence not only in the councils of the alliance itself, but among decision-makers in Washington and other capitals abroad; that it continued to fortify the morale of the Europeans and in particular made it easier for European statesmen to ward off the anti-NATO criticisms of their more sceptical domestic constituents; and more recently, that it contributed to the potential strength of western bargainers in approaching the

Soviet Union with a view to securing a mutual and balanced reduction of forces.

The difficulty with these arguments was that the very factor that made them essential as a rationale for existing Canadian policy—namely, the relative insignificance of the Canadian military contribution—also damaged their credibility in the eyes of the government's critics. Given the modesty of the Canadian military dues, was it reasonable to expect so bountiful a collection of advantages in return? Since there was no decisive way of settling such a question, the doubts expressed by opponents of the government's policies tended to persist.

The proliferation of independent states in the "third world" had similar implications for Canada in the United Nations, and to a lesser extent in the Commonwealth. The Canadians, like the Australians, had attempted at the San Francisco Conference in 1945 to secure alterations in the Dumbarton Oaks proposals which—by strengthening the General Assembly, the Economic and Social Council, and the Secretariat, and by reducing to some extent the privileges of the great powers in the Security Council—would have enhanced the role and influence in the organization of powers of the "middle" rank.[5] By placing considerable rhetorical stress on the "functional" aspects of United Nations activities, the Canadian Prime Minister, Mackenzie King, originally intended to ensure that the responsibilities of individual members would be related directly to their respective capabilities and interests. From the beginning it was hoped that the organization would provide an area within which the international behaviour of the larger states would be constrained by the free play of multilateral influences. In such a context, Canada, as the largest of the middle powers, might be expected to assume a leading role. In this way the maximum advantage could be drawn from the happy coincidence between the interests of Canada in a secure and peaceful international environment, and the fundamental purposes of the United Nations Charter.

This perception of the Canadian role subsequently achieved its purest fulfilment in the diplomacy of the Korean War, in which Canadian policy-makers aligned themselves in diplomatic combination with the representatives of other powers in constraint of the United States, but it was evident in a number of other contexts as well. Its viability depended, however, on the character of the issues that were brought before the organization, and on the susceptibility of the membership to the pragmatic, problem-solving approach to international conflict resolution which was (and still is) so typical of Canadian diplomatic practice.[6] Both these conditions were weakened by the dramatic increases in United Nations membership in the 1960s, which had the effect not merely of modifying the *style* of UN diplomacy, but also of shifting the substantive emphasis of the proceedings away from "east-west" politico-security issues to "north-south" socioeconomic issues. From the Canadian point of view, the General Assembly was thus converted from a place of diplomatic opportunity to a source of insistent, and sometimes embarrassing demands (as on the question of southern Africa). Certainly it was no longer a gathering that could readily be mobilized in subtle constraint of the United States. The issues were now too alien, the style too raucous, the Americans to indifferent, and the Canadians too powerless.

In some degree the same sort of pattern has been evident in the Commonwealth, although here it has less significance because the Commonwealth, as an institution, is less a vehicle for the making of decisions than an arena for quiet "exchanges of views." The attempts, moreover, of some of its newer members to revise and expand its role have not been received with great enthusiasm in Ottawa. As the British connection grows more faint, as the problem of French-English relations within Canada becomes more severe, and as the Commonwealth itself acquires a more varied (and less interdependent) membership, the interest in its affairs of even the most attentive of Canadian foreign policy publics seems gradually but inexorably to fade.

A third very obvious, if incomplete, transformation in world affairs has posed in recent years a more direct challenge to the orientation of post-war Canadian foreign policy by casting doubt upon one of its central premises. This is the assumption that the USSR is a "revisionist" power—predatory, aggressive, ready to take acquisitive advantage of any western display of irresolution or impotence. To challenge this assumption is potentially to challenge one of the most vital foundations of Canada's role in the international system. The NATO alliance, for example, might well reflect a community of needs and interests extending beyond the primitive requirements of collective defence (although the point is contentious), but its structure and purposes are predicated nonetheless on the assumed hostile intent of the Soviet Union. The same preoccupation underlies Canada's participation in American arrangements for North American defence (notably the North American Air Defence Command, or NORAD), the "western" orientation of Canadian voting patterns in the United Nations, and a host of other foreign policy linkages. The increasing evidence of "pluralism" within the Soviet *bloc*, therefore, together with the general development of east-west *détente*, served in the 1960s to reinforce the argument that Canada's external relationships were in need of an overhaul. The merits of this view were weakened, for some, by the Soviet intervention in Czechoslovakia in 1968, but the setback was only temporary and the view that the government ought to reflect upon the possibility of expanding its involvements with states outside the western world therefore continued to be heard.

Throughout the entire period, the constant (and growing) reality of Canada's external environment was of course the looming presence of the United States. More than any other single factor, this determined the parameters of Canadian foreign policy. In virtually every sector of Canadian life—capital investment, imports, exports, industrial management, mass media, cultural affairs, consumer habits, education, technological development, travel, natural resources—the level of American penetration is always in evidence, and sometimes dominant. The range of Canadian options in external affairs is consequently limited not merely by the explicit machinations of the American policy community (both actual and anticipated), but by subtle processes of integration which affect the values and perceptions of Canadian publics and policy-makers, and the structure and substance of their politics. The increasing awareness of the scope and intensity of these influences has generated in recent years a national "independence" debate of considerable political importance, and the protagonists on either side have tended accordingly to evaluate the practices of Canadian diplomacy in terms of their real and/or symbolic significance for this overriding issue.[7] Ironically, the drive for a re-examination of Canada's role in external affairs was in this way rooted ultimately in the need to reconsider the character of the American connection—"ironically," because this was the one major area of foreign policy that was neglected in the official review.

Internal Pressures

To observe, however, that changes in the external environment had raised the possibility of dysfunctional obsolescence in Canadian foreign policy is not sufficient in itself to explain the government's initiative. The casual chain must have domestic links. For a Canadian academic, it is naturally tempting to conclude that the most significant domestic input came from the small community of foreign and defence policy specialists housed in the universities, and indeed a superficial examination of the evidence would lend impressive support to such a thesis. The number of policy-oriented books and articles published in Canada on subjects related to external affairs accelerated rapidly in the 1960s, and most of them were composed by university faculty.[8] Academic "experts" were frequently invited (if they did not volunteer) to offer briefs to the appropriate Standing Committees of the House of Commons and the Senate, and the views of many were expressed on repeated occasions in the mass media, in the conferences and publications of the Canadian Institute of International Affairs, and in policy-development sessions organized by the major political parties. Most, although by no means all, of this input was critical of the *status quo*. The bulk of the arguments centred on four interrelated advocacies: (1) greater independence from the United States in the general conduct of foreign policy: (2) a reduction in the Canadian contribution to, and even complete withdrawal from, the North Atlantic alliance (an argument sometimes extended to include NORAD); (3) more extensive involvement in the problems of the "third world," and an expansion in particular of the government's external aid programme; and (4) a liberalization of the practices of so-called "quiet diplomacy." Some of these themes were taken up in varying degrees by the news media and other "leaders of opinion," but the academic ingredient was sufficiently dominant to lead in 1967 to the creation within the Department of External Affairs of a section devoted solely to "Academic Relations"—a signal flattery afforded to no other private domestic interest.

But it is easy in politics to make too much of what is merely most visible. As a group, the academic specialists may well have contributed to the growth of a general sense of dissatisfaction with existing policy, and it is conceivable that some, at least, of Canada's professional foreign service officers were mildly distressed by the alienation of so many of their more sophisticated domestic constituents. Academics, however, wield few votes, and while they may occasionally influence the opinions of their countrymen, it is not the normal habit of Canadian electors at large to govern their peacetime politics by the distant vagaries of foreign affairs. Hence, while the professorial critics were joined in their assault by the editors of a number of major newspapers and periodicals, and by prominent members of the three largest political parties, it is difficult to quarrel with Professor Peyton Lyon's observation that "the Trudeau government could certainly have persisted with prevailing policies had it wished to do so."[9]

If in fact the Prime Minister had decided on such a course, he would have received great encouragement from the permanent civil service, where there was a predictable distrust of radical change. A three-month review of foreign and defence policy conducted within the Department of External Affairs at the request of Prime Minister Pearson in the autumn and winter of 1967-68 had produced a classified report which recommended in effect that existing postures be continued without serious alteration, and that an attempt be made to propagate at home an awareness of the limitations of Canadian capabilities.[10] This tendency to defend the *status quo* was later evident also in the early phases of the Trudeau review, and it was not until the summer of 1969 that the Department's senior officials began to realize that their conservatism was weakening their credibility with the political leadership.

The Role of the Prime Minister

In the end, therefore, it was the Prime Minister himself who triggered the review. His May 1968 announcement began by paying tribute to the record of his predecessor, Mr. Pearson, but it went on to observe that a re-assessment had become necessary "because of the changing nature of Canada and of the world around us." The recovery of Europe, the emergence of the "third world," the growth of pluralism among the Communist powers and of *détente* in east-west relations, the increasingly evident problems of the developing countries, the isolation of the People's Republic of China—and all suggested the need for "a thorough and comprehensive review." The government's approach would be "pragmatic and realistic." In its examination of Canada's fundamental interests and capabilities, it would "take a hard look" at the Canadian role in NATO and NORAD. At the same time, it would consider ways of joining with the Europeans "in new forms of partnership and co-operation in order to strengthen international security, to promote economic stability on both sides of the Atlantic and in other regions of the world, [and] to balance our own relations in the Western Hemisphere." It had also "a major aim of maintaining mutual confidence and respect in our relations with the United States...without diminishing our Canadian identity and sovereign independence." An attempt would be made "to explore new avenues of increasing our political and economic relations with Latin America," and to consider ways of expanding the impact of Canadian aid programmes in the developing countries generally. The government would continue its support for the United Nations and its agencies, but some benefit might be derived from an (undefined) "shift of emphasis." It would seek also "to recognize the People's Republic of China Government as soon as possible and to enable that government to occupy the seat of China in the United Nations, taking into account that there is a separate government in Taiwan." Throughout, it would be looking "systematically, realistically, pragmatically" for "new approaches, new methods, new opportunities."[11]

It is important for an accurate understanding of the real functions of the review to recognize that while the Prime Minister's statement was intended as an announcement of an exercise that had only just begun, it actually contained the essence of the substantive decisions that were ultimately to emerge. The recognition of the regime in Peking; the government's subsequent support for the admission of mainland China to the United Nations; the partial withdrawal of Canadian military forces from Europe; the modest expansion of the external aid programme; the careful deflation of expectations that Canada would continue to play a major role in the *politiques de grandeur* of the United Nations; the concentration on the functional and technical aspects of international co-operation; the attempt to cultivate a new and more amicable relationship with the USSR; the ill-defined pursuit of expanded relations with the countries of Latin America, Europe, and the Pacific—all of these developments were expressed or implied in Mr. Trudeau's declaration. The ensuing official review eventually provided a generalized rationale for these initiatives, and it performed the ancillary functions of encouraging public debate, promoting (on a somewhat abstract level) the participation of other ministers in the making of foreign policy, and disturbing the tranquil complacency of the Departments of External Affairs and National Defence, but in itself it did not lead to the making of new decisions. In the end these came from the Office of the Prime Minister.

Nowhere was this illustrated with more dramatic effect than in the context of the review of Canada's relations with NATO. Under pressure not to leave its allies too long in doubt, the government was compelled in this area to accelerate the policy process. By March 1969 it had before it not merely the observations of academics and others who had seized an opportunity to express their views, but also three documents. The first was a 400-page report from an inter-departmental Special Task Force on Relations with Europe (STAFFEUR). Although acknowledging that alterations in Canada's commitment to the alliance might have to be considered when existing stores of military equipment became obsolete, it apparently recommended that no changes be introduced for the time being.[12] The second was a shorter report developed jointly by the Departments of External Affairs and National Defence. Its conclusions were virtually identical with those of STAFFEUR. The third was a hastily assembled report from the House of Commons Standing Committee on External Affairs and National Defence. It concluded that Canada's current role in NATO should be maintained "at least until such time as the main items of equipment for its Air Division and Mechanized Brigade require replacement." The Committee considered, however, that the matter should be "kept under periodic review."[13]

There was small comfort here for the supporters of innovation. What was obviously required was a report from someone who knew what the Prime Minister wanted. Mr. Trudeau's special assistant, Ivan Head, was assigned the task, and after a few days of secret labour with an informal committee, he produced a document entitled, "Canadian Defence Policy—A Study," in time for a Cabinet meeting on March 29. Neither the Secretary of State for External Affairs nor the Minister of National Defence, much less their bureaucracies, knew of its existence for more than a few hours before it became the focus of the Cabinet's deliberations.[14]

It soon became the basis of its decisions. On April 3 the Prime Minister announced that while the government had "rejected any suggestion that Canada assume a non-aligned or neutral role in world affairs," it intended "to take early steps to bring about a planned and phased reduction of the size of the Canadian forces in Europe." More generally, Canadian defence priorities were to be re-ordered in such a way as to give special emphasis to the protection of the home front. The designated functions of the military establishment were, first, "the surveillance of our own territory and coastlines"—i.e., the protection of our sovereignty; second, "the defence of North America in co-operation with United States forces"; third, "the fulfilment of such NATO commitments as may be agreed upon"; and fourth, "the performance of such international peace-keeping roles as we may, from time to time, assume."[15]

The practical implications of this announcement were at first obscure, but not for long. In June, the Cabinet imposed a three-year freeze on defence expenditures, with an annual ceiling, later slightly relaxed, of $1,815 millions. In September, it announced the redeployment and reduction by half of Canadian forces in Europe, the decommissioning of the country's only aircraft carrier, the phasing out in the early 1970s of the bulk of Canada's participation in the manning of nuclear weapons, and a substantial lowering of manpower levels in the active forces and reserves.

These could hardly be described as radical shifts of policy. Even in the slightly elaborated form in which they reappeared in the defence "white paper" of August 1971,[16] they suggested little more than a compromise between the major opposing positions, governed as much by considerations relating to the drive for economy in government spending as by new principles of foreign policy behaviour. In effect, at a time of European prosperity and international *détente* the bureaucracy was unable to convince a sceptical political leadership that the maintenance of a relatively expensive military establishment overseas offered significant advantages in return.[17] In these circumstances it could be argued that security begins at home (where it is cheaper), and that linkages with foreign powers can be pursued with greater profit by other means.

From the vantage point of the career civil servants the truly alarming feature of these announcements was not so much their substance, but the extent to which they revealed an erosion of the bureaucracy's influence. The contributions of the "professionals" to the NATO review had been peremptorily dismissed as the unimaginative outpouring of an inflexible machine, and replaced almost casually by inputs solicited from the Prime Minister's personal staff. As it happened, the foreign service was already under heavy attack. The Department of External Affairs not long before had been ordered to reduce its annual expenditures by $7,500,000, a cut of 13 per cent, and to provide convincing justifications, on a cost-benefit basis, of those that remained. In addition, several of the papers which it had drafted in other areas of the policy review were being criticized in the Cabinet for their failure to deal with fundamental assumptions.[18] With this mounting evidence of their vulnerability before them, they quickly moved to recover the initiative. The result was the creation of a Policy Analysis Group, responsible through its Chairman directly to the Under-Secretary of State for External Affairs. It was charged with the overall management of the review in general, and with the compilation of a "conceptual" paper on Canadian foreign policy in particular. The latter was to be written with the rhetoric and predispositions of the Prime Minister specifically in mind.[19]

The ultimate result was the publication on June 25, 1970, of *Foreign Policy for Canadians*, a "white paper" consisting of six brightly produced pamphlets ranging from 21 to 42 pages in length. The first—and longest—dealt with Canadian foreign policy in general. The other five were devoted to specific subjects (the United Nations, International Development) or to geographical areas (Europe, Latin America, the Pacific). Except for one or two passing references, Canada's relations with the United States were not explicitly considered—presumably because they were sufficiently important to be politically contentious.[20]

The White Paper

This last observation reflects the basic inadequacy of the white paper, which is its unrelieved commitment to innocuous generalities. Doubtless this results in part from its being a public document, but it derives also from the government's insistence upon dealing in terms of "fundamentals." For in the conduct of foreign policy, first premises often have little useful meaning; it is their implementation that counts. The difficulty is illustrated most dramatically in the first of the six pamphlets, which begins with an argument to the effect that the pursuit of external affairs "should be directly related to national policies pursued within Canada, and serve the same objectives," and proceeds from there to a definition of Canada's "national aims." There are said to be three: "that Canada will continue secure as an independent political entity": "that Canada and all Canadians will enjoy enlarging prosperity in the widest possible sense"; and "that all Canadians will see in the life they have and the contribution they make to humanity something worthwhile preserving in identity and purpose." The national aims are naturally pursued by "national policy," of which foreign policy is both an extension and a part. Canada's national policy is said to have "six main themes"—namely, fostering economic growth, safeguarding sovereignty and independence, working for peace and security, promoting social justice, enhancing the quality of life, and ensuring a harmonious natural environment. "The shape of foreign policy at any given time," the paper argues, "will be determined by the pattern of emphasis which the Government gives to the six policy themes. It is shaped as well by the constraints of the prevailing situation, at home and abroad, and inevitably by the resources available to the Government at any given time." Since in any specific situation it may not be possible to pursue all six of the objectives at once, "hard choices" and "trade-offs" are often involved in the making of decisions.[21]

In some respects this was an ingenious compilation, and it reflected careful attention to some of the Prime Minister's most familiar rhetoric (the concept of "social justice," for example, appears to have been derived from Mr. Trudeau's electoral commitment to the pursuit of what he calls "the just society"). The distinction, however, between the three "national aims" and the six "policy themes" was subsequently the source of considerable confusion among both politicians and publics alike, and it seems improbable that the general pamphlet performed the "educative" function for which it was partly designed. More seriously, the paper's opening generalities, while in some sense "true," were also unhelpful and distracting because they failed to provide clear indicators of the government's intentions. Later in the pamphlet there is a statement to the effect that of the six policy themes, economic growth, social justice, and quality of life would have the highest priority, and throughout there are comments suggesting that in the light of altered conditions at home and abroad, the government would concentrate to a greater extent than before on the pursuit of more narrowly conceived "national interests." Except, however, by reference to decisions that had already been taken (for example, the reduction of Canadian forces assigned to NATO, and the initiation of negotiations leading to the establishment of diplomatic relations with the government in Peking), the precise implications of these changes in emphasis were not further defined. The critics of the review were therefore compelled to deal in generalities also.[22]

The five "sector" papers added flesh to the bones, but not in large quantities. The European pamphlet, for example, placed heavy emphasis on the need "to strengthen...ties with Europe, not as an anti-American measure but to create a more healthy balance within the North Atlantic community and to reinforce Canadian independence."[23] In the context of considerable Canadian alarm over the development of the EEC and other regional trading blocs, the paper focused on the advantages that would ensue from an expansion of economic relations and from an increase in co-operative exchanges in the fields of science, technology, and cultural affairs. The previously announced decisions with regard to NATO were simply reaffirmed.

Similar reflections, based in large degree on the case for a diversification of Canada's linkages abroad as a way of offsetting the preponderant influence of the United States, were offered in support of the objective of strengthening relations with Latin America and the Pacific, although the means of doing so were given little more than general definition. The Latin American paper indicated that the government had reconsidered the perennial question of whether Canada should join the OAS, but for the time being it had decided not to do so on the ground that it would diminish the flexibility of Canadian policy without generating a significant advantage in return. In the Pacific, the major development was the approach to Peking, but of course this had been initiated very early in the Trudeau administration. At the same time, the pamphlet on International Development announced a modest increase in the size of the government's development assistance programme and the partial removal of a number of procurement and other "strings." It also indicated that a somewhat larger proportion of the total aid budget than before would be distributed through multilateral agencies.

In a review which ultimately amounted more to flavour than substance, however, perhaps the most revealing paper was the pamphlet on the United Nations. The fundamental theme of the entire review was the need to bring Canadian aspirations in foreign affairs more nearly in line with the country's eroded capabilities. "What Canada can hope to accomplish in the world," the general paper argued, "must be viewed not only in the light of Canadian aspirations, needs and wants but in terms of what is, from time to time, attainable." In the context of "a rapidly evolving world situation," it was "a risky business to postulate or predict any specific role," and it was "even riskier—certainly misleading—to base foreign policy on an assumption that Canada can be cast as the 'helpful fixer' in international affairs."[24] The Canadian people, in sum, ought not to expect their government's mediatory enterprises in the high diplomacy of "power politics"—as in Korea, Suez, the Congo, Cyprus, and elsewhere— to persist indefinitely and by self-appointment in the international community of the 1970s.[25] Foreign policy ought to relate in any case to domestic needs, and under contemporary conditions these pointed to the performance of important, if inglorious, new tasks—tasks associated above all with economic growth, social justice, and quality of life.

The natural result in the context of the paper on the United Nations was a reversion to the functionalism of Mackenzie King (although the departed Prime Minister was not invoked in its defence). With a slight touch of melancholy, the paper observed that while the UN originally had "51 members, mostly Western European, Latin American and Asian," there were now (Spring 1970) 126. "The African, Asian, and Latin American representatives, if they join forces, have a commanding majority. Canada, as one of the 22 Western nations, thus finds itself coping with the problem of being one of a permanent minority." The dominant coalition, while divided on many issues, was "united in a pre-eminent aim to overcome the problems of under-development, in opposition to the residue of colonialism, and in the desire to avoid involvement in East-West differences." The latter in the meantime had been profoundly affected by further developments in weapons technology, which made it "virtually impossible" for the super-powers "to contemplate general or total war." There was still the danger of war by miscalculation or as a result of outbreaks in the Middle East and other peripheral areas, but the great powers had shown themselves to be acutely aware of the problem and they had tended to deal with it on a bilateral basis. It was true that in the past the Security Council sometimes had been called upon to act in constraint of local disturbances, but the most probable forms of conflict in the future—"civil strife, indirect aggression, guerilla warfare supported by liberation movements"—did "not readily lend themselves to UN intervention." Henceforth, peacekeeping demands on the UN would therefore "take the form mainly of requests for the establishment of military observer missions." Under these circumstances Canada would continue to support the development of peacekeeping procedures, although the government's response to specific requests would "be decided in each instance in the light of its assessment of whether the UN can play a useful role"[26]—a qualification rooted in the unsettling history of the operations in Suez, the Congo, and Cyprus.

With the prospects for future enterprises in UN peacekeeping thus diminished, the paper could concentrate on less glamorous issues: contributing to social and economic development; working to stop the arms race; taking measures to prevent further deterioration in the human environment; promoting international co-operation

in the peaceful uses of satellite systems; promoting international co-operation in the use of the seabed beyond the limits of national jurisdiction; promoting observance of human rights, including adherence to and respect for various United Nations conventions; contributing to the progressive development and codification of international law; and contributing to the institutional development of the United Nations as a centre for harmonizing the actions of nations. These tasks, the paper observed, "give maximum opportunity to Canada for self-realization in terms of Canadian resources and capabilities."[27] Perhaps so, but the list suggests nonetheless a workman's view of world affairs. In place of the heady politics of peace and security, there is the quiet pursuit of "an equitable use of the radio-frequency spectrum for all space communications and an adequately-planned means of ensuring the fair sharing of synchronous orbit positions."[28] Mackenzie King would have rejoiced.

The Paper's Critics

Once published, the white paper was inevitably subjected to heavy attack. Those who had been content with the practices of "Pearsonian" diplomacy complained that the review had gone much too far in redefining the parameters of Canada's role in the international system. Those, on the other hand, who had been critical of existing preoccupations and alignments considered that it had not gone far enough. For others, the complaint was that the paper as a whole had no substance, and hence could not be taken seriously. Still others, who were prepared to accept the paper at face value and to deal with it in its own terms, commented, variously, that it revealed an excessively self-seeking preoccupation with the pursuit of parochial national interests, and a dispiriting indifference to the wider problems of the international community; that by giving so much emphasis to economic growth, it displayed an avaricious attachment to the ignoble fruits of commerce; that its de-emphasis of peace-keeping and the general diplomacy of conflict resolution was morally reprehensible and based in any case on an exaggerated view of the decline in Canada's diplomatic currency, that its analysis of the possibilities for diversification of Canadian contacts in Latin America, the Pacific and elsewhere was too optimistic (or too pessimistic); and so on. Yet another battery of complaints centred on particular issues: the changes in the external aid programme were insufficient, the decision not to initiate aggressive economic and diplomatic action against South Africa was neither ethical nor prudent; the failure to apply for membership in the Organization of American States reflected an inaccurate perception of Canadian interests in the western hemisphere. Above all, there was the recurrent charge that the government had failed to deal explicitly with the vital problem of Canada's relations with the United States.

The underlying premise of much of this comment was that the principal function of the white paper was (or should have been) to provide a blueprint or "grand design" for the present and future construction of Canadian foreign policy. The difficulty is that in the real world of foreign policy there is little room for grand designs—at least for countries like Canada, which are relatively small, are basically in pursuit of the peaceful maintenance of the *status quo*, and are governed by a liberal pluralist conception of politics. In this sort of context the practice of foreign policy- makers is to react to new problems and changing circumstances incrementally, treating each case on its own merits, and with reference to

functional criteria. Pragmatists, not visionaries, populate the Canadian foreign policy community. To ask them to rationalize their pragmatism is to invite a response which concentrates on methods rather than on substance (hence the prolonged debate in Canada on the merits of "quiet diplomacy"), or alternatively indulges in the most innocuous of generalities (hence the "conceptual framework" of the foreign policy review).

To repeat, the white paper does in fact suggest a change of emphasis. The alteration is rooted, however, not in the emergence of new values or goals, but in an empirical analysis of changes in the external environment. On the basis of such an evaluation, to de-emphasize (for example) Canada's role as a mediator in the resolution of international conflicts does not necessarily imply that the government will in fact "mediate" any less readily should an appropriate opportunity arise.[29] It merely means that the policy-makers believe such opportunities will in future be rare. Similarly, to exchange diplomatic representatives with the government in Peking signifies not a fundamental re-orientation of Canadian external relations, but a simple calculation that under contemporary conditions of relaxing Sino-American tensions, the benefits of recognition at last outweigh the costs. Again, to treat with the Soviet Union on economic, scientific and other issues represents not an alteration in Canadian alignments abroad, but the pursuit of a functional advantage that has been made more feasible by the progress of *détente*. The real transformations are thus in the international community, not in the domestic actor, and one is left at the end with the uneasy reflection that—minor differences in timing aside—the policy outputs would have been the same had Mr Pearson remained in office, and had the review never been held.

NOTES

1. Thordarson, Bruce, *Trudeau and Foreign Policy: A Study in Decision Making*, Oxford University Press, Toronto, 1972, p. 124.

2. Canadian Institute of International Affairs, *Annual Report, 1968-1969* and *1969-1970*. Of the four conferences, the Secretary of State for External Affairs, Mitchell Sharp, attended three.

3. Thordarson, *op. cit.*: D. C. Thomson and R. F. Swanson, *Canadian Foreign Policy: Options and Perspectives*, McGraw-Hill Ryerson, Toronto, 1971; and Peter C. Dobell, *Canada's Search for New Roles: Foreign Policy in the Trudeau Era*, O.U.P. for the Royal Institute of International Affairs, London, 1972. The Thordarson volume is a study of the review itself; the other two were largely stimulated by the review and make frequent reference to it, but they are also intended to perform more broadly as general introductions to Canada's external relations.

4. Canadian defence estimates show a total of $1,942.7 millions, indicating that the 1953 figure of $1,907 millions will be exceeded in absolute terms for the first time in 1972-1973. In real terms, however, and as a per cent of GNP, the figure is much smaller. See Department of National Defence, *Defence 1971*, Information Canada, Ottawa, 1972, p. 7.

5. For the fullest account to date, see Soward, F. H., and McInnis, Edgar, *Canada and the United Nations*, Carnegie Endowment, New York, 1956.

6. It has often been argued that the pluralistic pragmatism which appears to be characteristic of Canadian diplomacy is a product of domestic political culture. See, for example, McNaught, Kenneth, "Ottawa and Washington Look at the UN," *Foreign Affairs*, Vol. XXXIII, No. 4, July 1955, pp. 663-678; and Hockin, Thomas. "Federalist Style in International Politics," in Clarkson, Stephen, ed. *An Independent Foreign Policy for Canada?* McClelland and Stewart, Toronto, 1968, pp. 119-130.

7. Unfortunately for the decisive resolution of the issue, much of the evidence can be taken as "proof" of either position. Participation in NATO and NORAD, for example, can be seen on the one hand as an indicator of abject neo-colonialism, and on the other as an effective means of amplifying Canadian influence over American policy-makers. For statements of the former view, see many of the articles in Clarkson, *op. cit.* The most lucidly presented case for the other side is in Lyon, Peyton V., *The Policy Question: A Critical Appraisal of Canada's Role in World Affairs*, McClelland and Stewart, Toronto, 1963.

8. For a brief overview of book-length titles, see Stairs, Denis, "Publics and Policy-Makers: The Domestic Environment of the Foreign Policy Community," *International Journal*, Vol. XXVI, No. 1, Winter 1970-71, pp. 229-232.

9. Lyon, Peyton V., "A Review of the Review," *Journal of Canadian Studies*, Vol. V. No. 2, May 1970, p. 35. This general perception of the limits of academic influence is shared by Harold von Riekhoff. See his "The Recent Evolution of Canadian Foreign Policy," *The Round Table*, No. 245, January 1972, p. 64.

10. Thordarson, pp. 26-27. Those responsible for the review felt that the prominent Canadian role in United Nations peacekeeping operations had unduly inflated the expectations and aspirations of the Canadian public.

11. Department of External Affairs, *Statements and Speeches*, No. 68/17.

12. Thordarson, p. 136; Lyon, "A Review of the Review," p. 37.

13. Canada, House of Commons, Standing Committee on External Affairs and National Defence, *Proceedings*, No. 35, *Including Fifth Report to the House*, Wednesday, March 26, 1969, pp. 14-15.

14. Thordarson, p. 137.

15. Department of External Affairs, *Statements and Speeches*, No. 69/7.

16. Macdonald, Donald S. Minister of National Defence, *Defence in the 70s*, Information Canada, Ottawa, 1971.

17. Evidence that Mr. Trudeau was asking probing questions can be found in an address which he delivered in Calgary on April 12, 1969 on "The Relation of Defence Policy to Foreign Policy." See Department of External Affairs, *Statements and Speeches*, No. 69/8.

18. Thordarson, p. 177.

19. *Ibid.*, pp. 179-180.

20. This omission was the cause later of much adverse comment. The government's reply was that Canada's relations with the United States were so pervasive that they could not be isolated for separate treatment. In this sense, the entire review was by implication a review of Canadian-American relations.

21. Sharp, Honourable Mitchell, *Foreign Policy for Canadians*, Queen's Printer, Ottawa, 1970, pp. 9, 10, 14, 17.

22. For a representative sample, see "Foreign Policy for Canadians: Comments on the White Paper", *Behind the Headlines*, Vol. XXIX, Nos. 7-8, August 1970.

23. *Foreign Policy for Canadians (Europe)*, p. 14.

24. *Foreign Policy for Canadians*, pp. 6, 8.

25. This tendency to dampen public expectations can be explained in part by the desire of policy-makers to ensure that their constituents would not measure their performance against unduly high criteria of achievement, and in part by the need to prevent the creation in the international community of an artificial image of Canadian knight errantry. Self-advertisement in such matters is counterproductive, and often disqualifies. As in the case of Mr. Trudeau at Singapore, however, mediatory roles are sometimes difficult to avoid.

26. *Foreign Policy for Canadians (United Nations)*, pp. 6-7, 17.

27. *Ibid.*, p. 10.

28. *Ibid.*, p. 23.

29. As the Singapore experience, again, demonstrates.

SUGGESTED READINGS

Canada, *Foreign Policy for Canadians*, Ottawa: Queen's Printer, 1970.

Dobell, Peter C., *Canada's Search for New Roles: Foreign Policy in the Trudeau Era*, Toronto: Oxford University Press, 1972.

Lyon, Peyton V., "The Trudeau Doctrine," *International Journal*, Vol. 26, No. 1, pp. 19-43 (1971).

Thordarson, Bruce, *Trudeau and Foreign Policy: A Study in Decision Making*, Toronto: Oxford University Press, 1972.

"Trudeau and Foreign Policy," *International Journal*, Vol. 33, No. 2, 1978, pp. 267-456.

Von Riekhoff, Harald, "The Recent Evolution of Canadian Foreign Policy," *The Round Table*, Vol. 62, No. 245-248, 1972, pp. 63-76.

c h a p t e r 13

PROTECTING THE CANADIAN ARCTIC: THE *MANHATTAN* VOYAGES, 1969-1970

John Kirton and Don Munton

On 8 April 1970 the government of Canada introduced into the House of Commons the Arctic Waters Pollution Prevention bill. Designed to prevent the pollution of waters adjacent to the mainland and islands of the Canadian Arctic, it asserted offshore jurisdiction within a 100-mile pollution prevention zone. An accompanying bill amended the Territorial Sea and Fishing Zones Act to authorize the establishment of new fishing zones in areas of the sea adjacent to the coast of Canada. The Canadian government was thereby empowered to establish control zones behind fisheries closing lines across the entrances to bodies of water requiring fisheries conservation and to which Canada had geographic, economic, and historic claims. In this bill, the government also replaced its existing three-mile territorial sea and nine-mile exclusive fishing zone with a twelve-mile territorial sea.

Together these measures represented a carefully constructed, three-tiered approach to protecting the sovereignty and marine environment of the Canadian Arctic. At the outer 100-mile perimeter the government asserted jurisdiction for the specific purpose of pollution control. Within the archipelago formed by the Arctic islands it strengthened its ability to secure jurisdiction for further purposes in the future. And in the vital core of the Northwest Passage, it enlarged Canadian control over the critical eastern and western gateways at Barrow and Prince of Wales straits, where the channels were less than 24 miles wide. With these moves the Canadian government effectively protected its fragile Arctic maritime environment from the ecological threats presented by the U.S. supertanker S/T *Manhattan* in its summer 1969 transit of the Passage and prospective voyage in the spring of 1970.

These bills also constituted one of the largest geographic extensions of the Canadian state's jurisdiction in the country's history. Moreover, by acting unilaterally, by exempting its pollution and fisheries measures from the compulsory jurisdiction of the International Court of Justice (ICJ), and by avoiding an American alternative plan for a multilateral conference on the Arctic environment, the Canadian government broke decisively with the liberal-internationalist traditions that had dominated Canadian foreign policy since the Second World War.

. . .

In its performance the Canadian government was far from the sluggish, passive, and timid entity portrayed in much of the existing literature on this case.[1] Rendering this portrait inaccurate, and the government's international success all the more remarkable, were the fundamental char-

Don Munton and John Kirton, "The Manhattan Voyages and Their Aftermath," from F. Griffiths (ed.), *Politics of the Northwest Passage*, Montreal, McGill-Queens University Press, 1987. Portions of the text hasve been deleted. Some footnotes have been removed; those remaining have been renumbered.

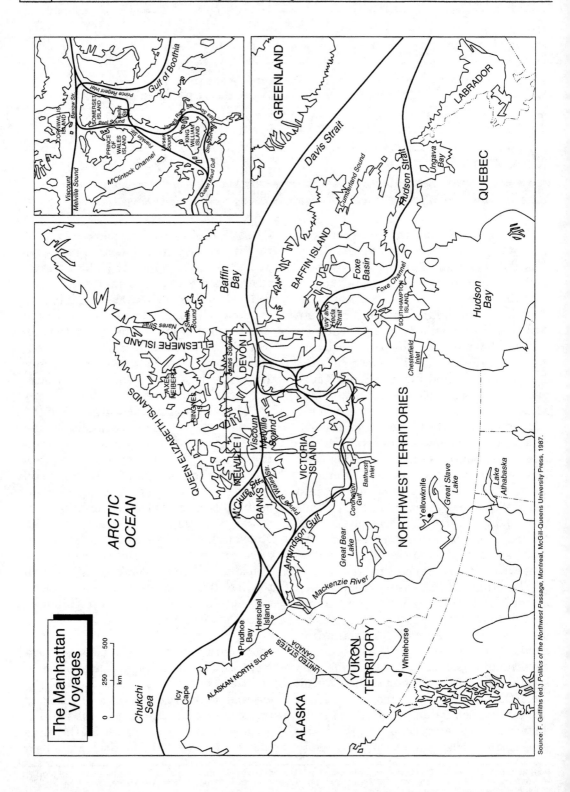

The Manhattan Voyages

Source: F. Griffiths (ed.) *Politics of the Northwest Passage*, Montreal, McGill-Queens University Press, 1987.

acter of the issues and the profound divisions existing within Ottawa over their resolution. These divisions reflected a basic ideological cleavage over principles central to Canada's national beliefs and its role in world affairs. This cleavage emerged and was resolved over a period of a year and a half, as a new dominant tendency in Canadian foreign policy evolved to replace the traditional liberal internationalism that had prevailed, largely without challenge, for decades.[2] Ultimately, the Arctic Waters Pollution Prevention Act and its supplementary legal reinforcements were the product of a strong Canadian state redefining its foreign policy to complement its emerging new position in the world.[3]

The Opening Gambit: October-December 1968

The 1968 discovery of commercially significant quantities of oil at Prudhoe Bay on the Alaskan North Slope led to intense study of the most cost-effective means of getting it to the lower 48 states. Various tanker and pipeline schemes were mooted, and in October 1968, Humble Oil, a private U.S. company acting on behalf of the giant multinational EXXON, announced that it would send a refitted tanker, the *Manhattan*, through Canada's portion of the Northwest Passage in the summer of 1969 to test its feasibility as a delivery route. The *Manhattan* left an eastern port on 25 August 1969, to begin its Arctic journey, and broke through to ice-free waters off northern Alaska on 14 September. It returned for a second voyage, confined to the area north of Baffin Island, in April-May 1970.

From the start, Humble's project presented Canada with both threats and opportunities. The *Manhattan*'s voyage might lead to regular commercial transits of the

Passage, thereby enhancing its status in law as an international strait (as the U.S. government argued it was), and increasing the chance of oil spills in the vulnerable Arctic environment. Yet it was more likely that the *Manhattan* experiment would show the Northwest Passage to be a poor transportation route, thereby sustaining Canada's case that the special ice-related qualities of the Passage gave it a different international legal status.[4] Moreover, by being prepared to notify Ottawa of the transit (even though this was not an established legal necessity), and by asking Ottawa for information on ice conditions, Humble seemed willing to recognize Canada's jurisdictional rights and operational position in the Passage. And because it was the beneficiary of a very small amount of U.S. government money for research to be conducted as part of the experiment, Humble's co-operation with Canada could be taken indirectly as recognition by the U.S. government of Canada's claims.

Moreover, the U.S. Coast Guard volunteered to let Canada help in the experiment, and, in keeping with past practice, informed its Canadian counterpart that it would send a ship to escort the *Manhattan*. But Washington refused to respond to a suggestion from Ottawa that the U.S. Coast Guard request permission to accompany the *Manhattan*.

Even before the first Prudhoe Bay discovery, the government's leading bureaucratic body for Arctic affairs, the Advisory Committee on Northern Development (ACND), was aware that intense oil exploration could be anticipated in northern waters, that Canadian control over foreign shipping was inadequate, that the U.S. Coast Guard had an interest in research on northern transportation, and that there were potential benefits for Canada of northern oil discoveries. By late November 1968 Department of Transportation (DOT) officials anticipated a possible U.S. request for a joint Canadian-U.S. development agency in the Arctic and searched for navigational safeguards to protect Canada's position.

Because pipelines, which had few implications for Canada's sovereignty, were the early favourites as the means of transportation, many in Ottawa shared the hope of the Department of Indian Affairs and Northern Development (DIAND) and EMR that the Prudhoe Bay discoveries would enhance Canada's northern economic development and balance-of-payments situation through increased Canadian oil exports to the United States by joint pipeline systems. No discrepant signals came from a new Prime Minister and Cabinet preoccupied with the far more direct and acute threat to Canadian sovereignty arising from Quebec's separatist efforts. Thus DEA's informal suggestion to Washington that the U.S. Coast Guard ask for permission to accompany the *Manhattan* was at most an attempt to further Canada's Arctic sovereignty claims without much ado, and at least a signal from the start that these claims would be firmly asserted in a new era of Arctic marine transportation.

Ottawa quickly followed with practical moves to facilitate the *Manhattan* experiment, ensure de facto Canadian sovereignty, and enlist co-operation from the United States. Ottawa decided to have DOT co-operate fully with the *Manhattan*'s voyage, to send the icebreaker *John A. Macdonald* to accompany it, and to suggest that icebreakers of both countries travel with the *Manhattan* in both Canadian and American waters. Simultaneously the government created a new internal body, the Task Force on Northern Development (TFNOD), to provide advice on the issues in a co-ordinated and comprehensive manner.

These decisions were catalysed by the U.S. failure to respond to Canada's informal suggestion of an official request for U.S.

icebreaker transit. Yet with the Canadian public still unaroused, Ottawa's decisions were largely defined by the perceptions of Canadian officials. These officials recognized that the United States was sensitive to restrictions on the mobility of its naval and commercial vessels and that Canada's international legal position on the Arctic was not widely supported. They further identified a possible danger to Canada's oil exports to the United States from the actual delivery of Alaskan supplies to the lower 48 states and from possible U.S. oil import restrictions in retaliation for a lack of Canadian co-operation in delivering U.S. supplies. Finally, they saw that U.S. interest in a special continental energy relationship with Canada might be used to maximize both Canada's oil export objectives and its sovereignty claims.

The policy of practical co-operation with the *Manhattan* voyage was thus designed to avoid or delay a major confrontation or even bilateral diplomatic talks with the United States over sovereignty, to reinforce Canadian claims to effective occupation of the Passage, and to solidify the support of the U.S. companies for Canada's regime. It also gave TFNOD time to define Canada's energy objectives and to construct an internationally defensible legal position. A desire to enhance Canadian economic development through practical co-operation with the United States, and to respect existing international law, dominated the government's thinking and appeared able to support Canada's particular sovereignty concerns.

Declaring Determination: January-May 1969

By the spring of 1969, however, Ottawa began publicly to signal its determination and to set its position on the sovereignty issue. Prime Minister Trudeau and Secretary of State for External Affairs Mitchell Sharp noted that Canada was discussing with other countries Canadian continental shelf rights and the possibility of straight baseline legislation, which would extend Canada's territorial waters outward from lines that ran from headland to headland, rather than following the sinuosities of the coastline. In early March the Prime Minister indicated that he had asked concerned departments to review Canada's international legal position on the Arctic waters, noting that the key issue was the distinction between a territorial and inland sea.[5] In March, he informed U.S. President Nixon of Canada's concern over territorial sea and fishing rights issues and his hope that Canada would take a position that would be respected by the entire international community. Further, he described Canadian oil as secure, continental oil and agreed to further discussions on a continental oil policy.

A much stronger emphasis on sovereignty appeared soon after. On 27 March the government announced a tour of the Arctic by Governor-General Roland Michener, to take place 22 April to 4 May. On 3 April, the Prime Minister presented Canada's new defence priorities, which emphasized surveillance of Canadian territory and coast lines and protection of its sovereignty.[6] On 22 April, the government introduced a bill to amend the Territorial Sea and Fishing Zones Act to allow all waters above the continental shelf to be declared fishing zones exclusively for Canadian fishermen (while respecting traditional rights). DIAND Minister Jean Chrétien further noted that drilling on Melville Island by government-controlled Panarctic Oil was being undertaken to show Canadian sovereignty in the Arctic.

Then, in a major speech on 15 May, the contents of which were delivered to the United States in a diplomatic note, the Prime Minister declared Canada's

sovereignty over the Arctic lands, its exclusive rights to the Arctic continental shelf, and its view that Arctic waters were national terrain. He added, however, that differences over the waters' status "should not be settled in an arbitrary way but in scrupulous respect of the established principles of international law."[7]

It was events abroad that had prompted Ottawa to begin devising a long-term Arctic policy. The frenzied pace of oil exploration in Alaska and the Canadian Arctic suggested that the *Manhattan*'s voyage could represent a real threat. Yet the creation by the U.S. government in February 1969 of a Task Force on Oil Policy to review the American oil import program indicated that Washington had still to determine how large a role expensive Arctic supplies would play in meeting U.S. energy needs. Moreover, discussions with Canada about a continental oil policy, continued at the official level on 12 April, held forth the promise of a non-confrontational solution. Washington's position on the sovereignty issue was also muted. In February, U.S. officials stated in Calgary that extension of Canadian territorial waters beyond the three-mile limit then accepted by Washington was not likely to be challenged. Moreover, both the United States and the Soviet Union appeared willing to engage in a broader effort to define further the law of the sea on a multilateral basis.

Domestically, however, significant pressures for an outright Canadian declaration of sovereignty were beginning to develop. Late February witnessed an article in the Toronto *Globe and Mail* that evoked public concern over northern sovereignty, worrying testimony before the House of Commons Standing Committee on External Affairs and National Defence (SCEAND), and complaints in the Commons. In the ensuing months Liberals were joined by Conservative and New Democrat MPs in the demand for a forthright declaration of sovereignty. In mid-March the government of Alberta and the Independent Petroleum Association demanded that Ottawa maintain U.S. market access for Albertan rather than Alaskan Arctic oil. By May, Arctic sovereignty had become the parliamentary cause célèbre. On 1 May, SCEAND announced that it was considering a review of the issue.

Despite rising public concern and the Cabinet's focus on the issue, the government remained largely free to shape the contents of the Prime Minister's 15 May statement. The statement was based on reviews, carried out primarily by TFNOD, of the legal status of the sea areas, of Canada's military presence in the north, and of the oil and gas situation. In March 1969, TFNOD's first memorandum to Cabinet "stressed the urgency of increased activities of the relevant departments to ensure 'effective occupation' of the high Arctic," rather than recommending a proclamation of sovereignty.[8] By late April recommendations had been made to Cabinet to upgrade the Canadian Rangers, while an interdepartmental study group of National Defence and other departments reviewed Canada's military presence in the north.

Narrowing Alternatives: June-October 1969

By early autumn the emphasis on sovereignty had intensified. In a June 1969 note to the United States, DEA highlighted the Prime Minister's views that Canadian jurisdiction was not affected by the *Manhattan* voyage, even as it warned that Canada "had inevitably the greatest interest in Arctic waters in the Northwest Passage given historic, geographic, climatic and economic factors."[9] At a joint Canadian-U.S. ministerial meeting in June, Canada

agreed to hold discussions with the United States before it made a definitive claim to sovereignty over Arctic waters. As September opened Trudeau was still stating that the *Manhattan*'s voyage was a positive development. On 11 September he promised a sovereignty statement and more precise acts during the current parliamentary session. He added that the impending statement would avoid a court challenge, undue offence to the United States, and a prolonged international legal battle. Given the evolution of international law, he argued, time was on Canada's side.

Yet a week later, a sharp shift in tone took place. On 18 September, four days after the *Manhattan* had made its way through the Passage, a *Globe and Mail* article by Mitchell Sharp declared: "Canada's sovereignty over Arctic waters is being steadily strengthened by developing concepts of international law and by our own activities."[10] Sharp argued that the extensive icebreaker support required for the *Manhattan* voyage demonstrated that the Passage was not an international strait. He concluded that "general principles of international law may have to be applied in a special way in the case of frozen waters" and that Canada had the best claim to contribute to the development of international law in this regard. Canada's Arctic waters were, however, open as a transportation route to all nations, for peaceful purposes, by suitable vessels "operating in accordance with minimum standards of safety."[11] On 6 October, Northern Development Minister Jean Chrétien indicated that the government was planning anti-pollution legislation for the Arctic. Minister of Transport Don Jamieson revealed that a federal task force was exploring the unification of civilian and military naval and air operations in the Arctic. Minister of Defence Léo Cadieux announced a distinctive defence role of surveillance of Canada's territory and coast lines, the creation of a task force to consider a headquarters for Mobile Command in the far north, and an increase in Arctic sovereignty patrols by long-range aircraft.

These developments were provoked in part by external pressures. In early June, a U.S. State Department official had described Canadian extension of its territorial sea and fishing rights as contrary to international law and a bad model for others. At bilateral talks later in the month between Alexis Johnson, the third-ranking official in the State Department, and Mitchell Sharp, there was wide disagreement over Canada's claims. The two sides agreed to meet in the autumn to consider Arctic waters issues and related matters before a definitive Canadian statement on sovereignty was made. The message was clear—Washington would resist Canada's sovereignty claims but was as anxious as Ottawa to avoid, or at least delay, a confrontation. This duality was still evident in late September. U.S. officials told visiting Canadian MPs that the United States held North America's Arctic waterways, including Prince of Wales Strait and Lancaster Sound, to be an international strait connecting high seas, that a Canadian claim would lead to a reference to the ICJ, and that the entire issue might best be resolved in a new international convention to extend coastal state authority for certain narrowly defined purposes. Such a convention might specify three maritime bands, with the third extending 50 miles from shore to meet coastal state responsibilites for navigational assistance and pollution control, but with the right of innocent passage preserved. By October it was clear that the U.S. Department of Defense would strenuously resist unilateral declarations that would establish precedents harmful to its strategic interests in Southeast Asian waters

(Indonesia and the Philippines) and in the Mediterranean and Middle East (the straits of Gibraltar and Hormuz). Canada's legitimate but subordinate pollution concerns in the Arctic could be taken care of by concerned international action, probably through the Intergovernmental Maritime Consultative Organization (IMCO).

If the U.S. government's statements provided no immediate need for bold Canadian action, the progress of the *Manhattan* did. In August and September the *Manhattan*, accompanied by the powerful Canadian icebreaker *John A. Macdonald* and the lighter U.S. Coast Guard icebreaker *Northwind*, steamed to and through the Northwest Passage, breaking into clear water on the western end on 14 September. There was much in the voyage that sustained Canada's jurisdictional case. The tendency of the two U.S. ships to get stopped in ice and to rely on Canadian support showed that the Passage was not like the high seas and that Canada's presence was essential to successful transit. Moreover, a weather-induced shift in the *Manhattan*'s route from the broad but ice-infested M'Clure Strait to the more hospitable but much narrower Prince of Wales Strait indicated that a commercial waterway would probably have to include sea lanes less than 24 miles across, which Canada could claim as territorial waters. Finally, the damage done to the U.S. ships and their reluctance to test the polar ice pack on the return voyage demonstrated just how difficult routine commercial transportation would be.

This damage also showed how severe might be the threat of oil pollution, in the highly vulnerable Arctic environment, should tanker traffic become frequent. And Humble spokesmen were suggesting it would. By early September, it was rumoured that Humble, Arco, and British

Petroleum were each preparing tankers for Arctic oil transportation and that the *Manhattan* would probably return to the Arctic between March and May 1970. On 13 September, Humble declared its $39 million *Manhattan* experiment a success in proving the feasibility of commercial shipping through the Northwest Passage and announced its calculation that tanker transport would be 60 cents per barrel less expensive than pipeline alternatives. At the same time, Humble officials continued to participate in the Mackenzie Valley Pipeline study, explore tanker submarine designs, and look at the Trans-Alaskan Pipeline System (TAPS), which would start snaking across Alaska that winter if U.S. government permission were given. Moreover, in early September Humble indicated that it would accept Canadian standards for vessel construction and manoeuvrability.

Other international developments were also encouraging to Canada. The Soviet Union tacitly signalled its support for Canada's efforts to enhance coastal state control of Arctic waters. Other states and Canada discussed convening another law of the sea conference to deal with fishing zones and territorial waters. And by September Canada was also securing signs of interest in a United Nations system of marine pollution control.

Within Canada, however, pressures to act unilaterally were becoming sharper. During the summer, opposition leaders continued to demand an immediate, forthright declaration of Arctic waters as internal waters subject to Canadian sovereignty. By September Toronto's *Globe and Mail*, *Telegram*, and *Star* all editorially demanded a declaration of sovereignty. Former Prime Minister Lester Pearson suggested an assertion of Canadian sovereignty to keep the north nuclear-free. Public ap-

prehension had been fuelled in August, when two supply barges were sunk in the Arctic, raising the spectre of a pollution disaster. And in early September, after an "inspection tour" of the *Manhattan* by 11 of its members, the chairman of the House of Commons Standing Committee on Indian Affairs and Northern Development (SCIAND), Ian Watson, demanded measures "to assert sovereignty over these waters for pollution control and navigation control," given the imminent use of the Passage for shipping.[12]

External Affairs legal officers had, by September, concluded that the *Manhattan*'s voyages, while not directly challenging Canada's sovereignty, showed the need for a definitive legal statement. As transit through the Passage would require Canadian aid and pollution and navigational controls, the department wanted to consider the waters internal, but with a potential for innocent passage as long as Canadian pollution and navigation regulations were followed. Following the 1958 UN Convention on the Law of the Sea, these regulations would apply to all waters within the Canadian Arctic archipelago and would offer other states open, maintained, assisted, and regulated passage. Canada should probably assert its claim by unilateral declaration accompanied by domestic legislation for anti-pollution and other regulations. However, DEA officials were worried about the overall friction level in bilateral Canadian-U.S. relations and about the consequences if Canada had to start seizing vessels that deliberately ignored the declared rules. They were also fearful that Canada might not win a court case.

These judgments were debated in a three-hour Cabinet meeting on 11 September 1969, the results of which were unveiled in the Prime Minister's and Mitchell Sharp's September statements. It was clear that Ottawa had gone far in developing its position and that its approach differed from the dominant positions abroad and at home. Yet within Ottawa, two competing tendencies were emerging. The first led by Sharp, assigned high priority to economic development, to applying existing international law to ice-covered waters, and to doing so in a way that corresponded to the slowly evolving international consensus on this subject. Critically, this tendency saw domestic law as having to meet the test of international acquiescence. In Sharp's words, "Action taken internally must therefore be either compatible with the current state of international law or at least be defensible in a court of law."[13] This position was modest in its geographic extent, its functional comprehensiveness, and its limitations on the traditional doctrine of innocent passage.

The second and competing tendency was centred on the Prime Minister and those close to him. It gave priority to pollution control, to creating new international law in areas such as ice-covered waters where little or none existed, and in leading rather than remaining abreast of or following the international consensus. This tendency was far less concerned about international legal acquiescence and ready to contemplate a geographically and functionally ambitious regime.

Despite this divergence, Ottawa had already moved a considerable way from the traditional ideological foundations of liberal internationalism and the demands of those at home and abroad. It had publicly affirmed its view that the waters of the archipelago were Canadian (though not made a formal, legal claim), its need to assert jurisdiction for the functions of navigation, safety, and pollution control, and the priority of these tasks over the traditional doctrine of innocent passage.

Defining the Policy: October-December 1969

The last three months of 1969 saw the Canadian government move tentatively towards answering these questions. Its basic approach—national jurisdiction reinforced by international co-operation—was unveiled on 23 October 1969 in the Speech from the Throne, which announced legislation for measures to prevent pollution in Arctic waters. Speaking in the debate the next day, the Prime Minister elaborated a policy of strictly regulated use of Arctic waters to prevent pollution through Canada's exercise of authority over the use of the waters and through the setting of standards for ships and cargoes therein. He also promised that Canada would seek international agreement on Arctic pollution prevention measures, beginning with a prime ministerial visit to UN Secretary General U Thant. The Prime Minister declared, "We invite the international community to join with us and support our initiative for a new concept, an international legal regime designed to ensure to human beings the right to live in a wholesome natural environment."[14] The government thus switched the focus of debate from sovereignty to pollution and the form of its claim from possession to custodianship. Yet it also suggested that national legislation would proceed regardless of international co-operation. The Prime Minister warned that Canada "would not bow to the pressure of any state."[15]

The Canadian government now sought international support. Trudeau met with U Thant on 11 November 1969 to discuss his idea for an "international regime" to protect the Arctic's natural environment and to call for a co-ordinated, urgent effort to develop international control for the non-Canadian portion of the Arctic. Simultaneously, Minister of Transport Don

Jamieson delivered a strong speech to the Brussels IMCO conference on pollution of the sea by oil.

On his visit to Ottawa, Soviet Foreign Minister Gromyko spoke with Mitchell Sharp about the possibility of Canadian-Soviet co-operation in the Arctic. At IMCO's International Legal Conference on Maritime Pollution Damage, held in Brussels 10-28 November 1969, Canada sought without much success support for rules that would protect against pollution of maritime waters, beyond the voluntary regime recently created by some major tanker owners to establish shipowners' responsibility to national governments that incurred expenditures in avoiding or alleviating damage from pollution.[16] Prime Minister Trudeau, meeting with U Thant, was assured that no UN member then had an objection to Canada's plan to set anti-pollution and environmental control standards for the waters of the Arctic archipelago. Thant added that the UN system was unlikely to devise an appropriate international regime in the near future.

At home the pressures were intensifying. In November Panarctic Oils, in its first wildcat well, hit gas at Drake Point on Melville Island in what seemed to be a commercially viable find if economic transportation were available. In mid-December, 44 oil companies, including the Canadian subsidiaries of the U.S. Alaskan permit holders, formed Operation Polarquest, a four-year exploration and date-gathering venture in over 100 million acres of Canada's Arctic Islands. Industry interest bred parliamentary vigilance. On 16 December, the Liberal-dominated SCIAND urged the government to declare sovereignty immediately over the waters of the archipelago in order to protect Canada's Arctic environment. The committee demanded "that the Government of Canada take whatever steps are necessary, consistent with international law, to assume recognition of Canadian Sovereignty by all vessels, surface and submarine, passing through the Arctic Archipelago."[17]

"Consistent with international law" was, however, beginning to become less of a sacred principle within some parts of the executive branch. The Prime Minister himself had already asserted Canada's responsibility to itself and the world to impose some controls on the use of this uniquely vulnerable environment, the world's last large natural reserve. As only Canada could take the lead in protecting its portion of this reserve, it would have to do so as an ecological or conservation trustee on behalf of the world community, until the latter was able to assume the responsibility. As the trusteeship role explicitly took precedence over "freedom of the seas" and economic development, the conflict with established international law, and traditional domestic priorities, was clear.

While the Prime Minister's instincts were certain, their dominance in the internal government debate was not. By late October the government had not yet decided how expansive Canadian authority would be. Three primary options had emerged. The most geographically ambitious was enclosure of the entire archipelago as internal waters by drawing straight baselines around the perimeter, with or without a right of innocent passage within. The least geograpically assertive option was, in accordance with the 1958 Convention, to extend the Canadian territorial sea from three to twelve nautical miles, with a right of innocent passage, and thereby place key chokepoints in Barrow Strait and Prince of Wales Strait explicitly within Canadian sovereignty. The third option was to convene an international conference to seek multilateral agreement on more innovative concepts of international law, perhaps by proceeding with general national legislation and seeking international agreement on a special pollution zone of up to 50 miles.

The task of meshing these various perspectives into a single strategy began late in the autumn of 1969 in the deliberations of a very senior group of officials.[18] At its first meeting this group tentatively decided to limit the "target" by excluding from the proposed legislation measures to control pollution of Canada's coastal seas as a result of atmospheric factors such as nuclear fallout. By early November it decided upon a new law based on Canada's concern over the pollution of its coastal seas, from such vantage points as the protection of fisheries and other resources of the sea, and safeguarding the welfare of Canada's aboriginal peoples and those living by, or depending for their livelihood on, the sea. The group thus agreed upon an act focused on the pollution threat posed by new resource exploitation and transportation technology to the Arctic waters and on the consequent need for determined Canadian government action as part of a larger problem of growing global concern. The act envisaged government-designated special "pollution control zones," which might be announced in advance of formal legislative action (so other countries and parties might object) but that would not be subject to parliamentary review. To these zones would be applied prohibitions, preventative requirements, and financial responsibility and liability provisions.

The Hard Choices:
January-February 1970

The new strategy was unveiled on 22 January by Mitchell Sharp. Avoiding a direct claim or declaration of sovereignty over the Arctic Waters, Canada would give priority to the prevention of pollution damage from oil tankers by imposing regulations on Arctic shipping in the form of a bill to establish pollution controls for the entire archipelago. In February Sharp, accordingly, welcomed a return of the *Manhattan* to the Arctic, as Canada needed to know more about the conditions under which "Canadian waters" could be used. Sharp later announced that Canada would provide icebreaking assistance to the *Manhattan* if asked but would enact laws against oil pollution in the Arctic before approving voyages through the Passage of any tankers actually carrying oil.

On 19 and 20 February, the Canadian position strengthened considerably. Sharp declared of the Arctic archipelago: "These are our waters."[19] Trudeau added that the *Manhattan* could not proceed until Canada was satisfied that there was no risk of oil pollution. Transport Minister Jamieson noted that Canada could bar tankers from journeying through the Passage by simply refusing to provide icebreaker assistance. Canada informed Humble and Washington of its position. Meanwhile it continued negotiating with other governments to establish territorial limitations on coastal waters, drawing up a headland-to-headland straight baseline system, and preparing to introduce a bill in the next few weeks.

A week later Canadian demands increased. Mitchell Sharp ruled out the use of non-Canadian icebreakers for the *Manhattan* voyage. Don Jamieson added that Humble's *Manhattan* would have to comply with the anti-pollution regulations of the legislation not yet passed or even introduced into the House, or else no Canadian icebreaker assistance would be provided. Ottawa was using the one physical resource on which it had a temporary monopoly—the specialized capability of a heavily powered icebreaker—to force an impatient multinational company to accede to a set of anti-pollution standards and procedures of an as yet unenacted Canadian law.

Canada's escalation was certainly not the result of any relaxation in the U.S. government's position. In mid-January, a press leak from Washington and a statement by former U.S. Secretary of State George Ball had suggested that the United States, as part of its revised oil import program, would press for a continental energy policy with Canada that would include unimpeded transit rights through the Passage. On a diplomatic level, Washington pressed its aide-mémoire, delivered on 6 November 1969, that welcomed Prime Minister Trudeau's invitation to the international community to support Canada's initiative for an international regime regarding the Arctic and the protection of its environment. Washington pressed for bilateral talks on the subject focused initially on the Arctic environment but then broadening to include the future development of Arctic resources and the operational aspects of transportation. It specifically suggested a discussion of the requirements for keeping the sea lanes open all year through "the North American Arctic."[20] The United States asked Canada's views on the desirability of extending the proposed bilateral talks to include other circumpolar states and interested countries. It requested an early Canadian response.

The sense of urgengy rose in February. A Liberian oil tanker, the *Arrow*, ran aground off Nova Scotia, placing one million gallons of oil on the shoreline and causing widespread coastal damage. Humble formally notified DOT of the second *Manhattan* voyage, which was planned to test the ship, without cargo, against the much stronger spring icepack in April. On 18 February, President Nixon, in his State of the World address, referred to the need to "head off the threat of escalating national claims over the oceans."[21] Shortly thereafter he announced that he was authorizing the State Department to pursue with Canada a continental energy policy that included access to the Passage for U.S. tankers. He did so on the basis of a report that recommended also that until negotiations were completed, oil imports from Canada should be cut back to 615,000 barrels a day, beginning 1 July. As Canadian oil exports to the United States were already running at levels one-third higher than permitted under previously negotiated arrangements, the report offered an exceedingly attractive carrot and highlighted an easily available American stick.

As external pressures intensified, so too did domestic ones. For months Progressive Conservative and NDP MPs had maintained a daily ritual of criticizing the government on the Arctic sovereignty issue and expressing fears that government negligence over the second *Manhattan* voyage would sell Canadian sovereignty short. The opposition parties did succeed in forcing a Commons debate on 21 January over the report of the Northern Development Committee and may have helped inspire Mitchell Sharp's sovereignty statement. Moreover, the Cabinet came under heavy pressure from the Liberal caucus and party to force Humble to ask for permission for a second voyage. Yet the parliamentary debate seemed primarily to strengthen the government's hand.

Outside Parliament, positions were even more strident. Led by the *Toronto Star*, with the *Globe and Mail*, the *Telegram*, and the *Ottawa Journal* following, editorialists constantly applauded the expansion of Canada's Arctic presence, while demanding further action and a straight-forward Arctic Waters sovereignty declaration. The anti-pollution concerns of the press were shared by groups such as the Canadian Wildlife Federation, which declared its 175,000 members to be in favour of a moratorium on Arctic energy development. And 51 per cent of the Canadian public in a January poll thought that Canada owned the North Pole. While these pressures may have tempered business influence in favour of rapid economic development, neither the moratorium nor the declaration acquired any major advocates within the government.

Translating the government's position into legislation provided the occasion for these differing approaches to become serious disagreements. As January opened, the Cabinet was considering five interrelated pieces of water and water-pollution legislation, including two versions of draft amendments to the Territorial Sea and Fishing Zones Acts and a proposed new Arctic Waters Pollution Prevention Act. The first version of the revised Territorial Sea and Fishing Zones Act authorized the creation of wider coastal fishing zones and extended the zones to Arctic waters. The second and stronger version, based on a proposal approved by Cabinet prior to the 1969 Speech from the Throne, extended the width of Canada's territorial sea from three to twelve miles. The package of a special Arctic pollution prevention zone with a 12-mile territorial limit had thus to contend with the far more limited option of a mere extension of fishing zones legislation into the Arctic. This latter option, its advocates argued, markedly lessened the chances of evoking U.S. retaliation or running afoul of international law.

Cautious voices arose over other issues as well. Transport proved reluctant to press ahead with an interim National Contingency Plan for the Arctic. Its minister, Don Jamieson, envisaged an approach based on

accepting the Brussels coastal state jurisdiction convention, extending the Canada Shipping Act to the high seas, and introducing new legislation on liability in the case of major incidents. EMR argued, in opposition to a 12-mile territorial limit, that Canada should merely assert jurisdiction over activities connected with the exploration and exploitation of the continental shelf outside territorial limits. EMR urged Cabinet to reexamine its approach to the Arctic in the light of the effects on Canada's oil exports to the United States.

The real battle came over the issue of whether the Arctic Waters Pollution Prevention bill, now entailing a 100-mile zone, would be sacrificed to maintain Canada's traditional support for international law and its central institutional embodiment, the ICJ. On 19 January 1970, Prime Minister Trudeau himself recommended Cabinet approval for preparation of Arctic pollution prevention legislation to be introduced as soon as possible in the current session of Parliament. Yet the deep divisions on this issue were revealed by a simultaneous direction for the Secretary of State for External Affairs, Mitchell Sharp, to prepare a memorandum to Cabinet recommending action to deal with possible international reaction to the proposed legislation. Sharp was also to consider, in consultation with the Prime Minister, the extent, nature, and timing of discussions with other countries that might react to the legislation. Moreover, the Prime Minister also forwarded an alternative course of action that would confine the application of the legislation establishing pollution control over ships to an outer limit of twelve miles, thereby establishing a nine-mile contiguous pollution control zone beyond the three-mile territorial sea.

The next day, 20 January, Sharp concluded before Cabinet that Canada need not protect itself over ICJ action regarding a 12-mile contiguous zone or a 12-mile territorial sea but would need a reservation for an assertion of pollution control jurisdiction over the waters of the Arctic archipelago. He also recommended that Canada should inform the United States before announcing legislative action on any of the alternatives.

Thus when the Cabinet Committee on House Planning and Legislation met to consider the Arctic-related bills, the basic alternatives were clear: a wide Arctic waters pollution control zone with a reservation on the jurisdiction of the ICJ, as forwarded by the Prime Minister; and a narrow 12-mile pollution control zone without an ICJ reservation, sponsored by Sharp.[22] In reference to the Prime Minister's recommendation, the Committee felt that it went beyond international law and would require at least a temporary ICJ reservation. In reference to Sharp's position, it accepted his recommendation for Cabinet to consider, simultaneously with the Prime Minister's proposal, a 12-mile territorial sea without a reservation.

Although Sharp's position had shifted to the 12-mile territorial control zone proposal, overall legislative policy was still very much in doubt when Cabinet met on 4 February to consider the matter. It was still in doubt afterward. Cabinet did decide to introduce during the current session Arctic pollution prevention legislation, to apply to a 100-mile zone, and to make no claim at that time to a 12-mile territorial sea. But this clear victory was accompanied by a decision that the Cabinet Committee on External Policy and Defence consider and report back to Cabinet on the issue of a reservation to Canada's acceptance of compulsory ICJ jurisdiction, the timing of such a measure, and, in the same context, changes in Canada's exclusive fishing zones.

When the External Policy and Defence Committee met on 10 February, Sharp took full advantage of the opportunities that his chairmanship allowed. Although supposed to focus on the narrow issue of whether Canada should make its ICJ reservation at or just before enactment of the Arctic waters bill and the Territorial Sea and Fishing Zones Act, the Ministers returned to the broader issue of what method would best assert Canadian jurisdiction over Arctic waters. It was a prolonged, wide-ranging, and heated discussion. Led by Paul Martin and Sharp, there was a trend back toward the 12-mile territorial sea proposal on the grounds that it required no ICJ reservation. Sharp concluded that as the ICJ reservation was an important question which the Committee could not decide, Cabinet might well reopen the whole subject. The one individual firmly opposed to proceeding without an ICJ reservation covering all elements of the Canadian approach was Allan Gotlieb. He argued that given the uncertain state of international law on the territorial sea, following the failure of the 1960 Law of the Sea Conference, the United States might be under no obligation to recognize a decision on Canada's part to enact a 12-mile territorial sea limit and could, therefore, possibly be in a position to take Canada to court over any enforcement action against its vessels.[23] While his opposition prevented a clear-cut decision being made, the majority present, led by Sharp, Martin, and Jean-Luc Pepin, were loath to recommend any ICJ reservation. They argued that such an action would be seen domestically and internationally as inconsistent with Canada's professed respect for the rule of law in international affairs.

So the big issue went back to full Cabinet. With it went a report that *if* Cabinet decided to proceed with the Arctic waters bill, it would be necessary to subit an ICJ reservation before or on the day the legislation was introduced. Here again discussion was both passionate and prolonged, extending through a Priorities and Planning Committee meeting and the Cabinet session of 19 February.

The dispute centred on the fundamental principle involved in Canada exempting its Act from the compulsory jurisdiction of the ICJ, thereby avoiding the risk of the United States opposing it in the Court. The individual most strongly in favour of Canada reserving its position before the Court was Donald Macdonald, a Toronto lawyer and government House Leader. While Macdonald understood the importance of building the international legal system through the use of the Court, he argued that Canada's interests were more important than the system in the particular case at hand. In addition, he had consulted a number of academic international lawyers and found agreement with his views.

Macdonald's major antagonist was Pual Martin, who was very strongly opposed to an ICJ reservation.[24] Martin argued that it was inconceivable that Canada would break away from its belief in the international order, of which the Court was a vital part. As an international lawyer himself, Martin felt that the weight of academic international legal opinion would be behind him. And he argued that Canada could persuade the Japanese, who might be asked by Washington to act as a surrogate in taking Canada to the ICJ, not to challenge the Canadian act.

The Prime Minister's position appeared to be more neutral.[25] Trudeau recognized that it was dangerous to weaken the Court with a reservation. Indeed, he spoke on several occasions to indicate the importance of Martin's argument and the significance of Canada's membership in the United Nations. Yet as the debate continued he did not oppose Macdonald's view and gradually accepted it. In this he followed most of his Cabinet, who had easily accepted Macdonald's view.[26] Finally, the Prime Minister went around the cabinet table and asked his ministers where they stood. Only Sharp and Martin voted against, standing alone with the internationalist principles they had done so much to promote and defend over the preceding decades. It was left only for Cabinet at its 26 February meeting to mandate External Affairs to consult rapidly with the United States over the Arctic and fisheries zones legislation in order to respond to U.S. requests for such consultations and to secure information as to possible U.S. reactions.

Finale: March-April 1970

The succeeding two months provided the dénouement. Here again Humble's compliance provided a needed opening. During the first week of March, Sharp informed the House that Canada had agreed to a second *Manhattan* voyage to begin 1 April, but had established anti-pollution rules that the ship must obey. DOT would inspect the ship's hull, navigation aids, and other equipment. The Canadian government would again have an agent aboard, but this time with additional duties. Most important, by early Arpil a letter from DOT to Humble established that the captain of the Canadian icebreaker accompanying the Manhattan would have the ultimate responsibility, in liaison with Canadian authorities, for ending the voyage if necessary. Thus before the legislative initiatives of early April were introduced into the House of Commons, their anti-pollution provisions and the underlying principle of Canadian jurisdiction had been given a successful field test.

Tensions were rising between Ottawa and Washington. Canada's blunt refusal to accede to American requests in early March when Trudeau sent Ivan Head and Alan Beesley (head of the External Affairs legal division) to brief U.S. officials. On 20 March, a U.S. negotiating team journeyed to Ottawa for talks with Sharp, Chrétien, and senior officials. On 8 April, the government introduced into the House of Commons a bill to establish the Arctic Waters Pollution Prevention Act and a bill to amend the Territorial Seas and Fishing Zones Act. These bills established a 100-mile control zone in the waters around the Canadian Arctic archipelago, within which Canada would exercise jurisdiction in specified ways to prevent pollution. The 100-mile limit followed the prevailing international legal standard applying to oil pollution from tankers. The size of the zone had only an indirect functional rationale. It was, however, "legal" enough to appeal to the international community, large enough to satisfy the appetite of the Canadian public, and limited enough to sustain the distinction between full zonal sovereignty and purpose-specific jurisdiction—and hence to complicate the diplomatic response of the U.S. government.

The government's bills also extended the territorial limit of Canada's coastal waters from three miles (with an additional nine-mile fishing zone) to twelve miles. This action increased the size of Canadian territory by one-eighth and brought Canada into line with the 56 other countries claiming a 12-mile territorial limit. Most important, the extension created territorial waters "gates" of less than 24 miles in Prince of Wales Strait and in Barrow Strait, thus asserting additional control over the Passage even if M'Clure Strait at the western end would one day prove to be regularly navigable.

Finally, immediately prior to introduction of the legislation, the government informed the United Nations that Canada was reserving from the compulsory jurisdiction of the ICJ "disputes arising out of or concerning jurisdiction or rights claimed or exercised by Canada in respect of the conservation, management or exploitation of the living resources of the sea, or in respect of the prevention or control of pollution or contamination of the marine environment in marine areas adjacent to the coast of Canada."[27] Although this was Canada's fourth reservation to the jurisdiction of the Court, it was the first dealing with a subject area category. It could thus be viewed as a repudiation of support for international law which Canada had provided since the establishment of the Court.[28]

Equally innovative were the concepts the government stressed in its ensuing public diplomacy campaign.[29] Canada argued that the threat posed by oil-laden tankers in the fragile Arctic environment made their passage inherently non-innocent and thus required an assertion of coastal state jurisdiction. It asserted that there was no international law covering the pollution threat from advanced technology in ice-infested areas and that merely because international law and the Court had traditionally been dominated by maritime powers, legal development of this kind ought not to be foreclosed. Canada claimed that it was engaged in an act not of asserting or extending sovereignty but of exercising purpose-specific jurisdiction, as with fishing or aircraft identification zones, in its role as a custodian of a global resource for the world community. It declared that it would not be swayed by the opposition of the United States, which was said to have been the largest obstacle to the creation of an international law of the sea effective in preventing marine pollution. And finally, the government stressed that it believed fully in international law, was searching for an international, multilateral, or bilateral agreement on the pollution prevention issue, supported the American call for an international conference on territorial sea limits, and would accept ICJ jurisdiction over Canada's extension to 12 miles (an area where international law did exist). Armed with these arguments, Canada held firm in the face of the predictable U.S. response.

In early March, Humble acquiesced by requesting the assistance of a Canadian icebreaker for the *Manhattan*'s second voyage, inviting a Canadian government representative to be on board, and fulfilling the Canadian pollution prevention standards. It also identified the ship's route as being merely an excursion into the waters of Baffin Bay. On 18 March, Humble agreed to post a bond and accept responsibility for the voyage. And on 26 March, Humble agreed to give Canada ultimate control over the *Manhattan*'s voyage.

The reaction of the U.S. government was strikingly different. It bombarded Ottawa with notes asking for more talks. And on 10 March President Nixon declared that "as a means of interim control during the period of transition to an alternative United States-Canada energy policy," oil imports from Canada for 1 March to 31 December east of the Rockies would be reduced by 20 per cent.[30] Although this measure was produced by the U.S. Assistant Secretary of State for Economic Affairs to secure Canadian agreement to the prized Continental Energy Plan (CEP), the Arctic access dimensions of the latter gave it a direct relevance to the issue at hand. The CEP and Arctic issues were also joined on 11 March, at the 13th meeting of the Interparliamentary Group, where the U.S.

delegation insisted again that the Northwest Passage was an international strait. This refrain was repeated at a meeting of Canadian and U.S. officials on 20 March. With Canada holding firm, the mood did not improve. On 1 April, the *Manhattan* began its voyage, just as a U.S. Federal District Court judge granted a temporary restraining order preventing the issuance of permits for the construction of TAPS. Simultaneously the U.S. Congress approved the construction of the most powerful non-nuclear icebreaker in the world, one that promised to be far superior to anything Canada possessed. Its sister ship, the *Polar Sea*, was to appear in Canadian Arctic waters amid renewed controversy 15 years later. U.S. government protests, in diplomatic notes and a presidential phone call, produced little, despite press reports from Washington indicating that the United States was considering economic sanctions or a navy submarine transit of the Passage to show Canada's lack of effective control.

The Aftermath

After the introduction of the Arctic legislation on 8 April 1970, the government was free to concentrate on the task of convincing audiences at home and abroad and of coping with persistent U.S. efforts to lure Canada into a less unilateral and ambitious approach. The frustrations faced by domestic and external actors throughout the *Manhattan* episode were underlined by the ease with which the government accomplished these tasks. The domestic demand for a straightforward declaration of sovereignty died almost instantly, as the public responded enthusiastically to Ottawa's creativity and cleverness. Within Parliament, the Conservatives unleashed a barrage of condemnation, but its effectiveness was greatly reduced by its striking inconsistency.

Dealing with the Americans and the rest of the international community proved only somewhat more difficult. The appeal of the anti-pollution principle, the creative approach to international law, and a carefully orchestrated campaign of public diplomacy did much to dampen the opposition of attentive Americans.[31]

Washington's suddenly sophisticated multilateral diplomacy proved to be a more formidable challenge. In a 14 April note and in a 15 April aide-mémoire, the United States proposed to convene in Washington during the fourth week of June 1970 a multilateral conference to establish an international regime for Arctic areas beyond national jurisdiction. It invited the Canadian government to join in the call for a conference. The multilateral alternative, American sponsorship, and the implied willingness to proceed without Canadian cosponsorship each constituted a major problem, particularly as the Canadian government's bills had not yet been enacted into law.

In a 16 April note and a subsequent aide-mémoire of 28 April, Canada indicated that it had no intention of submitting issues of territorial limits and national jurisdiction to the conference but welcomed multilateral discussions on agreed rules of environmental protection and the safey of navigation in the Arctic waters. On 6 May, the United States accepted Canada's willingness to participate in the multilateral discussions Canada specified and suggested immediate bilateral consultations to prepare for and determine the participants of the conference. The United States stressed its desire for a consensus approach at the conference, its lack of interest in provoking a jurisdictional dispute, and its agreement with Canada that the question of

rules for the Arctic environment and Arctic navigation transcended traditional concepts of sovereignty. Despite these alluring signals, Canada remained concerned about U.S. unwillingness to rule out other agenda items at the proposed conference. Canada thus sought to delay the conference, restrict its agenda, and shape its membership by lining up supporters for its April measures, even as the United States enlisted adherents to its multilateral conference approach.

In the end Canada proved able to secure the support of enough of the key states to block the U.S. approach. Canadian victory was in sight. While most diplomats judged the United States to have a strong legal case against Canada and recognized the self-interest in Canada's measures, most also felt that Canada would win the battle for world public opinion. Their judgment rested on the appeal of environmental protection, the acknowledged cloudiness and bias of the international law of the sea with regard to pollution, and Canada's effective use of the precedent of U.S. President Truman's unilateral 1948 extention of jurisdiction over the continental shelf. Perhaps more important was the desire of other countries, particularly coastal states, to break the three-mile territorial sea regime.

In its competition with the United States over the April measures themselves, Canada did lose, in varying degrees, all of the large Western countries—such traditional Canadian associates as the Netherlands and Belgium and the old dominions (notably Australia). Yet it secured the support of the critical circumpolar Scandinavian states of Sweden, Norway (an important shipping power), and Iceland. More important, it obtained the support of the other Arctic superpower, the Soviet Union, with a visit by Ivan Head to Moscow in June 1970. Moscow treated the U.S. conference proposal with suspicion and reserve and evinced no desire to see international discussions develop that might disturb the existing situation in the Soviet Arctic.

Thus, with the possible exception of Denmark and Finland, which remained noncommittal, all Arctic powers apart from the United States had gravitated to the Canadian side. The intellectual leader of the UN-sponsored Law of the Sea Conference, Malta, was sympathetic as well. Led by Brazil, all the Latin American coastal states backed Canada. Moreover, the two major flag-of-convenience shipping states that the United States invited to its proposed conference (Panama, which claimed a 200-mile limit, and Liberia, the only African country invited) both had expressed sympathy for the Canadian legislation.

Most important, of the 14 states (apart from Canada) that the United States was known to have approached with invitations to its proposed conference as of early May, only the Dutch seemed in favour, with the Spaniards and Finns noncommittal. Japan, Britain, Belgium, and Denmark refused to accept until the terms of reference were clarified by the United States and/or the conference was limited to technically based aspects of pollution and navigation. Italy went further, saying that any conference without Canadian participation would be worthless and Italian involvement in it a hostile act toward Canada. The Soviet Union, Iceland, Norway, and Sweden were opposed to the U.S. conference proposal. Indeed, Sweden considered the proposal a ganging-up operation and suggested that Canada call a counter-conference to develop an international regime based on the Canadian legislation.

Thus by the summer of 1970 it became clear that the United States no longer had an international constituency for its efforts

to shape the development of international law in this area. And despite the formidable array of unilateral economic, military, and political instruments at Washington's disposal, it chose not to deploy them alone on behalf of the old regime. By 1970, the United States was unable to define the new and unwilling by itself to defend the old international order in the field.

Conclusion

The voyages of the *Manhattan* through the Passage were the occasion of significant change in the Canadian government's foreign policy behaviour. They evoked competing tendencies that defined anew the alternative courses of action available to the state. Canada's response to the *Manhattan* transits illuminates the process of change in Canadian foreign policy itself, and ran against deeply held convictions backed by pervasive belief systems, with none more powerful than the classic liberal internationalist ideology that was created and applied during the Pearson-Martin era in Canadian foreign relations. And it suggests that Trudeau's revolution in Canadian foreign policy was neither the passing concern of an international neophyte nor an easy, unthinking repudiation of a gracious internationalism in favour of national greed. What we see in the *Manhattan* episode is instead an effort to build an international order more in keeping with the broader values and responsibilities of a Canada that had become more powerful than in the initial phases of the post-war era.

It is wrong to see this case as a choice between sovereignty and pollution prevention goals, with the latter serving only as a convenient cover for the former. Canada's pollution concerns were real and in some respects determining. They arose as a major element in the government's thinking as early as October 1969. They provided the general legislative context in which the Arctic measures took shape. And when reinforced by the damage done to the *Manhattan* on its first voyage and the accidents to barges and tankers elsewhere, they led to measures far more forceful, and far more focused on pollution, than those originally contemplated. Moreover, the concern with pollution was not a transitory, fashionable theme, nor a simple response to environmentalist pressure. Rather it was a direct committment of the Prime Minister and his closest associates to the integrity and legitimate interests of dispossessed communities.[32] For Pierre Trudeau, pollution *prevention* was essential to protect the distinctive way of life of Canada's northern native communities. It was a fellow French Canadian and Minister of Indian Affairs, Jean Chrétien, who first signalled the pollution-prevention approach. And the Prime Minister himself went to considerable personal effort to ensure that the Third World states within the global community would not see Canada's pollution prevention initiatives as merely a rich man's luxury, let alone a convenient cover for national greed.

Nor was this a simple choice between "internationalism" and "nationalism." Rather the interests of the international community were compelling throughout the period.

Uniting the concern with pollution and the interests of the global community was the concept of custodianship—a doctrine that appears to have had a real moral force in the minds of its progenitors. This doctrine conceived of Canada's Arctic waters as an essential component of the global ecological system and as part of the common heritage of humanity. The concept of Canada as an agent, par excellence, of the international system linked the Arctic initiatives to the finest traditions of the liberal-internationalist era in its most creative phase. Indeed, the belief that Canada must exercise leadership, unilaterally and multilaterally, on behalf of a global community incompletely knit together by the existing array of regimes, institutions, and great power managers suggested that the immediate legacy of the Arctic initiatives of April 1970 would lie in an effort to shape a new UN convention on the law of the sea.

NOTES

1. Notably Edgar Dosman, *The National Interest* (Toronto: McClelland and Stewart, 1975); Edgar Dosman, ed., *The Arctic in Question* (Toronto: Oxford University Press, 1976); and Richard Rohmer, *The Arctic Imperative* (Toronto: McClelland and Stewart, 1973). On the basics of the case see Maxwell Cohen, "The Arctic and the National Interest," *International Journal* 26, no. 4 (Winter 1970-1), 52-81, and Thomas Tynan, "The Role of the Arctic in Canadian-American Relations." PhD dissertation, Catholic University of America, 1976.

2. The precepts of traditional liberal-internationalism are specified in David Dewitt and John Kirton, *Canada as a Principal Power* (Toronto: John Wiley, 1983).

3. In additon to published sources and press accounts, this article is based largely on confidential inverviews and colloquia on Canadian-U.S. relations, involving both authors, extending over the past decade, supplemented more recently by selective documentary and interview evidence dealing with the *Manhattan* case.

4. On the legal status of the Passage see Donat Pharand, *The Law of the Sea of the Arctic* (Ottawa: University of Ottawa Press, 1973), and Donat Pharand, "The Legal Regime of the Arctic: Some Outstanding Issues," *International Journal* 39, no. 4 (Autumn 1984), 742-99.

5. In legal and geographical terms, the more precise distinction is that between "territorial" and "interal" waters, both of which give the coastal state exclusive jurisdiction, but only the latter of which allows it to control rights of passage.

6. "A New Defence Policy for Canada," Statement to the Press by the Prime Minister, Mr. Pierre Elliott Trudeau, 3 April 1969.

7. John Dafoe, *Globe and Mail*, 16 May 1969.

8. Dosman, *The Arctic in Question*, 42.

9. *Ibid.*, 46.

10. Mitchell Sharp, "A Ship and Sovereignty in the North," *Globe*, 18 September 1969.

11. *Ibid.*

12. "MPs Urge Full Claim to Waters of Arctic," *Toronto Star*, 8 September 1969.

13. Sharp, "A Ship and Sovereignty."

14. Peter Thomson, "MP Won't Allow Arctic challenge," *Telegram*, 25 October 1969.

15. "Trudeau Will Meet U Thant to Discuss Arctic Pollution," *Globe and Mail*, 25 October 1969.

16. For a full account of the Brussels process see R. Michael M'Gonigle and Mark Zacher, *Pollution, Politics, and International Law: Tankers at Sea* (Berkeley, Calif.: University of California Press, 1979).

17. "Claim Waters of Arctic Now, MPs of All Parties Urge," *Globe and Mail*, 17 December 1969.

18. The group comprised Ivan Head, Allan Gotlieb, and officials from the Privy Council Office, External Affairs, Justice, DIAND, Forestry and Fisheries, EMR, and Transport.

19. John Doig, "Arctic Pollution," *Toronto Star*, 20 February 1970.

20. By this phrase was meant both the Alaskan and Canadian portions.

21. John Aitken, "U.S. Prepares for Arctic Legal Fight?" *Telegram*, 18 February 1970.

22. The possibility of a 12-mile territorial sea limit, without an ICJ reservation, rested in between.

23. Allan Gotlieb had served formerly as the legal adviser in External Affairs and was, in 1969 and 1970, deputy minister of the Department of Communications.

24. Paul Martin had studied international law and international affairs at Cambridge University, where he had been taught by Arnold McNair, who, in 1970, was serving as president of the ICJ. Moreover, as a product of the inter-war generation, Martin believed that the wars against the Kaiser and Hitler had been fought in order to construct an international system centred in the United Nations and the ICJ. And as an international lawyer his commitment to the Court was as intense as that of his contemporary, Lester Pearson, to the United Nations. See Paul Martin, *A Very Public Life* (Ottawa: Deneau, 1983).

25. As another lawyer with exposure to international law, Trudeau fully understood the argument and felt the obligation to resist a small transitory national advantage in favour of the larger task of building the international system. Indeed, as he sat next to Martin at Cabinet he could be overheard whispering his private support for the internationalist position. Also evident was Trudeau's fear that Martin might resign over the issue. Yet

Trudeau's Jesuitical approach, and his position as head of the government, affected his views when he saw that the majority of the Ministers favoured a reservation. In addition he felt the Arctic waters were Canada's, recognized the pollution problem, saw the Act as a practical step, and felt that Canada could reduce the damage to the international system by withdrawing its ICJ reservation at a later stage. Finally, he wanted to settle the issue and found it difficult to repudiate a policy that he had introduced and which had been developed by his close associate Ivan Head.

26. Most other Ministers were primarily concerned that Canada not lose any ICJ case. And as none of the major Ministers was a lawyer who understood international law, they did not feel keenly about building up the international system. Their approach was more pragmatic.

27. "Documents Concerning Canadian Legislation of Arctic Pollution and Territorial Sea and Fishing Zones," *International Legal Materials* 9 (May 1970), 598-9.

28. The other three reservations concerned disputes dealt with in other forums, disputes with Commonwealth members, and disputes exclusively within the jurisdiction of Canada.

29. For a scholarly statement of these concepts, directed at the American legal community, see Allan Gotlieb and Charles Dalfen, "National Jurisdiction and International Responsibility," *American Journal of International Law* 67, no. 2 (April 1973), 229-58.

30. Dewitt and Kirton, *Canada as a Principal Power*, 295.

31. For example, editorial support in the United States was evenly balanced between the Canadian and U.S. position.

32. Ivan Head, "The Foreign Policy of the New Canada," *Foreign Affairs* 50, no. 2 (January 1972), 237-52. See also Harald von Riekhoff, "The Impact of Prime Minister Trudeau on Foreign Policy," *International Journal* 33, no. 2 (Spring 1978), 267-86.

SUGGESTED READINGS

Cohen, Maxwell, "The Arctic and the National Interest," *International Journal*, Vol. 26, No. 1, (1970-71), pp. 52-81.

Dobell, Peter, *Canada's Search for New Roles: Foreign Policy in the Trudeau Era*, London: Oxford University Press, 1972.

Emanuelli, Claude, "La pollution maritime et la notion de passage inoffensif," *Canadian Yearbook of International Law*, Vol. XI, (1973), pp. 613-36.

Gotlieb, A. and C. Dalfen, "National Jurisdiction and International Responsibility," *American Journal of International Law*, Vol. 67, No. 1, (1973), pp. 229-58.

Griffiths, Franklyn (ed.), *Politics of the Northwest Passage*, Kingston: McGill-Queen's University Press, 1987.

chapter 14

RECOGNIZING CHINA, 1970

John D. Harbron

On 13 October 1973, the third anniversary of Canada's recognition of the People's Republic of China, Prime Minister Pierre Elliott Trudeau was toasting Premier Chou En-lai in the Great Hall of the People in Peking. It was his promise during the 1968 Canadian election campaign which had led to recognition and he now expressed sentiments which he felt are shared by both Canada and China: "We, too, seek creative and satisfying lives for all our people. And in the pursuit of those goals, many of the values demonstrated by the Chinese people are found as well in Canada."

Some Canadians still take strong exception to the association of Canadian values with the world's largest communist social and political system by a Canadian prime minister. But organized opposition to diplomatic relations between Canada and China, never strongly articulated by any important sector of Canadian society, was virtually non-existent by the autumn of 1970 when they were established.

In Peking, Pierre Trudeau was performing as a western head of government who had visited China twice before as a private citizen. In 1949 he was an itinerant student traveller in Shanghai shortly before the Communist armies entered that city in triumph. In the fall of 1960 he returned to China as a guest of the Chinese government for a tour of several weeks, later recorded with whimsy and humour in a book of casual comment appropriately titled *Deux Innocents en Chine Rouge*.[1]

At the banquet in honour of Premier Chou, Prime Minister Trudeau deviated from his prepared text to comment on his earlier visit to China as a university professor: "Thirteen years ago I sat in this Great Hall thinking some day we should recognize this great nation. I saw at a distance and with admiration the leaders of China...and for me it is a great pleasure to be host to some of these leaders."

Mr Trudeau's intention to proceed with recognition was part of the programme he put forward when seeking the leadership of the Liberal party in 1968. As early as March, while still minister of justice in Mr Pearson's cabinet, he told a press conference at Vineland, Ontario, that he would offer diplomatic recognition to China if he became prime minister.[2]

...

Mr Trudeau's views on new foreign policy directions had grown in part out of discussions in the spring of 1968 among a small group of Mr Trudeau's associates, including Ivan Head who would become his principal adviser as prime minister. The result of these meetings, as well as informal discussions with the Minister of Justice on other occasions, was the drafting of a doc-

John D. Harbron, "Canada Recognizes China: The Trudeau Round 1968-1973," *Behind the Headlines*, Toronto, Canadian Institute of International Affairs, 1974. Portions of the text have been deleted. Some footnotes have been removed, those remaining have been renumbered

ument on a procedure for recognition of Peking as well as proposals for other new orientations in Canadian foreign policy. This informal policy group, working on the assumption Mr Trudeau would be chosen Liberal leader in April and thus become the next prime minister, did not consider the recognition of China as the only or even the most essential new foreign policy move, but looked at it in relation to other proposed changes, chiefly a de-escalation of Canada's existing military role in the North Atlantic Treaty Organization (NATO) and a re-assessment of Canadian commercial connections with western Europe. "In those days," Mr Head has said, "Mr Trudeau knew exactly what he wanted to do with foreign policy."[3]

. . .

On 29 May 1968, during the election campaign which closely followed his selection as Liberal party leader and his assumption of the prime ministership, Mr Trudeau issued his first major policy statement on foreign affairs, "Canada and the World."[4] The vocabulary and intentions were clearly those of Mr Head in the first instance and the new Prime Minister in the second.

During the campaign, the categorical yet informal manner in which Mr Trudeau said he would proceed to recognize China— his only firm election promise—sometimes left the impression he would try to do so without consideration of China's uncertain future in world affairs (on the heels of the receding chaos of the Cultural Revolution) or, more important, without regard for how the Canadian government would cope with the problem of Taiwan. But in the document of 29 May the Prime Minister said of China's future as a world power: "...China continues to be both a colossus and a conundrum. Potentially, the People's Republic of China poses a major threat to peace largely because calculation about Chinese

ambitions, intentions, capacity to catch up and even about actual developments within China have to be based on incomplete information—which opens an area of unpredictability." And on recognition and the handling of the Taiwan problem: "Our aim will be to recognize the People's Republic of China Government as soon as possible and to enable that Government to occupy the seat of China in the United Nations, taking into account that there is a separate government in Taiwan."

Moreover, from the beginning, Mr Trudeau always recognized the possibility that China might reject his approach. He had said so publicly in advance of the 1968 Liberal leadership convention and repeated his concern in private as late as the spring of 1969 when negotiations on recognition between the Canadian and Chinese embassies in Stockholm were moving slowly. "We pursued it then," Ivan Head has said, "knowing we might be rebuffed. But his [Trudeau's] instructions were to go ahead."

The election promise to recognize China did not create much stir among either dissenting Liberals or the opposition parties. If anything, the New Democratic party (NDP) was upstaged, since the party's foreign policy platform, like that of its predecessor, the Co-operative Commonwealth Federation (CCF), had always included a strong recommendation for Canadian recognition of the People's Republic. During the 1968 campaign a few fringe groups of the radical right did publish a spate of "hate literature" attacking the new prime minister. These pamphlets warned the voter against a leader who had long been personally sympathetic, so they insinuated, to the political philosophies of Chairman Mao, Fidel Castro, and the Soviet leaders.

One pamphlet, intentionally printed on deep pink paper in an effort at wry humour about the Prime Minister's enthusiasm for

Chinese communism, was distributed widely in suburban Toronto supermarkets during the 1968 campaign by the radical-right John Birch Society. It listed Mr Trudeau's academic and political associations, tying them to his visits to the Soviet Union (1952) and China.

But there was not in Canada an articulate, anti-communist, American-style China lobby, able with its powerful friends, adequate financing, and access to the press, to block all approaches by government to Peking. Indeed, in the Canada of the 1950s and 1960s, anything resembling a China lobby had been doing the direct opposite, pressuring governments and political leaders for early recognition of China. Former missionaries from the "old" China who had become supporters of the social doctrine of the Chinese Communists which they justified by calling it "Christian socialism," many of the trade unions, the CCF and its successor the NDP, American ex-diplomats and academics with an earlier China experience who had recently come to Canadian universities, all badgered Ottawa in print and privately to go the whole route and recognize Peking. While newspaper editorial writers tried to push successive prime ministers over the brink by criticizing their cautious statements that recognition would come some day, scholarly journals in both English- and French-speaking Canada were publishing articles assessing the value and need for recognition.

There were other voices as well, such as that of Chester Ronning, the Chinese-born Canadian who had been on the staff of the Canadian embassy at the time the Communists came to power and whose friendship with Chou En-lai extended back to 1945 when the two had met in Chungking. Mr Ronning had been present at a meeting called on 1 October 1949 in Nanking by the Director of the Foreign

Nationals Bureau, predecessor of the Foreign Ministry of the People's Republic. The purpose of that meeting was to invite countries still represented in China to recognize the new régime on its founding day.

Curiously, the Protestant churches, and especially the United Church of Canada which takes such strong positions on controversial Third World problems, were initially opposed to many of the favourable views of their returning missionaries regarding the social gospel of Chinese communism.

The United Church finally came to accept, and indeed to promote, the views of their missionaries and to take a position in favour of recognizing Peking, chiefly through the editorials of the *United Church Observer* in the later 1950s and 1960s, which also criticized successive federal governments for their failure to do so.

More than any other issue of foreign policy, Ottawa's delay in recognizing Peking came to be seen by critics as the main example of Canada's failure to develop a so-called "independent foreign policy." Not even Canada's continued membership in the "military alliances" of NATO and NORAD, which became a cause of controversy during the 1960s in Canada, raised the ire of foreign policy critics as much as the delay in recognizing China. For them, this had to be the classic example of feet dragging or, worse, of hidden opposition to the move by governments and the Department of External Affairs.

However, neither successive governments nor the department were opposed to the ultimate recognition of Peking. But, given the constantly changing relations of China with the outside world after the creation of the People's Republic on 1 October 1949, beginning with the impasse of Canada's participation in the Korean War (1950-3) and the subsequent belligerent positions of China in world affairs, a Canadian move toward Peking was always hedged with difficulties. At the multilateral level, in the United Nations, Canada continued to vote against the annual resolution proposing the seating of mainland China until 1966 and at the bilateral level it felt in part that its hands were tied by the prospect of pressure on Ottawa from the strongly anti-communist American governments of the years following the Korean War.

The classic prime ministerial assurance (until Mr Trudeau changed the rules) that Canada would go the entire route some day began with a statement from Prime Minister Louis St Laurent following his return from a trip to Asia in 1954. In early March Mr St Laurent said it was not yet time to act and that it would be unwise to promise commitments that might make recognition impossible or difficult at a later date. Mr Pearson, as secretary of state for external affairs, dared to move a little further when he added, in August 1955, "that the time is coming—and soon—when we should have another and searching look at the problem.[5]

In the 1960s world problems of a different kind emerged to impede a Canadian decision, in particular the growing political and cultural pressures of China on its Southeast Asian neighbours. Between 1959 and 1964 two successive secretaries of state for external affairs, the Conservatives' Howard Green and the Liberals' Paul Martin, shunned any change in Canadian policy toward China, given its possible effect on the ability of countries in Southeast Asia to resist the new Chinese pressures on their region.

John Holmes, whose excellent essay "Canada and China: The Dilemmas of a Middle Power" covers in detail the Canada-China relationship between 1950 and 1965, emphasizes, however, that the Canadian reticence over a move to establish relations

with Peking (or mainland China, the popular phrase of the time) was founded on a basis different from that of the hard line taken by Washington.[6] "Free Asia" to the Americans meant their Asian client powers, South Korea, Taiwan, South Vietnam, Thailand, and the Philippines. But "free Asia" to Canadian foreign policy planners of those years implied the Commonwealth Asian countries, India, Pakistan, and Ceylon. While Washington was heeding warnings about Chinese aggression from its "free Asian" allies to whom it had supplied weapons and, in the case of Korea, South Vietnam, and Thailand, in which it was establishing bases and stationing American troops, Canada's "free Asian" partners in the Colombo Plan were plying Ottawa with reasons why Canada should not follow the American posture on China. After all, three of them—India, Ceylon, and Pakistan—had recognized the People's Republic of China within months of its official establishment.

Nonetheless, Canadian disquiet about China's menacing international postures also undoubtedly influenced the Canadian decision to continue to vote against the annual United Nations resolution calling for Peking's seating. On 17 November 1965 Mr Martin articulated this concern about China's world activities as well as reiterating Canada's continued desire to respect the rights of Taiwan (the Republic of China) as one of the founding members of the United Nations.

Given all these understandably restrictive factors which would have made recognition difficult in the period 1949-68, the comment of the present Under-Secretary of State for External Affairs, A. E. Ritchie, made long after the event in September 1973 still makes sense: "recognition is easy, but recognition in the right way is not."

Nevertheless the single all-important element had been missing during that same unsettling and frustrating time. This was the political will of a Canadian prime minister and his government to approach the Chinese regardless of all the known hazards. "We needed a prime minister to 'grasp and nettle,' make the act of political will to proceed to recognize, worry later about the reaction from the United States and how to deal with the Taiwan problem. And Mr Trudeau was that man"—as a senior Department of External Affairs Chinese specialist has put it recently.

In the fall of 1968 Prime Minister Trudeau gave instructions to the department to prepare a working document on which the Canadian embassy in a selected nation that already recognized China could base its approach to the Chinese. This was not requested in limbo, but "in parallel," as Mr Head puts it, with a request for new thinking from the department on a reduced Canadian NATO commitment and new Canadian roles in this hemisphere.

Of the final document which went out to the Canadian embassy in Stockholm at the end of 1968, Mr Head has said: "External Affairs drafted it. Mr Trudeau polished it up. He knew his own goals...he wanted to break old, established patterns in the department..." Mr Head's comments were confirmed by the Prime Minister during his 1973 visit to China. He said: "Yes, I had to push them on it. They kept sending me memos on reasons for delay and I kept sending them back saying I wanted to move." The problems centred around timing had thus been resolved by the Prime Minister's impatience and Arthur Andrew, Canadian ambassador to Sweden, was instructed to commence contact with the Chinese embassy in Stockholm.

The most critical problem which had made the Canadians shy away from approaching Peking and which would now have to be faced squarely by the negotiators in Stockholm was the determined effort of the Chinese diplomats to win Canadian acceptance of the claim of Peking to Taiwan as the main condition for recognition. On the other hand, fast-moving political events in the United States meant that the perennial threat of United States opposition to Canadian efforts to approach China would fade in the winter of 1968-9. Already it was clear to Ottawa that the republican administration of President Nixon which would take office in January 1969 was going to attempt some dramatic shifts in foreign policy toward the two superpowers of the communist world, including proposed major rapprochements with Moscow (for a military détente) and an attempted "opening" with the People's Republic. Washington would therefore encourage Canadian efforts at Stockholm during 1969-70 to see how successfully the Canadians could negotiate with the Chinese, before sending their own feelers toward a long-hostile Chinese régime.[7]

Still there were other worries for Ottawa in the Stockholm meetings. Would the Chinese rebuff Canada's efforts, a fear always in the back of the Prime Minister's mind? And if so, would such a setback interfere with the long-time and, for western Canada, very profitable feed grains export business to China which had begun under the Conservative government of John Diefenbaker and had already brought about $3 billions into Canada's economy. The wheat trade with China had after all been conducted without establishing diplomatic relations. Did the Chinese have a priority list of countries from which they considered recognition important? If such a list concentrated on those countries centred around Taiwan such as Japan, Singapore, and Malaysia, it would necessarily exclude Canada.

But Canada's chief fear had to be: would the Chinese use Canada as the test case for major acceptance in the West of

Peking's claim to Taiwan by making it the prerequisite for recognition? For if the Canadians did fall into line, presumably a tier of European, African, and Latin American nations would follow, thus bringing immense prestige to Chinese diplomacy. Canada, however, would not accept the claim, as the many cautious statements on China by Prime Ministers St Laurent, Diefenbaker, and Pearson had made clear.

The rocky and long unresolved "two-China" issue was best put by John Holmes in 1964: "Taiwan remains the heart of the Canadian dilemma on China policy...For most Canadians, this issue is the critical barrier to recognition and acceptance of Peking into the United Nations."[8] Nor would the Chinese have found much satisfaction at the negotiating table in the view of the former Secretary of State for External Affairs, Paul Martin, that Canada had a "one-China, one-Formosa solution." This always was a semantically awkward statement and ideologically impossible for the Chinese to swallow at any time.

It was hoped that the original plan among Commonwealth countries to approach Peking shortly after official creation of the new régime would be counted in Canada's favour. Under this scheme, which it was believed the Chinese knew about, the Asian Commonwealth countries would seek recognition first (India recognized the People's Republic on 30 December 1949, Pakistan on 5 January 1950, and Ceylon on 7 January 1950). The British who had serious reparations problems about properties and other assets to negotiate with the new Peking government would follow (Britain recognized China on 6 January 1950), then Canada would make its overtures.

The reasons that have always been given for Canada's delay in doing so during the period from January to June of 1950 are Canada's preoccupation with its new Asian role under the emerging Colombo Plan which took Mr Pearson as secretary of state for external affairs to Ceylon and its opening meetings in January of that year and, of course, the outbreak of the conflict in Korea on 25 June 1950. The Ming Sung affair could have been a minor irritant, but certainly not a major reason for the long Canadian delay in approaching Peking.[9]

Another factor in Canada's favour in the Stockholm negotiations were the direct relations established with the Chinese in the course of the latter's many wheat purchases, which were initiated in 1959 as a result of visits to China by Alvin Hamilton, minister of agriculture in the Diefenbaker cabinet. So too were such cultural events as the Canadian tour of the Peking Opera.

Apart from the continued wheat sales, Canada's other commercial interests in China were also felt to be an important asset in the approaching negotiations. Not only had hundreds of Canadian businessmen visited the many Canton industrial fairs over the years but prominent Canadian industrialists and politicians had visited China, all of them returning home to praise the régime and call for early recognition of Peking. Among the well-known visitors of the late 1950s and early 1960s were James Duncan, former president of Massey-Ferguson Limited, James Muir, then president of the Royal Bank of Canada, and Walter Gordon, later minister of finance under Lester Pearson, all of whom strongly recommended recognition. Indeed, Mr Duncan wrote a book about his Chinese visit, an unusual departure for reticent Canadian tycoons.

Following the establishment of the People's Republic, Canada had maintained its embassy in Nanking as well as a newly opened consulate general in Shanghai for some time, until late 1951 in the latter case.

Nor did Canada ever open an embassy in Taiwan, though the Republic of China had an embassy in Ottawa from 1942 to 1970. It was hoped that this less than precipitate withdrawal might also help create a favourable attitude among the Chinese to the negotiations.

Negotiations began in Stockholm with a good deal of apprehension on the part of the Canadians. Their uncertainties were increased by the absence of any information on how much authority Peking had given to its diplomats in Sweden or, worse, who they were. In May 1969 Ambassador Arthur Andrew was still expressing his personal concern about his lack of knowledge of the Chinese diplomats in Stockholm and of their intentions.

Liu Chi-tsai, a commercial official, was acting chargé d'affaires of the Chinese embassy because the new ambassador, Wang Tung, did not arrive until mid-June 1969. He was also in charge of the Chinese negotiators during the on-and-off weekly meetings with the Canadians.

Canadian diplomats involved in the Stockholm discussions during 1969-70, other than Arthur Andrew, included Chinese-speaking Robert Edmonds, son of a Canadian missionary to China, who did much of the interpreting for the Canadians and John Fraser who was later to open Canada's embassy in Peking and serve as its chargé d'affaires. Mr Andrew returned to Canada a few months after the new Chinese chief of mission arrived in Stockholm and the balance of the negotiations were carried through by his successor, Margaret Meagher.

The arrival of the Chinese ambassador brought a toughening in attitude by the Chinese, as well as a negotiator who had briefed himself thoroughly on all the numerous statements regarding recognition made by prime ministers from St Laurent to Trudeau. Mr Wang referred to these so often that at one point Mr Andrew reminded him the Canadians were dealing with contemporary events, not on the basis of past prime ministerial speeches on the subject under discussion.

The first meeting took place on 21 February 1969 in the Chinese embassy; the twenty-first and last on 10 October 1970 when Miss Meagher and Mr Wang, as representatives of Canada and China, finally signified their approval of the documents of recognition.

The meetings during 1969 and 1970 were conducted against the backdrop of several statements by the Secretary of State for External Affairs, Mitchell Sharp, which gave some idea of the direction Canada was taking in the negotiations. On 12 February 1969 he said in the Commons: "I doubt very much that the Canadian government would recognize or challenge the sovereignty of Peking over Formosa." On 29 May, prior to a Scandinavian visit, Mr Sharp stated: "Canada has a one China policy, and since the nationalist government purports to be the government of China, we cannot recognize both Peking and Taiwan at the same time."

On returning from his trip to the Scandinavian countries, which he said did not include an overview of the Stockholm talks, Mr Sharp spoke again in the House of Commons on developments in Stockholm. On 16 July he reported that "negotiations are tough and may continue for some time." And he elaborated further on Canada's position on 21 July: "We are not promoting either a two-China policy or a one-China, one Taiwan policy. Our policy is to recognize one government of China. We have not asked and do not ask the government of the People's Republic of China to endorse the position of the government of Canada on our territorial limits as a condition to

agreement to establish diplomatic relations...We do not think it would be appropriate, nor would it be in accordance with
international usage, that Canada should
be asked to endorse the position of the government of the Peoples' [*sic*] Republic of
China on the extent of its territorial
sovereignty."

Meanwhile the weekly meetings were
temporarily postponed from mid-July to-
late August 1969 because the Chinese ambassador had said "he needed to consult
Peking."[10] Then from October 1969 through
the winter and spring of 1969-70 Chinese
drafts and Canadian counter-drafts moved
back and forth between the two parties.
During this protracted exchange it became
clear the Chinese wanted a statement of
Canada's position with respect to Taiwan.
The Canadian view was that such a requirement was out of place in a communiqué basically concerned with recognition
and an exchange of missions. As a
Department of External Affairs document
succinctly puts it: "the problem this presented was to find an adequate means of
expressing its [Canada's] own 'non-position'
on Taiwan."

The end to the semantic log jam came
from a Canadian proposal to use a simple
innovative phrase which has since become
known worldwide as "the Canadian formula." The phrase is "takes note." Prime
Minister Trudeau gave full credit to Mr
Sharp for coming up with the expression.
It appears as follows in the declaration issued jointly by Canada and China on 13
October 1970 establishing diplomatic relations: "The Chinese Government reaffirms
that Taiwan is an inalienable part of the
territory of the People's Republic of China.
The Canadian Government takes note of
this position of the Chinese Government." A
lesser publicized phrase from Mr Sharp's
accompanying statement was also crucial

to success in these negotiations. "the
Canadian Government does not consider it
appropriate either to endorse or to challenge the Chinese Government's position
on the status of Taiwan."

In the end, a middle-of-the-road approach to a prickly diplomatic problem had
been used in the most prickly one of all,
recognition of China. By applying the
phrase neither to endorse nor to challenge
Mr Sharp had brought to bear a Canadian
foreign policy position established in the
years of Pearsonian diplomacy: namely,
that Canada expected no statement from a
foreign power either supporting or opposing Canadian territoriality claims (especially in the Arctic regions) and that
Canada in return would not be required to
make similar declarations concerning the
territoriality issues of other states. This
policy had resulted from earlier approaches
by other states to invite a Canadian position
or statement on the future of Gibraltar (a
Spanish-British crisis) and in the territorial water limits dispute over the Straits
of Malacca (an Indonesian-Malaysian crisis).

In the end those impatient exponents
of Canadian recognition of China who had
attacked Canadian diplomatic "go-slow"
methods as a major roadblock to bringing it
about saw the application of traditional
Canadian diplomatic method to help break
the potential deadlock in Stockholm. In a
speech to the Canadian Junior Chamber of
Commerce in Toronto on 14 October 1972,
Mr Sharp summed up: "This formula, or
one something like it, has been used during the last two years by most of the countries which have followed Canada in
establishing relations with Peking. The
Sino-Canadian communique of October 13,
1970 was the world premiere of a performance repeated many times since. The formula we worked out with the Chinese has

entered the jargon of specialists as 'the Canadian formula.' Like so many important things, it all seemed so simple once it had been worked out. But remember: working out this simple formula took almost two years of steady work."[11]

Recognition of Peking necessarily brought an abrupt change in Canada's official position regarding who should occupy China's seat at the United Nations.

It is true that in 1966 and the years following Canada had abstained on the Albanian resolution rather than voting against it, but until we voted in favour of China's entry in November 1970, our position relative to the Republic of China remained the same as outlined in a statement of 17 November 1965 by the Secretary of State for External Affairs, Paul Martin. It emphasized that Canada supported the position of the Republic of China as a founding member of the United Nations and would not disregard the claim of Taiwan "to play their full and honourable part in the life of the international community." He continued: "Canada, for one, could not agree that it would be in accordance with the principles of the United Nations to support an arrangement which would result in a denial of that claim."

The measure of Canada's change of position after recognition of Peking is found in comparing the words of Senator Martin with those of his successor six years later. Speaking to the Twenty-Sixth General Assembly of the United Nations on 29 September 1971, Mitchell Sharp reiterated the view put forward by Canada the year before: "The Canadian position is clear— the government that has the responsibility for the overwhelming majority of the Chinese people must now take its proper place here, the Government of the People's Republic of China."[12]

NOTES

1. *Deux Innocents en Chine Rouge* (Montreal 1961); translated by Ivon M Owen and published as *Two Innocents in Red China* (Toronto 1968).

2. "Recognize China...Trudeau," *Toronto Telegram*, 4 March 1968.

3. This study was made possible as much by interviews with officials directly involved with the recognition of the People's Republic, 1968-70, as from published and other available sources.

4. Canada, Department of External Affairs, *Statements and Speeches* 68/17.

5. "St Laurent sure Red China regime to be recognized," *Globe and Mail*, 8 March 1954; *Statements and Speeches* 55/30, 25 August 1955.

6. John W Holmes, "Canada and China: The Dilemmas of a Middle Power," in A M Halpern, ed, *Policies Toward China: Views from Six Continents* (New York 1965), pp. 108-9.

7. A senior official in the Department of External Affairs told the author that William Rogers, the incoming secretary of state in the Nixon administration, was, in February 1969, "respectful of our position." At the same time he speculated how difficult Washington could have been in early 1969 if Dean Rusk had still been secretary of state, given his strong support of President Johnson's escalation of the war in Vietnam and his resistance to efforts by "allies of the United States" to attempt openings towards China, North Vietnam's chief ally in Asia and major arms supplier.

8. Holmes "Canada and China," p. 110.
9. During the years 1947-9 several Canadian shipyards built seven coastal passenger ships for the Ming Sung Industrial Company Limited of Montreal to be used in the Chinese coastal trade. The $12,750,000 loan from Canadian banks to build them was guaranteed by the Chinese Nationalist and Canadian governments. In 1951 the government of the People's Republic of China and the Ming Sung Company defaulted on principal and interest payments and the Canadian government was obliged to carry out the guarantee and pay off the Canadian banks. On 3 June 1973 Canada and China signed an agreement under which Peking paid the full amount of $14,469,183 with accrued interest.
10. "Canada's talks on ties to Peking appear stalled," Jay Walz, *New York Times*, 8 August 1969.
11. "Canada and a New World Power—China," *Statements and Speeches*, 72/21, 14 October 1972.
12. "Chinese Representation in the United Nations," *ibid*, 65/28, 17 November 1965; "A Turning-Point in World History," *ibid*, 71/25, 29 September 1971.

SUGGESTED READINGS

Canada, "Canadian Recognition of the People's Republic of China," *External Affairs*, Vol. 22, No. 12, December, 1970, pp. 414-17.

Holmes, John W., "Canada and China," in John W. Holmes, *The Better Part of Valour: Essays on Canadian Diplomacy*, Toronto: McClelland and Stewart, 1970, pp. 201-217.

Molot, Maureen A., "Canada's Relations with China Since 1968," in N. Hillmer and G. Stevenson, *Foremost Nation: Canadian Foreign Policy and a Changing World*, Toronto: McClelland and Stewart, 1977, pp. 230-67.

Quo, F.Q. and Akira Ichikawa, "Sino-Canadian Relations: A New Chapter," *Asian Survey*, Vol. 12, No. 5, 1972, pp. 386-98.

Ronning, Chester, *A Memoir of China in Revolution: From the Boxer Rebellion to the People's Republic*, New York: Pantheon Books, 1974.

Sharp, Mitchell, "Establishment of Diplomatic Relations With the People's Republic of China," *Statements and Speeches*, No. 72/21, October 14, 1972.

c h a p t e r   15

R E D U C I N G V U L N E R A B I L I T Y : T H E T H I R D O P T I O N , 1 9 7 0 s

Peter Dobell

The new economic policy announced by the United States president, Richard Nixon, on 15 August 1971 has been aptly termed "the Nixon shocks." The phrase was not used only in Canada; Japan and Mexico were each in their own way as shaken by the decision. It is no exaggeration to suggest that the effect in Canada of these short-term measures and of the negotiations that followed their introduction produced a national catharsis.

The crisis itself lasted barely six months. The immediate reaction in Ottawa was to act as if, as on several occasions in the past, the United States had adopted a policy without appreciation for the special position of Canada. A ministerial delegation was hastily dispatched to Washington to point out that Canada was not guilty of the deficiencies which the measures were intended to overcome. It was the denial of an exemption to Canada and the discovery that Canada was a prime target of United States policy which forced Ottawa to recognize that it faced a major problem. The government found itself obliged to respond to American pressures for trade concessions in a situation where it lacked a sense of what Canada's long-term relationship with the United States should be. Even before the exemption request had been rejected, the cabinet directed the secretary of state for external affairs to undertake an over-all policy review of Canada's relations with the United States.

It is difficult to appreciate the atmosphere of shock and uncertainty which prevailed during the hectic months of August and September 1971. The cabinet and its senior advisers found an uncompromising harshness in Washington which had no precedent in their experience of dealing with the United States. For some weeks Ottawa echoed with disbelief and self-questioning. The country found itself in a national therapy session, forced to re-evaluate its traditional assumptions of friendship with its neighbour to the south. As the weeks passed, the government recovered a sense of direction. Arguments and statistics to meet the American challenges were marshalled and decisions taken on how to respond both in the multilateral monetary negotiations and in the bilateral exchanges on trade questions. The international situation began to improve: the Smithsonian agreement of 16 December produced a realignment of the major currencies; Japan and the European Community offered trading concessions in February 1972; and the United States balance-of-payments position began to improve.

For Canada there was no dramatic end to the crisis, no event which marked its close. Slowly, almost imperceptibly the tension dissipated and by the summer of 1972

Peter Debell, "A Fundamental Reassessment," *Canada in World Affairs, 1971-1973,* Toronto, Canadian Institute of International Affairs, 1985. Portions of the text have been deleted. Some footnotes have been removed; those remaining have been renumbered.

Canada and the United States had ceased their confrontation. While for the United States this simply meant that the government was turning to face new problems, in Canada the whole episode profoundly shook the national psyche for some years.

The Nixon Measures

On 15 August, President Nixon announced to a startled world a series of drastic measures designed to stem the haemorrhage in the United States balance of payments and to revive the national economy. These were a special surcharge of 10 per cent on a wide range of [imported] products, a halt to the convertibility of the dollar, an accelerated investment tax credit on machinery and equipment purchased from domestic suppliers, and a proposal to establish Domestic International Sales Corporations (DISCS) to provide a tax incentive to American companies to increase their domestic production for export rather than to establish production facilities abroad. Stressing that the aim was to achieve quick results, the announcement indicated that these measures would remain in effect only as long as the "unfair" treatment of American exports continued.

The United States action created problems for all its major trading partners, but none felt more threatened than Canada because of its dependence on exports to the American market. The Canadian cabinet was called into emergency session, with many ministers rushing back to Ottawa from vacation. The prime minister, who was holidaying on the Adriatic coast, returned in haste, cancelling meetings with President Tito of Yugoslavia and Prime Minister Heath of the United Kingdom. Emphasizing the unexpectedness of the measures, Mitchell Sharp, the secretary of state for external affairs and acting prime

minister, told the press on 16 August that Canadian ministers had not been consulted or informed prior to the American action. Officials had been told that the president was about to make a statement, but the first notification of its content was a call Mr. Sharp had received from the White House just before the president's broadcast. Having just completed a transatlantic flight, he was awakened by the call and commented: "I thought it was part of a dream."[1] Indeed it would not have been easy to recognize the reality of the harsh American measures in the light of traditionally friendly bilateral consultations.

The government's most immediate attention was focused on the [import] surcharge. Canada's exports to the United States in 1970 had amounted to over $10.5 billion, a colossal 13 per cent of the entire gross national product (GNP). It was hurriedly estimated that at least 25 per cent or $2.5 to $3 billion worth of exports would attract the new tax, representing more than 4 per cent of the GNP. While all depended on how long the surcharge remained in force, initial government calculations suggested that the consequent unemployment might run between 40,000 and 100,000. It was also feared that the "Buy America" tax changes and the DISC proposal, if implemented, would have a further drastic effect on employment in view of the number of American-owned subsidiaries in Canada which would find it advantageous to transfer operations to their United States plants.

The first instinct of ministers, as they tried to understand the full implications of the Nixon action, was to find out whether Washington had again made a mistake. Three times previously, in 1963, 1966, and 1968, the United States had introduced measures to restrain the flow abroad of American capital. Each time Canada had pointed out that the policies had been drafted without consideration of the drastic effects on the Canadian economy, and in each case the United States had decided that it was in the American interest to exempt Canada from their application. The scale of the potential impact on employment in Canada, and therefore indirectly on Canada's capacity to continue to take American exports, naturally led the cabinet in August 1971 to assume that the United States had again left Canada out of its calculations and would accordingly agree to yet another exemption. Besides, Ottawa judged that "in the President's own terms, the import surcharges should not apply to Canada." As Mr. Sharp said at the 16 August press conference: "[The measures] are supposed ... to induce countries to change their unfair exchange rates or to remove discriminatory restrictions against American imports. We're not guilty on either count."[2] Another important factor in the initial Canadian response was the perception, widely held by the Canadian public, that a special relationship existed between the two countries and that, based on past performance, an exemption was obtainable. Given the public expectation as well as the ministerial conviction that Canada was not guilty on any of the points advanced, the cabinet decided to send a ministerial delegation to Washington. On 18 August Mr. Sharp announced that Edgar Benson, the minister of finance, accompanied by Jean-Luc Pepin, the minister of industry, trade and commerce, would go to Washington to try to persuade the Americans that Canada was being unjustly "penalized" and that it was contrary to the United States' own interest to apply these import surcharges against Canada.

At a Washington press conference Mr. Benson and Mr. Pepin amplified the case which they had energetically put to John Connally, the secretary of the treasury, and

other American officials.[3] Whereas President Nixon sought by his policy to bring about a realistic currency alignment and a liberalization of trade and investment policies on the part of his nation's trading partners, the Canadian emphasized that "Canada has already taken steps which the President was seeking to have other nations take." The Canadian dollar had been floating freely since June 1970 and by August 1971 had appreciated in relation to the United States dollar by some 6 per cent. Canada had speeded up the implementation of the Kennedy Round trade liberalization scheme under the General Agreement on Tariffs and Trade (GATT). It was pointed out that "the tremendous integration ... that exists between the two economics" had meant that "companies have taken for granted that they could establish in Canada or in the United States and provide and supply the total North American market." Furthermore, the Canadians sought to demonstrate that "when the Canadian economy is in difficulty ... imports into Canada from the United States go down ... and the end result is that they damage themselves as well as damage us in the process of implementing this 10% surcharge." Finally, while acknowledging the sizable trade surplus of 1970 with the United States, the delegation sought to point out that Canada still had "a small current account deficit last year, because the balance of trade ... was ... offset by interest and dividend payments to the United States.

The arguments of the Canadian delegation failed. Ottawa was forced to recognize that a new global doctrine was evolving in Washington and that Canada was, in fact, one of its prime targets. Within the United States administration the guiding perception was that in the past the United States had been generous to the point of disavowing its own self-interest, but that it could not be expected to carry the world's burdens indefinitely. Its friends and trading partners, having benefited from American generosity and assistance in the past and now comfortably placed, should be willing to share the burden. The deterioration in its balance of payments was one symptom of the malaise which Washington decided needed correction. The inventory of Canadian sins included not only unbalanced trading arrangements in automotive and defence products, but industrial policies such as that which encouraged a company like Michelin to locate in Canada from whence to supply the whole North American market.

Faced with what amounted to a rejection of its first bid for exemption, the government decided to take its case to the public. On 20 August, only a day after returning to Canada, Prime Minister Trudeau made a nationwide radio and television broadcast.[4] Warning that the surcharge could cause large-scale unemployment in Canada, he continued: "a weak Canadian economy is no help to the United States. Unemployed Canadians cannot afford to buy U.S. goods." Canada understood the American problem, however, and sympathized with its goal of a healthy economy. It was not in Canada's interest "to retaliate and set in motion the destructive spiral of an international trade war." "Everyone," Mr. Trudeau said, "would be the loser in those circumstances." Canada would therefore continue to press the United States government to re-examine the surcharge as it applied to Canada.

Washington's cool reception to Canada's request for exemption from the surcharge was not taken as a final answer. A few days later, on 26 August, a delegation of senior officials, armed with more detailed figures, was sent to Washington to renew the appeal. The government released these statistics simultaneously in Ottawa, showing the potential damage of the measures, inter alia, to Canadian exporters of animal and vegetable products, textiles, fibres, metals, machinery, and equipment. Overall, it was anticipated that US $2.7 billion in Canadian exports to the United States were likely to be affected.[5] The delegation returned empty-handed, but with a renewed awareness that the application of the surcharge to Canada was not an oversight. On the contrary, it was now evident that Canada was a principal target in the United States campaign to staunch the drain on its foreign-exchange reserves. Washington was disturbed by Canada's exceptional trade surpluses in 1969 and 1970, which represented a shift in Canada's favour of some $2 billion. Faced with a presidential order to turn about the massive United States payments deficit, the hawks in the Treasury, led by Secretary Connally who was the dominant force in the administration at that time, had concluded that Canada should be a major target. Canada, it was inferred, had profited too long from the Automotive Agreement and the defence production sharing arrangements, and the terms of these pacts should be adjusted. In fact, the Treasury Department had gone so far as to include in its press release the announcement that the United States had decided to terminate the 1965 Automotive Agreement. Julius Katz, an assistant secretary in the State Department, who first saw the release minutes before it was due in the White House, succeeded in persuading the Treasury to delete this from the text, using the argument that the Canadian government should not learn of this decision from a press release. As it turned out, the Treasury's objective was to re-negotiate the agreement rather than to terminate it, and this drastic strategy was not pursued. Canadian authorities were of course completely unaware of this drama.[6]

By late September, as the implications of the tough and unbending American stand sank in, a new, firmer tone was evident in the speeches of Canadian ministers. On separate occasions, the prime minister, the secretary of state for external affairs, and the minister of industry, trade and commerce suggested that a fundamental re-assessment of Canada's relations with the United States would be necessary if the American attitude did not change.[7] Speaking on television on 23 September, Mr. Trudeau attacked in blunt terms what appeared to be the American unwillingness to allow Canada to foster its secondary manufacturing industries and increase employment:

If (the Americans) just want us to be sellers of natural resources to them and buyers of their manufactured products... we will have to re-assess fundamentally our relations with them, trading, political, and otherwise.

. . .

Meanwhile, to mitigate the effects of the surcharge, the government had introduced in the House of Commons on 7 September a programme of temporary employment support designed to prevent layoffs or closures. Under this legislation $80 million was set aside in grants for firms that had exported at least 20 per cent of their 1970 production to the United States. The bill provided subsidies that offset up to two-thirds of the surcharge applicable to exports to the United States from these plants based on 1970 figures.

The legislation involved the risk of United States retaliation, and, indeed several days after the bill was introduced, there were rumblings of dissatisfaction from Washington. The under secretary of the treasury told a Senate Finance sub-committee that if the Canadian employment support measure were found to be merely an effort to get around the surtax, the United States government would consider action to nullify its effect either through countervailing duties or through anti-dumping measures. Representations were immediately made to Washington explaining why Canada's action should not justify countervailing measures. In a letter to Mr. Connally,[8] Mr. Benson defended the Canadian action as ameliorative and stressed that it was "intended only to ease the harsh impact on Canadian employment which would otherwise result from the effects on Canadian production and employment of your import surtax. It is not a condition of obtaining the grants that exports to the U.S. be maintained." In the end no retaliatory American action was taken.

Meanwhile it was reported that a senior American Treasury official had made the even more disturbing suggestion that the removal of certain safeguards in the Automotive Agreement was an item to be negotiated before the surcharge would be cancelled. Mr. Connally had already mentioned the removal of the safeguards as one of the contributions which Canada could make toward resolving the dollar crisis and getting the surcharge removed. Canadian ministers responded that the government could not agree that changes in the auto pact should be a precondition for the removal of the surtax; they repeatedly asserted that there had been no formal request from Washington to this effect.[9]

Shortly after these denials, the *Chicago Tribune* of 11 October reported that United States Treasury officials had "a shopping list" of grievances against Canada, whereupon the prime minister, the minister of industry, trade and commerce, and the secretary of state for external affairs all insisted in the Commons that the government had never received such a list.[10] Mr. Sharp said that Canada would like to enter into negotiations on such matters because "we also have our list" and gave as examples the United States ban on the import of uranium as well as certain restrictive features of American copyright and immigration laws, and the United States selling price on petrochemicals. However, the government strongly asserted that any negotiations on these issues should not be linked with talks regarding the removal of the surcharge. Following a visit by a group of American officials to Ottawa in early November, Mr. Sharp put the Canadian viewpoint even more bluntly in the Commons: "... the United States does not have the right to put on a surtax and say, 'Now you must bargain your way out of it.'"[11]

Preoccupied with their massive deficit and determined to achieve quick results, the American authorities in the Treasury were not particularly interested in Canada's longer term payments problem. Throughout the autumn, therefore, Canadian ministers and officials concentrated on explaining the ABCs of the Canadian situation to Washington. Canada had traditionally had unfavourable trade and payments balances with the United States, which were covered by favourable balances with other regions of the world and by United States capital inflows for investment in Canada. The large trade surplus of 1970 was exceptional. In only three years between 1900 and 1968 had Canada enjoyed such a surplus. Moreover, even the surpluses of 1968, 1969, and 1970 were insufficient to cover expenditure on invisibles and to service United States investments in Canada. In spite of the trade surplus of $1.1 billion which so troubled the Americans, Canada had actually run a small deficit of $165 million in

its current account in 1970 (Table 1). This pattern was subsequently repeated in 1971 and 1972, with increased current account deficits. At first discussions with the Americans remained unproductive because each side was talking about different problems. Dialogue was made still more difficult because United States and Canadian statistics told quite different stories. Thus, American figures for 1970 showed Canada with a merchandise trade surplus of $2 billion. The Canadian figures showed a trade surplus of just over $1 billion with the United States, leaving a gap of almost $1 billion.[12]

To counter United States pressures on Canada to revalue its dollar—the approach which the Americans were adopting with each of their major trading partners—the government stuck unwaveringly during the autumn to the position first formulated when the crisis began. The Canadian dollar had been floating freely since June 1970. Unlike the major European and Japanese currencies, which were floated for the first time on 23 August and which appreciated fairly rapidly in terms of the United States dollar, the adjustment of the Canadian dollar had already taken place in the preceding fifteen months and by September it had found a natural level at 7 per cent over the American dollar. Canada therefore, strongly resisted United States pressure to repeg the dollar at a higher rate, indicating that it intended to maintain a floating currency, and insisted that international monetary reform had to be negotiated multilaterally.

Continued American insistence, repeated in every discussion, on Canadian concessions to reduce the merchandise trade surpluses of 1969 and 1970 began to arouse suspicions that the United States was even unwilling to contemplate the possibility of future Canadian surpluses. In an interview in late October Prime Minister

| TABLE 1 | CANADA'S BALANCE OF PAYMENTS WITH THE UNITED STATES 1964-73 (CDN$ MILLION) |

Year	Balance on merchandise trade	Balance on non-merchandise trade	Current account balance
1964	-808	-827	-1635
1965	-1041	-896	-1937
1966	-993	-1037	-2030
1967	-569	-773	-1342
1968	+389	-1136	-747
1969	+472	-1317	-845
1970	+1121	-1286	-165
1971	+1209	-1491	-282
1972	+1233	-1687	-454
1973	+814	-2071	-1257

NOTE: United States statistics on trade with Canada differed significantly from Canada's.

SOURCE: Statistics Canada. *Canada Year Book* 1972: Quarterly Estimates of the Canadian Balance of Payments, Fourth Quarter, 1973, 49, and Fourth Quarter, 1974, 35.

Trudeau succinctly explored the implications of such a policy, given the already high concentration of American investment in Canada:

The United States is now telling us that it doesn't want to have a trade deficit with us. We are saying "if we don't have a trade surplus with you, how are we going to pay the interest and dividends which we have to pay you every year? We want an answer to this: Are you saying that you will continue to want to receive from Canada and indeed from all the world, interest and dividends coming back into the United States every year, and not let the rest of the world and Canada pay for that by selling more goods to you because you still want to sell more goods to them, therefore, are you saying that you must export long-term American capital to all the countries of the world? In other words, are you saying that your economic system is leading you to try and buy up as much of the world as possible."[13]

By November a number of developments had produced a new assurance among Canadian ministers. The surcharge was not having the drastic effect anticipated: the maximum numbers of unemployed which could be expected were being revised downward. Exports to the United States had held up extraordinarily well; indeed exports in 1971 were slightly higher than in 1970. The government had now had sufficient time to assess fully the merits of the United States demands, and it had concluded that there was no justification for unilateral Canadian concessions. Progress was being made in the international monetary talks.

A focus of Canadian resentment was John Connally. The secretary's strong temperament led him to pursue aggressively President Nixon's directive to reverse the outflow of United States dollars. The combination of his assignment and his energy resulted in the Treasury Department displacing the State Department as the executor of American foreign policy on questions linked in any way to the balance of payments. Mr. Pepin gave the flavour of Mr. Connally when he recalled later that the secretary had told him bluntly that the president and he had decided, "to shake the world. And that, brother, includes you!"[14] Mr. Connally was out to restore the economic strength of the United States, and he communicated his energy and determination to his staff. For their part, many of them had little previous experience of Canada. Canadian negotiators found them woefully ignorant of basic facts about the Canadian economy and of the pattern of the bilateral relationship. As an ascendant political figure and a potential vice-president, Mr. Connally and his department carried a lot of weight in Washington.

The problem for the Canadian government was how to reach out beyond Mr. Connally. In an attempt to make the Canadian case to a broader audience in the United States, both the secretary of state for external affairs and the minister of industry, trade and commerce gave speeches in the United States during the autumn. These efforts appear to have made some headway, for on 7 November a *New York Times* editorial sympathetically set forth the Canadian arguments on its floating dollar and its non-discriminatory trade policy and spoke of "a chronic ignorance of—and indifference toward—this northern neighbor and ally."[15]

Nor was Congress ignored.[16]

The government's major initiative to circumvent the power of Secretary Connally was revealed on 30 November, when it was announced that the prime minister would fly to Washington for a one-day meeting with President Nixon on 6 December. During the preceding months he had been continually urged by the opposition to make personal or telephone contact with the pres-

ident. The Progressive Conservatives gave political edge to their advocacy of a meeting by charging that Mr. Trudeau's past neglect of relations with the United States, while courting the Russians and Chinese, was responsible for the tough attitude of the Americans. They also said that the surcharge was a retaliatory gesture. The prime minister termed these charges "just not true" and "completely ridiculous."[17] However, it was not opposition pressure that provided the primary impetus for the trip. During November the government had become aware that Washington was arranging a series of bilateral meetings between President Nixon and the leaders of other major trading partners to discuss the United States measures and possible readjustments. There had been no request for a meeting with Canada. In taking the initiative to seek one, the government decided to avoid the normal channels involving the State and Treasury Departments and to have the prime minister's foreign affairs adviser, Ivan Head, contact Henry Kissinger, the president's special assistant for national security affairs, directly. Mr. Kissinger, apparently surprised that no meeting was being organized with the prime minister, undertook to set one up.

. . .

The meeting between the two leaders in the Oval Room at the White House lasted a little over two hours, attended only by one adviser from each side, Henry Kissinger and Ivan Head. At the same time, in the neighbouring Cabinet Room, the ministers of finance and industry, trade and commerce, Messrs. Benson and Pepin, and Canadian officials met Secretary Connally, the secretary of commerce, Maurice Stans, and other United States officials. The ministers reviewed the issue of the trade balance and the specific items which had been under discussion between officials since

August including the auto pact safeguard clauses, tourist duty-free allowances, Canadian uranium exports, and the defence production sharing arrangements. The Canadians met the same intransigent attitude on the part of the secretary of the treasury as before, and exchanges apparently became quite heated. Little progress was made in resolving the trade irritants although the Canadian side agreed to look at the auto pact with a view to suspension of certain safeguards.

The meeting in the Oval Room, however, progressed much more favourably. Although the general international situation including the India-Pakistan conflict and the Middle East was touched on, the main topic was Canadian-American relations. One of Mr. Trudeau's arguments, which had been honed in interviews during October and November and in an article Mr. Head had prepared for the influential American journal, *Foreign Affairs*,[18] drew on the writing of the American economist, Paul Sweezy. The prime minister suggested to the United States administration that they had not thought through the implications of their actions which could be interpreted as economic imperialism. At the televised press conference after the Washington meeting, Mr. Trudeau indicated he had used this approach with Mr. Nixon and Mr. Kissinger.[19]

In Ottawa, he told the house his purpose had been "to seek reassurance from the President, and it can only come from him, that it is neither the intention nor the desire of the United States that the economy of Canada become so dependent upon the United States in terms of a deficit trading pattern that Canadians will inevitably lose independence of economic decisions."[20]

The president may well have been somewhat taken aback by this interpretation of his August measures. But the strategy drew the answers the prime minister had sought. This response, the prime minister concluded, was "a total answer" to the concerns he had expressed. In glowing, almost extravagant terms, Mr. Trudeau told the press how understanding the president had been in comparing present Canadian dependence on American capital with earlier American dependence on European capital before the First World War and how he had recognized that Canada must be free to take only as much capital as it wished. This represented to Mr. Trudeau "a fantastically new statement in the mouth of the President of the United States ... the President's statement was, in my mind, a real breakthrough in that it recognized the entire freedom of Canada (to do things its own way)." The talks showed, he said, "that the United States not only want to respect our political identity but our economic identity. And the breakthrough is almost, I would say not philosophical, but expressed in terms of destinies of two countries."

. . .

While Mr. Trudeau waxed eloquent over the president's understanding of the future of the relationship, he was strangely silent about the more immediate concerns of the surcharge or the auto pact safeguards. There was nothing to announce "at this time" but perhaps "it was just as well," he said, because the re-establishment of a stable international monetary system to be worked out at the upcoming Group of Ten meeting should be given prior consideration.[21]

This was as much as he said publicly. But privately he carried back with him to Ottawa Mr. Kissinger's startling assurance to Mr. Head at the end of the meeting that the surcharge would be lifted in a matter of weeks, that the validity of Canada's floating dollar was recognized, and that Canada would not be penalized in the forthcoming settlement. Obviously any public hint of this exemption for Canada would have jeopardized the concessions the United States still wished to wring from its European trading partners and Japan in the next few weeks.

This situation led to a puzzled, somewhat sceptical, reaction from the opposition, the press, and the general public in Canada about just what had been achieved in Washington.

. . .

Washington too may have been some The White House press briefing following the meeting had spoken of "cordial relations" between the two countries, but was very matter of fact in tone. It is unlikely that President Nixon himself fully realized the long-term implications for Canadian economic independence which Mr. Trudeau saw in his statements. As for Mr. Connally, his tough uncompromising attitude at the ministerial talks suggests that he too may have been surprised at Mr. Trudeau's reaction, at least until Mr. Kissinger told him of Mr. Nixon's decision in effect to exempt Canada.

Two weeks later, on 18 December, the Smithsonian meeting of the Group of Ten in Washington reached an agreement on a realignment of currencies, and the United States government undertook to terminate the surcharge and the related provisions of the investment tax credit. Under the accord, the United States government agreed to propose to Congress a devaluation of the United States dollar through an increase in the price of gold from US\$35 to US\$38 an ounce. The dollar, however, was to remain inconvertible into gold. Other countries of the Group of Ten, Canada excepted, agreed on a set of exchange-rate parities for their currencies, with an enlarged margin of fluctuation of $2^{1}/_{4}$ per cent above and below the new fixed rates. The accord was accompa-

nied by an understanding that the major trading nations would proceed to resolve their trade differences with the United States through negotiations as soon as possible.[22]

A smiling Mr. Benson reported to the Commons on 20 December that Canada's case for maintaining a free float had been accepted and that Canada was alone in being exempted from repegging its currency. "There is no doubt," he claimed, "that the meeting two weeks ago between our Prime Minister ... and President Nixon contributed to [this] satisfactory outcome."[23] Indeed it had, and the key members of the cabinet had known for twelve days that this major battle had already been won.

. . .

Outlining The Options

Ottawa [nonetheless, had been] quite disoriented by the refusal of the United States government to [initially] exempt Canada from the import surcharge. To gain a sense of direction the cabinet had decided immediately after the request for an exemption had been clearly rejected, that is, before the end of August 1971, to direct the secretary of state for external affairs to prepare an overall assessment of Canada's relations with the United States, including an analysis of alternative policy options.

It had been surprising that *Foreign Policy for Canadians*, the 1970 set of booklets outlining the Trudeau government's rationale for a contemporary and anticipatory Canadian foreign policy, had not included a booklet on relations with the United States: "like playing *Hamlet* without the Prince of Denmark," the NDP foreign affairs critic, Andrew Brewin had remarked at the time.[24] The response to such criticism had been that the relationship with the United States was so persuasive and complex that it could not be treated comprehensively in a single booklet. Instead, the drafters maintained that the United States formed the central if largely unanalysed reality with which Canadian foreign policy always had to cope and was therefore an underlying thread. And indeed the first booklet had laid down some general propositions about the relationship. However, faced with the United States demands of August 1971 for which it was admittedly unprepared and which *Foreign Policy for Canadians* had not anticipated, the government felt an acute need for the "missing" booklet.

By the end of September Mr. Sharp was able to submit a memorandum to his colleagues outlining three approaches for dealing with the United States: continuing the present ad hoc policies, seeking closer integration, and a third option involving the pursuit of "a deliberate, comprehensive, and long-term strategy designed to develop and strengthen the Canadian economy." By late November cabinet had decided upon the third option, in time to provide a background for Prime Minister Trudeau's December meeting with President Nixon.

The government also decided that it wanted an inventory of current issues between Canada and the United States, which was to be updated regularly. At the same time, studies were undertaken of the international setting for the bilateral relationship and of the effect on it of the changing perspective in Washington. This work was reviewed in cabinet and consolidated in time for President Nixon's visit to Ottawa in April 1972. At that point, with the crisis over, the sense of urgency disappeared. Although during the summer the Department of External Affairs sought comments on the revised policy paper from other government departments, there was little response. Mitchell Sharp, as the minister most directly concerned, was faced with a choice: to accept the delays and compromises necessary to secure an interdepartmentally agreed text which could be presented as a white paper or to seek some other, less official, way of making the paper public.

Later, in describing how the paper had evolved, Mr. Sharp revealed:

> there were some misgivings in Government circles about opting for any particular direction in our relations with the United States. Why take a public position? Why not play it by ear? Why not leave all the options open? Why give the Opposition something else to criticize? ... but we finally came to the conclusion that a sense of direction had to be given to our relations with the United States.[25]

While this explains the initial resolution to commission a strategy paper, it does not account for the unusual decision to release it under the minister's name in the form of a special autumn 1972 issue of *International Perspectives*, a journal of opinion published by the Department of External Affairs.[26] Mr. Sharp decided against the white paper route and explained his decision this way some months later:

> To submit (to public examination) a tentative proposal or options being examined helps the Government make up its own mind and enables the public to take part in the decision-making process.
>
> In the paper on Canada-U.S. Relations ... the Government came out in favour of what has been termed the Third Option ...
>
> Is this the right direction for Canada? This Government thinks so. But do the Canadian people? The question can only be answered if it is put before the people.[27]

But this reasoning still begs the question. On one line the minister spoke of "a tentative proposal or options" and yet two lines later he asserted that "the Government came out in favour of ... the Third Option." The latter statement is even more interesting in that the article itself only implied, and did not claim, governmental endorsement of the third option.

There may also have been a link between the method of publication and the October election campaign. The Liberal party platform for the 1972 election promised that a Liberal government would present a policy option for Canada in its relations with the United States to "retain the benefits of this association ... [and] also insure the maintenance of Canadian sovereignty."[28] But when the paper appeared two weeks before the election, it received little notice in the press and did not become a subject of debate, as Mr. Sharp ruefully noted later. Four subsequent speeches by the minister and the opening of the columns of *International Perspectives* to academic comment generated little more public interest.

The policy paper itself was notable for an articulate and logical approach to the problem of dealing with the enormously complex bilateral relationship. It analyzed the history of the Canadian-American relationship from the time the United States had been viewed as a military threat to the postwar era of the "special" relationship and the contemporary period marked particularly by the continental pull in the economic field. The relationship was then set in the perspective of the changing international context: "In the new scheme of things both Canada and the United States saw a relatively diminished role for themselves" (page 6). Both countries had recently related their foreign policy objectives more to their own national interest than in the past. In the United States there was a new perception of its problems, a concentration on domestic difficulties combined with a disenchantment with foreign involvement. In Washington, there was "a strong disposition to believe that the United States has not been tough enough in trade and economic negotiations in the past" (page 10). Canada was bound to be affected by policies that reflected a narrower interpretation of the United States national interest. In Canada there was a growing awareness of the issue of economic independence and a new willingness to support reasonable measures to assure greater Canadian independence. For Canada, distinctness could have only one meaning in recent years: distinctness from the United States.

The paper then described the three broad options available to Canada, each of which delineated general directions of policy and could be supported by a varied assortment of policy instruments:

- Canada can seek to maintain more or less its present relationship with the United States with a minimum of policy adjustments.
- Canada can move deliberately toward closer integration with the United States.
- Canada can pursue a comprehensive long-term strategy to develop and strengthen the Canadian economy and other aspects of its national life and in the process to reduce the present Canadian vulnerability (page 1).

The advantages and disadvantages of each option were weighed. The first, which would call for steering a pragmatic course to maintain something of a "special relationship" was judged risky in that, in the end, Canada might find itself drawn more closely into the American orbit. This would be "a substantially reactive posture on Canada's part" (page 21). The second option could mean the pursuit of limited continental arrangements or might involve a free-trade area or customs union. The former might generate pressures for increased sectoral arrangements like the auto pact in which Canada might have difficulty over time maintaining an equal voice with the United States. A free-trade or customs union arrangement would, "to all intents and purposes, be irreversible for Canada once embarked upon" (page 15). This option was judged likely to be costly in terms of Canadian identity; moreover it was doubtful "whether this option, or any part of it, is politically tenable in the present or any foreseeable climate of Canadian public opinion" (page 16).

The aim of the third option would be, "over time, to lessen the vulnerability of the Canadian economy to external factors, including, in particular, the impact of the United States and, in the process, to strengthen our capacity to advance basic Canadian goals and develop a more confident sense of national identity" (page 17). There would be no basic change in Canada's multilateral trade policy or any distortion of traditional trading patterns. The United States would remain by far Canada's most important market and source of supply. The object would be to create a less vulnerable economic base for competing in the domestic and world markets. It would be necessary to encourage the specialization and rationalization of production and the emergence of strong Canadian-controlled firms, and it might be desirable to foster the development of large, efficient, multinational Canadian firms which could compete effectively on world markets. "Fiscal policy, monetary policy, the tariff, the rules of competition, government procurement, foreign investment regulations, science policy may

all have to be brought to bear on the objectives associated with this option" (page 18).

The paper stated that "no prescription for Canada is likely to be complete that did not attempt to cover the cultural sector" (page 19) as well as the economic. Here, the essential choices may already have been made, for Canada had in recent years applied two policies to counter the threat of cultural integration. One was regulatory where the intention was to ensure that, when the standards of the product are equal, the Canadian one is not ruled out by terms of competition that are unequal. This was the general philosophy that had guided the Canadian Radio-Television Commission and was probably applicable to other areas such as film, record, or publication, even though the control of the distribution system was not in Canadian hands. The other prescription was to give direct support, both in terms of financial assistance and institutions, to cultural activity in Canada. These policies, in the report's judgment, had been followed "with reasonable success." Although the cultural sector remains vulnerable, it concluded, "perhaps we have already turned the corner" (page 20).

Summing up, the paper stated that "if Canadians say they want a distinct country ... it is because they want to do the things they consider important and do them in their own way" (page 20). In its implicit approval of the third option, the paper looked to "the mutually-reinforcing use of various policy instruments to achieve greater Canadian distinctness" (page 21). Although there was clearly no possibility of Canada surmounting overnight its heavy dependence on the United States for trade, investment, and technology, there was no reason, the paper asserted, why Canada should not aim "in the context of an expanding economy and expanding trade prospects, to achieve relative shifts that, over time, could make a difference in reducing Canada's dependence on a single market and, by extension, the vulnerability of the Canadian economy as such" (page 23).

There is little evidence that the policy paper itself has had much influence since its publication. In May 1973 Mr. Sharp made the cautious claim that the paper was "beginning to have some effect upon the direction of Canadian Government policy." But to make his point he explained that "just the other day for the first time, a report to Cabinet passed my eye which referred to the Third Option in support of its recommendations."[29] As this was eight months after the paper's publication, it was hardly a convincing illustration of government commitment. The lack of response by other departments to the request from the Department of External Affairs for comment on the draft paper and the background studies conveys a similar impression of disregard and resistance to policy direction, even though these departments accepted the main thrust of government policy. The foreign investment review bill introduced in January 1973 was, it is true, designed to resist the intercorporate "continental pull" which the paper had spelled out and could be considered a partial implementation of a national industrial strategy in line with the third option; but the study of the problem of foreign ownership had been commissioned before the option paper was conceived. In respect to cultural policy, the option paper itself recognized that policies countering cultural integration had already been launched. And while the Cabinet Committee on Economic Relations did decide early in 1973 to carry "Canada-United States relations" as a regular item on its agenda, that committee only met sporadically at the time and the practice was subsequently dropped.

It would be a mistake, however, to conclude that the whole exercise was without significance. At least until the end of the decade, the third option concept remained a viable argument and continued to be summoned up to tilt government decisions in one direction rather than another. Furthermore, at the time of its preparation, a broad review of Canadian relations with the United States in terms of national goals had undoubtedly been helpful to the harried and worried cabinet members who had to respond to Nixon's new economic policy and to take tough decisions while under strong American pressure. Discussion of the options in cabinet did aid the government to gain "a sense of direction" and to resist United States demands for Canadian concessions.

Foreign Investment Review

The principal area of government concern about foreign control during this period lay in investment and ownership of Canadian industry. The Watkins Report of 1968 and an earlier royal commission of 1957 chaired by Walter Gordon had begun to alert public opinion to this issue.[30] During 1970 several highly publicized takeovers or attempted takeovers (Denison Mines, Home Oil, W.J. Gage, and Ryerson Press) had focused more public attention on the issue of foreign ownership than at any time since the Mercantile Bank case of 1965. Although the government naturally approached the subject in terms of ownership by any foreign national, the primary concern was with ownership and control by Americans, who were the major foreign shareholders in all sectors of industry. Opinion polls revealed that a growing number of Canadians considered the level of American investment in Canada was too high. In June 1971, the Committee for an Independent Canada had handed Prime Minister Trudeau a petition with 170,000 signatures urging the government to enact stronger policies on foreign ownership.

To guide it in handling this difficult and sensitive subject—affecting employment, the development of an industrial strategy, relations with provincial governments and with foreign governments, especially that of the United States—the government had appointed in March 1970 yet another task force to study the whole question. To underline the government's serious intent, a cabinet minister, Herb Gray, minister without portfolio, was appointed head of the group... [It] would not be until 4 April 1974 that the first phase of the Foreign Investment Review Act was actually proclaimed, some four years after the Gray task force began its work.

Even without the United States action in August 1971, there would likely have been delays and modifications in the government's handling of this complex subject. Already in June, for example, there were rumours in Ottawa that reaction to Gray's first report to cabinet had exposed deep divisions among ministers although it was later revealed that an agreement in principle had been reached at this time. That it was a thorny problem was acknowledged by the prime minister when he said in October that his colleagues had already "spent many many days and nights of Cabinet Committees on it."[31] But the American surcharge and the demands for trade concessions from Canada forced the government to postpone further consideration while it reassessed Canada's goals and their implications for relations with the United States in the broadest possible sense. The prime minister himself acknowledged that the surcharge and unemployment had influenced the government's action:

I dare say if we had made a decision six months ago it might have been marginally different than a decision we might make in six weeks ... I do know that since the Nixon measures and ... since the latest unemployment figures have been made known to the country, ... that there's much greater circumspection in Canada on the degree of toughness with which we want to treat foreign capital here.[32]

While it delayed discussions on legislation, the government nonetheless continued to express its concern over the difficulties, and even dangers, which foreign investment posed for Canada. In interviews the prime minister repeatedly linked the American demand for the elimination of Canada's bilateral trade surplus with the problem of how Canada was to make the interest and dividend payments to American investors in Canada. "I think it is more than a billion and a half net outflow ... every year," he said in late October and asked the Americans: "How are we going to pay for it if it's not by selling you goods? And if it's not by selling you goods, are you going to buy up more and more of our country? So this is the Herb Gray problem." Citing the high degree of American control in certain sectors of Canadian industry, he reiterated that "as a government, our minimum posture is to maintain the status quo."[33] Given the well-publicized fact that American takeovers of Canadian companies were being financed at an accelerated rate by the retained earnings of American firms in Canada [and thus, these takeovers did not involve new capital entering Canada], this statement appeared to indicate a determination of the government to act.

While the United States actions in August 1971 led to caution and reassessment on the part of the government, they had exactly the opposite effect on Canadian nationalists. In circumstances where they saw the need for strong and speedy action to limit foreign investment, they feared the government was actually slipping into greater and greater dependence on the United States. The *Canadian Forum* devoted its December 1971 issue to a leaked version of the Gray Report.[34] The *Forum* version apparently lacked the last two chapters of the original report but it made a strong case for some form of direct intervention by the government designed to exploit the opportunities provided by foreign investment while resisting the most undesirable results and suggested that the most desirable form of such intervention would be a screening mechanism with broad authority to investigate takeovers, new investment, licences and franchises, and the expansion of existing foreign-controlled firms in Canada.

...

The leak in the *Canadian Forum* had alerted the provinces to the government's thinking, and several provincial leaders immediately expressed dismay. By accident the publication had occurred just prior to a federal-provincial meeting of first ministers. The conference revealed wide disagreement among the provinces, a factor which probably further delayed federal action on the question. Certainly the prime minister, in justifying the eventual legislation which emerged, gave the provinces a central role in the process and repeatedly referred to provincial opposition to restrictions on investment capital inflows.

Nearly six months were to elapse before the government was finally able to submit a bill to Parliament. Finally, on 2 May, before an expectant audience in the Commons, Mr. Gray, now minister of national revenue, tabled the task force report entitled *Foreign Direct Investment in Canada*.[35] At the same time, he unveiled a draft bill which, two days later, was re-produced as bill C-201, the Foreign Takeovers Review Act. The product of two years' work, *Foreign Direct Investment in Canada* noted that the level of foreign control constituted a very high proportion of Canadian corporate activity, was higher in Canada than in any other industrialized country, and was likely to increase. Since 1954 there had been significant and rapid growth in the degree of foreign ownership and control in selected Canadian industries. The areas of greatest concentration were manufacturing and natural resources. In manufacturing, non-resident control by 1967 was estimated at 57 per cent, in petroleum and natural gas at 74 per cent, and in mining and smelting at 65 per cent. In these industries residents of the United States controlled 80 per cent or more of the capital employed that was controlled by all non-residents. Using another form of measurement, the study reported that in the petroleum and coal products industry, over 98 per cent of the assets, sales, profits, and taxable income were accounted for by non-resident ownership. Other industries with 80 per cent of their assets owned by non-residents were rubber products, transport equipment, chemicals, and tobacco. The data also made clear that high-technology industries were generally dominated by non-residents.

Analysing the situation in Canada, the report warned against an across-the-board protectionist policy on foreign investment which, it argued, could "close Canada off from new developments and technology elsewhere and preclude Canada from access to some foreign markets for certain products. It can also be unduly protective of Canadian management so that it will be under little pressure to innovate and constantly improve its efficiency" (page 439). The report judged the acquisition of majority ownership on Canadian industry on a large scale to be too costly for Canadians since foreign ownership was so widespread and noted as well that "Canadian control of a business is not in itself a guarantee of sound performance" (page 437). Instead, the report argued that the appropriate Canadian response to the problem should be a "flexible administrative intervention which could vary from case to case and time to time" (page 439).

Specifically, the report proposed a review agency which could screen not only takeovers but also new direct investment both by existing foreign controlled firms in Canada and by firms abroad. It would "marshall Canadian bargaining power in an effort to obtain the maximum benefits possible for Canada from foreign direct investment" (page 453). Criteria for the review agency's decisions might include the benefits which takeovers or investment would bring Canada in terms of contributions to productivity and industrial efficiency, to levels of economic activity and employment, to the location of activity in slow-growth areas, to the degree of competition in an industry, and to other spillover benefits including the training of Canadian managers and workers. The report stressed that the review agency should be flexible in its screening and focus on specific elements such as research and development or industrial structure to promote economies of scale which would vary from industry to industry and case to case.

It was explicitly stated in the foreword that the Gray Report was not a statement of government policy, nor had the government endorsed all of it. This lack of commitment became abundantly clear in the proposed legislation which covered only a narrowly defined portion of the total foreign investment picture, namely foreign takeovers of Canadian firms valued at more than $250,000 or with revenues above

$3 million. New foreign direct investment or investments using retained earnings of existing multinationals in Canada or borrowings from Canadian sources were not to be included.

The main objective of the legislation was to give the government—through a review process under the authority of the Department of Industry, Trade and Commerce—the leverage to ensure maximum benefits from foreign takeovers, with power to permit them or block them. The criteria to determine whether the takeover would bring "significant benefit" to Canada reflected in the main the Gray Report's recommendations. Five factors were to be considered: the impact on the level of economic activity and employment; the degree of participation by Canadians; the effect on productivity, industrial efficiency, technological development, and production innovation and variety in Canada; the impact on competition in Canada; and the compatibility of the acquisition with Canadian industrial and economic policies.

That there were serious differences among the cabinet ministers over the imposition of restrictive measures on foreign investment had long been surmised during the delays and leaks of the preceding months. Indeed, Donald Macdonald, now the minister of energy, mines and resources, made no bones about the problem of reaching a consensus, describing the decision to limit the review's mechanism as "the lowest common denominator of agreement within the Cabinet."[36] The bill was a cautious move on the government's part, in a complex and politically delicate area, falling well short of the expectations of many Canadians including the nationalists and Mr. Gray himself.

While some voices in the provinces and in business expressed relief at the moderation of the proposed measures, parliamentary and public opposition was sharp and outspoken. David Lewis [the NDP leader], in an angry speech, called the bill "one big zero" and "a betrayal of what we had all waited for and expected." Even some of the Liberals were critical. At the hearings on the bill before the Standing Committee on Finance, Trade and Economic Affairs,[37] the economic nationalists were angry in their denunciation of the bill's narrow focus, and the representatives of the business community argued forcefully that certain of its provisions would prove unworkable or unintentionally restrictive to desirable business transactions.

Defending the limited application of the government's bill, the minister of industry, trade and commerce said "the provinces would have damned us if we'd gone further. Business would have been unhappy. We'd have provoked a big national conflict."[38]

...

After the October [1972] election, in which the problem of foreign ownership had not been an important issue, the [minority] Liberal government, with its now tenuous hold on power, conceded that changes in the legislation would probably be necessary to gain support for its passage.[39] In the debate on the Speech from the Throne in January 1973 Mr. Gillespie, the new minister of industry, trade and commerce, revealed the proposed changes: a review agency, headed by a senior official as commissioner, which would have responsibility for screening foreign takeovers, registering and screening new foreign investment, and, ultimately, the registration of licensing and technology transfer arrangements affecting Canadian business. The first part of bill C-132 introduced on 24 January, the Foreign Investment Review Act, resembled its stillborn predecessor. What was new was the power to be given to a Foreign Investment Review Agency to

screen new foreign direct investment and the expansion of foreign-controlled companies already established in Canada into "unrelated" businesses. This part of the bill was to be proclaimed separately, allowing the agency to expand its responsibilities gradually, gaining experience first with the screening of takeovers and then proceeding into the other fields.

The thrust of the new bill resembled that of the earlier one in that takeovers or the establishment of new businesses would be allowed if they would result in "significant benefit" to Canada.

After second reading, the new bill was referred to the Committee on Finance, Trade and Economic Affairs where it again received extensive hearings. Business interests, labour interests, provincial representatives, and economic nationalists again had the opportunity to present their views which varied from outspoken opposition to commendation and support. The main point of criticism was over the limited application of the bill in not covering the expansion into "related" as compared to "unrelated" fields of business by the existing operations of foreign-controlled resident firms. In July 1973 the bill was reported back to the house where its progress was again overtaken by the summer recess. The act finally passed the House of Commons and the Senate in November 1973 and received royal assent in December 1973, even though the first phase of the act would not be proclaimed until 9 April 1974.

What had caused the government to change its mind and extend the application of the review process to new foreign investment? The new minister, Alastair Gillespie, was thought to be more convinced than his predecessor, Mr. Pepin, of the desirability of a more extended application of the regulations. At the same time, the political realities of minority government led many to conclude that the changes owed something to the need for NDP support. Mr. Gillespie's explanation was that "a great many Canadians, including a number of provincial premiers, stated that the government's decision ... did not go far enough."[40] While remaining conscious of the job-creating role of foreign capital, many of the provinces themselves were realizing the need for some controls, and several had actually introduced their own restrictive legislation in related fields such as land ownership and Canadian participation on the boards of directors of subsidiary companies.

The relatively calm public acceptance of the strengthened bill provided a marked contrast to the earlier heated debates and vociferous criticisms. Clearly there had been an opinion shift in the government and in the country. It was no longer generally questioned that dependence on the United States economy constituted a danger and that American ownership and control of Canadian industry involved risks, although naturally differences remained over the appropriate means for handling the problem.

Conclusion

Canada-United States relations reached their "lowest point in many years" in the wake of President Nixon's abruptly imposed economic measures in August 1971.[41] From Ottawa's viewpoint, the American action then and in subsequent months appeared harsh, unjustified by the policies which Canada was pursuing, and inexplicable against the background of the special relationship which had prevailed at least since the Second World War. The Canadian government felt impelled to undertake a fundamental reassessment of its relations resulting in a prescription intended to reduce the country's vulnerability to the United States: the doctrine of the third option. In terms of relations with the United States, the longer lasting expressions were the development of more nationalist policies to control American investment in Canada and a determined backing away from any continental energy link.

While Canadian disenchantment with and opposition to a variety of American foreign and domestic policies—bombing in Vietnam, underground testing in the Alaskan islands, the Watergate affair—sharpened the cutting edge of Canadian reactions, the main impulse in the bilateral controversies derived from different and sometimes conflicting perceptions of national interest. The mutuality of interest which had made the harmonization of postwar policies relatively easy temporarily evaporated.

NOTES

1. Canada, Prime Minister's Office (PMO), transcript of press conference, Mitchell Sharp, acting prime minister, 16 August 1971.

2. *Ibid.*

3. PMO, transcript of press conference, Edgar Benson and Jean-Luc Pepin, Washington, 19 August 1971.

4. PMO, transcript of radio and television statement, 20 August 1971

5. Department of Industry, Trade and Commerce (ITC), news release, 26 August 1971.

6. Information based on private conversations with former State Department and White House officials.

7. PMO, transcript of television broadcast, 23 September 1971. See also: Canada, Department of External Affairs, Statements and Speeches 71/23, 21 September 1971; and ITC, transcript of speech, Houston, Texas, 29 September 1971.

8. Tabled by Mr. Pepin in hearings before the House of Commons Standing Committee on Finance, Trade and Economic Affairs, 16 September 1971.

9. See Canada, House of Commons, *Debates*, 1 October 1971, 8348, for example.

10. *Ibid.* 12 October 1971, 8580. On 14 October 1971, the *Toronto Daily Star* printed the list of eleven items set out in the *Chicago Tribune*'s article of 11 October.

11. *Debates*, 15 November 1971, 9560.

12. Statistics Canada, *The Reconciliation of U.S.-Canada Trade Statistics*, 1970, a report by the U.S.-Canada Statistics Committee (Ottawa 1973), 11.

13. PMO, transcript of interview, 26 October 1971, 13-14.

14. Senate Committee on Foreign Affairs, *Proceedings*, 25 March 1975, 18.

15. *New York Times*, 7 November 1971.

16. Peter Dobell, "The influence of the United States Congress on Canadian-American relations," *International Organization* 28 (autumn 1974).

17. PMO, press release, 12 November 1971. Earlier, on 3 November, the Progressive Conservatives had moved a non-confidence motion against the government, condemning what they claimed to be deteriorating relations between Canada and the United States.

18. The article, entitled "The foreign policy of the new Canada," appeared in mid-December in the January 1972 issue of *Foreign Affairs*.

19. PMO, transcript of press conference, Washington, 7 December 1971.

20. *Debates*, 7 December 1971, 10205.

21. PMO, transcript of press conference, Washington, 7 December 1971.

22. International Monetary Fund, communiqué, Washington, 18 December 1971.

23. *Debates*, 20 December 1971, 10600.

24. Canada, House of Commons, Standing Committee on External Affairs and National Defence, *Minutes of Proceedings and Evidence*, 28th Parl, 2nd sess, no. 28, 12 May 1970, 13. The fourth report of the committee on the policy papers (June 1971) criticized the omission and called for a paper on Canada-United States relations.

25. Canada, Department of External Affairs (DEA), Statements and Speeches 73/14, 2 May 1973, 4.

26. "Canada-U.S. relations: options for the future," International Perspectives, special issue (autumn 1972).

27. DEA, notes for an address, 2 May 1973, 5.

28. "Together, the Land is Strong: the Work the Next Parliament Must Do for Canadians," the Liberal party campaign platform for 1972 as quoted in Geoffrey Stevens' column, *Globe and Mail*, 14 May 1974.

29. DEA, notes for an address, 2 May 1973, 4.

30. The report of the task force, headed by Professor Mel Watkins, entitled *Foreign Ownership and the Structure of Canadian Industry* (Ottawa: Queen's Printer 1968), had been neither accepted nor rejected by the government. The royal commission under Walter Gordon, charged with examining Canada's economic prospects, had warned of the danger of continued foreign takeovers of Canadian industry. Government of Canada, *Royal Commission on Canada's Economic Prospects, Final Report* (Gordon Report) (Ottawa: Queen's Printer, 1957). See also: *Eleventh Report of the Standing Committee on External Affairs and National Defence Respecting Canada-U.S. Relations*, Second Session, 28th Parliament (Wahn Report) (Ottawa: Queen's Printer, 1970).

31. Canada, Prime Minister's Office (PMO), transcript of interview, 26 October 1971, 12.

32. PMO, transcript of press conference, 17 November 1971, 16, 17.

33. *Ibid.*, transcript of interview, 26 October 1971, 14, 17.

34. "A citizen's guide to the Herb Gray report," *Canadian Forum* 51 (December 1971).

35. *Foreign Direct Investment in Canada* (Ottawa: Information Canada 1971). Supervised by the Hon. Herb Gray, the task force which prepared the report was headed by Joel Bell, Montreal economist and lawyer.

36. *Time*, 15 May 1972.

37. Canada, House of Commons, Standing Committee on Finance, Trade and Economic Affairs, *Minutes of Proceedings and Evidence*, 28th Parl, 4th sess, 7 June to 22 June 1972.

38. *Debates*, 29 May 1972, 2632; *Time*, 15 May 1972.

39. PMO, transcript of press conference, 1 November 1972.

40. *Debates*, 10 January 1973, 154.

41. The *New York Times*, editorial, 7 November 1971.

SUGGESTED READINGS

Holsti, K.J., *Why Nations Realign*, London: Allen and Unwin, 1982, pp. 73-104.

Munton, Don, and Dean Swanson, "Rise and Fall of the Third Option," in Brian Tomlin, ed., *Canada's Foreign Policy: Analysis and Trends*, Toronto: Methuen, 1978, pp. 175-213.

Munton, Don and Dale Poel, "Electoral Accountability and Canadian Foreign Policy: The Case of Foreign Investment," *International Journal*, Vol. 33, No. 1, Winter 1977-78, pp. 217-247.

Nossal, Kim Richard, "Economic Nationalism and Canadian Integration: Assumptions, Arguments and Advocacies," in Denis Stairs and Gilbert Winham, eds., *the Politics of Canada's Economic*

Relationship with the United States, Volume 29, Royal Commission on the Economic Union and Development prospects for Canada, Toronto: University of Toronto Press, 1985, pp. 55-90.

Sharp, Mitchell, "Canada-U.S. Relations: Options for the Future," *International Perspectives*, Special issue, Autumn 1972.

Von Reikhaff, Harald, "The Third Option in Canadian Foreign Policy," in Brian Tomlin, ed., *Canada's Foreign Policy: Analysis and Trends*, Toronto: Methuen, 1978, pp. 87-109.

chapter 16

RE-WORKING EUROPEAN SECURITY IN THE 1970s: THE CSCE

Peyton Lyon with Geoffrey Nimmo

The second phase of the Conference on Security and Co-operation in Europe opened in Geneva on 18 September 1973; the addition of Monaco brought the number of states represented to thirty-five. Through twenty-two months of intense and difficult negotiations, the agenda and mandates agreed to in the Multilateral Preparatory Talks (MPT) in Helsinki in 1972-3 were transformed into the Final Act that would be formally approved in Helsinki on 31 July-1 August 1975.

Journalists and scholars alike have found it easy to overlook Canada's participation in these negotiations. Even in one Canadian study of the subject, not only is Canada rarely mentioned but the study concludes that "narrow considerations" appear to have inhibited the "bridge-building function" that Canada should have fulfilled.[1] In the minds of most of the Canadian negotiators, by contrast, their part in drafting the Final Act ranks among the major achievements of Canadian diplomacy. The Act itself they regard as a great historic accomplishment, and they claim an important share of the credit for it.[2]

The principal Canadian contribution was not the bridge-building characteristic of Canada's postwar foreign policy.[3] Nor was it more stable relations with Moscow, one of Prime Minister Trudeau's oft stated aspirations. Although careful to keep in step with their European allies on most points, the Canadians were frequently encouraged to take the lead. They emerged as among the toughest advocates, and quite probably the most effective, of squeezing every possible concession out of the Kremlin and its allies. They vigorously and consistently urged their associates to make and maintain maximum demands—"to press détente to its outer limit"—and to avoid any hint of allied disunity or impatience.

For the Geneva negotiation Ottawa fielded a strong team composed on average of eight officials. There was a good deal more continuity in its membership than in most other delegations. During the first year the delegation was led by Michael Shenstone. He was succeeded in September 1974 by W.T. Delworth. Like Shenstone, he was known for an exceptional command of the English language as well as for militant anti-communism.

This relatively youthful delegation was exceptionally energetic, inventive, spirited, and cohesive. Both Shenstone and Delworth inspired great enthusiasm as they strove to maintain Western solidarity and resolve.

The length of the conference, and the obscurity and apparent triviality of many of the disputes, discouraged interest on the part of the Canadian press, parliament, and government. Neither Mitchell Sharp, the secretary of state for external affairs,

Peyton Lyon and Geoffrey Nimmo, "Canada at Geneva, 1973-5," from Conference on Security and Cooperation in Europe, Toronto, Centre for International Studies, 1984. Portions of the text have been deleted. Some footnotes have been removed; Those remaining have been renumbered.

nor A.E. Ritchie, the undersecretary, appears to have followed events closely. Other departments were kept informed but rarely displayed much interest beyond worrying that the economic provisions would cut across other commitments such as the General Agreement on Tariffs and Trade (GATT). Still less was heard from provincial governments, although they too were kept in the picture, especially on provisions concerning eduction and culture.

A general, but deceptive, statement of Canada's aims at the CSCE was drafted by the department just prior to Stage Two. Following the pattern of *Foreign Policy for Canadians*, the 1970 statement of basic aims by the Trudeau government, objectives were expressed in terms of the celebrated "six themes"—economic growth, social justice, an improved environment, the quality of life, global peace, and independence. In fact, higher priority was given "humanitarian questions and the development of human contacts." Mr Sharp had stated at the opening session in Helsinki that Canada attached "highest importance" to the "freer movement of people," and on the eve of Geneva a policy statement again described human contacts as "the single most important item for Canada" (EAD).[4]

Mr Sharp later contended that the central objective of the CSCE was "progress in East-West détente." Although it is not obvious that the Canadian negotiators considered "détente" to include, as a matter of definition, increased contacts and respect for individual rights, several public statements by government leaders support this interpretation. A second position, implied in other statements, holds that such contacts and rights are not part of détente, but rather essential conditions if détente, understood as a stable relationship between states, is to be achieved. Some Canadians, by contrast, conceded that demands in

human rights were likely to impede détente, but worth pursuing none the less. The Canadian delegation commented from Geneva that: "'Human contacts' will not go away. Whether it is a factor of improved relations between East and West, or a source, at least for a time, of acrimony (which we tend to believe it will be), it should represent a permanent and decisive addition to the landscape of détente."[5] Whatever their understanding of "détente," the Canadians were unanimous in enthusiastic support of the Western position that the WTO members must accept, as part of the "détente process," substantial and specific commitments to the freer flow of people and ideas.

Canada's success in promoting family reunification, along with its strong opposition to any wording in the Final Act that might imply sanctification of the territorial status quo, was certain to please Canada's ethnic communities and thus give substance to the Trudeau doctrine that foreign policy should be the extension abroad of domestic concerns. The government, notably Mr Sharp, were keen to win back for the Liberals the ethnic voters who had been lured away in the early sixties by the rhetoric of Prime Minister John Diefenbaker, and those who were unhappy with Trudeau's alleged softness on communism. The officials were probably correct in assuming that the politicians regarded family reunification as the principal Canadian interest in the CSCE.

Mr Sharp also saw in both the CSCE and the parallel negotiations on Mutual and Balanced Force Reductions (MBFR) opportunities for Canadian co-operation with the countries of Europe, and in particular Canada's partners in NATO. Indeed a primary objective was to strengthen Canada's independence by restoring its credentials as a reliable ally and active participant in "the world of Europe" (EAD). There is no more insistent note in the communications between Ottawa and Geneva than the need to avoid antagonizing the nine members of the European Community, or greater satisfaction in any accomplishment than in indications that the "Nine" appreciated Canada and would continue to regard it as a part of the wider community of European nations. Many Canadians, especially in the Departments of External Affairs and National Defence, had been acutely embarrassed by the Trudeau government's early disregard for allied interests and sensibilities manifested in the post-1969 reduction of Canadian forces in Europe. By 1973, as part of its Third Option strategy, the government acknowledged that Canada needed strong countervailing ties with third countries in order to lessen its dependence on the United States. The principal source of this counterweight could only be Europe. To strengthen transatlantic ties it was necessary to recover Canada's standing within NATO. For Canadian diplomats, being tough with the Soviet Union was an obvious means to persuade the allies to forget recent history and to recognize Canada as a loyal and useful member of the alliance. Through most of Stage Two, Washington's passive attitude to the CSCE afforded the Canadians a golden opportunity to show that they were not only different from the Americans but also more sympathetic to the concerns of the West Europeans.

The Geneva negotiations settled down early into what a departmental memorandum described as "careful sparring," principally, although not exclusively, between East and West. Beyond different conceptions regarding the shape and content of the concluding document, almost from the beginning a majority in the West felt compelled to resist WTO pressure for rushing into early drafting which would cut short efforts to secure acceptable terms. "Allied consultation and concerted action has been vitally important and has worked effectively," ran another memorandum prepared for the minister on the eve of the 10-11 December 1973 NATO ministerial meeting in Brussels (EAD). Information obtained from outside the conference halls in Geneva, including some gleaned during a ministerial visit to the USSR, had also "confirmed that we must be prepared patiently and without time constraints—real or imagined—to resist urgings to accept less than we need and take what appears to be the last WTO offer" (EAD). Even at this early date the possibility that there might be no summit meeting as a finale (as Moscow wanted), or even no final conference, was being considered in Ottawa. But Ottawa officials viewed the early weeks of the Geneva negotiations "with relative satisfaction." This, the minister was told, "is largely a credit to the Western negotiating approach combining firmness with avoidance of polemics, as well as to flexible but close consultation amongst allies."

At Geneva, as in the Helsinki MPT, the Canadian delegation tried to avoid siding with the United States when there were transatlantic disagreements, and it generally refrained from pushing Canadian points of view too hard on the infrequent occasions when they differed from the West Europeans lest they come to share the French reticence about Canadian participation. Although they never admitted it to others, the Canadians were always conscious that they were guests at the CSCE who must not wear out their welcome.

One problem the delegation faced was a major effort by the nine members of the EC to maintain a common position. As that position generally became the position of the NATO Fifteen, a constant Canadian preoccupation was to prevent the hardening of an EC position before there had been meaningful consultation with the NATO partners from "outer space"—the Canadians, Norwegians, and Americans. During Stage Two of the CSCE, however, the problem did not become as acute as it did during the later Belgrade review conference. Those from "outer space" were sometimes joined by disaffected elements within the Nine, frequently the Dutch, the West Germans, or the Danes, who welcomed NATO consultations as a "court of appeal," and saw to it that the Canadians were kept informed. They would often tell the Canadian delegation what had been or was going to be decided, and would sometimes join the Canadians on the grounds (or pretext) that the prior decision of the Nine was no longer valid because of a change in the tactical situation. The Americans were less concerned about EC versus NATO consultation because they were less easily left out of the equation.

The problems raised by the EC caucus were also eased by a "buddy" system by which one of the Nine was detailed to keep one "outsider" informed. The system worked well for Canada, as the "buddy" delegated to it was Britain. The Canadians were irate when the British, along with the French, Americans, Russians, and Germans, insisted upon a "Berlin" clause couched in such general terms that it appeared to weaken the hard-won texts on non-interference.[6] In the later stages they were concerned at the British delegation's anxiety to bring proceedings to a close while additional gains could be won. They admired the general competence of the British negotiators, however, and especially their leadership on confidence-building measures (CBMS), in the tricky information field, and in the package deal on contacts.

Among the most ardent "Europeans" were the Belgians and Italians. Their re-sistance to follow-up proposals, on the grounds that these might be exploited to weaken West European cohesion, was a second source of difficulty for the Canadian delegation. But Canada's interest in follow-up provisions that would enable it to remain active within a new European forum was not allowed to become a bone of contention with its European allies. To the Canadians it was clear that the Russians would insist on some sort of follow-up, and there was thus no need for the issue to become a source of strife in the NATO caucus.

Although hardly the most "European" in action, the French were by far the most difficult. Relations between Ottawa and Paris were strained over French encouragement of Quebec separatism, and one senior official speculated that the French delegation to the CSCE appeared to have instructions to block every Canadian initiative. The Canadians hesitated to oppose the French on issues that divided the Nine. They were less inhibited, however, in resisting French views on Western negotiating strategy. They were willing to acknowledge that the French were strong concerning the principles that mattered most to their German partner, and gave effective leadership in the field of culture. Moreover, as long as the Americans remained passive, the French assumed the leadership of the West and played a major part in the "global" deals with the Soviet Union. In Canadian eyes, however, the French were often overly anxious to protect their bilateral relationship with the Soviet Union and, consequently, were too reluctant to press demands that the Kremlin might find difficult. In fact, there seemed at times very little to distinguish French and Soviet positions. The Canadians and the French also differed frequently over specific issues, such as national self-determination. Relations between members of the two delegations were not unpleasant, nor were they close and productive. It was perhaps fortunate for the Canadians that excessive self-assurance and tactical miscalculations combined to limit French influence within the conference.

The Canadian delegation stayed close to the West Germans, who were already emerging as the strongest element in the European Communities and the most helpful to Canada in its quest for a "contractual link."[7] Though the German delegation was frequently embarrassed by the receipt of contradictory instructions from their chancellor and foreign minister, occasional difference over tactics did not seriously disturb the relationship with Canada. The Canadians were delighted when, early in Stage Two, the Bonn delegation suggested that Canada manage the NATO text on family reunification, an issue that mattered a great deal more to Germany than to Canada since there were probably 1000 German families involved for every Canadian. This shared interest provided a good means to demonstrate to the West Germans the utility of Canada as an ally. A more surprising means was the exceptional Canadian effort to obtain formulations in Basket 1 that would strengthen Bonns' claim that the reunification of Germany had not been foreclosed. On several key points, indeed, the Canadians emerged as more German than the Germans in the struggle to keep alive the theoretical possibility of German unity.

Even though the Canadians favoured a tougher negotiating strategy, they found it easy to co-operate with their traditional Scandinavian allies. They were particularly appreciative of the Danish lead on human contacts. The Canadians were more critical of the Norwegians as being too ready to make concessions to Soviet pressure, no-

tably on timing, but they were brought together by being outside the caucus of the Nine and by a common interest as suppliers of energy and raw materials. The only delegation consistently tougher than the Canadian was the Dutch. While admiring their stand on human rights, the Canadians considered the Dutch too doctrinaire to be effective, and relations with them were not especially close.

The Canadians shared the widely held view that the four main neutral participants—Austria, Finland, Sweden, and Switzerland—constituted a "curious but immensely important caucus" (EAD). They considered from the start that inter-bloc negotiations with the participation of the neutral and non-aligned (NNA) would be useful. The Canadians were often effective in mediating differences between the Alliance and the NNA.

At times the Canadians found themselves close to the Swedes, and collaboration with them was rewarding. The Canadians were disappointed, however, that the Swedes were not more assertive in drafting controversial texts, notably those on principles, human contacts, and information. Australia, the "Western neutral" which chaired the informal negotiating group on family reunification, appeared more sensitive to Soviet demands when performing a similar function with respect to CBMS, but collaboration with the Canadians remained easy and productive. The unusual Swiss role also earned the praise of the Canadians, who supported their proposals for peaceful settlement of disputes, even though they were certain they would be rejected by sovereignty-conscious participants in both East and West. As Finland had a major stake in the successful outcome of the conference, it was used by both sides. Its contribution was viewed by the Canadians as competent and constructive. The Canadians realized that the Finns were the furthest "left" of the neutrals, but this did not stand in the way of close co-operation.

The Canadians also admired the aggressive and highly visible diplomacy of the Yugoslav delegation for its stress on arms control and disarmament, for keeping the "global dimension" to the fore, for combating the Brezhnev doctrine, and for insisting on a meaningful follow-up. Despite early disagreement over the right of Israel to be heard at the conference, the Canadians and Yugoslavs interacted well.

Relations with Malta, by far the most active and aggressive of the mini-powers, were complicated by its ardent championing of Arab interests. Canada did not want the Middle East to become an issue in the CSCE, and to defeat Malta's demands at Stage One it had followed, on the basis of prior ministerial direction the domestically popular course of insisting on equal participation of Israel alongside the Arab states. When the issue again arose in the first week at Geneva, the Canadian delegation was no less firm in support of equal participation. On both occasions most other delegations agreed with Canada's approach but were happy to let the Canadian delegation take the heat virtually alone.

Although the Canadian team prided itself on being the toughest in the West when bargaining with the WTO participants, several key members have nevertheless maintained that the Soviet delegation had more respect for them than for almost any other. This is not an easy claim to test. The head of the Soviet delegation did not spend more time in conversation with his Canadian counterpart than with other non-communist ambassadors. Canadian reports of their encounters, however, suggest that the Soviet delegation took the Canadians seriously. The Canadians gave the Soviet side

both an accurate account of Western concerns and informed estimates of the probable price the USSR would have to pay for an agreed final text and a thirty-five-nation summit as a finale. In turn they were treated to what appears to have been a frank explanation of the problems faced by the Soviet delegation, including the mounting impatience in the Kremlin with the slow pace of negotiations. Although at times the Russians unsuccessfully tried to draw the Canadians into concessions by accusing them of intransigence, on one occasion their leader assured Mr Delworth that they did not consider Canada to be among the most unreasonable participants (EAD). Nor were Canadian assessments of Soviet CSCE objectives unduly harsh. In several communications a certain similarity with some of Canada's objectives was noted, such as the claim to be involved in a regular manner in determining European affairs. The Canadians also interacted constructively with most other WTO delegations.

Even when it chose to be inactive, the United States could not help being an essential element in the CSCE. The Canadians found it easy to work with individual members of the large and able United States delegation. On the whole, however, they were disappointed by the lack of co-ordination and commitment of the United States delegation. They realized that its relatively low-key activity in Stage Two was largely a reflection of Secretary of State Henry Kissinger's pessimism about a useful outcome and, as his memoirs reflect, his unwillingness to spend time familiarizing himself with CSCE matters.[8] It was also clear that he was sceptical about individual rights as a subject for international negotiation. More particularly, Kissinger appeared to be mainly concerned that the CSCE should not be allowed to complicate bilateral United States-USSR talks on such matters as arms control, and he shared a good deal of the Kremlin's impatience to wind up Stage Two.

Much as the Canadians deplored American indifference towards the CSCE, they welcomed the opportunity to exploit Stage Two to underscore Canadian identity and independence. Repeatedly the delegation stressed in their telegrams that the American attitude enabled them to demonstrate Canada's distinctiveness and greater "Europeanness," and the advantages to the Europeans in ensuring that an independent Canadian voice continued to be heard in European deliberations.

The Canadians, more than most of the Fifteen, complained about American attempts to accelerate negotiations. The communiqué following the June 1973 Nixon-Brezhnev meeting on the eve of Stage One had been judged disastrous because it had granted, virtually without compensation, the Kremlin's demand for a summit finale. The Canadians warned the Russians that since thirty-four other states were involved it would be unwise to assume that an agreement with the United States would necessarily mean an advance. The American proposal to define CSCE priorities, put forward just before the 1974 summer break, was considered especially harmful by the Canadians. They felt that it weakened the West's ability to extract Soviet concessions by suggesting that the West was not prepared to hold out for a comprehensive agreement.

The Canadians, although not at the time eager to stress "the special relationship," won considerable credit for helping in the successful attempt to educate Kissinger. No active participant or close observer could fail to discern the marked difference in the Canadian and American approaches to the CSCE. However, whenever the interest and the tactical judgement of the two did coincide, the Canadians were not so foolish as to act differently simply to foster the image of being different.

The Canadian delegation at Geneva introduced few texts. Its contribution was generally made within the NATO caucus or in informal sessions with the WTO or NNA delegations. The delegation was particularly adept at putting together texts which incorporated a number of individual "last ditches," and as a result the wording of a considerable number of resolutions was largely Canadian. Given their position as an "honoured guest" at a European feast, the Canadian delegation frequently followed the tactic of advancing a suggestion, sitting back, and, beyond the occasional nudge, letting others take the lead and win the plaudits.

Of the specific Canadian contributions during Stage Two, the best publicized was the successful management of the controversial text on family reunification. It was the one item for which the leader of the delegation assumed direct responsibility. Virtually every feature of the draft which was worked out jointly with the other NATO delegations, particularly that of West Germany, found its way into the Final Act over the stubborn resistance of the Soviet Union and East Germany.

Canada's agreement to lead on family reunification indicated a willingness to become involved in serious controversy with the WTO. Lack of agreement on the issue was in fact the primary reason bilateral relations had not been established between East Germany and Canada. The initial Canadian statement was given on 4 October 1973 and accepted as the definitive NATO position. It first established that the reunification of separated families was an essential condition of increased cooperation, and then laid down the means of implementing this principle. Canada's formal text, tabled on 20 November, was accorded strong support from almost all the allies and NNA countries. The WTO states objected to the raising of what they regarded as a matter best left to bilateral negotiations. The text, they also complained, favoured the rights of the individual over those of society, and "immigrant" countries like Canada as opposed to those of emigration. Presumably to stir up trouble within the West, they demanded that the Canadian text be broadened to include the rights of migrant workers whose families were denied entry by such countries as Switzerland and West Germany. All participants realized that pushing issues such as family reunification was intended to demonstrate the superiority of the liberal democracies over Marxist-Leninist régimes. Not surprisingly they met with stubborn resistance. At one point the Canadian delegation became pessimistic. Ottawa, however, was persuaded by information received from the Russians outside the Geneva process that an acceptable text could be won if the negotiation-weary delegation could just carry on a little longer.

Despite pride in their achievement, complaints arose within the delegation that family reunification had come to loom too large. Towards the end of Stage Two, the delegation repeatedly requested that it be authorized to shift emphasis to issues of more central concern to the whole Alliance. Since the Canadian negotiators had emphatically not neglected the major political and security issues, the request simply underlined the importance they attached to the CSCE as a means of improving credibility among their allies.

The Canadians were also active in negotiating other texts in basket III, notably those on family visits and marriage, but they largely avoided culture and education. Ostensibly this was to avoid complications with the provinces, but it may also have had something to do with French leadership in these fields. The Canadians did succeed in inserting a positive reference to the joys of "cultural diversity," although only five words of the original draft survived into the Final Act. While concerned about facilities for journalists, the Canadians were conscious that information was ideologically the most difficult area and were happy that the informal division of labour among Western delegations gave this subject to the British (EAD). The worry within Canada about the impact of American media upon Canadian culture, and the steps being taken to counteract this flow, strengthened the delegation's reluctance to become seriously involved.

Another textual contribution to the Final Act was in Basket II and dealt with protection of the environment. Canada won acceptance of a text calling for "the progressive development, codification and implementation of international law as one means of preserving and enhancing the human environment, including principles and practices...relating to pollution and other environmental damage..." This wording was a watering down of the original wording in the face of Italian and Belgian reluctance to undertake what could become expensive obligations, and of the familiar objections of less developed countries raised by Romania, but it retained all the "essentials." The reference to co-operation in research into problems of life in the Arctic contained in the agreements on science and technology was of Canadian origin. The delegation also got into the Final Act approving references to the work of the United Nations Environment Programme and to the Stockholm Declaration which most of the WTO had not previously accepted. Environment, however, was not an East-West issue, and less resistance came from the Soviet bloc delegations than from some of Canada's allies.

Although Canada submitted no draft texts in Basket I, the delegation's proudest achievement was its contribution to the decalogue of principles and to the passages on CBMS.

Canadian negotiator Gabriel Warren's most celebrated contribution was to provide the phrase that ended a long stalemate over Principle III. Here the Russians had resisted any suggestion that only violent violations of frontiers were to be excluded. Warren claims that he ultimately suggested as a "joke" the notion that frontiers must not be "assaulted." Its ready acceptance by the Soviet Union demonstrated, he believes, that their earlier objections had not been "sincere."

Another Canadian achievement in drafting the decalogue was the insertion of a comma into the statement providing for the possibility of peaceful change of frontiers. The Germans, to whom the issue was vital, had inadvertently accepted, in addition to the two conditions, "by peaceful means, and by agreement," the proviso that any change be "in accordance with international law." Warren instructed the Germans in the subtle use of the comma and persuaded them that one immediately in front of this phrase would eliminate it as a third and possibly awkward condition. This in turn became one of the changes that Chancellor Helmut Schmidt requested Kissinger to pursue in his talks with Gromyko late in Stage Two. Kissinger obliged, and even succeeded.

A solid tribute to Warren was the conference decision to designate him chairman of the informal negotiating committee on the decalogue for its decisive second reading. This was the only time that a representative of an aligned country was entrusted with such a responsibility.

Drawing on his impressive knowledge of the tentative agreements and of potential trade-offs, as well as on his considerable knowledge of United Nations resolutions and of international law on the subject, Mr Warren was able to guide the second reading to completion within three days, to widespread surprise and relief.

Captain John Toogood, the Canadian representative on the subcommittee dealing with CBMS, not only served as chairman of the NATO caucus on security matters but became at least in Canadian eyes, its most effective spokesman. His "Canadian matrix" had been picked up by several neutral delegations and became the basis for breaking a serious impasse with the Soviet Union. This involved the linkage of numbers, space, and time; if it was proposed to alter one, changes in the others would necessarily follow; for example, the higher the minimum number of troops in the manoeuvres to be reported, the wider the area to be covered, and/or the longer the required notice.

Canadian participation in Stage Two also helped to head off several formulations in the Final Act that would have been contrary to Canadian interests. The principle of self-determination, for example, might well have been stated in terms that could be exploited by Canadian separatists. The delegation had initially assumed that the Soviet Union and others, acting in their own interests, would see to it that the principle was "balanced" by one in favour of "territorial integrity." When this assumption proved wrong, the help of Spain was enlisted in rounding up the support necessary to restore the "balance." Premier René Lévesque of Quebec still cited the Helsinki Final Act to support his cause, but less persuasively than would have been the case without the delegation's effective intervention.

Similarly, when it seemed possible that the Nine would obtain a provision favouring the secure supplies of energy and raw materials, the Canadian delegation, with assistance from the Norwegians, was able to ensure a formulation more consistent with supplier interests. Some members of the Nine also seemed likely to accept the WTO's insistent demand that they be granted most-favoured-nation tariff treatment without effective reciprocity. The Canadians were relieved when, with the collaboration of the United States and others, the threat was overcome. Apart from External Affairs and National Defence, the few Ottawa departments (notably Finance) that displayed interest in the CSCE did so in terms of economic threats rather than of opportunities. External Affairs was pleased to be able to show that it had headed off these dangers.

If one agrees that Canada did play a significant role in Stage Two of the CSCE, how can that achievement be explained? Canada, after all, is not geographically a European power. Little of its very considerable foreign trade is with Eastern Europe, and of its relatively modest military forces, in 1973 only 5000 men were based in Europe. One peculiarity of the CSCE, however, was that on most points such considerations did not matter. Strictly military issues were largely excluded from the agenda, and, while economic questions loomed large in Basket II, it was generally regarded as the least significant or controversial. As noted earlier, the passive role of the United States, the pretensions of the French, and the inconsistency of the West German performance left a vacuum to be filled by other allies. The rule that all decisions must be taken by consensus permitted even the smallest participants to be heard, to make a significant input, and to ensure that the unacceptable was not accepted. Even after the broad lines of compromise had become evident, a great deal of ingenuity was required to obtain wording that all thirty-five would accept. The talents and drive of individual negotiators frequently mattered more than national or bloc affiliation. Any country able and willing to field a strong negotiating team, and to grant it reasonable room for manoeuvre, might make a serious contribution.

The Canadians also sought to avoid causing irritation. Because there were few specifically Canadian axes to grind, and because of the general directive to seek West European favour, this was relatively easy.

Few other delegations can have been instructed by their governments to concentrate more of their efforts on furthering the common interest. This was, of course, the common interest as perceived by the Western allies, but pursuit of it did not impede Canada's co-operation with the NNA. It also appears likely to have enhanced the interest in the Canadian position shown by the WTO delegations.

Despite the Canadian delegation's resolve to maintain a low profile, and its consistent opposition to any suggestion that the conference be hurried, when the time did come to wind up proceedings, Mr Delworth played a prominent role in the tense and tricky negotiations that proved necessary. On 24 June the foreign ministers of the Nine meeting in Luxemburg called for the holding of Stage Three, the formal conclusion of the negotiation, at the end of July. The Canadians concurred that all feasible objectives had been attained and, in any case, did not wish to oppose the unanimous wish of their European allies. A Swedish proposal that the date be set for 28 July appeared to enjoy general acceptance until the French ineptly circulated the word that the Big Four had decided that this would be the date. Tempers frayed, and the Western caucus was in disarray.

Mr Delworth, having privately ascertained that 30 July would be acceptable to the Americans, and probably to the Finns, now proposed this date conditional upon all outstanding questions being settled by 15 July; if this could not be accomplished, the financial and political consequences would be shared by all the participating states. This initiative—"the right proposal at the right time," according to the Danish ambassador—was adopted on 12 July and served as a "psychological bulldozer" in accelerating the work of the conference (EAD).

All hurdles were cleared and Stage Two wearily came to a halt at 4:00 AM on the morning of 21 July.

For most Canadians involved in the CSCE at Geneva or in Ottawa, the Final Act represented not only a diplomatic triumph but a victory for humanity. Members of the Canadian delegation also maintain that the successful outcome of Stage Two justified their original optimism and the tactics they adopted. The Soviet government, they believe, always expected the West to be tough and demanding. Early in Stage Two, Soviet concessions confirmed that they were prepared to pay a substantial price both for an agreement and for a summit finale. The Canadians were impatient with delegations, such as the French, which frequently argued against presenting certain texts or amendments on the grounds that the USSR might refuse to accept them. Occasionally the Canadians themselves complained of Soviet intransigence and, for a brief period in 1974, contemplated the possibility that the CSCE might break down. On the whole, however, they remained confident.

Most Canadian negotiators contended that in the end the Soviet Union had won on no important point. One expressed pleasure that the West had rarely been obliged to retreat to its prepared fall-back positions.

As the conference proceeded, the delegation became convinced that the Soviet side knew it had been bested and was disenchanted with the entire proceedings. Only its long-standing advocacy of a European security conference, and the engagement of Brezhnev's personal prestige in the process, they felt, had persuaded the Kremlin not to abandon the conference.

This victory, in their eyes, was not entirely deserved. They had often deplored the lack of Alliance unity on such matters as the appropriate follow-up. They had bemoaned the passivity of the Americans and the decidedly unhelpful moves by Messrs Kissinger and Nixon. Both the French and the Germans were criticized for making private deals with the Soviet Union. At times the delegation was also critical of the Nine for their failure to consult adequately with the other members of NATO. On the whole, however, Canadian reports on Stage Two praised the high degree of Western solidarity, and to this they attributed the success of the conference.

In justifying the claim that the West had emerged the clear victor, the Canadians generally stressed the ways Soviet aspirations had been frustrated. For example, the reaffirmation of the inviolability of frontiers was described as "so brief, so exotically phrased and so totally swamped by masses of other text pointing away from immutability," that it could hardly be considered an advance by East Germany, Poland, or the Soviet Union (EAD). The principle of peaceful change, although not as strongly placed as the Canadians had wished, was adequate to keep alive the theoretical possibility of German reunification. The thrust of the Final Act was change rather than maintenance of the status quo. The Brezhnev doctrine had been weakened by the emphasis on non-intervention in the affairs of other states, including those that possessed similar social systems. The stress on relations between individuals and groups was itself contrary to the conservative, state-centric philosophy of the communist régimes. And the modest but specific obligation to reduce impediments to the flow of ideas and people would, if fulfilled, tend to modify the way in which the Soviet system operates.

On the other hand, the USSR had ensured that the principle of non-intervention would not be allowed to rule out alliance commitments that could erode the ability of the WTO governments to maintain tight control over their populations. Moreover, as the Canadians were very well aware, there was no guarantee that principles aimed at easing the flow of peoples and information would be honoured. Nevertheless, especially in view of the fact that the Final Act was a unique document, signed at the heads of government level, the Canadians were persuaded that violations or delays would be far from cost-free. The long and favourable build-up of the CSCE by the WTO would make it difficult to dismiss the Final Act lightly. Simply by signing the document the USSR had accepted the novel and vital proposition that a state's treatment of its citizens could be the legitimate concern of other states, and the follow-up procedures could provide the means to ensure that violations would not be unnoticed.

The Canadians regarded many other features of the Final Act as Western successes. These include rejection of the notion of a *lex specialist* for Europe, and the repeated references to the authority of the UN Charter and the relevant declarations on human rights and friendly relations. They also thought that the Fifteen's solidarity, often joined by the NNA group, had taught the Kremlin a useful lesson concerning the West's seriousness about liberal values.

Throughout the twenty-two months of Stage Two, Canada had played the role of NATO militant rather than the moderator or mediator that had become its postwar speciality. Moreover, the delegation's toughness was inconsistent with the softer line towards the Soviet Union repeatedly enunciated by the prime minister. Neither in Ottawa nor in Geneva does there appear to have been concern that Canada was acting contrary to its traditional roles.

A case may be made, moreover, that by playing the role of militant, and helping to fill the leadership gap, the Canadians were serving a wider interest. A decade earlier, the principal obstacles to a lessening of East-West tension, the search for negotiated solutions, and the development of East-West co-operation appeared to Canada to lie in Washington and Bonn. By the early seventies, however, the United States required no prodding to engage in serious negotiations with the Kremlin to reduce the risks of nuclear war. And Bonn's *Ostpolitik* had progressed to the point where the West Germans had acquired a huge stake in the continuance of détente. The French, while aspiring to leadership in Western Europe, persisted in nurturing their special relationship with Moscow in ways that aroused suspicion as well as resentment among their allies. The British, although tougher towards the Soviet Union, were too handicapped by domestic weakness, both economic and political, to provide strong leadership. Canadian militancy, along with that of the Dutch and Italians, may thus have served the Western cause.

There seems little doubt, however, that more narrowly national concerns provided the principal motivation for Canada's energetic CSCE diplomacy during the years 1973-5. This was in accord with *Foreign Policy for Canadians*, which had stressed that foreign policy should be the projection abroad of national interests. Foremost among these was the restoration of Canada's credibility with its European allies, who were perceived as the primary source of the external counterweight necessary to contain the generally benign but overwhelming influence of Canada's superpower neighbour. Doubts about its willingness to shoulder its share of Alliance burdens were reduced, and individual allies, most notably the Germans, were given cause to be grateful for Canada's active involvement in Europe. This facilitated the negotiation with the European Communities of the "Contractual Link" of 1976 that was intended to strengthen ties between Canada and Europe.

The most important domestic objective of Canada's political leadership appeared to be the appeasement of those ethnic groups which attached great weight to human rights within the Soviet bloc, increased contacts, and refusal to legitimize the territorial status quo in Europe. This objective was also largely attained, and it is notable that the interest of Canadians in the CSCE picked up greatly after publication of the Final Act, and the demonstration by Soviet dissidents that it might be exploited at least to publicize the denial of individual rights in the WTO countries.

One may question the costs of a significant role reversal to a nation seeking to establish a distinctive international identity. Nor is it self-evident that the West served the general interest in détente, most notably limitation of the nuclear arms race, by pressing the Soviet régime so vigorously for commitments that, if honoured, would weaken its control over its citizenry. Beyond doubt, however, is the fact that the Canadian negotiators saw in Stage Two of the CSCE a splendid opportunity to advance their nation's interest. They made the most of that opportunity.

NOTES

1. François Carle, "Consensus Formation at the Conference on Security and Cooperation," Master's thesis (Carleton University 1976), 92.

2. External Affairs Documents (hereafter cited in text as EAD). This chapter is based on the study of Department of External Affairs files for the period 1973-5, as well as interviews with virtually all the officers involved in the CSCE in both Geneva and Ottawa.

3. For data on Canada's roles in international affairs, see Peyton V. Lyon and Brian Tomlin, *Canada as an International Actor* (Toronto 1979), chap. 2. Surveys conducted in 1975 and 1983 have established that the most prevalent image of Canada held by foreign experts is that of mediator.

4. Department of External Affairs, *Statements and Speeches*, 73/71, 4 July 1973.

5. Cited in Jeanne Kirk Laux, "CSCE and the Search for Cooperation," *International Perspectives* (September/October 1974), 26.

6. The Canadians held that if Berlin had been specified in the text the Russians would have had less opportunity to cite it to justify interference elsewhere.

7. "Contractual link" was the popular term for the agreement on economic co-operation with the European Communities which the Trudeau government was eagerly pursuing during the Geneva negotiations.

8. Henry Kissinger, *The White House Years*, (Boston, Toronto 1979), 412-13, 534, 948, 966-7.

SUGGESTED READINGS

Carle, François, "Consensus Formation at the Conference on Security and Co-operation," M. A. Thesis, Carleton University. 1976.

Crean, J.G., "European Security—The CSCE Final Act: Text and Commentary," *Behind the Headlines* 33 (1976).

Karsgaard, David, "European Security: A Review of the Conference's First Stage," *International Perspectives* (September/October 1973).

Laux, Jeanne Kirk, "CSCE and the Search for Co-operation," *International Perspectives* (September/October 1974).

Page, Donald, "Canada and European Détente," pp. 37-62, in Norman Hillmer and Garth Stevenson, (eds.), *Foremost Nation: Canadian Foreign Policy and a Changing World*, (Toronto: McClelland and Stewart, 1977).

Spencer, Robert, "The Curtain Rises: Canada in Stage One. Helsinki, July 1975," pp. 102-109, in Robert Spencer, (ed.). *Canada and the Conference on Security and Co-operation in Europe*, Toronto: University of Toronto Centre for International Studies, 1984.

c h a p t e r   17

MOVING THE EMBASSY
TO JERUSALEM, 1979

George Takach

O n 25 April 1979, halfway through
Canada's 1979 federal election campaign and just minutes before a
meeting with the Canada-Israel Committee
(CIC) at a Toronto hotel, the leader of the
Progressive Conservative party, Joe Clark,
announced to the press that if elected he
would be prepared to transfer the Canadian
embassy in Israel from Tel Aviv to
Jerusalem. Only a few months before, while
on a trip to the Middle East, Clark had refused to make such a commitment, on the
grounds that it might adversely affect the
Egyptian-Israeli peace negotiations. On 5
June 1979, at his first press conference as
prime minister, Clark reaffirmed the
Conservatives' new Middle East policy by
indicating that it was definitely the intention of the new government to move the
embassy to Jerusalem. Yet on 29 October
Clark effectively abandoned this initiative
when he announced in the House of
Commons that his government no longer
intended to move the embassy, at least until
such time as a just, comprehensive, and
lasting peace settlement between Israel and
its Arab neighbours had settled the status
of Jerusalem. This chapter explores these
two policy reversals within the context of
domestic interest group activity, international power politics, and government decision-making.

Initiative

Canadian involvement in the Jerusalem
issue dates from the creation of the state
of Israel in 1948. A Canadian, Ivan Rand,
was one of the eleven members of the
United Nations Special Committee on
Palestine which recommended that
Jerusalem be constituted an international
city for ten years, at which time its status
would be reviewed. Following the Arab-
Israeli War of 1948, Canada called for the
internationalization of the holy places
rather than of the whole city and, prior to
1967, gave de facto recognition of Jerusalem
as a part of Israel by conducting some diplomatic business there, while keeping its embassy in Tel Aviv. The Canadian position
changed during the Six-Day War in 1967
when Israel captured the West Bank, East
Jerusalem, and the Old City formerly occupied by Jordan. Until Clark's initiative
Canada had not recognized this Israeli annexation and, like most nations, regarded
East Jerusalem and the Old City as Israeli-
occupied territory. Since 1967, however, it
had been a major thrust of Israeli foreign
policy to secure international recognition
of its annexation of Jerusalem and to have
states confirm that recognition by transferring their embassies from Tel Aviv to
Jerusalem. In 1976 the Democratic party

This article is an abridged version of a chapter titled "Clark and the Jerusalem Embassy Affair: Initiative and Constraint in Canadian
Foreign Policy" in D. Taras (ed.), *The Domestic Battleground: Canada and the Arab-Israeli Conflict*, Montreal, McGill-Queen's University
Press, 1989. Numerous deletions have been made by the editors.

in the United States adopted as part of its election platform the position that the American embassy in Israel should be moved to Jerusalem. In 1980, several months after the resolution of the Clark embassy affair, thirteen countries withdrew their embassies from Jerusalem and moved them to Tel Aviv in response to the passage of a bill in the Knesset which established as a basic law earlier administrative orders declaring Jerusalem the capital of Israel.

Prime Minister Clark had several options in the wake of his election pledge. He could have ignored his promise, as the American president, Jimmy Carter, had done with regard to his party's pledge in 1976. Alternatively, he could have postponed the implementation of his promise. Clark, however, boldly chose to pursue both de jure recognition of Israeli claims to Jerusalem and a de facto move of the embassy.

Jerusalem and the Jewish Community

The idea of moving the embassy from Tel Aviv to Jerusalem first emerged as a major issue within the Canadian Jewish community during the visit to Canada of Israel's prime minister, Menachem Begin, in November 1978.[1] Begin urged the Canada-Israel Committee to take action on a number of issues important to Israel including the Arab boycott, the prevention of recognition of the Palestine Liberation Organization (PLO), and the transfer of the embassy in Israel. The Israeli prime minister was particularly anxious to see the CIC mobilize on the embassy issue.

While the leadership of the CIC agreed unanimously with Begin on the justice of the case for moving the embassy and readily committed itself to promoting the move, there was a marked lack of consensus

within the Canadian Jewish community with regard to timing and tactics. Some Jewish leaders were extremely reluctant to make the embassy transfer a high priority because they foresaw opposition from Christian leaders who favoured a form of shared jurisdiction of Jerusalem and from Canadian business interests fearful of retaliation from Arab governments. From the contending approaches, the CIC leadership fashioned a compromise whereby it agreed to undertake an educational campaign on Jerusalem aimed at both Jews and Canadians generally.

The dissolution of Canada's thirtieth parliament on 22 March 1979 and the ensuing federal election reopened the debate within the Canadian Jewish community. After much discussion, the CIC launched a campaign, focused on Jerusalem and other issues of concern to the Jewish community, to contact all parties and candidates. Several prominent Jewish Conservatives who did not hold official leadership positions in Jewish organizations openly lobbied Ron Atkey and Rob Parker, two Tory candidates in Toronto, for a Conservative commitment on the embassy initiative. At the same time Eddie Goodman, an influential Jewish Conservative (also from Toronto), advised the Conservative party against any public announcement. Most importantly, several Jews on Clark's election team, such as Reva Gerstein and especially the Toronto lawyer, Jeff Lyons, exerted significant influence by virtue of their close personal and professional access to Clark and were crucial in persuading the Tory leader to make his pledge.

. . .

Explaining the Initiative

Clark had not met with Begin during the Israeli prime minister's trip to Canada in

November 1978. Shortly after Begin's visit, however, individual Jews identified with the Conservative party began to make representations to the leader of the opposition and to Conservative party officials and members of parliament, urging them to adopt a policy favouring the embassy transfer. It was also at this time that Atkey became the Tories' expert on the issue. A lawyer and former member of Parliament for St Paul's, a Toronto riding with a significant Jewish population, Atkey had a wealth of experience dealing with matters of concern to the Jewish community. For example, in 1976 he had drafted, with the assistance of Eddie Goodman, Ontario's anti-Arab boycott legislation. Early in January 1979, Atkey prepared a brief on the embassy question for Clark's world tour which was delivered to the Conservative leader en route to Israel. The report was mainly factual in tenor, dealing with the demographic, administrative, and legal aspects of Jerusalem. While it advocated the transfer of the embassy from Tel Aviv, the report did not discuss tactics, timing, or the political ramifications of such a move.

In Israel, Clark was subjected to different pressures on the embassy issue. Begin spent half of his meeting with Clark urging the Tory leader to make an immediate commitment in support of moving the embassy. Several Conservative party colleagues who had flown to Tel Aviv to meet Clark, including Atkey, Parker, Lyons, and Irving Gerstein, also urged Clark to incorporate the embassy move into Tory policy but argued that the announcement of an initiative should be delayed until his return to Canada. Finally, in an intensive briefing with Edward Lee, Canada's ambassador in Tel Aviv, Clark was advised strongly against moving the embassy. Clark was also given a briefing document on Jerusalem prepared by the Conservative

party's research bureau and Douglas Roche, the Conservatives' foreign policy critic, which outlined more than a dozen reasons for not moving the embassy. Clark charted a careful course between these approaches both in Israel and at his final press conference of the tour in Amman, Jordan, by maintaining that any decision on the embassy would require further review in Canada and a successful resolution of the Egyptian-Israeli peace process.[2] Several months later, however, Clark made his electoral pledge, and after his victory in the 1979 election he reaffirmed his intention to move the embassy to Jerusalem.

Any explanation of Clark's embassy initiative must take into account three distinct yet interrelated factors. First, both Clark and his senior advisers considered the transfer of the embassy to be a foreign policy initiative justifiable on historic, moral, and especially legal grounds. Second, the electoral dimension must be considered. Whether or not there is a "Jewish vote" in Canadian politics, Clark's election team certainly perceived there to be one and believed that it could be induced to support the Conservatives by a promise to move the embassy. The 5 June 1979 statement of the new prime minister introduced a third element—namely, the use of the embassy issue as a vehicle by which the Conservative government could impose itself on the Ottawa civil service which Clark's transition team perceived as strongly Liberal in orientation.

The Conservative party, from at least the time of Diefenbaker's government, had taken a consistently sympathetic view toward Israel. Similarly, throughout his time as leader of the Conservative party, Clark's perception of the Middle East was weighted in favour of Israel. In a speech to the CIC shortly after becoming leader of the opposition, Clark stated that "Israel's right to exist is simply not open to discussion," and he implored the Liberal government of the day not to be blackmailed by the politics of oil with respect to the survival of Israel. A month after this speech, the "Delorme" incident during the federal by-election in the Quebec riding of Terrebonne reinforced Clark's pro-Israel sentiments. Roger Delorme, the Conservative candidate, gave a pro-Palestinian speech at an election campaign meeting at which Clark and many other high-ranking Conservative officials were present.[3] The fact that Clark did not disown Delorme caused a great stir in the Canadian Jewish community. Several observers have mentioned Clark's desire to make up for the Delorme incident as a factor in his 25 April promise.

Clark's pro-Israel sympathies, which were based at least in part on his religious background as well as his view of Israel as an island of liberal Western democracy in a sea of autocratic, Soviet-manipulated regimes, were shared by his senior advisers. Bill Neville, Jim Gillies, and Lowell Murray had long been on record as highly sympathetic towards Israel.

Finally, Clark's emotional attachment to Israel was strengthened during his trip to the Middle East in January 1979. Clark was greatly impressed by what he saw in Israel. Clark was treated graciously in Tel Aviv and Jerusalem. By contrast, Jordan's King Hussein made Clark and his entourage wait a lengthy time in Amman before receiving them. This seemingly minor affair led both Clark and his wife to contrast Arab inhospitality with Israeli friendliness as they disembarked from their plane in Ottawa.

The embassy transfer was thus viewed by Clark and his team as a measure of unequivocal support for the people and government of Israel. There was, of course, a very detailed intellectual argument put forth as to the justice of the transfer. Clark believed that moving the embassy would simply confirm Middle East reality; hence the statement in the press release of 25 April 1979 that "this foreign policy initiative is only a recognition of the political, administrative, and legal realities of Jerusalem in 1979." The signing of the Camp David Accords in March 1979 gave further credence to Atkey's argument in the minds of Clark and his advisers; again, Clark's team believed, as stated in the press release, that this event had settled the controversy surrounding Jerusalem and had opened "the way for Canada to take positive initiatives in the Middle East."

This was a misreading of the Camp David Accords by Clark and his advisers. Far from settling the status of Jerusalem, these accords had only set the stage for deliberations on this and other fundamental issues such as the future of the West Bank and the Palestinian question. Given the critical state of Arab-Israeli negotiations in the spring of 1979, Clark could not have found a more inopportune time to announce a transfer of the embassy.

Clark's people had played down the potential negative ramifications of the new policy. It was argued that the Arab world would not be overly upset because, for them, Jerusalem ranked third behind Mecca and Medina as a place of religious significance. Clark's advisers also dismissed the possibility of domestic repercussions on the grounds that the policy was intended for a very particular constituency and that it would not even be noticed, let alone be of interest, to Canadians other than those of the Jewish faith. The risk factor, as far as Clark's entourage was concerned, was also decreased by the very slow timetable envisaged for the embassy transfer; his advisers considered it at best a four-year project. Moreover, Clark planned to move Canada towards eventual recognition of the importance of involving the Palestinians in the Arab-Israeli peace process. This second prong of Conservative Middle East policy, which never got on track because of the controversy over the embassy proposal, was seen by Clark as balancing this first initiative.

...

During the election campaign, any discussion of the merits of the embassy issue became increasingly difficult as electoral concerns came to overshadow intellectual ones. One factor in the Conservatives' decision to use the embassy issue was a desire to put policy distance between themselves and the Liberal party. Moreover, Clark's election team knew that it was facing a close contest. Few if any Conservative inroads would be made in Quebec and Ontario thus became fundamental to Clark's election strategy. Winning Toronto's "swing" ridings was critical. Among these were three ridings with substantial Jewish populations: Eglinton-Lawrence and Willowdale, where candidates Parker and Bob Jarvis were the incumbent Conservative members of parliament, and St Paul's, where Atkey, the Conservative candidate in 1979, had been the member of parliament between 1972 and 1974. The Jewish vote was also a factor in Don Valley East. Parker had urged his leader to consider making a commitment to the Jewish community on his return from the Middle East in January 1979 and had asked Roche to do the same at the time of a CIC meeting in February 1979. During the election he warned that the Liberals, who were experiencing trouble with the Jewish community because of the negative comments on the anti-boycott bill of the minister of industry, trade and commerce, were about to announce their own embassy policy. The decisive pitch was made at a breakfast on 25 April before Clark's meeting with the CIC, at which it was decided to announce publicly a Conservative policy favouring the transfer of the embassy. Throughout the deliberations on timing, Parker insisted that a positive policy on the embassy would deliver the Jewish vote to the Conservatives.

After the election the embassy issue took on added significance. During the transition period, Clark was in Jasper, Alberta, drawing up a cabinet and reading government briefing papers. One document, drafted jointly by the Department of External Affairs and the Privy Council Office, concerned Jerusalem. It warned the prime minister-elect not to proceed with his election promise. This warning went unheeded, partly because Clark intended that the new Conservative government use the embassy issue to impose its will upon what he perceived to be the Liberal-oriented bureaucracy in Ottawa. Acting on the long-held Conservative assumption that Diefenbaker's government had been sabotaged by the lack of co-operation and often questionable loyalty of civil service mandarins, Clark wanted very early in the thirty-first parliament to establish effective political control over the senior personnel in the civil service. Accordingly, in reply to an innocuous question about the embassy promise at his press conference on 5 June 1979, Clark launched into a lengthy speech about the new relationship he envisioned between cabinet and the bureaucracy:

...And (Secretary of State for External Affairs) Miss MacDonald will be indicating to officials at External Affairs that we will be expecting from them recommendations fairly directly as to how it can be accomplished...these questions are now beyond discussion as to their appropriateness and that what we will be seeking from the public service will be indications as to how we accomplish what we have undertaken to do.

The tone of Clark's response was earnest and defiant. Further evidence of the bureaucratic imperative underlying Clark's announcement was his telephone call to a close friend that same evening during which he asked: "Do you think they got the message?" In effect, he hoped to make clear to officials of External Affairs and indeed throughout the federal civil service that they had a new boss.

Constraint

Arab Reaction

Canada's Arab community and the rest of the Arab world were quick to respond to Clark's election pledge and affirmation of 5 June. Iraq took a very hard line while the PLO condemned the embassy policy as an "act of aggression." A more moderate approach was taken by the council of Arab ambassadors in Ottawa which met on 6 June in an emergency session to co-ordinate the official Arab response to Clark's initiative. One telling response to Clark's remarks at the press conference came from Egypt's representative in Canada, Hassan Fahmy. Interviewed by the CBC on the morning of 6 June, he stated that on the question of the embassy, Egypt was going to remain firmly in the Arab camp.

On 8 June, at the request of the council of Arab ambassadors, the secretary of state for external affairs, Flora MacDonald, met with the representatives of Morocco, Algeria, Iran, Tunisia, Jordan, Saudi Arabia, Lebanon, Somalia, and Sudan. Following this meeting a spokesman for the Arab League Information Office in Ottawa publicly suggested that Canada send a goodwill mission to the Middle East. On 16 June the Arab Inter-Parliamentary Union called upon Clark to reverse his decision as did the Islamic Conference meeting in

Rabat. The French-Canadian press reported an alleged Arab-Quebec understanding whereby Quebec City would not recognize the federal government's transfer of the embassy to Jerusalem if in turn the Arabs would support Quebec's aspirations for independence.

Canadian-Arab relations were further strained by remarks made by Ron Atkey, the new minister of employment and immigration, during an appearance on CTV's "Question Period" on 17 June. Arguing that "the same sort of threats were made by Arab ambassadors to Ontario business," Atkey concluded that the "Arabs' bark is worse than their bite." The Arabs interpreted the reference to barking dogs as particularly degrading inasmuch as the dog is considered a lowly creature in Arab culture. In Ottawa the nine Arab ambassadors met again and their spokesman met once more with MacDonald. Several days later, in an unprecedented series of meetings, Prime Minister Clark received the nine Arab ambassadors as well as the Egyptian and Israeli ambassadors. Then, on 23 June, several hours before his departure for the summit in Tokyo, Clark announced what became known as the Stanfield mission.

In addition to the verbal barrage directed at the Conservative government during the summer of 1979, at least three concrete measures were taken by the Arab world against Canada. The first was the decision of the Arab Monetary Fund (AMF) to suspend dealings with Canadian financial institutions. The second was an Iraqi oil embargo imposed against Canada. The third involved the cancellation of several Canadian contracts by Arab buyers. Officials of the Departments of Industry, Trade and Commerce and External Affairs argued that each case was a "straw in the wind," sample of bigger things to come. For example, what worried Ottawa officials and

Canadian bankers most about the AMF's action was that Kuwait, and especially Saudi Arabia, were shareholders in the AMF. If these two countries were to follow the AMF's lead, then Canada would suffer serious economic damage indeed.

Canada's vulnerability vis-à-vis the Arabs in terms of oil supply was patently clear. During 1979 Arab crude accounted for 30 per cent of Canadian imports and 14 per cent of total Canadian supply. It was in light of these facts that the minister of energy, Ray Hnatyshyn, ordered the petroleum utilization group of his department's emergency program section to prepare a special study of a potentially severe oil shortage arising from a complete Arab oil embargo.

Another source of weakness was the $4.5 billion of Arab investment capital in Canada. While this amount was little more than a 4 per cent of the Arabs' US $100-billion global pool at the time, a massive dumping of Canadian currency by Arab holders would have depressed the Canadian dollar by at least three cents, and perhaps by as much as six cents, in relation to the American dollar.[4] Finally, the Middle East and North Africa had become an important market for Canadian goods in the preceding decade, especially in manufactures which comprised 97 per cent of all exports to this region at the time. In 1979 Canada sold nearly $800 million in goods and $500 million in services to the Middle East. While this was less than 3 per cent of Canada's total exports, trade officials as well as many businessmen believed the Arab states of the Middle East and North Africa were the single most promising market for future Canadian exports.

...

The embassy issue was extremely divisive in Canada. Apart from the obvious rift between domestic Jewish and Arab groups and the business community's strong reaction to the Clark initiative, it is telling that even within the Jewish community opinion was divided as to the appropriateness, and especially the timing, of the embassy promise. Moreover, a Gallup poll taken during the summer of 1979 indicated 15 per cent of the respondents in favour of the transfer of the embassy and 70 per cent opposed.[5]

...

The Clark government, having greatly underestimated the intensity of Arab reaction, was forced into a defensive position. Clark's lack of expertise in foreign affairs, coupled with the Conservative government's inexperience in exercising power, added to the uncertain posture taken by Clark in dealing with the Arabs. The embassy affair was a harsh introduction to the realities of international power politics for which the Tory leader and his new cabinet were clearly ill prepared.

Domestic Reaction

Spirited negative reaction to the embassy initiative was not confined to the Arab world. Groups such as the United Nations Association of Canada and several university professors opposed the proposed transfer because they felt it would mean a departure for Canada from responsible international citizenship in its Middle East diplomacy. Initial press comment following Clark's 5 June statement was cautious, but by 8 June, with front-page headlines proclaiming "Arabs threaten economic 'war' against Canada" and "Arabs' reply could cost 55,700 jobs," most editorial comment turned against the initiative. Interestingly, when Arab pressure began to make itself felt, some Canadian newspapers, while maintaining that the embassy policy was improper, argued against giving in to Arab blackmail, thereby attempting to transform the embassy issue into one of Canadian sovereignty. Finally, Liberal party reaction was predictably negative during both the election campaign and the ensuing parliament; the leader of the opposition, Pierre Trudeau, was particularly vehement and accused Clark, among other things, of undermining Canadian credibility in the Middle East.

The Canadian corporate community was deeply disturbed by the Arab world's reaction to Clark's initiative. Three sectors of Canadian business were particularly anxious to make their opposition known to the Clark government; oil-importing companies, banks and other financial institutions, and manufacturers with export contracts in the Arab world. Besides individual corporations, several trade associations, and especially the Canadian Export Association, were active after 5 June in making the business community's concern known to the government. The business lobby also acted in concert with Arab interests; in a startling meeting, Bell Canada's president, Jean de Grandpré, flew to Ottawa from Montreal two days after Clark's press conference to reassure Arab ambassadors not to worry about Clark. Bell Canada was especially concerned because it had a contract to help install a large telecommunications network in Saudi Arabia.

The business community's lobbying of the government began with a corporate storming of the Department of Industry, Trade and Commerce. Every conceivable means, at every possible level, was employed. As well, the business lobby gave considerable attention to several other ministers and departments and the prime minister received numerous personal representations. The most significant meeting took place on 22 June when Clark invited thirteen leading Canadian businessmen to 24 Sussex Drive. It was the next day that Clark announced the appointment of Robert Stanfield as the government's representative to study the embassy move and other Canadian-Middle East questions.

The Stanfield Mission

Clark's appointment of Robert Stanfield on 23 June 1979 as Canada's special representative and ambassador-at-large was an important development. The choice of Stanfield is generally credited to MacDonald. The choice was a wise one. As a public figure who enjoyed widespread admiration, Stanfield was able to command the respect of those with whom he spoke, and he likewise was assured that the Clark government would consider his recommendations seriously. There was, however, substantial debate among Clark, External Affairs, and MacDonald about Stanfield's terms of reference. Clark wanted him to find out how best to implement the embassy transfer and to determine its costs. By contrast, the department saw the mission as a means to dump the policy altogether, while MacDonald hoped Stanfield could provide the government with a breathing space in which it could weigh all the ramifications of the policy. Stanfield's final terms of reference were a mix of the three positions: he was asked to examine ways in which to enhance Canada's bilateral relationships with the countries of the Middle East and North Africa, to determine how Canada could contribute to a just and lasting peace settlement in the Middle East, and "to examine ways and means of implementing the Government's policy on Jerusalem in a manner that will be compatible with efforts to achieve such a peace."[6]

In carrying out his mandate, Stanfield consulted with numerous groups and individuals both interested in and expert on questions relating to Canada-Middle East relations. In speaking with and accepting written and often very detailed briefs from academics, bureaucrats, members of the Arab diplomatic corps in Ottawa, and representatives of the Canadian business and Jewish communities, Stanfield was exposed to all the arguments surrounding the embassy controversy. As well, in the fall of 1979 he visited several Arab countries, Israel, France, the United Kingdom, the Vatican, Italy, Washington, the United Nations in New York, and four provincial capitals. Stanfield's first trip overseas coincided with the opening of Parliament and this had the effect of bringing the embassy issue into the House of Commons where Conservative Middle East policy was subjected to persistent attack by the Liberals. Disgruntled Conservatives believe that the negative publicity induced by this scrutiny reinforced Clark's image of incompetence and thereby contributed to the defeat of the Conservatives in the February 1980 federal election. Conversely, those in the Ottawa foreign policy community who were anxious to improve Canadian-Arab relations considered the Stanfield mission a success. Officials in the Departments of Industry, Trade and Commerce and External Affairs have maintained that Stanfield made a major contribution to rebuilding a healthy rapport between Canada and the Arab world.

In his interim report, Stanfield approached the embassy question from the perspective that Canada's contribution to a just and lasting peace in the Middle East was more important than Canada's economic interests in the region. Accordingly, because the Camp David Accords had not resulted in a comprehensive peace settlement, especially with regard to the future of Jerusalem, Stanfield recommended against

the transfer of the embassy. Given the complex negotiations on Jerusalem and the sharply differing positions of the Israelis and Arabs, he maintained that a transfer of the embassy would have an exceedingly negative impact upon the peace process:

> To use effectively whatever influence we may have in the area to encourage moderation and compromise we must retain credibility with both sides as a fair minded interlocutor. We could not do this if we were to move our Embassy to Jerusalem.... I do not think that Canada should pursue any course of action which erodes the credibility of the Camp David Accords by creating the impression that they have strengthened the position of one of the parties on a key issue yet to be addressed in negotiations.

Explaining the Reversal

At least a dozen factors must be weighed when considering Clark's decision to postpone indefinitely the embassy transfer. Officials had, at least initially, the least effect on Clark. Indeed the bureaucracy's warnings had the opposite effect because of Clark's perception of External Affairs as a bastion of civil servants sympathetic to the Liberals. In his view this had been borne out by the department's handling of the initial Arab response to his 5 June statement; a senior Clark adviser was particularly startled by how the External Affairs official in Jeddah, Saudi Arabia, sent back to Ottawa hysterical cables during the summer of 1979. Indeed, Clark's advisers have maintained that External Affairs encouraged Arab reaction by letting it be known that the cabinet was divided over the embassy issue and that pressure exerted upon certain ministers would have a significant effect. In short, Clark believed that his Middle East policy would have worked, had the department spent as much time supporting as criticizing it.

There is evidence that soon after 5 June Clark developed somewhat of a siege mentality. The front-page headlines trumpeting dangerous Arab retaliation at first served only to harden his resolve and later he refused to acknowledge the "bad press" he was getting by simply not reading any more damaging newspaper reports. By contrast, editorial sentiment to the effect that Canada ought to stand up to Arab "blackmail" pleased Clark greatly.

Clark's hostile reaction to the criticism of Ottawa's bureaucrats, academics, and the press was certainly due in part to the fact that the embassy issue was his first major policy initiative. Cognizant of the need to look capable and decisive, Clark made a conscious effort to act "prime ministerial" from the moment he was elected. This was particularly true with regard to foreign policy, where Clark was perceived to be far less adept than his predecessor. The cumulative weight of these factors made him resistant to any quick policy reversal on the embassy issue. After trips to the Tokyo Summit and the Commonwealth Conference in Lusaka, however, Clark began to give credence to the foreign policy specialists. He came to realize that External Affairs was supportive of his government and his confidence in their advice grew to the point that by the autumn of 1979 Clark was ready to follow their counsel on the embassy issue.

One of the important factors which influenced Clark's reconsideration of the embassy initiative was the massive, unyielding, continuing Arab opposition to his policy. The only group to enjoy greater effectiveness was the business community. Against the Arab groups and the business community, the Canadian Jewish community and the Israeli government stood practically alone in urging Clark to remain firm. Prime Minister Begin telephoned Clark on 7 June to thank him for his initiative; he also said that he expected Clark to follow through on his pledge. Some prominent Canadian Jews publicly warned Clark not to back down in the face of Arab and corporate pressure and these efforts were not without effect. Moreover, Arab and business criticism initially served only to strengthen Clark's pro-Israel position. Indeed, inasmuch as the Arab and business lobbies called for an immediate reversal of the embassy policy, the Stanfield appointment and Clark's disagreement with External Affairs over its terms of reference indicate the degree to which Clark was still intent on transferring the embassy prior to his Tokyo trip.

A discussion that Clark had with President Jimmy Carter of the United States at the Tokyo Summit had an impact upon the development of Clark's thinking on the embassy affair. Carter confronted Clark on his Middle East initiative and impressed upon him the negative repercussions it would have on the delicate Camp David peace process. Several other factors then conspired to allow Arab and business reaction to hit their mark more effectively. Cabinet and the Conservative caucus became increasingly opposed. Clark had already resigned himself to receiving little or no support from his party when at the second caucus meeting after the election he took the burden of responsibility for the policy upon himself. By the time Parliament convened on 8 October 1979, Clark clearly was thinking of putting the embassy policy into the deep freeze. The incessant pummelling from opposition members in the House of Commons was difficult to withstand. Clark, a Commons man, took the debate seriously.

The unexpectedness and urgency with which Stanfield submitted his interim report seems to have provided the final factor in Clark's reversal. It was announced originally by Clark's office that Stanfield would not be heard from until autumn 1980 at the earliest. In September 1979 Stanfield himself did not envisage producing a report until "some time early next year." Indeed, upon Stanfield's return from his first trip abroad in October 1979, Clark's office issued a release stating that an early report was not anticipated. Three days later Stanfield delivered his Interim Report to Clark, stating that "appropriate recommendations regarding the location of the Embassy in Israel seem so clear following the consultations I have already held that I wish to submit them to you." The next day, 29 October, Clark announced in the House of Commons that he no longer intended to proceed with the embassy initiative.

Conclusion

The conventional view of the embassy affair is that Clark made an electoral promise at the behest of the Jewish community, found the resulting Arab and domestic corporate pressure compelling, and consequently appointed the Stanfield mission in order to abandon the initiative. In fact, the emergence and resolution of the embassy affair were far more complex and problematic. The Canadian Jewish community was divided over the political course to follow and, most importantly, the issue's emergence exemplifies not so much an interest group demanding policy action from a political party as it does a political party using an ethnic group for what was perceived to be possible electoral gain. As for the issue's resolution, the business community did not consider the appointment of Stanfield a victory because Clark did not comply with its

demand for an immediate reversal of policy. Furthermore, because Stanfield's terms of reference did not herald explicitly a reversal of Conservative Middle East policy, the business community initially viewed its appointment as a setback. Indeed, the conflict over Stanfield's terms of reference, coupled with the fact that Stanfield treated his endeavour as a truly independent mission of inquiry, is further proof that Stanfield was not appointed merely to help the Conservatives jettison the embassy policy.

The embassy affair brought into sharp relief several important themes in Canada's Middle East Policy. One is the paramountcy of the prime minister in determining the direction of foreign policy. Clark's pro-Israel sympathies played a role in the embassy affair, first in helping to inspire the initiative and then in impeding the eventual reversal of the decision.

Another recurring theme in Canadian-Middle East relations is the role of the Jewish community as a domestic source of policy. While there are cleavages within this ethnic group, its overriding concern with the survival of Israel remains an important factor in the formulation of Middle East policy. This is so for several reasons: the Jewish vote—or, more precisely, the major parties' perception of its existence—the presence in Ottawa of a very expert lobby, and, magnifying the effect of both, the lack of a countervailing Arab electoral or domestic organization presence. Certain events in the Middle East, however, such as the 1973 war, President Sadat's peace mission to Jerusalem in 1977, and, more recently, Israel's involvement in Lebanon, have tended to diminish the ability of the Jewish community to have an impact upon the Canadian foreign policy process. The effectiveness of the Jewish community in Ottawa has also been tempered by the increase in commercial exchanges between Canada and the Arab world since the early 1970s which has resulted in the increasing influence of the Arab point of view.

Stanfield's mission and his two reports stand out as a positive outcome of the embassy affair. Genuinely impressed by the diplomatic role Canada might be able to play in the Middle East, Stanfield argued for a policy of scrupulous evenhandedness. This includes, in Stanfield's estimation, recognition of the Palestinian issue as central to the Arab-Israeli conflict and of the fact that worthwhile negotiations towards a settlement will only occur with Palestinian involvement in the peace process. The embassy affair also raises several important questions about the Canadian public policy process generally. It highlights the predicament of a party too long in opposition; namely, a lack of access to information and expertise, a pronounced vulnerability to special interest groups, and, on achieving power, a lack of experience in governing. In retrospect, the Conservatives have taken the lesson from the embassy af-

fair that a two-week whirlwind tour, even one punctuated with briefings by officials, is insufficient to prepare a leader of the opposition for the intricacies and nuances of world politics.

It is when a party long in opposition comes to power that its inexperience in world politics and its tendency to adopt potentially dangerous policies really take their toll. Distrustful at first of the foreign policy bureaucracy that seemed so unhelpful to it while in opposition, the new government is likely to adopt a posture of confrontation towards its senior civil servants. By the time the new government comes to grips with the levers of power, major errors are likely to have been made. Had Prime Minister Clark found a means other than the embassy transfer with which to exert his dominance over the bureaucrats, and had the embassy issue arisen several months after his first prime ministerial press conference, conceivably Clark already would have learned enough about initiative and constraint in Canadian foreign policy not to proceed with the electoral pledge.

NOTES

* Most of the information in this chapter was gathered in confidential interviews during the winter of 1979 and the spring and summer of 1980. Some of the ideas in this chapter were previously expressed in a master of arts thesis submitted by the author to the Norman Paterson School of International Affairs, Carleton University, Ottawa.

1. See H. Adelman, "Clark and the Canadian Embassy in Israel," *Middle East Focus* 3 (March 1980).
2. *Globe and Mail*, 16 January 1979.
3. D. Humphreys, *Joe Clark: A Portrait* (Ottawa: Deneau and Greenberg 1978), 250-1.
4. *Financial Post*, 30 June 1979.
5. *Toronto Star*, 18 August 1979.
6. Order-in-Council, P.C. 1979-1843.

SUGGESTED READINGS

Adelman, Howard, "Clark and the Canadian Embassy in Israel." *Middle East Focus* 3 (March 1980): 6-18.

Canada, Special Representative of the Government of Canada and Ambassador at Large, *Final Report of the Special Representative of the Government of Canada Respecting the Middle East and North Africa*, Ottawa: 1980.

Cox, David, "Leadership Change and Innovation in Canadian Foreign Policy: the 1979 Progressive Conservative Government." *International Journal*, Vol. 37 (Autumn 1982): 555-582.

Dewitt, David and John Kirton, *Canada as a Principal Power*, Toronto: John Wiley, 1983, pp. 355-402.

Simpson, Jeffrey, *Discipline of Power: the Conservative Interlude and the Liberal Restoration*, Toronto: Personal Library, 1980, pp. 145-159.

Troyer, Warner, *200 Days: Joe Clark in Power*, Toronto: Personal Library, 1980, pp. 54-73.

chapter 18

SANCTIONING THE SOVIETS: THE AFGHANISTAN INTERVENTION, 1979-80

James Bayer

The Soviet invasion of Afghanistan on December 26, 1979 precipitated what American President Jimmy Carter described as the worst international crisis since the Second World War. Canada, along with the United States and other NATO allies, responded to this unwarranted act of Soviet aggression by imposing a number of economic, political, cultural, and athletic sanctions on the Soviet Union. The Canadian government's desire to punish the Soviet Union for its aggression in Afghanistan was determined by a mixture of domestic political consideration related to the ongoing 1979-80 winter federal election, as well as by traditional Canadian foreign policy objectives related to NATO unity and the need to support the United States in a major confrontation with the Soviet Union. The aim of this article is to outline the origin and evolution of Canada's policy towards the Soviet invasion of Afghanistan in the final months of the Clark administration.

If the Russian invasion of Afghanistan was the most serious international crisis since the Second World War, the fact was initially lost on Canadians. The press carried no banner headlines or front-page stories announcing the aggression. Indeed, in the days immediately following the Soviet invasion of Afghanistan, the front pages of Canadian newspapers remained dominated by the ongoing Iranian hostage crisis, the

Canadian federal election, the run-away price of gold, and even the defeat of the New York Rangers by a visiting Soviet hockey club.[1] News stories related to the invasion were, for the most part, tucked away on the back pages of the paper alongside local news and fashions. The reason for this apparant lack of concern was reflected in the few editorials to appear on the subject. These interpreted Soviet motives for the invasion as nothing more sinister than a desire to prevent an unpopular Marxist client regime in Kabul from falling prey to a ragtag collection of fundamentalist Moslem guerrillas.[2] Certainly there was no hint on the part of editorial writers at this time that the invasion was part of a wider Soviet plot to dominate Iran and the Persian Gulf area.

The Canadian public was not alone in its apparent indifference to the Soviet invasion.[3] The immediate official reaction from Ottawa, Washington, and the capitals of European NATO countries was so low-keyed that it prompted the editors of the *Toronto Star* to appeal for "someone—why not Canada?—[to] bring this matter before the United Nations since...at least it would alert the world to this brazen military intervention."[4] In Ottawa, the short-lived minority government of Conservative Prime Minister Joe Clark faced a general election in February following the unexpected de-

This is an original article.

feat of its budget in the Commons on December 13. The first official response was a short statement issued on December 28 by the Minister for External Affairs, Flora MacDonald. In it she expressed "deep regret" at the Soviet intervention, fearing it would adversely affect East-West relations and the passage of the SALT II treaty in the American Senate, encourage those in the United States who favoured direct military intervention to free the American hostages in Iran, and add to the general instability of the explosive Iran-Pakistan region.[5] Notably the Canadian government did not see the invasion as the first step in a wider Soviet plan of conquest in the area.

One reason for the subdued Canadian and international response to the Afghan situation appeared to be the lack of clear immediate information as to what exactly had happened in Kabul over the previous few days, and the extent to which the Soviet military was responsible for events. Certainly this was the case in Ottawa. An External Affairs official noted on the initial cable reporting that Hafizullah Amin had been replaced in a coup by Babrak Karmal: "This is curious—We know little about Karmel[sic], whether militare[sic] or civilian or what."[6] Moreover, even after the extent of Soviet military involvement became clearer, there appeared no reason to think Western interests were threatened by the invasion. Initially, Soviet objectives for the invasion were believed to lie within the borders of Afghanistan and not beyond in areas more sensitive to Western interests. This assumption was reflected not only in editorial analyses but also in diplomatic reports from overseas Canadian missions. The Canadian mission in Islamabad, for example, concluded that Soviet intervention was motivated primarily by a desire to force a more efficient prosecution of the counter-insurgency campaign in Afghanistan:

All available evidence supports the view that recent USSR military build-up and introduction of combat troops in strength with massive supplies of equipment into Afghanistan was for purpose of engineering coup to oust Amin and place in power leader who would be completely under Soviet control. It is commonplace that USSR has been profoundly unhappy with Amin's failure to establish firmly based regime and to deal effectively with growing opposition. This could mean that Soviet Union intends that Babrak regime carry out much more rigorous prosecution of counter-insurgency operations and more severe policy of repression. But it could also mean that USSR intention is to have new regime adopt more conciliatory posture in expectation that this will help to mollify outraged Islamic and tribal sensibilities of population and thus to reduce gradually opposition to formation of communist state in Afghanistan.[7]

Finally, the subdued Canadian and international response appeared explained by the fact that most observers believed that the Afghan guerrillas would be crushed within months if not days by the powerful Soviet Red Army, and that there was little Canada or the West could do to prevent this inevitable outcome.

By January 4, the attitude of the Canadian government towards the Soviet invasion of Afghanistan had hardened considerably. At a press conference that afternoon, a somber Prime Minister Clark now warned Canadians that the true objective of the Soviet invasion was not Afghanistan but the Persian Gulf and Indian Ocean, and that only tough and determined action on the part of the Western alliance could deter the Soviets from such a dangerous military adventure.[8] Towards this end Clark announced that his government planned an immediate review of Canadian-Soviet relations to see what actions might be taken to help force the Soviets out of Afhanistan.

At the same time he indicated that it was his intention to withhold diplomatic recognition from the new Afghan government, to suspend the Canada-Afghanistan bilateral aid development program worth $3 million, to press the United Nations Security Council for action, and to write personally to President Brezhnev to protest the attack. Notably, however, Clark rejected the suggestion that Canada boycott the Olympics scheduled for Moscow in the summer of 1980 on the grounds that such a boycott would have no practical effect on the Soviet Union.

This assertive new Canadian reaction towards the Soviet invasion of Afghanistan was in direct response to the changing mood in the United States. At the end of December, it became clear to Ottawa that the Carter administration planned to take a much tougher line towards the Soviet invasion.[9] Two factors had prompted this hardened response in Washington. First, by late December the Carter administration appeared convinced that the true motive for the Soviet invasion was not to preserve the Marxist regime in Kabul but to acquire warm water ports on the Indian Ocean, to gain control of the oil-rich Persian Gulf area, and to sever the West from its critical supply of Middle East oil. A hard-line response was clearly necessary to deter this threat to vital Western interests. Secondly, in late December the Carter political advisors also concluded that a hard-line policy towards Soviet aggression was desirable from the point of view of President Carter's bid for re-election in 1980. A tough response towards the Russians was viewed as likely to rally the American people behind Carter and help dispel his image as weak, vacillating, and ineffective in the handling of foreign policy. The new tough approach had been unveiled by the Carter administration at a NATO emergency meeting called by

Washington on December 31 to consider how best to respond to the Soviet aggression "in terms stronger than mere protest." Though no consensus emerged on how NATO might best respond to the invasion, it was clear that the Americans, supported by the West Germans, wanted the alliance to take tough retaliatory action against the Soviets including commercial sanctions and a possible boycott of the 1980 Moscow summer Olympics.

From the Clark government's point of view, there were a number of reasons to bring the Canadian policy towards the Soviet invasion into line with that of the United States on the afternoon of January 4. First, it was considered necessary in order to maintain NATO unity on an issue considered of great importance to the alliance leader. More importantly, it was necessary in order to forestall politically damaging domestic criticism of Clark. The flurry of diplomatic activity in Europe and Washington associated with the emergency NATO meeting had served to spark a rush of commentary on the Afghan situation in a Canadian press which only the week before had virtually ignored the invasion. Canada's major newspapers suddenly swelled with angry editorials and commentaries which not only echoed the Carter administration's view that the Persian Gulf and Indian Ocean were the ultimate targets of Soviet aggression, but also called for a resolute Western response, including sanctions, to deter future Soviet military adventures.[10] The Conservative government, in adopting what appeared to be a tough and timely Canadian response to Soviet aggression, denied the NDP and Liberals an issue which they might use as part of their strategy to focus on Clark as a weak and inept leader—a perception already widely held by the Canadian public.[11] Finally, by announcing Canada's tough new response to Soviet aggression on the afternoon of January 4, several hours before Carter was scheduled to go on American television to outline the American response to Soviet aggression, Clark avoided the impression of merely tagging along with the United States.

The sanctions outlined by President Carter on the evening of January 4 surprised the NATO allies in terms of their severity. Carter curtailed Soviet fishing privileges in American off-shore waters, restricted American commercial credits, limited Aeroflot service to the United States, banned the sale of American high technology to the USSR, delayed the opening of new consular offices in Russia, banned further American grain sales to the Soviet Union, requested that other major grain producers, like Canada, not make up the shortfall in grain deliveries, and finally, warned that the United States intended to boycott the Moscow Olympics if these measures failed to get the Soviets out of Afghanistan.

In Ottawa a pledge not to make up the shortfall in American grain deliveries to the Soviet Union came swiftly. It was easy to make. It furthered NATO unity, immunized the government against charges of being unsupportive of the Americans, and came at no cost to Canadians. In reality Canada was in no position to make up the shortfall in American grain deliveries: its domestic transport system was too inefficient; its sales commitments to Japan and China too great; and the volume of grain involved too large for Canada to contemplate making up.[12] But if the shortfall in American grain deliveries was an easy question to deal with, the same could not be said for the actual sanctions announced by Carter. They were much more problematic in that they threatened to place the Conservatives in a "no win" political situation from an electoral point of view.

On the one hand, it was clear from the reaction in the press that a growing number of citizens wanted the government to "teach the Soviets a lesson" by imposing sanctions on the Soviet Union identical to those adopted by the Americans.[13] Editorial opinion nationally showed strong support for a grain embargo against the Soviet Union (provided the government compensated farmers for lost income), as well as support for a boycott of the Moscow Olympics, a ban on Soviet fishing activity in Canadian waters, a ban on Aeroflot service to Canada, and a ban on export credits and the export of high technology to the Soviet Union. On the other hand, it was also clear that special interest groups central to the Conservatives' re-election strategy were equally opposed to the imposition of such sanctions. Farmers in the West, as well as associated business interests and trade unions, adamantly opposed a grain embargo for fear of losing one of Canada's best grain customers.[14] Opinion in the Atlantic provinces strongly opposed a ban on Soviet fishing activities in Atlantic waters and on Aeroflot services to Gander because of the severe negative impact these measures were likely to have on an already depressed regional economy.[15] The Canadian Olympic Association, arguing that a boycott would kill the Olympic movement, received widespread public support in its campaign to keep politics out of sports.[16] There was also opposition, though less widespread, to restrictions on high-tech exports and credits to the Soviet Union. Indeed, it was clear from the government's own review of relations with the Soviet Union at this time that American-style sanctions would do more harm to Canada than to the Soviet Union, particularly in grain and fishing-related industries.[17]

The dilemma for the government evolved around its electoral strategy. The Conservative party had entered the general election campaign 19 percentage points behind the Liberals in the Gallup polls. The Conservatives hoped to elect at least a minority government on February 18 by holding on to seats in the Maritime provinces while making gains in the West to offset likely losses in Ontario.[18] Their strategy had experienced a major setback early on in the campaign when the opposition parties successfully made Joe Clark's leadership the main election issue and thwarted Conservative plans to re-kindle the public's old animosity towards Pierre Trudeau, who had been coaxed out of retirement to lead the Liberals once again.[19] Now suddenly the sanctions question threatened to add to their difficulties. If they failed to copy American sanctions, it would alienate a large number of Canadians and lend credibility to Liberal charges that Clark was an unfaithful ally of the United States. On the other hand, if they replicated American sanctions, it would alienate important elements of public opinion in key electoral areas like the Prairies and Atlantic Canada.

On January 11, Prime Minister Clark came up with a solution when he presented Canada's much awaited sanctions policy to the nation. On the surface it appeared as tough as that imposed by the Americans: grain sales were to be restricted to "traditional levels" (defined as 3 million metric tonnes per annum) and compensation paid to farmers; the International Olympic Committee would be urged to move the 1980 Games outside the Soviet Union, possibly to Montreal; other Western nations would be approached to cooperate in "tightening up" the export of strategic and high-tech goods to Russia; a long-term credit agreement currently under negotiation with Moscow would be delayed; Aeroflot would be denied extra flights into Gander during the busy summer season (though no actions would be taken to prevent the Soviets from fishing in Canadian waters); scientific and cultural exchanges with the Soviet Union would be severed; and a ban would be placed on high-level visits between the two governments.

While the sanctions announced by Clark appeared as tough as those imposed by the United States, in reality they were crafted in such a way as to ensure no economic costs were imposed on regional interest groups of electoral importance to the Conservative party. In defining Canada's "traditional level" of grain sale to the Soviet Union as 3 million metric tonnes per annum, the government actually placed the Wheat Board in a position to expand rather than contract grain sales to the Soviet Union! The figure of 3 million tonnes represented a volume twice that shipped to the Soviets in 1979 (1.4 million metric tonnes) and approximately 600,000 metric tonnes greater than the annual average of Canadian grain exports to the Soviet Union over the previous decade.[20] Similarly, the ban on extra summer season flights into Gander in reality amounted to only one flight per week, while the proposal to move the Olympic Games out of the Soviet Union catered to those who wanted to punish the Russians as well as those who wanted Canada to participate in the Games. The commitment to tighten exports of strategic and high-tech goods to the Soviet Union was also not as severe as it appeared; most Canadian exports to the Soviet Union were not of a high-tech nature and to have a new item placed on the list of goods which the Western allies agree not to export to the Soviet Union was notoriously difficult owing to the rule of unanimity.[21] Finally, the termination of export credits for the Soviet Union was more apparent than real—since credits were to remain available, albeit on a case-by-case basis. Indeed the most effective ban announced by Clark was that which affected two groups of little political consequence: the artistic and academic communities.

If the aim of Clark's policy was to prevent the question of sanctions from becoming an election issue, he succeeded admirably. It generally appeared to satisfy the Canadian press as well as those special interest groups most directly affected by the sanctions. Most groups offered no comment except to request additional information as to what technologies would be affected and how compensation payments would be calculated for grain farmers. As for the Liberals and NDP, they remained silent. Any opportunity to use the policy as evidence of Clark's disloyalty to the United States disappeared when the American Ambassador to Canada expressed his government's pleasure at Ottawa's measures.[22]

Indeed, in the weeks that followed the sanction announcement, the government quietly clarified domestic uncertainties regarding the application of policy, met with other major grain producers in Washington to establish procedures for monitoring the flow of the international grain trade, and sounded out foreign and domestic opinion on the possibility of moving the Olympics from Moscow to Montreal.[23] The response to the Montreal initiative was not encouraging. In Canada, the Canadian Olympic Committee refused to support the proposal, the Mayor of Montreal showed little interest in hosting the games, and privately, a committee of government experts questioned the feasibility of holding the games in that city at such short notice. Abroad, only the United States and Britain favored moving the Olympics to Canada. Others, including the President of the International Olympic Committee, either rejected the proposal or remained non-commital.

The government attitude towards the Afghan crisis altered dramatically in late

January when it suddenly adopted a much harder line on the sanctions question in a deliberate effort to make the Soviet invasion the main election issue. Once again electoral considerations appeared primarily responsible for the shift in attitude and policy. On January 23, it became obvious that the Clark government faced certain defeat on February 18 unless the Conservative party could work a political miracle. A Gallup poll released that day, the first since the defeat of the government in December, showed the Liberals had actually increased their lead over the Conservatives from 19 to 21 points.[24] That Afghanistan held the key to a possible political miracle appeared obvious from electoral developments in the United States. Two days earlier, on January 21, President Carter had stunned political observers when he defeated fellow Democrat and presidential challenger, Senator Edward Kennedy, in the first of the American presidential primaries. Two months earlier Carter, who like Clark was widely regarded as a weak, irresolute and ineffective leader, had been so unpopular with the American people that he appeared all but certain to lose the Democratic nomination to Kennedy. Carter's sudden political resurrection appeared directly attributable to his tough response to the Soviet invasion and the instinct of the American people to rally around the President in time of international crisis.[25] To Conservative strategists it seemed possible that such a political resurrection might be worked in Canada. It definitely seemed worth the gamble, given the lack of effective options and the looming specter of electoral defeat.

Certainly one of the prerequisites needed to work such a political miracle already existed in Canada. By late January, public opinion in Canada reflected a mood of Cold War hysteria every bit as strident as that in the United States. Protesters in Toronto and Montreal demanded that the Soviets get out of Afghanistan; auto-dealers in Vancouver banned Ladas from a major auto exhibition; and newspapers across the land bristled with anti-Soviet rhetoric.[26] Private Tory party polls showed that Canadians favoured a strong allied response to Soviet aggression and viewed the threat of war as second only to that of inflation.[27] Indeed the only ingredient missing from a Carter-style political miracle in Canada was a Conservative campaign strategy that made a hard-line Canadian response to the Soviet aggression the main electoral issue; a campaign strategy that exploited the anti-Soviet mentality of the Canadian people, dispelled Clark's image as a weak and irresolute leader, seized the campaign initiative from the Liberals and the NDP, captured the attention of the media, deflected attention away from the Conservative's vulnerable record on domestic policy, and above all, offered the prospect of electoral victory.

Prime Minister Clark unveiled the new hard-line approach to the Soviet Union on January 26 in a speech to a Toronto crowd of 2,500 cheering Ukrainians. The new approach was characterized by anti-Soviet rhetoric, declarations of loyalty to the United States, and even a little Canadian saber rattling, as Clark, "the Cold Warrior from High River,"[28] toured the nation in the weeks following, warning that further Soviet expansion would find Canada willing to stand up and be counted alongside its American ally.

Amid the fevered rhetoric, two new anti-Soviet initiatives emerged from Ottawa. On January 26 Clark announced that Canada would boycott the Moscow Olympics unless the Soviets withdrew from Afghanistan, or, unless the International Olympic Committee moved the games from Moscow. This brought Canadian policy into line with that of the United States. On January 20 the Carter administration had appealed to the leaders of over one hundred nations, including Canada, to support a boycott of the Olympics if the Soviets remained in Afghanistan after February 20. Clark, by supporting Carter on the boycott question, clearly contrasted his position with that of the Liberals and the NDP who had rejected Carter's call for a boycott of the Moscow Olympics. This, it was hoped, promised to have a positive impact on Canadian public opinion which not only applauded the American decision to boycott the Olympics but now appeared overwhelmingly in favor of a similar Canadian policy.[29] At the same time, it would put Trudeau and Ed Broadbent, the leader of the NDP, on the defensive, for suddenly, it would be they, not Clark who appeared unsupportive of the Americans.

The second new hard-line initiative introduced by Clark focused on defence policy, where, once again, the government sought to duplicate popular policy measures announced by the Carter administration. On January 23 Carter had outlined a tough new anti-Soviet defence policy in his annual State of the Union Address to Congress. In it he declared the Persian Gulf to be an area of vital interest to the United States (the Carter Doctrine), created a rapid deployment force for possible dispatch to the Middle East, increased defence spending, and reintroduced draft registration. In Canada, public opinion generally praised Carter's decision to "draw the line" at the Persian Gulf and argued that the same tough measures should be adopted "by all friends and allies of the United States."[30] Ottawa would not disappoint them.

In a series of fiery speeches delivered in late January, Clark, like Carter, declared the Persian Gulf to be "vital to Canada and

Western interests" (the Clark Doctrine?); he declared Canada's willingness to station troops in the Persian Gulf area, or alternatively, to bolster Canada's military presence in Europe; and he announced a 17 percent increase in defence spending over the coming fiscal year as part of a "decade of dedication to Canada's own defence capabilities and of dedication to renew our commitment to Canada's defence partners..."[31] The only American defence measure not adopted by Clark, for obvious historical reasons, was draft registration. Instead Clark promised to expand Canada's armed forces by 16,000 over four years and to introduce a third infantry battalion in the Middle East, if the Persian Gulf situation further deteriorated.[32]

Although the Olympic boycott and new defence policy formed the heart of the Conservatives' hard-line policy, the government took a number of other initiatives at the end of January to accentuate and publicize its tough new attitude. On January 28, the Canadian Track and Field Association, bowing to pressure from its major source of funding—the federal government, announced that Russian athletes were to be banned from competing in the forthcoming Second International Indoor Games sponsored by the *Edmonton Journal* newspaper.[33] Two days later the Department of External Affairs announced that the Soviet research vessel Victor Bugav which was conducting oceanographic studies in the North Atlantic, would be denied permission to enter Halifax "as one more concrete manifestation of the government's response to the situation in Afghanistan."[34] Finally, in early February, Canada and the Soviet Union became engaged in a well-publicized round of diplomatic expulsions.

To the delight of Conservatives, the new strategy appeared to work. Clark dominated the media in late January, partly

because of his anti-Soviet policies and partly because of his government's role in the daring rescue of six American hostages from Iran. Press reaction towards the hard-line policy was predominantly positive and opinion polls showed a shift away from the Liberals and the NDP.[35] A Gallup poll taken at the end January showed a three-point increase in Tory popularity, while private Conservative party polls reported a "massive shift of voters away from the Liberals into the undecided category."[36] Other opinion polls also indicated a softening of Liberal support especially in the key area of metro Toronto.[37]

Indeed, the shift in public opinion appeared significant enough to put the opposition parties on the defensive for the first time in the campaign. The Liberals sought to regain the initiative by having Trudeau cancel a campaign swing through PEI in order to give a major foreign policy address in Toronto on January 29, a week earlier than scheduled.[38] The speech turned out to be a disaster. His claim that Clark had not given the Americans' sufficient support during the Iran hostage crisis appeared ridiculous in light of the disclosure made earlier in the day of the government's role in freeing six American hostages from Tehran. Similarly, his insistence that Canada must take the lead among allied nations in supporting the United States when it "cried out for help" appeared cynical if not hypocritical given his own refusal to support Carter's call for an Olympic boycott unless a majority of Western nations agreed first to do so.

The Conservative hard-line offensive was even more devastating on the NDP. Broadbent, in an attempt to overcome the dovish image of his party and bring NDP foreign policy more into line with the hawkish temperament of the Canadian people, made a number of bellicose speeches which suggested a major shift to the right in NDP foreign and defence policy.[39] Specifically he announced his support for Carter's new military measures, declared his readiness to wage war if necessary to defend the non-aligned states in the Middle East, and called upon Canada to renew its commitment to NATO—a position which flatly contradicted his party's 1969 resolution calling on Canada to get out of NATO. The problem was that Broadbent apparently made these statements without first consulting his parliamentary colleagues; the result was open division within the party. Pauline Jewitt, the NDP critic for External Affairs, immediately disavowed Boadbent's hawkish pronouncements, pointing out that they did not represent party policy: "We do not support military action or saber rattling," she declared.[40] Eventually Broadbent was forced to retreat from his hard-line position but not before Robin Sears, the National Director of the NDP, feverishly spent what he described as "the worst day of my life" attempting to close the rift between the left and moderate wings of the party.[41]

In the meantime the Clark government soldiered on. With the success over Afghanistan and Iran, it appeared on the verge of yet another foreign policy triumph in early February when the State Department announced that it was "within shot" of convincing a majority of countries to support moving the Moscow Olympics to Canada.[42] Thirty-six nations reportedly favored moving the games to Canada and this number was expected to swell to between fifty and sixty when the International Olympic Committee met on February 9 at Lake Placid, the site of the Winter Olympics, to consider the boycott question. The State Department was confident that the IOC would bow to international pressure to move the games to Montreal, par-

ticularly if key countries such as West Germany responded to the intense pressure being applied by the Americans to "get onside."[43]

When the IOC met on 9 February it came under unprecedented direct pressure from the United States government to move the games to Montreal. Secretary of State Vance himself appeared before the Committee to warn that the United States was determined to prevent the games from being held in Moscow while Joseph Onek, a White House Counselor reportedly warned the Committee that the Carter administration would "destroy the IOC" if it refused to move the Olympics.[44] But the strong-arm tactics failed if only because most committee members were not controlled by their respective governments. On February 12 the IOC voted unanimously to hold the Olympics in Moscow, in the face of a Western boycott if necessary. Back in Canada, Clark labeled the IOC decision as "clearly wrong" and warned the Canadian Olympic Committee that it would be denied government funding if it defied the Canadian boycott of the Moscow Olympics.[45]

The setback at Lake Placid coincided with the end of the Conservatives' anti-Soviet offensive. During the final week of the election campaign, the party returned to its original theme of asking Canadians for a fair chance to govern the country. What prompted this abrupt reversal in strategy is not clear. Perhaps the party felt the public's attention span for foreign policy issues had been exhausted. Perhaps Clark felt uncomfortble in the role of the "Cold Warrior from High River." Maybe the Party ran out of policy initiatives that were sufficiently bold to gain the attention and support of the electorate and media. Whatever the reason, it seemed a mistake for it allowed the Liberals and the NDP to regain the initiative and again make Clark's leadership record the main election issue.

The Conservatives' defeat on February 18 shocked few Canadians. The only surprise seemed to be that the margin of defeat was not greater than 10 percent; a Gallup Poll taken a few days before the election again showed the Conservatives 20 points behind the Liberals.[46] Clark's hard-line policy may have been responsible for narrowing the gap, given the positive impression it made on Canadians in the weeks before the election. Whether Clark could have defeated the Liberals had he continued his hard-line strategy for the last week of the campaign is doubtful. What may be concluded is that far from costing the Conservatives the election, as is sometimes suggested,[47] the hard-line policy towards the Soviet invasion of Afghanistan was sufficiently appealing to Canadians that it likely reduced the size of the Conservative defeat in February 1980 and perhaps fleetingly offered Clark the prospect of victory.

Canadian economic sanctions against the Soviet Union during this period of the Afghan crisis appeared to have had three objectives. First, they were intended to help force the Soviet Union out of Afghanistan; second, they were intended to satisfy the widespread desire on the part of Canadians to punish the Soviet Union and in so doing protect, if not further, the electoral fortunes of the Conservative government; and third, Canadian sanctions were intended to demonstrate support for the United States, maintain NATO unity, and deter possible further Soviet aggression in the area. The extent to which the Canadian government was able to achieve these objectives reflects a number of the wider problems associated with the use of economic sanctions in the international arena.

The Canadian government, indeed the Western community as a whole, failed to achieve the first objective in applying sanctions against the Soviet Union, that is, the withdrawal of Soviet forces from Afghanistan. Economic sanctions are not effective tools of diplomatic coercion if the target state is not dependent on trade with the imposing states, if alternative sources of supplies are readily available to the target state because of the lack of broad international support for sanction measures, or if there is a lack of resolve on the part of the imposing state to apply full sanctions for fear of damaging its own economy. Certainly these factors undermined the effectiveness of Canadian sanctions against the Soviet Union in the case of Afghanistan. Not only was the level of trade between Canada and the Soviet Union inconsequential, but the goods and services imported from Canada could be readily secured by the Soviets from other sources. Canadian sanctions therefore had little impact on the Soviet economy. Indeed, the application of sanctions threatened a more adverse impact on the Canadian economy than on the Soviet economy because of the dependence by certain Canadian industries to continued access to the Soviet market. The Canadian government, aware of this, diluted sanctions so as to minimize damage to the Canadian economy as well as to special interest groups critical to its re-election chances. The experience of the Canadian government in the Afghan case was not uncommon. Economic sanctions often do more damage to the economy of the imposing state than to the intended target, and seldom succeed in altering offensive behavior.

This leads to the second and third objectives for Canadian sanctions. More often than not sanctions are imposed not with the expectation that they will force the target state to alter objectionable behavior, but rather as a means to satisfy the desire of domestic and internatinal opinion "to do something" to punish aggressions, and as a means to demonstrate support for alliances and international organizations. Certainly this was evident in the case of Canadian sanctions against the Soviet Union. The primary motive behind Canada's sanction policy was to satisfy domestic opinion in order to protect, if not further, the Conservatives' re-election hopes. In this regard the policy was a success. It satisfied those Canadians who wanted to punish the Soviet Union but not at the expense of those in Canada who were most vulnerable to a sanctions policy. Indeed, although public support for the hard-line sanctions policy was not sufficient to re-elect the Conservative government in February 1980, it certainly seemed responsible for narrowing their margin of defeat.

NOTES

1. A banner headline in the *Globe and Mail* on 21/12/79 read "Soviets Defeat Rangers 5-2."
2. See editorials in the *Toronto Star*, 28/12/79; the *Victoria Daily Colonist*, 29/12/79; the *St. John's Evening Telegram* and *Montreal Gazette*, 31/12/79.
3. Ian Urqhart, "Death for Detente," *Maclean's*, 14/1/80, p. 27.
4. Editorial, *Toronto Star*, 28/12/79.
5. *Globe and Mail*, 29/12/79.
6. "Reported Coup in Afghanistan," 27/12/79, *Department of External Affairs* (hereafter *DEA*), 2-Afghan-1-4, GPS-0743. The unpublished government documents cited in this paper were obtained under Access to Information legislation.
7. Canadian Embassy (Pakistan) to External Affairs (Ottawa), 28/12/79, *DEA*, 20-Afghan-1-4.
8. *Globe and Mail*, 5/1/80.
9. Jimmy Carter, *Keeping Faith: Memoirs of a President*, Toronto: Bantam Books, 1982, p. 471-2; Cyrus Vance, *Hard Choices: Critical Years in America's Foreign Policy*, New York, Simon and Schuster, 1983, p. 388; Zbigniew Brezezinski, *Power and Principle: Memoirs of the National Security Adviser 1977-1981*, New York: Farrar, Straus Giroux, 1983, p. 432.
10. For example, see editorial in the *Globe and Mail*, 1/1/80, 2/1/80; the *Winnipeg Free Press*, 2/1/80, the *Victoria Daily Colonist*, 2/1/80, 3/1/80; the *Calgary Herald*, 2/1/80, 3/1/80; the *Montreal Gazette*, 3/1/80; the *Toronto Star*, 3/1/80; the *St. John's Evening Telegram*, 3/1/80; the *Vancouver Sun*, 3/1/80; the *Halifax Chronicle-Herald*, 4/1/80.
11. William Irvine, "Epilogue: The 1980 Election," in *Canada at the Polls 1979-80: A Study of General Elections*, edited by Howard Penniman, Washington: American Enterprise Institute, 1981, p. 358.
12. Co-ordinator, Grains group to Minister Responsible for Wheat Board, Possible Trade Embargo-USSR-Grains, 4/1/80, *DEA*, 37-16-1- USSR. The 17 million metric tonne shortfall involved in the American grain boycott represented a volume of grain nearly equal to that exported by Canada to all parts of the world the previous year.
13. For example, see editorials in the *Globe and Mail*, 8/1/80; the *Regina Leader-Post*, 7/1/80, 11/1/80; the *Calgary Herald*, 7/1/80; the *Montreal Gazette*, 8/1/80; the *Vancouver Sun*, 11/1/80.

14. *Toronto Star*, 4/1/80, 11/1/80; *Vancouver Sun*, 8/1/80, 11/1/80; *Globe and Mail*, 8/1/80, 10/1/80, 12/1/80; *Winnipeg Free Press*, 10/1/80; *Regina Leader-Post*, 10/1/80.

15. For example, see editorial, *St. John's Evening Telegram*, 9/10/80. Also see *Globe and Mail*, 8/1/80.

16. *Victoria Daily Colonist*, 3/1/80; *Le Devoir*, 5/1/80; *Montreal Gazette*, 3/1/80.

17. Soviet Trade with the West and Canada, 7/1/80, *DEA*, 37-16-SU; Co-ordinator, Grains Group to Minister Responsible for Wheat Board, Trade Embargo-Grains, 4/1/80. *DEA*, 37-16-1-USSR.

18. Jeffrey Simpson, *Discipline of Power*, Personal Library, Toronto, 1980, pp. 336-7.

19. *Ibid.*, p. 332.

20. *Financial Post*, 19/1/80.

21. *Loc. cit.*

22. *Globe and Mail*, 15/1/80.

23. *Montreal Gazette*, 19/1/80. Clark formally offered Montreal as a site on 16 January.

24. *Gallup Report*, 23/1/80.

25. Brzezinski, *Power*, pp. 432, 437.

26. *Montreal Gazette*, 14/1/80; *Vancouver Sun*, 15/1/80; *Toronto Star*, 21/1/80.

27. *Maclean's*, 4/2/80, p.15-16.

28. Geoffrey Stevens, *Globe and Mail*, 19/1/80.

29. *Globe and Mail*, 22/1/80. A Gallup survey conducted during the first few days of February showed 61 Percent of Canadians felt the Games should be boycotted, moved or cancelled. Only 30 percent favoured holding the Games in Moscow, while the rest offered no opinion. Indeed pro-boycott opinion was so strong in the electorally important Toronto area in late January that a majority of the thirty-two Conservative candidates running in Metro called upon the government to boycott the games. *Toronto Star*, 22/1/80, 25/1/80.

30. For example see the editorials in the *Winnipeg Free Press*, 25/1/80; the *Calgary Herald*, 24/1/80; the *Regina Leader-Post*, 29/1/80.

31. *Globe and Mail*, 26/1/80.

32. *Ibid.*, 29/1/80, 30/1/80, 9/2/80.

33. *Ibid.*, 28/1/80.

34. *Ibid.*, 30/1/80.

35. For example see editorials in the *Globe and Mail*, 28/1/80; the *Calgary Herald*, 28/1/80; the *Victoria Daily Colonist*, 29/1/80; the *Winnipeg Free Press*, 29/1/80; 5/2/80; *Le Devoir*, 30/1/80, the *St. John's Evening Telegram*, 1/2/80.

36. *Gallup Report*, 9/2/80; *Globe and Mail*, 4/2/80; *Regina Leader-Post*, 6/2/80.

37. Simpson, *Power*, p. 346; *Canadian News Facts*, Vol. 14, No. 2, p. 2261.

38. *Loc. cit.*

39. *Globe and Mail*, 27/1/80; Jim Turk, "Left Debates," *Canadian Dimension*, 1980, Vol. 7, 1980, p. 25.

40. *Globe and Mail*, 29/1/80.

41. Turk, "Debate," *Canadian Dimension*, p. 25.

42. *Globe and Mail*, 9/2/80.

43. *Ibid.*, 30/1/80, 1/2/80, 2/2/80, 12/2/80; *Financial Post*, 9/2/80.

44. *Globe and Mail*, 11/2/80.

45. *Ibid.*, 13/2/80, 16/2/80.

46. *Gallup Report*, 16/2/80, 3/2/80.

47. Richard Gwyn, *The Northern Magus*, Toronto: McClelland and Stewart, 1980, p. 355-6. Gwyn argues that the Soviet invasion of Afghanistan helped save the Liberals from defeat because it prompted Clark to switch from "Trudeau-bashing to Red-baiting" just at that point when the attacks on Trudeau were starting to have an impact on the electorate.

SUGGESTED READINGS

Bromke, Adam, "Detente or Cold War II: East-West Relations After Afghanistan," *Behind the Headlines*, Vol. 38, No. 2, (1980).

Cox, David, "Leadership Change and Innovation and Canadian Foreign Policy: The 1979 Progressive Conservative Government," *International Journal*, Vol. 37, No. 4, Autumn 1982, pp. 555-83.

Doxey, Margaret, "Oil and Food and International Sanctions," *International Journal*, Vol. 37, No. 2, Spring 1981, pp. 311-34.

Paarlberg, Robert L., "Lessons of the Grain Embargo," *Foreign Affairs*, Vol. 59, No. 1, Fall 1980, pp. 144-62.

Skinner, G.R., "Soviet Invasion of Afghanistan Calls for Strategic Reappraisal," *International Perspectives*, March/April 1980, pp. 7-11.

Troyer, Warner, *200 Days: Joe Clark in Power*, Toronto, Personal Library, 1980.

chapter 19

CANADIANIZING OIL AND GAS: THE NATIONAL ENERGY PROGRAM, 1980-83

David Leyton-Brown

In October 1980, the Canadian government introduced the National Energy Program (NEP), a set of policies, federal-provincial agreements, legislation, and regulations that would change many aspects of the country's oil and gas activities from exploration to pricing and taxation. Although the NEP was designed to achieve domestic policy goals of security of supply, greater Canadian participation in the petroleum industry, and changes in revenue sharing among governments, it also had a major impact in the United States and resulted in a dispute that dominated the bilateral relationship during the 1980-83 period.

The issue's origins can be attributed to several factors: rapid changes in world oil market conditions, Canadian domestic politics that were influenced by bitter federal-provincial relations and an increase in nationalist sentiments about energy policy, and a philosophical divergence between the Canadian and U.S. governments. The resulting dispute was not about energy *per se* but about investment and, to a lesser extent, trade.

Managing the resolution of the dispute over the NEP was, at first, very difficult. Inflammatory public statements and threats of retaliatory action contrasted sharply with the traditional practice of quiet diplomacy and longstanding norms of conduct between the two countries. But the central concern of the United States was to prevent any departure from the established principle of "national treatment" of foreign investors embodied in a declaration by the Organisation for Economic Cooperation and Development (OECD). In pursuing this goal, it chose primarily to use multilateral institutions to influence Canada's policies.

The purpose of this chapter is to describe the origins of Canada's policy in more detail and to analyze the factors that mainly determined how the bilateral issues were managed and partially resolved.

The NEP was developed in response to dramatic changes in world oil market conditions. Despite the fact that a large quantity of petroleum is produced in Western Canada, the high cost of transporting it to Eastern Canada had made foreign oil imports more economical in that part of the country. After the first sharp increase of oil prices in 1973 and 1974, the international price of oil continued to rise and many Canadians became uneasy. When world oil prices more than doubled in 1979-80 the reaction of oil importers became more urgent. The NEP explicitly reflected this mood.[1]

Canada's policymakers anticipated unstable and rising prices over the next decade, accompanied by supply shortages

David Leyton-Brown, "The National Energy Program," from *Weathering the Storm: Canadian-U.S. Relations, 1980-83*, Toronto; Washington, D. C.: Canadian-American Committee, 1985.

in the world oil market. Their approach was to try to insulate the Canadian economy from the rising cost of oil imports, to ensure that the federal government and not the oil producers would receive any windfall gains resulting from higher world oil prices, and to assert greater federal control over Canadian energy policy.

Such an approach led almost inevitably to domestic conflict. Federal-provincial conflicts over energy pricing and taxation had marked the 1970s. The government of Alberta, the main producing province, wanted high domestic oil and gas prices so as to generate high revenues for itself and to bring about the long-desired economic growth of the province and region. Alberta also staunchly maintained its constitutional right to control natural-resource production within its boundaries. The federal government, on the other hand, wanted to see a much slower increase in domestic oil and gas prices so as to ease the impact of rising world prices on energy consumers and on the central Canadian manufacturing base.

The Canadian tax and royalty systems channelled most petroleum revenues to the industry and to the governments of the producing provinces. As world and Canadian oil prices continued to rise, the substantially foreign-owned Canadian oil industry became wealthier and so did the oil-producing provinces. The federal government, however, faced increasing expenditures to subsidize imports of high-priced foreign oil so that Canadian consumers would be cushioned from the impact of high world prices.

In negotiations with Alberta, the federal government sought to increase its share of energy revenues and to increase its control over development of the oil and gas industry. It also sought to reduce the high level of foreign ownership and control of the Canadian oil and gas industry.

In the mid-1970s, the Minister of Energy, Mines and Resources had announced the objective of moving toward higher levels of Canadian ownership of the oil industry, though effective measures to implement it had not been introduced.[2] The sharp price increase in 1979 renewed the fears of federal policymakers. They had a general concern that multinational oil corporations might disregard Canadian interests in exploration or production decisions or in some future world energy-supply crisis. More specifically, the federal government was concerned that because more than 70 percent of sales of Canadian oil and gas were made by foreign-owned or foreign-controlled firms, non-Canadians would reap the major financial benefits of increased prices. If those profits were repatriated, there would be a drain on the Canadian economy. If they were reinvested in new exploration, then opportunities for new Canadian participation would continue to be limited.

When its negotiations with Alberta broke down in July 1980, the federal government decided to act unilaterally, as part of an autumn budget. The fact that these Canadian domestic policy moves would have a major impact on the United States was largely ignored in the rush to prepare the program. Canada's multilateral obligations under the General Agreement on Tariffs and Trade (GATT) and commitments with the OECD were also little considered.

Because the NEP was to be introduced as part of the forthcoming budget, budget secrecy applied. Consultation with outside experts from industry, provincial governments, or the public at large was not possible even if it had been considered desirable. A small circle of policymakers, who clearly favored expanded federal intervention in the energy sector, designed the program within the parameters set by the Minister Of Energy, Mines and Resources, Marc Lalonde.[3] The normal process of interdepartmental consultation was not followed. Entire departments, such as External Affairs, and even some key individuals in other departments such as Finance, and Industry, Trade and Commerce were frozen out of the preparatory process.

From the evolution of policy in the late 1970s and from the 1980 throne speech, the United States was familiar with the philosophy and objectives on which the NEP was based. But U.S. leaders first heard the details of the policy when they received phone calls from angry oil-company executives asking what Washington was going to do about the program then being announced in Ottawa.

The lack of prior consultation with or even of notification of the U.S. government had serious consequences. Canadian policymakers had been deprived of a source of information about the effects of certain features of the NEP and the likely reaction to them. Even worse was the creation of a climate of surprise and disappointment in which the increasingly emotional and bitter reaction between the two governments would develop in the months ahead.

The NEP had three broad goals: energy security, fairness in energy pricing and revenue sharing, and increased Canadian participation in the oil and gas industry.

The first of these goals, *energy security*, was to be attained by making Canada self-sufficient in oil by 1990. Independence from world oil markets was to be achieved through a combination of oil conservation, a shift to alternative energy sources, expanded domestic production, and the reduction or elimination of imports.

The second goal was that of *fairness in energy pricing and revenue sharing*. As the

Liberals had promised during the 1980 federal election campaign, oil price increases were to be held down for consumers and manufacturers in Eastern Canada. The distribution of revenues was restructured so as to increase the federal government's share from 10 to 25 percent, leaving 43 percent for the governments of the producing provinces and 33 percent for industry.

The third objective of the NEP was to *increase Canadian participation in the oil and gas industry*. The specific objective was to reduce the level of foreign ownership of the industry to less than 50 percent by 1990 and to establish Canadian control over a significant number of large, foreign-owned oil and gas firms. The NEP thus restricted permits for oil and gas production on territory under federal jurisdiction to companies that were at least 50 percent Canadian-owned.

A second Canadianization measure was the introduction of preferential grants for Canadian firms. The Petroleum Incentives Program (PIP), paid direct subsidies for exploration and development on a scale reflecting the degree of Canadian ownership of the company.

The third method of Canadianization imposed "strict requirements for use of Canadian goods and services in exploration, development and production programs on the Canada Lands, and in major non-conventional oil projects."[4]

A more direct role for the federal government in the energy sector through state-owned enterprise was also expected to Canadianize the industry. The government was encouraged by public support for government-owned Petro-Canada as a window on the industry, a stimulus to activity, and a supporter of domestic industries that provide goods and services to the energy sector.

The NEP envisaged an early increase in the federal government's ownership of the oil and gas sector. In addition to increasing Petro-Canada's investment activity, the program introduced a special tax to finance the government's purchase of foreign oil companies.

The most controversial Canadianization measure of the NEP was the Crown Interest provision. Under it, any company, whether Canadian- or foreign-owned, that held an oil or gas lease on the Canada Lands had to yield to the federal government (as represented by Petro-Canada or some similar Crown corporation) a 25 percent equity in that lease.

The Canadian government's attempt to restructure the entire Canadian oil and gas industry was announced just days before the 1980 presidential elections in the United States. With its diminution of the role of foreign—principally U.S.—energy companies, the NEP ran headlong into the free-market orientation of the Reagan administration. U.S. concerns focused on four main areas of the NEP: the oil-pricing policy, the procurement provisions, the Crown Interest provision in oil and gas leases, and the discriminatory treatment of foreign-owned companies.

The United States charged that the maintenance of Canada's domestic oil price below world levels was, in effect, a subsidy to Canadian industry. The U.S. government raised the possibility of countervailing duties against Canadian exports and suggested that the administered price level might have adverse consequences for the NEP's goal of energy security.

These concerns were, however, largely alleviated by the federal-provincial pricing agreements of September 1981, which provided for prices to rise closer to world levels.

The United States saw the NEP's favoring of Canadian suppliers of goods and services as a restraint on U.S. export opportunities and called it a violation of

Canadian obligations under the GATT. The Canadian government intended the procurement provisions to stimulate Canadian industry by overcoming a perceived tendency of multinational corporations to deal with their traditional suppliers and giving domestic companies and labor fair access to major projects in Canada.

The procurement section of the bill was changed to provide that, although Canadian goods and services had to be considered, they were to be assessed on a competitive basis. U.S. officials have taken some of the credit for bringing about this change. It appears, however, that some Canadian government departments that had not been consulted before the legislation was drafted were equally concerned about the original language and argued for the change during the interdepartmental consultations that followed the announcement of the NEP.

The United States did not object to the Canadian government's reserving an interest in future exploration leases. The main bone of contention was the imposition of a 25 percent interest in oil and gas already discovered but not yet in production on the Canada Lands. The United States saw the provision as changing the rules in the middle of the game, as a form of expropriation that required prompt, adequate, and effective compensation, in line with international standards.

The Canadian government was insistent that the Crown Interest provision applied to all nonproducing areas of the Canada Lands, irrespective of the nationality of company ownership or the date of the exploration license, and that the reservation of Crown rights should not involve the payment of compensation.

The Canadian Senate Committee on Banking, Trade and Commerce saw it rather differently:

The Committee agrees that a royalty or tax may be imposed or increased and, as such, it may have retroactive effect. The Crown's share is not, however, a royalty or tax. It is the acquisition of someone else's rights.[5]

This was also how the U.S. government perceived the situation. It argued that companies, such as Mobil Corporation, Gulf Canada Limited, and Standard Oil Company of California (through its Canadian subsidiary, Chevron Canada Ltd.), operating in the large Hibernia oil field off Newfoundland should be either exempted from the retroactive provision or given full compensation for the value of their lost holdings.

In an attempt to respond to the U.S. government and the angry oil companies, the Canadian government amended the legislation to provide for *ex gratia* payments, although it was quite explicit that they were not to be considered compensation for the Crown Interest. Rather, the payments would be tied to past exploration costs, payable to permit-holders who had begun drilling before December 31, 1980 and had wells qualified as significant discoveries before the end of 1982.

· · ·

The issue of the *ex gratia* payments proved a microcosm of the faulty communication and perception that plagued the bilateral interaction over the NEP. The Canadian government considered that the introduction of such payments represented a sincere and substantial gesture of flexibility in response to the concerns of the United States. It believed it had been assured that such a move would be well received, and it emerged from the exercise feeling betrayed because its concession was unappreciated. The U.S. government, on the other hand, considered that the *ex gratia* payments did not constitute the sort of concession that

had been discussed. It was satisfied neither in principle nor in adequacy of compensation, and it felt betrayed in that the promised degree of Canadian flexibility had not been forthcoming. The retroactive nature of the Crown Interest provisions continued to be the U.S. government's outstanding complaint regarding the NEP.

Of all the U.S. complaints, the one that generated the most heat was that the NEP's favoring of Canadian-owned companies, through such measures as PIP grants and the Crown Interest provision, amounted to a massive derogation from the principle of national treatment of foreign investors enunciated in the 1976 OECD *Declaration on International Investment and Multinational Enterprises*, which Canada had signed. The *Declaration* provides that member nations will:

accord to enterprises operating in their territories and owned or controlled directly or indirectly by nationals of another Member country...treatment under their laws, regulations and administrative practices, consistent with international law and no less favorable than that accorded in like situations to domestic enterprises.[6]

Canada had, in fact, expressed a qualification when it ratified the *Declaration*. It had noted that "elements of differentiation in treatment between Canadian and foreign controlled enterprises" existed in Canada, so that Canada would "continue to retain its rights to take measures, effecting foreign investors, which we believe are necessary given our particular circumstances."[7]

The *Declaration* provides that exceptions to the principle of national treatment must be reported and explained to the OECD. Canada did provide such an explanation for the NEP.

Such an explanation was, however, insufficient for the U.S. government. One of its primary goals was to maintain a stable environment for international investment, and the principle of national treatment was crucial to that objective. It was particularly concerned that a major threat to that stability should appear to come from Canada, a country that it believed ought to be defending rather than subverting the principle.

Throughout 1981 the United States became increasingly concerned that the NEP was setting a precedent for the discriminatory treatment of foreign investors in other Canadian sectors and in other countries.

The United States initially expressed its criticism of the NEP almost entirely through diplomatic channels. The issue rapidly became more visible and more inflammatory, however, as it came to be linked in U.S. eyes with a spate of unfriendly takeover attempts of U.S. parent companies by Canadian firms in the spring and summer of 1981.

In none of these episodes could the U.S. firm involved make a counteroffer to acquire the smaller Canadian company (a standard countermeasure in U.S. takeover battles) because of the existence of the Foreign Investment Review Agency (FIRA), the Canadian federal agency that must approve all foreign takeovers of Canadian companies. The U.S. companies thus resorted to other weapons at their disposal, including legal challenges and appeals to their government. In Congress, these companies found a receptive hearing for the view that the discriminatory treatment of U.S.-owned companies under the NEP was driving down their asset values so that Canadian companies could pick them up at "fire sale" prices, while FIRA prevented U.S. firms from investing in Canada.

Increasingly, the issue became not just the provisions of the NEP, but Canadian investment policy in general. Even so, the U.S. executive branch and Congress differed somewhat in their emphasis. The administration was most concerned with the impact of the NEP and its implications for foreign investment world-wide. Congress responded primarily to the wave of takeover attempts the NEP seemed to have precipitated.[8]

FIRA and the NEP came to be referred to in a single breath for three reasons: first, because of FIRA's apparent association with the NEP; second, because of the cumulative effect of FIRA's recent regulatory practices; and third, because of the Canadian government's announced intention of broadening and expanding FIRA's powers in a fashion the United States saw as discriminatory.

The United States' entanglement of objections to the NEP and objections to FIRA was not a linking of two totally unrelated issues. Rather, it was a broadening of the agenda that proved an impediment to smooth management of the bilateral relationship. The two sides often had different expectations about the specific subjects to be discussed during negotiations, and it became difficult to ensure that individuals with the appropriate expertise were brought into contact with one another.

In response to the NEP, the United States took action on three fronts. First, it used multilateral machinery to try and affect Canadian policies. Second, it threatened several kinds of retaliation. Third, it used bilateral diplomatic negotiations to seek modifications to the NEP.

In Canadian-U.S. relations historically, it is the Canadian government that has tended to rely upon membership in multilateral institutions to enhance its effectiveness in dealing with its superpower neighbour.[9] Now, in an interesting, though not unprecedented, reversal of roles, the United States resorted to multilateral forums, including two OECD committees, the International Energy Agency (IEA) and the GATT, in attempts to resolve the disagreements over both the NEP and FIRA.

In March 1981, at the initiative of the U.S. government, the OECD Committee on International Investment and Multinational Enterprises (CIME) met in the first formal use of consultation provisions of the 1976 *Declaration* on national treatment and its associated guidelines. At that and subsequent meetings of CIME and its Working Group on International Investment Policies, the U.S. government criticized the extent to which parts of the NEP departed from the principle of national treatment. In response, the Canadian government explained the NEP to CIME members and reaffirmed its commitment to the national-treatment principle. It promised to fulfil its obligations to report and explain to the OECD any elements of the NEP that might be exceptions to this principle.

In the IEA, the United States raised questions about the impact of the NEP's pricing, taxation, and production policies on Canadian energy supplies and about the ability of Canada to meet its IEA undertakings. By voicing these concerns, the United States pressured Canada to change its policies and mobilized other countries to express their concerns.

On the broader question of interference with the free flow of trade and investment, the United States persuaded the OECD's Trade Committee to begin a study of trade-related performance requirements and the OECD's Investment Committee to study both this subject and the issue of investment incentives. Discussions of investment policy and discriminatory practices exemplified by, but not limited to, Canadian policies were also raised in a variety of other multilateral forums, including the OECD and GATT ministerial meetings and the economic summits.

The most dramatic multilateral move by the U.S. government was to launch a formal complaint under the GATT against the alleged trade-distorting effects of FIRA's performance requirements. In January 1982, it used the GATT mechanism to request formal consultations with Canada on complaints that FIRA's export and local-content requirements for investment approval were contrary to the GATT articles regarding restrictions on imports, national treatment, and import substitution.

These consultations failed to produce a mutually acceptable resolution of the problem. The U.S. government then moved to the next step, appealing under the GATT for a binding decision by an international panel. In July 1983, the panel found that the requirement that FIRA take into account the effect a proposed investment will have on the use of Canadian parts, components, and services constituted a violation of Article III(4) of the GATT. At the same time, however, the panel rejected another U.S. complaint.[10]

The full 88-member governing council of the GATT adopted the panel's report on February 7, 1984. Prior to the final council ruling, however, Canada's Minister for International Trade, Gerald Regan, announced that his government would accept the finding and adjust the wording of the act to conform with the decision.[11]

All in all, dealing with these trade and investment issues through multilateral institutions helped move the bilateral disputes to a less politically charged arena. Nevertheless, use of the multilateral forums did not result in substantial changes; in general they are of greater importance in constraining behavior in advance, rather than remedying a problem after the fact.

The other notable way in which Canadian-U.S. interaction over the NEP (and FIRA) issue differed from the traditional pattern of bilateral relations was in the United States' active consideration of retaliation against Canada.

Most of the retaliatory measures contemplated by the Reagan administration were expressed to the Canadian government through diplomatic rather than public channels, although occasional press reports appeared. These measures ranged from disruption of the auto pact or Defense Production Sharing Arrangements to action under Section 301 of the U.S. *Trade Act of 1974*. The threat that apparently had the greatest impact in Ottawa was that of excluding Canada from participation in a meeting of international trade ministers scheduled for mid-January 1982 in Key Biscayne, Florida. The grounds were that Canada's failure to live up to its international commitments made it no longer worthy to be a member of the group of advanced countries engaged in such negotiations. At the last moment, the United States reversed its position, and Canada took part in the meeting.

The greatest pressure for retaliation, however, came not from the U.S. administration but from Congress. Alarmed by the acrimonious Canadian takeover attempts in the spring and summer of 1981 and concerned that the administration's bilateral negotiations had failed to bring about fundamental changes in the NEP, several members of Congress seized the public initiative.

All their measures lost much of their immediacy when the wave of takeovers ebbed. The takeovers involved a massive outflow of funds that began to threaten the level and stability of the Canadian dollar. On July 29, 1981, the Minister of Finance, Allan MacEachen, asked the Canadian chartered banks to reduce substantially the amount of funds they would lend to finance Canadian takeovers of U.S. companies. In short order the Canadian-U.S. aspect of the takeover issues became moot.

. . .

Though repeated U.S. threats of unilateral retaliation poisoned the public and diplomatic climate from mid-1981 to early 1982, no actual retaliation occurred. Try as they might, the various branches of the U.S. government could not find any measure sufficiently punitive to compel the Canadian government to change its policies that would not at the same time rally nationalist Canadian public opinion and impose counterproductive economic and political costs on the United States itself. In addition, the U.S. administration was concerned that it not be seen as departing from the principles and practices it was struggling to defend.

In brief, the United States could take no retaliatory action against Canada without jeopardizing its own interests. But threats alone may have been sufficient to harm the bilateral relationship.

The use of diplomatic channels constituted the U.S. government's third general approach to seeking modifications of the NEP. After the announcement of the program, an ongoing series of letters, meetings, and speeches registered U.S. concerns and sought modifications in both the NEP and FIRA.

The diplomatic exchanges involved some clearly understood posturing, but also a failure of communication and mismatch of expectations. U.S. officials went to meetings with their Canadian counterparts hoping to negotiate some compromise in the subjects on the agenda and believing that flexibility had been promised, only to be lectured once again about the nature and purposes of the NEP. Some key individuals felt personally betrayed when their perception of promised flexibility turned out to be unfounded. Canadian officials attended meetings expecting to clarify the nature and intent of Canadian policy and perhaps to explain some recent amendment to the regulatory legislation that they saw as substantial indication of flexibility, only to be confronted with more complaints about features that they had repeatedly said were nonnegotiable.[12]

The frustrations arising from these unsatisfactory interactions were compounded by the fluid nature of the agenda. U.S. complaints about FIRA were really quite separate from those about the NEP, but they tended to be lumped together as the agenda grew. By December 1981, a supposedly definitive list of U.S. complaints covered the entire range of Canadian foreign direct investment policy.

...

In 1981 and early 1982 Canada did modify some portions of the NEP that had bilateral implications. On May 14, 1981, the government changed the language on procurement of Canadian goods and services to conform to GATT obligations and introduced the *ex gratia* payments in connection with the Crown Interest provisions. The original preference for Canadian-owned firms in authorizing gas exports was eliminated on February 14, 1982. The "constrained shares" provisions, which would have empowered companies to drive out foreign shareholders by buying out their shares so as to increase their Canadian ownership rating, were withdrawn on April 7, 1982.

These modifications resulted in part from the various multilateral and bilateral interactions, but more importantly from internal Canadian developments, including interdepartmental consultation and pressures from the private sector and from provincial governments.[13] And 1983 saw a

number of other major modifications to the NEP—most notably to the Canada-Alberta price agreement—as it became clear that the pricing assumptions on which the NEP was based failed to conform to the real world.[14] Nevertheless, the Canadian government has held firm to those aspects of the NEP to which the U.S. government objected most strongly: the retroactive nature of the Crown Interest and the discriminatory treatment of foreign-owned companies.

Canada's most significant action came in the budget speech of November 12, 1981, when the government declared that the Canadianization measures of the NEP would not be applied in other sectors. As for its previously announced intention of expanding the powers of FIRA to publicize foreign takeover bids, to seek Canadian counterbidders, and to conduct performance reviews of existing foreign-owned companies, the government said, "for the time being, no legislative action is intended on these measures."[15]

Interpretations of the reason for this move differ. One analyst described it as the outward sign of the Canadian government's inward collapse in the face of U.S. pressure and retaliatory threats.[16] An alternative view would be that as the recession worsened, the mood in Canada began to shift away from one receptive to economic nationalism.

By the middle of 1982, both Canada and the United States had clearly come to a realization of the need to manage bilateral tensions better. Over the summer, officials of both governments made public statements downplaying irritants and reinforcing the tone of goodwill.[17]

Prime Minister Trudeau gave a series of interviews to prominent U.S. journalists and met with a group of U.S. businessmen, demonstrating statesmanship and moderation far removed from the image of predatory economic nationalism fostered in the inflammatory rhetoric of the previous year. By a happy coincidence, both countries changed foreign ministers, and the warm personal rapport, common pragmatic approach, and regular meetings between George Shultz and Allan MacEachen became a valuable influence moderating the tone of the whole relationship.

To ease the concerns of foreign investors and the U.S. government and to improve the investment climate in Canada during a time of recession, the Canadian government tried to ease criticism of FIRA in a variety of ways. More investments became eligible for review under streamlined procedures for "small business," and some legal aspects were clarified. In September 1982, Edward Lumley replaced Herb Gray as the minister responsible for FIRA—a move widely regarded as signalling a more pragmatic approach by the agency.

By the end of 1983, the U.S. government was embarked on a policy of patience with the NEP and FIRA.

The U.S. government did, however, continue to speak out about the retroactivity of the Crown Interest provision. However, the disagreement was purely one of principle since the Canadian government did not convert its 25 percent carried interest in Hibernia or any of the significant smaller fields, nor was it likely to do so until some company sought to convert its existing exploration permit to a production licence. Meanwhile, the U.S. government and the oil companies concerned were striving to effect a change in Canadian policy before the various exploration permits in Hibernia expired in the mid- to late 1980's.[18]

The controversy over the NEP set the tone for bilateral relations during the 1980-83 period. The NEP triggered a storm of protest in the United States and subsequent threats of retaliation. FIRA also became embroiled in the dispute because of a wave of contested takeover bids in the energy industry.

By the end of 1983, some of the differences between the two countries had been resolved through, for example, appealing the trade issues to the GATT. The Canadian public's mood had shifted away from the economic nationalism, and a more pragmatic attitude on the part of the federal government allayed many U.S. concerns. In spite of such relaxation of tensions, however, important aspects of the NEP remained on the bilateral agenda.

NOTES

1. See Canada, Department of Energy, Mines and Resources, *The National Energy Program* (Ottawa: Supply and Services Canada, October 1980), p. 7.
2. Canada, Department of Energy, Mines and Resources, *An Energy Strategy for Canada: Policies for Self-Reliance* (Ottawa: Supply and Services Canada, 1976), p. 146.
3. See G. Bruce Doern, "Energy, Mines and Resources, the Energy Ministry and the National Energy Program," in G. Bruce Doern, ed., *How Ottawa Spends Your Tax Dollars: Federal Priorities 1981* (Toronto: James Lorimer, 1981), pp. 56-61.

4. Canada, Department of Energy, Mines and Resources, *The National Energy Program*, p. 103.

5. Canada, Parliament, Senate, Standing Committee on Banking, Trade and Commerce, *Proceedings*, 1st Session, 32nd Parliament, no. 75, December 16, 1981, p. 13.

6. OECD *Observer 82* (July/August 1976), p. 9.

7. Allan J. MacEachen, "Investment Issues and Guidelines for Multinational Enterprises" (Notes for a Statement by the Secretary of State for External Affairs, at the OECD Ministerial Meeting, Paris, June 21, 1976), p. 2. The Canadian government did not regard its statement as a formal reservation, but merely a qualification.

8. The intention to expand the scope of FIRA was announced in the throne speech of April 14, 1980. It may seem ironic that an agency that had been established in 1973 should not have become a bilateral issue until 1981. There had, however, been earlier U.S. complaints about the FIRA process and the legal undertakings it required of firms. One long-standing complaint was the extraterritorial reach of FIRA in subjecting to review a corporate transfer in Canada that arose from a merger in the United States.

9. John W. Holmes, *Life with Uncle: The Canadian-American Relationship* (Toronto: University of Toronto Press, 1981), p. 7.

10. This second U.S. complaint concerned the FIRA requirement to export a certain amount or proportion of production.

11. Failure to comply with the GATT finding would have resulted in the possibility of retaliation by Canada's trading partners. Moreover, the GATT ruling did not affect provisions of the act regarding the effect of a proposed investment on the economy and on employment, so FIRA could continue to pursue its underlying objectives.

12. See Myer Rashish, "North American Economic Relations," *Department of State Bulletin 81* (November 1981), p. 24-28.

13. In the early days of the NEP, for example, the Alberta government not only threatened but executed retaliation against the federal government in the form of a series of reductions in authorized oil production.

14. Edward A. Carmichael and James K. Stewart, *Lessons from the National Energy Program*, Observation no. 25 (Toronto: C.D. Howe Institute, 1983), p. 2.

15. Government of Canada, *Economic Development for Canada in the 1980s* (Ottawa, November 1981), p.13.

16. Stephen Clarkson, *Canada and the Reagan Challenge*, (Ottawa: Canadian Institute of Economic Policy, 1982), pp. 41-42

17. Richard J. Smith, "Quiet vs. Public Diplomacy in U.S./Canadian Relations" (Notes for presentation by the Minister of the U.S. Embassy, Ottawa, at the Campobello Conference, August 6, 1982).

18. The new Canadian government of Prime Minister Brian Mulroney announced its intention of altering the Crown Interest provision. See Hon. Michael H. Wilson, Minister of Finance, *Economic and Fiscal Statement* (Ottawa, November 8, 1984), p. 9.

SUGGESTED READINGS

Canada, Department of Energy, Mines and Resources, *The National Energy Program*, Ottawa: Supply and Services Canada, October 1980.

Canada, Department of Energy, Mines and Resources, *The National Energy Program, Update 1982*, Ottawa, Supply and Services Canada, 1982

Clarkson, Stephen, *Canada and the Reagan Challenge: Crisis and Adjustment, 1981-1985*, Toronto: James Lorimer, 1985, pp. 55-82.

Doran, Charles, *Forgotten Partnership: U.S.-Canada Relations Today*, Baltimore: The Johns Hopkins University Press, 1984, pp. 211-250.

Wonder, Edward, "The US Government Response to the Canadian National Energy Program," *Canadian Public Policy*, Vol. 8, October 1982, pp. 480-493.

RE-INVOKING INTERNATIONALISM

As had been the case before, the broad pattern of Canadian foreign policy underwent no sudden, fundamental shift with the election of the Progressive Conservative government of Brian Mulroney in 1984. However there were election campaign calls for changes, particularly in Canada's relations with the United States and in Canada's defence preparedness. The Conservatives had taken special aim at the way in which Trudeau and the Liberals had handled—or mishandled—this aspect of external affairs. But some changes here would have been likely anyway had John Turner's very brief 1984 tenure as Prime Minister lasted longer. Indeed, given the troubled state of the bilateral relationship in the early 1980s, and the spirit of the second Reagan administration, some sort of movement toward a more cooperative mood was likely.

The first comprehensive statement of the new government was a "green paper" released in May 1985 as the start of a parliamentary-based foreign policy review process. The world was a complex and dangerous place, it said, and Canada's capabilities were modest. Thus its aims must be correspondingly modest, especially in contrast to those of a pre-eminent United States. The paper, conceived as a discussion paper, generally reflected in its realistic and pragmatic approach its origins in the External Affairs bureaucracy.

The reaction among foreign policy watchers was almost unanimously critical. The most basic criticism was that the scope for intitative was not as narrow as the paper portrayed. The paper, many argued, failed to recognize the potential for Canada to contribute constructively in the solution of international problems and to offer outlets for the idealism of Canadians. The government, perhaps thus finding its own true instincts, and reflecting the increasing influence of Secretary of State for External Affairs Joe Clark, quickly adjusted. A special parliamentary committee, under the guidance of co-chair Tom Hockin, identified "constructive internationalism" as the watchword of Canadian foreign policy and developed an innovative and ambitious set of policy proposals. The special parliamentary committee issued an interim report in 1985 which cautiously recommended against official Canadian involvement in Reagan's strategic defence initiative (or SDI) and in favour of the pursuit of a freer trade arrangement with the United States. In the government's little noted "blue" paper of December 1986, entitled *Canada's International Relations*, the Mulroney cabinet under Joe Clark's determined urging, accepted the Hockin report.

There was, however, one area where the Clark emphasis on vigorous internationalism in the wider world took second place to the Prime Minister's instinct to create "super" relations with the United States. This was the issue of free trade. The Reagan economic vision was embraced by Brian Mulroney shortly after his election as leader of the Progressive Conservative Party. Free trade was finally ratified by the Canadian Parliament after a hard-fought election on the issue in the autumn of 1988. As Michael Hart, a participant in the free trade negotiations, describes in his chapter written for this volume, the government moved cautiously but steadily from its consultations with Canadian business, through its decision to open talks with the United States, its initialing of a final agreement and its re-election campaign, to the final exchange of letters on the agreement in January 1989.

In other areas where Mulroney's Conservatives adopted foreign policy decisions different from those of the Liberals, they renewed previous Progresive Conservative positions. The clearest case was their leadership in the international campaign against apartheid in South Africa. Inspired by the legacy of John Diefenbaker's role in the Commonwealth on this issue in the early 1960s, Brian Mulroney and Joe Clark moved quickly, against British opposition and American reluctance, to mobilize the Commonwealth and the major industrial democracies in a campaign of ever-tightening sanctions. As Clarence Redekop describes, Canada used its strategic position in several critical international institutions to tighten steadily the noose around a South African government which soon singled out Canada as their major adversary abroad. Although Canada never implemented the Prime Minister's pledge to break diplomatic rela-

tions entirely if necessary, Canada's role in arousing coordinated international pressure was sufficiently effective to help induce South Africa by 1989 to pursue a radially more accommodating approach.

Canada's leading role against apartheid in the Commonwealth and la Francophonie was reinfored by its relatively generous approach to development assistance. Despite its concern with controlling the large federal fiscal deficit it had inherited from the Liberals, and an early, short-lived effort to cut the aid budget, aid expenditures expanded steadily during the early Mulroney years. As David Morrison describes, the 1987 aid policy review was an effort to marry continued generosity with an updated philosphy. Using the parliamentary-based review mechanism that had served it so well in its general foreign policy review, the government produced a policy that met with the approval of most affected constituencies. It was later in 1989, however, to succumb to the budgetary pressures and cut aid funds along with defence expenditures.

Among the elements of the Mulroney strategy for restoring good relations with the US had been a de-escalation of the mounting Canadian criticism of American unwillingness to take action against acid rain. The Trudeau and Clark governments had both made this issue a priority and had both carried the message to American audiences in Washington and elsewhere. After September 1984, the focus of Canada's acid rain diplomacy became the newly instituted annual "Shamrock" summits of the Prime Minister and President. The shift was more one of style than substance, however; the pursuit of a bilateral accord with commitments to reduce those emissions that lead to acid rain remained the objective. Neither the harsh public diplomacy of the Trudeau era nor the quiet personal approach of Mulroney proved very effective. As the chapter by Don Munton and Geoffrey Castle shows, the movement toward such an accord came after environmental issues re-emerged at the top of the US domestic political agenda and after a new, effective Clean Air Act passed the American congress in 1990.

As Canada approached the final decade of the twentieth century, its foreign policy focus slowly turned to the new post-Cold War agenda that followed the opening of the Berlin Wall in November 1989, the unification of Germany, the destruction of the Soviet bloc, and the incipient disintegration of the Soviet Union itself. However Saddam Hussein's August 2, 1990 invasion and annexation of Kuwait rapidly threw Canadian leaders back to confront issues they had last addressed in constructing the United Nations in 1945 and resisting aggression by force in Korea in 1950. As John Kirton recounts in his chapter on the Persian Gulf crisis, Canada moved in the vanguard of the international community to condemn the invasion, introduce sanctions against Iraq, and dispatch naval and air forces to the region. As a non-permanent member of the Security Council, Canada also helped obtain approval of a resolution authorizing the use of force against Iraq if it did not withdraw completely from Kuwait by January 15, 1991. Canada was once again, as in Korea fully four decades earlier, forced to confront the challenge of using its armed forces in combat to support its internationalist ideals.

N E G O T I A T I N G
F R E E - T R A D E , 1 9 8 5 - 8 8

Michael Hart[*]

The picture of weak and timid Canadian negotiators being pushed around and browbeaten
by American representatives into settlements
that were "sell-outs" is a false and distorted one.
It is often painted, however, by Canadians who
think that a sure way to get applause and support at home is to exploit our anxieties and ex-
aggerate our suspicions over US power and
policies.

Lester Pearson, *Memoirs*

The process that led to the conclusion
of a bilateral free-trade agreement
with the United States started on
September 4, 1984, the day the Tories led
by Brian Mulroney swept to victory in a
wave of public enthusiasm for a change
from the perpetual Grits. The new prime
minister had made economic renewal and
refurbished relations with the United
States key elements in his platform. As a
symbol of the new approach, he made a
whirlwind visit to Washington on
September 26, nine days after being sworn
in, to confirm to a smiling Ronald Reagan
that the days of confrontation were over
and the era of cooperation about to begin.
Toronto *Globe and Mail* reporter Bill
Johnson, in a remarkably prescient article,
speculated that the visit also marked the
opening shot in the quest for free trade.[1]

Johnson's speculation was not as
strange as it might at first seem. Despite
the prime minister's curt dismissal of free
trade during the election campaign, once
in office he had to confront the stalled sectoral trade initiative introduced by his pre-
decessors.[2] Debate in the country had
already moved beyond that initiative and
both provincial politicians and business
spokesmen were calling for serious examination of the free-trade option. Additionally,
refurbished relations with the Americans
required a serious look at the management
of bilateral trade relations and more than a
reiteration of Liberal policy. Whatever their
personal predilections, free-trade was one
issue the new ministers had to face from
the moment they took office.[3]

Canadian Interest in a Bilateral Agreement

Canada is a trading nation. A third of its
wealth is derived from trade. Close to half
of the goods produced are exported; more
than half of the goods consumed are imported. In order to survive, Canada needs
open and secure access to world markets.

For years, Canadians traded largely
with Britain and the United States and concentrated their trade in a narrow range of

* The author was director of the Centre for Trade Policy and Law at Carleton University and the University of Ottawa. From 1982
through 1987 he was intimately involved in the preparation for and conduct of the Canada-US negotiations. The views expressed
are those of Mr. Hart and do not necessarily reflect the views of the Government of Canada. (This is an original article.)

commodities.[4] Almost two-thirds of Canada's exports are based on resources and many are sold at low stages of processing. Outside of the auto industry, which has benefitted from the integrating forces of the autopact, Canadians sell only a small amount of finished goods abroad. Canadian manufacturers concentrate on the domestic market. They compete with imports. If they are to export and compete on world markets, Canada has to develop a more competitive, more outward-oriented economy relying on more than the resource industries.

Over the years, the Americans have proven Canada's most reliable customer for finished and semi-finished goods. The Europeans and Japanese may be important sources for finished goods, but they are not major buyers of anything other than Canadian resources, reflecting geography, business practice, attitudes and protection. The European and Japanese markets are more inward-looking than the American market and thus frustrate enterprising Canadians who want to do business there. Efforts to change that in the 1970s with framework agreements did not lead to any significant breakthroughs.

Critics of the FTA tend to belittle the importance of the Canada-US trade and economic relationship. But it is a relationship that cannot be ignored. More than $200 billion in goods and services are exchanged annually. Canadians and Americans have invested billions in each other's economies. Millions of Canadians and Americans cross the border every year. A relationship of this size and complexity generates dozens of problems and irritants annually. But the rules and machinery for managing the relationship have not kept pace with these developments.

For the private sector, it is less a question of rules than the proliferation of barriers old and new that stand in the way of rational economic decisions. Business people have long concluded that doing business in Canada is a gamble and that the prudent course is to hedge ones bets by expanding in the larger market and serving the smaller market from there. Thus for Canada, the problem is not only one of management, but of finding a policy framework that will make investment in Canada more attractive and less of a gamble.

For forty years, Canada sought to achieve access to a large market though GATT negotiations, supplemented, when it suited, by bilateral deals with the Americans, Europeans and Japanese. Some progress was made but not enough. The GATT process has become increasingly slow and considerably more complex. It takes a long time to build consensus among 96 countries and that consensus is likely to be the lowest common denominator, only remotely related to the specific objectives of any one country. For Canada and the United States, GATT has become an insufficient instrument to settle bilateral issues.

Over the past few years, some progress has been made in bringing the GATT up to date, but not nearly enough. While Canada and the United States began and concluded their bilateral negotiations, the GATT countries were also at work, but at a more sedate pace. Hardening resistance to adjustment and the wide disparity in economic development and attitudes among the participating countries suggest that if and when consensus is finally reached, it is likely to be considerably less ambitious than the objectives set for the negotiations by either Canada or the United States.

Canada and the United States are major players at GATT but both Canadians and Americans have become increasingly conscious of GATT's limitations. If it ever was, it certainly is no longer a sufficient instrument for managing the largest bilateral trade and economic relationship in the world. That is why the two countries entered into the autopact, into the defence production sharing arrangement, a safeguard agreement and many more bilateral deals and why they entered into negotiations for a comprehensive agreement in 1985.

There was an even more urgent reason. Canadians had become increasingly reliant on the American market as the main outlet for their exports. But that market was turning inward. Americans were frustrated by their lack of access to the markets of Japan, Europe, Korea, Brazil and elsewhere and by the increasing flow of imports from these countries. Their frustration was turning into anger and Canadians found themselves sideswiped by this anger. Canadians also found themselves the direct targets of protectionist fervour. Thus Canadian entrepreneurs, ready to break out of the constraints of the Canadian market, found the one foreign market that traditionally welcomed their goods no longer a reliable or predictable market.

In 1983, the Liberal government of Pierre Trudeau concluded, after the failure of the GATT ministerial meeting of the previous year, to see if a range of outstanding issues between Canada and the United States could be resolved by negotiating sectoral free-trade agreements. Both governments attacked the problem with enthusiasm but at the end of a year concluded that while the objective was sound, the means were inadequate. It was too difficult to find a match of sectors where both countries saw advantages. Only in a broadly based negotiation is it possible to make cross-sectoral trade-offs. They concluded that what they were doing could not be squared with their GATT obligations. The initiative was dead in the water by the summer of 1984. The issue was whether to give up or expand the talks into a broader initiative.

Prologue

Unencumbered by the policy baggage of twenty years in office, the new government proved it was ready to take a serious look at the full free-trade option. Over the next twelve months, without any strong preconceptions, it consulted widely and listened to every Canadian with an idea. It studied the issue from every angle and cautiously, step-by-step, shaped the debate and indicated its interests and opinions.

The first key statement came from finance minister Michael Wilson. In his November 8, 1984 economic statement, *A New Direction for Canada*, he set out the main government themes, including:

> The government will examine, as a matter of priority, and in close consultation with the provinces and the private sector, all avenues to secure and enhance market access. This will include a careful analysis of options for bilateral trade liberalization with the United States in the light of various private sector proposals, as well as preparations for and opportunities provided by multilateral trade negotiations.[5]

Three months later, Wilson's colleague, minister for international trade James Kelleher, issued a Discussion Paper, *How to Secure and Enhance Canadian Access to Export Markets*, which set out the government's thinking on the emerging multilateral and bilateral trade agenda and invited Canadians to tell the government whether they favoured a continuation of the sectoral bilateral initiative, preferred some other form of bilateral cooperation or were prepared to go further and endorse pursuit of a comprehensive free-trade agreement. The paper carefully avoided casting multilateral and bilateral negotiations as alternatives, insisting that "the choice for Canada is not between multilateral or bilateral approaches to trade but how both avenues can be pursued in a mutually reinforcing manner"[6] to secure more open and secure access to foreign markets. At the same time, other aspects of the government's economic agenda emerged, suggesting a strong preference for private enterprise and a suspicion of government intervention measures.

After five months of internal debate, the government now joined a public debate that had already attracted considerable attention. An April 1984 Environics poll suggested that more than three-quarters of Canadians favoured free-trade with the United States. Kelleher, during a cross-Canada tour to gauge reaction to his Discussion Paper, heard from a broad spectrum of Canadians confirming that view.[7]

While Kelleher toured the country, a special task force of officials prepared the ground for a meeting of the prime minister and president in Quebec City March 17-18. The prime minister had indicated that the meeting afforded a solid opportunity to put improvement in trade relations front and center on the bilateral agenda. The president agreed and in their March 17 Quebec Declaration on Trade in Goods and Services, the two leaders took the next critical step on the road to free trade. Declaring themselves "convinced that an improved and more secure climate for bilateral trade relations will encourage market forces to achieve a more rational and competitive production and distribution of goods and services," they charged their two trade ministers "to establish immediately a mecha-

nism to chart all possible ways to reduce and eliminate existing barriers to trade and to report to us within six months."[8]

Trade minister Jim Kelleher and the United States trade representative Clayton Yeutter set to work and over the next six months they and their officials looked at the alternatives. On September 17, 1985 they recommended that the two governments proceed in the negotiation of a comprehensive bilateral trade agreement and set out their respective agenda.[9] By then momentum had carried the issue much further in Canada. Meetings with the provincial premiers and trade ministers had demonstrated a strong federal-provincial consensus favouring negotiations, with only Ontario cautious. Confidential consultations chaired by former senior official Tom Burns had indicated strong support in the business community.[10] The same message had been conveyed to a special parliamentary committee established to hold hearings over the course of the summer. In an August 23, 1985 report it recommended that the government proceed to negotiations.[11] Finally, on September 5, 1985 the long-awaited report of the Macdonald Royal Commission strongly urged the negotiation of a comprehensive bilateral free-trade agreement.[12] Based on three years of hearings and detailed study, the report, ratified by twelve of the thirteen commissioners, was met by a wave of equally strong endorsements in editorials across the country.

When the prime minister finally rose in the House of Commons on September 26, his announcement that the government would proceed to explore with the Americans the feasibility of a bilateral agreement appeared anticlimactic. The following week formal letters were exchanged between the prime minister and the president setting out their views of the negotiations.[13]

Preparing for Negotiations

The next logical steps were to appoint two negotiating teams, establish the necessary consultative and analytical resources and prepare for formal negotiations. But first the president had to obtain authority from the Congress to pursue the negotiations under the so-called fast-track authority. The authority was grounded in the 1979 *Trade Agreements Act* and the 1984 *Trade and Tariffs Act*, both of which had a specific authority to negotiate bilaterally with Canada. This authority ran out on January 3, 1988, placing a time limit on the negotiations, but one considered to be well within reason. The prime minister and president were both determined to conclude any agreement within their respective mandates.

Over the course of the summer of 1985, Canadian officials had made it clear that Canada would only be prepared to negotiate a comprehensive trade agreement pursuant to the fast-track authority. Memories of the aborted East Coast Fisheries treaty earlier that decade and of the congressional penchant for unilaterally amending agreements through legislative changes (as it had done in implementing the 1967 Anti-dumping Code negotiated during the Kennedy Round of GATT negotiations) made the fast-track process the only acceptable basis for the negotiations.

Preparations were thus set in train for a start to negotiations early in 1986, in the confident expectation that the necessary procedural steps would be completed by then. After all, preliminary soundings by the administration over the course of the summer had indicated that the members of the two principal committees concerned (Finance and Ways and Means) were well disposed toward Canada and welcomed the negotiations. Unfortunately, this was not the way the scenario was played out.[14]

It took the administration more than two months of internal wrangling to send the necessary notice to the two committees. The administration and the Congress were seriously at loggerheads over trade policy and some committee members were looking for an opportunity to show their displeasure. As a result, some in the administration counselled delay in the notification until there had been some progress in the negotiations. This was rejected by others with Canada's full support. Canadian ministers made it clear to their American colleagues that without clear fast-track authority, there could be no negotiations.[15]

Notice was finally sent December 10, 1985 and received without fanfare by the two committee chairmen just before the Christmas recess. Informal consultations in January and February suggested that the two committees would be content to let the necessary ninety days elapse without comment and thus allow negotiations to proceed. This was what happened in the House Ways and Means Committee where Congressman Sam Gibbons, chairman of the trade subcommittee, indicated he was a strong supporter of the negotiations. In the Senate, however, strong displeasure with administration management of trade policy led to an unexpected brouhaha and a cliff-hanger tied vote not to disapprove the negotiations. The committee appeared initially inclined to disapprove the request by a substantial margin and the president had had to use all of his powers of persuasion to achieve the close vote. Approval to proceed finally came on April 23, but not before sending strong alarm bells ringing in Canada about the capacity of administration officials to manage all aspects of the negotiations.

During the intervening seven months between the decision to proceed and congressional approval, the two sides had picked chief negotiators and prepared for negotiations. Canada had decided to go with Simon Reisman, a retired deputy minister of finance with a long and distinguished record as a trade negotiator, while the United States chose its ambassador to the GATT, Peter Murphy.

Reisman had long been on record as strongly favouring a bilateral free-trade agreement and, together with his crusty, no-nonsense reputation and experience made him an eminently acceptable choice to take on what by then had been dubbed the most important negotiation in Canada's history.[16] The prime minister told Reisman that the full resources of the federal government were at his disposal and in his first six months in office, Reisman set out to test the prime minister's word. By May of 1986 he had assembled a team of nearly a hundred advisors, specialists and support staff and housed them in a penthouse suite in downtown Ottawa. Responsible for both multilateral and bilateral negotiations, Reisman had inherited Sylvia Ostry as his deputy for the MTN and appointed Gordon Ritchie to be his deputy for the bilateral negotiations. Below them, a team of assistant negotiators took charge of federal-provincial relations, industry liaison and analysis, legal advice, and the details of the negotiations. With all this expertise housed under one roof and directly responsible to him, Reisman had a team that could deliver on all the necessary analysis and technical advice and be independent of the various departmental fiefdoms.

At the same time, trade minister Jim Kelleher had established a forty-member International Trade Advisory Committee (ITAC) and fifteen Sectoral Advisory Groups (SAGITs) to provide Reisman with industry advice. Modelled on the US private sector advisory system, it would pro-vide business with direct access to the negotiators. As negotiations proceeded, senior members of Reisman's team would periodically brief the SAGITs and seek their advice on particular issues. The minister, accompanied by Reisman or Ritchie, met regularly with the ITAC. Additionally, the issue of provincial participation had been resolved by establishing a Continuing Committee on Trade Negotiations made up of senior officials from each of the provinces and the two territories who would meet on a monthly basis with Reisman to be briefed on progress and to share ideas. The prime minister had also agreed to meet regularly with the premiers (over the course of two years, he met with them on twelve separate occasions to discuss the trade negotiations, each occasion providing the media with a circus of pertinent and irrelevant comments as Canadian federal and provincial politicians played the perennial federal-provincial relations game). Finally, a special cabinet committee had been struck to oversee the negotiations and provide Reisman with detailed instructions. Originally chaired by secretary of state for external affairs Joe Clark, it was taken over by new trade minister Pat Carney when she replaced Jim Kelleher in July, 1986.

By May of 1986, Reisman and his team were as ready as they would ever be. They had analyzed the issues, widely solicited advice, continued consultations and obtained a general mandate. After an initial round of discussions with the Americans, they would be ready to seek detailed negotiating instructions.

The Americans in April had formally appointed Peter Murphy, US ambassador to the GATT in Geneva, to take charge of the American negotiating effort. Housed in the office of the United States trade representative, the US team opted for a very different negotiating apparatus. Rather than the highly hierarchical and tightly structured Canadian team, Murphy was given a personal staff of three, including Bill Merkin, the senior USTR officer who had been responsible for much of the preparatory work, and for the rest would have to rely on the resources of USTR and other agencies interested in trade. Those officials who joined Murphy's team would pursue the negotiations in tandem with their other responsibilities.

Preliminary Sparring

Between the end of May and the end of September of 1986, Reisman and Murphy and their senior advisors met five times, twice in Washington, and other times in the boardroom of the Trade Negotiations Office in Ottawa, at a lodge in Mont Tremblant, Quebec and at the cabinet retreat in the Gatineau Hills outside Ottawa. These five sessions were billed as a preliminary round needed by the two teams to establish the negotiating agenda and priorities, forge a working method, gain each other's confidence and generally set the ground rules for the more serious negotiations to follow. Each session lasted two days and was devoted to two or three main negotiating issues. Each side took turns presenting its views of the issues in an effort to set out the parameters within which the negotiations would be pursued.

Each plenary session sought to advance the discussion far enough to establish a working or fact-finding group to pursue more detailed discussions and prepare draft negotiating proposals for consideration by the plenary sessions chaired by the two chief negotiators. By the end of September, the two sides had set up working groups on intellectual property, customs matters, agricultural trade, services, government procurement and subsidies as well as fact-finding groups on automotive trade, energy, fisheries and state and provincial barriers. As negotiations proceeded, groups were also established to deal with financial services, investment, dumping, safeguards, dispute settlement, alcoholic beverages and, finally, a legal group to integrate the work of the other groups and prepare the draft text of an agreement. The establishment of some groups came only after much tactical maneuvering to determine whether sufficient progress had been made on other issues to warrant further consideration on a matter of greater interest to one side or the other. Investment, financial services and contingency protection (subsidies, dumping and safeguards), for example, all involved such jockeying.

Two other aspects of the negotiations had also become clear by the end of the summer. Federal-provincial wrangling during the spring over the provincial role in the negotiations had already demonstrated the intense media interest in the negotiations, but nothing had prepared either Reisman or Murphy for the media circus that would dog them as negotiations proceeded. Murphy and Reisman would become household names in Canada. Unfamiliar with the issues under negotiation, the media concentrated on personalities and on the sensational, aided in their quest, often unwittingly, by the mercurial Reisman and the laconic Murphy. If nothing else, reporters could file a story comparing the different styles of the two chief protagonists.

Never had a trade negotiation been reported in such breathless detail and never before did a government have to manage its trade agenda under such relentless scrutiny. The detailed media attention soon began to influence the conduct of the negotiations and the approach to the issues. There was endless debate whether the autopact was on the table or off it, whether culture and social programs would be effected by the negotiations, whether agricultural supply management programs would be compromised, whether investment would be included and whether Canada would gain exemption from US trade remedy laws. Endless media speculation fed and was in turn fed by the regular antics of Question Period in the House of Commons. On an almost daily basis, Canadians were informed of one piece of nonsense after another. All the public airings required briefs, spooked the development of negotiating positions and generally affected the professional pursuit of a good agreement.

A further complicating factor was that the government had simultaneously to conduct negotiations and manage the usual range of trade irritants. The media hype of the negotiations led to much more detailed scrutiny of these irritants and ministers were called on to explain complicated technical issues as if the very essence of Canada depended on how the issue was resolved. During the preliminary period, US decisions involving shakes and shingles and softwood lumber, consideration of the highly protectionist US Omnibus Trade Bill, and unguarded comments about the exchange rate all threatened to derail the negotiations. As negotiations proceeded, other issues would regularly crop up to provide a fertile field for mischief, particularly culture, the autopact and agricultural supply management measures.

Used to negotiating in the quiet isolation of Geneva, Canadian and US negotiators had never before confronted such a carnival atmosphere. The barrage of media attention began to assume a place at he table, often occasioning sharp exchanges between the negotiators as to who had been indiscreet. Both chief negotiators began to use press scrums to stake out positions or to attack or discomfort the other, often inadvertently reducing their room for maneuver and complicating the negotiations. At the same time, the veil of secrecy was increased. Dire warnings were issued to any official caught being indiscreet, either publicly or to officials not directly involved in the negotiations. No notes of plenary sessions were kept for fear of leaks, although participants at the technically more important working sessions did keep detailed notes.

Review

At the end of the September, 1986 session, Reisman and Murphy agreed that they would not meet again until after the US mid-term elections in November. They reasoned that they needed to give the working groups time to make some progress before bringing any issues back to plenary for further broad policy consideration. In addition, they wanted to sit back and consider what they had learned from the preliminary sessions and what they needed to do to ensure that they were in a position to conclude a mutually acceptable agreement a year later.

The six-week break in the negotiations offered an opportunity to take stock. On the Canadian side, preliminary conclusions were not very optimistic. Both the first five plenary sessions as well as opening meetings of the various working groups had revealed a very wide gap in approach and philosophy between the two teams. Reisman came armed with a single vision of a comprehensive agreement that would establish the rules of the game for Canada-US trade relations for the next few generations. He wanted to establish national treatment as the norm for the movement of virtually all goods and services between the two countries. If the US was prepared to accept his vision, he was prepared to extend this principle of non-discrimination to the US priorities of investment and intellectual property. In pursuing his vision, he saw an agreement that would proceed from general principles to the details necessary to make it work. This was a vision he had explained to the federal cabinet, to provincial ministers and officials, to the business community and to anyone prepared to listen. All that remained was for the Americans to agree and translate the vision into the detail of an agreement.

Murphy, on the other hand, had not come armed with any vision. Indeed, even after five sessions it was difficult to devise any plan to his approach. He seemed to be driven by the pressures generated by individual irritants, by the views of special interest groups and by the worry of possibly unhelpful precedents for America's worldwide trade interests. More than anything else, he seemed risk-averse, determined not to make any early commitments. Unsure of the degree of support he could count on from within the administration, he constantly worried about the views of congressmen and senators. His team, led by middle-level officials from other agencies, appeared to be equally concerned about congressional opinions and determined not to sacrifice any of the powers and authorities of their home agencies. Rather than the leader of a tightly knit group, Murphy appeared to be no more than the nominal chairman of a collection of individualists, each with his own agenda.

The differing importance of the negotiations in the two capitals seemed thus directly to have influenced the makeup of the two teams and the approach to the issue. By now the centrepiece of the Mulroney government's agenda, the bilateral negoti-

ations seemed to have all the necessary resources and ideas to carry them to a succesful conclusion on the Canadian side whereas on the American side, the negotiations appeared a poorly prepared orphan able to command only meager resources and virtually bankrupt of ideas and vision. With these differences clearly apparent by the end of the five preliminary sessions, the way forward from an Ottawa perspective appeared to be decidedly uphill.

One positive development during this period was that Reisman and his senior officers were able to complete the process of obtaining clear and detailed mandates and gain the full support for that mandate from provincial officials. By the time the two teams were ready to engage again at the end of the year, every issue had been thoroughly considered. Not since the King government had ministers been so intimately involved in the detail of a trade negotiation.[17] Despite the seeming public wrangling in Canada, the official effort was in good shape.

Serious Negotiations

With this pessimistic analysis to fortify them, the Canadian team soldiered on. Plenary sessions were scheduled every month and working groups told to meet more frequently. Between the sixth plenary session in November and the twentieth plenary on the banks of the St. Lawrence River in Cornwall in mid-August, each main negotiating issue was given at least two or three thorough airings at the level of the chief negotiators. As spring gave way to summer, the pace quickened and over the course of the summer, plenary meetings were held almost on a weekly basis. Some working groups met even more frequently. Even if progress was uneven, there was no shortage of effort as the deadline of the end of September loomed ever larger.

By late winter all the issues had been discussed at least once and the main negotiating issues clearly defined. Many technical issues had been thoroughly discussed and the main problem areas determined. What had not been achieved was any clear consensus on the shape of any final agreement. With the exception of a few relatively uncontentious issues, Canada continued to propose while the Americans lay in the weeds. Even for issues on which the US was the main demandeur, such as services, intellectual property and investment, US proposals proved woefully inadequate, being either poorly thought out or insensitive to Canadian concerns. On issues critical to Canadian interests, such as contingency protection and dispute resolution, the US team had by mid-summer yet to put forward any detailed positions.

Given the inadequate response by Murphy and his team, the Canadian team began to explore alternative ways to get the message across and cut through Murphy's reticence. In December, 1986, trade minister Pat Carney invited new Senate Finance Committee chairman Lloyd Bentsen to visit Canada with some of his colleagues so that ministers could explain the issues directly to them and gauge their interest. Bentsen expressed himself as keenly interested in a very comprehensive agreement and confident that such an agreement would be welcomed by the Congress. In January, the prime minister invited vice-president George Bush and treasury secretary Jim Baker to Ottawa for a tongue lashing on the inadequacy of the US response. The result was an assurance in the State of the Union message that the president attached the highest priority to the conclusion of an agreement. In early April, the prime minister discussed the

issue with the president and his senior advisors during the third bilateral summit in Ottawa and once again received assurances that the US understood Canada's concerns and would be responsive to them. The president used the occasion of an address to the joint houses of Parliament to assure Canadians directly of the priority he attached to the negotiations. In June, at the Venice Economic Summit, the prime minister once again appealed to the president to give the issue more priority and received assurances that he would. At periodic meetings between Joe Clark and secretary of state George Schultz and between Pat Carney and USTR Clayton Yeutter, the message was repeated.

Each time Canada raised the political stakes, it received the necessary assurances as well as heavy media attention, but the messages did not penetrate to the level of Peter Murphy and his colleagues. The responses and ideas remained inadequate. By mid-summer, the two sides were no closer to an agreement than they were a year earlier. To the negotiators, there seemed a puzzling disconnect between Murphy and his colleagues and their political masters. Other explanations were even less assuring: were Murphy and his team carrying out instructions to stall or were the Canada negotiations too low on the agenda to warrant more serious political attention? Whatever the explanation, frustration mounted, particularly in the face of continued battering by the media who had long given up hope of any serious breakthrough.

Despite the slow progress in reaching consensus on any issue, Murphy and Reisman determined that they would exchange complete drafts of an agreement in mid-August, based on the labours of the working groups but also clearly setting out each other's position. A week-long drafting session at the Transport Canada Training Centre in Cornwall would then finally clear away the underbrush and delineate the crunch issues. A Canadian team had been assigned to the preparation of such a text as early as January and by midsummer had produced a workmanlike draft agreement that was true to the Reisman vision but also took account of American sensitivities and discussion at plenary sessions and working groups. Intense negotiations inside the Canadian team had further honed the text. Many of the cherished ideas of individual team leaders had been ruthlessly discarded in order to weld together a single, integrated text for the next stage of the negotiations.

The Americans, in order to avoid having to work from a Canadian text, quickly set to work to produce a similar text. In a matter of two weeks, the US legal team stapled together a text from various proposals tabled by US team members or prepared by them for eventual tabling. The two texts were exchanged the third week of August. The Canadian draft presented a fully integrated text proceeding from the principle of national treatment and prepared in a single drafting style. The US draft presented a collection of disparate texts that in places contradicted each other and had little in common. For the first time, a complete picture of the difference in approach and attitude between the two sides stood out in sharp relief.

The two sides made a valiant effort at Cornwall to bridge the obvious gap but to little avail. By the end of a week the only solid achievement was recognition by the Americans that they had a long way to go. Rather than an intensive drafting session, the various US members of the working groups for five days in a row had to stick to their task without the usual distractions. But there were no breakthroughs. The two

sides remained as far apart at the end of the week as they had been at the beginning.

Impasse in September

By the beginning of September 1987 Reisman and Murphy had presided over twenty plenary negotiating sessions. Some dozen working groups had held numerous technical meetings. Canada had made dozens of negotiating proposals and finally had tabled a complete text of an agreement. Almost two years of preparations and more than a year of negotiations had resulted in a detailed appreciation of the issues. Public debate and controversy had sharpened public awareness. It was now or never.

Reisman had also met some eighteen times with the Continuing Committee on Trade Negotiations, and the prime minister had met six times with the provincial premiers. Dozens of consultations with the ITAC/SAGIT advisory system had honed Canadian positions. Weekly meetings with ministers had kept them engaged in the detail of the negotiations. By now all these groups were becoming somewhat impatient at the lack of visible progress. While Reisman may have assured them that the negotiations were on schedule, he too had become increasingly disappointed. With only a month to go, it was clear that the negotiations had reached an impasse. Something dramatic was required to rescue the initiative. If it could not be rescued, a plan was necessary to disengage with grace and repair the damage of failure.

On four special occasions, the prime minister had raised concern about the lack of tangible progress in the negotiations with the president. As well, ministers had expressed uneasiness during their regular contacts with their US colleagues. On each occasion, US political leaders assured their

Canadian counterparts that the US was taking the negotiations seriously. By September, the prime minister and his key ministers and advisors concluded that it did not appear that Reisman and Murphy could successfully wrap up the negotiations. Further political appeals were unlikely to lead to results any different from previous appeals. What was needed was a second front. To this end, Reisman was encouraged to continue trying but if by the third week of September he had not achieved a breakthrough, he was to suspend negotiations. Meanwhile, the prime minister's chief of staff, Derek Burney, working together with finance minister Michael Wilson and trade minister Pat Carney, was to begin to make exploratory soundings on a political settlement.

Reisman presided over two more negotiating sessions, both in Washington. They came to nought and on September 23, he staged a dramatic walkout and declared the negotiations over. "The United States is not responding on elements fundamental to Canada's position. I have therefore suspended the negotiations." While Reisman's walkout occupied center stage, Burney and Wilson had already flown to Washington to meet with treasury secretary James Baker. In an exchange of letters with White House chief of staff Howard Baker, Burney had been told that Jim Baker was the President's point man. On Saturday, September 19, Jim Baker had been confident that Reisman and Murphy could still succeed. On the phone to Burney on the following Thursday he was less sure.

While the Americans at first considered Reisman's walkout a media stunt, they now put their crisis team into full gear. As Reisman watched, Burney and the two ministers made two more pilgrimages to Washington to explore the parameters for reconvening the negotiations with Baker,

Clayton Yeutter and their closest advisors. On Thursday, September 29, they concluded that the negotiations were over; the Americans were not capable of delivering on Canada's basic requirements regarding dispute settlement and contingency protection.

But the next day Burney, Wilson and Carney, accompanied by the whole of the negotiating apparatus, flew back to Washington and in a dramatic series of events hammered out the elements of an agreement. Baker, following further consultations with the Congress, agreed that the US was now prepared to work on a compromise proposal first advanced by congressman Sam Gibbons that would allow appeals of trade remedy cases to be decided by a bilateral panel. A breakthrough on this issue was the bellwether that would allow breakthroughs on many other issues.

Given the tight time frame, the two political teams decided they could not afford a return to the normal negotiating process. Instead, they agreed to work together as long as it would take to draft a series of brief one-page statements setting out the basis for agreement on each of the major elements of the agreement. In effect, they would draft a memorandum of instructions for the two legal teams who would then be given the time to draft the actual legal text. If the first part of this task could be completed by Saturday midnight, October 3, the deadline imposed by the fast-track procedure would be met and the details worked out later.[18]

Breakthrough

The two teams worked at breakneck speed all weekend. Several times it looked as if an agreement would again escape them but finally minutes before midnight on October 3, the final breakthrough came. While many details remained to be worked out, Canada and the United States had concluded an agreement. Despite the conviction only a few days earlier that it could not be done, they had succeeded. US determination not to fail and Canadian adherence to the bottom line had paid dividends. It was clear that the US attitude had changed dramatically. Driven by a desire not to fail, US officials had been prepared to make compromises in areas where previously they had only reluctantly considered Canadian demands. While the focus of hard bargaining over the course of the weekend had been trade remedies and dispute settlement, many other intransigent issues had been settled.[19]

Balancing the US desire not to fail had been Canada's determination that it had to have an agreement that made economic sense and would stand the test of time. Canada had been prepared to compromise on the short-term issues on which the US needed to be seen to be making progress while insisting that the basic agreement be sound. The tariff would be eliminated over ten years and most other access issues had been resolved to the mutual benefit of both countries. The security of access issue, so important politically, had been only partly resolved, but a good basis had been laid for making things better. Canadian sovereignty had been protected by the establishment of a good general dispute settlement mechanism. A start had been made on services trade, access had been eased for business travel to the US market and balanced commitments had been concluded on investment.

Consolidation

Over the next eight weeks the two legal teams, supplemented by policy advisors where necessary, translated the 35-page memorandum of instructions into a 250-page legal text. In addition, tariff experts completed the final details of the more than two thousand pages of tariff annexes. It took, however, one more session at the political level to tie up loose ends. The weekend of December 2-3, Burney worked with deputy treasury secretary Peter McPherson to work out the final details which could not be resolved through legal drafting.

Finally, on December 11, 1987, the final package was released for public scrutiny. On January 2, 1988, the president and the prime minister signed the final text of the agreement. For the negotiators, the task was completed.

It had been a long and tough challenge. But an even larger challenge lay ahead. Despite the public character of the negotiations and five years of debate, the details of the agreement remained a mystery to most Canadians. Public debate, if anything, took on an even more fevered and unreal pitch. Most of what was said and written about the agreement shed little light on the issues.[20]

Objectives and Results

Canada had sought three overriding objectives:

- the most important, if least publicized, was to effect *domestic economic reform* by eliminating, at least for trade with the United States, the last vestiges of the National Policy and constrain the more subtle new instruments of protection. By exposing the Canadian economy to greater international competition while simultaneously improving access to the large market to the south, Canadian firms would have an incentive to restructure and modernize and become more efficient and productive.

- the most publicized was to provide a *bulwark against US protectionism*. By gaining more secure and open access to the large, contiguous US market, Canadian business would be able to plan and grow with greater confidence.
- finally, the agreement was meant to provide an improved and more *modern basis for managing the Canada-US relationship*. Since 1948, the GATT had served this function but had increasingly proved inadequate. New and more enforceable rules combined with more sophisticated institutional machinery were needed to place the relationship on a more predictable and less confrontational footing.

The agreement reached on October 3 and signed on January 2, 1988 meets these three fundamental objectives. The preamble and first chapter set out the basic aims and objectives of the two governments and provide the philosophical framework within which the whole agreement must be viewed. The heart of the agreement can be found in Chapters 3 to 13 establishing a sound but conventional free-trade agreement, fully consistent with GATT article XXIV. They take a set of basic rules and strengthen them. Where either side was not prepared to go as far as the other, provisions are made to continue negotiations, but within a new and more secure framework. These chapters also eliminate various barriers to trade, including the tariff, and thus give Canadians more open access to that large market of 270 million people they have long sought.

The link to GATT cannot be overemphasized. Many of the clauses of the agreement are drawn directly out of the GATT or provide agreed interpretations of GATT provisions. A good illustration is afforded in the energy chapter. That chapter is in most respects identical to the provisions of chapter four dealing with tariffs and customs administration and both chapters incorporate GATT provisions. The controversial requirement that Canada cannot arbitrarily restrict exports of energy to the United States and must share resources in the event that it does impose restrictions is a more explicit statement of an existing GATT requirement. It is an obligation that Canada and the United States accepted forty years ago.

Chapters 14 to 17 make a cautious start on the so-called new issues of services, business travel, investment and financial services. They recognize that international commerce is more than a matter of shipping goods to one another. The two governments decided to freeze the status quo and promise that any future laws and regulations will be based on the premise of fairness. Canada and the United States will treat each other's service providers and investors and business travellers as they treat their own. The two countries made a similar commitment with regard to trade in goods in 1935 and then gradually rolled back and eliminated areas where they did discriminate, a job they finally finished in 1987. They have agreed that they will try to do the same for the service industries and investors under the FTA.

Agreeing to be fair should not be confused with agreeing to do things the same way. Canada and the United States will continue to set their own rules and priorities. Investors and service providers will have to satisfy Canadian rules in Canada and US rules in the United States. But they can count on being treated fairly—on being treated the same as their domestic competitors.

The 1935 and 1938 bilateral trade agreements between Canada and the United States were an important precedent for the world and formed the basis for later multilateral negotiations. The 1987 FTA does the same for the new issues. The Australians and New Zealanders have been the first to follow this lead. In 1989 they updated their bilateral agreement along similar lines. The 96 members of GATT are trying to do the same in the Uruguay Round. The Europeans are looking forward to consolidating their common market by dealing with these issues as they move forward to a more integrated market by 1992.

Thirdly, chapters 18 and 19 achieve a Canadian quest of long standing—a contractual, institutional basis for managing the trade and economic relationship. Chapter 18 takes well-established GATT practice, commits it to a clear body of rules and procedures, and applies these to the rights and obligations of the agreement as a whole—to the enhanced and improved GATT-like rules dealing with trade in goods as well as the new rules dealing with services, investment and business travel. For the first time, there exists a clear mechanism that puts Canada and the United States on an equal, one-on-one footing. The agreement as a whole provides the rules—chapter 18 provides a neutral referee to enforce those rules.

Chapter 19 deals with the thorny issues of trade remedies. Here the United States recognizes for the first time that disputes between the two countries are not a matter for the application of domestic law and unilateral decisions alone, but should also be subject to bilateral dispute settlement. They provide an important beginning. While both countries will continue to rely on their respective trade remedy laws, they have agreed to replace judicial review of domestic decisions by bilateral review. Canadians will sit on panels to determine whether US

law was properly followed and whether any changes in US law are consistent with GATT, the GATT Codes and the FTA. These provisions combined are an important shield against abuse and harassment.

Finally, the agreement provides a framework for the negotiations of the future. At least ten articles throughout the agreement anticipate continued negotiations. The most important of these relate to subsidies and government procurement. The two sides tried to come to a common understanding on subsidies but did not reach it. Not because the Americans attacked social programs and other policies that are important to Canadians, but because the issues are exceedingly complex and difficult. GATT has tried to reach a definition of subsidies for forty years and not succeeded. Perhaps it may eventually prove less difficult on a bilateral basis to agree on which kind of direct industrial assistance is trade distorting and impose disciplines on these practices. If the two sides cannot agree, at least they will continue to work on finding better ways to resolve disputes and defuse one of the most corrosive issues in bilateral trade.

The government procurement provisions of the agreement are a disappointment. It had been Canada's hope to eliminate preferences and discrimination by state, provincial and federal governments in the awarding of government contracts and thus place government business on the same basis as private transactions. This did not prove possible except for a slight improvement in the coverage provided by the GATT procurement agreement.

Political Reality

Throughout the preparations for the talks and the negotiations, despite strong and unrelenting criticism, the idea of a free-trade agreement with the United States enjoyed strong, popular support in Canada. Indeed, even though the Conservatives took a disastrous tumble in the polls in 1986, free trade continued to be supported by more than half of the Canadian people. An articulate opposition at times suggested that it was tremendously unpopular but poll after poll demonstrated the opposite. The worry of the negotiators and their political masters from 1984 through 1987 was not whether Canadians would support a trade deal but whether the deal would be the victim of protectionism and indifference in the United States.

During the course of 1988, both governments took the necessary steps to implement the agreement in domestic law and anticipated bringing the agreement into force on January 1, 1989. In the United States, some opposition to the agreement was mounted by protectionist critics, but none found much resonance in either the Senate or the House. Skillful drafting of the implementing legislation as well as careful administration-congressional consultation and cooperation disarmed all but the most rabid critics. All the legislative committees of record made their contributions and by the end of September 1988 all the necessary legislative hurdles had been cleared and the president could sign the agreement into law. The only remaining step was for him to determine that Canada had also satisfied this final challenge and was ready to bring the agreement into force.

In Canada, similar legislative steps were taken. An omnibus implementing bill amending some 29 statues was tabled in the House of Commons in May and, after second reading, sent to Committee for detailed study. The House and Senate foreign affairs committees had already held weeks of hearings and, given the overwhelming majority enjoyed by the government in the House of Commons, there should have been

no difficulty in meeting the January 1, 1989 deadline.

Opposition to the agreement, however, mounted steadily. Proponents of the agreement appeared to have lost their enthusiasm for the constant backbiting that had characterized the previous two years and decided that their job was largely done. Opponents, however, concluded that their job had only just begun. Loosely allied in a Pro-Canada Network and made up of organized labour, church groups, environmental coalitions, economic nationalists, the artistic community and other veterans of dissent, they determined that the very future of Canada was at stake. With this as their holy grail, all reverence for truth and fairness went out the window and their fight became a crusade for the future of Canada.

With an increasingly vocal extra-parliamentary opposition carrying the battle, the two opposition parties each set out to prove that it was the better and more reliable opponent to free trade, adding mounting political and rhetorical excesses. As a result the final weeks of the campaign became a nailbiting event for both sides. The election came down to one issue: free trade. While the government eventually carried the day, it did so only after a bitter and divisive campaign. It is fair to ask, therefore, why Canadians, who throughout the negotiations supported the idea of free trade for at least six months appeared to endorse the actual agreement negotiated, suddenly displayed cold feet. For many analysts, the issue appeared to come down to a failure to communicate what the agreement is and is not.

An electoral campaign is a particularly poor moment to try to sway voters on the benefits of a technically complex idea. The communications challenge, therefore, had to be met well before the election and Canadians in general had to be convinced that despite their perceived historic reluctance to entertain a bilateral free-trade agreement with the United States, domestic and international developments made such an agreement necessary, desirable and workable in the 1980's. That challenge was not met. Efforts to make Canadians feel comfortable with the idea of a free-trade agreement received a set-back at the starting gate when an early version of a communications strategy was leaked, initiating a sterile debate that spooked the government about the need to communicate the issue aggressively and forthrightly. Nevertheless, by being in the 1988 election, the government ended by winning the only battle that really counts and thus winning the war.

Government efforts today to reach the people must be channelled through the media. The government may put out pamphlets and booklets explaining its policies and programs, take out advertising and sponsor seminars. All these efforts reach targeted, specialized audiences and, for some issues, are sufficient to garner the necessary support and disarm all but the most vocal critics. But the free-trade negotiations dominated the public policy agenda throughout the four years of the Conservatives' electoral mandate. For an issue of such critical political importance, the targeted audience is all Canadians and all Canadians can only be reached through the popular media, particularly the electronic media. Unfortunately, free trade proved an issue particulary difficult to communicate positively through the electronic media.

In the age of charisma, television and specialization, complicated truths are easily buried under an avalanche of half-truths and innuendo. For opponents, on the other hand, the communications strategy was clear and simple: portray the government as slick and manipulative. It was a message that television found easy to carry and with which most reporters for the electronic media were comfortable. It fitted in with their generally left-of-centre orientation. In Canada, this manifests itself in mild but uncritical economic nationalism, anti-Americanism, suspicion of big business and similar attitudes. It soon became clear that reasoned editorials or columns in the print media could not undo the steady diet of negative images projected by the electronic media.

Related to this problem of media orientation is the perception that "fair" journalism requires that both sides of an issue get equal billing and that any criticism of the government, whatever the source, is news. Thus, if 250 economists issue a statement indicating their support for the FTA, a dissenting economist must be found and given equal prominence stating why the agreement is not good for Canada. Curiously, criticism of government policy is not subject to the same standard. Thus, if a coalition of minor environmental groups issues a statement indicating that it fears the FTA will undermine efforts to protect the environment, no dissenting voice is heard in the same story—even though Pollution Probe, one of the largest and most respected environmental groups and not known for its support of the government, welcomed the agreement as a step toward environmental sanity. Over time, balance may be restored by means of editorials, op ed pieces and the columnists—but this is a balance that is available only to the dedicated and inveterate newspaper reader. For the general public, the image left is that some legitimate and influential group has found fault in one way or another with government policy, reinforcing the subliminal message that the government is trying to keep Canadians in the dark.

The journalistic task in Canada is immensely simplified by Question Period. Every day that Parliament is in session, the opposition parties are given 45 minutes to grill the government. For three years, most questions revolved around free trade. Few questions were friendly. For journalists, Question Period now provides the main feed for political news. Ironically, the reverse is also true: for the politicians, the news media provide the fodder for their questions. Thus, reporters and opposition politicians jointly reinforced a negative image, suggesting a greater degree of controversy and concern than was in fact the case. The fact that Parliament is now televised gives the electronic media ideal fifteen- or thirty-second political "bites" to put on the evening news. Most are negative.

For three years, the free trade issue was subjected to this kind of journalism and political jousting. Day in day out, it demanded at least one story every day in the print media, at least one probe in Question Period and at least one serious mention every few days in the electronic media. The basic message projected to Canadians was that free trade was a very difficult and controversial issue, that the government's handling of the negotiations left a lot to be desired, that the government was reluctant to take Canadians into its confidence and that a lot of experts drawn from a wide spectrum of opinion and expertise had grave doubts about the wisdom of the idea. Nevertheless, despite this generally negative perception, polling suggested that Canadians continued to give broad support to the idea of free trade in general and, eventually, to the particular agreement negotiated by the government. The long-term effect of this negative press, however, was to build unease about the venture, an unease waiting to be exploited.

The Roots of Dissent

This negative public image was in part aided by the disappearance of trade policy from public debate, university study and broader understanding. Interest in and knowledge of trade policy issues have not always been at the low level they are today. Until the 1930s, trade policy was a principal focus of political debate in Canada. Elections were fought and won on the basis of the tariff—as they were in the United States. Indeed, until the 1960s, trade policy was an important part of the university economics curriculum.

A number of factors since then have contributed to the current state of affairs. One was the development of a cadre of professional trade policy practitioners. Until the 1935 and 1938 bilateral negotiations with the United States, negotiations were conducted by ministers with the occasional help of their advisors, most of them generalists with little specialized expertise in trade policy. A minister was as likely to turn to a university professor for advice as to a civil servant. Not surprisingly, trade policy was an intensely partisan issue. The Tories were generally perceived as the party of protection and the special interests of the manufacturers, while the Grits portrayed themselves as the party of free trade and farm and consumer interests. During the 1930s and 1940s, however, trade policy was increasingly designed and executed by an exceptional group of public servants. By the time they retired from the trade policy field in the early 1950s, they had firmly established that trade policy making and trade negotiations should be left to professionals operating within a general policy framework established by ministers. They had also made trade policy a boring, nonpartisan issue. Canada benefitted by gaining remarkable continuity and stability in its trade policy; it lost when, as a result of an almost non-existent public profile, public understanding of and interest in trade policy disappeared.

The obscurity into which trade policy had descended paid its dividends during the free-trade negotiations. The government could count on no more than a handful of informed Canadians who could comment convincingly and independently on its principal public policy issue. The media had little knowledge upon which to base its analysis. Even worse, it could find few commentators outside of government who had the depth of understanding to explain the issues in simple terms. Government officials continued to be unavailable for this task.

The way was thus eased for the triumph of emotionalism and anti-intellectualism. Two popular publications illustrated the problems. Since 1984, a plethora of conferences and seminars resulted in a deluge of books and articles by learned commentators on various aspects of free trade. While trade policy practitioners might well be dissatisfied with much of this literature, it did lend an air of seriousness to the debate before, during and after the completion of negotiations. These books have all enjoyed a modest success. Some have sold as many as two or three thousand copies. Most have sold no more than a few hundred. Two books, however, enjoyed a phenomenal success. One of them sold 20,000 copies in the space of five days.

The first is *If You Love This Country*, a collection of essays by Canada's glitterati.[21] David Frum described it as follows in *Saturday Night*:

What's wrong with (their views) isn't that they are overwrought or vituperative; it's that their authors simply do not consider themselves bound by the customary standards of evidence ex-

pected in controversies over matters of urgent public policy.[22]

This book enjoyed wide circulation in Canada, selling thousands of copies, merrily undermining confidence about the very concept of free trade and ordered trade relations with the United States. But its impact was nothing compared to a 100-page analysis of the agreement by a retired family judge from Edmonton, Marjorie Bowker. Even the *New York Times* reported on the Bowker phenomenon. Billing herself as an ordinary grandmother and concerned Canadian, she set out to satisfy herself whether the FTA is in Canada's interest. Her homespun analysis came to the conclusion that the FTA is neither free trade nor in Canada's interest. It is akin to the local butcher preparing a detailed assessment of the Income Tax Act—undoubtedly fun reading but not very enlightening.

The Bowker analysis would not have been a problem if her manuscript had not become the darling of the media. A number of widely read columnists informed Canadians that here was what they had been waiting for—an unbiased, disinterested analysis of the agreement which confirmed all their worst fears. An enterprising publisher took the manuscript, cleaned it up a little, removed some of the most egregious howlers, gave it a catchy title—*On Guard for Thee: An Independent Review of the Free Trade Agreement*—and gambled that a low price would pay off with high volume.[23] The gamble paid off. Bookstores could not keep up with the demand.

To cap this campaign of anti-intellectualism, the anti-free-trade coalition produced a comic book featuring simple-minded analysis and vitriolic cartoons and distributed it to 2.2 million households in Canada as a supplement to their daily newspaper. It was written by a skilled craftsman—writer Rick Salutin—and finished the job of confusing concerned Canadians already reeling from the claims and counterclaims of the politicians and the negative media images. A much more sober counter effort sponsored by the pro-business Alliance for Trade and Job Opportunities was immediately dismissed by the media as no more than special pleading by big businesses, most of whom, Canadians were confidently told, take their orders from head offices in the United States.

The FTA is a complex document. A skillful demagogue can, without much difficulty, isolate texts that give comfort to the most outrageous claims. Serious analysis of the agreement, on the other hand, requires careful reading of the whole text and its antecedents, such as the GATT, in order to bring out the various interrelationships and qualifications. It requires some acquaintance with the underlying policy issues as well as the rights and obligations contained in other, related trade agreements and their interpretation over the years. It is, after all, a legal document. Its analysis is aided by some appreciation of history, law and economics. In short, it was not written for amateur analysts. The discipline and knowledge required for this kind of analysis, however, was dismissed by the anti-free-trade forces as illegitimate. They insisted that all commentaries are equally valid and that those worried about the future of Canada have a special claim to truth.

Competing Views of Canada

Of course, the critics would not have been able to sustain their essentially negative and destructive message if there were not

deeper feelings and views underpinning their arguments.

First, proponents of free trade have had to come to terms with the enduring appeal of mercantilism or what British economist David Henderson has termed do-it-yourself economics.[24]

Second, the free-trade negotiations ran into abiding anti-Americanism. Canada was founded as a nation that rejected the American dream. Part of that rejection required that the dream be characterized as a nightmare. Anti-Americanism in Canada is thus often expressed by harping on the negative qualities of American life and insisting that these are the essence of America, while all the time protesting that its proponents are not anti-American but pro-Canadian. The most eloquent expression of Canadian angst about the ability to survive as a separate nation on the North American continent can be found in George Grant's *Lament for a Nation*. Wrote Grant: "To be a Canadian was to build, along with the French, a more ordered and stable society than the liberal experiment in the United States."[25] Maintaining this Canadian dream requires vigilance against the inroads of American commerce, entertainment, culture, and political values. The FTA, from this perspective, erodes the will to resist and will eventually suck Canada into the American nightmare.

Third, Canadians have long prided themselves on being internationalists. But the truth of the matter is that the more Canadians learn about the rest of the world, the less they want to have anything to do with it. Noted political scientist Gil Winham:

The FTA is a magnet in Canada for those who oppose modern economic life, and for those who oppose the preponderant presence of the United States in Canadian life. Neither the effects of modern economic life nor American influence will be reduced by rejecting the FTA. In all nations today, people are facing the internationalizing of the domestic economy, as well as increased competition on a world scale. These changes are painful, but they are not a result of the FTA or any other trade agreement. Instead, the FTA is an intelligent response to these pressures, because by removing trade protectionism it removes incentives to be inefficient.[26]

In sum, the debate reflected two visions of Canada and of the role of government in society—the one characterized by economic nationalism and an emphasis on the need for an active interventionist government to direct our economic life, the other by economic internationalism and a reliance on market forces to order our economic life. The first wanted to isolate Canada from the world and feared the wider implications of economic interdependence and integration; the second wanted Canada to take an active role in the world and its confident Canadian values and priorities will survive closer economic integration.

Conclusions

In spite of the difficulties posed by American indifference and insensitivity, the differences proved surmountable. The agreement, despite some obvious flaws and shortcomings, represents a prudent course for the future. It solves many of Canada's bilateral problems with the United States and establishes a better basis for tackling the problems of the future. It places Canada at the cutting edge of international trade policy-making and gives Canada once again the influence it enjoyed in this area thirty and forty years earlier. It is an agreement that will lead to an economically stronger, richer and more self-confident Canada.

More difficult to resolve will be the wounds opened in Canada as a result of the domestic debate. Even dismissing the excesses of that debate, the agreement responds to the beliefs, hopes and aspirations of only one group of Canadians. For a smaller but more articulate group, the agreement symbolizes everything it does not like about the demands of the modern world. It bespeaks a vision of Canada that they reject. In the coming decade, as the technical aspects of the agreement are implemented and enforced, allowed to strengthen Canada's economic performance and diffuse trade problems with the Americans, the bigger challenge of soothing the anxieties of at least some of these Canadians will also have to be met. Until then, only one set of differences will have proven reconcilable; until the second set reaches the same stage, the agreement will continue to prove controversial and thus vulnerable to political upheaval.

NOTES

1. "The most portentous issue Prime Minister Brian Mulroney will deal with today when he meets President Ronald Reagan is that of free trade." Toronto *Globe and Mail*, September 26, 1984.

2. In 1983, as part of his department's trade policy review, international trade minister Gerald Regan had introduced the idea of negotiating a number of sectoral arrangements with the United States along the lines of the 1965 autopact.

3. Most of the material in this article is drawn from a much more detailed treatment of the negotiations I have prepared in collaboration with my colleagues on the Canadian negotiating team, Bill Dymond and Colin Robertson. Canadian deputy negotiator Gordon Ritchie, in addition to speeches and public testimony, has published two accounts of the negotiations from his perspective in John Crispo, ed., *Free Trade: the real story* (Toronto: Gage, 1988) and in an introduction to Jon R. Johnson and Joel S. Schachter, *The Free Trade Agreement: A Comprehensive Guide* (Toronto: Canada Law Book, 1988). As well, Ambassador Ritchie's detailed testimony before the Senate Foreign Affairs Committee in the fall of 1987 and spring of 1988 adds further detail. The account that follows differs to some extent in its detail, in part because of my longer association with the issue than Ambassador Ritchie and because of a different perspective on what was taking place.

4. Recent treatments of the historical background to the FTA can be found in Randall White, *Fur Trade to Free Trade: Putting the Canada-U.S. Trade Agreement in Historical Perspective* (Toronto: Dundurn Press, 1988); J. L. Granatstein, "The Issue That Will Not Go Away: Free Trade between Canada and the United States," in Denis Stairs and Gilbert R. Winham, *The Politics of Canada's Economic Relationship with the United States* (Toronto: University of Toronto Press, 1985); and David J. Bercuson, "Canada's Historic Search for Secure Markets," in John Crispo, ed., *Free Trade: the real story* (Toronto: Gage, 1988).

5. Department of Finance, *A New Direction for Canada: An Agenda for Economic Renewal* (Ottawa, 1984), p. 33. Wilson had signalled his views as Tory trade critic some six months earlier. In an interview with the *Globe and Mail*'s Patrick Martin, he criticized the stalled sectoral initiative as "not moving fast enough ... we must move more quickly to get a deal because the protectionist influences in the United States are moving quickly." Toronto *Globe and Mail*, March 16, 1984.

6. Department of External Affairs, *How to Secure and Enhance Canadian Access to Export Markets* (Ottawa, 1985), p. 3.

7. Mr. Kelleher's report on his consultations is reproduced in Department of External Affairs, *Canadian Trade Negotiations: Introduction, Selected Documents, Further Reading* (Ottawa: Supply and Services, 1985), pp. 15-18.

8. The Quebec Declaration is reproduced in External Affairs, *Canadian Trade Negotiations*, pp. 13-14.

9. Their reports are reproduced in External Affairs, *Canadian Trade Negotiations*, pp. 65-72.

10. See External Affairs, *Canadian Trade Negotiations*, pp. 57-64.

11. Special Joint Parliamentary Committee on Canada's International Relations, *Interim Report* (Ottawa: Supply and Services, 1985). For the conclusions and recommendations of the report, see External Affairs, *Canadian Trade Negotiations*, pp. 43-48.

12. Royal Commission on the Economic Union and Development Prospects for Canada, *Final Report* (Ottawa: Supply and Services, 1985). For the conclusions and recommendations of the Report, see External Affairs, *Canadian Trade Negotiations*, pp. 49-56. The dissenting commissioner was Gerard Docquier.

13. The text of the prime minister's statement in the House and the exchange of letters can be found in External Affairs, *Canadian Trade Negotiations*, pp. 73-78.

14. A detailed American account of the process leading up to Senate consideration of fast-track authority in April 1986, based on interviews with all the participants has been prepared by Glenn Tobin, a Ph.D. student at Harvard University. I am grateful to Mr. Tobin for sharing the manuscript with me.

15. Problems between the administration and the Congress over trade are discussed in detail in I. M. Destler, *American Trade Politics: System Under Stress* (Washington: Institute for International Economics, 1986).

16. See, for example, Simon Reisman, "The Issue of Free Trade," in Edward R. Fried and Philip H. Trezise, eds., *U.S.-Canadian Economic Relations: Next Steps* (Washington, Brookings Institution, 1984).

17. I am drawing here on research in progress being used in a book on the historical development of Canadian trade policy.

18. For an account of these dramatic events through American eyes, see Peter McPherson, "Political Perspectives," in Jeffrey J. Schott and Murray G. Smith, eds., *The Canada-United States Free Trade Agreement: The Global Impact* (Ottawa and Washington: Institute for Research on Public Policy and Institute for International Economics, 1988).

19. Including government procurement, investment, alcoholic beverages, intellectual property and financial services.

20. The FTA and the debate preceding and during the negotiations has generated a lively and growing literature in Canada. Among commentaries on the Agreement and its implications, see Murray G. Smith and Frank Stone, eds, *Assessing the Canada-U.S. Free Trade Agreement* (Halifax: The Institute for Research on Public Policy, 1987); Jeffrey J. Schott and Murray G. Smith, eds, *The Canada-United States Free Trade Agreement: The Global Impact* (Ottawa and Washington: Institute for Research on Public Policy and Institute for International Economics, 1988); William Diebold, Jr., ed., *Bilateralism, Multilateralism and Canada in US Trade Policy* (New York: Council on Foreign Relations, 1988); Richard G. Lipsey and Robert C. York, *Evaluating the Free Trade Deal: A Guided Tour through the Canada-U.S. Agreement* (Toronto: C. D. Howe Institute, 1988); Donald M. McRae and Debra P. Steger, eds., *Understanding the Free Trade Agreement* (Halifax: Institute for Research on Public Policy, 1988); and Rick Dearden, Michael Hart and Debra Steger, eds., *Living with Free Trade* (Ottawa and Halifax: Centre for Trade Policy and Law and Institute for Research on Public Policy, 1990).

21. Laurier LaPierre, ed., *If You Love This Country* (Toronto: McClelland and Stewart, 1985).

22. David Frum, "Free for All," *Saturday Night*, April, 1988.

23. Marjorie Bowker, *On Guard For Thee: An Independent Review of the Free Trade Agreement* (Hull: Voyageur Publishing, 1987).

24. David Henderson, *Innocence and Design: The Influence of Economic Ideas and Policy* (Oxford: Basil Blackwell, 1986).

25. *Lament for a Nation*, Carleton Library Edition (Toronto: McClelland Stewart, 1970). p. 4. Grant's more up-to-date views can be found in Laurier LaPierre, ed., *If You Love this Country* (Toronto: McClelland and Stewart, 1987), as well as in testimony before the 1985 Joint Parliamentary Committee in Halifax summarized at page E-9 of its Interim Report.

26. Gilbert R. Winham, *Trading with Canada; The Canada-U.S. Free Trade Agreement* (New York: Priority Press, 1988), p. 71.

SUGGESTED READINGS

Cameron, Duncan, ed., *The Free Trade Papers*, Toronto: James Lorimer, 1986.

Gold, Mark, and David Leyton Brown, eds., *The Canada-U.S. Free Trade Agreement*, Toronto: Carswell, 1988.

Granatstein, J. L. "Free Trade Between Canada and the United States: The Issue That Will Not Go Away," in Denis Stairs and Gilbert Winham eds., *The Politics of Canada's Economic Relationship with the United States*, Vol. 29, (MacDonald) Royal Commission on the Economic Union and Development Prospects for Canada, 1985, ch. 2, pp. 11-54.

Laxer, James, *Leap of Faith*, Toronto: James Lorimer, 1986.

MacDougall, John, "The Canada-US Free Trade Agreement and Canada's Energy Trade," *Canadian Public Policy*, Vol. 17, March 1991, pp. 1-13.

Tomlin, Brian, "The Stages of Pre-negotiation: The Decision to Negotiate North American Free Trade," *International Journal*, Vol. 44, No. 2, Spring 1989, pp. 254-279.

Wannacott, R. J., "Canada's Future in a World of Trade Blocs: An Appraisal," *Canadian Public Policy*, Vol. 1, Winter 1975, pp. 118-130.

Wilkinson, Bruce, "Canada-United States Free Trade: The Current Debate," *International Journal*, Vol. 42, No. 1, Winter 1986-87, pp. 199-218.

c h a p t e r 21

SANCTIONING
SOUTH AFRICA, 1980s

Clarence G. Redekop

After the landslide election of Brian Mulroney and the Progressive Conservative party on 4 September 1984 the problems of Africa came to play an unexpectedly central role in Canadian foreign policy. Although the Canada-United States relationship in all its complexity clearly lies at the heart of the Mulroney government's foreign policy concerns, international events and domestic forces have conspired to propel African issues onto the foreign policy agenda. To this the Mulroney government has responded in a surprisingly forceful and creative way. The first massive response to the Ethiopian famine came from Canada.

The Mulroney government was also one of the first to announce a moratorium on African debt repayments. Africa has also been designated as an area of high priority by the Canadian International Development Agency.

In this welter of African concerns, the issue of apartheid in South Africa stands out because of its complexity, intractability, and longevity. International outrage over the treatment of a black population of some 24 million has swelled with the rising tide of civil unrest and ruthless repression within the country.

Until the government imposed new and more stringent censorship controls on the domestic and foreign media, there were al-most daily accounts of police brutality in crushing black demonstrations and at funeral services, police torture in prison cells, and police aid for black vigilantes whose purpose it is to eliminate those who oppose the government. Although reporting of such incidents became difficult, there was no reason to believe that the incidents became fewer or any less harsh. And internal repression was accompanied by external aggression as the South African government did not hesitate to extend its military might to the territory of its neighbouring states, particularly Angola, Mozambique, Botswana, Zambia, and Zimbabwe, purportedly to strike at the bases of the African National Congress, but even more to destabilize further the fragile social, political, and economic structures of these states.

The repressive domestic policy and the aggressive foreign policy were not accompanied by any significant reform in the rigid racial structures of the apartheid system.

. . .

The South African government recognized how emotionally charged the concept of apartheid became in the world beyond its borders, and therefore, sought to bury it under a barrage of reformist rhetoric. Most Western governments, including that of Canada, realized, however, that the pace of meaningful reform slowed to a virtual standstill (if indeed it ever got started) and

 Clarence G. Redekop, "The Mulroney Government and South Africa: Constructive Disengagement," from *Behind the Headlines*, Canadian Institute of International Affairs, 1986. Portions of the text have been deleted. Some footnotes have been removed; those remaining have been renumbered.

that the power structure remained basically intact. The real problem for the Western world was to determine how to stimulate or encourage genuine change in the face of steadfast South African intransigence backed by military might and nearly forty years of experience in deflecting international criticism and pressure.

Shortly after the resounding electoral victory of the Progressive Conservative party in September 1984, the secretary of state for external affairs, Joe Clark, announced that a general review of Canadian foreign policy would be carried out, the purpose of which was, no doubt, to permit the new government to put its own stamp on an area which had for so long been dominated by Pierre Trudeau and the Liberal party. The result of this exercise, a green paper entitled *Competitiveness and Security: Directions for Canada's International Relations*, was published in May 1985.[1] Its tone was cautious and platitudinous while its policy thrust was directed towards the United States and the enhancement of trade. Only one paragraph was devoted to Southern Africa, the tone of which was so detached as to suggest that the official outrage, such as it was, over institutionalized racism in South Africa had burned itself out.

Although the green paper failed to indicate the direction of the new government's thinking on the issue of South Africa, it would have been logical to expect an explicit endorsement of the policy of constructive engagement emanating from Washington and also from London. The ideological kinship between Canada's new prime minister and President Reagan and Prime Minister Thatcher was striking: all appeared to believe in the liberating effect of free enterprise, deregulation, and free trade. Logically, it might have been expected that the new Canadian policy would

be even less sympathetic to the disruption of normal business relationships than had been the policy of the previous government. In addition, there were the traditional arguments against economic sanctions of the businessmen, the timid bureaucrats, and the cautious politicians: sanctions were ineffective because they were partial, unenforceable, and non-universal, and they were counter-productive because they strengthened the resolve of the target state and created unintended victims.

The response of the Mulroney government to the problem of South Africa however, confounded these expectations: the government in the first two years of its existence began to formulate a policy of what might be called constructive disengagement. In so doing it brought forward new sanctionist policies and sided with Third World African states in opposition to the United States and British policies. There are several factors which may account for this behaviour.

On the domestic side, the pressure groups of the "counter-consensus," such as the Christian churches and the Canadian Labour Congress, maintained constant pressure to bring about some measure of Canadian disengagement from South Africa. The pressure for more decisive action from Ottawa also came from Desmond Tutu, Archbishop of Cape Town and head of the Anglican church in Southern Africa, who made two highly publicized trips to Canada, in December 1985 and May 1986, and who called publicly for the termination of all economic links between Canada and South Africa. Those favouring the status quo appeared to be more on the defensive as the racial problems in South Africa escalated. On the international side there were pressures from members of the Commonwealth, particularly the front-line states, who demanded an effective response to the growing crisis of violence in Southern Africa. In addition, there were policy expectations confronting the new government—expectations which had been created by several decades of creative and sympathetic diplomacy on the part of Canadian governments towards Commonwealth problems and, in particular, Southern African problems.

These domestic and foreign pressures appear to have reinforced the perceptions and concerns of key members of the Department of External Affairs, the secretary of state for external affairs, and the prime minister himself. South Africa's policies of external destabilization, internal repression, and rigid intransigence on issues of meaningful reform demonstrated that constructive engagement, as practised in Washington, amounted to little more than a euphemism for tacit acquiesence in, or even support for, apartheid. The only alternative to such a policy of ineffective moral suasion was one of disengagement, or sanctions, whether partial or complete. By the time of the Commonwealth conference in Nassau in mid-October 1985, the Mulroney government appeared to have accepted the view that economic sanctions offered the one remaining method of exerting international influence on South Africa (although without any necessary guarantees of success), that the issue of economic sanctions would remain on the international agenda as long as the South African problems remained unresolved, and that the process of instituting sanctions against South Africa had entered a new and probably irreversible stage. A year later, on 3 October 1986, the United States Congress signalled its agreement with the Canadian government when it set aside President Reagan's policy of constructive engagement and instituted a series of new economic sanctions.

The Liberal government under the leadership of Pierre Trudeau had reviewed its policies towards South Africa on two occasions—in 1970 and 1977. The fact that the Mulroney government, after only two years in office, moved through four phases in its policy towards South Africa was testimony to the turmoil in the area and the fluidity of the political situation. The first phase ended with the completion of a review of Canadian policy towards South Africa and an announcement on 6 July 1985, of a number of additional measures to be taken.[2] The scope of the selective economic sanctions was to be expanded and the administration tightened. The government moved to end the few remaining export programmes still in effect, such as the Programme for Export Market Development, designed to promote the sale of Canadian products to South Africa. In addition, the government moved to ban the sale of computers and other sensitive equipment to the South African police and security forces, and it undertook to tighten the administration of its compliance with the voluntary United Nations arms embargo. The government announced that it would act to discourage the continued sale of the South African Krugerrand in Canada, ban the importation of Namibian uranium by Eldorado Nuclear Limited, a federal crown corporation, after its existing contract expired in 1988, and ban the importation of South African arms.

Although the monetary value of these actions was not large, the measures were significant. The termination of all government-funded export activity finally brought to completion a policy process begun in 1977. The actions in the grey areas of dual purpose equipment such as computers came on the heels of a charge, levelled by the Taskforce on the Churches and Corporate Responsibility, that the government had permitted the export of computers to South

Africa which could be used specifically for the development of jet fighters. The Taskforce also charged that rebuilt used tanks had been shipped to South Africa, thereby giving further evidence of the sieve-like nature of the Canadian arms embargo. The government's request to Canadian banks to refrain from selling Krugerrands proved to be very effective, and the market for the gold coins collapsed almost immediately. The boycott of Namibian uranium, shipped to Canada for reprocessing and then re-exported, involved a contract valued at only $5 million; however, without a similar boycott on South African uranium, this measure would be easy to circumvent.

The government also announced the termination of the Canada-South Africa double taxation agreement, a move long opposed by the business community and by trade and finance officials in the government. Furthermore, the voluntary code of conduct for Canadian business operations in South Africa, introduced in 1978, was to be made more effective by the appointment of a special administrator whose function would be to monitor corporate behaviour and report to Parliament. Heretofore the code had been little more than a farce; only one company—Alcan Aluminium Limited—had ever bothered to file the requested reports. A mandatory code was rejected because of the problems of extraterritoriality which would result and the consequent inevitable weakening the Canadian ability to prevent the extraterritorial application of United States laws in Canada. Other measures announced on 6 July included a reaffirmation of the sports boycott and the establishment of a $5 million education aid package for South African blacks.

The measures announced by the secretary of state for external affairs, Joe Clark, failed to impress the South African authorities. On 21 July 1985 the South

African government imposed a state of emergency enabling it to arrest and detain people without charge for up to two weeks, to censor the media, to control internal travel, to seize property, and to establish curfews.

As a result, the international perception of South African policy as one characterized fundamentally by repression without reform was confirmed. The French government recalled its ambassador and banned new investment in South Africa. The foreign ministers of the European Communities were summoned home for consultations. The Scandinavian countries devised new measures of economic sanctions. The Canadian response, however, was more muted. Ottawa did not respond to the new state of emergency until 24 July, a day after most other Western countries had registered their protests. Moreover, Mr. Clark went out of his way to indicate that although the Canadian ambassador to South Africa had been recalled on 21 July, this should not be considered a diplomatic protest; rather, his presence was required in Ottawa for the ongoing policy review and policy-making process. The new South African ambassador to Canada also routinely presented his credentials in Ottawa on 15 August while the South African ambassador-designate to the United States returned to his country in July after being diplomatically snubbed for two months as a demonstration of United States disapproval of South African military raids into Botswana.

The apparent hesitancy displayed by the Mulroney government was actually the prelude to the second phase of its policy towards South Africa. On 22 August the prime minister indicated that "further steps" were being contemplated. A few weeks later, on 10 September 1985, Joe Clark went so far as to state that the

Canadian government was prepared to undertake the "full disruption of economic and diplomatic relations" with South Africa if lesser measures proved ineffective in bringing about meaningful change.[3] Just three days later further sanctions were announced. An embargo was placed on the shipment of oil and oil products to South Africa. Canadian investment in South Africa was to be limited by a voluntary ban on loans to the South African government and its agencies. A former Canadian diplomat, Albert Hart, was appointed as the administrator of the business code of conduct and new consultations were to be held between the government and the business sector on means of improving co-operation in this area. The government also undertook to create a central registry of voluntary steps taken against apartheid by provincial and municipal governments, companies, and individuals. Travel between Canada and South Africa was to be discouraged by a mandatory ban on air traffic, and, lastly, an additional $1 million was set aside to assist families of political prisoners in South Africa.[4]

A number of these measures were designed more for their public relations value than for their potential impact on the policies of the South African government. Canada, for instance, exported no oil to South Africa and it was inconceivable that it ever would. Direct air contact between the two countries was also non-existent although in the past there had been a number of direct charter flights. The voluntary ban on loans to the South African government could be significant provided that the banks were prepared to comply with the government's wishes. The unstable financial and political climate in any case made such loans unwise, and the bankers indicated to the secretary of state for external affairs that they intended to wind down their estimated

$200 million in outstanding loans. The changes in the administration of the code of conduct were potentially very important since, for the first time, compliance records were made public. The first report, released by Albert Hart on 18 June 1986, indicated that three of the seventeen Canadian companies operating in South Africa had not bothered to file reports and that another five paid wages below the level set by researchers at the University of South Africa. The report concluded that, although most of the firms were not bad corporate citizens, their record was not as good as that of companies based in the United States.[5] Should the voluntary system fail, Joe Clark threatened to "secure the legal right to impose mandatory compliance."

The Commonwealth Heads of Government Conference, held in Nassau in the Bahamas from 16 to 22 October 1985, ushered in the third phase of the government's policy towards South Africa. A major, not unexpected, split developed between the frontline states, which demanded comprehensive sanctions, and the British government, which favoured minimal, if any, sanctions. A compromise formula was eventually hammered out which called for the establishment of a Commonwealth Group of Eminent Persons which would attempt to influence the South African government in the direction of such reforms as the release of Nelson Mandela and other political prisoners, the termination of the state of emergency, and the legalization of the African National Congress. Should these discussions produce no tangible reforms, the heads of government committed themselves to implementing a series of sanctionist measures including a ban on new investments in South Africa and a boycott of South African agricultural products.

The Group of Eminent Persons, which included Archbishop Edward Scott, the primate of the Anglican Church of Canada, departed from South Africa with the realization that its mission had been an utter failure. In its report, released on 11 June, it called for the imposition of economic sanctions against the South African regime. Failure to do so, it suggested, could mean missing "the last opportunity to avert what could be the worst bloodbath since the Second World War."[6] The following day, on the eve of the tenth anniversary of the 1976 Soweto riots, the South African government reimposed the state of emergency which it had lifted in March 1986.

On the same day the Mulroney government announced further sanctions against the South African government. It imposed a voluntary ban on the promotion of South African tourism in Canada, it cancelled the Canadian credentials of four South African diplomats based in the United States, it ended its internal purchases of South African goods—valued at around $1 million—and it increased by $2 million the fund set aside for the education of South African blacks.[7] Of these four measures only the voluntary ban on tourist promotion raised controversy, particularly after the South African Tourism Board placed a half-page advertisement in the 5 September issue of the *Globe and Mail* for a $3,000 two-week "see the real South Africa" tour. This action led to an immediate request by the secretary of state for external affairs to South African Airlines to close its offices in Montreal, Toronto, and Vancouver by 1 November.

The fourth phase of the Mulroney government's policy towards South Africa covers the period from the publication of the report of the Group of Eminent Persons to the implementation of a further round of Commonwealth sanctions on 1 October 1986. During this sixteen-week period the Commonwealth was yet again threatened

with disintegration and yet again it managed to survive. The Nassau compromise had called for a mini-summit to discuss the Group's report and to co-ordinate the implementation of the sanctions agreed to in October 1985. The British government under Prime Minister Thatcher was, however, resolutely opposed to the whole concept of economic sanctions. The summit, held in London from 3 to 5 August 1986 and attended by Australia, The Bahamas, Britain, India, Zambia, Zimbabwe, and Canada, eventually agreed to disagree. The British agreed to a voluntary ban on new investment and the promotion of tourism—which Prime Minister Thatcher held to be ineffective—and to an embargo on South African coal, iron, steel, and gold coins, if the European Communities agreed to such an embargo. The EC, under the influence of the West German and British governments, actually dropped coal from the list—the only item of real significance since the Community absorbs 80 per cent of South Africa's coal exports—when it adopted sanctions on 15 September 1986.

The other six countries, including Canada, endorsed eleven measures, eight of which had already been approved at Nassau. Measures which had previously been implemented by the Canadian government included the ban on air links and the promotion of tourism, the termination of all government-assisted export programmes, government purchases of South African goods, the cancellation of the double taxation agreement, and a ban on new bank loans to South Africa. New measures included an embargo on agricultural imports and on imports of coal, iron, and steel, a ban on new investments and the reinvestment of profits earned in South Africa, and the withdrawal of all consular facilities in South Africa except those dealing directly with one's own nationals.

Although the list of actions taken against the South African government was steadily lengthening, Canadian leverage was limited. The value of Canadian investment in South Africa stood at about $135 million and had in fact declined in recent years. Imports in 1985 were valued at only $228 million; of this, 35 per cent was accounted for by agricultural products ($80 million) and 8 per cent by steel ($12 million), coal ($1 million), and uranium ($5 million).[8] Eldorado Nuclear, the crown corporation which processed the South African uranium for re-export, forfeited a "substantial part of its current operations" when the existing contracts came to an end; nevertheless, government officials expected that the economic impact of the new sanctions would be four or five times greater on South Africa than on Canada. While it was unlikely that this action would cause great unease in Pretoria, the real significance of the new measures was that it was the first time that the Canadian government prohibited trade in the private sector in goods of a peaceful nature. The arms embargo was supplemented by a mandatory boycott of South African products which accounted for nearly half of total Canadian imports from that country.

The policy of the Mulroney government towards South Africa evolved from one of excessive caution—as typified by the ethos of the green paper—to one of much greater dynamism and creativity—as typified by the Report of the Special Joint Committee on Canada's International Relations. Released in June 1986, it called for "an approach based on constructive internationalism" which "would impart both a vision and sense of purpose to Canadian foreign policy."[9] While the Reagan administration pursued its policy of "constructive engagement," the policy of the Mulroney government evolved rapidly towards one of "constructive disengagement." While the former was based on efforts to enhance the economic and political interaction of the United States and South Africa in order to exert influence, the latter sought to exercise influence through the curtailment of such interaction. The former viewed the South African government as amenable to friendly persuasion, sweet reason, and good example; the latter held that the rigid intransigence of the South African government over several decades demonstrated that the inducements for change held out to Pretoria must include punitive measures. By the mid-1980s the bankruptcy of the policy of constructive engagement was beyond doubt, as was the need for a new, as yet largely untried, policy of constructive disengagement.

Several elements of this policy became apparent during the first two years of the Mulroney government. The Canadian diplomatic presence in South Africa appears to have been enhanced by the new policy initiatives and by an activist Canadian ambassador. Although both the prime minister and the secretary of state for external affairs have indicated that the Canadian government would be willing to sever diplomatic relations in the absence of meaningful reform, they were aware that creative diplomacy would not happen in the absence of diplomats. Political, as well as economic, disengagement would largely eliminate the possibility of constructive political action: without a diplomatic presence in South Africa, the Canadian government would be dependent upon other states for information and political assessments, and it would, therefore, hardly be in a position to influence either the policies towards South Africa of other Western states or the government of South Africa itself. To break off diplomatic relations with South Africa would be to opt out of one of the central problems confronting Canada, Southern Africa, and the world; it would be a negation of constructive internationalism and of the best elements of postwar Canadian foreign policy.

Along with a more activist diplomatic presence in South Africa, the Mulroney government moved to endorse the use of economic sanctions as a policy instrument in a way qualitatively different from that of previous Canadian governments which were long on rhetoric but short on actions which actually had a discernible impact on the economic relations between the two countries. It is, of course, possible that the new government was merely exhibiting the vigour and energy characteristic of young governments before the reality of unsolvable problems sank in to produce a lethargic cynicism. It was also possible—indeed likely in this case—that the escalation of the South African crisis convinced the Mulroney government that the intransigence of the South African regime nullified the effectiveness of any policy of appeasement, and that, in the words of Malcolm Fraser, the former Australian prime minister and co-chairman of the Commonwealth Group of Eminent Persons: "sanctions ... represent[ed] the only path remaining to bring the South African government to negotiate the dismantling of apartheid."[10] For the first time, a Canadian government accepted the contention that economic sanctions should be for Ottawa a central policy instrument in the effort to bring about the elimination of apartheid.

For maximum impact on South Africa, economic sanctions should ideally be comprehensive, mandatory, and universal in their application. The Mulroney government, however, recognized that sanctions could also be effective in the absence of these three conditions. The strategy of the government was to expand the use of eco-nomic sanctions on an incremental basis rather than to opt for a complete rupture of economic relations. Although the Special Joint Committee on Canada's International Relations recommended that "Canada should move immediately to impose full economic sanctions,"[11] the government opted for a gradual escalation of Canadian economic pressures even though the potential leverage to be gained was very small. The strategy was closely related to the concept of constructive disengagement since each act of economic disengagement would be evaluated for its political impact. According to Edward Lee, the Canadian ambassador to South Africa, the threat of sanctions could sometimes be more effective than their application. In addition, the government deemed it wise to keep the sanctions option open—in terms of greater or lesser pressure—in view of the fluid political situation in South Africa.

Similarly, the strategy of the government was to call for voluntary sanctions in areas where a domestic or international political consensus on mandatory sanctions did not exist. There was also a recognition that informal sanctions, driven by commercial imperatives rather than by political or moral concerns, could perhaps be even more effective in applying pressure on the South African regime than policies of economic disengagement directed by the government. In August 1985, for example, the combination of prolonged economic recession, inflation running at about 17 per cent, black unrest, government repression in the absence of meaningful reform, and a high foreign debt of US$19 billion led to a chain of events which seriously damaged foreign confidence in the South African economy. Over the previous eighteen months there had been a net capital outflow of over $2 billion and the rand had sunk in value from 85 cents to 35 cents (US). Western banks then triggered the South African debt crisis by refusing to renew short-term South African loans. Pretoria responded by closing the foreign exchange and stock markets for three days, by imposing a four-month freeze on the repayment of its foreign debt, and by establishing a two-tier currency to stem the outward flow of capital. The governor of the South African Reserve Bank made an emergency trip to Europe to consult with Western bankers, and eventually, in February 1986, a compromise formula was reached for the rescheduling of South Africa's foreign debt. The long-term result of these developments was to seriously erode Western business confidence in the South African economy and the government in Pretoria. Mandatory economic sanctions, backed by national and international law were very important in any disengagement strategy; at the same time, the impact of voluntary or informal sanctions should not be underestimated.

The Mulroney government further sought to increase Canadian influence and the impact of economic sanctions on South Africa by attempting to encourage other states, especially Britain and the United States, to join in a multilateral effort to impose sanctions. If Britain were brought on line, it would have access to the policy-making machinery of the twelve-nation European Community with its large economic stake in South Africa while the United States would presumably have greater influence over Japan and its growing economic links with South Africa. The key to the Mulroney government's sanctions strategy, therefore, lay not in Pretoria, but in London and Washington.

The British and United States governments, however, were resolutely opposed to economic sanctions. Prime Minister Thatcher was not to be swayed from her position and she coldly rejected the repeated efforts of Prime Minister Mulroney to mediate the growing split within the Commonwealth after the Nassau conference and the report of the Group of Eminent Persons. The August Commonwealth mini-summit thus resulted in deadlock; Prime Minister Thatcher proved to be as intransigent as the government in Pretoria. In the United States events took a different turn. The United States Congress overwhelmingly overturned the presidential veto on sanctions and placed the country squarely in a leadership role on the issue of economic disengagement from South Africa. Among other measures Congress banned the importation of South African uranium, coal, textiles, iron, steel, agricultural products, and military equipment. New investments, both portfolio and direct, were prohibited, the arms embargo was strengthened, and the landing rights of South African aircraft in the United States were terminated. Although the interventions of Prime Minister Mulroney with the United States administration had been unsuccessful, the end result was even better than hoped for in Ottawa.

A final element in the evolving policy of constructive disengagement was to increase the level of economic assistance to the frontline states which depended so heavily on the South African economy and which were consequently so vulnerable to South African economic sanctions. The most effective counter-sanctions weapon in the South African arsenal was the threat to cripple their economies, and any Western sanctions policy must therefore have incorporated an aid and development package for these states. In early 1984 the Canadian International Development Agency (CIDA) announced a five-year programme worth $125 million in transportation, communications, energy, and agricultural development to the member countries (Angola, Botswana, Lesotho, Malawai, Mozambique, Swaziland, Tanzania, Zambia, and Zimbabwe) of SADCC, the Southern African Development Coordination Conference. This funding was additional to the $125 million per year of bilateral development assistance to Southern Africa, which was itself an increase of nearly 50 per cent since 1983.[12] Economic disengagement from South Africa would logically entail greater involvement in the fragile economies of the frontline states.

The Mulroney government's policy towards South Africa placed it within the best traditions of postwar Canadian foreign policy. It was mediatory within the Commonwealth; the actions of Mulroney and his special emissary, Bernard Wood, were reminiscent of those of Trudeau and his emissary, Ivan Head, some fifteen years earlier. It was flexible and creative in its search for workable approaches to seemingly insoluble problems. Much more, however, could have been done. Multilateral action should have focused not only on Britain and the United States but on coordinating policies with such like-minded states as the Nordic countries, the Netherlands, and even France. In addition, "constructive internationalism," according to the Special Joint Committee, "by no means precludes taking unilateral initiatives," and striking out alone in a leadership role should never be rejected out of hand.[13]

NOTES

1. Joe Clark, Secretary of State for External Affairs, *Competitiveness and Security: Directions for Canada's International Relations* (Ottawa 1985), 42.
2. Department of External Affairs. "Statement on South Africa by the Right Honourable Joe Clark, Secretary of State for External Affairs," Baie Comeau, 6 July 1985, Statement 85/37.
3. Ian Mulgrew, "PM plans sanctions against South Africa," *ibid.*, 22 August 1985: "Clark says end of all relations with South Africa possible," *ibid.*, 10 September 1985.
4. Department of External Affairs, "Statement in the House of Commons by the Secretary of State for External Affairs. The Right Honourable Joe Clark, on South Africa," 13 September 1985, Statement 85/50.
5. Code of Conduct Concerning the Employment Practices of Canadian Companies in South Africa, *Annual Report 1985* (Ottawa 1986).
6. Commonwealth Group of Eminent Persons. *Mission to South Africa: the Commonwealth Report* (London: Commonwealth Secretariat 1986). 141.
7. Department of External Affairs. "Notes for a Statement in the House of Commons by the Secretary of State for External Affairs. The Right Honourable Joe Clark," 12 June 1986, Statement 86/35.
8. Canada, Statistics Canada, *Imports by Country*, 1985.
9. Report of the Special Joint Committee on Canada's International Relations, *Independence and Internationalism* (Ottawa 1986), 137.
10. Malcolm Fraser, "Sanctions seen as West's last chance." *Toronto Star*, 5 August 1986.
11. *Independence and Internationalism*, 110.

12. Steve Godfrey, "Canadian sanctions and Southern Africa," *International Perspectives* (November/December 1985), 14.

13. *Independence and Internationalism*, 138.

SUGGESTED READINGS

Brown, Chris, "Canada and Southern Africa: Autonomy, Image and Capacity in Foreign Policy," pp. 206-224, in Maureen Molot and Fen Hampson, eds., *Canada Among Nations: The Challenge of Change, 1989*, Ottawa: Carleton University Press, 1990.

Canada, Department of External Affairs, "Canada Against Apartheid," *Canadian Foreign Policy Series*, October 1987.

Godfrey, Steve, "Canadian Sanctions and South Africa," *International Perspectives* (November/December 1985): 13-16.

Munton, Don and Timothy Shaw, "Apartheid and Canadian Public Opinion," *International Perspectives* (September/October 1987): 9-12.

Nossal, Kim, "Out of Steam: Mulroney and Sanctions," *International Perspectives* (November/December 1988) 13-15.

c h a p t e r 22

EVALUATING DEVELOPMENT ASSISTANCE, 1987

David R. Morrison

onflict between the North and the South has not been as visibly intense in the 1980s as it was in the 1970s. In the previous decade, the countries of the South were able to work out a common agenda for international structural change despite their growing economic differentiation and ideological and regional conflicts. The self-confidence that culminated in the demand for a more equitable New International Economic Order (NIEO) reflected an overestimate by the South of its bargaining strength, as the rather indifferent response of the industrialized countries to the "North-South dialogue" indicated. However, any hope for an NIEO evaporated in the early 1980s in the wake of the worst global recession in fifty years, the collapse of oil and other commodity prices, an enormous debt overhang in Africa and Latin America, growing trade protectionism among governments in the North, and, within many of the latter, a neo-conservatism interested in international development only if state interventionism yields to the "magic of the marketplace."

Many of the impressive economic gains of the earlier period have been lost, living standards among the relatively privileged in many countries have declined, the magnitude of rural and urban poverty, already growing, has intensified, and efforts to achieve enhanced democratization and human rights are endangered. Meanwhile the destruction of the human habitat in both North and South continues apace, often in ways that make it appear as though developmental and environmental goals are antithetical to one another. The challenge of finding viable pathways to sustainable development with dignity and justice is greater than ever.

Canada's modest role in confronting that challenge changed very little in the late 1980s. However, it was a time for significant fresh thinking about policies and priorities. Parliamentarians rather than bureaucrats played the leading role in this process. In 1987 the House of Commons Standing Committee on External Affairs and International Trade (SCEAIT) completed a far-reaching assessment of Canadian policies and programs in the sphere of official development assistance (ODA); its recommendations and the government's response to them will be examined here in some detail. The chapter will then turn to a discussion of evolving Canadian positions on the international debt problem (the subject of yet another parliamentary study undertaken by SCEAIT's Senate counterpart), trade with the Third World, refugees, and the report of the World Commission on Environment and Development (WCED). The chapter concludes with an assessment of the Mulroney government's record in the sphere of North-South relations.

David R. Morrison, "Canada and North-South Conflict," from B. W. Tomlin and M. Molot (eds.), *Canada Among Nations, 1984: A Time of Transition,* Toronto, James Lorimer & Company Ltd., 1985.

New Directions in Official Development Assistance?

ODA is but one vehicle for financing international development. In fact, it will never be more than a marginal supplier of the external capital needed; trade, direct investment, and commercial loans will remain much more important in aggregate terms. Canadian ODA, currently running at $2.7 billion (Cdn.), makes Canada the fifth-largest donor among the industrial country members of the Organization for Economic Cooperation and Development (OECD), but that sum represents only about 6 per cent of OECD aid, which in turn accounts for only a fraction of North-South capital flows. However, development assistance does create opportunities for particular sorts of capital and human-resource transfers that many developing countries, especially the poorest, are not able to obtain through other means. In addition, ODA has now assumed a special saliency in the context of the international debt crisis as one means of offsetting the dramatic reversal of resource flows between North and South. Thus, the issue of aid effectiveness is a critical one.

Aid effectiveness is the principal concern of *For Whose Benefit?*, issued by the House of Commons Standing Committee on External Affairs and International Trade in May 1987.[1] Chaired by William Winegard, a former university president elected as a Conservative member of Parliament in 1984, the committee embarked upon the study in the wake of the African famine and the questions that it raised about the efficacy of Canadian aid efforts. Various parliamentary committees and subcommittees had examined aid issues on a piecemeal basis over the years. The most recent was a special House-Senate committee, which reported a year earlier; though concerned with all aspects of Canada's external relations, it was inundated with submissions on North-South issues.[2] However, more than a decade had elapsed since the last comprehensive public review of the ODA program.

Some of the earlier parliamentary studies (notably one in 1981 on Canada's relations with Latin America and the Caribbean) had failed to achieve agreement between parliamentarians from all three major parties who espouse an internationalist perspective and those who hold a more confrontational, Reaganite vision of the world. This time some of the latter were so heavily involved in projects such as restoring the death penalty that they left SCEAIT in the hands of the former. What emerged was a rather remarkable non-partisan consensus that was closely attuned to the concerns of the many non-governmental organizations (NGOs), community and church groups, and educational and other institutions that testified.

The report suggested that "the aid program needs a fresh jolt of political energy." Noting several positive aspects in Canada's performance, it nonetheless concluded that "the aid program continues to betray an ambivalence of purpose and design" (SCEAIT 1987:3). The mandate of ODA is quite simple:

> to help the poorest people and countries in the world to help themselves. Only by discharging that mandate does assistance serve Canada's long-term national interests, be they defined in the humanitarian, political or commercial terms. At the same time, there are many pressures on the aid program to serve other short-term interests, not all of which are consistent with the central purpose of Canada's official development assistance. (p. 12)

This is a refreshing approach in that it rejects the glib assumption often enunciated by governments that there is a necessary complementarity of interest in ODA between developmental and other concerns such as the support of Canadian industries and exports. As far as the committee was concerned, this is an empirical question that must be answered on a case-by-case basis, with basic developmental objectives taking precedence in the event of a conflict. The report recommended that Parliament adopt a legislative mandate for development assistance, in the form of a parliamentary charter, and made proposals for changing priorities, linking aid to human-rights performance, untying more ODA, improving aid organization and strengthening evaluation.

New and Clearer Priorities

A Development Assistance Charter. The Winegard Committee suggested the following as the text for a parliamentary charter:

- The primary purpose of Canadian official development assistance is to help the poorest countries and people of the world.
- Canadian development assistance should work always to strengthen the human and institutional capacity of developing countries to solve their own problems in harmony with the natural environment.
- Development priorities should always prevail in setting objectives for the ODA program. Where development objectives would not be compromised, complementarity should be sought between the objectives of the aid program and other important foreign policy objectives. (SCEAIT 1987: 12)

The government response accepted these three principles and added a fourth:

- Development assistance should strengthen the links between Canadian citizens and institutions and those in the Third World. The Government will therefore endeavor to foster a partnership between the people of Canada and the people of the Third World.[3]

While rejecting legislative enactment, the government did promise to "enshrine" the charter in a public statement of policy. At this stage, one can only speculate about the likely impact. However, the fourth principle, laudable at one level and perhaps seemingly innocuous, may be used to justify the primacy of Canadian goods and services, perhaps in certain cases offsetting the intended steering effect of other principles.

A Greater Emphasis on Human-Resource Development. Historically, Canada's bilateral aid program has been skewed heavily towards the provision of food aid and major capital projects, particularly in the spheres of energy, transportation, and agricultural equipment. With the emphasis in the mid-1970s of the World Bank and other international development agencies upon meeting basic needs, the Canadian International Development Agency (CIDA) began to move more into rural development, health, education and housing. In 1980 CIDA adopted human-resource development as one of three sectoral priorities alongside energy and agriculture. However, bureaucratic inertia and a program tied heavily to Canadian procurement had precluded any dramatic movement in this direction five years later.

In advocating a much greater emphasis upon human-resource development, the Winegard Committee criticized what it saw as "a strong tendency to treat expenditures on capital equipment and infrastructure as productive investments, while expenditures on people, especially the poorest people, are regarded as unproductive social costs" (SCEAIT 1987: 9). The report identified needs for expanded efforts in strengthening the role of women in development (already a strong CIDA priority), improving primary health-care delivery systems and supporting educational development, especially at the primary and post-secondary levels (pp. 24-30).

The government again accepted these recommendations, although the text of the response suggests that the reorientation of practice will not be as substantial as the committee advocated. It also expressed some hesitancy about becoming heavily involved in primary health care, literacy and primary school education (Government of Canada 1987: 43-45). More enthusiasm was expressed for expanded occupational, university and in-house business educational and training programs—all areas where Canadian expertise can be readily called upon and the tying of aid more easily accommodated.

Food Aid and Agriculture. Ever since the Ethiopian famine of 1984-85, the Canadian government has formally acknowledged what critics had been saying for some time: that "food aid *can* be incorporated in a rational development plan, which, by means of judicious technical and structural changes in the agrarian sector, has among its objectives the eventual elimination of the need for such aid."[4] However, the Winegard Committee found Canadian performance still wanting. For the most part, the report noted, food aid is used as a "quick disbursing program transfer that also satisfies high Canadian tying requirements." It went on to recommend that non-emer-gency food aid not exceed 10 per cent of the ODA budget, and that more resources be devoted to agricultural development (SCEAIT 1987: 57-58).

In response, the government indicated that it intended to continue increasing the food aid budget by 5 per cent a year. Clearly, this use of Canadian surpluses (largely of wheat) is deemed to be too important to domestic interests to consider jeopardizing it. However, the response temporized slightly by agreeing that "food aid is not always the best form of development assistance" and promising to announce shortly "a new food aid policy framework" (Government of Canada 1987: 70).

Reorientation of Country Focus. The Winegard Committee also tackled the question of how to select the countries that would be the primary focus of the Canadian aid program. The existing three-tier system, established in the early 1980s, was subjected to harsh criticism. Ostensibly designed as an attempt to achieve greater concentration of impact and greater coherence of effort in some countries, "the country classification system as now constituted is over-extended." The committee called for the abolition of the existing system and the designation of no more than thirty core program countries on the basis of developmental criteria (SCEAIT 1987: 675-67). The government accepted the recommendation (Government of Canada 1987: 75).

Human Rights. The other major recommendation for a shift in priorities reinforced the earlier call by the Special Joint Committee for a more explicit link between aid and the human-rights performance of recipients. While mindful of the political and ideological controversy embedded in debates about human-rights violations,

SCEAIT came down in support of a set of guiding principles for informing ODA policies (SCEAIT 1987: 26-27). The government expressed skepticism about the possibility of establishing operationally effective criteria, both because international standards are so general and because of the "diversity of legal systems, social values and traditional structures in the countries in which CIDA functions." For similar reasons, and because judgments would be "too subjective," the government rejected a recommendation to establish a public human-rights country classification grid in favour of using diplomatic channels and less formal means of responding to concern about violations (Government of Canada 1987: 50, 52). However, a commitment was given to make respect for human rights a "top priority" in ODA policy and to place more emphasis on human-rights performance in deciding whether or not to proceed with development programs. The government also accepted recommendations to establish a human-rights unit within CIDA and to give CIDA personnel training on human-rights issues (Government of Canada 1987: 50-56; CIDA 1987: 2).

In response to the Special Joint Committee, the government had earlier agreed to set up an International Institute of Human Rights and Democratic Development and had commissioned a special study by two academics.[5] The Winegard Committee asked for assurance that the institute would be an independent body like the International Development Research Centre, and not a mere substitute for a comprehensive human-rights policy (SCEAIT 1987: 30). This recommendation was accepted. Subsequently, the special study was published and officials from External Affairs and CIDA began drafting legislation (News Release, Government of Canada, November 13, 1987).

While the committee's recommendations for establishing clear standards for judging human-rights performance and a public classification system were perhaps based on naive assumptions, one can respect its desire to develop a way of making human-rights conditionality meaningful. However, even though the significance of the new policy remains to be judged, it will meet opposition from elements in the business community worried about a potential loss of Canadian export markets.

Tied Aid

Another form of conditionality has a long history. The debate between proponents and opponents of "tied aid" has been going on for over twenty years. Critics of the requirements tying Canadian bilateral ODA to the purchase of at least 80 per cent of required goods and services from Canadian sources (with at least two-thirds Canadian content) claim that the resulting technological bias, real costs and lost opportunity costs weaken the value of aid. The North-South Institute commented in a recent publication: "The bald fact is that the poorest countries and people and the projects that benefit them are rarely the most attractive markets for most Canadian industries, universities and other institutions."[6]

In addition, cogent arguments and research (including some internal government studies) have been advanced to show that much greater untying could be achieved without a resulting detrimental impact upon the Canadian economy. However, policy makers have not been convinced and claim that tying aid does serve the mutual interests of donor and recipient. In any case, so many domestic interests have become dependent upon the ODA program that it is difficult to foresee any dramatic change.

However, while careful to maintain a balance among competing claims, the Winegard report took quite a radical stand in relation to existing government policy. Tied aid should act "as an incentive, not an alternative, to achieving the goal of Canadian international competitiveness...From a development point of view, even more crucial than competitiveness is appropriateness" (SCEAIT 1987: 37). The committee proposed that the 80 per cent rule be relaxed to increase flexibility for developing-country procurement, with the untied authority being gradually raised to 50 per cent of the bilateral budget; that tying requirements be waived for some of the least developed countries in sub-Saharan Africa; and that greater untying of food aid be permitted when a neighbouring country has exportable food surpluses (p. 39).

Not surprisingly, the government had trouble with these recommendations, but it did give a little ground. The proposal on food aid was essentially rejected, but the government agreed to adapt the policy on tying "while ensuring that the Canadian private sector continues to be involved in development co-operation through the provision of goods and services." Accordingly, the response accepted moving to a level of 50 per cent untying in sub-Saharan countries and some other least developed countries, and to 33 1/3 per cent elsewhere (Government of Canada 1987: 57-58).

Improving Aid Organization and Delivery

Decentralizing CIDA. The Winegard Committee made several recommendations for improving the organization and delivery of Canadian ODA. Potentially the most significant one advocated decentralization to the field. Critics had long been saying that CIDA was far too Ottawa-centred in terms of both decision making and personnel, a theme that ran through much of the testimony to the committee. Noting that CIDA itself had been actively studying and debating the issue for some time, the committee urged movement from discussion to action, arguing that decentralization would do much to streamline a cumbersome, rigid and delay-prone organization that requires a loop through headquarters for almost every decision. A more field-based operation would also permit greater flexibility and responsiveness to local conditions, involve recipients in all stages of the process, foster a greater orientation towards human-resource development and secure more effective coordination of aid efforts with Canadian NGOs and institutions and other donor countries (SCEAIT 1987: 82-84).

In pressing for decentralization, the committee recognized that CIDA's personnel resources are limited and that the exercise has to be undertaken in a cost-effective manner. It suggested creating five or six regional offices in Africa, Asia and the Americas, each headed by a senior official who would have considerable project-approval authority (pp. 86-90). The government accepted the recommendation "in principle" (Government of Canada 1987: 82-84), and has given every indication of "biting the bullet." In the short run, decentralization will be energy-absorbing and could well lead to decreased effectiveness and lessened attention to the other reforms emerging from the review. However, the potential gains are well worth the risk, provided that regional offices and employees are not so lavishly endowed as to force a cutback in real aid.

There is another aspect of decentralization that is not discussed by SCEAIT, but that continues to be a source of concern for those who want to strengthen Canada's ODA effectiveness. More and more of the

delivery of the Canadian bilateral aid program has been contracted out to private
consultants and firms. While undoubted
benefits flow from tapping energies outside
public agencies for many types of projects,
privatization in certain instances can add
an additional layer of red tape to an operation and runs the risk of excessive frag-
mentation of effort. There has not been a
careful analysis assessing the true comparative costs and benefits of employing
public servants or private consultants in
any given situation.

Other ODA Channels. SCEAIT endorsed
Canada's long-standing commitment to the
international financial institutions and other
international agencies, recommending that
about one-third of the ODA budget continue
to be allocated to multilateral programs
(SCEAIT 1987: 58-60). The report was also
enthusiastic about the work of NGOs and
other non-profit private institutions, and
proposed a substantial increase in funding
for them (pp. 91-99, 104). The government
responded positively (Government of
Canada 1987: 85-89, 91-92).

SCEAIT consistently asserted that the
primary thrust of ODA ought to be towards
Third World development, and only secon-
darily towards Canadian commercial and
other objectives if these do not conflict with
the primary thrust. However, it did suggest that

> the business community is the most underutilized
> resource in Canadian official development as-
> sistance....The Committee ... would especially
> like to encourage initiatives that involve a more
> lasting business commitment to developing
> countries. The Committee is deeply troubled by
> the apparent tendency on the part of some busi-
> nesses to look upon CIDA as a convenient source
> of tied aid contracts where the partnership ends

> as soon as the money runs out. This is not good
> enough. (SCEAIT 1987: 99-101)

Long-term commitments were needed
through a continuing Canadian commercial presence in some countries. The committee urged greater use of the programs
offered by CIDA's Industrial Co-operation
Division (INC) that support private sector
initiatives aimed at establishing joint ventures or other forms of collaboration leading
to investment flows and technology transfer. The government accepted a series of
recommendations calling for increased
funding for a stronger and more flexible
CIDA-INC that would "not sacrifice developmental criteria in the bargain" (p. 103;
Government of Canada 1987: 90-91). With
a few exceptions, Canadian businesses have
seldom set their longer-term horizons beyond Canada and the United States.

Improving Evaluation. Another potentially
significant section of the report focused on
improving the evaluation of aid effectiveness by better and more-targeted long-term
planning, a more open and self-critical policy-making process and a greater use of
arm's-length evaluations (SCEAIT 1987:
115-19). The government's reply was generally positive (Government of Canada
1987: 97-101), but it remains to be seen
whether the protectiveness and defensive-
ness that have characterized CIDA in the
past will change. There has been an un-
derstandable nervousness about the
prospect of embarrassing findings reaching the media or the parliamentary opposition. However, for the most part,
reservations have been more a reflection of
the characteristic caution of the Canadian
public service. This trait has an under-
standable place in many government activities, but it is certainly inappropriate if
evaluation is to become a tool for improving

ODA performance and for creating more public confidence in that performance. The embarrassing reports already have a way of emerging, but better planning and evaluation could help to ensure that the incidents leading to them would occur less often.

The Debt Crisis

The Third World debt crisis has now been with us for a decade. Soon after the Mexican bubble burst in 1982, country after country announced that it could not pay its foreign debts on schedule. After initial fears of a global financial panic were assuaged, governments in the dominant countries of the North, led by the United States, took the position that each situation would be best handled on a case-by-case basis, with the principal remedy being the conventional program of adjustment through austerity under the guidance and leadership of the International Monetary Fund (IMF). There was no shortage of suggestions for more-integrated multilateral approaches, but these were generally rejected as unworkable or too costly.

Meanwhile, drastic import strangulation and disastrous drops in living standards occurred within both "epicentres" of the crisis: some seventeen middle-income countries, principally in Latin America, that together owe upwards of $400 billion, mostly to commercial banks; and three dozen low-income countries, mostly in Africa, that owe only about one-tenth of that amount, largely in concessional loans from multilateral agencies and donor countries. The worst crisis is "that of the disadvantaged—the people who have lost jobs, seen their limited purchasing power decline, experienced a deterioration in their already inadequate access to health care and unpolluted water, and so on."[7]

By 1985, it was clear that conventional adjustment strategies were not leading to recovery. The so-called Baker initiative, named for James Baker, the U.S. secretary of the treasury, represented an important breakthrough in American thinking about the debt crisis. While still emphasizing a case-by-case approach, Baker prescribed policies for middle-income debtors that would achieve some growth along with balance of payments adjustment and control of inflation; an ongoing key role for the IMF, but with enhanced involvement in structural adjustment lending by the World Bank and regional development banks; and increased lending by the World Bank—however, the emphasis for the World Bank was even more on adjustment and less on growth. Not surprisingly, there was also a strongly Reaganite edge to Baker's call for more reliance on the private sector, supply-side market reform and increased foreign private investment.

Canada's policy on the debt crisis has mirrored that of the United States since the election of the Mulroney government, with perhaps three notable exceptions. First, Canada has been more prepared to carry its proportionate share of funding increases for the IMF and the World Bank; second, a number of measures have been taken to lessen the burden of official debt to Canada of several African countries and a few others as well; and third, Canadian banks have been forced to set aside greater provisioning to cover their portfolios in countries with serious debt problems. In 1987 the Standing Senate Committee on Foreign Affairs (SSCFA) suggested that Canada's stake has several dimensions: lessening the strains on domestic banks (with their $26-billion exposure to problem debtors in Latin America and the Caribbean); strengthening financial institutions and markets around the world; enhancing trade (the value of Canadian exports to the Third World fell from 12.1 per cent of total exports in 1982 to 8.2 per cent in 1985); reducing the risk that processes of democratization in debtor countries will be reversed; and improving Canada's capacity to promote international development.[8]

The Senate committee's general recommendations included a call for a more integrated international strategy for handling the debt problem that would guide the case-by-case approach, much more direct involvement by creditor-country governments, including Canada, increased flows of funds from creditor countries and the international financial institutions, consequent higher funding levels for the debt-related programs of the IMF and the World Bank, more effective coordination of Fund and Bank policies, and improved market access to Canada and other OECD countries for the exports of indebted developing countries (SSCFA 1987: 69, 92, 94, 108, 110, 111). While generally supportive of Fund and Bank initiatives, the Senate committee offered a cautionary note on the American-induced ideological bias of conditionality: "It will be important ... to temper the conditions that are pressed on debtor countries to adopt economic policies favouring a market economy with an understanding of the differing traditional values and systems of some developing countries" (p. 67).

Addressing the problem of middle-income debtors, the Senate report supported the broad outlines of IMF and World Bank adjustment programs (p. 14). At the Canadian end, it recommended building up the provisioning of domestic banks beyond the level of 10 to 15 per cent of exposure to high-risk debt ordered by the inspector general of banks in 1984. It was noted that some European banks had set aside reserves of about 50 per cent, while the

Japanese figure was around 20 per cent; only the American level was lower than the Canadian (principally because American banks are not allowed to write off any provisions as a business expense, compared to about one-fifth in Canada and high levels elsewhere). The committee suggested that Canadian provisioning be increased to 18 to 20 percent by 1989 and that this be facilitated by enabling the banks to write off a greater proportion as taxable expenses (SSCFA 1987: 39-40, 84-86). "The banks must carry an appropriate share of the cost of handling the bank debt problem, but maintaining the health of the domestic and international economies justifies governments in relieving them of some of that burden" (p. 85). Ultimately, it is likely that much more of the commercial debt will be dealt with in this way by governments.

Turning to the African and other least developed countries, the Senate committee applauded steps that successive Canadian governments had taken to lighten the debt burden of several low-income debtors: the decision in 1977 to forgive the ODA debt of the least developed countries and from that date to put all CIDA projects in these countries on a straight grant basis; the offer in 1986 of a fifteen-year moratorium on payments of principal and interest of the ODA debt of other African countries where Canada had continued to make concessional loans rather than grants; and the decisions of Canada and some other donor countries, also in 1986, to provide all future aid in the form of grants and to convert to grants the non-utilized parts of development assistance loans. The committee recommended further debt-relief measures, including outright forgiveness in the case of some least developed countries and the extension of support to some non-African countries (SSCFA 1987: 41, 97-98). The government did subsequently forgive the debt of several African countries, announcing these decisions at the Heads of Government Conferences of la francophonie in Quebec and the Commonwealth in Vancouver. (These steps elicited generally favourable responses in the press, except for a questioning of the human-rights record of some of the beneficiaries, such as Zaire). Also, consistent with its earlier efforts to strengthen the capacity of the IMF and the World Bank to assist low-income debtors, Canada was one of the first Western countries to pledge a full share to the IMF Structural Adjustment Facility.

North-South Trade

While there have been several positive aspects of Canada's performance on the debt question, at least as it relates to the least developed countries, there has been little movement on trade. The latter is an issue at the forefront of the South's demand for an NIEO in the mid-1970s and remains a matter of intense conflict even though much of the unity and optimism within the Third World has been dissipated by events in the 1980s. What happens in the sphere of world trade is crucial for the recovery of the major debtors and for development more generally. As the Winegard report noted critically, "we still hear far more about how aid can support our exports than about how trade with us can support their development" (SCEAIT 1987: 43).

Canada imports less from developing countries as a proportion of total imports than any other industrial country, and our national policy has been among the more protectionist. One standard explanation for these facts is that the external trade profile of the Canadian economy is closer to that of many Third World countries than to the industrial country norm; Canada wants less of what the developing world has to offer,

and has not had much success in capturing markets in the South for what Canada has to offer. Also, domestic political forces continue to ensure that many more resources are devoted to protecting labour-intensive industries such as clothing and footwear than to the retraining and adjustment policies that would be needed in the wake of trade liberalization in these sectors. Canada was again a prime mover behind the renegotiation in 1986 of the Multi-Fibre Agreement (MFA), "the GATT-endorsed system of restraints that discriminates against Third World textile and garment exports to industrialized countries."[9]

Although the Winegard Committee recognized the constraints upon any significant change in Canadian performance in the near future, it urged making import promotion a declared objective of ODA policy, particularly in core countries. It also recommended a reduction in protectionist barriers (SCEAIT 1987: 44). The government "accepted" these recommendations, but, as in the reply to the Special Joint Committee a year earlier, the official rhetoric was more positive than what the government can actually be expected to deliver (Government of Canada 1986: 65; 1987: 61-62). However, perhaps judgment should be deferred until we are further into the current Uruguay Round of trade liberalization talks within the General Agreement on Tariffs and Trade (GATT). Heading into these, Canada did help to achieve a modest success that could well redound to the interest of many agricultural exporters in both the North and South: the so-called Cairns Group of fourteen countries managed to persuade the European Community to include agriculture on the agenda, provided that it is not given undue priority.

The emphasis of the Winegard Committee on import promotion was part of a concern to put both sides of the trade ledger into a longer-term perspective, to see trade as a means of promoting development for the poor majorities in the poorest countries with the expectation nonetheless "that a strategic increase in aid and trade involvement in some countries can and should repay long-term dividends to Canada" (SCEAIT 1987: 35). The report was critical of the emphasis in Canadian policy upon immediate returns for domestic interests. It also stressed the danger that a narrow focus upon using ODA for trade promotion may downplay or ignore human-rights considerations. Without these broader concerns, an aid/trade policy "can risk becoming subsidy for mainly commercial transactions that really ought to pay for themselves" (p. 35).

This position reflected an interesting convergence within the committee of "small c" conservative opposition to public subsidies for business and the left-liberal/social democratic critique of how ODA is distorted when it is used as a vehicle for immediate commercial gain. We have already seen how this convergence informed the proposals for greater untying of aid and a longer-term commitment by business to Third World ventures. Other recommendations called for stronger Canadian action within the OECD to discourage mixed credits (a mix of subsidized concessional and commercial terms) for Third World export promotion and for a commitment not to count as ODA any concessional export-financing package unless it meets the criteria of the proposed development assistance charter (p. 42).

Again the government "accepted" the recommendations, but once more the cutting edge of the committee's recommendations was blunted by a response making it clear that practice would not change appreciably (Government of Canada 1987: 59-

60). While it is true that Canadian participation in concessional trade financing has been a reluctant response to the aggressive use of this practice by others, notably France and Japan, the general use of aid for trade promotion is simply too strongly entrenched in a web of vested interests to expect otherwise. The government's decision in 1986 to defer action on a proposed aid/trade fund (inherited from the previous Liberal administration) was a reflection more of deficit cutting and backtracking on aid targets than of any change in policy.

The Plight of Refugees

The recent Canadian record on refugees is also a mixed one. There are now over ten million refugees worldwide; most of them are from countries of the South and many of these have fled from civil wars, other manifestations of intense regional, ethnic and religious conflict, and abuses of human rights. Although Canada's contribution to easing the problem has been modest in terms both of admitting refugees to Canada and of relief work abroad, the performance was deemed sufficiently praiseworthy that the country was awarded the international Nansen Medal in 1986 in recognition of national efforts to help refugees. Clearly, this award reflected much good work and human caring, but its announcement came at a time when there were almost daily reports of muddled policies and procedures, of bureaucratic delays in processing refugee claims and of other instances of official insensitivity.

Then in 1987, just when the government strengthened its pledge to make international development policies more attuned to human rights, it also introduced legislation aimed at curbing bogus refugee claims through means that have been criticized as conflicting with the Geneva

Convention on refugees, other international covenants and our own Charter of Rights and Freedoms. The catalyst of course was the arrival in Nova Scotia in July of a boatload of 174 Sikhs from India claiming refugee status; a year earlier 155 Tamils from Sri Lanka had waded ashore to Newfoundland in similar circumstances. Both events generated popular outrage against those who arranged the transport and organized the trips, giving the government an opportunity to demonstrate leadership by clamping down on human trafficking for profit. However, the cabinet also capitalized on the popular perception that these people were illegal immigrants trying to jump the queue rather than people with genuine claims for sanctuary.

Parliament was recalled in mid-August, five weeks early, and was asked to give speedy approval to the Deterrents and Detention Bill (C-84). Its passage was seen as a higher priority than approval for Bill C-55 (introduced earlier in the year), which was designed primarily to simplify and speed up the refugee determination process, a generally agreeable objective, but which had been criticized sharply for proposing to give to Canadian officials the right to turn back refugee claimants at the border and to deport them to "safe third countries."[10] Bill C-84 met with general support from the opposition and the media for its intent to impose heavy penalties upon illegal commercial smugglers such as those who organized the boat trips for the Tamils and Sikhs, but was denounced for applying these penalties equally to church and other humanitarian groups that have been active in assisting potential refugees to come to Canada. It was attacked as well for provisions that would enable authorities to board and turn back suspicious ships without a hearing, to detain for lengthy periods and without a hearing people who arrived without proper identification and documentation, to deport, again without a hearing, claimants who were deemed to be security risks, and to exercise sweeping search and seizure powers.

The chorus of protests extended to the United Nations high commissioner for refugees, the Tory MP chairing the Standing Committee on Immigration (who was subsequently removed), and several individuals and groups who have said they will proceed with legal challenges under the Charter of Rights. However, the government refused to back down on any of these measures and after some months secured passage of the bill in the House of Commons.

Environment and Development: A Preliminary Response to Brundtland

Of all of the challenges that arise in the domain of North-South conflict, none is as important for the future of humankind as developing a more active and better-balanced global strategy for achieving sustainable economic development that respects the limits of nature. *Our Common Future*, the 1987 report of the World Commission on Environment and Development says little that is new for students of environment and development.[11] Rather, its importance lies in the fact that it speaks on behalf of an eminent group of people from North and South who served on the commission, chaired by Gro Brundtland, the prime minister of Norway.

In 1972, when the first United Nations Conference on the Environment was held in Stockholm, concern for the environment was viewed by many Third World leaders as a luxury they could ill afford until their countries were much further along the path to industrial development; some complained, not without cause, that the logic of environmentalism in the North appeared to condemn the South to the continuing poverty associated with being "hewers of wood and drawers of water." The Brundtland report reflected considerable political and educational work since then to forge a consensus that the preservation of the environment and the development of the Third World, far from being contradictory, are inextricably linked. This change of consciousness has also obviously been facilitated not only by industrial disasters such as Bhopal and Chernobyl, but also by growing knowledge about the human impact on rural environments that has intensified desertification and deforestation. It is too soon to predict whether the Brundtland report will go the way of the earlier Pearson and Brandt reports on international development, both of which generated considerable discussion but little action as they moved into the archives of history. Stephen Lewis, Canada's ambassador to the United Nations, stressing the urgency of seizing the moment, regretted that some Third World governments were afraid that the report would be used as a club to keep them from the fruits of industrial development, while some Western governments opposed what they saw as recommendations for meddling with free enterprise.[12] Environment Minister Tom McMillan was one of the first national spokespersons to participate in the United Nations' debate on the report in October 1987. He avoided taking positions on many of Brundtland's specific recommendations, but his speech reflected a strong rhetorical commitment to its fundamental premises:

> Surely, the policies of the industrialized world are fundamentally flawed when the interest payments of many Third World countries are larger than the amounts they receive from us in aid. We may not ourselves strip their rain forests of virgin timber. But we certainly bear some responsibility for the conditions that compel those who do.[13]

McMillan outlined existing Canadian policies and initiatives, but the only new announcement was an offer to hold an International Conference on Environment and Sustainable Development in Canada in 1992, the twentieth anniversary of the Stockholm Conference (p. 13).

Within the sphere of Canadian ODA, this sort of rhetoric is now informing policy at a general level. While CIDA lagged behind many other major OECD donor agencies (including the American) in establishing procedures for environmental monitoring and assessment,[14] the government did announce in July 1986 the introduction of what was billed as a comprehensive environment and development strategy for CIDA. A further commitment to put a central priority upon ecological concerns was made in June 1987, and details were spelled out in the government's response to the Winegard report (Government of Canada 1987: 74-75), although some criticized the report itself for a failure to highlight environmental issues.[15] It is too soon to determine what impact the new policy will have upon practice, other than adding a new layer of bureaucratization. However, it may help to reinforce a movement away from larger capital projects towards the greater emphasis on human-resource development advocated by SCEAIT.

Beyond the specific question of how to ensure that Canadian aid is geared to sustainable development is the broader one raised by Ted Schrecker.[16] "If relatively rich Canada cannot get its internal act together, our pronouncements on environmental questions will neither have nor deserve much credibility with poor countries which face far harsher tradeoffs between short-term economic policy and resource management objectives." Obviously, the record to date in forest, soils and fisheries management leaves much to be desired, as does the performance in respect to non-renewable resources and energy. Schrecker is pessimistic about the future, in large measure because of the resource dependence of most of the country's regional economies.

> The result is to hasten ecological degradation and inappropriate resource uses: both individual resource users and governments which depend on resource-related revenues for continued solvency, and the superficial health of resource-based economic activities for continued electoral success, neglect long-term conservation measures which are associated with significant short-term (economic or political) costs.

There is another dimension to the issue of whether Canada will or can give leadership on environment and development. The Brundtland Commission stated: "Among the dangers facing the environment, the possibility of nuclear war, or military conflict on a lesser scale involving weapons of mass destruction, is undoubtedly the greatest" (WCED 1987: 290). It also claims that "four of the most urgent global environmental requirements—relating to tropical forests, water, desertification, and population—could be funded with the equivalent of less than one month's global military spending" (p. 303). This question of budgetary trade-offs was discussed in the special United Nations Conference on Disarmament and Development in August [1987]. Secretary of State for External

Affairs Joe Clark endorsed the goals of arms reduction and increased ODA, but rejected as simplistic a proposal for a new international agency that would channel military savings into extra development assistance. He noted that while Canada's military spending is four times greater than aid expenditures, twenty-five times more is spent worldwide on arms than on development: "If the rest of the world were operating under the same rules that Canada is operating under, we'd have significantly fewer problems."[17] Canada, though hardly "clean," is a relatively minor player in international arms trafficking. However, the Mulroney government is committed to increasing domestic military expenditures more rapidly than ODA, and official regulations governing Canadian participation in the arms trade, such as they are, have become more lax.

Conclusion: An Assessment of the Mulroney Government and North South Conflict

Although there remains a considerable agenda for reform in Canadian North-South policy, the Mulroney government has taken a more consistent interest in this domain than its Liberal predecessor. Pierre Trudeau tended to blow hot and cold on Third World issues, often leaving a series of undistinguished secretaries of state for external affairs to muddle through when his attention was focused elsewhere. Some of the credit for the change must go to Joe Clark, whose steady hand at the helm has been in marked contrast to that of many of his ministerial colleagues: remarkably, he also retreats to the background on occasions when Mulroney wants to appear on the global stage. Moreover, despite the gov-

ernment's preoccupation with the trade negotiations with the United States (or perhaps because the prime minister has
pre-empted this issue for himself), Canada's
current foreign posture under Clark had a
strong multilateral orientation, in which
Canada's leadership in North-South matters is a key component.

It was not clear that this would be the
case in 1985 when in its Green Paper,
Competitiveness and Security, the new government "tended to interpret Canada's economic and security interests ... in a
predominately bilateral, North American
framework."[18] However, a year later the official response to the Special Joint
Committee supported the strong multilat-
eralist position of the committee
(Government of Canada 1986: 5). In the
meantime, the appointment of Stephen
Lewis as Canada's ambassador to the
United Nations had given the country a
strong and principled voice there, and someone who would go on to play a key role in
international initiatives to deal with the
human and ecological disasters of Sub-
Saharan Africa. Although the response to
the Ethiopian famine in 1984 was, as elsewhere, "too little, too late," the government
eventually responded creatively both by
matching private generosity with government funds and by mounting a large-scale
relief operation coordinated by David
MacDonald. MacDonald, subsequently appointed ambassador to Ethiopia, has helped
to keep the continuing African crisis in the
consciousness of the public, and CIDA has
devoted considerable energy to Africa 2000,
a program aimed at improving long-term
developmental prospects on the continent.

While Canada has long been a key actor
within the Commonwealth and has become
the largest donor to Commonwealth technical assistance programs, the strong stand
that Clark and Mulroney have taken on

South Africa, especially in the context of
British Prime Minister Thatcher's firm opposition to further economic sanctions, has
enhanced Canada's stature among Third
World members. Canadian policy still falls
short of the complete sanctions and the
break in diplomatic relations sought by the
anti-apartheid movement, but it is no
longer correct to characterize it by the epi-
thet "commerce over conscience" that
Redekop used to describe the record of the
Trudeau era.[19] It is of course easier for a
Canadian government to take a stronger
stance now than it was a few years ago.
The domestic resistance within South Africa
is much stronger, solidarity movements in
Europe and North America have continued
to grow, and campaigns for corporate dis-
investment have met with considerable success. However, the government's position
is remarkably hard-edged considering the
strength of opposition to it among some
Tory backbenchers.

The current government's efforts have
been instrumental in creating a stronger
institutional basis for la francophonie, the
organization of French-speaking countries
that may become, like the Commonwealth,
an important organization for bridging interests and mediating conflicts between
North and South. Canadian credibility in
Third World eyes was further strengthened
during the summit of la francophonie in
Quebec City in September, just as it was
when the Commonwealth Heads of
Government meeting was hosted in
Vancouver in October. The government's
stance on South Africa was significant in
both cases, as were the debt forgiveness
measures and new promises for cooperation in distance education and other
spheres.

The policy on Central America has been
cautious and ambivalent in contrast with
that on South Africa and the associated com-

mitment to increasing support for the Front-Line States. To some extent the Canadian position reflects a polarization within public opinion that is as sharply divided as it is on Southern Africa, but that has many more shades of viewpoint between pro-Nicaragua and pro-U.S. (administration) positions. What has emerged has been fairly soft-spoken support for various efforts to facilitate a peace process (albeit with a more vigorous enunciation late in the year on behalf of the Arias peace plan). In this respect, the government has consistently but rather quietly opposed all foreign military intervention in the region, whether it be American, Cuban or Soviet, and has signalled its "neutrality" by sponsoring modest aid programs in Guatemala, Honduras, El Salvador and Nicaragua. None of this has been very adventurous when set alongside the political and developmental challenges within Central America. Nevertheless, in terms of political realities, the policy has been at odds with President Reagan's pet project at precisely the time when the major external agenda for the Canadian government has been the achievement of a free trade agreement with the United States.

In sum, the Mulroney government's record on North-South matters has been mixed. During the past three and one-half years, Canada has projected a forceful presence in the United Nations, while in the Commonwealth and la francophonie it has focused upon developmental priorities, human rights and creative conflict resolution. Policies on the debt crisis of the least developed countries and on the survival needs of sub-Saharan Africa have been

creditable. However, the response to other aspects of the debt problem has been inadequate. If the renewed efforts of the major Latin American debtors to develop a common strategy in the wake of the November 1987 Acapulco Commitment are successful, Canada and other OECD countries may soon regret not having taken a more comprehensive course of action. Also, as has been argued above, Canadian policies on trade and refugees leave much to be desired. There is considerable potential for playing a high-profile role in the Central American peace process, but its realization will likely depend as much upon domestic American politics as upon events within the region itself. Whether the rhetoric on the environment will have much significance in practice remains to be seen.

As far as the Winegard proposals for reform are concerned, the initial government response suggested that muddled objectives will continue to characterize the aid program. In trying to cater to all interests, the response blurred the sharp focus of the SCEAIT report, which judged all activities first and foremost by developmental criteria. However, some key elements of the report have become a new orthodoxy—the emphasis on human-resource development and human rights, the desirability for CIDA to decentralize, and the need for more-coherent planning and evaluation of ODA programs. The constituency concerned with international development is vocal and articulate, but it is small. Thus, action on some of the recommendations may be delayed unless Joe Clark sees them as important for the legacy of his stewardship.

NOTES

1. SCEAIT (House of Commons of Canada. Standing Committee on External Affairs and International Trade), *For Whose Benefit?* Ottawa: Queen's Printer, 1987.

2. *Canada's International Relations, Independence and Internationalism*, Ottawa: Supply and Services, 1986.

3. Government of Canada, *Canadian International Development Assistance: To Benefit a Better World*, Ottawa: Supply and Services, 1987.

4. David R. Morrison, "The Mulroney Government and the Third World," *Journal of Canadian Studies*, Vol. 19, No. 4, 1985, p. 7.

5. Gisele Côté-Harper and John Courtney, *International Cooperation for the Development of Human Rights and Democratic Institutions*. Report to the Right Honourable Joe Clark and the Honourable Monique Landry, Ottawa: External Affairs, 1987.

6. North-South Institute, *Review '85 Outlook '86: Multilateralism Still the First Option for Canada*, Ottawa, 1986.

7. Morrison, p. 10.

8. SSCFA (Senate of Canada, Standing Senate Committee on Foreign Affairs), *Canada, the International Financial Institutions and the Debt Problem of Developing Countries*, Ottawa: Supply and Services, 1987.

9. North-South Institute, *Review '86 Outlook '87: Canada's Foreign Policy: Testing Our Resolve*, Ottawa, 1987, p. 10.

10. Michael Schelew, "Misguided bills pose a threat to true refugees," *Globe and Mail*, August 13, 1987.

11. World Commission on Environment and Development (WCED), *Our Common Future*, New York: Oxford University Press, 1987.

12. *Globe and Mail*, "Lewis says UN must grab chance to take on environmental woes," October 19, 1987.

13. Environment Canada. "Canada's Perspective on Global Environment and Development," Notes for an address by the Honourable Thomas McMillan to the United Nations General Assembly, Ottawa news release, October 19, 1987, p. 4.

14. David Runnals, *Environment and Development: A Critical Stocktaking*, North-South Institute briefing paper, Ottawa, 1987.

15. Janine Ferretti, Letter to the Right Honourable Joe Clark on behalf of Pollution Probe, September 14, 1987.

16. Ted Schrecker, "Responding to Brundtland," Report prepared for the Canadian Environmental Advisory Council, Peterborough, September 1987, p. 8, 34.

17. *Ottawa Citizen*, "UN's swords-to-plowshares plan simplistic: Clark," August 25, 1987.

18. North-South Institute, *Review '86 Outlook '87: Canada's Foreign Policy: Testing Our Resolve*, Ottawa, 1987.

19. Clarence G. Redekop, "Commerce over Conscience: The Trudeau Government and South Africa, 1968-84." *Journal of Canadian Studies*, Vol. 19, No. 4, 1985, pp. 82-105.

SUGGESTED READINGS

Canada, *Canadian International Development Assistance Agency: To Benefit a Better World*, Ottawa, Supply and Services, 1987.

Gillies, David, "Commerce over Conscience? Export Promotion in Canada's Aid Programme," *International Journal*, Vol. 45, No. 4, Winter 1989-90, pp. 138-169.

House of Commons, Canada, Standing Committee on External Affairs and International Trade, *For Whose Benefit?*, Ottawa, Queen's Printer: Supply and Services Canada, 1987.

Morrison, David R., "The Mulroney Government and the Third World," *Journal of Canadian Studies*, Vol. 19, No. 4, pp. 3-15.

North-South Institute, *Review '85 Outlook '86: Multilateralism Still the First Option for Canada*, Ottawa, 1986.

North-South Institute, *Review '86 Outlook '87: Canada's Foreign Policy: Testing Our Resolve*, Ottawa, 1987.

Pratt Cranford, "Ethics and Foreign Policy: The Case of Canada's Development Assistance," *International Journal*, Vol. 43, No. 2, Spring 1988, pp. 264-301.

chapter 23

REDUCING ACID RAIN, 1980s

Don Munton and Geoffrey Castle

"Acid rain" was first brought publicly to Canada's foreign policy agenda in June 1977 by federal environment minister Romeo LeBlanc. It was, he said, "an environmental time bomb," indeed, "the worst environmental problem [Canada has] ever had to face." LeBlanc warned that there was no time "to wait for final research before beginning politiucal action"; what was needed were negotiations with the United States to "draw up new rules which could allow one nation to tell the other to turn off the pollution at the source."[1] These negotiations, he expected, would commence within "a few weeks." The minister was decidedly over-optimistic. It would be not weeks but years before serious negotiations began and almost a decade and a half before any new rules came into effect. And even then only some of the pollution would be halted.

The popular term "acid rain" has come to stand for a complex set of physical and chemical phenomena by which gases, especially sulfur and nitrogen oxides, are emitted as a result of combustion and other processes, transformed into acidic compounds while being transported through the atmosphere, and then deposited on land and water surfaces.[2] Given that other substances, particularly toxic chemicals, are also emitted and transported long distances through the atmosphere and pose signifi-

cant environmental hazards, the term "long-range transport of air pollution" might also be used.

Acid rain was not the first Canada-United States air quality dispute. Closely related air pollution problems had appeared on the bilateral agenda long before the 1970s. Principal among them was the now famous Trail Smelter case. American farmers and then the American government complained about the deleterious effects of "fumes" from the Cominco smelter at Trail, BC, near the Canada-US border in the 1920s.[3] The two governments asked the International Joint Commission (IJC) to investigate the problem. Eventually they arrived at a settlement; the company was required to pay compensation and to reduce drastically its emissions of sulfur dioxide (SO_2). The principal established by the IJC tribunal was that "no state has the right to use or permit the use of its territory in such a manner as to cause injury by fumes in or to the territory of another or the property or persons therein, when the case is of serious consequence and the injury is established by clear and convincing evidence."[4]

Unlike the Trail Smelter case, both the United States and Canada contribute to continental acid rain. LeBlanc recognized the shared responsibility for the problem in his 1977 speech:

Despite all cooperation that exists between Canada and the United States, I believe we have both been negligent in this area. What we have allowed to happen, innocently enough perhaps, is a massive international exchange of air pollutants, and neither party to this exchange is free of guilt.[5]

While the minister may have wanted not to be quoted personally in ascribing relative blame for the problem, newspaper reports of his speech noted that "it was estimated" that US sources in fact contributed five times as much transboundary air pollution as Canadian sources.[6]

Carter, Canada and Acid Rain

The initial dialogue on acid rain between Canada and the United States proceeded cautiously. The Carter White House, while much more concerned with environmental issues than the Reagan administration would prove to be, did not consider the problem of acid rain a matter of great national importance. A telling example of the Democratic administration's attitude towards controlling acid rain was the coal conversion plan announced in 1979, only months after committing to negotiate an air quality agreement with Canada.

In the interest of reducing America's dependence on foreign oil, the Carter administration proposed to Congress a $10 billion program to convert oil-fired power plants to run on domestic coal—a plan which would have as a side-effect a massive increase in SO_2 pollution. Canadian officials interpreted the step as being "totally out of keeping" with the mutual effort toward bilateral talks on acid rain; indeed it was a "deliberate action to make the problem worse."[7] Canadian officials flew to Washington "to raise hell." They received,

not unexpectedly, little more than a polite hearing. Those with whom they talked could do little. The Environmental Protection Agency (EPA) had not been consulted by the Department of Energy (DoE) officials during the proposal and then had been unsuccessful during an inter-agency battle over whether the plan would include stronger environmental safeguards. As one Agency official admitted, "The DoE won at the White House. EPA lost."[8]

The United States had, however, shown early signs of willingness to cooperate on transboundary acid rain, following LeBlanc's "time bomb" speech. Prompted by their scientists and by LeBlanc's concerns, Canada and the United States formed, in early 1978, what became known as the Bilateral Research Consultation Group on the Long-Range Transport of Air Pollutants (BRCG). The group was composed of researchers from both federal governments. Though Ottawa had greater hopes, Washington's intention was merely that it should coordinate research. Indeed the two governments could not even agree on the group's formal terms of reference until after it was established and underway.

A new pressure for actual negotiations was created in the fall of 1978 when the US Congress passed a resolution requiring the State Department to enter into talks with Canada toward an air quality agreement. The key figures behind this unexpected move were a small group of border state Congressmen whose constituents were concerned, not about acid rain, but about potential air pollutants from new developments in Canada. In particular, the concern was focused on two coal-fired power plants being planned for sites just across the international boundary in southern Saskatchewan (Poplar River project) and northwestern Ontario (Atikokan project).

Two bilateral meetings were subsequently held, but they did not progress beyond the exploratory discussion stage. The initiative soon died, without fanfare, in quiet diplomatic fashion.

The election in May 1979 of a Conservative government created another impetus. The new environment minister, John Fraser, a lawyer with a deep interest in pollution problems, seized the acid rain issue. His efforts were assisted in early July by the publication of reports from the IJC's Great Lake Water Quality Board and its Science Advisory Board, both of which warned of possible serious environmental and health effects from acidic pollution.[9] But the most the two governments could manage was an agreement a few weeks later on a general statement of principles on which a formal air quality agreement might be based.

The BRCG report was released in October 1979.[10] The Group concluded that "irreversible" damage was being done to lakes, rivers, and fish through acidification. The BRCG identified thermal generating plants in the US and non-ferrous smelters in Canada as the main sources of emissions.[11] It also confirmed what Canadian officials had been saying about the two countries' relative contributions; American emissions of sulfur dioxide were estimated to be five times greater than the Canadian ones and American emissions of nitrous oxides ten times greater. While both countries polluted their own and the other's territory, overall the US produced about 70-80% of transboundary air pollution.

Based on the new research, a consensus had formed in Ottawa around the objective of reducing by half the SO_2 and NO_x emissions in North America which lead to acid rain. Washington's various and competing centres of power, to say the least, showed little sign of a similar consensus.

On 13 November 1979, Canada and the US did join thirty-two European countries in signing the Convention on the Long Range Transport of Air Pollution (LRTAP), negotiated under the auspices of the Economic Commission for Europe (ECE). The convention was a modest result of long-standing but largely unsuccessful pressure by the Scandinavian countries on their European neighbours. The agreement called for, but did not require, the reduction of air pollution, and especially the reduction of long-range transboundary pollution associated with acid rain.[12]

John Fraser, representing Canada, and American EPA head Douglas Costle met at the signing ceremony in Geneva. They agreed at a private meeting to accelerate their mutual timetable toward negotiations for a bilateral agreement. At a further meeting in January 1980 they made progress concerning the form and content of such an agreement and on a working group mechanism, similar to the process which led to the Great Lakes Water Quality Agreements of 1972 and 1978. The earlier gap between the two sides' perceptions of the main problem to be negotiated had given way to a general recognition that near-border sources and long-range transport problems must both be covered. A gap remained on the nature of the commitments to be made on reductions. It was agreed to meet in two months time to pursue discussion of commitments and possible interim concrete measures.

Though much of the initial Canadian effort in seeking acid rain reductions was made through direct dialogue with the US executive branch, it was always evident that any eventual cuts in US emissions of SO_2 and NO_x would need enthusiastic support on Capitol Hill. In the latter stages of the Carter Presidency, Congress was not able or disposed to strengthen the Clean Air Act to deal with acid rain. In the preceding decade, the Act had proven an effective instrument for dealing with the problem of urban air pollution. During the 1970s the air quality in most US urban centres improved markedly, meeting tough ambient air quality guidelines laid down by the EPA. However, some of this improvement in local air quality was obtained through the construction of tall smokestacks, which served to exacerbate the problem of long-range transport of acid rain. Though the next logical step might have been to address these new pollution problems, by the end of the 1970s the political will to create new environmental laws in the US had largely evaporated. The pressures of slow economic growth and high inflation, which were partly responsible for the conservative shift apparent in the 1980 American elections, contributed to the pressure to *reduce* environmental regulations. As longtime advocate Senator Edmund Muskie observed in 1980, the "momentum behind (US) environmental laws...is fast running out of steam, I guess."[13] A Congressional aide agreed. "Don't expect any Congressional initiatives against acid rain in the near future," he said. "It's a good time to circle the wagons and protect what environmental legislation we have."[14]

The key underlying factor—which worked against both the enforcement of existing Clean Air legislation and against improving it—was the powerful political opposition mounted by industrial interests, including coal-mining companies, electric power utilities, and their affected labour unions. These interests were closely allied with a number of large coal-producing, coal-using states in the American mid-west. This area, particularly the Ohio River Valley, is responsible for the bulk of US sulfur dioxide emissions because of a large number of old, unregulated power plants burning lo-

cally-produced, high-sulfur coal. The economic interests of these "coal states" alone dictated opposition to sulfur dioxide emission controls. And, because their bedrock and soils are well "buffered" against acidification, they themselves suffer little from acid rain. In contrast, the major US recipients of acid rain, especially New York and the New England states, have low bicarbonate soils with little or no buffering capability. (Many areas of Ontario, Quebec and the Atlantic provinces are in the same predicament.) The political problem for American federal authorities vis-à-vis domestic polluters, therefore, as well as the political problem for Canada vis-à-vis the US, is thus compounded because the major source areas are not the major recipient areas. The former therefore stand to pay a great deal for, and benefit little from, reductions in their own emissions. The position of former Ohio governor Rhodes, for example, was summed up his statement that "You're talking about some fish in the northeast, while in Ohio we've got 22,000 unemployed coal miners."[15]

The stakes for the power companies were also high. Estimates of the overall cost of fitting "scrubbers" and similar control equipment on major US sources, sufficient to effect a 50 percent cut in SO_2 emissions, ranged from one to two billion dollars per year to tens of billions annually.

The alliance of coal-burning industry and midwest politicians was much in evidence at Congressional hearings held during the spring of 1980 to review the Carter oil-coal conversion bill, as were the regional differences within the United States. Representatives from the coal-burning, electric power industry systematically questioned the adequacy and validity of existing scientific studies on acid rain. Many speakers insisted acid rain was not a serious problem. "It would be premature," one cautioned, "to base control action ... on speculation."[16] The whole issue, said an Ohio spokesman, had been created by "no-growth environmental extremists." "Blaming Ohio for acid rain" he suggested, "is like blaming Florida for hurricanes."[17]

The Memorandum of Intent

In 1980, the pursuit of a Canada-US air pollution accord gathered pace, in part due to a fear that the forces opposing controls were about to gain the upper hand. Costle's speech to a June conference of American pollution-control professionals—entitled "A Law in Trouble"—was a frank warning that the existing US Clean Air Act was in danger of being "substantially gutted." He called on their help to defeat the expected challenge by industry, anti-environmental interests, and many newly formed conservative political action groups when the Act came up for review by Congress in 1981.

Following the conference, Costle and Roberts met over dinner and the EPA head was apparently able to convince his Canadian counterpart that his agency and the Carter White House were, in fact, seriously committed to combatting the problem of acid rain. The meeting, following on the heels of discussions between officials a few days earlier, put the finishing touches on a procedural breakthrough. In August 1980 the two countries signed a joint "Memorandum of Intent" (MOI) committing themselves to negotiate an acid rain agreement, and to begin within one year.

The MOI outlined the major features of the prospective accord and committed both governments, albeit only rhetorically, to pursue vigorous enforcement actions under existing statutes. It also established five technical-level working groups to lay the groundwork for the start of negotiations, a process patterned after the suc-

cessful negotiations on the Great Lakes Water Quality Agreement almost a decade earlier. But even as the document was being signed, in the midst of the 1980 presidential election campaign, the US commitment was being put in doubt. "This all goes to hell," a senior American official noted quietly, "if Ronald Reagan gets in."[18]

The Carter people and Canadian officials had agreed that, regardless of the result of the US presidential election in November, a progress report from the working groups would be made public in early January. The US administration representatives had further indicated that a Reagan victory would prompt a stronger commitment from them in that statement. The purpose would be to try to bind the incoming anti-environment Republican administration as much as possible to negotiating an eventual agreement.

In the transition period after Carter's electoral defeat, his EPA officials sought other ways to force the incoming administration into taking some action on acid rain. In cooperation with the Canadian government, a last-gasp effort was mounted by invoking a little-used section of the US Clean Air Act. The international protection clause, section 115 of the 1977 Act, authorized the EPA Administrator to order state governments to revise their air quality plans if air pollution from the United States "may reasonably be anticipatd to endanger public health or welfare in another country." There were only two requirements: first, that this danger be determined by "a duly constituted international body" and, second, that the injured country offers reciprocal legislative treatment to the United States. To this end, the Canadian Parliament, on December 16, 1980, passed an amendment to the Canadian Clean Air Act the explicit intention of which was to satisfy the reciprocity requirement of section 115 of the

US Act. Following the Canadian legislative action, and in the final week of the Carter presidency, EPA Administrator Costle wrote to Secretary of State Edmund Muskie, indicating that the necessary conditions for invoking section 115 had been established by the 1979 IJC report in the case of transboundary acid rain.

It was a game try. Costle's "finding" served as the basis for a series of legal proceedings over the ensuing years. Several eastern US states, as well as the province of Ontario, claimed that the Reagan EPA was bound by Costle's decision to order reductions in emissions causing environmental harm to Canada. In 1986, however, the DC Circuit Court ruled that Costle's hasty finding had been arrived at without following necessary administrative procedures, and was thus void.[19] Even if the court had upheld the Costle finding, however, the responsibility for implementing pollution abatement to protect the "welfare" of Canadians would still have been that of Reagan's political appointees at EPA—not a promising scenario for action, to say the least. Emissions reductions through the US courts, thus, proved to be a dead end.

Reagan, Canada and Acid Rain

The impact of the Reagan White House on relations with its northern neighbour was soon felt. Its list of Canada-US "irritants," beginning with the Foreign Investment Review Agency and the National Energy Program, was as long as, if not longer than, that of the Nixon administration in 1971.[20] Conspicuously missing from the new administration priorities list was controlling acid rain. Indeed, the Reagan administration's crusade to reconstruct the American economy and unshackle American indus-

try from governmental interference meant that environmental *deregulation* was the priority. What followed from the bold and uncompromising ideological premises was a quiet campaign to cripple the EPA and effectively undermine long-standing federal environmental policies and regulations—especially regarding air pollution. Budget cuts made during 1981-1982, and those of subsequent years, significantly reduced the EPA's programme and research funding.[21]

To be sure, the changes wrought were not solely the work of what Charlie Farquarson, the creation of Canadian humourist Don Harron, once referred to as the "encumbrance" in the White House. Reagan was no more directly involved in this aspect of his administration than he was in most others; indeed he seems to have been less involved. The changes were largely the work of the appointees put in charge of US environmental policy—a crop of pro-industry figures, aggressive in their pursuit of deregulation and government withdrawal from pollution control and research. Although the Reagan appointees were quickly attacked by leading US conservation and environmental organizations, they succeeded in the first few years of the administration to weaken substantially both American pollution policies and the EPA itself. In this crusade they were not lacking powerful allies.

Efforts in Congress by senators, such as George Mitchell of Maine, to reduce acid rain were strenuously resisted by the administration and by affected interests, especially the coal and utility companies. A number of proposed congressional amendments to the Clean Air Act mandating emission cuts of around ten million metric tons were dismissed by administration spokespersons as premature at best. As it was, the White House did not feel much public pressure for action. Public awareness in the United States lagged well behind that of Canadians, let alone that of scientists.[22]

Despite administration rhetoric about desiring to cooperate with Canada, little cooperation emerged. First, American representatives delayed and frustrated the process of the bilateral working groups established by the 1980 Memorandum of Intent. US scientists on the groups who were regarded by Mr. Reagan's appointees as "untrustworthy," for example, were replaced or ordered not to attend scheduled group meetings. Then, when the research reports looked a mite too definitive, senior Reagan officials set about re-writing the scientists' conclusions. The final BRCG report bore the scars.[23] Even the most optimistic of Canadian officials was coming inescapably to agree with the aide to a Republican senator who said: "The administration's real position is to do nothing about acid rain."[24]

Never having gotten out of low gear, the bilateral negotiating process ground nearly to a halt in mid-1982. A few negotiation sessions were subsequently held but there was no progress. The most the Americans were willing to offer was an agreement on further cooperative research and some experimental liming of particularly damaged lakes. There were to be no new controls on American emissions. It was not enough for the Canadians. They continued to insist on reductions in the range of 50 percent.

Following a disultory negotiation session in June 1982, Canada's environment minister, John Roberts, went public and bluntly accused the United States of "stalling." Given what he called the Americans' "stuck in the mud stance," Roberts questioned "whether the talks are serving any useful purpose" and hinted Canada might even withdraw from the bilateral process.[25] Such public criticism and

threats were almost unprecedented in Canadian-American negotiations.

Canada's political tactics had already begun to change somewhat, and the process was accelerated by the stalemate in the official diplomatic negotiations. Good science and persistent diplomacy were clearly not enough. The battle was going to be won or lost in the political arena. Breaking with the longstanding tradition of conducting "quiet diplomacy," officials in Ottawa and at the Canadian embassy on Washington's Massachusetts Avenue began to carry their arguments more often and more directly to the US Congress, to US opinion leaders, and to the American public—much to the chagrin of some government officials south of the border. The counselor for environmental affairs at the embassy and other Canadian officials were made available to any US group wanting a speaker, and to some who did not know they wanted one. Ottawa broke precedent and supplied Canadian government scientists to testify at congressional hearings on the Clean Air Act. They arranged a series of tours to Canada for politicians and journalists to see first-hand the damage caused by acid rain.[26] The embassy sponsored lunches for small groups of senators and congressmen. And Canadian customs officers handed out "stop acid rain" brochures to American tourists driving into Canada.

Ottawa was not alone in its public relations efforts. The Canadian Coalition on Acid Rain, a private organization with substantial funding from Canadian governments, was also active in Canada and the US during the 1980s. The Coalition's primary objectives were to provide public information and assistance to the staffs of sympathetic or strategic members of Congress. (Senator George Mitchell of Maine was one of the Coalition's closest contacts in Washington.) The CCAR also did some advertising and brought their message to a variety of American audiences, often working the "fish and gun show" circuit. Recognizing the rather modest levels of concern about Canada in the United States, the Coalition's public emphasis in the US was always on the danger of acid rain to Americans and the American environment.[27]

In addition to its public diplomacy efforts, Ottawa pursued two other strategies, one domestic and the other international. Both were designed in part to strengthen Canada's diplomatic hand. Domestically, federal environment officials slowly patched together an agreement with the seven eastern provinces to reduce Canadian emissions by half. Although some provincial governments had SO_2 control programs, no comprehensive national abatement policy on acid rain precursors existed in Canada before 1985. While the federal government had earlier promulgated guidelines for SO_2, the provinces were under no obligation to meet these standards. In February, 1984, Liberal Environment Minister, Charles Caccia, announced the federal government's commitment to a 50 percent reduction in SO_2 emissions from the 1980 levels. In 1985, a federal-provincial emissions reductions agreement was signed, involving all provinces from Manitoba eastward. The agreement specified a 50 percent cut in SO_2 as its target, and required all provinces to commit to the more stringent US NO_x emission standards on vehicles. The vehicle emission cuts were to enter into force by the 1987 model year, while the SO_2 reduction was to be completed by 1994.[28]

The provinces came on-side, some more reluctantly than others. The least keen were the provinces of Nova Scotia and New Brunswick, both heavily dependent on coal-generated electricity. In October 1987, however, New Brunswick Premier Hatfield's

signature was obtained, just days before handing over power to the incoming Liberals. The last provincial government to sign on—that of coal-producing and coal-burning Nova Scotia—finally did so, reluctantly, in February 1988.

Internationally, the "feds" were instrumental in forming, at a major meeting in Ottawa in early 1984, what became known as the "30% club"—a group of developed states committed to reducing SO_2 emissions within their own territories by at least 30 percent. The club, needless to say, did not include the United States, although the embarrassed Americans insisted they be invited to the meeting as observers.

The Canadian federal election of September 1984, as well as sounding the death-knell for the Foreign Investment Review Agency and the National Energy Policy, brought about a decline in Ottawa's bilateral "public diplomacy" campaign on acid rain. All were judged as inconsistent with new political realities as well as being out of keeping with Prime Minister Brian Mulroney's vision of a new cooperative era in Canadian-American relations. In the pursuit of "super relations" with the United States, the negative rhetoric of the Trudeau period had to give way.

The central symbol of this new era was the series of annual presidential-prime ministerial get-togethers that began with the "Shamrock Summit" of February 1985. Although the Prime Minister had dutifully identified acid rain as a top Canadian concern, it was not that for the United States, and certainly not a concern at all for the Reagan administration. Destined to make no breakthroughs on this issue, the leaders' image-makers and political salvage teams came up with a face-saving action—the appointment of two "special envoys" to investigate the problem for a year and to report back at the next meeting. Acid rain action went on hold, a captive of the summitry schedule.

The envoys, Bill Davis, former premier of Ontario, and Drew Lewis, former transportation secretary in Ronald Reagan's cabinet, conscientiously took on their task and brought their report as bidden to the following year's summit in Washington. They concluded that acid rain was, indeed, a real problem, not a myth, but did not recommend immediate emission reductions. Instead they proposed a major and long-term $5 billion cooperative investment program by industry and government into research, development and demonstration of "clean coal" technologies, methods by which coal could be burned with fewer emissions.[29] Both the Prime Minister and the President accepted the report.

"Clean coal," however, turned out to be more promise than prospect, let alone imminent reality. Despite the summit promises, it was only after forceful Canadian representations during a visit by Vice-President George Bush to Ottawa the following year that the White House finally sought funding for the program. The third annual Reagan-Mulroney summit of April 1987 added only a meaningless Ronald Reagan pledge that he "agreed *to consider* the Prime Minister's proposal for a bilateral accord on acid rain" (italics added). After three face-to-face meetings, it was not much.

It was not even enough to get the formal talks going again in any productive fashion. The next month a team of Canadian officials arrived in Washington for a one-day meeting with American counterparts—the first such formal meeting during the tenure of the Mulroney government. There, and again at two follow-up meetings in the next months, it became evident that the fundamental opposition of the administration to any sort of new legislated emission reductions remained unshaken.

Ironically, the Reagan administration moved extremely quickly in late 1986 and early 1987 to conclude an international air quality agreement with Mexico. Why the contrast? The fundamental difference between the Canada-US and Mexico-US cases is that in the latter it is the United States who is the major recipient of transboundary pollution. The major air pollution problem along the Mexican-American border is a new, very large, Mexican smelter: it is thus a problem of long-range transport of air pollution *into* the United States. And it is thus a problem which the Reagan administration, not surprisingly, found little research was needed and on which action was taken immediately.[30]

The duplicity of the Reagan administration over acid rain may have reached its height in the series of events surrounding the release of the long awaited National Acid Precipitation Assessment Program (NAPAP) interim report of 1987. Comprising over 800 pages, ten substantive chapters, and four volumes, the first of which was an Executive Summary largely written by the White House-appointed NAPAP director, Dr. J. Lawrence Kulp, the report was accompanied by an administration-prepared press release. In general, the Summary and the press release left the impression that the damage due to acidic deposition is largely unproven, slight and not widespread where proven, and probably not getting worse. Release of the Interim Assessment was greeted with what one industry journal termed "a crescendo of criticism."[31] Canadian environment minister, Tom McMillan reacted quickly, calling a press conference the day after the NAPAP assessment was released, and branded it "voodoo science."

What had been documented in volumes of credible scientific research, what had been addressed in a 1980 Memorandum of

Intent, and what a president, a prime minister, their environment ministers and two special envoys had collectively declared at a 1986 summit meeting to be an important transboundary environmental concern, was clearly not going to broach the walls of the Reagan White House. "Canada," one American official observed, "got snookered again."[32]

Bush, Canada and the Agreement

The American presidential election of November 1988 was remarkable in a number of respects, perhaps particularly for its vicious negative advertising. It was also remarkable in the extent to which the heir of the Reagan legacy, George Bush, sought to outdo his Democratic opponent, Michael Dukakis, in promises to clean up America's pollution. A bold initiative this was not; it was clear to all that in late 1988 the public was aroused. The country's mounting environmental ills were squarely and firmly back on the national political agenda. The victorious Bush then symbolically broke with the eight years of Reaganism in appointing a well-known environmentalist as administrator of the EPA, and by committing his administration to formulating a new Clean Air Act, one with significant ammendments aimed at reducing sulfur dioxide emissions that produce acid rain. The new administration's proposals were forwarded to Congress in July 1989.

Another important political development was the replacement as Senate majority leader of Senator Robert Byrd of coal-dependent West Virginia, an arch opponent of acid rain controls, with George Mitchell of Maine, a strong proponent of such controls. After a careful weighing of the balance of forces, Mitchell and his supporters made a pact with the White House on a sweeping set of improvements to the Act with which both sides could live, and proceeded through the early months of 1990 to gain Senate approval for them. Included in the set were requirements to reduce the precursors of acid rain by 10 million tons or approximately 50 percent from 1980 levels—a figure which had become accepted by most of the players on all sides of this issue as well as by Canada. Major electrical generating plants in the midwest states were specifically targeted for reductions. The costs of the war on acid rain, which had once appeared so formidable, were actually dwarfed by other costs to clean up America's air. In May 1990 the House of Representatives passed a similar bill, and in the fall both the Senate and House approved a common version of the much strengthened Clean Air Act. The US administration now had, at last, the necessary statutory basis for dealing with the acid rain problem and thus for proceeding to negotiate the kind of international agreement which Canada had long sought.

Bilateral consultations between Washington and Ottawa were actually initiated during the summer months of 1989, even before the amendments were considered by Congress. Formal negotiations commenced in August 1990. Congress finalized it and did not take long. Nor did they add much to what was already in place. Given that both countries had initiated domestic emission control policies, there were few substantive issues to discuss. The major hurdles were a Canadian demand that the agreement commit each side to dealing with transboundary pollution (not just to reducing emissions domestically) and an American demand that Canada make commitments to a national SO_2 "cap" on emissions and strengthened standards on other pollutants. The text of the air quality agree-

ment was agreed to and initialed by officials before the end of the year. The long-
awaited accord then waited a little longer,
until the hostilities of the Gulf war had
ended, but was finally signed by the Prime
Minister and the President during a short
visit by Bush to Ottawa in March 1991.

The first ever Canada-US Air Quality
Agreement features SO_2 and NO_x emission
reduction commitments by both sides, establishes a research and monitoring network, and creates a bilateral coordinating
group. It also provides a framework within
which other, emerging transboundary air
pollution problems might be addressed. In
contrast to the Great Lakes Water Quality
Agreement, after which it was modeled,
however, the new accord does not mandate
the International Joint Commission to act
as a watch-dog over the implementation
process. The governments themselves will
decide whether or not they are meeting
their commitments.

Conclusion

Two questions stand out. First, how can we
explain the achievement of this landmark
accord? And second: why did it take so long?
Let us take these questions in reverse
order.

The reasons for the long delay, of
course, have to do with the many constraints that were to be found—especially in
the United States—for a long time, the lack
of public awareness, the continuing and
strenuous resistance of the affected industries, the lack of interst in the Reagan
White House, and so on. Perhaps the dominant and fundamental factor underlying
many of the obvious constraints has to do
with the essential nature of the problem;
in a phrase it has to do with who pollutes
whom, who pays what, and who benefits.
The nature of the transboundary problem of

acid rain is that most of the pollution orig-
inates in the US and that Canada is more
affected by emissions from the US than the
US is affected by emissions from Canada.
And thus, the bulk of the clean-up costs
will be American while much of the benefit
from that clean-up will go to Canada. The
situation can therefore be characterized as
one of "environmental dependence" for
Canada but not for the US.[33] In the same
sense as a country can be economically dependent, the quality of its environment can
depend more on external factors than domestic ones. With respect to acid rain, as
with respect to pollution of the Great Lakes,
this is the Canadian dilemma. Two simple
examples will underscore this point.

The first example is the Reagan administration's very active pursuit of an air
quality deal with Mexico, while at the same
time referring the Canadian complaints
about acid rain to an interminable period
of study. The second example is that of the
Trail Smelter case of the 1920s and 1930s.
Here again the problem was one of pollution originating outside the US affecting
those within. And in this case, it was the
American government waging a determined
battle and the Canadian government resisting for years before agreeing both to pay
compensation and to reduce the emissions.[34] In short, environmental dependence
leads to a country being the demander in
an international issue, and the greater the
dependence the fewer the bargaining chips
it has to play and the longer the issue will
likely take to be resolved. In this way, acid
rain is not unique but rather characteristic
of environmental relations between these
two neighbours.

Among the factors which led to this
landmark agreement, Canadian diplomatic
influence was not one of the more important, for the reasons outlined above. The
emergence of the issue and its accession to

that of a priority problem in each country had much to do, first of all, with the development of a consensus among scientists on the nature and seriousness of the problem and its solution. The driving force of scientific evidence was crucial. The subsequent emergence of a public consensus flowed from this basis of scientific evidence, although it was delayed much longer in the US than in Canada due to the strength of the opposition forces. But with substantial efforts by environmental groups such a consensus did emerge eventually. The relatively non-controversial inclusion of acid rain provisions in the 1990 Clean Air Act are evidence of the extent of that consensus. The support, and indeed the push, that the Bush administration gave to this legislation cannot be denied, but ought not to be exaggerated. The emergence of American acid rain reductions in 1990 is less a testament to the impetus provided by the Bush administration than to the roadblocks imposed by its predecessor. Acid rain had clearly, and finally, made it to the American domestic policy agenda. The uncertainties of policy implementation, as well as the history of other Canada-US environmental issues, suggest it is likely to remain there and on the bilateral agenda for some time.

NOTES

1. Ross Howard, "Industrial Pollutants 'Time Bomb' LeBlanc Warns," *Toronto Star*, 21 June 1977, p. B2.

2. For a non-technical introduction to the science of acid rain, see G. E. Likens and F. H. Bormann, "Acid Rain," *Scientific American*, Vol. 241, No. 4, 1979, pp. 43-51.

3. D. H. Dinwoodie, "The Politics of International Pollution Control: The Trail Smelter Case" *International Journal*, Vol. XXVII, No. 2, 1972, pp. 219-35.

4. Decision Reported on 11 March 1941 to the Government of the United States of America and to the Government of the Dominion of Canada by the Trail Smelter Arbitral Tribunal. The Trail case had involved on the part of the IJC an earlier report on findings (28 February 1931) and then an initial tribunal decision (16 April 1938). On the Commission itself, see Robert Spencer, John Kirton and Kim Richard Nossal, *The International Joint Commission, Seventy Years On*, Centre for International Studies, University of Toronto, 1981, and especially the chapter by William Willoughby,"Expectations and Experience," pp. 24-32.

5. Howard, "Industrial Pollutants," p. B2. For a useful discussion of air pollution control technology and of the various available techniques for reducing emissions, see R.A. Barnes, "The Long Range Transport of Air Pollution: A Review of the European Experience," *Journal of the Air Pollution Control Association*, 29, 1979, pp. 1219-35.

6. While the above noted 21 June article (note 1) did not cite LeBlanc personally as having provided this estimate of relative contributions, a 23 October 1977 article in the same newspaper does cite him.

7. Confidential interview, Ottawa, June 12, 1980.

8. EPA official Lowell Smith was quoted in Harrowsmith Staff Report, "The Acid Earth," *Harrowsmith*, 4 (27), April 1980, pp. 32-41, 93.

9. International Joint Commission, Great Lakes Water Quality Board, *Seventh Annual Report*, July 1979, Windsor, Ontario; and International Joint Commission, Great Lakes Science Advisory Board, *Annual Report*, July 1979, Windsor, Ontario.

10. Canada-United States Research Consultation Group on the Long-Range Transport of Air Pollutants, "The LRTAP Problem in North America: A Preliminary Overview," Ottawa and Washington, 1979.

11. The largest single point source of sulfur dioxide in North America is the "superstack" at the Inco smelter outside of Sudbury. On the other hand, the combined emissions of the power plants and other industries in a number of midwest US urban centres, including St. Louis, Cincinatti, and Pittsburgh, are each greater than Inco's.

12. Gregory Wetstone, "Air Pollution Control Laws in North America and the Problem of Acid Rain and Snow," *Environmental Law Reporter*, 10, 1980, pp. 50001-20.

13. United States, Senate, Committee on Environment and Public Works, Subcomittee on Environmental Pollution, *Hearings on Environment Effects of the Increased Use of Coal*, Ninety-Sixth Congress, Second Session (Washington: US Government Printing Office, March 19 and April 21 and 24, 1980), Serial No. 96-H45, p. 187.

14. *Toronto Star*, 16 October 1979.

15. Cited in *Globe and Mail*, 7 May 1981.

16. William H. Megonell, "Atmospheric Sulphur Dioxide in the United States: Can the Standards be Justified or Afforded?" *Journal of Air Pollution Control Association*, 25, 1975, pp. 9-15.

17. *Globe and Mail*, 7 May 1981.

18. *Globe and Mail*, August 1980, p. 1.

19. See John L. Sullivan, "Beyond the Bargaining Table: Canada's Use of Section 115 of the US Clean Air Act to Prevent Acid Rain" *Cornell International Law Journal*, Vol. 16, No. 1, Winter 1983; D. R. Wooley, "Acid Rain, Canadian Litigation Options in US Court and Agency Proceedings" *University of Toledo Law Review*, Vol. 17, Fall 1985; and Carol Garland, "Acid Rain over the United States and Canada" The DC Circuit fails to Provide Shelter under Section 115 of the US Clean Air Act while State action Provides a Temporary Umbrella," *Boston College Environmental Affairs Law Review*, Vol. 16, No. 1, 1988.

20. On US Complaints in 1971 about the policies of its economic allies and on the Foreign Investment Review Agency, see Chapter 15, "Reducing Vulnerability: the Third Option" in this volume. On the National Energy Program, see Chapter 19.

21. The effects were felt in other departments as well; the Office of Environmental Quality in the Department of Agriculture, which was directly involved in the Canada-U.S. scientific work on acid rain, was entirely eliminated.

22. Acid rain gained the dubious distinction of being rated, by a panel of media jurors, as one of the ten "best censored" stories in the US (cited in Elizabeth C. Agle, "Why Acid Rain Must be a Top Environmental Priority for the 97th Congress," *Environmental Forum*, Vol. 2, No. 2, pp. 12-15). As a result, in contrast to the 60-80 percent or more of Canadians who were aware of acid rain in the early 1980s, the corresponding figures for the United States were 10-25 percent at best (*Globe and Mail*, 30 September 1981). Even for those Americans in the most seriously affected areas, awareness came relatively late.

23. Ernest J. Yanarella and Randal H. Ihara, *The Acid Rain Debate: Scientific, Economic and Political Dimensions*, Westview Press: Boulder, Colorado, 1985, p. 40.

24. *Cleveland Plain Dealer*, 6 February 1982.

25. James Rusk, "US blamed as talks on acid rain stalled," *Globe and Mail*, 16 June 1982, p. 1.

26. When told US acid rain was seriously damaging Canadian lakes, an Ohio state legislator on one of the trips sponsored by the Canadian government responded unambiguously: "I don't believe you," he said. During a similar trip an American reporter was almost as sceptical; it would have been more impressive, he suggested, "if they had taken a bunch of fish and stuck them in a lake and brought them up dead" (*Globe and Mail*, 30 September 1981). Nor was the public relations effort received well by all who observed the new tactics. Administration officials classified a National Film Board on acid rain as "foreign propaganda," sought to pressure Ottawa into cancelling the testimony of its scientists at the congressional hearings, and were to "complain bitterly" about the private lunches.

27. "One of the first things we discovered when we started going down there," said Executive Director Michael Perley, "was that interest in Canada stops at the border." (Interview with M. Perley, March 15, 1990).

28. See Susan Milburn-Hopwood, "The Role of Science in Environmental Policy-Making: A Case Study of the Canadian Acid Rain Policy" Unpublished MA Thesis, University of Toronto, September, 1989.

29. Serious analyses of the "clean coal" option for reducing acid rain found that its promise was, essentially, too little, too late. See, for example, Philip Jessup, "Strategies for Reducing the Cost of Acid Rain Controls: Electricity Demand-side Management and Clean Coal Technologies," Environmental and Energy Study Institute, Washington, 1988.

30. The "Agreement of Cooperation between the United States of America and the United Mexican States Regarding Transboundary Air Pollution Caused by Copper Smelters on their Common Border," was negotiated as a result of American concern over a new copper smelter in Nacozari, just south of the Rio Grande. The document is carefully worded so as not to contradict US government positions on the "uncertainties" of long-range transport, and instead focuses on environmental problems "in the border area."

31. Lois Ember, "Acid precipitation program head resigns" *Chemical and Engineering News*, October 12, 1987. p. 15.

32. Personal interview, Washington, D.C., October 14, 1987.

33. Don Munton, "Dependence and Interdependence in Transboundary Environmental Relations" *International Journal*, 36 (1), 1980-81, 139-184.

34. The main difference between the processes which resolved the Trail Smelter case and that of the problem of transboundary acid rain is that the Trail settlement was brought about largely as a result of external pressure from the injured party. (Washington suggested to Ottawa the lack of a settlement would result in trade reprisals.) In the case of acid rain, significant action was not taken by the US until acid rain had become a highly important domestic issue, one which would almost certainly have received Congress's attention regardles of Canadian complaints.

SUGGESTED READINGS

Howard, Ross and Michael Perley, *Acid Rain: The North American Forecast*, Toronto: Anansi, 1980.

Likens, G.E., F. H. Bormann and N.M. Johnson, "Acid Rain," *Environment*, Vol. 14, No. 1, 1972, pp. 33-39.

Likens, G.E. and F. H. Bormann, "Acid Rain: A Serious Regional Environmental Problem," *Science*, Vol. 184, 1974, pp. 1176-79.

Likens, G.E., Richard F. Wright, James Galloway and Thomas J. Butler, "Acid Rain," *Scientific American*, Vol. 241, No. 4, 1979, pp. 43-51.

Munton, Don, "Dependence and Interdependence in Transboundary Environmental Relations," *International Journal*, 36(1), 1980-81, p. 139-184.

Schmandt, Jurgen and Hillilard Roderick (eds.), *Acid Rain and Friendly Neighbours: The Policy Dispute between Canada and the United States*, Durham: Duke University Press, 1985.

Weller, Phil and the Waterloo Public Interest Research Group, *Acid Rain: The Silent Crisis*, Kitchener, Ontario: Between the Lines, 1980.

Wetstone, Gregory and Armin Rosencranz, *Acid Rain in Europe and North America*, Washington, D.C., Environmental Law Institute, 1983.

c h a p t e r 24

LIBERATING KUWAIT: CANADA AND THE PERSIAN GULF WAR, 1990-91

John Kirton

In the summer of 1990, for the first time in forty years, Canada went to war. On August 10 the Progressive Conservative government of Prime Minister Brian Mulroney announced the deployment of three warships to the Persian Gulf, as part of a multinational force assembled in response to Iraq's August 2 invasion of Kuwait. On September 14 Ottawa despatched 18 CF-18 fighters to provide air cover for these vessels. It subsequently filled out its force with a command, communications and security unit in late October, and a KC-135 aerial tanker and six additional CF-18s on January 11, 1991.

Four days later these forces went into combat. Under the authority of a United Nations Security Council resolution whose passage Canada had helped secure on November 29, Canada refuelled American aircraft attacking Iraq on January 16, authorized its CF-18's to conduct sweep and escort missions over Iraq, and sent a mobile field hospital to the Gulf. On February 20, three days before the start of the coalition land offensive to liberate Kuwait, Canada's planes were authorized to conduct ground attacks on Iraqi forces. With the cessation of hostilities on February 27, Canada's forces emerged victoriously, with no lives and equipment lost.

For a country which had sent 21,000 troops and suffered 300 combat deaths in the four-year-long Korean War forty years earlier, this deployment of 3,700 troops in an eight-month operation was a relatively small affair. Moreover, in sharp contrast to the Korean venture, no Canadian land combat forces were ever sent to the Gulf. And Canada's actual waging of war—by conducting offensive attack missions—involved only a week's worth of effort, and came only after verbal condemnation, economic embargo, diplomatic mediation, and the threat of force had been tried and seen to fail.

Yet despite the small, limited and incremental nature of Canada's commitment, Ottawa had decided at an early stage in the crisis that if necessary, it would use force. And its ability to deliver on its determination, in the face of international uncertainty and domestic division, ultimately placed it, along with only the United States, Britain, France and Italy, in a very exclusive club of the world's principal powers.

Among the significant countries that contributed to the coalition against Saddam Hussein, Canada's position was quite distinct. Unlike its co-combatants, the United States, Britain, and France, Canada was not a permanent member of the United Nations Security Council nor a country that sent its forces outside the NATO area for tasks other than peacekeeping and minor military training. Unlike the Arab coali-

This is an original article.

tion combatants, Canada did not feel directly threatened by Iraq, and had few material interests in the Gulf region. Yet unlike major industrial democracies such as Japan and Germany, and internationally-minded middlepowers from around the world, Canada did more than merely send money and naval forces. When the time came, Canada, along with Italy, fought in the air, in offensive attack roles, as well. For a peaceable kingdom, proud to be the world's premier peacekeeper and practitioner of mediatory diplomacy and international law, going to war was an unfamiliar, unexpected, and unwanted task.

Why did Canada go to war to liberate Kuwait? A close look at the causes of Canada's critical initial decisions to deploy military forces, and a more general review of the subsequent decisions to employ them suggest that the cause of Canada's combat involvement in the Gulf does not lie primarily in Washington. For while Canada would certainly not have fought without the United States, if only America and a handful of its small associates had gone to war, Canada would have probably, as in Vietnam three decades earlier, sat the conflict out. While Prime Minister Mulroney was, along with British Prime Minister Margaret Thatcher, one of President Bush's closest confidants throughout the war, Canadian advice was given to the President, and carefully weighed by him, before rather than after the critical US decisions were taken. Moreover, Canadians were able to resist US requests, notably for ground forces, that Canada was unwilling to provide.

Nor does the cause of Canada's combat role lie in New York, at the United Nations. Despite the emphasis in the few existing accounts of Canada's participation in the war, Canada's credentials as a middlepower

devotee of United Nations-centred multilateralism were of secondary importance. Indeed, the United Nations' seal of approval for the coalition's use of force was not even a necessary condition for Canada's combat role. Although the quest for UN approval shaped Ottawa's approach within the coalition and, when secured, made its task of securing support at home much easier, both Prime Minister Mulroney and Secretary of State for External Affairs Joe Clark made it clear that Canada would use force even without an authorizing United Nations Security Council resolution.[1]

Finally the key causes do not lie in the demands of any bellicose domestic consensus. Canada's political parties, interest groups, media, and public opinion were badly divided on the correct course to follow at most critical junctures in the crisis. They were united only in never demanding that the government use more force than it had already decided, at each stage, to deploy.

The central cause of Canada's combat commitment lies instead in the steady succession of atrocities perpetrated by Saddam Hussein, as they impacted a Canadian government conscious of its role in defending internatinal order in concert with the world's other principal powers. Here the willingness to fight on the part of all Canada's fellow 1945 victorious allies (the United States, Britain, France and Italy), and the financial and material support of the remaining major inudstrial democracies (Germany, Japan and the European Community), were decisive. Yet in order to sustain domestically what the Mulroney government quickly concluded it must do internationally, it was necessary for the government to manage with extraordinary skill the interpretations of the war and Canada's role offered by a suspicious media and public. And while Saddam Hussein's actions facilitated the task, ultimate success came only through the Canadian government's ability to mobilize the embedded distinctive values of Canadians, to go to war through the right processes, for the right purposes.

Sending the Ships, August 10, 1990

Canada's first major step on the road to war came eight days after Iraq's August 2nd invasion of Kuwait. On Friday August 10 Prime Minister Mulroney announced at a nationally-broadcast news conference that two destroyers (the *Athabaskan* and *Terra Nova*) and a supply ship (the *Protecteur*) would be sent to the Persian Gulf as part of a hastily assembled multinational force. The ships, to be fitted with new weapons, would arrive in the Gulf by mid-September, at which time Parliament, scheduled to resume sitting on September 24, could debate and approve their role.

The decision to send the ships came after a week of verbal condemnation and economic sanctions. On August 2 Secretary of State for External Affairs Joe Clark, travelling in Asia, had called the invasion of Kuwait "totally unacceptable aggression" and urged an immediate withdrawal of Iraqi forces. Simultaneously Canada announced support for a United Nations Security Council resolution of condemnation. The next day Clark froze all Kuwaiti assets in Canadian financial institutions, announced Canada's support for any UN sanctions, indicated the government would consider other sanctions, and told Iraq's ambassador that Canadians trapped in Kuwait by the invasion must be allowed to leave.

On Monday, August 6, Canada co-sponsored and voted for sweeping United Nations Security Council economic sanc-

tions against Iraq. That evening Prime Minister Mulroney announced in Washington that Canada would support a military blockade of Iraq to enforce these sanctions. The following day Canada imposed a complete embargo on all trade and financial transactions with Iraq. On Friday, August 10 Clark attended an emergency meeting of NATO foreign ministers in Brussels, immediately after which Canada's decision to dispatch the ships was announced.

A week prior to the NATO meeting, Clark, when asked at a news conference if military action were being contemplated, had replied, "No. Certainly not by Canada." However in Washington on Monday evening, August 6, Prime Minister Mulroney had implied that Canada's CF-18 aircraft in Europe might be available to defend Turkey, a NATO member. Before entering a cabinet meeting on Wednesday, August 8, Clark told reporters "I think the most important steps we can take are diplomatic steps." However Prime Minister Mulroney subsequently told a news conference that Canada would offer military help if NATO foreign ministers meeting in Brussels on Friday decided it was needed. The Prime Minister noted "We don't have the military might and military reach to accomplish the things that others seek to do," and pointed to the absence of a specific request for help from Saudi Arabia or the United States. But he declared that the brutality of the Iraqi aggression was now clear, that it had major political and economic repercussions for the world and Canada, and that the world was united as it has been at "few times in history." He added: "...we're not entirely bereft of equipment. We're capable of participating—as we do with peacekeeping forces—in other initiatives that may or may not be taken by allied governments." In rapidly moving toward military involvement the government was certainly not driven by any domestic demands. While the opposition Liberal and New Democratic parties had generally supported the imposition of economic sanctions, they harshly criticized the dispatch of the ships, charging that Canada's peacekeeping tradition was being violated and that United Nations authorization should have been sought. They also demanded that Parliament be recalled immediately to debate the move.

Similarily, while the Canadian Bankers Association had assisted the government in imposing financial sanctions, western grain farmers and their allies in the Canadian Wheat Board opposed the imposition of food sanctions, and asked for full compensation for their losses. From the intellectual community, Fred Crickard, the former deputy commander of Maritime Command had warned against sending the navy to the Gulf, on the grounds the ships were so worn out they could not operate effectively.

Among the editorialists, only Canada's elite financial daily, the *Financial Post*, called from the start for a naval blockade by members of the United Nations Security Council. English Canada's elite daily, the *Globe and Mail*, Francophone Canada's elite daily, *Le Devoir*, and the *Calgary Herald* asked only for economic sanctions. Canada's largest circulation daily, the *Toronto Star*, explicity warned against the use of force, then endorsed a show of force only by the United States, Britain and France. The government's announcement that the ships would be sent did win a limited, lukewarm endorsement from *Le Devoir* and the *Toronto Star*, and more hearty plaudits from the *Globe and Mail*, *Calgary Herald*, the *Vancouver Sun* and the *Halifax Chronicle-Herald*. However the *Ottawa Citizen*, much read by those in Canada's capital, remained steadfastly opposed.

Although no public opinion polls on the Gulf were available, Gallup's results showed that the government began August with an unprecedentedly low reservoir of public trust. Seventy-one percent of Canadians were dissatisfied with the direction of the country. Only 14% believed Mulroney would make the best Prime Minister. Only 19% declared they would vote Progressive Conservative in the next election. Only 17% professed a great deal or a lot of respect for federal authorities in Ottawa. And only 24% (compared to the Liberals 31%) believed the Conservatives were best able to handle international affairs. With so few Canadians willing to give the Mulroney government the benefit of the doubt, it is all the more surprising that the decision to send ships to the Gulf was retroactively endorsed by 69% of Canadians and 62% of Quebecers in Angus Reid's September poll, and 67% of Canadians in a Longwoods poll sponsored by the Department of National Defence the same month.

This rush to "rally" behind the Canadian government's decision was fuelled by media coverage of the invasion. The media provided saturation coverage and highlighted Iraqi atrocities. Moreover it largely ignored Prime Minister Mulroney, who allowed other more trusted leaders, notably Secretary of State for External Affairs Joe Clark, and senior American figures, to present the Canadian government and coalition case.

It was thus the external causes that were critical. The sheer shock of Iraq's militarily unprovoked aggression against its much smaller and defenceless sovereign neighbour, the brutality of its ensuing occupation, its evident reluctance by August 8 to allow trapped Canadians to leave Kuwait, and Saudi Arabia's request the same day for US forces to come to the Kingdom to deter the Iraqi troops massing on its border all produced a strong incentive for a military response. The United

Nations' August 6 passage of unprecedentedly comprehensive United Nations sanctions suggested a political consensus and rationale, if not a precise authorization or actual demand, for the dispatch of military forces. Iraq's August 8 announcement that it was annexing Kuwait, and its August 10 order to countries, including Canada, to close their embassies in Kuwait City within two weeks provided further outrage. Also of considerable importance was President's Bush's White House meeting with Prime Minister Mulroney on the evening of August 6. The two discussed "all appropriate action that might be taken," and the American dispatch over the next two days of air and ground forces to Saudi Arabia.

But Iraqi aggression, United Nations decisiveness, and American initiative were not sufficient to prompt Canada to send its ships. That required, in addition, the August 7 decision of Egypt, Morocco, and even the critical Arab "swing state" of Syria to commit troops to Saudi Arabia's defence, and the sending of ships to the Gulf by major powers Britain and France, and middlepowers Australia and Belgium. The final element, however, was the decision at the Brussels meeting on August 10 by Italy and even Germany to contribute forces, outside of any NATO umbrella, to the coalition effort in the Mediterranean and the Gulf. With these two countries on board, all of the major industrial democracies save Japan were engaged, however cautiously, in the military effort in the Gulf.[2]

Committing the CF-18s, September 14, 1990

Five weeks after Canada decided to send its ships, Prime Minister Mulroney announced he was committing an 18-plane squadron of state-of-the-art CF-18 fighter aircraft to the coalition forces in the Gulf. Canada simultaneously placed its three ships on combat status (formally "active service") and concentrated them at the dangerous northerly end of the central zone inside the Gulf. Moreover, it offered an additional $75 million to assist refugees from Iraq and to help Jordan, Turkey and Egypt enforce the trade embargo against Iraq.

The move to reinforce the ships with fighter aircraft was a significant shift from the United Nations-oriented diplomacy of constraint that Canada had emphasized in August. On Monday August 13 Canada joined fellow Security Council members France, the Soviet Union and Malaysia in insisting that the United Nations rather than the United States should decide if a military blockade should be enforced against Iraq. Canada declared it would participate only in a UN-sanctioned blockade and insisted its ships were currently heading toward the Gulf only to monitor, and not enforce, UN sanctions. The Prime Minister urged President Bush to give sanctions time to work, contacted King Hussein of Jordan, and gave the Jordanians $2.5 million in emergency refugee relief.

At the same time Canada was forced to cope with an Iraqi demand, issued on August 10, that all diplomatic missions in Kuwait be closed by August 24. Canada refused, advised the estimated 800 Canadians trapped in Kuwait to remain in their homes, and demanded their release from the Iraqi authorities. On August 14 Prime Minister Mulroney warned Saddam Hussein to back off plans to close the embassy. Three days later, Mulroney refused to rule out a larger Canadian force in the Gulf. On August 29 Clark rejected swapping food and messages for trapped Canadian women and children that Saddam Hussein already said he would release. On September 14, as Clark normally protested Iraq's incursion into Canadian diplomatic premises in Kuwait, Mulroney announced the dispatch of the CF-18s. While many other middle and minor powers had and would commit naval vessles to the Gulf, the dispatch of fighter aircraft placed Canada among the far more select ranks of the five extra-regional major powers (the United States, United Kingdom, France, and Italy) who contributed in what was to prove to be the militarily decisive way.

The first sign that Canada might expand its military involvement came on August 23 when Prime Minister Mulroney, following an emergency cabinet meeting, stated that it was unlikely that diplomatic efforts would succeed in securing an Iraqi withdrawal from Kuwait. However during the following two months he put his public emphasis on diplomatic efforts, and as late as September 7 termed Canada's three ship commitment "adequate for the moment." Following the decision to dispatch the aircraft, taken at a cabinet meeting on the morning of Friday, September 14, the Prime Minister spoke of the need to provide maximum protection to the Canadians on board the three ships, Canada's "obligation to international solidarity," requests from Kuwait and Saudi Arabia, and the United Nations economic embargoes against Iraq. He also carefully avoided stating whether cabinet had taken a position on whether Canada would actually participate in an attack to liberate Kuwait.

Once again there were few domestic pressures pushing the government to deploy more force in general, or to dispatch aircraft in particular. Both opposition parties, supported by former UN ambassador Stephen Lewis, continued to call for a recall of Parliament, UN approval for (and command of) the ships, and a clear statement of Canada's military commitments.

But with Parliament not in session, and Canadians distracted by summer vacations, these complaints had a limited audience. They thus had little effect, apart from a government briefing given to the opposition parties in late August and a two-day delay in the arrival of the Canadian ships in the Gulf to respect statutory and Parliamentary deadlines.

Parliamentary criticism was backed by societal caution. The families of Canadians trapped in Kuwait soon expressed concern about the plight of their loved ones. However no complaints about Ottawa's dispatch of the ships came from them or their returning relatives, who instead spoke eloquently of the brutality of the Iraqi occupation. Iraqi Canadians spoke out against any use of force. Haligonians offered their departing warships a tearful, rather than belligerent, farewell. Among the community of defence commentators, Martin Shadwick and retired Commodore Ronald Cocks advised against deploying the ships too close to Iraq, even as retired admiral Crickard declared that the ships' rapid refit had left him "completely satisfied."

On September 13, Joe Clark, in the first of many journeys to universities across Canada during the Gulf crisis, travelled to the University of Toronto to defend Canada's actions in the Gulf in a Hart House debate.[3] Here he declared that Canada was "actively" considering a request for more aid. His arguments help win the ensuing debate for the government's supporters by a two-to-one margin. But even here, as elsewhere, no one of consequence demanded that more Canadian forces be sent.

The same was true among the country's major editorialists. In the five weeks preceding the decision, there were repeated demands for UN consensus, the use of diplomacy, stronger sanctions, major refugee relief, and, above all, the recall of Canada's Parliament. But only the *Financial Post* spoke vaguely of communications and command specialists as a possible alternative Canadian contribution. And no one even implied that more Canadian military deployments should be made. Yet once the decision was made, it was approved in passing by all editorialists, as they rushed to demand yet again that Parliament be recalled. Similarly, a Decima poll in September revealed that defence ranked last as a government spending priority, even though Canadians believed, in a Longwoods poll begun in September for the Canadian Institute of International Peace and Security, that the danger of war was at the same high levels as in the early 1960s.[4] Once the decision was taken, however, 58% of Canadians (responding through a Gallup poll taken September 12-15) approved of Canadian Armed Forces being sent to the Gulf, even as their abhorrence of the Mulroney government in general continued unabated.

But if no one at home was asking for more Canadian military force, many abroad were. The most notable was US Secretary of State James Baker. Two weeks after the United Nations Security Council authorized enforcement of the embargo against Iraq, and two weeks after Mulroney and Bush held a regularly scheduled summit at Kennebunkport, Maine, Baker requested (on September 10) increased international participation in the Gulf operation. The United States' request was immediately acceded to by the critical coalition partners, led by the vital "swing state" of Syria, which pledged a full armoured division.

While the US request and international compliance were important, the decisive catalyst was the expanding set of atrocities Saddam Hussein was mounting directly against Canada. During August Saddam Hussein refused the release of Canadians trapped in Kuwait, paraded his civilian hostages (including a British child on television) and asked for food and medicine in return for the release of women and children he had already agreed to let go. At the same time he began to use force against the Canadian government itself. On August 10 he ordered the Canadian embassy in Kuwait closed within two weeks. On August 24, when Canada refused to comply, he surrounded it with troops and cut off its supplies, in an effort to starve it out. Perhaps emboldened by the Scandinavian, Japanese, and Greek compliance with his demands, on September 13 he sent his troops into the diplomatic premises of Canada (as well as those of France, Belgium and the Netherlands) and forcibly carried off a Canadian consul, Jean Gauthier. As diplomatic premises are considered part of their occupant's national territory, the Iraqi move constituted not only a direct assault on the most elementary foundation of international order—the integrity of the system of diplomatic immunity. It also represented, in a sense, an invasion of Canada itself. Combined with an Iraqi announcement on September 13 that singled out Canada (and Australia) for hostile actions, the invasion of the Canadian ambassador's residence in Kuwait directly catalyzed Canada's decision to escalate its military involvement in the Gulf.

Limiting Ground Forces, October 1990

Having joined the lofty reaches of the coalition's principal powers, however, Canada proved reluctant to take the next step of sending combat forces on the ground. On September 21 Clark publicly left open the possibility that Canada might send such forces. But five days later, in his "co-oper-ative security" speech to the UN General Assembly, he repeated a message, previously delivered to James Baker, that the coalition should use diplomatic resources rather than military action and act within the auspices of the UN.[5] On September 27, after meeting Soviet Foreign Minister Shevardnadze, Clark called for a pause for Saddam Hussein to consider a voluntary withdrawal, and looked to Jordan's King Hussein to find the basis of a peaceful settlement.

Diplomacy outside Iraq continued to be backed—for a while—by determination within. By October 10, Canada again stood alone with its principal power partners on the diplomatic as well as military front when it, along with the US, Britain and France were left as the only countries with functioning embassies in Kuwait. However nine days later the Canadians abandoned their embassy, leaving only the three western permanent members of the Security Council in Kuwait. Canada's reluctance to stand out everywhere with the big four was further evident on October 23 when Clark announced that Defence Minister Bill McKnight, and not Prime Minister Mulroney, would visit Canadian troops in the Gulf for Remembrance Day. Simultaneously the government promised it would secure Parliamentary approval before taking military action.

This same caution was evident in late October when Canada made its ground force contribution, limited to 250 communications and command specialists. While Canada was ready to soar with Italy in the air as a minor major power, it proved unwilling to join the historic great power triumvirate of France, Britain and the United States in the dirty world of combat forces on the ground. The reluctance was fuelled by a lack of directly relevant military capa-bilities, by painful memories of the military and political traumas that historic dispatches of expiditionary ground forces had caused (notably in Hong Kong, Dieppe, and the conscription crises of World War I and II), and by the absence of any new Iraqi atrocity abroad of sufficient magnitude to overwhelm the painful memories at home.

Setting the Deadline, November 29, 1990

One month later, however, Canada made it clear it was prepared to use such forces as it had sent. On November 29 Canada voted as a non-permanent Security Council member to use "all necessary means" to dislodge Saddam Hussein from Kuwait if he had not left by January 15, 1991. In so doing Canada was in good selective company, for a full twelve of the Council's fourteen members voted, in effect, to set a dealine and then use force.

However while this United Nations' legitimization was nice to have, the Canadian government had made it clear that it was not necessary. On October 24, Clark told Parliament that Canada would join a military offensive without United Nations authorization. On November 11, as Ambassador Yves Fortier continued working to secure agreement on a UN resolution backing the use of force, Prime Minister Mulroney promised "substantial additional funding" to Canada's military contingent. The following day he refused to rule out sending ground troops. On November 13, Defence Minister McKnight arrived in Saudi Arabia on the first leg of a four-country Gulf tour while his officers, reading the mood of their political masters, worked on a contingency plan to deploy a mechanized brigade. On November 23 the Department of National Defence was granted an additional $350 million dollars, in part for Gulf-related expenditures.

The mood was not all bellicose. In early November Clark reluctantly offered the services of the Canadian embassy in Baghdad to assist three Canadian MPs on an unauthorized, and largely unsuccessful mission to beg Saddam Hussein to release the Canadian hostages. On November 14, Mulroney himself met with five Edmonton-area wives of Canadians trapped in Kuwait and Iraq to demonstrate the government's concern. Meanwhile Clark visited London, Prague, Moscow, Jordan, Israel, Turkey and Egypt, in an attempt to find a negotiated settlement. On November 24, after meeting Jordan's King Hussein, Clark voiced some hope, but rejected linking the Palestinian and Kuwait issues. Two days later he offered Israel aid in settling Soviet Jews in Israel. Such diplomacy, however, ultimately proved ineffective. Thus, on November 29, despite Clark's initial reservations over the wisdom of setting a deadline, Canada voted to allow the use of force. It was a step taken in the hope that the collective thrat to use force might succeed, where Canada's own internationally vigorous and domestically visible diplomatic mediation had failed.

Reinforcing the Squadron, January 11, 1991

Having threatened to use force, Canada turned to preparations for using it, in a six-week-long sequence that culminated in the January 11 dispatch of six more CF-18s and supporting forces to the Gulf. The process began on December 1 when Canadian Squadron 412 left for the Gulf to transport coalition VIPs. By late December Canada's embassy in Israel had developed plans to evacuate Canadians, and issued a travel

advisory warning of rising tension in the Middle East. A new crew for the *Protecteur* left Halifax on January 1. The navy announced plans for a mid-July replacement of the two destroyers on January 2. And the *Huron* departed Victoria to relieve sister destroyer crews in the Gulf on January 4. Over the next few days the government announced it would give gas masks to Canadian civilians in the Gulf, and sent a new nerve gas antidote to its troops in the theatre. And on January 8 Mulroney said Canada would consider moving from a defensive to a more active role in the Gulf if Iraq refused to comply with the UN deadline.

Last minute diplomatic efforts also intensified. In early December Clark had written Baker saying Saddam Hussein must be given room to withraw without feeling his survival was threatened and be allowed to negotiate his grievances with Kuwait directly or in an international forum. On January 7, Canada formally protested to an anxious Israel the remarks made by its Defence Minister about Canada's lack of support. On January 9, Clark flew to New York to meet with Peres de Cuellar to discuss possible arguments to use in de Cuellar's last-chance visit with Saddam Hussein in Baghdad. The meeting, which the government said it had intended as a private encounter, was uncovered by the American television network CNN, and was quickly aired on all Canadian newscasts and highlighted in newspaper reports.

Two days later, any hope for a diplomatic solution was all but dead. On January 11 Canada closed its embassy in Baghdad and evacuated its four remaining diplomats. The Prime Minister announced Parliament's recall and postponed his planned visits to Britain and Germany. Clark announced that Canadian forces had been authorized to defend themselves if attacked. Most importantly Canada added to its Gulf task force six CF-18s, a Boeing 707 in-flight refueller, and 130 support staff, in order to be able to do northern Gulf combat air patrols 24 hours a day, and be available for other duties as required.

Canada's decision to use force was driven ultimately by its judgement that it must make good on its threat, and accept its responsibility as a major power (even if one no longer on the United Nations Security Council as a non-permanent member) to use force once the threat of force had so clearly failed. Its determination was reinforced by the steady increase in Iraqi military preparations to defend Kuwait, new evidence of Iraqi brutality (including stories verified by Amnesty International), the visible sign of any Iraqi flexibility in Iraqi Foreign Minister Tariq Aziz's news conference following his January 9 meeting with James Baker in Geneva, and Aziz's threat to attack Israel should the coalition move to liberate Kuwait. Yet the decision ultimately required that Canada itself try, and fail, in one last visible attempt to find a negotiated, and peaceful settlement to the conflict.

Expanding into Sweep and Escort, January 16, 1991

It quickly became apparent what the other duties of the additional forces sent on January 11 would be. Five days later Defence Minister McKnight announced that Canada's CF-18s had been authorized to move from defensive "combat air patrols" over the Gulf itself, to more offensive "sweep and escort" missions for American aircraft over Kuwait. While the aircraft would remain under Canadian command,

they would come under the tactical control of US forces during their missions. At the same time, Defence Minister McKnight announced Canada would provide a mobile field hospital with 130 medical and 350 support personnel (including a protective infantry company), and Chief of Staff General Jean de Chastelain announced he would send 30 more soldiers to Qatar as security for CF-18s.

These military moves followed a flurry of diplomatic activity as the January 15 deadline approached and passed. On January 14, Mulroney told the visiting James Baker in Ottawa that Canada was committed to use force. He also declared that the international community should keep searching for a diplomatic solution, even after UN Secretary General Peres de Cuellar returned from Baghdad to declare failure in his last-minute mediatory mission. The next day Mulroney declared support for all last-minute peace initiatives, including that of France, which was particularly visible in Francophone Canadian coverage of the crisis. Mulroney then led off the debate asking Parliament to re-affirm "its support of the United Nations in ending the aggression by Iraq against Kuwait." Immediately after, and long before the Commons passed the resolution, cabinet approved the new sweep and escort role.

The government's determination to go on the offensive may have been strengthened by the reminder of the fragility of the carefully constructed UN-approved coalition that came on January 12, when Mikhail Gorbachev's secret police opened fire upon and murdered civilians in Vilnius. But it depended as well on Saddam Hussein's all-too-apparent refusal to compromise at all, even after exhaustive and continuing coalition and UN efforts at a negotiated settlement.

Going to Ground Attack, February 20, 1991

There followed six weeks of war, during which Canada's CF-18s played a full part in the air assault which dominated the campaign. On February 20, with the skies cleared of hostile Iraqi aircraft and serious ground-based fire, and with the land offensive about to begin, Canada shifted its CF-18s from escorting US bombers in the sky to directly attacking Iraqi targets on the ground.

The decision, while potentially divisive at home, was accompanied by a growing Canadian effort to set forth a comprehensive and far-reaching set of proposals to guide the postwar peace settlement and reconstruction in the region. It was also almost immediately overshadowed by a flurry of discussion about whether to accept the terms for a conclusion to hostilities offered first by Saddam Hussein, and then, more seriously, by the Soviet Union.

Canada, with increasing reluctance, stood with its coalition partners, in insisting on nothing less than full compliance with all United Nations resolutions. At the same time, Canada both hinted that it might send more forces, while, in a visible divergence from Washington, insisting that the war be ended immediately upon Iraq's ejection from Kuwait.

The risks inherent in being forced to chose between these positions were nicely avoided by February 27, when the coalition partners agreed to accept a temporary ceasefire with a defeated Iraq. By that time, support for continuing the war in Canada had largely evaporated, as even the consistently supportive *Globe and Mail* demanded that Canada not go beyond the UN-sanctioned objectives that it judged to have been already met.

The Aftermath

With the hostilities over, Canada turned to the challenge of translating its more-than-middlepower military contribution into an equally energetic and effective effort to build a durable postwar order in the Gulf. It did so amidst broad approval in public and editorial opinion for its handling of the war. Indeed, the polls showed a significant, war-driven rise in the government's overall approval rating. While the increase was only from 15 to 20%, it was the first sign in over a year that a recovery in political popularity was possible. Such domestic support helped sustain a significant government effort to shape the postwar peace, notably through a Prime Ministerial proposal for a world summit to control arms transfers in the region. While the idea received a non-committal response from President Bush on his visit to Ottawa the following month, he was to give it generous praise as a foundation for his own proposal for Middle East arms control announced at the end of May. The tribute was further testament to the ability of Canada to design a Gulf policy in accordance with its own traditions and calculations of international requirements, and to implement this policy in concert with the principal powers of the world.

NOTES

1. Accounts emphasizing such factors, written along with this chapter during and immediately after the conflict without the advantage of detailed interview research, can be found in Martin Rudner, "Canada, the Gulf Crisis and Collective Security," in *Canada Among Nations 1990-91: After the Cold War*, (Ottawa: Carleton University Press, 1991), and Andrew Cooper, Richard Higgott, and Kim Nossal, "Bound to Follow? Leadership and Followership in the Gulf Conflict," Paper presented to the International Studies Association, Vancouver, March 22, 1991.

2. In partial contrast, it has been argued that neither Mr. Clark nor Mr. McKnight were in Ottawa when the invasion took place, and that the decision to act militarily "was made unilaterally by Mr. Mulroney either during or shortly after his quick visit with U.S. President George Bush on Monday, August 6." (Hugh Winsor, "Three ships sailing eastward with little sense of direction," *Globe and Mail*, August 24,1990, p. A1).

3. See also Joe Clark, "Canada in the World: Foreign Policy in the New Era," *Statements and Speeches* 90/11, Ottawa, Ontario, September 13, 1990.

4. Don Munton, "Old Thinking, New Thinking: CIIPS Public Opinion Survey 1990," *Peace and Security* (Spring 1991): 14-15.

5. "Notes for a speech by the Right Honourable Joe Clark, Secretary of State for External Affairs to the Forty-fifth Session of the United Nations General Assembly," *Statements and Speeches* 90/13, New York, September 26, 1990.

SUGGESTED READINGS

Cooper, Andrew, Richard Higgott, and Kim Nossal, "Bound to Follow? Leadership and Followership in the Gulf Conflict," Paper presented to the International Studies Association, Vancouver, British Columbia, March 22, 1991.

Rudner, Martin, "Canada, the Gulf Crisis and Collective Security," pp. 241-280, in Fen Osler Hampson and Christopher J. Maule, (eds.), *Canada Among Nations, 1990-91: After the Cold War*, (Ottawa: Carleton University Press, 1991).

CHRONOLOGY OF MAJOR EVENTS IN POSTWAR CANADIAN FOREIGN POLICY

1 September, 1939
Germany invades Poland; World War II begins. Canada declares war 10 days later, ending a period of quasi-isolationism.

7 December, 1941
Japan attacks U.S. military base at Pearl Harbour; U.S. declares war on Japan and Germany.

9 July, 1943
Prime Minister Mackenzie King sets forth in the House of Commons the so-called "functional principle" of representation in international organization.

1 November, 1943
Moscow declaration of U.S., USSR, U.K. and China supports a postwar international organization.

20 November, 1943
Canadian Gallup poll released indicates that 78% support active Canadian involvement in maintaining world peace.

9 March, 1944
Canada and the United States consider the prospect of cooperatively developing the Columbia River.

6 June, 1944
D-Day: Allied troops invade Normandy.

1 July, 1944
Canada participates in Bretton Woods conference which establishes principles and institutions of the postwar international financial system.

6 October, 1944
Great powers agree on Dumbarton Oaks Proposals for the postwar United Nations.

8 May, 1945
Germany surrenders, ending war in Europe.

12 May, 1945
U.S. President Franklin D. Roosevelt dies; Harry Truman becomes president.

11 June, 1945
Liberal government of Mackenzie King re-elected.

25 June, 1945
United Nations Charter approved at San Francisco conference.

15 August, 1945
Japan surrenders, ending World War II, after atomic bombs are dropped on Hiroshima and Nagasaki.

14 December, 1945
Parliament approves the Bretton Woods Agreements Act; Canada joins the International Monetary Fund and, later, the World Bank.

30 October, 1946
23 nations, including Canada, sign the General Agreement on Tariffs and Trade.

13 January, 1947
Secretary of State for External Affairs Louis St. Laurent outlines principles of Canadian foreign policy in "Gray Lecture."

12 March, 1947
Truman Doctrine announced; containment becomes basic principle of U.S. policy toward USSR.

5 June, 1947
Marshall Plan of U.S. economic aid to Europe announced.

15 August, 1947
India and Pakistan become independent.

25 February, 1948
Communist coup in Czechoslovakia solidifies Soviet influence.

22 March, 1948
Intergovernmental negotiations for a North Atlantic defence treaty begin in Washington.

11 November, 1948
Harry Truman wins U.S. presidential election.

15 November, 1948
Louis St. Laurent becomes Prime Minister as Mackenzie King resigns.

4 April, 1949
North Atlantic Treaty signed into effect, forming NATO alliance.

1 June, 1949
Apartheid is instituted by the ruling Nationalist Party of South Africa.

27 June, 1949
Liberal government of Louis St. Laurent re-elected.

21 September, 1949
People's Republic of China established.

9 January, 1950
Commonwealth Foreign Ministers meet in Colombo to establish the Colombo Plan for Cooperative Development in South and Southeast Asia.

25 June, 1950
North Korean troops cross 38th Parallel, starting Korean War. United Nations Security Council resolution calls for immediate halt in hostilities and withdrawal of North Korean forces.

27 June, 1950
U.S. commits troops to stop North Korean invasion of South Korea.

30 June, 1950
Canada sends three destroyers to Korea; later sends air transport planes.

7 August, 1950
Canadian government decides to send "special force" ground troops to fight in Korea.

11 September, 1950
U.S. President Truman and UN General Assembly give MacArthur authorization to proceed into North Korean territory.

26 November, 1950
Chinese troops enter the Korean War; UN forces driven back.

31 January, 1951
Canadian government decides to send ground and air forces to Europe as part of NATO commitment.

10 July, 1951
Korean armistice negotiations begin.

4 November, 1952
Dwight D. Eisenhower wins U.S. presidential election.

5 March, 1953
Joseph Stalin dies; Nikita Khrushchev eventually becomes Party Secretary and Premier.

27 July, 1953
Armistice signed ending the Korean War.

10 August, 1953
Liberal government of Louis St. Laurent wins re-election.

21 July, 1954
Geneva accords signed ending French colonial rule in Indochina and dividing Vietnam into North and South; Canada named member of international truce supervision commissions.

14 May, 1955
Soviet-led Warsaw Pact formed in response to admission of West Germany to NATO.

5 October, 1955
Lester B. Pearson begins first tour to USSR of a western foreign minister.

26 July, 1956
Egypt nationalizes the Suez Canal, precipitating the Suez Crisis.

29 October, 1956
Israel attacks Egypt through the Sinai Peninsula; British and French intervene, sending troops to the Suez Canal.

1 November, 1956
Lester B. Pearson, Canadian Secretary of State for External Affairs, proposes formation of the first UN peacekeeping force in General Assembly.

10 June, 1957
Progressive Conservatives under John Diefenbaker win general election with minority.

4 October, 1957
USSR launches *Sputnik*, the first satellite.

1 January, 1958
European Economic Community comes into effect.

31 March, 1958
Conservative government under John Diefenbaker wins election with majority.

23 September, 1958
Diefenbaker announces a review of the Avro Arrow interceptor project and the acquisition of the U.S. Bomarc anti-bomber missile, which will be equipped with nuclear weapons.

1 January, 1959
Fidel Castro's revolution overthrows Cuban government.

20 February, 1959
Diefenbaker announces Canada will scrap the Avro Arrow.

20 February, 1959
Diefenbaker officially announces that Canada is discussing with the U.S. the acquisition of nuclear weapons for Canadian forces as well as the storage of nuclear weapons in Canada.

26 June, 1959
St. Lawrence Seaway, joint Canada-U.S. project, is opened.

2 July, 1959
Canadian government announces purchase of U.S. F-104 fighter aircraft to fulfil a nuclear "strike-reconnaissance" role in NATO; nuclear weapons considered standard equipment.

29 March, 1960
Defence Minister Pearkes announces Canadian troops in Europe to acquire U.S. "Honest John" rocket system equipped with nuclear warheads.

1 May, 1960
American U2 spy plane is shot down over the USSR.

22 June, 1960
Liberals under Jean Lesage win Quebec election, ushering in the "Quiet Revolution."

19 October, 1960
U.S. imposes embargo on trade with Castro's Cuba.

1 November, 1960
John F. Kennedy wins U.S. presidential election.

17 January, 1961
Columbia River Treaty is signed in Washington, despite lack of a general agreement between Ottawa and British Columbia on implementation and financing.

16 March, 1961
U.S. Senate approves the Columbia River Treaty.

19 April, 1961
Attempted invasion of Cuba by U.S.-backed Cuban exiles at Bay of Pigs fails.

12 June, 1961
Canada acquires U.S. F-101B (Voodoo) fighter aircraft for North American defence; U.S. version of this plane is nuclear equipped.

12 August, 1961
Soviet and East German forces begin building the Berlin Wall.

14 November, 1961
President Kennedy escalates U.S. involvement in Vietnam; direct military support for South Vietnam begins.

18 June, 1962
Progressive Conservative government of John Diefenbaker re-elected with minority.

14 October, 1962
American U2 spy plane photographs construction of USSR ballistic missile sites in western Cuba.

22 October, 1962
U.S. President Kennedy discloses Soviet missile sites in Cuba, demands their removal and announces naval "quarantine" of the island.

22 October, 1962
Diefenbaker in House of Commons urges calm and suggests UN inspection of Cuba; Canadian forces put on alert by Defence Minister Douglas Harkness.

25 October, 1962
Diefenbaker declares missiles in Cuba a threat to Canada and offers support for U.S. actions.

28 October, 1962
Cuban missile crisis resolved: Khrushchev agrees to withdraw missiles and Kennedy

promises not to invade Cuba and, secretly, to withdraw American missiles from Turkey.

3 January, 1963
General Norstad, retiring NATO commander, states in Ottawa that Canada has committed itself to acquiring nuclear weapons.

12 January, 1963
Lester Pearson announces a Liberal government will accept existing Canadian commitment to acquire nuclear weapons.

8 April, 1963
Liberals under Lester B. Pearson win general election with minority.

8 July, 1963
Canada-British Columbia Agreement, resolving major issues of contention over the Columbia River Treaty between the federal and provincial governments, is signed.

5 August, 1963
Nuclear test ban treaty is signed by Britain, the U.S., and USSR.

16 August, 1963
Pearson government accepts nuclear weapons for Canadian armed forces; later approves storage in Canada of nuclear weapons for U.S. forces.

30 August, 1963
The "hot-line" establishes direct communication between Moscow and Washington.

22 November, 1963
U.S. President Kennedy assassinated; Vice-president Lyndon Johnson becomes president.

16 September, 1964
Columbia River Treaty is ratified in Canada.

1 October, 1964
Soviet premier Khrushchev deposed; Brezhnev and Kosygin named party secretary and premier, respectively.

1 November, 1964
Lyndon Johnson wins U.S. presidential election.

2 April, 1965
Prime Minister Pearson, speaking at Temple University, calls for a pause in U.S. bombing of North Vietnam at an appropriate time.

1 July, 1965
President Johnson increases U.S. commitment to Vietnam sending 125,000 troops.

1 November, 1965
Rhodesia unilaterally declares independence from Britain to maintain white control of government; in response, UN imposes economic sanctions.

8 November, 1965
Liberal government of Lester B. Pearson re-elected with minority.

1 April, 1966
"Cultural revolution" begins in China.

1 July, 1966
France withdraws from the military command of NATO.

22 March, 1967
Thailand allows the U.S. to use bases inside its territory for raids on Vietnam.

1 May, 1967
Nigerian civil war begins as Biafra province declares secession.

1 June, 1967
"Six Day War" erupts between Israel, Egypt, Jordan and Syria.

24 July, 1967
French President De Gaulle appears to endorse the Quebec separatist movement in Montreal speech.

30 January, 1968
Tet offensive launched by communist forces in Vietnam.

5 February, 1968
Quebec, on invitation from Gabon, participates in a Conference of Educational Ministers from Francophone countries.

4 March, 1968
Canadian government suspends diplomatic relations with the Republic of Gabon.

1 May, 1968
New Prime Minister, Pierre Elliott Trudeau initiates a comprehensive foreign policy review.

10 May, 1968
Preliminary peace talks to end the Vietnam War begin in Paris.

29 May, 1968
Trudeau, in a major "Canada and the World" statement during election campaign, announces that Canada will move to recognize People's Republic of China and support its membership in the UN.

25 June, 1968
Liberals under Pierre Trudeau win general election with majority.

1 July, 1968
Nuclear nonproliferation treaty signed.

1 September, 1968
Soviet and other Warsaw Pact forces intervene in Czechoslovakia, ending reform movement.

1 November, 1968
Richard Nixon wins U.S. presidential election.

21 February, 1969
Recognition negotiations begin between Canada and China in Stockholm.

1 March, 1969
Soviet and Chinese forces clash along their border.

3 April, 1969
Trudeau announces Canada will remain a member of NATO, but will reduce the size of its forces in NATO.

15 May, 1969
Trudeau declares Canada's sovereignty over the Arctic lands, exclusive rights to the Arctic continental shelf, and jurisdiction over Arctic waters.

8 June, 1969
President Nixon announces the beginning of a phased withdrawal of U.S. forces from Vietnam.

25 August, 1969
U.S. tanker, the *Manhattan*, begins the first of two Arctic voyages through the Northwest Passage.

16 September, 1969
Canadian Defense Minister announces Canada's NATO forces will be cut by half, and Canada will begin a disengagement from nuclear role in Europe.

23 October, 1969
Canadian government announces legislation for pollution prevention measures in the Arctic.

7 January, 1970
Civil war in Nigeria ends leaving two million dead.

1 April, 1970
Manhattan begins second voyage after Canadian anti-pollution requirements are met.

8 April, 1970
Canadian government passes the Arctic Waters Pollution Prevention Act.

23 June, 1970
First ministerial-level meeting concerning Great lakes pollution problems in the history of Canada-U.S. relations discusses possible bilateral agreement.

25 June, 1970
"Foreign Policy For Canadians," a government White Paper, is published; it promotes idea of foreign policy as pursuit of national interests.

5 October, 1970
FLQ kidnaps British trade commissioner James Cross, starting the "October Crisis"; Quebec cabinet minister Pierre Laporte later kidnapped and murdered.

13 October, 1970
Canada and China establish diplomatic relations.

15 August, 1971
President Nixon announces new economic measures, including surtax on manufactured imports from Canada.

1 October, 1971
People's Republic of China admitted to UN; Canada votes in favour.

15 April, 1972
Great Lakes Water Quality Agreement is signed by Prime Minister Trudeau and President Nixon.

1 May, 1972
Strategic Arms Limitation Treaty signed by U.S. and USSR.

20 May, 1972
Nixon and Brezhnev sign a treaty limiting anti-ballistic missile systems.

11 August, 1972
U.S. withdraws last of its ground troops from Vietnam.

3 October, 1972
Strategic Arms Limitation Treaty (SALT I) signed by U.S. and USSR.

30 October, 1972
Liberal government of Pierre Trudeau re-elected with minority.

27 January, 1973
U.S., North and South Vietnam and the Viet Cong agree to end the Vietnam War

1 June, 1973
West and East Germany establish diplomatic relations.

18 September, 1973
Second phase of the Conference on Security and Cooperation in Europe (CSCE), involving 35 countries including Canada, opens in Geneva.

1 October, 1973
"Yom Kippur" War breaks out between Israel, Egypt and Syria.

1 November, 1973
OPEC embargo on oil to western nations initiated; world oil prices begin to jump.

17 January, 1974
Egypt and Syria sign armistice agreements with Israel; a UN-patrolled buffer zone is established in the Suez Canal zone.

1 May, 1974
India explodes a nuclear device; technology supplied by Canada employed.

8 July, 1974
Liberal government of Pierre Trudeau re-elected with majority.

9 August, 1974
U.S. President Nixon resigns over Watergate scandal; Vice-president Gerald Ford becomes president.

1 May, 1975
Vietnam war ends with collapse of South Vietnam government.

31 July, 1975
The Final Act of the CSCE is approved in Helsinki.

1 August, 1975
Agreement on Security and Cooperation in Europe ("Helsinki" accord) signed by 35 countries including Canada.

16 June, 1976
Soweto uprising results in the worst racial violence in South Africa's history.

15 November, 1976
Jimmy Carter wins U.S. presidential election.

15 November, 1976
Parti Quebecois under René Lévesque wins Quebec election.

20 June, 1977
Environment minister Romeo LeBlanc calls acid rain an "environmental time bomb" and calls for reductions in Canada and the U.S. of its sources.

3 November, 1977
French President Giscard D'Estaing publicly affirms his support for self-determination in Quebec.

4 November, 1977
UN Security Council votes to impose a mandatory embargo on arms and military material to South Africa.

17 September, 1978
Camp David Accords make Egyptian recognition of Israel official and begin the peace negotiations between the two countries.

1 November, 1978
A second Great Lakes Water Quality Agreement, with more emphasis on industrial pollutants, is signed into effect.

22 May, 1979
Progressive Conservatives under Joe Clark win general election with minority.

22 May, 1979
John Fraser, the new Canadian environment minister, begins a campaign to publicize talks with the U.S. about the acid rain problem.

1 June, 1979
SALT II treaty signed by U.S. and USSR (but subsequently not ratified).

5 June, 1979
Prime Minister Joe Clark announces that the government does not intend to move its embassy from Tel Aviv to Jerusalem.

29, October 1979
Clark, reversing an earlier decision, announces that the government does not intend to move the Canadian embassy until the status of Jerusalem is settled.

13 November, 1979
Canada, the United States, and 32 European countries sign an agreement in an effort to reduce air pollution.

12 December, 1979
NATO agrees to deploy intermediate-range nuclear missiles in Europe.

21 December, 1979
Following negotiations in London, the white minority government of Rhodesia agrees to black majority rule.

26 December, 1979
Soviet forces intervene in Afghanistan; new government installed.

4 January, 1980
U.S. President Carter orders economic sanctions against the U.S.S.R., suggests boycott of Moscow Olympics, and delays ratification of SALT II treaty.

4 January, 1980
Clark announces the Canadian response to the Soviet invasion, including the withholding of recognition from the new Afghan government and the suspension of bilateral aid to Afghanistan.

26 January, 1980
Clark announces Canadian sanctions against USSR and a boycott of the Olympic Games in Moscow unless the USSR withdraws from Afghanistan.

28 January, 1980
Canadian embassy in Tehran arranges escape of six Americans after U.S. embassy is taken over.

18 February, 1980
Liberals under Pierre Trudeau win election with majority after Conservative government's defeat in House of Commons.

22 May, 1980
Quebec voters oppose negotiation of "sovereignty-association" in Quebec referendum.

1 August, 1980
The Carter administration and the Trudeau government sign a joint Memorandum of Intent committing the two governments to reach an acid rain agreement.

1 October, 1980
The Canadian government introduces the National Energy Program as part of its budget.

1 November, 1980
Ronald Reagan wins U.S. presidential election.

1 April, 1981
OECD committee on International Investment and Multinational Enterprises meets on the initiative of the United States in order to discuss the issue of national treatment for the first time.

7 June, 1981
Israeli aircraft bomb a nuclear reactor in Iraq.

14 December, 1981
Israel annexes the Golan Heights captured from Syria in the 1967 war.

17 August, 1982
Constitutional amendment power is transferred from Britain to Canada with the termination of the 1867 BNA Act.

6 March, 1984
Cruise missile tested over northern Canada for the first time.

30 June, 1984
John Turner succeeds Pierre Trudeau as Liberal leader and Prime Minister.

4 September, 1984
Progressive Conservatives under Brian Mulroney win general election with record majority.

6 November, 1984
Ronald Reagan is re-elected President of the United States.

17 March, 1985
At Quebec City "Shamrock Summit," Prime Minister Brian Mulroney and President Ronald Reagan commit their countries to pursuing trade liberalization, and issue Canada-U.S. Declaration on Goods and Services.

14 May, 1985
Secretary of State for External Affairs Joe Clark releases the government's Green Paper on Foreign Policy, "Competitiveness and Security"; it prompts widespread criticism.

21 July, 1985
The South African government imposes a state of emergency.

10 September, 1985
Canada warns it is prepared to cut all economic and diplomatic ties with South Africa if there is no meaningful change in that country.

16 October, 1985
Commonwealth Conference opens in Nassau; Mulroney government is committed to keeping the issue of sanctions against South Africa on the agenda, despite British opposition.

7 January, 1986
U.S. President Reagan calls for economic sanctions by U.S. and allies against Libya for terrorist-related activities.

18 April, 1986
Prime Minister Mulroney and U.S. President Ronald Reagan accept a report of their envoys on need to deal with acid rain.

3 August, 1986
Commonwealth mini-summit in London agrees to a further round of sanctions against South Africa.

27 November, 1986
U.S. exceeds (unratified) SALT II limits on nuclear missiles; USSR confirms continued Soviet adherence to treaty limits.

4 December, 1986
Clark tables the government's response to a special joint House of Commons-Senate committee report on Canadian foreign policy.

6 April, 1986
President Reagan visits Ottawa for third annual summit meeting, but only agrees "to consider" the idea of acid rain action.

1 May, 1987
House of Commons Standing Committee on External Affairs and International Trade releases "For Whose Benefit," a report evaluating official Canadian development assistance efforts.

26 November, 1987
Canadian parliament votes in favor of ratification of the "Meech Lake" constitutional accord.

8 December, 1987
U.S. and the USSR sign the Intermediate-Range Nuclear Forces Treaty, eliminating land-based medium- and shorter-range missiles.

2 January, 1988
Prime Minister Mulroney and President Reagan sign the final text of the Free Trade Agreement.

15 May, 1988
USSR begins withdrawal of military forces from Afghanistan.

26 October, 1988
Canada elected to a two year term on United Nations Security Council.

1 November, 1988
U.S. and twenty-four major industrial countries sign protocol to freeze emission rates of nitrogen oxides.

8 November, 1988
George Bush wins U.S. presidential election.

21 November, 1988
Progressive Conservative government of Brian Mulroney re-elected to form majority government.

1 January, 1989
Canada-United States Free Trade Agreement signed into effect.

9 November, 1989
East Germany opens Berlin Wall and lifts all restrictions on emigration and travel to West Germany.

12 December, 1989
U.S. Secretary of State James Baker outlines proposals for the transformation of NATO from primarily a military organization to a political alliance.

3 February, 1990
South African President F.W. de Klerk reveals a package of reforms which include lifting the 30-year ban on the African National Congress.

7 February, 1990
Soviet Communist Party agrees to surrender its monopoly on political power in favor of a more democratic system.

10 February, 1990
South African black leader Nelson Mandela is released from prison.

12 February, 1990
East-West conference of foreign ministers in Ottawa; troop level reductions in Europe and framework for negotiating German reunification agreed upon.

2 May, 1990
South African government initiates constitutional talks with ANC.

2 June, 1990
U.S. President Bush and Soviet President Gorbachev commit to cuting stockpiles of long-range nuclear arms and most chemical weapons during a summit meeting in Washington.

11 June, 1990
U.S.A. and Mexico agree in principle on negotiating a free trade agreement; Canada later joins talks.

22 June, 1990
The Meech Lake Accord fails after the three-year deadline for ratification expires.

1 July, 1990
Prime Minister Mulroney and U.S. President Bush announce negotiations on Canada-U.S. air quality accord to begin.

1 July, 1990
Economic union between East and West Germany takes place.

2 August, 1990
Iraq invades Kuwait.

2 August, 1990
UN Security Council condemns Iraqi invasion of Kuwait, demands immediate and unconditional withdrawal, and threatens to invoke mandatory sanctions if Iraq does not comply.

3 October, 1990
East and West Germany are united.

29 November, 1990
UN Security Council authorizes military action if Iraq does not withdraw from Kuwait by January 15, 1991.

16 January, 1991
U.S. led coalition launches air attacks on Iraq.

24 February, 1991
U.S.-led coalition launches ground offensive against Iraq.

27 February, 1991
Iraq withdraws from Kuwait. Military offensive against Iraq ends.

12 March, 1991
South African government proposes to end all restrictions on black property ownership by end of June, 1991.

13 March, 1991
U.S. President Bush and Canadian Prime Minister Mulroney sign the first Canada-U.S. Air Quality Accord, committing both countries to reduce emissions causing acid rain.

INDEX